CW01262824

The Law of Landlord and Tenant; to Which is Added an Appendix of Precedents

THE

LAW

OF

LANDLORD AND TENANT;

TO WHICH IS ADDED,

AN APPENDIX OF PRECEDENTS.

BY WILLIAM WOODFALL,

OF THE MIDDLE TEMPLE, ESQ. BARRISTER AT LAW.

THE FOURTH EDITION,

WITH CONSIDERABLE ALTERATIONS AND ADDITIONS.

London:

PRINTED FOR J. BUTTERWORTH AND SON, FLEET-STREET;
AND J. COOKE, ORMOND QUAY, DUBLIN.

1814.

TO

THE RIGHT HONOURABLE

JOHN LORD ELDON,

BARON ELDON OF ELDON IN THE COUNTY PALATINE OF DURHAM,

LORD HIGH CHANCELLOR OF GREAT BRITAIN

&c. &c. &c.

THIS WORK IS DEDICATED,

WITH THE MOST PROFOUND RESPECT,

FOR HIS LORDSHIP'S EXTENSIVE KNOWLEDGE

AND DISTINGUISHED TALENTS

AS A LAWYER,

AND INTEGRITY AS A MAN,

AND

WITH GRATEFUL REMEMBRANCE

OF HIS LORDSHIP'S PERSONAL KINDNESS;

BY HIS LORDSHIP'S

MOST OBEDIENT HUMBLE SERVANT,

WILLIAM WOODFALL.

A 2

ADVERTISEMENT

TO THE FOURTH EDITION.

Since the publication of the last edition of this work, many important Cases have been decided, affecting the Law of Landlord and Tenant.—These have been carefully collected and added to the text. Several passages have been omitted, which did not appear to have a proper relation to the subject of this treatise, and much new matter has been introduced.

An entirely new Index has been framed, upon a more concise and simple plan than the former one, and which, it is presumed, will be found greatly to increase the facility of reference; on which the utility of a publication of this nature so much depends. In other respects, attention has been paid to the revision and correction of the work; and it is hoped that "*The Law of Landlord and Tenant*" is now presented to the public in a more improved and perfect state.

Trinity Vacation,
1814.

ADVERTISEMENT

TO THE SECOND EDITION.

THE Patronage, with which this Treatise has been honoured by the Public, is so fully evinced by the rapid sale of the First Edition, and by the approbation of those who are most competent to judge of its merits; that every feeling of gratitude has in the present instance confirmed the principle of emulation, which induces an Author to endeavour to render his Work as useful and complete, as his means and capacity will allow.

Under these impressions, this Second Edition of THE LAW OF LANDLORD AND TENANT has been very carefully revised; and, besides other necessary augmentations to the several subjects as they originally stood in the Work, *three new Chapters have been added*, which treat 1. Of the remedy for a forcible entry. 2. Of the remedy for any infringement of a right of way. 3. Of the right to accommodation in the Parish Church, and of the liability to bear the expences incident to the Church Establishment.

The Appendix has also been rendered more perfect, by the introduction of some accurate and useful Precedents.

Middle Temple,
Trinity Term, 1804

CONTENTS.

CHAPTER I.

CHAPTER II.

CHAPTER III.

Of the Parties to a Lease; wherein by whom a Lease may be made.

x

CONTENTS.

CHAPTER X.

Of the general Incidents to Leases (continued).

CHAPTER XI.

CHAPTER XII.

CHAPTER XIII.

Of the Remedies for and against Landlord and Tenant.

CHAPTER XIV.

Of the Remedies for and against Landlord and Tenant, wherein

CONTENTS.

CHAPTER XX.

Of the Remedies for Tenants against Landlords (continued).

CHAPTER XXI.

Of the Remedies for Tenants against Third Persons.

CHAPTER XXII.

Of Remedies against Third Persons; wherein of

CHAPTER XXIII.

Of Remedies against Third Persons; wherein of

CHAPTER XXIV.

APPENDIX OF PRECEDENTS.

THE

LAW

OF

LANDLORD AND TENANT,

&c. &c. &c.

CHAPTER I.

SECTION I. *Introductory Observations on Leases in general.*

DEFINITION *of a Lease.*—A lease is a contract for the possession and profits of lands and tenements on the one side, and a recompense of rent or other income on the other, or it is a conveyance of lands and tenements to a person for life, or years, or at will, in consideration of a return of rent or other recompense. The party letting the land is called the lessor or landlord, and the party to whom the lease is made, the lessee or tenant.

Antiquity of Leases, &c.—It has generally been supposed, that the connection between landlord and tenant has gradually improved from that of master and slave into a state of total independance, and mutual interest in the soil. In support of this opinion, we are told (*a*) that lands were originally occupied by bondmen, but as these men derived no profit from their labour, and had consequently no interest in being industrious, it became necessary to have a free man to manage the farm, who probably at first had some acres set apart to him for his maintenance and wages. In progress of time, it was found more politic to give him an interest in the produce, first, by allowing him a certain proportion in place of wages, and ultimately, by reserving to the master a yearly quantity certain, and permitting the servant to retain the overplus. One further step, necessary to bring this contract to its due perfection, was to give the servant a lease for years, without which he was not secure that his industry would turn to his own profit. By a

(*a*) Kaims' Hist. Law Tracts.

contract in these terms he acquired the name of tenant, because he was entitled to hold the possession for years certain

But the notion that the cultivation of the ground was formerly carried on by slaves alone, is contradicted by the evidence afforded by the records and monuments of the middle ages, (*a*) which prove, that while slavery existed in this country, there were also tenants and free labourers of the ground, who held their lands under lease It appears that the practice of letting lands was known among the antient British. a proprietor of lands being permitted to let them for a year at his pleasure, though he could not alien or charge them. (*b*) Those who formerly held large districts and tracts of land being unacquainted with the arts of husbandry and tillage, found it their interest to lease out their demesnes, which, for want of care and cultivation, lay waste, and afforded them little or no profit. These leases were granted for years; this mode of letting being thought best to answer the designs and intentions of the lord, as well as the expectations of the tenant. for if they had let them for life, this had given the tenants too great a power over the lord, because then they would have had a property in the freehold, and by suffering disseisins or feigned recoveries to be had against themselves, might have shaken or endangered the inheritance of the owner; and on the other side, if they had leased their land only at will, few would have chosen to bestow any great pains or industry upon so precarious a possession, which the arbitrary will and pleasure of a peevish lord might have defeated (*c*).

(*d*) Thus, these estates were originally granted to mere farmers or husbandmen, who every year rendered some equivalent in money, provisions, or other rent, to the lessors or landlords, but in order to encourage them to manure and cultivate the ground, they had a permanent interest granted them, not determinable at the will of the lord Their possession, however, was esteemed of so little consequence, that they were rather considered as bailiffs or servants who were to receive and account for the profits at a settled price, than as having any property of their own they were, therefore, not allowed to have a freehold estate, but their interest, such as it was, vested after their deaths in their executors, who were to make up the accounts of their testator with the lord, and his other creditors, and were entitled to the stock upon the farm The lessee's estate might also, by the antient law, be at any time defeated by a common recovery suffered by the tenant of the freehold, which annihilated all leases for years then subsisting, unless afterwards renewed by the recoverer, whose title was supposed to be superior to his by whom those leases were granted

While estates for years were thus precarious, it is no wonder that

(*a*) See Bell on Leases, [illegible]

(*b*) 1 Whit. March. s. 4 p. 377

(*c*) Bac. Abr. tit. Lease

(*d*) 2 Bl. Com. 141

they were usually very short, like our modern leases upon rack rent, and indeed, we are told that, by the antient law, (*a*) no leases for more than forty years were allowable, because any longer possession, (especially when given without any livery declaring the nature and duration of the estate, might tend to defeat the inheritance. Besides, such leases were only made to serve the occasions and exigencies of the lord in cultivating and improving his demesnes, (*b*) not to borrow money upon, or to raise portions for daughters, or such other uses as are now made thereof: therefore there was no need to extend them to any great length of time, since they might be renewed as often as occasion required; the lessees likewise, if they were evicted, being only to recover damages, it would have been fruitless to prolong leases for the term of a thousand years, when the persons who would have to possess under such leases had no remedy for their damages but by recourse to the representatives of the original lessor. The law, however, that restricted the duration of leases for years to forty years, if it ever existed, was soon antiquated. (*c*) for we may observe in Madox's Collection of Antient Instruments, some leases for years of an early date, which considerably exceed that period, and long terms for three hundred years, or a thousand, were certainly in use in the time of *Edward* III. and probably of *Edward* I. But undoubtedly when by the statute 21 *H.* 8. c. 15. the termor (that is, he who is entitled to the term for years) was protected against these fictitious recoveries, and his interest was rendered secure and permanent, long terms began to be more frequent than before, and were afterwards extensively introduced, being found extremely convenient for family settlements and mortgages.

But though, at this day, terms for years are multiplied to a much longer duration than they were formerly, and there is ample remedy to recover the term itself, yet the succession continues the same (*d*) for besides the reason already given, it would be inconvenient to have had one rule of property for short terms, and another for those that were longer, being all of the same nature, and still no more than leases for years. The difficulty, also, of fixing the just bounds to any precise determinate number of years occurs, since one or two years, more or less, would have made very little difference in reason, were the bounds affixed to leases of never so long a continuance, and long or short are only terms of comparison, as a lease for forty years is long with respect to one of eight or ten years, and yet short with respect to another of a hundred years, therefore, that there might be an uniformity in the law, all leases for years are held to be of less value than estates for life, as being originally of much shorter duration, and also because they were under the power of the tenant of the freehold to destroy, and therefore are considered only as chattels, and cast upon the executor.

(*a*) 2 Bl. Com. 142.
(*b*) Bac. Abr. Tit. Leases.
(*c*) 2 Bl. Com. 142.
(*d*) Bac. Abr. Tit. Leases.

Section II. *Of the Requisites to a Lease, and how it may be made.*

In every lease it is requisite that there should be, 1. A lessor able to grant it. 2. A lessee capable of accepting it. 3. A subject-matter that is demiseable. 4. There must also be the needful ceremonies, &c; as where a freehold estate is created by lease, livery of seisin must be given to the lessee; and where a lease is for a term of years there must be an entry by him.

No lease is good unless it contains a sufficient degree of certainty, as to its beginning and ending; though it may determine prior to the period for which it is granted, in consequence of a proviso or condition; and all modern leases contain a proviso enabling the lessor to re-enter and determine the lease on non-payment of rent, or breach of the covenants (*a*). It is immaterial whether any rent be reserved upon a lease for life, years, or at will, or not, except only in the cases of leases made by tenant in tail, husband and wife, and ecclesiastical persons: of which hereafter.

By what words made.—The usual words, (*b*) whereby a lease is made, are "demise, grant, and to farm let," and whatsoever words amount to a grant may serve to make a lease. Farm, ferme, fearme, *firma*, is derived of the *Saxon* word "feorman" to feed, or relieve, because, in antient time, they reserved upon their leases, cattle and other victual and provision for their sustenance, so that a farmer, *firmarius*, was one who held his lands upon payment of a rent or feorme, though at present, by a gradual departure from the original sense, the word "farm" is brought to signify the very estate or lands so holden upon farm or rent. and this word "farm," in a will is sufficient to pass a leasehold estate, if it appear to have been the testator's intention that it should so pass (*c*).

Here, it may be laid down for a rule, that whatever words are sufficient to explain the intent of the parties, that the one shall divest himself of the possession and the other come into it, for such a determinate time, whether they run in the form of a licence, covenant, or agreement, are of themselves sufficient, and will, in construction of law, amount to a lease for years as effectually as if the most proper and pertinent words had been made use of for that purpose.

Thus the word "*demise*" is said to be a sufficient word to make a lease for years (*d*).

So, a licence to inhabit amounts to a lease (*e*).

If therefore one "license" another to enjoy such a house or land from

(*a*) Cruise Dig. Lease. (*b*) Co Lit. 45. Ibid 5. 2 Black. 318.
(*c*) 6 T. R. 345. (*d*) Co Lit. 301 b.
(*e*) 4 Burr 2209. 1 Mod. 14. 11 Mod. 42. 1 Ld Raym. 431. 2 Salk. 223.

such a time to such a time, it is a lease; (*a*) for it is a certain present interest, and ought to be pleaded as a lease it may, however, be pleaded as a licence; and if it be pleaded as a lease for years and traversed, the lessee may give the licence in evidence to prove it.

The words "covenant, grant, and agree" that *A.* shall have the lands for so many years, are apt words to make a lease for years, and enure as a lease (*b*).

The word "covenant" will make a lease, though the words "grant and agree" be omitted (*c*).

So, a covenant, "to stand seised" entered into by the owner, is a lease (*d*).

Covenant and entry amount to a lease. but a lease merely does not vest the estate in the lessee, but only gives him a right to enter and possess it.

These words in an instrument, "be it remembered that '*A B.* hath let and by these presents doth demise, &c." were held to operate as a present demise, although the instrument contained a further covenant for a future lease (*e*).

So, when one by articles, covenants, grants, and agrees with *J. S.* that he shall have such lands, or have, hold, and enjoy such lands for so many years, these words are sufficient to shew a present contract for the lessee's enjoyment of these lands, (*f*) and therefore amount to a present lease of them. The difference is, where such articles by way of covenant, are made by him who is owner of the lands, and where they are made by a stranger, who has then nothing in the lands in the first case they amount to a present and absolute lease, but not in the other, because a man cannot be supposed to lease what he has not, or if it might be so supposed, yet when it appears in the very articles that he has nothing in the lands, his covenant then can have no other construction, but that he will procure the owner of the lands to permit the covenantee to hold and enjoy those lands

It is, indeed, settled, that words in an agreement "that *A* shall hold and enjoy, &c" if not accompanied by restraining words, operate as words of present demise (*g*).

A memorandum was entered into, whereby *A.* agreed to let, and *B.* agreed to take a piece of land for a certain term, at the yearly rent, &c. And for and in consideration of a lease to be granted, *B.* agreed to lay out a sum of money in building, and *A* agreed to grant a lease when the houses were covered in, and *B* to take such lease "The agreement to be considered binding till one fully prepared could be produced." This was held to amount to an actual demise, the intention appearing to be that the tenant, who was to expend so much capital

(*a*) Bac Abr Tit Leases (*b*) Cro Jac 91. (*c*) 2 Mod. 80
(*d*) 3 Burr 1446 (*e*) 5 T R 163 (*f*) Cro Jac 172 Cro Car 207
(*g*) 5 T R. 163

upon the premises within a given time, should have a legal interest in the term, though when a certain progress was made in the buildings a more formal lease, in which the premises might be more fully described, for the convenience of underletting or assigning might be executed (*a*).

So, where one agreed to let, and also upon demand to execute a lease of a term, &c. which lease was to contain the usual covenants, &c. but it was stipulated that the agreement should be binding until the lease should be executed—it was held to be a present demise, the agreement for a future lease with further covenants being for the better security of the parties (*b*).

A paper writing was entitled "Memorandum of an Agreement between *A.* and *B.* and signed by them, expressing that in consideration of 40*l.* *A.* doth agree to let, and *B.* doth agree to take a messuage, &c. at 40*l.* per annum rent, and it is further agreed that *A.* shall not raise the rent nor turn out *B.* so long as the rent is duly paid quarterly, and he does not sell any article injurious to *A.* in his business;" though the terms do not exclude the construction of actual demise, yet the import of the whole looking to some future instrument, and a more permanent interest, than from year to year, a demurrer to a bill, for specific performance against *A.* who had succeeded in an ejectment, was overruled (*c*).

A deed that the person shall "hold and enjoy the premises from seven years to seven years, for and during the term of forty-nine years," with a proviso "that it shall be void on payment of so much money," though intended only as a collateral security, amounts to a present lease (*d*).

One made his will in this manner: "I have made a lease to *J. S.* for term of twenty-one years, paying but 20*s.* rent," this was held a good lease, or demise by will, for twenty-one years; and that the word "have" should be taken in the present tense, as *dedi* is in a deed of feoffment, to comply with the intent of the testator (*e*).

A devise of "the issues and profits" of land passes the land itself, for to have the issues and profits and to have the land is all one (*f*). [*Quære*, Would not it be the same of a lease by such words, as they would be tantamount to "enjoy," especially if a rent were reserved?]

So, if a grant be made of a boilery of salt, the land passes, for that is the whole profit (*g*).

Any one may now lease or convey his land, and reserve to himself the right of entering to kill game without being subject to be sued as a trespasser [illegible]

Articles by which "it is covenanted and agreed that *A.* "doth let the

(*a*) 12 [illegible] R. 17. (*b*) 15 East R. 244. (*c*) 14 Ves. 156. 409.
(*d*) Cro. Jac. 172. 2 Mod. 8. (*e*) Bac. on Leases, 16.
(*f*) 1 Co. [illegible] (*g*) Co. L. 4 b.

said lands, &c." amount to an immediate lease (*a*) and a *proviso* that the lessee "shall pay to the said *A* annually, &c." is a good reservation of rent, and not a condition. one of the judges, however, held it to be a reservation and a condition also, as in another case, where a *proviso* joined with words of covenant made it a condition and a covenant also.

So, an agreement to grant a lease, whereby the lessor did let and set for twenty-one years from a future day, shall be a lease *in præsenti*, if the circumstances shew the party's intent so to be (*b*).

But although no specific words are necessary to create a lease, yet there must be words used which shew an intention to demise.

Therefore where a lessee of tithes agreed with the owner of lands, for certain collateral considerations, not to take tithes in kind from the tenants of their lands for twelve years, but to accept a reasonable composition not exceeding 3*s* 6*d* per acre; this was adjudged to be no lease. (*c*) for 1st, the rent affected to be reserved is uncertain; under this agreement it is at the option of the party either to pay tithes in kind, or to tender the reasonable value of the tithes, which may be under 3*s*. 6*d*. per acre, 2dly, the owner of the lands, the person with whom the agreement is made, is neither to enjoy any thing nor pay any rent, it cannot therefore be a demise to him. It can, at the utmost, amount to no more than a mere covenant with *A* that *B*. shall enjoy, and creates no lease to either.

So, where articles were drawn between *A*. and *B*. in this manner: (*d*) Articles agreed upon, *&c*. *Imprimis*, *A* doth demise such a close to *B* to have it for forty years, and a rent reserved with a clause of distress, *&c*. In witness whereof, *&c*. And afterwards was written on the same paper a memorandum, that these articles are ordered by counsel of both parties, according to due form of law: here because the intent of both parties appeared by that memorandum, and by a lease actually drawn by counsel, but never sealed, (upon some disagreement between the parties,) it was ruled by the court, upon evidence in ejectment, that these articles were not a sufficient lease, and the jury found accordingly.

So, where one made a lease for life, *&* *provisum est*, that if the lessee die within sixty years, then his executors and assigns, should enjoy the land in his right for so many years as should be behind of the sixty years from the date of the lease, this was held to be only a covenant and no lease, (*e*) for which divers reasons are assigned in the books; the best however seems to be, that he having in the first part of the deed made a lease in express and proper words, must be sup-

(*a*) Cro. Eliz. 486. 385. Cro. Car. 207. S. C.
(*b*) 2 Bl. Rep. 973.
(*c*) [illegible] 413.
(*d*) Bac. Abr. tit. "Leases," (K.)
(*e*) Ibid.

posed to mean something less in the last part of the deed, which varies so widely in the form of expression, and which has a natural and proper meaning of its own as a covenant, but cannot amount or come up to a lease, without violence and force done to the words, as well as the intent of the parties. This seems the more probable, because it is held clearly, that if it had been provided that if the lessor die within sixty years, that then he demised the land to another, (who was also a party to the deed) for so many of the sixty years as should be then to come, this would be a good lease; for here he comes into the very same form of expression made use of in the first part of the deed, which was an actual demise, and therefore must be supposed to mean the same thing in the latter part too, and consequently such words would make it an actual demise.

In one case it is said, that though a grant "to have and to hold" land for years be a good lease, yet a grant to "enjoy" lands in the same manner is but a covenant; (*a*) [but unless it be with reference to a stranger, it is conceived that this opinion is erroneous, if the case itself be rightly reported.]

For, a covenant "that a stranger shall enjoy such land for so many years at such a rent," does not amount to a lease, but a covenant (*b*).

It is said also, that a covenant "that he shall permit the covenantee himself to hold the land for so many years," does not amount to a lease, for it sounds only in covenant. (*c*) [but this seems doubtful at this day, not merely because a licence to inhabit amounts to a lease, but because the intention of the parties clearly is that the one grants and the other accepts a lease.]

An article (*d*) "that he is content *A.* shall have a lease for six years, that the rent shall be 10*l.*" does not amount to a lease; for it appears to be only instructions for a lease.

So, "I agree to let my land," this is no lease (*e*).

So, an agreement or covenant made between *A.* and *B.* that *C.* shall have such land for years, this being made between strangers, cannot amount to a lease (*f*).

So, if *A.* covenants with *B.* that his executors shall have such land for twenty one years, this cannot amount to a lease (*g*).

A Lease, how made.—A lease may be made, either, 1. by deed, 2. by writing without deed, or 3. by parol demise.

A deed is a writing sealed and delivered by the parties. Deeds are either deeds poll, or deeds indented. The former are commonly used where the granting party only seals, and there is no need of the other party's sealing a counterpart, the nature of the trans-

(*a*) Cro. Jac. [illegible]
(*b*) Ibid.
[illegible]
(*c*) Com. Dig. tit. Estates (G. [illegible]
(*d*) Cro. Eliz. 1[illegible]6.
(*e*) Ibid.
(*f*) Ibid. [illegible]

action requiring no covenant from him. It can therefore rarely happen that a lease is made by deed poll, since leases generally contain a variety of mutual covenants.—When a lease is granted by indenture, two parts or copies are made, one of which is executed by the lessor, and delivered to the lessee, and is called the *original*, the other is executed by the lessee, and delivered to the lessor, and is called the *counterpart*. Sometimes each part is executed by all parties, which renders them both originals.

As every lease is presumed to be by deed, till the contrary be shewn, so every deed that is pleaded shall be intended to be a deed-poll, unless it be alledged to be indented (a). Whenever a lease, therefore, is pleaded as an indenture, it must be so alledged (b).

Parts of a Lease.—A lease by deed indented consists of the following parts: 1. the premises, 2. the *habendum* and *tenendum*, 3. *reddendum*, or reservation, 4. covenants, and 5. provisoes or conditions.

The premises of a lease are all the parts that precede the *habendum* (c). The office of this part of the lease is rightly to name the lessor and lessee, and to comprehend the certainty of the thing demised, either by express words, or by that which by reference may be reduced to a certainty; and the exception, or thing excepted, if there be any. The recital also, if there be any, is for the most part contained in the premises.

(d) A lease to one for life *habendum* to his three sons successively, but omitting to mention the sons in the premises of the deed, was held to be for the life of the father only, and that the sons should not take in possession or by way of remainder: for it being limited to the father for his life, that was a greater estate than for the lives of others, and the three sons were named as persons to have an estate, and not to make a limitation of an estate.

The *habendum et tenendum* is that part of the lease, (e) which begins with "to have and to hold," and properly succeeds the premises. The office of the *habendum* is to name the lessee, and to limit the certainty of the estate. It may also abridge or alter the generality of the premises (f). The *habendum*, in short, limits, enlarges, ascertains, and fixes, the meaning of the premises, but it cannot contradict them. The *tenendum* was formerly used to denote the lord of whom, and the tenure by which, the estate was to be holden, which has long been unnecessary; it is retained merely by custom.

If a man have a lease for years of land, and he, reciting this, by the premises of the deed grants all his estate in the land, to have and to hold the land or the term after his death, or for part of the time only;

(a) 1 Str 555. (b) Cro Eliz 658. (c) Shep. Touch 75.
(d) Cro Eliz 58. (e) Shep. Touch 75. Com. Dig tit Fait (E.9.)
(f) Lofft 191.

in this case the *habendum* is void, and the whole estate passes immediately by the premises (*a*).

An exception is a clause in a deed, whereby the lessor excepts something out of that which he has granted before by the deed; and being the act and words of the lessor, shall be taken strictly against him (*b*). But (*c*) where an exception does not defeat the grant, or is contrary to it, it must stand. In every good exception, these things must always concur; 1. the exception must be by apt words, as "saving and excepting," &c. 2. it must be of part of the thing demised, and not of some other thing. 3. it must be part of the thing only, and not of all, the greater part, or the effect of the thing granted; an exception therefore, in a lease, which extends to the whole thing demised, is void; (*d*) 4. it must be of such a thing as is severable from the premises demised, and not of an inseparable incident; 5. it must be of such a thing as he that doth except may have, and which properly belongs to him. It must be of a particular thing out of a general, and not of a particular thing out of a particular thing; 6. it must be certainly described and set down: therefore, if one demise a manor excepting one acre, without setting forth which, or what acre it shall be, the exception is void. But (*e*) if a man be possessed of a new house and an old house, and make a lease with an exception of the new house for the use of the lessor when he pleases to reside there, and at other times for the use of the lessee, the new house is well excepted, which exception is not avoided by the words "at all times to be used by the lessee, when the lessor doth not dwell there," for that sentence doth not enure as an exception out of an exception, (which sets the matter at large,) but only as a declaration of the lessor's intention in making the exception. The latter words, however, make the lessee tenant at will.

So if a man lease his houses, excepting his new house, during the term, this exception is good; but if he except it during life, it is void; or if a man having a term of two houses for certain years, grant his houses, excepting one of them, for life, this exception is void; for the words "during life," qualify the exception, and shew his intent that the one house shall not be excepted during the whole term, and so is void (*f*).

The *reddendum* or reservation is a clause in the lease, whereby the lessor reserves some new thing to himself out of that which he granted before (*g*) and this commonly and properly succeeds the *tenendum*, and is usually made by the words "yielding and paying," and such like. In every good reservation, these things must always concur; 1. it must

(*a*) Shep. Touch. 114. 1 Salk. 346. S. P.
(*b*) 12 Mod. 15. Dyer 264 *b*. Hob. 173.
(*c*) [illegible] 4 Mod. 11. S. C.
(*g*) Shep. Touch. 80.

(*d*) Shep. Touch. 77.
(*e*) Cro. Eliz. 6.
(*f*) 12 Mod. 15.

be by apt words, 2. it must be of some other thing issuing or coming out of the thing granted, and not a part of the thing itself, nor of some thing issuing out of another thing, 3 it must be of such a thing whereunto the grantor may have resort to distrain; 4. it must be made to one of the grantors, and not to a stranger to the deed.

A covenant is a clause of agreement contained in the lease, whereby either party is bound to do, perform, or give something to the other.

A condition, or proviso, is a clause of restraint in the lease, which is commonly expressed by the words "provided," or "provided always," or words similar (*a*).

Formalities requisite.—It is requisite that the respective parties, the lessor and lessee, whose deed the lease is, should seal, and now in almost every case, sign it also: an instrument not under seal, is no deed, for a seal is essential to a deed (*b*). The neglect of signing, and custom of resting only on the authority of seals, remained very long among us, for it was held, in all our books, that sealing alone was sufficient to authenticate a deed. The common form of attesting deeds, "sealed and delivered," continues in great measure to this day; notwithstanding that the statute 29 *C.* 2 *c.* 3. commonly called "The statute of Frauds and Perjuries," revives the Saxon custom, and expressly directs the signing in all grants of lands and many other species of deeds: in which, therefore, signing seems to be now as necessary as sealing, though it has sometimes been held that the one includes the other.

The lease must also be delivered, either by the parties themselves, or their certain attorney or attornies, which delivery is also expressed in their attestation "sealed and *delivered*," for delivery makes it a lease (*c*). Almost (*d*) any manifestation, however, of the party's intention to deliver, if accompanied by an act importing the same, will constitute a delivery. If the date be false or impossible, the delivery ascertains the time of it. If another person seals the deed, yet if the party delivers it himself, he thereby adopts the sealing, and, by a parity of reason, the signing also, and makes them both his own. Every deed shall be intended to be delivered on the day it bears date, unless the contrary be proved.

The last requisite is the attestation or execution of the lease in the presence of witnesses, though this is necessary rather for the preservation of the evidence, than to constitute the essence of the deed. Ever since the reign of Henry VIII the witnesses have usually subscribed their attestation, either at the bottom or on the back of the deed but such actual subscription by the witnesses is not required by law, though it is prudent for them so to do in order to assist their memory when living and to supply their evidence when dead. A party (*e*) who has

(*a*) Co. Litt. 35 (*b*) 2 T. R. 695. 2 Bl. Com. 297. 3 Inst. 169

(*c*) Co. Litt. 36 2 Bl. Com. 307 (*d*) 1 Ves. jun. 206

executed a lease shall not be permitted to acknowledge it, but it must be proved by the subscribing witness and a subscribing witness to any instrument may be compelled to give evidence respecting it, for the person by subscribing his name as a witness, undertakes to give evidence at a proper time, and in a proper manner; and if he deny the deed, other witnesses may be called to prove it (*a*). But proof of the hand-writing of the contracting party may under some circumstances be sufficient, even where there is a subscribing witness, as if no intelligence can be obtained respecting the subscribing witness after reasonable inquiry has been made (*b*). Generally speaking, however, every instrument, whether under seal or not, the execution of which is witnessed, must be proved in the same manner, regularly by the witness himself, if living; if dead, by proving his hand writing, if residing abroad, by sending out a commission to examine him, or at least by proving his hand writing, which last, indeed, is a relaxation of the old rule and admitted only of late years.

A lease by deed may be avoided or rendered of no effect, if it wants either 1 proper parties and a proper subject matter; (*c*) 2. writing, (or printing) on paper or parchment duly stamped; 3 sufficient and legal words properly disposed, 4. reading, if desired, before the execution (*d*) for not reading a deed to a person in the rough draft, nor in the engrossment before execution, is a badge of fraud, 5 sealing, and by the statute of Frauds, in most cases, signing also, or 6 delivery (*e*). Without these essentials it is void *ab initio* It may also be avoided by matter *ex post facto*: as 1 By erasure, interlineation, or other alteration in any material part (*f*). If a deed be altered by a stranger, in a point not material, this does not avoid the deed; but otherwise, if it be altered by a stranger in a point material, for the witnesses cannot prove it to be the act of the party, where there is any material difference. an immaterial alteration, however, does not change the deed, and consequently the witnesses may attest it without danger of perjury. But if the deed be altered by the party himself, though in a point not material, yet it avoids it, [unless a memorandum thereof be made at the time of the execution and attestation. 2 *Bl Com.* 308.] for the law takes every man's act most strongly against himself. So, if there be several covenants in a deed, and one of them be altered, this destroys the whole deed, for it cannot be the same, unless every covenant of which it consists be the same also. 2 By breaking off, or defacing the seal, unless, indeed, it be done by accident Thus, on an indenture to guide the uses of a common recovery being offered in evidence, with the seals torn off, yet, it being proved to have been done by a little boy, the indenture was allowed to be read. 3. By delivering it up to be cancelled, that is, to have lines drawn over it in the form of lattice work, or *cancelli*, though the phrase is now used figuratively for any manner of obliterating or defacing it (*g*). 4. By the

(*a*) 10 Mod 333 1 Str 1 S C Cowp 845 Bull. N P 284.
(*b*) Doug 216 7 T R 266. (*c*) 2 Bl Com 308. (*d*) 2 Atk 32[illegible]
[illegible]

disagreement of such whose concurrence is necessary in order for the deed to stand as the husband where a feme-covert is concerned, an infant, or a person under duress, when those disabilities are removed; and the like (a). 5. By the judgment or decree of a court of judicature. This was antiently the province of the court of Star Chamber, and now is that of the court of Chancery; and is exercised when it appears that the deed was obtained by fraud, force, or other foul practice, or is proved to be an absolute forgery, in any of which cases, the deed may be avoided either in part, or totally, according as the cause of avoidance is more or less extensive.

The lease need not be proved in an action of debt, for the performance of covenants therein; for the party is estopped to say that the lease was not duly executed (b).

Of a Lease by writing without deed.

Although the court will presume the lease to be by deed, a lease for a term of years may be created by writing without deed (c). The statute 29 *Car.* 2. *c.* 3. *s.* 3. enacts, that "No leases, estates, or interest either of freehold or term of years, or any uncertain interest (not being copyhold or customary interest) of, in, to, or out of any messuages, &c. shall be assigned, granted, or surrendered, unless by deed or *note in writing*, signed by the party so assigning, granting, or surrendering the same, or their agents thereunto lawfully authorized by writing, or by act and operation of law."

In the case *d.* of *Fry* and *Phillips*, one *Jones* granted a lease for 99 years, if three persons should so long live. The executrix of the grantee assigned to one *Pennington* by indorsement on the lease in these words, "I assign all my title, &c. to Mr. *Thomas Pennington*, for six guineas," which writing was neither sealed, delivered nor stamped. *Pennington* entered, and exactly in the same manner assigned to one *Fry* who entered and was possessed; but in 1756 gave up the possession. The executrix of the grantee was then dead. Her executor had never entered or done any act of ownership but in 1770, he regularly assigned to *Fry*: at that time, however, *Phillips* was in possession under a grant from *Jones*, made by him on *Fry* giving up the possession. The question for the opinion of the court was, "Whether any thing passed to *Fry* by the last assignment made to him by the executor of the executrix of the grantee, which executor himself never was in possession?" which question the court did not determine, because, upon the whole of the case, *Fry* had a right. Lord *Mansfield* told the counsel that a point had occurred to the court which had not been mentioned in the argument. If the indorsement by the executrix carried a legal interest in the term to *Pennington* from *Elizabeth French*, and *Pennington's* indorse-

(a) 2 Bl. Com. 309. (b) 1 Esp. R. 153. (c) 1 Str. 555. 2 Wils. 26. (d) 5 Burr. 2827.

ment to *Fry* had a like effect, then *Fry* had the whole lease in him and by the statute of Frauds, 29 *C* 2 *c* 3 *s* 3 it may be assigned by a *note in writing*, and such a note in writing need not be either sealed, delivered, or stamped, as a deed must His Lordship mentioned a case in the Common Pleas, *Trinity* term, 1755, between *Farmer* and *Rogers*, in which it was resolved, " that by the statute of Frauds and Perjuries a lease for any term of years may be created by *writing without deed* and that the same may be surrendered by deed or note in writing: and the court held that there was no occasion for any stamp duty upon the note or indorsement, it not being by deed" (which however is now rendered necessary, it should seem, by stat 23 *G* 3 *c* 58] So, in the present case, the legal interest in this term might be assigned by a note in writing Mr Justice *Aston* was of the same opinion *Elizabeth French*, by writing under her hand, indorsed on the back of the indenture, assigned to *Pennington* This writing was neither sealed, delivered, nor stamped *Pennington* entered and then assigned in the same manner to *Fry* The executor of *Elizabeth French* had nothing to convey.—Lord *Mansfield* The court must take the whole of what is stated in the case, and upon the whole of the case the plaintiff has a right

Of a Lease by Parol Demise.

A lease may likewise be made by parol demise, or verbal contract. with respect to which, by the before-mentioned statute, 29 *C* 2 *c* 3. commonly called the statute of Frauds and Perjuries, several things must be evidenced by writing, of which, before that statute, parol evidence had been sufficient

By that statute, all leases, estates of freehold, or term of years, created by parol and not put into writing and signed by the parties making the same, or their agents thereunto lawfully authorized by writing, shall have the effect of estates at will only, except leases not exceeding three years from the making, whereupon the rent reserved amounts to two thirds of the improved value, and no such estate or interest shall be granted or surrendered but by deed, or note in writing

The meaning of the statute was, that such an agreement should not operate as a term (*a*)—A parol agreement, therefore, to lease lands for four years, creates only a tenancy at will: but what was considered as a tenancy at will at the time when the act passed, has been since properly construed to enure as a tenancy from year to year

So, a general parol demise at an annual rent, where the bulk of the farm is enclosed, and a small part of it lies in the open common fields, is only a lease from year to year, and not for so long as the usual course of husbandry extends (*b*)

A lease for three years, to commence *in futuro* by parol, is not warranted by the statute of Frauds (*c*).

(*a*) S T R [illegible] 3 T R. 16 4 T R 680
(*b*) 12 Mod. 612 2 T. R [illegible]
(*c*) 2 Bl. Rep 1172

But a lease by parol for a year and a half, to commence after the expiration of a lease which wants a year of expiring, is a good lease within the statute; for it does not exceed three years from the making (a).

If land be leased to *A* for a year, and so from year to year, so long as both parties shall agree, this is a lease for two years certain, and if the lessee hold on after two years, he is not a lessee at will, (as the old opinion was) but for a year certain, and his lease is not determinable till that year be ended; for his holding on is an agreement to the original contract: and such executory contract is not void by the statute of Frauds, for there is no term for above two years ever subsisting at the same time, and there can be no fraud to a purchaser, for the utmost interest that can be to bind him can be only for one year. But if the original contract were only for a year at 8*l.* *per ann.* rent, without mentioning any time certain, it would be a tenancy at will after the expiration of the year, unless there was some evidence, by a regular payment of rent annually, or half yearly, that the intent of the parties was that he should be tenant for a year (b).

If a landlord lease for seven years by parol, though the lease be void by the statute of Frauds, as to the duration of the term, the tenant holds under the terms of the lease in other respects, as to the rent, the time of the year when the tenant is to quit, &c (c).

So where the tenant holds over after the expiration of his term without having entered into any new contract, he holds upon the former terms (d).

SECTION III. *Of registering Leases.*

THE *registry of deeds* has been rendered necessary in particular parts of the kingdom, by certain statutes passed at various periods of time, in order to prevent the frauds which were practised by means of secret transfers and prior mortgages.

The statute 2 and 3 *Ann.* c. 4, enacts, that a memorial of all deeds and conveyances made and executed in the West-Riding of the county of *York*, after *September* 29, 1704; whereby any honors, manors, lands, &c. may be any way affected in law or equity, may, at the election of the party or parties concerned, be registered in an office to be kept at *Wakefield*, in the said Riding, for that purpose; which memorial must be written and directed to the register of the said office; and must be under the hand and seal of some or one of the grantors, or grantees, his or their guardians or trustees, attested by two witnesses, one whereof to be one of the witnesses to the execution of such deed or conveyance; which witness shall, upon oath before the said register or his deputy,

(a) Bull. N. P. 177. 1 Str. 651.
(b) Bull. N. P. 85. Cro. Eliz. 775. 2 Salk 414. 1 Wils. 262. (c) 5 T. R. 162.
(d) 1 T. R. 162.

prove the signing and sealing of the said memorial, and the execution of the deed or conveyance therein mentioned, and that every such memorial shall contain the date of such deed or conveyance, and the names and additions of all the parties thereto, with the places of their abode; and shall also mention the honors, manors, lands, &c contained in such deed, &c and the names of the parishes, &c wherein they are situated · every deed or conveyance that shall, at any time after such memorial is so registered, be made and executed of the honors, manors, lands, &c. or any part thereof contained in such memorial, shall be adjudged fraudulent and void against any subsequent purchaser or mortgagee for valuable consideration; unless such memorial thereof shall be registered as the act requires, before the registering of the memorial of the deed or conveyance under which such subsequent purchaser or mortgagee shall claim

The statute 6 *Ann* c. 35. contains provisions of a similar nature with respect to the East-Riding of the same county, and the town of *Kingston-upon-Hull*, and appoints the Register-office to be kept in *Beverley* in the said Riding.

The statute 8 *G.* 2 *c.* 6 contains provisions of a similar nature with respect to the North-Riding of the same county.

The statute 7 *Ann. c.* 20 contains provisions of a similar nature, with respect to the county of *Middlesex* The Master of the *King's Bench* to be the Register who may appoint a deputy, both of them to be under the controul of the *Lord Chancellor*, by whom rules may be made for the management of the office, which is to be kept in or near the Inns of Court or Chancery The registers to endorse a probate of every deed so registered, which certificate shall be allowed as evidence of such registry in all courts of record whatsoever. Upon certificate and proof made to the register that money due on a mortgage entered in the registry has been satisfied, the register shall make an entry thereof in the margin against the enrolment

By statute 25 *G* 2 *c.* 4 the deputy of the chief clerk of the *King's Bench*, is appointed a register for *Middlesex*, instead of the chief clerk.

By these statutes, deeds, conveyances, and devices by will shall be void against subsequent purchasers and mortgagees, unless registered before the conveyances under which they claim, also no judgment, statute, or recognizance, shall bind any lands in those counties, but from the time a memorial thereof shall be entered at the Register-office But the acts do not extend to copyhold estates, leases at a rack-rent, or to any leases, not exceeding twenty-one years, where the possession goes with the lease, nor to any chamber in the inns of court

The intention of the register act plainly is to secure subsequent purchasers and mortgagees against secret conveyances and fraudulent incumbrances (*a*).

(*a*) 3 Atk 651 2

Where a person had no notice of a prior conveyance, there the registering of his subsequent conveyance shall prevail against the prior; but if he had notice of a prior conveyance, then that was not a secret conveyance by which he could be prejudiced The enacting clause, which says "that every such deed shall be void against any subsequent purchaser or mortgagee, unless the memorial thereof be registered, &c." gives them the legal estate, but does not say that such subsequent purchaser is not left open to any equity which a prior purchaser or incumbrancer may have, for he can be in no danger where he knows of another incumbrance, because he might then have stopped his hand from proceeding.—The operation of the register act 7 *Ann c.* 20 and that for the inrollment of bargains and sales 27 *H.* 8. and the construction of them, are the same, and it would be a most mischievous thing, if a person taking advantage of the legal form appointed by an act of parliament, might under that protect himself against a person who had a prior equity, of which he had notice (*a*)

The register act is notice to every body, and the meaning of it was to prevent parol proofs of notice (*b*) It is only in cases of fraud that the court of Chancery have broke in upon the act, although one incumbrance was registered before another. and though clear notice is a proper ground of relief, suspicion of notice will not suffice.

A registered conveyance therefore of premises in Middlesex for a valuable consideration, was established against a prior devise not registered, the evidence of notice, which ought to amount to actual fraud, not being found (*c*)

But notwithstanding that it was said that the register act is notice to every body, registration in Middlesex of an equitable mortgage was held not presumptive notice of itself to a subsequent legal mortgagee, so as to take from him his legal advantage (*d*)

So, after an assignment of a mortgage, payments to the mortgagee without notice, must be allowed by the assignee, the registry, (the premises being in Middlesex) not being notice for this purpose (*e*)

Registering an assignment is not registering the lease. Therefore, where the defendant claimed under a lease made in 1730, which was soon after mortgaged, and in 1731, sold out and out to the defendant; the original lease was not registered, but the first mortgage of it, and the defendant's purchase were. and it not being a lease at rack-rent, the question was, whether this was a registry within the meaning of 7 *Ann c.* 20? and the Chief Justice (*Holt*) held it not to be sufficient for the act says the deed under which the party claims, with the witnesses' names, shall be registered, and of this a subsequent purchaser can have no notice by the bare registry of the assignment, and it is also required that the original be produced to the officer (*f*).

(*a*) 3 Atk 651-2 (*b*) 2 Atk 275 Ambl 436 s. c. (*c*) 3 Ves jun 478.
(*d*) Ambl 678 (*e*) 1 Ves jun 98) (*f*) 2 Str 1064

On a proviso in a lease of lands of the Duchy of *Lancaster*, according to stat. 27 *H.* 8. *c.* 11. that it should be enrolled with the auditor; the certificate of the auditor on the margin was held to be sufficient evidence of the enrollment (*a*).

If a memorial is executed by any party to a deed, resident in the metropolis, whether it be grantor or grantee, and it is convenient to the witness to attend at the registering office, the oath of such execution is administered verbally, in the following terms, "You swear that you saw this memorial signed and sealed, and the deed to which it refers duly executed by the party (or parties) thereto, whose execution you have attested" (*b*) and it is not necessary, in such case, to affix an affidavit stamp, or any other, to the parchment on which such memorial is written. But if the memorial is necessarily executed by all parties in the country, and there sworn, the affidavit must be engrossed on the proper stamp, and may be either written under, or annexed to, the memorial. It must be on parchment, and its form will be found among the precedents in the Appendix.

It being often found more convenient to obtain the registry of an instrument by a representative of a deceased party, under some one of the designations of heir, executor, administrator, guardian, or trustee than by any of the survivors, who if grantors may perhaps hesitate to do justice, and as the direction of the act does not convey a very distinct idea of the manner in which the registry by such representative is to be effected, it may be useful to premise, that the instrument to be registered, notwithstanding it is already sufficiently executed for general legal purposes, must, in addition, be sealed and delivered by the person requiring the registry, as if he was a party in his own right, (*c*) and such person must also sign and seal a memorial, which will be varied from the usual form where it refers to witnesses (see Appendix). An alteration in this case is to be written under, or indorsed on the instrument in the following terms, "Sealed and delivered by *C. D.* one of the executors" (or otherwise "of the within-named *A. B.*" for the purpose of registering) "in the presence of ——" In respect to the parties to deed residing out of town, if such deed appears properly executed and attested, the proof of its execution and that of the memorial by any one of the parties (consonant to the form of oath contained in the preceding paragraph) will render any affidavit from the country useless: neither is it material that the witness should see the same party execute the deed who signs and seals the memorial, for instance, if the deed be made from *A.* to *B.* and the witness attests the execution of the deed by the former, his seeing the memorial executed by *B.* will suffice. It will be requisite, however, in such memorial to recite the other attestation, (or attestations, if more than one) to the deed, with

(*a*) D. [illegible] (*b*) Reg. [illegible] Registering Deeds, 74. (*c*) [illegible]

the descriptions of all the witnesses. [For more particulars respecting these Acts, the reader is referred to M. *Rigge's* Observations on the Statutes for registering Deeds.]

A lessee of land in the Bedford Level cannot object to an action by his landlord for a breach of covenant in not repairing, that the lease was void by the stat. of 15 *Car.* 2d. *c.* 17. for want of being registered; and such act enacting that "no lease &c. should be of force, but from the time it should be registered," not avoiding it as between the parties themselves, but only postponing its priority with respect to subsequent incumbrances registering their titles before it.

[illegible]

CHAPTER II.

SECTION I. *Of Agreements for Leases and the Remedies thereon.*

SECTION II. *Of Stamps required to Leases, and Agreements for Leases.*

SECTION I. *Of Agreements for Leases, and the Remedies thereon.*

WE have already seen that where an agreement for a lease contains words of present demise, and there are circumstances from which it may be collected that the tenant was meant to have an immediate legal interest in the term, such an agreement will amount to an actual lease: but we shall now shew on the other hand, that, although words of present demise are used, yet if it appears on the whole, that no legal interest was intended to pass, and that the agreement was only preparatory to a future lease to be made, the construction will be governed by the intention of the parties, and the contract will be held not to amount to more than merely an agreement for a lease, which equity will enforce.

Thus an instrument, setting forth the conditions of letting a farm, the term to be from year to year, and the lands to be entered upon at a period fixed, &c. and that a lease was to be made upon these conditions with all usual covenants, at the foot of which instrument the intended lessee wrote, "I agree to take the premises at the rent of, &c. subject to the covenants," was held to be an agreement for a lease, and not a present demise, there being not only a stipulation for a future lease, but time being given to prepare it, before the commencement of the term, and no present occupation by tenant contracted for (*a*).

A agreed to let to *B* a farm at a certain rent, "and at and under all usual and customary covenants, as between landlord and tenants where the premises are situate." A proportionate abatement was to be made out of the rent in respect of certain excepted premises. This was considered, under the circumstances, as being only an agreement for a lease (*b*).

An instrument on an agreement stamp reciting that *A.* in case he should be entitled to certain copyhold premises on the death of *B.* would immediately demise the same to *C.* declaring "that he did agree to demise and let the same," with a subsequent covenant to procure a licence to let from the lord, operates only as an agreement for a lease, and not as an absolute demise (*c*).

(*a*) 13 East R. 18. (*b*) 3 Taunt. 65. (*c*) 5 T.R. 163.

So, though words in an agreement, that "*A* shall hold and enjoy, &c." if not accompanied by restraining words, operate as words of present demise, yet if they be followed by others which shew that the parties intended that there should be a lease in future, they constitute merely an agreement for a lease, for the whole must depend, in this and similar cases, on the intention of the parties (*a*).

An agreement to lease at a certain rent, and that the lessor should not turn out the tenant so long as he paid the rent, and did not sell, &c. any article injurious to the lessor's business, either purports to be a lease for life, and would then be void as not being creatable by parol; or if it operate as a tenancy from year to year, it must necessarily be determinable by either party giving the regular notice to quit (*b*).

Where *A.* by agreement in writing, but not stamped, articled with *B.* to grant him a lease for twenty-one years, and *B.* entered and continued in possession eighteen years, but no lease was ever tendered by *A.* or demanded by *B.* the agreement was held to be a good defence in an action of ejectment brought by *A.* (*c*).—This case, however, seems inconsistent with the principles upon which other cases similarly circumstanced have been ruled, and has indeed been since doubted (*d*). The rule certainly does not extend to the case of a purchaser.

The trustee of a term, for the benefit of creditors, not having notice of an agreement for a lease made previous to the grant of the term, has been permitted to maintain ejectment against the tenant in possession, under the agreement, on the ground that the title of the tenant being only a doubtful equity, could not be set up against the legal title of the trustee (*e*).

An agreement to make a lease is a good lease in equity, and a confirmation of such lease by him in remainder is a good lease. *Hamilton v. Lady Caudress, H. Brown's Cas. in Parl. by Tomlins.*

An agreement for a lease from a dean and chapter, executed by the dean for himself and chapter, though signed by him only, shall bind the chapter notwithstanding. Deans and chapters, for fear of incurring the penalties of the restraining statutes, (of which hereafter) have been careful of preserving the same description in their leases since, as they did before those statutes; and possibly at the time of the old leases there might be barns or antient buildings, which, after such a length of time, must have been long since decayed and gone: the court therefore will not decree a specific performance of covenants for repairs, but will leave the party to their action at law for the non-performance: neither will they decree that a tenant in such case shall deliver up, at the expiration of his lease, the premises with such buildings upon them, when there is not the least proof that they were in being at the making of the lease (*f*).

If an agreement be by *A. B.* and *C.* to make a lease, and it is exe-

(*a*) 2 T. R. 739. (*b*) 2 East 165. (*c*) Cow. 457. (*f*) 1 Bro. R. 397.

cuted by *A.* it shall be decreed that *B* and *C* who were the sons of *A* shall execute it, though the agreement was by parol, for it was out of the statute (*a*).

With respect to parol agreements, it is an established rule, (*b*) that a parol agreement, *part performed*, is not within the provisions of the statute of frauds, but will be decreed to be executed by a court of equity; for where a part of the agreement is performed on one side, it is but common justice that it be carried into execution (*c*). Plea, therefore, of the statute of frauds to a bill for discovery of a parol agreement part performed, will not be allowed. So a parol agreement confessed or in part executed, [illegible] (*d*).

As to what acts amount to a part performance, the general rule is, (*e*) that the acts must be such as could be done with no other view or design than to perform the agreement, and not such as are merely introductory or ancillary to it. A tender of conveyances, therefore, is not part performance of an agreement; it must be something in actual execution of the contract, not merely towards the execution: thus, in a letter, "I will give 16,500*l*." answer, "I will not take less than 17,000*l*." answer returned, "I will give 17,000*l*." this is not an agreement executed in writing within the statute of Frauds (*f*).

Delivery of possession, however, or payment of money, is a part performance of an agreement not reduced into writing: (*g*) for delivery of possession by a person having possession to the person claiming under the agreement is a strong and marked circumstance (*h*).

Thus, upon an agreement for the surrender of a term where the lessor accepts the key, he shall be bound to accept of the surrender (*i*). – But though taking possession, or such other act in pursuance of an agreement, is sufficient evidence to have the agreement decreed, yet the circumstance of vendees ordering conveyances to be drawn in pursuance of a parol agreement, and going several times to see the premises, and a letter from the vendor, mentioning the agreement, but not the price, will not induce the court to decree a performance; nor will sending an appraiser to value the things agreed for (*k*).

So in another case, it is said that where a man on promise of a lease to be made to him, laid out money in improvements, he shall oblige the lessor afterwards to execute a lease, because it was executed on the part of the lessee (*l*).

Therefore, (*m*) where a lessor made a verbal promise to his lessee, to secure him in the possession of the premises during the lessee's life, in consequence of which promise the lessee made considerable alterations and improvements, and after the lessor's death, a *memorandum* of this promise was found among his papers, wherein he expressed a

(*a*) 1 Vern. 210. (*b*) 2 Bro. R. 566. 2 Atk. 100. 2 Str. 783. (*c*) 1 Vern. 297.
(*d*) [illegible] 441. (*e*) Ambl. 586. Bro. R. 412. (*f*) Lofft 786. (*g*) 3 [illegible]
(*h*) [illegible] Ves. [illegible] 561. (*i*) 3 Vern. 113. 1 Atk. 12. (*k*) 1 Eq. Ca. Abr. 20.
[illegible]

hope that the same would be observed, Lord *Thurlow* held that the *memorandum* took the case out of the statute of Frauds, and directed a lease to be made for ninety-nine years, determinable on his life.

But the bare entry of a steward in his lord's contract book with his tenants is not in evidence of itself that there is an agreement for a lease between the lord and one of the tenants, but must be supported by other proof (a).

Plaintiff, pursuant to a parol agreement for a building lease of Wild-house, had proceeded to pull down part and build part. Before any lease executed, the owner of the soil died. The defendants, his representatives, knew nothing of the matter, and insisted on the statute of Frauds. The Lord Keeper dismissed the bill, but on appeal to the Lords in Parliament, his dismission was reversed, and a building lease decreed (b).

If there be a parol agreement for a lease for twenty-one years, and lessee enter and enjoy for several (as for example, six) years, he shall not, upon a bill brought to compel him to execute a counterpart for the residue of the term, plead the statute (c).

For an agreement, though not in writing, being executed on one part and an enjoyment accordingly, equity will not avoid it, as it has been already carried into execution (d).

But (e), where a bill was by a tenant of a farm for a specific performance of a parol agreement for a new lease, stating improvements made at a considerable expence and continuance of possession after the expiration of the old lease, and payment of an encreased rent under the agreement, the plea of the statute of Frauds was ordered to stand for an answer, with liberty to except.

Bill for specific performance of a parol agreement for a lease within the statute of Frauds charging possession taken under the agreement and other acts of part performance; plea of the statute and answer not denying the acts alledged as a part performance, but stating, that being advised that he entered as tenant at will, he gave notice to quit: plea overruled (f).

Though the agreement be by parol, yet if it be agreed to be *reduced into writing*, and part of the agreement is executed, but the reducing of it into writing is prevented by fraud, it may be good (g).

Therefore, an agreement to assign a term and goods, and that it should be put in writing, was decreed to be executed, it being part of the agreement, that it should be put in writing, and part of the money having been paid (h).

So, if a lease by *A* to *B* is agreed by parol, and drawn and ingrossed by the counsel of *B* and afterwards executed by *A* it shall not be avoided by *B* (i).

(a) 1 Atk. 499. (b) 2 Vern. 456. 1 Eq. Ca. Abr. 21. (c) 2 Str. 783. (d) Prec. Ch. 519. (e) 3 Ves. jun. 378. (f) 4 Ves. jun. 91. (g) 1 Eq. Ca. Abr. 19. (h) 2 Ch. Ca. 135, 6. 1 Vern. 151. (i) Ib. 221, 2.

Bills were to have an execution of parol agreements touching leases of houses, setting forth that in confidence of these agreements, the plaintiffs had expended great sums about the premises, and it was alledged, that it was agreed, that the agreements should be reduced into writing: the defendant pleaded the statute of Frauds. Lord *King* said, that the difficulty was, that the act makes void the estate, but does not say that the agreement itself shall be void; and therefore, he thought, that if that subsisted so as to entitle the party to damages at law, it might be decreed in equity, and directed that point to be tried, but as to the improvements made, his Lordship was clearly of opinion that for such as were of use and necessity, and not merely for humour and fancy, the party was entitled to have satisfaction (*a*).

Lease was not decreed upon expenditure in repairs and improvements under an alledged agreement proved by one witness, the answer containing a positive denial of the agreement, which denial was also confirmed by circumstances. No relief upon general equity from expenditure under the observation of the landlord by a tenant, but not under any specific engagement or encouragement (*b*).

Where there is an agreement by parol, and part of it executed, equity will decree specific execution of the whole, (*c*) but where there is an agreement by writing executed, evidence cannot supply any defect in that agreement, which was intended to be part of that agreement, but was not inserted in it: [unless, as is conceived, in case of fraud.]

Yet, if there is an agreement in writing for taking a house at 32*l.* the owner to put it in repair, and afterwards a parol agreement for 40*l.* the owner having rebuilt with the tenant's consent, and the lessee brings a bill for specific performance of the written agreement, parol evidence may be given of the new agreement to rebut the equity prayed (*d*).

So (*e*) if a bill is brought to carry into execution an agreement for the lease of a house, the defendant, the lessor, shall be admitted to parol proof that the plaintiff, who wrote the agreement, omitted to make the rent (which was reduced to 9*l.* instead of 14*l.* the former rent,) payable, clear of all taxes.

Sealing is not necessary in order to bring an agreement out of the statute of Frauds (*f*).

A *letter* takes a parol agreement out of the statute: but wherever a letter is relied on as evidence of an agreement, it must be stamped before it can be read, it must also furnish the terms of the agreement, or must at least refer to some written agreement in which the terms are set forth (*g*).

(*a*) 1 Eq. Ca. Abr. 20 (*b*) 12 Ves. jun. 78 (*c*) Bunb. 65 9 Mod. 6. (*d*) 2 Vern. 229
(*e*) 3 Atk. 388. (*f*) Prec. Ch. 17. (*g*) 2 Bro. R. 32 1 Str. 426 1 Atk. 12.

There have been cases where a letter written to a man's own agent, and setting forth the terms of an agreement as concluded by him, has been deemed to be a signing within the statute, and agreeable to the provision of it (*a*).

Therefore, (*b*) where there was a complete agreement in writing, and a person who is a party, and knows the contents, subscribes it as a witness only, he is bound by it, for it is a signing within the statute of Frauds, which was passed in order to prevent any thing depending either on the mistake or the perjury of witnesses.

If there be an agreement for a lease in the county of *N.* where the lessor usually repairs, at 30*l.* *per ann.* without saying who shall repair, if it appear that the land is of greater value, it shall be decreed, that the lessee shall take a lease and do the repairs, and pay 30*l.* *per ann.* without deduction, except for taxes by parliament (*c*).

Articles of agreement may be rectified by the minutes (*d*).

But though a formal mistake in a deed may be rectified by articles of which it purports to be an execution, essential additions cannot be made to a conveyance from articles of which it does not purport to be an execution; nor can the transaction be rescinded by the court (*e*).

The court will not relieve against a contract in writing, unless there is express proof of the mistake of the intention of the parties (*f*).

Effect of an indefinite representation by a vendor, as that a leasehold estate was nearly equal to freehold, being renewable upon a single fine, may, connected with certain circumstances, be fraudulent, and form a ground for rescinding the contract (*g*).

It has been held that if a bond is given with a penalty, a specific performance shall not be decreed; for the party has relied upon the penalty (*h*).

But this may well be doubted as a general proposition: (*i*) for it is clear that a bill lies for a specific performance though a remedy be at law, for the remedy by specific performance is superior in many cases to that of damages; and a penalty has never been held to release parties from their agreement, for though incurred they must perform it notwithstanding (*k*).

Thus where a proviso was in articles for the purchase of an estate, that if either party should break the agreement he should pay 100*l.* to the other, and the defendant on being offered two years' purchase more accepted it notwithstanding that agreement; Lord *Hardwicke* decreed a specific performance (*l*).

The constant doctrine of the court is, that it is in their discretion whether they will decree a specific performance, or leave the plaintiff to his remedy at law (*m*).

(*a*) 3 Atk 503. (*b*) Ibid. (*c*) 2 Vern 231. (*d*) 1 Ves jun 456. (*e*) 3 Ves jun 184. (*f*) 3 Ves jun 317. (*g*) 14 Ves jun 144. (*h*) Ch Ca 128. (*i*) 1 Ves jun 542. (*k*) 2 Atk 371. (*l*) Ibid. (*m*) Ibid. 389.

Specific performance of an agreement to build may be decreed if sufficiently certain: but a general covenant to lay out a certain sum in a building of a certain value cannot be so executed (*a*).

A. agrees for the lease of certain lands for three lives; the lease is prepared according to the agreement, except the insertion of a clause to restrain the tenant from alienation without the consent of the landlord: this clause being no part of the agreement, the landlord is bound to execute a lease without it (*b*).

On a covenant to build, the lessors are entitled to come into a court of equity for a specific performance, but not on a covenant to repair (*c*).

Specific performance may be decreed against one become a lunatic since the agreement, if the legal estate is in trustees (*d*).

In bills for specific performance, the court never gives relief where the act is impossible to be done, but leaves the party to his remedy at law (*e*).

If an agreement be otherwise than certain, fair, and just in all its parts, the court will not decree a specific performance (*f*).

Specific performance will not be decreed of an agreement to renew a lease in consideration of money previously laid out by the tenant; such promise is *nudum pactum*, nor will the case be varied by money having been expended by him after such promise.—But if previous to such promise the tenant had signified his intention to lay out money, and on that consideration the promise had been made, a specific performance would be decreed (*g*).

Specific performance of articles to grant a lease to the plaintiff decreed, though he had contracted to under let, contrary to those articles (*h*).

But the court will not decree a specific performance of an agreement to grant a lease, if under a clause for re-entry, the lease, when granted, would be at an end by the tenant's acts, except on the ground of there having been a waiver of the forfeiture, and upon an undertaking to give possession when required by the court, and to pay the rent due (*i*).

B treats with *A* for a piece of land, intending to build a mill, to which the consent of a corporation is necessary, but *A* refuses to treat on condition, *B* fails in obtaining consent. this failure in his speculation is no defence against a bill for specific performance (*k*).

A plea to a bill for a specific performance of an agreement for a lease to the plaintiff, and for an injunction against an ejectment, that the defendant had since the filing of the bill, taken the benefit of an insolvent act, was over-ruled (*l*).

So the bankruptcy of a person who has agreed to purchase does not discharge the contract. It must be a very strong case, however, that

(*a*) 3 Ves. jun. 184. (*b*) 1 Bro. C. in Parl. 334. (*c*) 3 Atk. 512. 3 Bro. R. 165.
(*d*) 1 Ves. jun. 82. (*e*) 1 Atk. 573. (*f*) 3 Atk. 386.
(*g*) 2 Br. Ch. C. 140. 1 Eq. Ca. Abr. 18. (*h*) 3 Ves. jun. 59.
(*i*) 1 Ves. & Bea. 68. (*k*) 1 Bro. 567. (*l*) 16 Ves. jun. 466.

will induce the court to carry into execution an agreement between landlord and tenant, the estate not being executed at law, where the person, who is to become the tenant, has become a bankrupt (*a*)

So, the court would not execute an agreement to grant a lease to a man who had committed felony (*b*)

An agreement may be decreed to be delivered up on the ground of surprise, neither party understanding the effect of it; as where there was an agreement for a lease, with a covenant for perpetual renewal, at a fixed rent of premises held under a church lease, renewable upon fines, continually increasing A single lease for 21 years was refused no terms of agreement for such an interest appearing, and under the circumstances permission to try the effect of it at law was also denied (*c*).

Bill for specific performance of an agreement to grant a lease to the plaintiff would, on evidence of his fraud, misrepresentation, and insolvency, have been dismissed with costs, if not compromised (*d*).

A lessee's bill for the specific performance of an agreement was dismissed, his interest being described as 50 years, the residue of a term free from incumbrances, but being, in fact, a few years only of an old term, and a reversionary term from another lessor, and old incumbrances not shewn (*e*).

A being in insolvent circumstances suffers another person to become the apparent owner of the farm (though under a secret trust for him,) *A*. shall not have against the landlord a specific execution of an agreement made by him with the trustee, the landlord supposing the trustee to have been the rightful owner and confiding in his honesty. 1 Sche. Lef 123

So, specific performance was not decreed where there was concealment on the part of the vendor (*f*)

Even where one party to an agreement trifles or shews backwardness in performing his part of it, (*g*) equity will not decree a specific performance in his favour, especially if the circumstances and situation of the other party are materially altered in the mean time

But the refusal of a tenant to execute a lease when tendered, declaring himself satisfied with the agreement, cannot be considered as repudiating the agreement, and is not a sufficient ground for refusing a specific performance (*h*)

Remedies at Law—If either of the parties to an agreement for a lease refuse to perform the stipulations which it contains, besides the relief which a bill in equity for a specific performance may afford him, the party injured has one of two remedies at common law, namely, an action of debt, or covenant if the agreement be by deed, or an action

(*a*) 3 Ves jun 255 (*b*) Ibid 167 (*c*) 16 Ves jun 72 (*d*) Ibid 163.
(*e*) 11 Ves jun 337 (*f*) 1 Bro 440 (*g*) 1 Bro. Cas. in Parl 126.
(*h*) 1 Ves jun. & Bea 73.

of debt, or special *assumpsit*, if it be either by writing without deed, or by parol, provided the contract be to be performed within a year from the making thereof (a).

Covenant.—A covenant is the agreement or consent of two or more by deed in writing, sealed and delivered, whereby either or one of the parties doth promise to the other, that something is done already, or shall be done afterwards. He that makes the covenant is called the covenantor, and he to whom it is made, the covenantee (b).

An action of covenant lies when a man covenants with another by deed to do something and does it not, and it lies upon a covenant in any deed, whether indented or poll. But covenant does not lie upon an agreement without deed; but an action upon the case, except in London, where covenant lies without deed, by custom (c).

In covenant all is recoverable in damages, and those will be what the party can prove that he has actually sustained, (d) therefore in covenant it is sufficient to assign the breach in the words of the covenant.

Assumpsit.—If the agreement be by writing without deed or by parol, damages for the breach of it may be recovered in an action on the case upon a special *assumpsit*.

By the statute of Frauds (e), no action shall be brought to charge, &c. upon any contract, or sale of lands or tenements, or any interest in or concerning them, or upon any agreement that is not to be performed within the space of one year from the making thereof, unless the agreement, or some *memorandum* or note thereof, be in writing, and signed by the party to be charged therewith, or by some other person by him thereunto lawfully authorized.

One contracts with the owner of a close for the purchase of a growing crop of grass there, for the purpose of being mown and made into hay by the vendee: this is a contract of sale of an interest in or concerning land, within the 4th section of the statute of Frauds, 29th of *Car.* 2. c. 3. (f).

If a party has entered into a parol agreement for a lease, and a draft of it is prepared (g), though the agreement is void under the statute of Frauds, yet an indorsement by the party, referring to the draft, admitting the agreement is sufficient within the statute.

An action may be brought in consideration that the plaintiff will make a lease according to a former agreement (h), for the agreement is not executed till the lease is made.

So if an agreement be to assign a term of years, as well as where it is for an interest created *de novo* (i).

But in an action upon an agreement to deliver possession for certain considerations subject to a forfeiture on failure by either party, the

(a) 29 C. 2. c. 3.
(b) Shep. Touch. 160.
(c) Com. Dig. tit. Covenant, (A. 1.)
(d) Bull. N. P. 161.
(e) 29 C. 2. c. 3.
(f) 5 East, 653.
(g) 5 Cop n. [illegible]
(h) 1 Rol. 12. l. 15.
(i) 1 Vent. 361.

person who was to deliver possession cannot sue for the forfeiture, without shewing in his declaration a possessory title in himself (a).

Action for money had and received on the common counts (b). Defendant was possessed of a lease for years, which he sold to plaintiff for sixteen guineas, and at the time of the sale observed that it was a good lease for seven years; it turned out afterwards that the lessor was tenant for life only and had no right to make a lease for a longer term than his own life; in consequence of which the plaintiff was turned out of possession in two years after the assignment of the lease had taken place, the lessor having died previously to the bargain between the plaintiff and the defendant. The plaintiff brought this action, therefore, to recover the money paid for the lease, as paid on a consideration which had failed. On *Leycester* objecting to plaintiff recovering on this declaration, which contained only the common counts, *Lawrence* J. referred to the case of *Crips* v. *Reade*, 6 T. R. 606. tried before him at *Oxford*, in which a lease had been sold by one as administrator, whose letters of administration were afterwards repealed, and there he permitted the plaintiff to recover on a similar declaration, and the court of King's Bench confirmed his opinion. Verdict for the plaintiff.

But a contractor for the purchase of an estate to which the title proves (without collusion) defective, is not entitled to any satisfaction for the loss of his bargain (c): for such contracts are merely on condition frequently expressed, but always implied that the vendor has a good title; if he has not, the return of the deposit, with interest and costs, is all that can be expected; the purchaser cannot be intitled to any damages for the fancied goodness of the bargain which he supposes he has lost.

An agreement, though not under seal, may be declared on specially, in which case it may be said to bind the parties by its own force: or the plaintiff may, in some instances, declare generally, and give the written contract in evidence (d).

Where money has been paid under an agreement, which has not been performed, it may be recovered in an action for money had and received: and though the agreement be in writing, the party need not declare specially (e).

Thus (f) *A.* having sold certain leasehold premises to *B.* assigned them by indenture containing a proviso that *B.* should not assign over until the whole of the purchase money should have been paid, and *B.* and *C.* covenanted for themselves, their executors, administrators, and assigns, for the payment of the money. The premises having been taken in execution for a debt of *B.* who had not paid the purchase-money, were sold by the sheriff to *D.* who paid down the deposit, and

(a) Doug. 620.

(b) Matthews v. Hollings, Cor. Lawrence, J. at Shrewsbury, Oct. [illegible] Cir. MSS.

(c) 2 Bl. R. 1078.

(d) 6 T. R. 319.

(e) 2 Esp. R. 637.

(f) 3 Bos. & Pul. 181.

agreed to complete the purchase on having a good title held, that the non-payment of the purchase-money by *B* was a sufficient objection to the title, and that *D.* might recover back his deposit in an action for money had and received

A. (*a*) agreed with *B.* to let him land rent-free, on condition that *A.* should have a moiety of the crops; while the crop was on the ground it was appraised for both parties; *A* declared in *indebitatus assumpsit* for a moiety of the crop sold to *B.* without stating the special agreement: and it was held that he might well do so, as the special agreement was executed by the appraisement, and the action arose out of something collateral to it *Semb* such an agreement need not be in writing, under the statute of Frauds.

A (*b*) agreed in consideration of 10*l* to let a house to *B* which *A* was to repair and execute a lease of within ten days; but *B.* was to have immediate possession, and in consideration of the aforesaid, was to execute a counterpart and pay the rent. *B* took possession and paid the 10*l.* immediately; but *A.* neglected to execute the lease and make the repairs beyond the period of the 10 days, notwithstanding which *B.* still continued in possession, held that *B.* could not by quitting the house for the default of *A.* rescind the contract and recover back the 10*l*, in an action for money had and received, but could only declare for a breach of the special contract.

A (*c*) agreed to under-let his house to *B.* the latter paying for the furniture at an appraisement, *A* at the time that he quitted the house, was in arrear for rent to his landlord: held therefore that *B* was excused from the performance of the agreement, for the furniture would be liable to be distrained for the rent due by *A.*

In an action (*d*) of *assumpsit* for non-performance of a contract for the sale of a house with counts to recover back the deposit, the plaintiff having in his first count alledged that the defendant who was to make a good title, had delivered an abstract which was "insufficient, defective, and objectionable," the court obliged the plaintiff to give a particular of all objections to the abstract arising upon matters of fact, for the party ought to specify every matter of fact which he meant to rely upon at the trial

A case (*e*) was sent to a jury by way of inquiry of damages by the court of *Chancery*, where it appeared that the parties who applied to the court for a specific performance of an agreement, had by their committee and surveyor, viewed without complaint, the progress of the party in repairing premises which they at last insisted on being rebuilt

A purchaser discovering an incumbrance, may retain so much for it as remains in his hands (*f*).

(*a*) 1 Bos & Pul 367. (*b*) 5 East, 55[illegible] (*c*) 3 Bos & Pul 172.
(*d*) Ibid 246 (*e*) 3 Atk. 517 (*f*) 1 Ves. 83.

SECTION II. *Of the Stamps required to Leases and Agreements, &c.*

A LEASE must be stamped *as a lease* by deed, though it be not by deed; for though not by deed, it falls within the words of the act that requires a stamp to leases, enumerated among other specialties. The statute 23 *G* 3. *c* 58 which imposes a stamp duty on "indentures, leases, and other deeds," applies to every instrument that operates as a lease, whether it be by deed or not; for the imposition of a duty is a mere matter of positive institution, and as a lease, by whatever means constituted, falls within the words, there is nothing in the nature of the thing to take it out of them (*a*)

A deed is good though executed before it be stamped, provided that when it is offered in evidence it be stamped, and with the proper stamp appropriated to the particular instrument (*b*) —The author remembers, however, Lord *Eldon*, when Chief Justice of the *Common Pleas*, to have spoken of an objection having been taken to an agreement being received in evidence, not being stamped, whereupon it was stamped during the trial, and then offered in evidence; but it was again objected to, as not being stamped at the time the cause of action arose.

Whether or not the instrument were valid, by the revenue being satisfied in point of amount of duty, though the particular stamp or stamps were not used, was a point on which the court had, at different times, held contradictory opinions. The most recent determinations, however, went to invalidate any instrument that had not been stamped with the peculiar stamp appropriated to it

Thus it was holden, that articles of agreement under seal could not be given in evidence unless stamped with a deed stamp, although the agreement stamp was of the same value but differently formed: Lord *Kenyon* observing, that it was absolutely necessary that the distinction of the several stamps should be preserved in courts of justice, as long as that distinction is kept up by the legislature, and that it had often proved the means of detecting forgeries, by comparing the stamp on forged instruments with those in use at the time (*c*)

On the same principle it was held (*d*), that a promissory note, written upon a stamp of greater value than the proper stamp required, could not be given in evidence, though the stamps were applicable to the same kind of instrument. In this case also Lord *Kenyon* said, However much it were to be wished that an *ad valorem* stamp would suffice in such cases, yet till the legislature so declare it, no other than the particular stamp, appropriated by the law to the particular instrument, can be

(*a*) 1 T R 737. 3 Burr 1763 (*b*) 1 Str 624. 2 Str 716.
(*c*) 6 T R 319 (*d*) 1 East's R 57

deemed sufficient; for the words of the stamp acts were express, and could admit of no other interpretation.

His Lordship's suggestion of the propriety of an *ad valorem* stamp has not escaped the attention of the legislature, for by stat. 43 *G.* 3. *c.* 127. which recites that, Whereas it is expedient to prevent the multiplication of stamps upon pieces of vellum, parchment, or paper, or other instruments, matters, or things, on which several rates are by several acts of parliament imposed, it is enacted that it shall be lawful for the commissioners for managing the said duties, instead of the distinct stamps directed to be provided to denote the several duties, to cause one new stamp to be provided to denote the said several rates and duties from time to time as they shall think needful, and to renew or alter the same as occasion shall require. *s.* 1.

And instruments not having the stamp of the proper denomination and value, though of equal or greater value, may be stamped without payment of the 5*l.* penalty imposed by the 37 *G.* 3. *c.* 136.—*s.* 5.

And it is further enacted, That every instrument, although stamped with any stamp of greater value than that required by law, shall be valid, provided such stamp be of the denomination required for such instrument. *s.* 6.

Though a parol lease for three years is good, yet if a man, through caution, will reduce it into writing, he must pay for the stamp, otherwise the court are inhibited from receiving it in evidence (*a*).

But where a party enters and continues in possession of premises for any long space of time, as for eighteen years, under articles of agreement for a lease, which were not stamped, and no lease ever tendered or demanded, the agreement was held to be a good defence against an ejectment, for though it is in law a lease, and therefore ought to be stamped, it would be set up in equity as an agreement. *tamen quære* the law of this adjudication (*b*)?

Where an instrument contains a written contract of demise in its general terms, with a several operation in respect to the different tenants who sign it for different estates, at the different rents set opposite their signatures, and one stamp only appears upon the paper, it is matter of evidence to which contract such stamp applies, and the circumstance of juxta-position of the stamp to the defendant's signature, which stood untouched, while the other names appeared to be cancelled, together with the date of the stamp office receipt for the stamp and penalty, which shewed that it had been affixed recently before the trial; and there being no evidence of a dispute with any other tenant, which could make the stamp necessary for another purpose, are evidence that it was intended to be applied to the contract with the defendant (*c*).

By the stamp act, 48 *G.* 3. *c.* 149. every lease for a term not exceed-

(*a*) Bull. N. P. 269. (*b*) Cowp. 174. (*c*) 13 East. 241.

ing twenty-one years, at a yearly rent of 10*l* or less, and without fine, is liable to a duty of 1*l*, and every lease for a life or lives, or for a term of years, determinable with a life or lives, or for a term absolute, not exceeding forty years, made in consideration of a fine not exceeding 20*l.* if the rent shall not exceed 40*s.* is liable to a duty of 1*l*, and if the rent shall exceed 40*s.* to a duty of 1*l* 10*s.* Counterparts of leases, on which a duty of 1*l* is imposed, are subject to the same duty, and of other leases, to a duty of 1*l.* 10*s* Assignments on the sale of any lease, or any interest therein, are made liable to an *ad valorem* duty, and other assignments to a duty of 1*l.* 10*s.*

By the same act every schedule, inventory, or catalogue of any lands, furniture, fixtures, or effects, or containing the terms and conditions of any lease, or regulations for the cultivation or management of any farm, lands, or other property leased, or agreed to be leased, or containing any other matter of contract or stipulation, which shall be referred to by, and be intended to be used as part of, any agreement, lease, &c. but which shall be separate and distinct therefrom, is charged with a duty of 1*l* and a further duty of 1*l.* for every 1080 words, above the first 1080 words.

CHAPTER III.

Of the Parties to a Lease, or hereby by whom a Lease may be made.

Section I. *Of the general Rule, and hereof of Leases by Tenants in Fee Simple.*

WITH respect to the persons who are capable, by the common law, of making leases, it may be laid down, that all those who are capable of alienating their property, or of entering into contracts respecting it, may make leases, which will endure as long as their interest in the thing leased, but no longer (*a*).

As an estate in fee simple is the largest estate which a man can have in lands, giving him a full dominion over property, with an absolute power of alienation, it necessarily includes the smaller power of granting leases, which, consequently, he may do without limitation or restraint.

Section II. *Of Leases by Tenants in Tail.*

An estate in fee tail, though an estate of inheritance, is of a limited nature, being a gift to a man and the heirs of his body, who are prohibited from alienation, except by particular modes prescribed by law.

If tenant in tail after the statute *de donis* had made a lease for years and died, the lease was not absolutely determined by his death, but the issue in tail was at liberty either to affirm or avoid it, as he thought fit.

Acceptance by tenant in tail of the rent or fealty, or bringing an action for the recovery thereof, or an action of waste, were each of them accounted as a confirmation of the lease, because these plainly manifested his intent to continue the lessee in possession upon the terms of his lease, and by consequence such issue could never afterwards avoid it during his own life (*c*).

If a tenant in tail had leased to *A* for twenty years, and the lessee make a lease to *B* for ten years, and then the tenant in tail die, [illegible] the issue accepts the rent of *B* [illegible] of the lease, because *B* was under no [illegible] to pay [illegible] to him, [illegible] [illegible] tenant in tail [illegible] [illegible] acceptance thereof [illegible] [illegible] mere stranger, and, by consequence, the issue in tail may enter and avoid the lease: but if the issue had accepted the rent, then [illegible] had amounted to a confirmation of the lease made to *A.* and by consequence he could not [illegible] the lease to *B.* which was derived thereout (*a*).

But if *A.* had assigned five acres of the land in lease to *B.* for the residue of twenty years, and the issue in tail had accepted the rent from *B.* this would amount to a confirmation of the entire lease to *A.* because the rent issuing out of the whole and out of every part of the land, *B.* as to the five acres, succeeded in the place of *A.* by having his whole interest [illegible]; and then the issue in tail, by acceptance of the rent from one whole part, as to him, was equally chargeable with the whole rent, having given his consent that the whole estate chargeable [illegible], though he chose to take his rent out of part only, for otherwise he would do injustice to *A.* [illegible] he would be liable to make recompence to *B.* for the overplus of the rent, and yet have no recompence himself, if the issue might defeat the residue of the lease remaining in his hands (*b*).

If a tenant in tail makes a lease for ten years, to begin ten years hence, and dies, and the issue within the ten years enters and makes a feoffment in fee, the feoffee, at the end of the ten years, shall have election either to affirm and make good such lease, or to avoid it, for upon the death of tenant in tail, the possession [illegible] and none had a right to enter but the issue in tail, for [illegible] lease [illegible] was not yet come, [illegible] his primary right was, in respect of [illegible], [illegible] in tail, [illegible] at that time to any other purpose, [illegible] in respect of the [illegible] to him [illegible] he makes a feoffment in fee to a stranger, [illegible] just in the [illegible] in tail [illegible] to [illegible], and [illegible] power [illegible] to [illegible] by [illegible] acceptance of rent [illegible].

If tenant in tail makes a lease for life, [illegible] out of the [illegible], and afterwards [illegible] grantor becomes tenant in tail again, [illegible] defeated, yet, because the grantor [illegible] clothed with a defeasible fee simple, the rent-charge remains good against him, but not against his issue (*c*).

A man seized in fee made a lease for ninety-nine years, if three per-

(*a*) [illegible] (*b*) [illegible] (*c*) [illegible]

[illegible] lo[illegible], then he settled the reversion upon himself in tail, with power [illegible] for [illegible]-one years, and then he made such a [illegible], who [illegible] the issue in tail, levied a fine and sold [illegible] determined, and the court thought that the cognizee [illegible] the [illegible] lease, because it never was in the [illegible] or his issue to avoid it, they having con[illegible] before this second lease was to commence, for [illegible] to commence *in præsenti*, and convey away [illegible], the cognizee must hold it charged with such lease; [illegible] to commence *in futuro*, it is otherwise, because it cannot be avoided before the commencement. Therefore, if tenant in tail makes a voidable lease for years or life, and dies, and the issue, before entry on the lessee, levies a fine to a stranger, the cognizee shall not avoid the lease, because such lease being only voidable by entry, when the issue before entry conveys over the land by fine, the power of entry, which was the only means of avoiding such lease, is by the fine destroyed and gone; for a right of entry cannot be transferred to a stranger any more than a right of action. So, if the tenant in tail himself after such lease, had levied a fine to a stranger, or even to the reversioner, and died, yet they could not avoid the lease ever after, because, if they could, it must be by reason of the right of entry transferred by the fine, which would have come to the issue if no such fine had been levied; and the law absolutely condemns all alienations of right only, whether it be right of entry or of action, and consequently in these cases, by such alienation, the lease is become absolute and unavoidable (*a*).

If tenant in tail makes a lease for thirty or forty years, rendering rent, and dies with issue, his wife *privement enceint*, with a son, and the donor enters, and as to himself avoids the lease, then the son is born, and the lessee re-enters; the son at full age may either affirm or avoid such lease as he thinks fit; for the lease was not absolutely determined or avoided, more than the estate tail itself, out of which it was derived, but only *usque dum quod*, and subject to be set up again upon the birth of the issue, which revived the estate-tail. But if such lease were made by the tenant in tail before marriage rendering rent, and then he married and died, leaving his wife *privement enceint*, and the donor enters, and as to himself avoids the lease, yet if the wife be afterwards endowed, the lease is revived as against her, because her estate is *quodam modo*, a continuance of the estate-tail of the husband, and therefore, revives all charges made by him before the marriage; but if the wife be after delivered of a son, and dies, now the issue may again avoid that lease or affirm it, as he thinks fit; or if such lease were made after marriage, and the wife being endowed thereof, avoids that lease, yet after her death the issue in tail may revive it, for in all these cases the avoidance

(*a*) Sec. Abr. Tit. "Leases," (D) 3 Salk. 336. 4 Mod. 1.

of such leases being only by those who had a temporary estate or interest in the land, it cannot bind those who succeeded to the inheritance thereof, but that they may, if they think fit, re-establish and set up such lease again, which, as to them, was at first only voidable, and not absolutely void. And herein a lease at common law by the tenant in tail differs from rent granted by such tenant which is void by the death of the grantor; whereas the lease is only voidable by the issue in tail, whose acceptance of rent amounts to a confirmation (a).

Power to lease by the enabling statute. — Thus, by the common-law, tenant in tail could make no leases which should bind his issue in tail, or the reversioner; to remedy which, the statute 32 *Hen.* 8. c. 28. commonly called *The Enabling Statute* (b), was passed.

By this statute, any person whatsoever, of full age, that hath any estate of inheritance in fee tail in his own right, of any lands, tenements, or hereditaments, may, at this day, without fine or recovery, make leases of such lands for lives or years, and such leases shall be good, so as these conditions following be observed:

1. Such lease must be by indenture, and not by deed-poll or by parol.

2. It must be made to begin from the day of the making thereof, or from the making thereof; therefore a lease made to begin from *Michaelmas*, which shall be three years after, for twenty-one years, or a lease made to begin after the death of the tenant in tail, for twenty one years, is not good. But a lease made for twenty years, to begin at *Michaelmas* next, it seems is a good lease [illegible]

3. If there be an old lease in being, of the land, the same must be expired, surrendered, or ended within a year of the time of the making of the new lease; and this surrender must be absolute and not conditional; also, it must be real, and not illusory, or in shew only. Therefore,

4. There must not be a double or concurrent lease in being at one time; as if a lease for years be made according to the statute, he in reversion cannot afterwards expulse the lessee, and make a lease for life or lives, or another lease for years according to the statute, nor *e converso*.

But if a lease for years be made to one, and afterwards a lease for life is made to another, and a letter of attorney is made to give livery of seisin upon the lease for life, and before the livery made the first lease is surrendered, in this case, the second lease is good.

5. These leases must not exceed three lives, or twenty-one years from the time of making them; for the words of the statute are to make a lease for three lives, *or* twenty one years, so that either the one or the other may be made, but not both. Therefore, if tenant in tail make a lease for twenty-two, or for forty years, or for four lives, this

(a) Cruise's Dig. tit. II. c. 2. s. 8. Bro. Abr. tit. "Grant" 1[illegible]. 2 Ld. Raym. 7[illegible].
(b) 32 H. 8. c. 28.

lease is void, and that not only for the overplus of time more than three lives, or twenty-one years, but for the time of three lives or twenty-one years also; and it hath been resolved, that if tenant in tail make a lease for ninety-nine years, determinable upon three lives, this is not a good lease. But if a lease be made by a tenant in tail for a less time, as for two lives, or for twenty years, this is a good lease. If a lease be made for four lives, and it happens that one of the [illegible] die before the tenant in tail dies, yet this [illegible] good, but [illegible] void be notwithstanding.

6. [illegible] leases [illegible] of [illegible], tithes, or hereditaments, ma[illegible] [illegible], whereto there need [illegible] be let, and whereout a rent by law may be reserved and received. Therefore, if a tenant in tail make a lease of such things as lie in grant, as an advowson, [illegible], [illegible], markets, or the like, out of which a rent cannot be reserved, especially if it be [illegible], the lease is void, [illegible] the thing [illegible] been [illegible] by law. A grant of rent-charge, therefore, out of such things is void; and if a tenant in tail make a lease for three lives of a portion of tithes rendering rent, this lease is unquestionably void, [illegible] it [illegible] be a lease of twenty-one years.—But now by the statute 5 Geo. [illegible] 17, a lease of tithes, or other incorporeal hereditaments, may be granted by any bishop, or [illegible] such ecclesiastical or other [illegible] corporation, and the same [illegible] recover [illegible] action of debt, which [illegible] have brought at common law.

7. [illegible] usually let [illegible] occupied [illegible] by the space of twenty years [illegible] had been let for eleven years, [illegible] twenty years before the [illegible] by copy [illegible] But [illegible] of an estate [illegible] charity [illegible], this will not serve to [illegible]

8. [illegible] lease [illegible] rever-sion [illegible] rent, [illegible] hath been [illegible] twenty [illegible] be [illegible] void. So, [illegible]

[illegible] acre which hath not been accustomably let, reserving the usual yearly rent, and so much more [illegible] the value of the [illegible], this is not a good lease by the statute. So, if the tenant in tail of two manors, the one at twenty pounds rent, the other at ten pounds rent, make a lease of both these [illegible] together, at thirty pounds rent, this is not a good lease within the statute. But if besides the annual rent, there have been [illegible] other things not annual, as heriots, fines or other profit, upon the death of the farmer, or profit out of another's soil, as [illegible] for a colt, &c. if upon the new lease the yearly rent be reserved, [illegible] these collateral reservations be omitted, yet these leases are good. So, [illegible] if there be more rent reserved upon the new lease than the rent that hath been anciently paid, the lease is good notwithstanding. So, [illegible] tenant in tail of land, let a part of it that hath been accustomably let, and reserve the rent *pro rata*, or more, this is good, for that is in substance the accustomable rent. Also, if two coparceners be tenants in tail of twenty acres, every one of equal value, and accustomably letten, and they make partition so as each have ten acres, they may make leases of their several parts of each of them, reserving [illegible] of the accustomable rent. If the accustomable rent had been payable at four days or feasts of the year, yet if it be reserved yearly, [illegible] it is sufficient, for the words of the statute are, to be reserved yearly. On a question, Whether the reservation of the [illegible] [illegible] tenant in tail, [illegible] than the statute, [illegible]

9. Such leases must not be made without impeachment of waste. Therefore, if a lease be made for life, the remainder for life, [illegible] this is not warranted by the statute, because it is dispunishable of waste. But, if a lease be made [illegible] during three lives, this is good, for the occupant, if any happen, [illegible] be punished for waste. [illegible] makes a lease for years, reserving the running of a colt, rendering rent, a new lease, rendering the same rent, without reserving the running of a colt, adjudged good, because [illegible] it [illegible] reservation, nor exception. But if a lease be of a manor, except the woods, rendering rent, and after the expiration of it, there is a new lease rendering the same rent without [illegible] exception, the second lease is bad [illegible].

By this statute, then, a tenant in tail is enabled to grant such leases as shall bind his issue in tail, though not those in remainder or reversion.

If tenant in tail make a lease for a term of [illegible] years, and the lessee assign over to another, but before such assignment tenant in tail male dies without issue male, no action of covenant upon the lease can be maintained against the representatives of the grantor by such assignee,

(*q*) Co. Lit. [illegible] [illegible] Mo. [illegible] [illegible]

the lease being void at the time of the assignment, and no interest passing under it (a).

Tenant in tail male, had issue two sons by divers venters, and died, the eldest son entered and made a lease for twenty-one years, reserving rent generally to him and his heirs and assigns, and died without issue, leaving two sisters his heirs at law; and if by this reservation, the rent belonged to the second brother, to whom the reversion descended, as heir male of the body of the father, was the question; for if not, then the lease could not bind him within 32 *H.* 8. c. 28. and it was adjudged to be a good lease, and that the rent should go along with the reversion; for the words of the statute are, that the rent shall be reserved to the lessor his heirs, or "to those to whom the lands would go if no such lease had been made," and here the intent was, that the rent should go along with the reversion, and so it may here, for rent naturally follows the reversion, and the second brother is heir to the intail and reversion, though not to the lessor (b).

Tenant in tail makes a lease for twenty years, rendering the usual rent, to begin from *Michaelmas* next ensuing; and this seems a good lease, though it do not begin from the making of the lease, according to the proviso 32 *H.* 8. c. 28. for the intent of the statute was only that the lease should not exceed the number of twenty-one years from the making, which this lease did not; and in the margent, a case is of *Thompson* and *Trafford*, *Pasch.* 8 [illegible] 35 *Eliz.* in *B. R.* cited to be adjudged, *per totam curiam*, that it was a good lease, and well warranted by the statute: though my Lord *Coke* lays it down for one of his rules, that leases upon this statute are not good if they do not commence from the day of the making, which perhaps may be reconciled upon the same diversity, where they are made twenty-one years and where not so, that from the time of the sealing and executing the lease, till the expiration thereof, there does not intervene more than twenty-one years. For, if the commencement of the lease be at such a distance, that between the time of the sealing and executing thereof, and the expiration, there do not intervene above twenty-one years, then such lease seems to be without any exception from the statute, though the time for commencement thereof in the possession of the lessee be under twenty-one years, for otherwise the tenant in tail might so prevent the commencement of the leases, as to have always the greatest part of the twenty-one years running out in the time of his issue, which the statute never intended to countenance.

So, where one made a lease for ten years, and after made another lease for eleven years, both these leases are good, because they do not in all exceed twenty-one years, and so the inheritance is not charged [illegible] which the statute allows (d).

C[illegible]

[illegible]

Section III. *Of Leases by Tenant in Tail after possibility of Issue extinct.*

This estate is where one is tenant in special tail, and the person from whose body the issue was to spring, dies without issue, or having issue that issue becomes extinct (a). The law looks upon this estate as equivalent to an estate for life only, and in truth the tenant is only tenant for life, and is permitted to exchange his estate with a tenant for life, an exchange that can only be made of estates that are equal in their nature.

His power to demise, therefore, will come more properly within the consideration of the next subject.

Section IV. *Of Leases by Tenant for Life, absolute or contingent.*

Tenant for life can make no leases to continue longer than his own life, for his leases are absolutely void at his death (b).

Thus (c) where tenant for life leased premises for twenty-one years, and before the expiration of that term died, the trustees of the remainder-man, then an infant, continued to receive the rent reserved, and he, on coming of age, sold the premises by auction, in the conditions of sale the premises were declared to be subject to the lease, and in the conveyance to the purchaser, the lease was referred to as in the possession of the lessee, and in the covenant against incumbrances, that lease was excepted, the purchaser mortgaged, and in the mortgage deeds the like notice was taken of the lease, and the mortgagee for some time received the rent reserved; held that the lease expired with the interest of the tenant for life, and that the notice since taken of it did not operate as a new lease.

Therefore a lease so rendered void against him in remainder, cannot be set up in a court of law by such remainder-man's acceptance of rent, and suffering the tenant to make improvements after his interest vests in possession (d).— But when the remainder-man lies by, and suffers the lessee or assignee to rebuild, and does not by his answer deny that he had notice of it, all these circumstances taken together, will bind him in a court of equity from controverting the lease afterwards.

Also, a lease executed by a tenant for life, in which the reversioner, who was then under age, is named, but which was not executed by him, is void on the death of the tenant for life, and an execution by

(a) 2 Bl. Com. 124. (b) Bac. Abr. tit. "Leases," (I) (c) 1 Bos. & Pull. 531.
(d) Doug. 50. Cowp. 482. Bull. N. P. 96. 7 T. R. 83. 478. 3 Atk. 393.

the reversioner afterwards is no confirmation of it, so as to bind the lessee, for it is not his covenant (*r*).

But if tenant for life makes a lease for twenty years generally, and afterwards he in reversion confirms this lease, and then the tenant for life dies, though this estate would have determined by the death of the lessor, yet the confirmation hath made it good for the whole term (*s*). But if the lease had been for twenty years, if the lessor or tenant for life should so long live, there, if the reversioner had confirmed this lease, yet it would not prevent its determination upon the death of the tenant for life.

The [illegible] which cases is this [illegible] that in the first case, the [illegible] twenty years, nothing appears to the [illegible] it was a good lease for the time [illegible], [illegible] the [illegible] which would determine it sooner, does not appear [illegible] when the reversioner, who [illegible] advantage [illegible] the lease [illegible] twenty years [illegible] it [illegible], [illegible] of the [illegible] would [illegible] his reversion [illegible] of the tenant for life being made the express limitation [illegible] of the twenty years [illegible], no confirmation of [illegible] limited can enlarge [illegible] to extend beyond the life of the lessor [illegible] the express determination affixed to it.—For although we [illegible] one case, where it is held, that if a man makes a lease for [illegible] years, if the lessee so long live, and afterwards the lessor and lessee join in a grant by deed of the term to another, after which the first lessee dies within the twenty-one years, yet the grantee shall enjoy it during the residue of the term absolutely. To reconcile this case with the other, it must be intended, that in the assignment no notice is taken of the express limitation affixed to the lease, but that they joined in an assignment of the lease, for the residue of the twenty-one years, and then it may be well construed to amount to a *confirmation of the lease* for that time, as the lessor may confirm the land to the lessee for any longer time, and thereby enlarge his estate or interest.

B tenant for the life of *C* and he in remainder or reversion in fee join in a lease for years by indenture (*u*), this during the life of *C* is the lease of *B* who then only had the present interest in the lands, and the confirmation of him in the remainder or reversion; but after the death of *C* then this becomes the lease of him in the reversion or remainder, and the confirmation of *B.*, for the lessors having several estates in them in several degrees, the lease shall be construed to move out of each one's respective estate or interest, as they become capable of supporting it, which is the most natural and useful construction of the

[illegible] 1 T. R. [illegible] [illegible] Leas. [illegible] lease, especially as there can be no estoppel in this case, by reason of the several [illegible] which passed from each. Therefore during the life of tenant for life, if the lessee, being evicted, should [illegible] a lease to both, [illegible] could [illegible] him, as was adjudged, because for that time it was only the lease of the tenant for life.

[illegible] makes a lease to *B* and *C* on condition that if they [illegible] *A* then the land shall revert to *A* without determining any estate [illegible] in the grant, all the estate passes under the condition, for [illegible] *A* was not received on default of *B* and *C* ([illegible]).

If tenant for life and he in remainder in tail join in a lease to *A* for years, remainder to *B* for life, and the issue in tail accepts the rent of *A* and [illegible], the lease in remainder is good, notwithstanding the [illegible].

Where lessee for life makes a lease for years, except all the wood, underwood, and trees growing upon the land, it is a good exception, although he has no interest in them but [illegible], because he remains the [illegible] tenant, and is chargeable [illegible]; therefore to prevent it, he may make the exception.—But if lessee for years assign over his term, with such an exception, it is a void exception ([illegible]).

Section V. *Of Leases by Tenants pour autre Vie.*

Where a person holds for the term of another's life, he is called tenant *pour autre vie*, and leases made by him of course determine on the death of the *cestui que vie*, or person during whose life he holds, but not on his own death; for by the statute of Frauds every estate *pour autre vie* is made devisable, and if not devised, it shall be assets in the hands of the heir, if limited to the heirs; if not limited to the heirs, it shall go to the executor or administrator of the grantee, and be assets in their hands.

Section VI. *Of Leases by Tenant by the Curtesy of England, and Tenant in Dower or Jointure.*

Tenant by the curtesy is where a man marries a woman seised of an estate of inheritance, and has by her issue born alive, which was capable of inheriting her estate ([illegible]). Tenancy in dower, is where the husband of a woman dies, with or without issue, in which case, the wife shall have the third part of all the lands and tenements whereof he was seised of an estate of inheritance at any time during the coverture,

([illegible]) Co. [illegible] 12.
([illegible]) Cro. Jac. 296.
([illegible]) Cro. Eliz. 252.
([illegible]) 2 Bl. Com. 126.

to hold to herself during the term of her natural life. Tenant in jointure is by the 27th *H.* 8. c. 10. commonly called the statute of Uses, by which dower may be barred by a jointure or by conveying a joint estate to husband and wife; but in common acceptation, it means a sole estate limited to the wife only (a).

As to the [illegible] estates, it will be sufficient [illegible] either of [illegible] this lease [illegible] heir or [illegible] *quid on mis[illegible]*, [illegible] yet it is a certain [illegible] or intermeddle with the inheritance, [illegible] charges fall off [illegible] they are derived, and the lessee is become tenant by sufferance by his continuance of possession after (b).

Section VII. *Of Leases under Powers.*

Lord *Mansfield* has observed, (c) that of all kinds of powers, the most frequent is that "to make leases." Though it may not now perhaps be the most frequent, it is certainly one of the most useful, as it is highly necessary for the encouragement of farmers to occupy, stock, and improve the land, that they should have some permanent interest. If the owner of the estate for life was not enabled to make a permanent lease, he could not enjoy to the best advantage during his own time; and they who came after must suffer, by the land being untenanted, out of repair, and in a bad condition. The plan of this power is for the mutual advantage of possessor and successor. The execution of it is checked by many conditions, to guard the successor, so that the annual revenue may not be diminished, nor those in remainder prejudiced in point of remedy, or other circumstances of full and ample enjoyment.

The limitation and modifying of estates by virtue of powers, came from equity into the common law with the statute of Uses (d): as therefore powers came into the courts of law with the statute of Uses, so the construction of them, by the express direction of the statute, must be the same as in courts of equity (e), for whatever is a good power or execution in equity, the statute makes good at law (f). As powers are derived from equity, and ought even at law to be construed equitably, so in the construction of powers originally in their nature legal, courts of equity must follow the law, be the consideration ever so meritorious.

(a) [illegible]
(b) [illegible]
(c) [illegible]
(d) [illegible] 1 C[illegible] 398.
(e) 1 B[illegible] 120.
(f) 2 L[illegible] 1146. 1 Bl. R. 28[illegible].

The circumstances attending the execution of such leases may be considered, 1. With respect to the lessor; 2. to the lessee; 3. to the subject on which the power is to operate; 4. to the quality and quantity of interest to be granted; 5. to the rent; 6. to the form of the lease (a).

1. With respect to the lessor.

He must, as we have observed, pursue the power strictly. If tenant for life, therefore, has a special power of granting leases for a longer term than his own life, upon his death the lease is void, unless he has strictly pursued the power (b). So, tenant for life, with power of leasing under certain conditions, must demise in strict conformity with those conditions (c). Indeed in respect to the execution of powers (d), courts of justice have always looked with a jealous eye to see that the conditions in favour of the next taker be pursued, not literally only, but substantially.

So, tenant for life, with power to make leases for three lives, or twenty-one years, cannot make such leases by letter of attorney, by virtue of his power (e), because such leases not being derived out of the interest of the tenant for life, but by an authority derived from the tenant in fee, and to charge the estate of third persons, the trust for that purpose is personal, and cannot be delegated to another.

It has also been determined, that where a power of leasing was given to the father, tenant for life, and after his decease, to the son, tenant for life, and the son obtained a grant from the father, of his life estate, (without noticing the power) subject to a certain rent, with a power of re-entry for non payment; the son, during the life-time of his father, could not lease under the power (f).

A power to make leases generally, extends only to leases in possession, and not to leases in reversion, or *in futuro* (g).

The grant of a lease need not be in actual possession, but a constructive possession, by the receipt of the rents and profits, is a sufficient compliance with the power. If actual possession were necessary, a leasing power could never be executed where the land is in the hands of a tenant (h).

Therefore, where a tenant for life, with power to grant leases, in possession for twenty-one years at the best rent, conveyed his life-estate to trustees to pay an annuity for his life, and the surplus to himself, the power was held to be not thereby extinguished, but he might still grant a lease agreeable to the terms thereof [illegible].

2. With respect to the lessee.

The lessee, in a lease under a power, must, it should seem, be a

(a) Po[illegible] Pow. 39[illegible] [illegible] 67.
(c) 6 Bro. Cas. in Parl. [illegible] [illegible] 2[illegible] 6[illegible]
(f) 13 East R. 11[illegible] (g) Cro. J[illegible] [illegible] (h) D[illegible]
[illegible]

re[illegible] be [illegible] at the time when it is made. For generally such leases cannot be made in reversion or in futuro; and it has been held, that if a power be to make leases to one, two, or three persons, the demise of the power cannot be made to commence after the death of the first son of J. S. because the [illegible] made under a power ought to be in possession.

I[illegible] [illegible] in consideration of [illegible] [illegible], with the power to [illegible], a lease to a stranger is void.

9. With respect to the [illegible] which the power is to operate [illegible] [illegible], a [illegible] power to grant building leases for [illegible] years, [illegible] the best improved ground rent, granted a lease on [illegible], which was not [illegible] to be a building lease, but which [illegible] a covenant by the lessee to keep in repair the premises [illegible] old houses on such [illegible] "Lessees should be building, [illegible]," held that [illegible] not a building lease within the power [illegible] granted by tenant for life, who had a limited [illegible] [illegible] void, and consequently not capable [illegible] confirmed [illegible] acceptance of rent.

[illegible] to be exercised only over hereditaments [illegible], [illegible] twice letten are included within the description [illegible].

But lands that have been but once letten, are not within such a [illegible].

So, if lands had been leased by virtue of a contract, from year to year for three years, they cannot be said to be usually letten, because there is but one lease, though renewable every year.

Any kind of demise is sufficient to [illegible] [illegible], there being no necessity that it should [illegible] demised by indenture; a demise by will, or by copy, is sufficient to make lands to be [illegible] usually demiseable (f).

[illegible] not demised for the space of twenty years before the execution of a power to demise, at the rent then [illegible], cannot be let under such power.

Thus, where there was a tenant for life, with power to [illegible] leases of all or any of the lands in the settlement, particularly mentioned, which at any time [illegible] had been usually letten or demised, for, and during the term of twenty-one years or under, in possession and not in reversion, reserving the rent thereupon then yielded or paid, or more [illegible] the premises mentioned in the [illegible], which had been let [illegible] for twenty-one years, but such term of twenty-one years had expired, and the premises had not been let [illegible] the space of [illegible].

[illegible]

years before the demise, under the power which was the subject of dispute. It was held, that what was not farmed at the time of the proviso made, nor twenty years before, could not be said to be at any time before commonly farmed, for those twenty years were a time before in which it was not farmed. Besides, the proviso was, that leases might be made for twenty-one years of any lands in the deed, reserving the rents thereupon reserved at the time of the deed made, which necessarily implied, that the land demiseable by that proviso must be land which then was under rent; for if no rent then was, the rent then thereupon reserved could not be reserved. But the premises in question had then no rent upon them, for they were not let of twenty years before, nor then, and therefore were not demiseable by that proviso. The words "or more," could not at all help the lessee, for the words "more" or "less," were words of relation, the one of addition to what was before, the other of diminution; for "more" or "less," must relate to something positive before, and could never be a relation to nothing.

A covenant to stand seised, as it is a lease if made by the owner, so also is it an evidence of the usual manner of demising (a).

It seems now to be settled, that the question, whether, under a power to lease lands, and other hereditaments, provided that such rent or more be reserved upon every lease as hath been reserved, or paid for it, within a given time, previous to the creation of the power—lands not before in lease may be demised, is a question of construction on the intention of the author of the power, to be collected from the instrument creating the power, or [illegible] (b).

Thus, where a power was to lease a manor, except the demesne lands, though copyholds, being within that description, could not be demised under such power, yet the rents and services of the manor might be, for it appeared to be the intent of the settlement, that part of the manor should be demiseable, and notwithstanding a qualification annexed to the power which said that the ancient rent should be reserved, and no reservation of rent could be upon a lease of rents and services, out of which no rent issues, yet the rents and services might be demised within the power; for it appeared, that part of the manor was intended to be comprised within the power, but that the demesne lands were not to be comprised, then the rents and services must pass, for the whole of the manor consists in demesnes, and rents and services, and if a man have a power reserved to him over one of two things, and the qualification [illegible] to the power [illegible] extend to one of these things, he may make a lease of the other without any regard to the qualification.

(a) [illegible] 2 R[illegible] 26, [illegible] K[illegible]
(b) [illegible]

Accordingly, where there is a power to make a lease of a manor, and every part thereof, so that such rent be reserved upon every lease as was paid for two years before, and it happens that some part of the land was not let at any rent within two years before; a man may make a lease of such land, reserving what rent he pleases, for the intent appears to be, that he might make leases of the whole manor (*a*).

So, also, where a man had power to make leases of a rectory, tithes, and other lands, reserving the ancient rent, it was held, that he might make leases of tithes, although no rent can issue out of tithes; but he might demise them without any rent if it pleased him, for it appeared, that tithes were within the power (*b*).

So, under a power to lease all manors, messuages, lands, &c. "so as there be reserved as much rent as is now paid for the same," such parts of the estate enumerated in the power as have never been demised, may be let (*c*).

But under a power in a family-settlement to make leases of all or any part of the premises, reserving the ancient rent, lands always occupied with the family seat cannot be demised; for in such case, the qualification annexed to the power, "that the ancient rent must be reserved," manifestly excluded the mansion-house, and lands about it *never* let: the nature of the thing in such case, speaks the intent (*d*).

So, under the settlement of an estate, with a power to the tenant in possession, to let all or any part of the premises, so as the usual covenants be reserved, a lease of tithes, which had never been let before, was held void.—In all these cases, the intention of the parties is to govern the court in construing the power (*e*).

Every power, in the construction of it, is to be taken with such a restriction, that the estate itself, which is subjected to the power, shall not be destroyed by the exercise of it. Therefore, in the case of *Winter* and *Loveday, Rokeby*, J. held that, had the express words used in that case, "so as it be not of the demesne lands" been left out, yet there would have been a restraint by implication from making leases of customary land held of the manor; for if the customary land might be demised, the manor would be destroyed, which, it must be presumed, was not the intent of the parties (*f*).

One who has a power to grant a concurrent lease within seven years of the expiration of the old, may grant a lease at any time on the surrender of the old one (*g*).

4. With respect to the quality and quantity of interest to be granted.

A lease for ninety-nine years of a charity estate, (a farm) as a hus-

(*a*) 5 Mod. [illegible] 378. 1 Com. R. 37, &c.
(*b*) [illegible] 294. &c. cited
(*c*) [illegible]
(*d*) [illegible]
(*e*) 8 Mod. 219 [illegible] 132
(*f*) 1 Powell on Pow. 407 [illegible] 5 Mod. 2[illegible]5, 378, &c.
(*g*) [illegible]

bandry lease, cannot stand without proof of a consideration, shewing that it is fair and reasonable, and for the benefit of the charity. Under the circumstances, long possession permitted, and the defendant being the personal representative, such a lease was set aside *without costs*, and without imposing an additional rent previous to the bill, but future cases will not be so treated (*a*).

Upon a general power to make leases, without saying more, the law adjudges, that the leases ought to be leases in possession, for if upon such power a lease might be made upon a lease, the party might, by making infinite leases, detain those in remainder out of possession for ever, which would be contrary to the intent of the parties and against reason (*b*).

So, a general power to make leases for one and twenty years, does not enable the party to make such a lease in reversion, by which a widow would be deprived of the benefit of her jointure, to secure which the land was settled by act of parliament: for, besides that jointures are favoured in law, the statute intended not to give him that liberty, and, it being a liberty and power, it must be strictly pursued (*c*).

If a man has power to make leases in possession or reversion, if he makes a lease in possession once, he shall never after make a lease in reversion, for he has an election to do the one or the other, but not both (*d*).

Devisee for life, with power to make leases for twenty-one years, whereupon the old accustomed rent shall be reserved, makes a lease for twenty-one years under the old rent, &c. and a year before the expiration of that lease, he makes a lease to another for twenty one years to begin presently; this lease seems to be good within his power as a concurrent lease, because it is no charge upon the reversion, nor is there any more than twenty-one years *in toto* against the reversioner: but this power would not warrant the making of leases in reversion, for then he might charge the inheritance *ad infinitum* (*e*).

But notwithstanding, where one having power to make leases for twenty-one years in possession, made a lease to *A.* for twenty-one years in trust for the payment of debts, but the lease was made to commence from a time to come, and so not pursuant to the power, yet being made for the payment of debts, it was supported in equity (*f*).

Under a power to lease in possession for one, two, or three lives, or for thirty years, or any other number of years determinable on one, two, or three lives, or in reversion for one, two, or three lives, or for

(*a*) 10 Ves 555.
(*b*) 1 Brownl 148. 1 Com R 39, & ante.
(*c*) Cro Eliz 5.
(*d*) Ld Raym 267.
(*e*) Powell on Pow 428. Bac Abr. tit "Leases," 42. Leon. 147, 8. Hard 412.
(*f*) Bac. Abr. Ibid, 428. Cha. Ca. 10.

thirty years, or any other number of years determinable on one, two, or three lives, a man cannot make an absolute lease in possession for thirty years, but an absolute lease in reversion, for thirty years, he may (*a*).

Where there is a power to grant leases in possession, but not by way of reversion or future interest, a lease *per verba de præsenti*, is not contrary to the power, although the estate at the time of granting the lease, was held by tenants at will, or from year to year, if at the time, they received directions from the grantor of the lease to pay their rent to the lessee (*b*).

So, (*c*) one under a power in a marriage settlement to lease for twenty-one years in possession, but not in reversion, grants a lease to his only daughter for twenty one years, "to commence *from* the day of the date," adjudged a good lease.—It was held that the word "from" may mean either inclusive or exclusive, according to the context and subject matter, and the court will construe it so as to effectuate the deeds of parties, and not to destroy them. But the authority of this determination has been much questioned.

Under a power in a will to lease in possession, and not in reversion, a lease for years, executed the 29th of March to the then tenant in possession, *habendum* as to the arable from the 13th of February preceding, and as to the pasture from the 5th of April then next, &c. under a yearly rent, payable quarterly, on the 10th of July, 10th of October, 10th of January, and 10th of April, is void for the whole, though such lease were according to the custom of the country, and the same had been before granted by the person creating the power (*d*)

Under a power to demise for twenty-one years in possession, and not in reversion, a lease dated in fact on the 17th of February, 1802, *habendum* from the 25th of March next ensuing the date thereof is good, if not executed and delivered till after the 25th of March, for it then takes effect as a lease in possession with reference back to the date actually expressed (*e*).

One had power in effect to make leases for the lives of *A B* and *C* and he makes a lease to them for their three lives, and the life of the longer liver of them and this was held to be sufficient within the power, because, for three lives generally, and for three lives, and the longer liver of them, is all one, since without such words it would have gone to the survivor.—So, a lease to one for three lives, or to three for their lives, is all one (*f*).

Where a man makes a settlement of the reversion of lands, demised

(*a*) Ld Raym. 267

(*b*) Doug. 565

(*c*) Cowp. 714. 2 Wils. 165.

(*d*) 2 East's R. 376.

(*e*) 10 East 427

(*f*) Bac. Abr. tit. "Leases." 3 Keb. 44.

for life or years, to the use of one for life, with power to make leases generally, he may make a lease during the continuance of a former lease, to commence after the former, as otherwise his power would be ineffectual (*a*).

So, *a fortiori*, if a power expressly enable one to make leases in reversion, such a lease will of course be good by virtue thereof (*b*).

Under a power to make leases "for ninety-nine years, or three lives in possession, or for two lives in possession, and one in reversion, or for one life in possession, and two in reversion," the party, during the continuance of the first lease, made a lease for life to *T.*, and the question was, Whether the latter lease, being made whilst the lives in the former lease were in being, was authorized by the power? By two of the justices, out of three, it was held, that had the words, "in possession," and the words of the power been generally to make leases, the case had been strong in favour of the lease, the settlement being of a reversion, but the power being expressly to make leases in possession, the lease in reversion was not within it; and they noticed the particular wording of the power to make leases, namely, "for two lives in possession, and one in reversion," or "one in possession, and two in reversion," so that it appeared, that the scope and intent was, never to have an estate above three lives in being at one time (*c*).

The nature of a lease in reversion is this. In the most ample sense, that is said to be a lease in reversion, which hath its commencement at a future day, and then it is opposed to a lease in possession, for every lease that is not a lease in possession, in this sense is said to be a lease in reversion. Where mention is made of leases in reversion of a power, this shall be intended of leases to commence after the end of a present interest in being; which is the second notion of a lease in reversion. But as a lease for life cannot be made to commence at a future day, where a power is given to make leases for one or two lives in reversion and to make leases for years, the very same expression (lease in reversion) will have a different signification in the same conveyance: being applied to a lease for life, it shall be intended of a concurrent lease, or a lease of the reversion, viz. a lease of that land which is at the same time under a demise, and then it is not to commence after the end of the demise; but hath a present commencement, and is concurrent with the prior demise; but being applied to a lease for years, it shall be intended of a lease which shall take its effect after the expiration or determination of a lease in being (*d*).

The law therefore, which is founded in reason and common sense, considers "possessory," and "reversionary," according to the natural and ordinary import of those terms, without annexing any artificial idea to them,) as including the simple ideas of time present, and time

(*a*) 1 Com. R. 315. (*b*) 8 Rep. 69.
(*c*) Powell on Pow. 420. 2 Lev. 167, &c. (*d*) 5 Mod. 245, 278. 1 Com. R. 39, &c.

to come: and consequently, that every subsisting interest, or time not present, is an interest or time to come (a).

The circumstance of a second lease for years being granted to the same lessee who holds under a former lease, to commence after the expiration of such former lease, does not operate to make the latter a continuation of the former lease, where the terms are granted by different deeds, although the residue of the time to come after the former lease, together with the period for which the latter lease is granted, do not in length of time exceed the limits fixed by the power: for the latter will, notwithstanding, be considered as a reversionary lease, as much as if it had been granted to a reversionary lessee (b).

But, if under a power to demise for fourteen years, a lease were made of lands, &c. *habendum*, for seven years, and so from seven years to seven years, the latter, it seems, would be but a continuance of the former term, and an addition to it, and not a remainder or future interest (c).

If there be a power to make leases in possession expressly, which attaches upon an estate, part of which is in possession, and other part thereof in reversion, at the creation of the power: the donee of the power may immediately make leases in possession of the estate in reversion, as well as of that in possession: for in such case, the word "possession," in the power, refers to the lease, and not to the land (d).

But it seems, that if a power enable any one to make leases in reversion, as well as in possession, and some part of the land subject to the power be in possession, and other part of it in reversion, he cannot make a lease in possession and another lease in reversion of the same land, but his power to make leases in reversion, will be confined to such land as was not then in possession: and note the distinction between these two cases (e).

If a power be created to enable a tenant for life, to make leases for one, two, or three lives, or for any term or number of years, determinable upon one, two, or three lives, in possession, &c. of such part and parts, and so much only of the manors, &c. of the creator of the power, as are then demised or granted for any such time, &c. no lands or hereditaments can be demised under such a power, but what are at the time of the execution of the power under lease for one, two, or three concurrent lives, or for any term of years, determinable upon one, two, or three concurrent lives; for the meaning of such restriction is, that the candles shall be all burning at the same time (f).

A power to make a lease for three lives was held not to be well executed in law, by a lease for ninety-nine years, determinable upon three lives. The reason seems to be, that the estates are different, one being

(a) Powell on Pow. 431. (b) 5 T. R. 568. (c) 1 Lev. 45. 3 T. R. 462.
(d) Powell on Pow. 4[illegible]. Pre. Assist. Lessees. Cro. Jac. 347.
(e) Powell on Pow. 42[illegible]. 2 Com. R. 59, arte. (f) Powell on Pow. 541. 7 T.R. 713.

a freehold, and the other a chattel. Such was the construction in *Whitlock*'s case, (*a*) and such seems now to be the settled rule of law, notwithstanding that the Judges, in 3 *Keb.* 746, thought the construction too nice, and contrary to the intent of the parties, and though determinations to the contrary are in the books (*b*).

An estate was settled on several tenants for life in succession with remainders in tail, with power to every tenant for life, from time to time by indenture to make leases for any term or number of years, not exceeding twenty-one years or for the life or lives of any one, two, or three persons, so as no greater estate than for three lives be at any one time in being in any part of the premises and so as the ancient yearly rent, &c. be reserved. Held first, that the power only authorised either a chattel lease not exceeding twenty-one years, or a freehold lease not exceeding three lives, and that a lease by tenant for life for ninety-nine years determinable on lives as it might exceed twenty-one years was void at law, and was not even good *pro tanto* for the twenty-one years; but the special verdict finding that the tenant in tail had received the rent reserved by such lease accruing after the death of the tenant for life who made it, and who had not given any notice to quit, Held secondly, that the receipt of rent was evidence of a tenancy the particular description of which it was for the jury to decide upon, and for the defect of the special verdict in this respect, a *venire de novo* was awarded; but the court intimated that under the circumstances of the case, and the disparity of the rent reserved being 4*l.* 2*s.*, while the rack rent value was 60*l.* a year (though one of the lessees had been presented by the homage as tenant after the death of the tenant for life, and admitted by the lord's steward, and the 4*l.* 2*s.* reserved was more than the ancient rent), a jury would be strongly advised, to decide against a tenancy from year to year (*c*).

Powers to lease, *habendum* for lives or years, may be either absolutely for one, two, or three lives, or for an absolute term of years, as for thirty years, or qualified, as for any number of years, determinable upon one, two, or three lives.

A man, having a power to grant leases, may do less than such power enables him to do, or, if he do more, it shall be good to the extent of his power.

Thus, where the city of London under a power granted by act of parliament to lease for one and one-and-twenty years, granted a lease for one and twenty, it was held no variance upon oyer of the indenture in which such power was recited (*d*).

So, if a man hath power to lease for ten years, and he leaseth for twenty years, the lease for twenty years shall be good for ten years of the twenty in equity, and so it has been settled several times (*e*).

So, where tenant for life had power to let leases for twenty-one

(*a*) 8 Rep. 70 B. 2 Str. 992 S. P. (*b*) 8 Com. 69, 70. Bac. Abr. Tit. "Leases." (*c*) 10 East, 158. (*d*) Bac. Abr. tit. "Leases." (*e*) 1 Chan. C. 23.

years in possession, and he made a lease for twenty-six years, without referring to the power, it was held that the first lease should be presumed to have been surrendered, and the remainder-man should be bound for twenty-one years of the new lease (*a*)

If a man pursues all the requisites within his power, though he does it by more deeds than are necessary, it will be good (*b*)

A power may be executed at different times, if not fully executed at first, provided that the party, in the whole execution, does not transgress the limits of the power (*c*).

Therefore if a woman, seised of an estate for life, with a power to lease for three lives, or twenty-one years, marries, and then she and her husband join in making the lease, and the husband and wife both die before the lease is expired; here, though the husband, in right of his wife, and she in her own, are possessed of an estate for life, and therefore can as owners make a lease, and there appears no intention of the parties, (imagining perhaps that they should have outlived the lease,) that this lease should be made by virtue of the power, yet because the lease, supposing it made by them as owners, cannot have the effect the parties intended, for some it would have (viz it would be a good lease during the lives of the husband and wife,) yet because it cannot have all, it shall be esteemed to be made by virtue of the power (*d*)

If the deed has not a full operation, except where it is in execution of his power, it will notwithstanding be good, as if tenant for life make a lease, without taking notice of his power, it shall be an execution of his power to make leases, for otherwise the lease will not have an effectual continuance (*e*)

5 With respect to the rent.

There are two methods of leasing in common use in this kingdom; at the best rent, and upon fines, which as the lives or leases drop, are considered among the annual profits.

The latter mode is not very common in England, where the power of leasing usually introduced in settlements requires the best rent to be reserved, and expressly prohibits the taking of any fine or premium (*f*)

Where a lease is made under a power requiring the best rent to be reserved, the question whether the best rent has been reserved must be left to a jury -- Improvements by the tenant will not authorize a lease at an undervalue, and if a fine be taken the lease cannot be supported, though the rent be ever so considerable The surrender of an existing lease, and the grant of a new one at an increased rent is not equivalent to taking a fine (*g*)

In a power to grant building leases, the term *best rent* must, although not so expressed, be understood to mean the best rent which can be

(*a*) Amb. 740 (*b*) Com. Dig. Tit. "Pow," (C 5)
(*c*) 1 Bl. R. 128; (*d*) 10 Mod. 36. (*e*) 1 Vern. 228
(*f*) Sugd. on Powers, 511 (*g*) Ibid 511, 512, 513

obtained with reference to the gross sum to be laid out by the tenant in buildings or improvements (*a*)

A lease at 43*l.* a year granted under a power, directing the best rent to be reserved cannot be impeached merely by showing that the lessor rejected at the time two specific offers, one of 50*l.* and another from 50*l* to 60*l.* from other tenants, though the responsibility of such other tenants could not be disproved; for in the exercise of such a power where fairly intended and no fine or other collateral consideration is received or injurious partiality plainly manifested by the lessor, all other requisites of a good tenant are to be regarded, as well as the mere amount of the rent offered, unless something extravagantly wrong in the bargain for rent be shewn The best rent means the best rack rent that can reasonably be required by a landlord, taking all the requisites of a good tenant for the permanent benefit of the estate into the account (*b*).

The sufficiency of the rent must be governed by the consideration on whom the *onus* of the repair is thrown (*c*).

A power was given to lease for twenty-one years reserving the best rent, so as the lease should not contain any clause whereby authority should be given to the lessee to commit waste, or whereby he should be exempted from punishment for committing waste, and so as such lease should contain, such other conditions, covenants and restrictions, as were generally inserted according to the usage of countries where the premises were situate. It was held that a lease was good, though the lessor thereby took on himself the repairs of the mansion house excepting the glass windows, and covenanted that if he did not repair it within three months after notice, the tenant might do so, and deduct the expense out of the rent reserved, and though the lessor covenanted in consideration of a large sum to be laid out by the lessee in the repair of the premises in the first instance, to renew during his the lessor's life, at the request of the lessee, his executors, &c. on the same terms, because this covenant only bound the lessor himself, and if the best rent were not reserved upon such renewal, the lease would be void against the remainder-man (*d*).

Therefore, if a power be to make leases, rendering the ancient rent, a lease which does not reserve it will be void as if the party leases two acres with other land, and reserves the rent of the two acres for the whole (*e*). By a reservation in a power to lease of the ancient and accustomed rent, is to be understood that which was reserved at the creation of the power, if a lease were *then* in being, or that which was last *before* reserved, if no lease were then in being, for he who created such a power intended no more than that the lessor and lessee should not be able to put the estate in a worse condition than it was in when the power was created, but should keep it in the same plight and con-

(*a*) Sugd on Powers, 513. (*b*) 10 East, 273 (*c*) 12 East, 305
(*d*) Ibid 305. (*e*) Com Dig. tit "Power," (C 6)

dition at least, as it was in when so settled. This was the opinion of Lord *Holt*, who also observed, that without a certainty, the power could not be executed even by reserving a sum in particular; and, therefore, he gave it as his opinion, that upon any settlement where a power was reserved to the tenant for life to make leases of the lands in that settlement, (which were anciently and accustomably demised, and whereof fines had been taken), at the ancient, usual, and accustomable rent, for three lives, for one and twenty years, or any other number of years determinable on three lives, that rent which was *then* or *last before* reserved upon a lease in being of the same lands, or on a lease which expired just before the time of the settlement made, must be the sum and no other (*a*).

But Lord *Cowper*, in the same case, doubted as to this point, and suggested, that suppose lands were leased once at a greater and twice at a lesser rent, he took the rent of the former lease to be the ancient rent: the last lease might be made by him that had the fee, who was not bound to reserve the ancient rent, but might let it for nothing if he pleased.—So, his lordship thought that this rule would likewise not apply to lands anciently demised, whereof fines had been taken; for there the rents were more or less, as the fines were higher or lower (*b*).

But it seems that, if the custom of the country where the lands lie be to lease partly on a rent, and to take a fine for the remaining value, then Lord *Holt's* mode of ascertaining the ancient rent is most reasonable.—So, if such power be to lease, reserving so much yearly rent, or more, as hath "been most accustomably" yielded or paid within twenty years next before such lease thereof made, the reserved within the twenty years must be the measure of the reservation upon leases made by virtue of such power, although a greater rent hath been reserved before the twenty years (*c*).

But if *several* rents have been reserved within the twenty years referred to, Lord *Holt's* rule seems in that case the most proper to go by: unless the leases on which the rent has been reserved within the twenty years have been sometimes with fines and sometimes without, in which case Lord *Cowper's* rule seems best (*d*).

Tenant for life under a power in a settlement to lease at the "usual rent" may demise upon reserving the usual fines and rent, where the usual profit has heretofore been made by fines; for if the trustees under the said settlement were obliged to let the lands at a rack-rent, it might be quite inconsistent with the nature of these estates (*e*).

If a lease be made under a power to demise, reserving the true and ancient rent, and the rent reserved be not conformable to that both in quantity and quality, and manner of reservation also, the lease (it is said) will be void (*f*).

(*a*) 3 Ch. Rep. 76; 2 Vern. 531, 542. Bac. Abr. tit. "Leases." (*b*) Ibid.
(*c*) Powell on Powers, 551. (*d*) Ibid. (*e*) 3 Burr. 1446.
(*f*) Powell on Pow. 552.

Thus where rent anciently payable in gold, was in a new lease under a power so restricted made payable in silver, such lease would not bind: for the variation may be prejudicial to the remainder-man. But a reservation of "eight bushels" where "a quarter of corn" was mentioned in the power, will be good: for the variation is only in words (*a*).

If a tenant in tail be of two farms, under a settlement, one of which has been always let at 20*l* rent, and the other for 10*l* rent, he may not, (it is said) by virtue of such power, make a lease of both for twenty one years, rendering an entire rent of 30*l* (*b*).

So, two farms, usually let to separate tenants, cannot be let by one lease to one tenant, by 32 *H.* 8. *c.* 28. though a greater rent be reserved (*c*).

For the intent of such reservation is, not only that the old sum of money shall be reserved, but that it shall be issuing out of the old land (*d*).

Improving the estate will not be considered such an alteration as varies the rent, by making it to issue out of other hereditaments than those certained in the power: as where the tenant entered and built a new house upon the land, and then made a lease for twenty-one years, reserving only the ancient rent, &c. the court would not suffer an objection to it to be argued (*e*).

If a power to lease be, provided that two parts in three of the improved value be reserved as a rent, the reservation may be made in the terms of the power; and the constant payment of such a sum as amounted to that at the time of making such a lease, will be good, whether the tenements that are the subjects of it rise or fall in value (*f*).

But in general, it seems necessary, that the sum intended to be reserved under such provisoes in family settlements and conveyances, should be *specifically* stated in the lease: for otherwise the remainder-man may be put to infinite trouble and expense. It hath, therefore, been held, that the reservation, may not be made in the same or as general terms as the power itself is, as, by simply transcribing the clause respecting the reservation of the ancient and accustomable rent, &c in the instrument creating the power to lease, into the lease, leaving the necessity of averring and proving what was the ancient and accustomable rent to the tenant for life or remainder-man (*g*). Tenant for life with power to make leases of all lands anciently demised, reserving the ancient rents or more, and of other lands reserving the best and most improved rents that could be got, makes a lease of part of the premises usually demised reserving "the old accustomed rents," and a lease of other part not usually demised, reserving "such sum of

(*a*) Resol. in 5 Rep. 3, 6. Mountjoy's Case. (*b*) Ibid. (*c*) Cro. Car. 23.
(*d*) Powell on Powers, 554. (*e*) 1 Leon. 147. (*f*) Powell on Powers 555. 2 Ch. R. 82.
(*g*) Powell ut ante. 3 Bro. Par. Ca. 248. Gilb. Eq. R. 45. S. C. 2 Vern. 531, 542.

money as should amount to the best and most improved yearly rent." both these leases held to be void as against the remainder-man, the first not being warranted by the power, and the other for the uncertainty of it (*a*).

So, where tenant for life had made a lease of the lands not usually letten, reserving therefore the best and most approved rents for the same, according to the words of the power, this was held to be so utterly uncertain, that nothing was offered to support it (*b*).

But where such rent is ascertainable, it is otherwise, for *id certum est quod certum reddi potest.*—Therefore, where a power was, by a settlement to make leases of land anciently demised, reserving at least 12*d.* for every Cheshire acre; and a lease was made of all the lands anciently demised, reserving all the rent intended to be reserved: though these words were very general and uncertain in themselves, the reservation was held good, because it might easily be ascertained by the reference of the 12*d.* at least for every Cheshire acre, for it is known what a Cheshire acre is; and that may by admeasurement be at all times ascertained, and depends not upon uncertain evidence (*c*).

If the lease be of lands subjected to a power, together with other lands not so subjected, and there be equivocal words, under which the reservation of the rent may be referred to, namely, whether to the premises on which the power attaches, or otherwise, and the lease cannot take effect unless the rent be to issue out of those premises. then the better opinion seems to be, that the reservation shall be taken as referable only to the premises subjected to the power, and that by that means the lease may be made good (*d*)

It seems that several leases may be made in the same deed, under such a power, if the reservations be several and certain.—Thus where a lease for a term of years was made of the manors of *A B* and *C* by indenture, rendering annually to the lessor, his heirs and assigns, for *A.* 10*l* for *B.* 6*l* for *C.* 4*l.* at the feast, &c. and payable at one place out of the manor, with a condition to re-enter into the said three manors for non-payment of the said rents, or any of them, or any part or parcel of them within a month after the said feast, &c. The lessor entered upon the lessee into all the three manors, for rent of one of the manors in arrear, and one point was, whether the several reservations of the rent, were several tenures, demises, reversions, and rents, and to be avowed for severally? Three of the justices held that they were: but *Dyer* J. held not, because they were not divers leases, but one lease to one person, and one limitation of an estate, and consequently that there was but one reversion to which the rent was incident, and that therefore, the several reservations of several rents could not change

(*a*) 6 Bro. Cas. in Parl. 145.

(*b*) Powell ut ante.

(*c*) Bac. Abr. tit. "Leases." 3 Ch. R. 61, 76.

(*d*) Powell on Powers, 567. 1 Vent. 338, 339. 1 Vent. 228, ante.

the nature of the reversion which was the principal, the rent being only accessary. *Ideo quære* (*a*).

If there be a difference as to the time of the payment of the rent, so that it be not payable at the same periods as anciently, that will vitiate a lease, under a power restricted to be made, rendering the true and ancient rent (*b*). Thus a reservation of the rent at two days, where the rent was formerly reserved and payable at four days, was held, in *Mountjoy's* case (*c*), to make the grant and render void; because it was *ad nocumentum*, to the injury of the heirs in tail, which was restrained by the statute that created the power: for it was more beneficial for them to have it paid at four feasts than two; and all beneficial qualities of the rent ought to be reserved and observed (*d*).

In this respect, leases under powers in settlements differ from ecclesiastical leases under 13 *Eliz.* (of which hereafter) for in them a reservation at two days when the rent was payable formerly at four days does not vitiate the lease, because the statute does not avoid such lease if the accustomed yearly rent or more be reserved (*e*).

The whole rent must be payable annually during the whole term; for the design of the donor is not answered, unless a continual revenue be yearly payable by compulsion of law, and not in expectancy, or *in futuro* (*f*).

But, under a power to make leases, reserving the ancient yearly rent annually, yet if it were reserved upon a day before the year was up, as if the year ended at *Christmas*, and it was reserved at *Michaelmas*, it would be well pursuant to the power (*g*).

Heriots and the like need not be reserved in a lease made under a power, restrained to be rendering the true and ancient rent; for they are casual and accidental services, and therefore fall not within the meaning of such restriction (*h*).

Although in common law conveyances, no rent can be reserved but to the lessor, donor, or feoffor, and his heirs, who are privies in blood, and not to any who is privy in estate, as, to him in reversion, remainder, &c. yet in the case of powers the reservation by tenant for life is good, and shall enure as rent to the remainder man, and he may distrain for it (*i*); and this, though it be reserved to such tenant for life, and his heirs; for powers take effect through the medium of the statute of Uses, which executes the possession according to the limitation of the use, and such lease, when made, takes effect out of the uses of the settlement by which it is created (*k*).

Thus, where a question was, whether the words of the reservation did not make that which was called a rent, to be only a sum in gross,

(*a*) Powell on Powers, 569. Dyer, 308. 6 Pl 75. Vide Postea.
(*b*) Powell on Powers, 571. (*c*) Ante. (*d*) 32 H. 8. c. 28.
(*e*) Cro. Jac. 76. (*f*) 1 Burr. 121. (*g*) 2 Ld. Ray. 2198.
(*h*) Cro. Jac. 76. 1 Com. R. 312. (*i*) Powell on Powers, 573. (*k*) 8 Rep. 70.

and not rent, and so turn the reservation of rent into a condition? the Court held that the land was distrainable for it as for rent, and that it was not a payment upon condition (*a*), one reason for which was, that it was not the *intent* of those who were parties to the indenture to make it a condition, but rather to make a limitation of the rent for the uses mentioned; and that it could not ensue the nature of a condition for it could not be taken as a condition at common law, because those in the remainder were mere strangers to the condition, and a condition united to the use of the term it could not be; for, if it were so, he in remainder being a stranger, could not in law take advantage of it but if it were rent, he immediately in remainder might distrain for the rent, when it incurred due, by reason of the statute 27 *H.* 8 *c.* 10 of Uses, by which it was enacted, "that the intent of the parties should be observed." Therefore, if the use were so limited that a stranger should have the rent, &c. he should have it, and might distrain for it (*b*).

6. With respect to the form of the lease.

In the usual power of leasing, besides the reservation of the best rent, it is commonly required that the lessee covenant for payment of the rent, that a clause of re-entry in default of payment be inserted, that the lessee be not made dispunishable for waste, and that he execute a counterpart, and if these conditions are required, and any of them be not complied with, the lease will be void. It should seem indeed that the circumstances usually made requisite in powers of leasing, must be considered as implied, although not expressly required (*c*).

Under a power to lease reserving a condition of re-entry for non-payment of rent for twenty-one days, a lease granted with a condition for re-entry for non-payment of rent within twenty days, in case no sufficient distress could be taken on the premises, whereby to levy the rent, &c. is not a good execution of the leasing power, because such conditional power of re-entry is less beneficial to the remainder-man than an absolute power of re-entry on non-payment of rent (*d*).

If contrary to the clause that the lessee be not made dispunishable for waste, he be impowered to work unopened mines (*e*), to fell timber, or the like, the lease is void, unless in the case of a building lease, where the clause would be deemed repugnant to the power, and the lessee might pull down old buildings, &c. in order to erect new ones (*f*).

Where a power to lease was restrained to be executed, reserving ancient, usual, and accustomed rents, heriots, boons, and services, a covenant "to keep in repair," was held to be "an ancient boon," and the omission of it was deemed fatal (*g*).

Under a power to a tenant for life to lease for years, reserving the usual covenants, &c. a lease made by him, containing a proviso, that in case the premises were blown down or burned, the lessor should rebuild,

(*a*) Ander. 278. (*b*) Stat. 27 H. 8. c. 10. (*c*) Sugd. on Powers, 527, 530.
(*d*) 13 East, R. 118. (*e*) Ambl. 740. (*f*) Willes, 169. (*g*) Cited ibid. 122.

otherwise the rent should cease, is void, the jury finding that such covenant is unusual (*a*).

What covenants are usual or not is a question of fact, it seems, for the decision of a jury. for *Buller* J. in the preceding case, observed, that "the Court were relieved from determining whether the covenant was usual or not;" because the jury had expressly found that it was unusual (*b*).

But if the covenants in a lease under such a power be upon the whole, such as leave the parties upon the same footing as under former leases, (as where it appeared that what was thrown on the landlord was compensated by what was paid by the tenant), their differing in trivial circumstances will not be material (*c*).

A renewable lease was held not to be inconsistent with a covenant to let and manage to the best advantage, with reference to the subject which was a trust for creditors (*d*).

It is no objection to a lease under a power "that it is in trust for him who executes the power," provided the legal tenant be bound during the term in all requisite covenants and conditions (*e*).

Livery is not necessary to a lease for lives, under a power, (though it be incident thereto at common law,) and it hath been held to be a forfeiture of the power; but Lord *Hale* conceived it was not a forfeiture, because a lease by virtue of a power, takes effect out of the settlement that gives the power, and by sealing the lease the power is executed, and then the livery comes too late to affect it.

If a power be to *A.* or his assigns, to make leases, &c. the power runs with the estate to the assignee in deed, or in law.—If, therefore, a power be given to a lessee for years and his assigns, to make leases for lives, such power goes to his executor, though only an assignee in law, or to the assignee of the executor. But a power to an executor to make leases does not extend to the executor of his executor (*f*).

A power under an Act of Parliament to lessee, his executors, administrators, and assigns, to grant building leases, does not extend to the tenant in a renewed lease, according to the usual course of church leases (*g*).

If *A* settles land to the use of himself for life, with power to make leases, and afterwards to *D* upon such trust as he shall afterwards declare; if *A.* declares the trust for payment of debts, and afterwards leases at a small rent, the lease is not defeated by the execution of his power, for it is precedent to it (*h*).

So, if a man having a power annexed to his estate, charge his estate, and afterwards executes his power, the estate which arises by the execution of the power shall be subject to the charge during the estate.

(*a*) 1 T R 705 (*b*) Powell on Powers, 579 (*c*) Ibid D.. 565
(*d*) 13 Ves. 547 (*e*) 1 Bau 124 (*f*) 1 Vent. 340. 2 Jo... 110
(*g*) 13 Ves. 255. (*h*) Skin. 427.

as if tenant for life, with power to make leases, grants a rent-charge, and afterwards makes a lease, the lessee shall take, subject to the rent-charge during the life of the lessor (a).

A lease under a power by a person having only a particular estate, if not conformable to the power, is not good at law, but when the persons granting the lease, have at law the inheritance, with directions only how they are to execute leases, the legal estate passes (b).

If there be a power of revocation, and a lease for years is made, such power is suspended *quoad* the term, but after it is good (c).

Section VIII. *Of Leases by Tenant for Years.*

As a lessee or tenant for years may assign or grant over his whole interest, so he may grant it for any fewer or lesser number of years than he himself holds it, and such derivative lessee is compellable to pay rent, perform covenants, *&c.* according to the terms agreed in such grant or assignment. Also it is said [in *Broke* title Distress 7,] that a termor so assigning may distrain for the rent, without any power reserved for that purpose, though a person who assigns his whole interest cannot, because he has no reversion (d).

But such derivative lessee is not liable (to the original lessor) for the rent reserved on the original lease, otherwise than as his cattle, (*&c.*) may be liable to a distress for rent-arrear to the original lessor, as any stranger's levant and couchant may be, for there is no privity between him and the original lessor, as there is between a lessor and an assignee, and therefore such an one, though he take the whole term except one day, shall not be liable to any of the covenants in the original lease (e).

Section IX. *Of Leases by Tenant from Year to Year; or for a less Term.*

Any one, possessed of a certain quantity of interest, may alienate the whole, or any part of it, unless restricted from so doing, by agreement with the party from whom he derives that interest or estate, or by the terms upon which he takes it.

In fact the tenant has it as a right incident to his tenancy to make a sub-tenancy, in order to do which, it is by no means necessary to have the first landlord's assent: the law gives him authority to assign his interest (*f*).

A tenant from year to year, therefore, may assign his term, or may

(a) Hard 415. (b) 13 Ves 582. (c) 1 Mod 114.
(d) Bac. Abr. tit. "Leases." (e) Ibid. (*f*) 1 East. R. 598. T.'s M. S. S. s. c.

under-let part of it, as for three quarters of the year, or so many months, *&c.* So, upon the same principle, one possessed of lands or tenements, for a less term, as for half a year, a quarter, or a month, or the like, may grant his interest, however small the quantity, or any portion of it, to another: for, while such interest endures, he has the absolute disposition of it, unless some agreement subsists between him and his lessor, that by circumscribing his power, qualifies that disposition.

A tenant at will, however, cannot lease, for there can be no such thing as an under-tenant to a tenant at will, the demise itself would amount to a determination of the will. Neither can he surrender, any more than he can grant, for, to surrender also, would be to determine his will, and relinquish his estate (*a*).

As a tenant at will cannot grant or surrender, so *a fortiori* cannot a tenant at sufferance.

Section X *Of Leases by Corporations*

With respect to what acts a corporation aggregate must do by deed, and what it may do without deed, it is a question which seems by the old books, to have been the subject of considerable controversy among the Justices. Some go so far as to say, that without deed, a corporation cannot do any act whatever. One makes a distinction, which seems to be founded in good sense, between the case of a corporation aggregate, consisting of many persons, one capable, and the other incapable, as abbot and convent, and corporations aggregate of many persons capable, as mayor and commonalty, or dean and chapter, the former, he seems to intimate, may do many acts without deed, because the abbot is the only person capable, and the oracle of the whole, the rest being incapable of any act, because they are dead in law; but corporations of the other kinds being composed of persons, all of whom are capable of action, there is no individual who can be considered as the oracle of the whole, and therefore they can speak only by their deed executed in due form (*b*).

They can neither make a disposition of their property, nor do any act relating to it, nor receive a grant, without deed thus they cannot, without deed, make a lease for years, nor grant a licence to take away their trees; and if a disseisin be made to their use, they cannot agree but by writing under their common seal (*c*).

But though they cannot make a lease without deed, yet before the statute of Frauds, a lease made by them might, without deed, have been granted over by the lessee.

(*a*) 1 Inst. 57. a Doug. 283 Cro. Eliz. 156 (*b*) Kyd on Corp. 259 (*c*) Ibid. 262

So, it is said, that if a lease for years be made to a corporation who cannot take without deed, and they grant it over, the grantee may entitle himself thereto, without shewing the deed, because, the lease of the thing in its nature, might have passed without deed, although the persons who took it could not take it without deed also, his possession is some privilege for his title (*a*).

If a lease for years be made to a corporation aggregate of many, they cannot make an actual surrender thereof, but by deed under their seal: but if they accept a new lease thereof, this is a surrender in law of their first lease, and may therefore, by the statute of Frauds, be without writing (*b*).

Neither can a corporation aggregate without deed, authorize their servant or agent to enter into land on their behalf, for a condition broken; though this does not seem to have been always free from doubt (*c*). In one place it is said, that a man cannot justify as servant to a corporation, without shewing a deed of retainer, and it is contrasted with the case of a man avowing as bailiff to a corporation, which may be done without deed. In another place, where it is reported to have been said by *Littleton*, that it was the opinion of all the Judges in the Common Pleas and King's Bench, that an assignment of auditors by a commonalty is good without deed, it is added, "and so of a justification by their commandment." In a third place, it is said to be the better opinion, that he who pleads the freehold of dean and chapter, and that he entered by their commandment, ought to shew a command in writing, and the same of a servant of mayor and commonalty. In another place, a distinction is made between a corporation which has a head, as mayor and commonalty, and a corporation without a head; in the first case, it is said, that a man may justify entering into land by the commandment of the mayor, without writing; in the latter, that a command to enter must be by writing.—*Rolle* lays it down as clear law, that "a corporation aggregate cannot command their bailiff to enter into land of their own leasing for years, for a condition broken without deed, for such commandment without deed is void (*d*)." and this is consonant to the principle, that, where the interest or title of the corporation is concerned, their officer must be appointed by deed.

It seems however to have been generally admitted, that a bailiff might be appointed to take a distress without deed. It is even said, that "it is not necessary that he should be made bailiff before he distrain; it is sufficient if the corporation agree to it afterwards, for that his being bailiff is not traversable, and a member of the corporation may distrain in right of the corporation, and justify as bailiff." Again,

(*a*) Cro. Jac. 110. (*b*) Bac. Abr. tit. Corporations, (E 3.) (*c*) Id. ib. 262.
(*d*) 1 Rol. 514.

it is said, a man may justify as bailiff to dean and chapter, and the like, without shewing the deed constituting him bailiff " and in more modern times, it has been laid down as a rule, that " a corporation aggregate may appoint a bailiff to distrain without deed or warrant, because the distress neither vests an interest in them, nor devests one out of them (a)."

Where any personal act is necessary in the case of a corporation, that act must be done by attorney appointed by deed under their common seal (b).

Thus, if they accept rent from the assignee of a lease made by them, that must be by warrant of attorney, in order to discharge the original lessee unless the corporation have a particular officer, whose business it is to manage the revenues, as is the case of the city of *London*. So, whenever delivery of a deed is thought necessary, that must be by attorney, who must have a letter of attorney for the purpose (c).

But in an ejectment by a corporation against a tenant from year to year, a notice to quit given by a person acting as steward of the corporation, is sufficient, without evidence that he had an authority under seal from the corporation for this purpose (d).

A dean and chapter made a lease for three lives, and a letter of attorney to deliver it on the land. *Twisden* J. thought the letter was void, the lease being a perfect lease by sealing, and the delivery afterwards impertinent, but *Hale* C. J. observed, that since he had sate in the court, it had been ruled, that the latter execution was good, and that the lease, on being sealed, was but an escrow, where the letter of attorney was delivered at the same time (e).

On evidence at a trial in ejectment, the case was this:—A dean and chapter having a right to certain land, but being out of possession, sealed a lease with a letter of attorney to deliver it upon the land, which was done accordingly, and this was held to be a valid transaction, on the ground, that though putting the seal of a corporation aggregate to a deed be equivalent to a delivery, yet the letter of attorney to deliver it on the land, suspends the operation of it till actual delivery of it by the attorney (f).

A deed by a corporation out of possession, containing a lease of land and letter of attorney, is not good under the common seal, if the attorney does not deliver it upon the land (g).

In ejectment, the plaintiff declared upon a demise made to him by the aldermen and burgesses of ——, without setting forth that it was by deed, or under the seal of the corporation, and on a writ of error, it was held well enough, for that this being a fictitious action to try

(a) Kyd on Corp. 260. (b) Ibid. 262. (c) Ibid. 263.
(d) 2 Campb. R. 96. (e) Kyd on Corp. [illegible] (f) Ibid. (g) Com. Dig. [illegible] Fait (A. 4).

the title, the demise need not now be set out to have been made by deed (*a*).

It is a general rule, that a corporation cannot take but by their corporate name. It is also a general rule, that it cannot grant but by its proper name of corporation, though every minute variation in the name is not material to avoid a grant (*b*).

As to naming the corporation, we shall only observe, that corporations *aggregate*, as dean and chapter, mayor and commonalty, warden and fellows, &c. may make or confirm leases, without expressing either the christian or surname of the dean, mayor, warden, &c. because in their politic capacity, as a corporation aggregate, they continue always the same, and are said never to die; but in leases or confirmations by a bishop, dean, mayor, &c. or other *sole* corporation, both their christian and surname, or at least their christian name, ought to be expressed, [as John bishop of P.] because they are subject to death and succession, &c. and therefore must be particularly named, to shew whose lease, &c. it was; and so, some hold too, in the first case (*c*).

Where a corporation, declaring in a covenant by their modern name, stated that citizens, &c. were from time to time immemorial incorporated by divers names of incorporation, and at the time of making the indenture by *A. B.* declared on, were known by a certain other name, by which name *A. B.* granted to them a certain water course, and covenanted for quiet enjoyment. Held that the deed granted the water course to them by such name was evidence as against the defendants, who claimed under the grantor, that the corporation was known by that name at the time, upon an issue taken on that fact (*d*).

A corporation aggregate may take any chattel, as bonds, leases, &c. in its corporate capacity, which shall go in succession, because it is always in being (*e*).

But regularly, no chattel shall go in succession, in case of a sole corporation. By custom, however, it may, as in the instance of the chamberlain of *London*.—Therefore, if a lease for years be made to a bishop and his successors, and the bishop dies, this shall not go to his successors, but to his executors (*f*).

A corporation cannot be sued in an action of *assumpsit*.

A covenant in a corporation lease, to renew upon the falling in "of one life for ever," there is no equity to extend it to the case where two are suffered to fall in, although a compensation be offered (*g*).

This subject is connected with that which follows; other information therefore will be found under the next article.

(*a*) [illegible] Jac. 61 [illegible] (*b*) [illegible]
[illegible] Bac. Abr. [illegible] (*c*) [illegible]
[illegible] Corporations (I. 3.) (*f*) [illegible] (*g*) [illegible] Bro. R. [illegible]

SECTION XI. *Of Leases by ecclesiastical Persons.*

As to leases by *ecclesiastical* persons, *bishops with the confirmation of the dean and chapter*, parsons or vicars with the consent of their patrons and ordinaries, archdeacons, prebends, and such as are in the nature of prebends, as precentors, chanters, treasurers, chancellors, and such like, also, masters and governors, and fellows of any colleges or houses (by what name soever called), deans and chapters, masters or guardians of any hospital, and their brethren, or any other body politic, spiritual and ecclesiastical, (*concurrentibus his quæ in jure requiruntur*) might, by the ancient common law, have made leases for lives or years, or any other estate of their spiritual or ecclesiastical living, for any time without stint or limitation (*a*).

By the before-mentioned statute, of 32 *H.* 8. *c.* 28. bishops and the rest of the said spiritual persons, (except parsons and vicars) may, at this day, *make leases of their spiritual living, for three lives, or twenty-one years, and such leases will be good both against themselves and their successors.* But, in order to be binding, they must have the effect of all the qualities or properties before-mentioned and required by the said statute, in the lease made by tenant in tail, and be made after that pattern. But with respect to the old lease being surrendered, there is an exception in favour of a bishop; for if he make a lease for twenty-one years to come to one man, and then, within a year after, make another lease to another for twenty-one years, to begin from the making of it, this, so as it be confirmed by dean and chapter, is resolved to be a good lease. A lease by a bishop, wherein more than the old rent was reserved, was held good, two of the Judges however, who were absent when the case was argued, were of a different opinion (*b*).

Next follows, in order of time, the *disabling* or *restraining* statute, 1 *Eliz.* c. 19 (made entirely for the benefit of the successor) which enacts, that all grants by archbishops and bishops, (which include even those confirmed by the dean and chapter, the which were good at common-law) other than for the term of one and twenty years, or three lives from the making, without reserving the usual rent, shall be void. Concurrent leases if confirmed by the dean and chapter, are held to be within the exception of this statute, and therefore valid, provided they do not exceed, together with the lease in being, the term permitted by the act. But, by a saving expressly made, the statute did not extend to any grants made by any bishop to the crown; the statute 1 *J.* 1. c. 3. however, extends the prohibition to grants and leases made to the king, as well as to any of his subjects.—Next comes the statute 13 *Eliz.* c. 10. explained and enforced by the statutes 14 *Eliz.* c. 11. & 14. 18 *Eliz.* c. 11. and 43 *Eliz.* c. 29. which extends the restrictions

(*a*) [illegible] c. 28.　　(*b*) 2 Mod. [illegible]

[illegible] by the [illegible] to certain other inferior corporations, [illegible].

The [illegible], in some respects altered by stat. 39 & 40 G. 3. c. [illegible] whereby it is enacted, that where part of the possessions of any [illegible], bishops, masters, and fellows, dean and chapter, [illegible], or any other person or persons, bodies politic or corporate, having any ecclesiastical living, [illegible] which was formerly demised [illegible] the ancient rent [illegible] shall be retained in the possession of the lessor, the [illegible] rents reserved on the separate demises of the specific parts shall [illegible] to be the ancient rents within the meaning of the statutes 32 *H.* 8. c. 28. [illegible] *Eliz.* c. 10. 13 *Eliz.* c. [illegible] and 14 *Eliz.* c. 11.

Section 2 provides, that no [illegible] shall be valid, unless the several rents reserved upon the separate demises of separate parts of tenements accustomably demised under one lease, or if part be [illegible] in the possession of the lessor or lessors, unless the rent reserved on the parts demised shall be at least so far equal to the whole amount of the ancient rent or rents, that the part not demised shall be sufficient to answer the difference.

Section 3 provides, that where the whole of such demises shall in future be demised in parts, the aggregate rents reserved shall not be less than the accustomed old rent, and so in proportion, where a part shall be retained in possession by the lessor.

Section 4 provides, that no greater proportion of the accustomed rent shall be reserved by any separate lease than the part of the premises demised will bear.

Section 5 provides, that where any specific things shall have been reserved by the lessor, it may be charged on a competent part of the premises; and in case such provision shall have been made for payment of any sum of money, stipend, &c. it shall be deemed lawful if the lands, &c. charged be of greater annual value, exclusive of the rent reserved.

Section 6 provides, that no lease shall be confirmed whereon no annual rent is reserved to the lessors, &c.

Section 7 provides, that the act shall not authorize the [illegible] of any rent, on any such lease, made by any master, &c. of any college, in any other manner than required by the 18 *Eliz.* c. 6.

Section 8 provides, that where payments have been reserved to vicars, curates, schoolmasters, and other persons than the lessor, provision shall be made in leases for the future payment thereof out of premises of three times the annual value, exclusive of the rent, except (section 9) such payment depends only on the will of the person granting or renewing the lease.

(a) 2 Bl. Com. 320.

Section 10. provides, that persons holding such leases in trust, or granting under-leases of specific parts under covenants of renewal, may surrender them, in order that separate leases may be granted to the original lessors to the *cestui que* trusts, and under-lessees, for the same terms, subject to the accustomed rent, or a rent ... such surrender, and the new leases granted thereupon, shall be good in law and equity, notwithstanding such under-lessees and *cestui que* trusts may be infants, issue unborn, or other persons incapacitated to act for themselves; provided such new leases be for their benefit, and such be expressly declared in the body of each lease [illegible].

From laying all which together, we may collect, that all colleges, cathedrals, and other ecclesiastical, or eleemosynary corporations, and all parsons and vicars are restrained from making any leases of their lands, unless under the following regulations 1. They must not exceed twenty-one years, or three lives, from the making 2. The accustomed rent, or more, must be yearly reserved thereon [illegible] respecting which, the first sections of 39 and 40 G. 3. are particularly explanatory. 3. Houses in corporations or market-towns may be let for forty years, provided they be not the mansion-houses of the lessors, nor have above ten acres of ground belonging to them, and provided the lessee be bound to keep them in repair, and they may also be aliened in fee simple for lands of equal value in recompense [illegible], therefore, a bond or covenant for rendering or making a lease within a city or town may be enforced [illegible]. 4 Where there is an old lease in being, no concurrent lease shall be made, unless where the old one will expire within three years [illegible]. Since the statute of Frauds and Perjuries, (29 C. 2. c. 3.) which requires all surrenders to be in writing, it was usual to have [illegible] the person or corporation to whom the surrender was made [illegible] they would, within such a time, make a new lease, under [illegible] such terms [illegible] the statute, however, does not extend [illegible] by taking a new lease [illegible]. No lease (by the equity of the statute) shall be made without impeachment of waste [illegible]. 6. All bonds and covenants, tending to frustrate the provisions of the statutes of 13 and 18 *Eliz.* shall be void [illegible].

As to leases, therefore, made by parsons, vicars, and others, having benefices or promotions with cure of souls, these things are to be observed, 1. That parsons and vicars are expressly excepted out of 32 *H.* 8. *c.* 28. so that they are not, as other sole corporations, enabled by that statute to make any leases to bind their successors without the confirmation of the patron and ordinary, but remain as they did, perfectly at common-law, for any thing in that statute. 2. That an annual rent must be reserved to the lessor or lessors, otherwise the lease cannot be confirmed. 3. That they are not restrained by 13 *Eliz.* c. 10. from

(*a*) H [illegible] 26)
(*b*) 39 & 40 G. 3. c. 41. s. 10
(*c*) 2 Bl. Com. 320.
(*d*) [illegible] Leases [illegible])
(*e*) 2 Bl. Com. 320

making leases for twenty-one years, or three lives. But then such leases must not only be confirmed by the patron and ordinary, but must also be made in conformity to the rules or qualities before mentioned, otherwise they will not bind the successor (a). They, as well as others, are restrained by 13 *Eliz.* c. 10. from making leases for any longer time, notwithstanding any confirmation, or conformity to those rules or qualities (b).

Another restriction occurs with regard to college leases (c), which is created by stat. 18 *Eliz.* c. 6. and is specially exempted from the operation of the 39 & 40 *Geo.* 3. c. 41. by s. 7 of that Act, by which it is directed, that one third of the old rent then paid, should for the future be reserved in wheat or malt, reserving a quarter of wheat for each 6s. 8d. or a quarter of malt for every 5s. or that the lessees should pay the same according to the price that wheat and malt should be sold for in the market next adjoining to the respective colleges, on the market-day before the rent becomes due. This sagacious plan is said to have been the invention of Lord Treasurer *Burleigh* and Sir *Thomas Smith*, then principal Secretary of State; who observing how greatly the value of money had sunk, and the price of all provisions risen, by the quantity of bullion imported from the newly found *Indies*, devised this method for upholding the revenues of colleges. Their foresight and penetration have, in this respect, been very apparent. This corn rent has made the old rent approach in some degree, nearer to its present value [illegible]; otherwise, it should seem, the principal advantage of a corn rent, is to secure the lessor from the effect of a sudden scarcity of corn.—The leases of beneficed clergymen were farther restrained, in case of their non-residence, by stat. 13 *Eliz.* c. 20. 14 *Eliz.* c. 11. 18 *Eliz.* c. 11. and 43 *Eliz.* c. 9. But by 43 *Geo.* 3. c. 84. s. 1. the 13 *Eliz.* c. 20. is repealed, together with every explanation, &c. thereof made by the 14 *Eliz.* c. 11. 18 *Eliz.* c. 11. and 43 *Eliz.* c. 9. and the penalties for non-residence are altered altogether. As far as the 43 *Geo.* 3. respects the present subject, it may be observed that by sect. 3, all contracts or agreements made after the passing of the Act, for the letting of houses of residence, or the buildings, gardens, orchards, and appurtenances necessary for the convenient occupation of the same, belonging to any benefice, donation, perpetual curacy, or parochial chapelry, to which houses of residence any spiritual persons shall be, by the order of the archbishop or bishop, required to proceed and reside therein, (a copy of such order being, immediately on the issuing thereof, transmitted to one of the churchwardens, who shall forthwith serve it on the occupier of such house of residence, or left at the same) shall be null and void; and any person continuing to hold such house or any such building, &c. or premises, after the day on which such spiritual person shall by the said order be directed to reside therein, and after service of such copy

(a) Bac. Abr. tit. Leases (F).   (b) 2 Bl. Com. 322.   (c) C[illegible] N[illegible]

as aforesaid, shall forfeit forty shillings for every day he shall, without the archbishop's or bishop's consent in writing, wilfully continue to hold such house, building, &c. the said penalty or penalties to be recovered by action of debt, bill, plaint, or information in any court of record at *Westminster*, or the courts of great sessions in *Wales*, and the whole to go to the person suing, together with costs. But in case of any contract before the Act, the person holding shall not be liable to any penalty for three calendar months from the service of such order as aforesaid; and sequestration for disobedience to reside shall not issue for three calendar months, to be computed from the service of such order of the archbishop or bishop. Neither shall any person be liable for non-residence while such tenant shall continue to occupy. s. 35.

At common law, if a parson had made a lease for years of his glebe land, to begin after his death, or granted a rent-charge in that manner, and such lease or grant were confirmed by the patron and ordinary, this would have bound the successor of the parson, because here were the consent and concurrence of all persons interested, and the lease or charge bound immediately from the perfecting of the deed by the parson, patron, and ordinary, though it was not to take effect in possession till after the parson's death: but now, no confirmation whatever will make such lease or grant good against the successor, by reason of the statutes made to avoid them (a).

If a person obtain a grant to build houses on church or college lands, which is confirmed, (in case where confirmation is necessary), yet this grant is no alienation against the statutes, but is only a covenant or licence, and nothing else; for the soil remains in the grantor, and by consequence the houses built thereon are in him (b).

In some cases, the confirmation of the patron is necessary, and in some not; wherein this diversity is taken in the books, That such sole corporations, who have *not* the absolute fee and inheritance in them, as prebends, parsons, vicars, and such like, if they make any leases or estates, there in order to bind their successors, the patron must confirm the same: but such sole corporations who *have* the whole estate and right in them, as bishops, abbots, &c. or such corporations aggregate, who have the whole fee and inheritance in them, as dean and chapter, masters, fellows, and scholars of any college, hospital, &c. these may make leases to bind their successors, without any confirmation of the patron or founder, though the bishop, abbot, dean, master, &c. were presentable; and the reason of this diversity appears in the nature of the right with which each is invested (c).

But if a parsonage or vicarage be a donative, then the confirmation of patron alone is sufficient to all leases, &c. made by the parson or

(a) Bac. Abr. tit. Leases (E). (b) Ibid. (c) Bac. Abr. tit. Leases (G 2).

vicar, and shall bind the successor without the confirmation of any other (a).

Yet, if there be a lord-paramount, as well as an immediate patron, confirmation of the immediate patron, without the other's confirmation, is not good; as if a parson be patron of the vicarage of the same church, and the vicar makes a lease confirmed by the parson and ordinary, this is not good without the confirmation of the patron of the rectory also, because both have an interest in the possessions of the vicarage (b).

As a patron may confirm expressly by his deed or writing, so may he also confirm by consequence of law; for, if a parson makes a lease for years to the patron, who grants or assigns it over to another, this amounts to a confirmation in law by the patron, because a confirmation being nothing but an assent under the hand and seal of the party confirming, such assent in this case sufficiently appears by his assigning over the lease to another (c).

Another difference observable in the manner of confirming such leases as we are treating of, is, as to their duration, or continuance: for, if a parson make a lease for twenty-one years at this day, and the patron and ordinary confirm his estate therein for seven years, or (after reciting the lease) "not beyond" that term, yet is the estate or lease well confirmed for the twenty-one years, for when they confirm the estate of the lessee, that is entire, and cannot be divided (d).

As to the estate which they who make such confirmation ought to have, to make the lease effectually binding upon the successors, this regards chiefly the patron, whose advowson or right of patronage, being a temporal inheritance, and considered as such, is to be governed by the same rules as other temporal inheritances are: his confirmation, therefore, being in nature of a charge upon the advowson, is to be directed by the estate which he hath in the advowson, and can continue no longer than that endures (e).

If, therefore, the patron had a conditional estate in the advowson, and he confirm a lease of the parson's, and afterwards the condition be broken, this defeats also his confirmation, so that the succeeding incumbent shall not be bound by it. So, if a church be full of a parson, and afterwards another is made parson, and he makes a lease for years, which is confirmed by the patron and ordinary, yet the lease is void, because he who made it was not parson, the church being full before (f).

As to the time of confirmation, generally speaking, it is not material whether it be before or after the making of the lease, which is to be confirmed, so it be made in the life-time of the parties who make the lease; for the confirmation is but an assent or agreement by deed, to

(a) Bac. Abr. tit. Leases, (G. 2.) (b) Ibid. (c) Ibid.
(d) Ibid. (e) Ibid. (G. 3.) (f) Ibid.

the making such lease or grant, and not a confirmation of the estate itself (*a*).

Thus, where a bishop made a lease to the second of *May*, which was confirmed the third of *May*, and sealed the fourth of *May*, this was held a good confirmation (*b*).

Yet it hath been holden on the contrary, that if a confirmation be made and delivered before the grant or lease be confirmed, that this is not a good confirmation, and, though after the grant or lease, the deed of confirmation be delivered again, yet that will not make it good, for that it was a deed by the first delivery, and the second delivery will not make it good as an assent, because the assent ought to be by deed, and the first delivery was void, but that confirmation may be made before the grant or lease be confirmed, the other cases are express (*c*).

If a bishop, parson, or any other sole ecclesiastical corporation, make a lease for years, which needs confirmation, his confirmation ought to be made in the life and during the incumbency of the lessor, for after his death, resignation, deprivation, or other amotion, the lease is become void for want of confirmation; and then, confirmation made after cannot revive it, though it be made in the vacation before any successor comes in (*d*).

But if a parson make a lease for years, which is not confirmed by the bishop or patron, then in being, but by the succeeding bishop and succeeding patron, this is a good lease, and shall bind the successor.

Section XII. *Of Leases by Trustees of Charities.*

Leases of charity lands are under the peculiar cognizance of the Court of Chancery, and where a lease is made by trustees at an under-value, by collusion between them and the lessee, the court can make a decree not only against the trustees, but also against the lessee for the surplus value (*e*).

The mode of granting leases of charity lands is sometimes prescribed by the founder, as that the term shall not exceed twenty-one years, that no fine shall be taken &c. and then the terms of the power must be strictly pursued: and sometimes power is given to the trustees to make leases generally, in which case they have a power both in law and equity, either to take fines or reserve rents, as is most beneficial for the charity (*f*). Where there is no power, the trustees must be guided by the general principles of the court, which will take care that a reasonable discretion is exercised (*g*).

Where the rules of the foundation directed that no lease should be

(*a*) Bac Abr tit Leases (G 3) [illegible] (*b*) Ibid (*c*) Ibid (*d*) Ibid
(*e*) High on Mort. 449 (*f*) Ibid. (*g*) 10 Ves Jun 555

granted for more than twenty-one years, and that at the old rent, taking a fine of two years' value, also a lease for twenty-one years at the old rent, with a covenant by repeated renewals to make it up sixty years, was decreed upon certain conditions, to be confirmed for twenty-one years from the last renewal, but the covenant for renewal was declared void, as rendering the lease no less prejudicial than an actual lease for sixty years (*a*).

A college restrained by its constitution from making leases, other than for twenty-one years, at a rack rent, made an entry in their order book, recommending it to their successors to renew a particular lease at less than the rack rent, the tenant having made great improvements. The court refused to decree the renewal, considering the parties who had signed the order for a breach of the college statutes (*b*).

Where long leases of charity lands have been procured upon terms very inadequate to their full value, the court has, in several instances, interfered to annul them, and to bring the lessees to a just account of the rents and profits (*c*).

An alienation for ninety-nine years of a charity estate, if it be a mere husbandry lease and without consideration, is a lease which the court will not permit to stand, unless it is shewn to be fair and reasonable, and for the benefit of the charity (*d*). A long lease of a charity estate is *primâ facie* a breach of trust, and a proof of the circumstances that make it a provident administration is thrown on those who take such a lease (*e*). Therefore, trustees of a charity cannot in general, unless specially empowered, grant a lease for seventy years, except for the purpose of building (*f*), for a case may occur in which the property cannot be made beneficial without building, and the trustees may have no fund.

In 1715 the trustees of a charity granted a lease of lands, theretofore let at 31*l. per annum*, for nine hundred and ninety-nine years, in consideration of 500*l.* to be laid out in improvements, and of 4*l. per annum* additional rent. The court considered this to be a sort of perpetuity, destructive to the charity estate, and therefore decreed the lease to be given up, but as the tenant had lately laid out 600*l.* in improvements, it was ordered that he should have just allowances made him in the account which was directed (*g*).

It is laid down in a recent case (*h*), that neither a lease of charity land for ninety-nine years, as a mere husbandry lease, upon terms and at a rent adapted to a lease for twenty-one years, nor a building lease of nine hundred and ninety-nine years upon an expenditure, commensurate to a term of ninety-nine years, can be supported.

But a lease of a charity of land for eighty years, was supported as to

(*a*) 2 Vern. [illegible] (*b*) [illegible] (*c*) 2 Ves. [illegible]
(*d*) 6 Ves. Jun. 452. 10 Ves. Jun. 555. (*e*) [illegible] (*f*) 13 Ves. Jun. 563.
(*g*) [illegible] (*h*) 17 Ves. Jun. 282.

the interest of a sub-lessee, who had given a fair consideration, and had no notice, except that the estate belonged to a charity (a), the court observing that its feelings upon the abuse of a charity estate must not carry it beyond what is just, even against those who are guilty, much less against other persons, and upon that ground the decree should be mollified with regard to the interests of sub-lessees having given a fair consideration, merely directing them to pay the rent to other persons than those to whom they had contracted to pay it. The interests of those persons may be very fair, as between them and those from whom they take, and the relief in these cases is to be adapted to the conduct of the parties, as the court finds them respectively to have acted fairly or not, towards the trust.

SECTION XIII. *Of Leases by married Women, and Husbands seised in right of them.*

By the common law, if a husband seised of lands of inheritance in right of his wife, make a lease thereof by indenture or deed-poll, reserving rent, this, though voidable, will be good, unless the wife by some act after the husband's death shews her dissent thereto, for if she accept rent which becomes due after his death, the lease is thereby become absolute and unavoidable.

If a widow chooses to avoid such lease, notwithstanding her having joined therein, then it is so absolutely defeated *ab initio* as to her, that she may plead *non demise*, because, as to any interest that passed from her she did not demise, nor in truth had any power to contract, but the whole interest passed from the husband, and the lessee is in merely by virtue of the husband's contract, and yet because the lessee, by his acceptance of such lease, admitted them both to have power to join therein, he must accordingly during the coverture declare of the lease by them both as an essential part of the description of the lease whereby he makes title (b).

But the indenture or deed-poll, whereby such lease was made, being no essential part either of the description or lease itself, because the husband, during the coverture, might have made it by parol only, therefore it is not necessary nor usual for the lessee in his declaration to make any mention thereof (c).

A lease made by husband and wife of the lands of the wife, and delivered by letter of attorney in both their names, will support a declaration in ejectment on a lease by the husband only; for the delivery by

(a) 17 Ves. Jun. 283. (b) Bac. Abr. tit. Leases (C 1.) (c) Ibid.

attorney being void as to the wife, it is the lease of the husband only (a).

But if the husband and wife join in a lease for years by parol of the wife's lands rendering rent, or if the husband solely make such parol lease, rendering rent, this determines absolutely by his death, so that no acceptance of rent, or other act done by the wife, will prevent its avoidance, for a lease for years being an immediate contract for, or disposition of the land itself, if the same appears in writing duly executed, so that there can be no variation or deviation therefrom attempted by the lessee after the husband's death, the law so far gives countenance to such lease for the encouragement of farmers and husbandmen, that the same shall continue in force till the wife's actual dissent or disagreement thereto, but because there can be no such certainty of the terms of a parol lease, when nothing appears in writing to manifest them, therefore they, like other charges of the husband, fall off and drop with his estate or interest therein (b).

If the husband and wife make a lease for years of the wife's land, without reservation of any rent, yet it hath been adjudged that this is a good lease by them both during the coverture, and that the wife, after the husband's death, may affirm the same by acceptance of fealty, or bringing an action of waste, so that the reservation of rent is not essential to the existence or continuance of such lease after the husband's death, but only a writing attesting the same, and the wife's allowance and approbation thereof, for as the husband made such lease at first without any reservation of rent, so the wife, if she thinks fit, may continue the lessee in possession after his death upon the same terms (c).

A husband seised in right of his wife cannot grant copies in his own name, but the wife ought to join (d).

But if a husband seised of a copyhold in right of his wife, make a lease not warranted by the custom, it is a forfeiture of the estate during the life of the husband only, for it is not a continuing detriment to the inheritance, or such an act as tends to the destruction of the manor, in which case it would bind the inheritance of the wife after the husband's death (e).

A husband letting copyhold lands of which he is seised in right of his wife, by indenture, will not destroy the custom of demising by copy, because the wife may enter after his death and avoid such lease (f).

A woman guardian in socage, marries and joins with her husband by indenture, in making a lease for years of the ward's land, yet after her husband's death she may avoid the same in right of the infant whose

(a) Cro. Jac. 617. (c) Bac. Abr. ut ante. (e) Bac. Abr. tit. Leases, (C 1.)
(b) Cro. Jac. [illegible] (d) Bac. Abr. ut ante, & Cro. Car. 7. (f) [illegible] Cro. Eliz. 45[illegible]

guardian she still continues to be, and to whom, when he comes of age, she must be accountable for the profits (*a*).

A husband, in whom a long term of years was vested in right of his wife, made an under-lease for the ten years, and upon borrowing money of the lessee, covenanted to grant him another lease after the end of the ten years, and to continue during the time he had any right, but died before he made such lease, it was decreed to be a good disposition of the term in equity (*b*)

Touching leases made by husband and wife, pursuant to the statute 32 *H* 8 *c* 28. [concerning which statute *vide ante*,] the husband may at this day, without fine or recovery, make leases of the lands, tenements, or hereditaments, whereof he hath any estate of inheritance in fee-simple or fee-tail in right of his wife, made before or after the coverture, so as there be in such leases observed the conditions or limitations before required in the leases made by tenant in tail, and so that the wife join in the same deed, and be made party thereunto, and seal and deliver the same deed herself in person for if a man and his wife make a letter of attorney to another to deliver the lease upon the land, this lease is not a good lease from the wife warranted by the statute, and yet then, as in other like cases, of leases not warranted by the statute, it is a good lease against the husband. When the lease is such an one as is warranted by the statute, it binds the husband and wife both, and the heirs of the wife, but if it be an estate-tail, it doth not bind the donor nor him in remainder (*c*).

Husband and wife, the husband purchased land to him and his wife, and their heirs, and afterwards he, without his wife, lets this land for sixty years, if they should so long live, rendering 28*l* *per ann.* rent at the two usual feasts, during the term, then the husband dies, and if this lease should bind the wife by the 32 *H* 8 *c* 28 was the question, and it was held by three justices that it should · for the wife is appointed to join only when she hath the sole inheritance by the appointment of the rent to be reserved to the heirs of the wife, and not when she hath a joint-estate, as in this case, and then clearly by the body of the act, the lease by the husband solely is good, and the proviso does not extend to it, in truth, the lease determined by the death of either of them (*d*)

Where a feme-covert has for many years been separated from her husband, and, during that time, has received for her separate use the rents of her own property, which accrued to her by devise after the separation, she shall be presumed to receive the rents, and acknowledge the tenancy, by her husband's authority (*e*)

A husband possessed of a term, in right of his wife, may dispose of the whole or any part of it.

(*a*) Cro Eliz 159 (*b*) 12 Mod. 43 (*c*) Shep Touch 28.
(*d*) Bac Abr tit Leases, (C. 1) (*e*) 1 Taunt 367

So, he may make a lease to commence after his death, and it will be good, though the wife survive; for, having an interest to dispose of in his life, he might dispose of all the term, and it should bind the feme; so, when he hath disposed by an act executed in his life of the interest of the term, and hath created a term in interest, this is as good as if he had granted all the term (a).

But, if the wife hath only the possibility of a term, the husband cannot dispose of it; as if there be a lease to a husband and wife for their lives, and afterwards to the executor of the survivor, the husband cannot grant this executory interest (b). Therefore he cannot grant a lease to endure beyond both their lives.

It is now settled that a man possessed of a term of years in right of his wife as executrix of her former husband has power to grant and convey the same; for the husband may administer in right of his wife without her consent, though she cannot administer without the consent of her husband; and if the husband can administer, *jure uxoris*, without her consent, it is incident to the power of administration to sell or dispose of a term of years (c).

If the husband possessed of a term for seventy years in right of his wife, make a lease of the [illegible] for twenty years, to begin after his death, this is good and shall bind the wife, because the term, being but a chattel, he had power to dispose of it wholly, and by consequence may dispose of any lesser interest thereout as he thinks fit; and this being a present disposition, which he cannot revoke, binds the interest of the lands immediately, though it takes not effect in possession till after his death. This differs therefore from a devise of such term, or any part thereof by the husband, by his will; for that not taking effect, nor binding the interest at all till after his death, comes too late to prevent the operation of law, which, at the instant of death, immediately casts it upon the wife surviving, and so defeats and destroys the operation of the devise (d).

But as to the residue of the term, whereof the husband makes no disposition in his life-time, the wife, if she survives, will be entitled to it, because as to that, the law is left to take place as it would have done for the whole, if he had not prevented it by such his disposition of part (e).

Yet if the husband demise for part of the wife's term, rendering rent, the rent shall go to his executor or administrator, though the wife survive (f).

Yet if the husband had granted away the whole term upon condition and died, though the condition were afterwards broken, and his executors entered for breach thereof, the wife would, notwithstanding, be

(a) Cro. [illegible] & [illegible] (B 2) 1 Cro. El. 287. (b) Co. [illegible]
(c) 3 V[illegible] 2 Bl. R. 801 [illegible] (d) Bac. Abr. [illegible] Baron & Feme (C 2)
(e) Ibid. (f) 1 Vern. 7 [illegible] 3 Atk. 1[illegible]

for ever barred to claim any interest in the said term, because there was a total disposition thereof by the husband in his life-time, and the breach or non-performance of the condition was perfectly contingent and uncertain; besides that, the breach of the condition happened not till after his death, and so the disposition continued perfect and unaltered during his life; for if the condition had been broken during his life, and he himself had entered for breach thereof, it might be a great question if the wife surviving should not have the term after his death, because by his re-entry for the condition broken he is restored to the whole term *in autre droit*, and then being possessed of it in right of his wife as he was before, it seems but reasonable that the wife should have it, if she survived the husband, as she would have had if no such disposition had been made, since that disposition is now defeated and gone (a).

Section XIV. *Of Leases by Infants and Guardians.*

With respect to the power that an infant possesses to grant a lease that shall be binding, the cases in the books are somewhat contradictory, and the point is liable to unsettled. The better opinion however seems to be, that leases made by infants are not absolutely void, but voidable on their attaining their majority.

"All gifts, grants, or deeds, made by infants, by matter in deed, or in writing, which do take effect by delivery of his hand, are voidable by himself, by his heirs, and by those who have his estate (b)." The words "do take effect," are the essential part of the definition, and exclude letters of attorney, or deeds which delegate a mere power and convey no interest (c).

All the books agree, that if an infant make a lease for years, he cannot plead *non est factum*, but must avoid it by pleading the special matter of his infancy, which favours the opinion of those who hold, that the lease is not absolutely void, for if it were absolutely void, there is no good reason why he should not plead *non est factum*, as a feme covert certainly may do in such a case, whose lease is absolutely void, so that no acceptance of rent after the husband's death can make it good (d).

An infant made a lease for years, and at full age, said to the lessee, "God give you joy of it," this was holden by *Mead* a good affirmation of the lease, for this is a usual compliment to express one's assent and approbation of what is done (e).

What seems decisive upon the question is, that "the lessee can in no case avoid the lease, on account of the infancy of the lessor," which

(a) Bac. Abr. Baron & Feme (C 2) (b) Perk s 12 (c) 3 Burr 1794
(d) Bac Abr. Leases (B) (e) Ibid

shews it not to be void, but voidable only, and it is better for infants that they should have an election (*a*).

It has long been settled that "an infant may make a lease without rent to try his title." In truth, very prejudicial leases may be made, though a nominal rent be reserved, and there may be most beneficial considerations for a lease, though no rent be reserved (*b*).

The court of Chancery will decree building leases for sixty years of infants' estates, when it appears to be for their good (*c*).

Where an infant makes a lease for years, reserving rent, and the lessee enters, the infant hath election to allow him to be his tenant, or to be his disseisor, whichever is most to his advantage: so, where one enters, and claims as guardian, and occupies, the infant may allow him to be either disseisor, or accomptant, whichever shall be for his best advantage (*d*).

In case there be no testamentary guardian [illegible] mother, if the infant has any socage land and is of the age of twelve if female, or fourteen if male, he or she is allowed to choose his or her guardian, as is frequently done on circuit, and is the constant practice, and what the court of Chancery frequently calls on infants to do, though this is still liable to any reasonable objection made to such choice (*e*).

A *guardian in socage* may make leases for years in his own name, and the lessee may maintain ejectment thereupon (*f*), for this guardian is a person appointed not by any special designation of the party, but by the wisdom of the law, in respect of the lands descended to the infant, so that where no lands descend, there can be no such guardian [illegible] and his office originally was to instruct the ward in the arts of tillage and husbandry, that when he came of age he might be the better able to perform those services to his lord, whereby he held his own land, and though the office now be in some measure changed, as the nature of the tenure itself is since the time that the socage tenants bought off their personal labours and services with an annual rent to the lord, yet it is still called socage tenure, and the guardian in socage is still only where lands of that kind (as most of the lands in England now are) descend to the heir within age; and though the heir after fourteen may choose his own guardian, who shall continue till he is twenty-one, yet as well the guardian before fourteen, as he whom the infant shall think fit to choose after fourteen, are both of the same nature, and have the same office and employment assigned to them by the law, without any intervention or direction of the parent himself, for they were appointed because the infant, in regard of his minority, was supposed incapable of managing himself and his estate, and consequently unfit

(*a*) 3 B[illegible] (*b*) [illegible] 2 [illegible] 22. (*c*) [illegible] 376.
(*e*) 2 [illegible] (*f*) Bac. Abr. tit. Leases, (I. [illegible]) (*g*) [illegible] 99.

their authority, not from the infant, but from the law, and that is the reason they transact all affairs in their own name, and not in the name of the infant, as they would be obliged to do, if their authority were derived from him. Indeed, if their authority were derived from him, it would by no means answer the intention of the law in appointing them, for then all acts done by virtue of such derivative authority could be of no more force than if done by the person himself who gave that authority, since none can communicate more power to another than he has himself, and that would invalidate all their contracts, and make them savour of the same imbecility as if made by the infant himself.

Therefore, to enable them to take especial care of the infant and his affairs, the law has invested them, not with a *bare authority* only, but also with *an interest*, till the guardianship ceases: and to prevent their abuse of this authority and interest, the law has made them accountable to the infant, either when he comes to the age of fourteen years, or at any time after, as he thinks fit; and therefore their authority and interest extend only to such things as may be for the benefit and advantage of the infant, and whereof they may give an account.

From what has been said, it appears that a guardian in socage hath not only *a bare authority*, but *an interest* in the lands descended, and therefore during that time may make leases for years in his own name, as any other who hath an interest in lands may do, for he is *quasi dominus pro tempore*. If he makes leases for years to continue beyond the time of his guardianship, such leases seem not to be absolutely void by the infant's coming of age, but only voidable by him, if he thinks fit; for they are not derived barely out of the interest of the guardian, or to be measured thereby, but take effect also by virtue of his authority, which, for the time, was general and absolute, and therefore all lawful acts done during the continuance of that authority, are good, and may subsist after the authority itself, by which they were done, is determined, and consequently the infant, when he comes of age, may by acceptance of rent, or other act, if he thinks fit, make such leases good and unavoidable (*a*).

A testamentary guardian, or one appointed pursuant to the statute 12 *Car.* 2. *c.* 24. *s.* 8, 9, 10, 11. is the same in office and interest as a guardian in socage.

But a guardian by nurture cannot make any leases for years, either in his own name, or in the name of the infant, for he hath only the care of the person and education of the infant, and hath nothing to do with the lands merely in virtue of his office, for such guardian may be, though the infant has no lands at all, which a guardian in socage cannot (*b*). But such guardian, it seems, may make leases at will. Though

(*a*) [illegible] Lease [illegible] (*b*) [illegible]

every guardian except a guardian in socage, is but tenant at will, and by consequence cannot make a lease for any certain time or number of years; yet if a lease be made by such guardian, the lessee is estopped to say, that being only tenant at will, he had no power to make the lease (*a*).

A lease renewed by a guardian for an infant's benefit, shall follow the nature of the original lease; and in general a guardian or trustee shall not alter the nature of the infant's property, so as to change the right of succession to it in case of the infant's death, unless by some act manifestly for the advantage of the infant at the time (*b*).

A devise to a person as guardian, that he may "receive set and let" for his ward, gives him an authority only, and not an interest (*c*).

Section XV. *Of Leases by Executors and Administrators.*

Executors and administrators, as they may dispose absolutely of terms of years vested in them in right of their testators, or intestates, so may they lease the same for any fewer number of years, and the rent reserved on such leases shall be assets in their hands, and go in a course of administration (*d*).

If administration be granted *general*, to one during the minority of an infant executor, the grantee has authority to make leases of any term vested in such infant, which shall be good till he comes of age; and, as it has been also holden by some, till he avoid them by actual entry (*e*).

Section XVI. *Of Leases by Mortgagors and Mortgagees.*

The mortgagor has no power of making leases to bind the mortgagee, but he may make leases which will bind his equity of redemption.

Where the mortgagor is himself the occupier of the estate, he may be considered as tenant at will: but he cannot be so considered if there be an under-tenant, that is a tenant in possession under a lease prior to the mortgage, for there can be no such thing as an under-tenant to a tenant at will, the demise itself would amount to a determination of the will (*f*).

If, therefore, a mortgagor, who continues in possession by consent of the mortgagee, makes a lease for years, and the lessee enters, claiming nothing but his lease, he is not a disseisor, but on payment and acceptance of his rent, a tenant at will, and if the mortgagor enter

(*a*) [illegible] 12 [illegible] (*b*) 3 P. Wms. 121 [illegible] (*c*) [illegible] 6-9 [illegible] (*d*) [illegible] (*e*) 6 Co. 67. Bac. Ab. "Leases," [illegible] (*f*) Doug. 2[illegible]

after the expiration of the lease, he shall be tenant at will again to the mortgagee, and his acts, being by permission of the mortgagee, shall not turn to his prejudice (*a*).

But if a mortgage be made with a proviso and agreement between the parties, that "the mortgagee, his heirs, and assigns, shall not intermeddle with the actual possession of the premises, or perception of the rents," until default of payment, the mortgagor is a tenant at sufferance to the mortgagee, and not a tenant at will, as he would have been on a covenant that he should take the profits till default of payment (*b*).

Indeed the legal interest of a mortgagor in possession, has been held to be inferior to that of a mere strict tenant at will (*c*). However, as to what in strictness is the interest of a mortgagor, after the usual time given for the payment is expired, the estate becomes absolute in the mortgagee at law.

As all leases, or other interests in the land, created by the mortgagor, subsequently to the mortgage, and before the foreclosure, are void against the mortgagee, he may treat the tenants under such leases, or persons claiming such interests, as trespassers, disseisors, and wrong-doers (*d*), or not, at his election; unless where the acts of the mortgagor have been done with the permission of the mortgagee.

If the mortgagee permits the lessee to enjoy his lease, the mortgagor may thenceforth be considered as a receiver of the rent, or, in some sort, a trustee for the mortgagee, who may at any time countermand the implied authority, by giving notice to the tenant not to pay the rent to the mortgagor any longer (*e*). But if the mortgagee elects the other alternative, the lessee may be turned out by ejectment (*f*).

Though the tenant be in possession under a lease prior to the mortgage, yet the mortgagee, after giving notice, is entitled to the rent in arrear at the time of the notice, as well as to what shall accrue afterwards, and he may distrain for it after such notice (*g*).

But where there is a tenant from year to year, and the landlord mortgages pending the year, the tenant is entitled to six months' notice, before he can be evicted by the mortgagee (*h*).

With respect to leases by the mortgagee, he cannot, before foreclosure of the equity of redemption, make a lease for years of the premises in mortgage to bind the mortgagor, unless to avoid an apparent loss and merely in necessity (*i*).

If mortgagor of a term join with the mortgagee in a lease for a shorter term, in which the covenants for the rents and repairs are only with the mortgagor and his assigns, and the interests of the mortgagor

(*a*) Cro. Jac. 660. (*b*) Ibid. 659. (*c*) Doug. 22.
(*d*) Powell on Mort. 22? Dougl. 21. (*e*) 1 Atk. 606. (*f*) Doug. 21.
(*g*) Doug. 279. (*h*) 1 T. R. 378. (*i*) 9 Mod. 1.

and mortgagee become extinguished during the lease by the reversioner acquiring their estates, still the mortgagor may maintain an action of covenant against the lessee, the covenants being in gross (*a*).

But if a mortgagor and mortgagee make a lease in which the covenants for the rent and repairs are only with the mortgagor and his assigns, the assignees of the mortgagee cannot maintain an action for the breach of these covenants on stat. 32 *H* 8 *c.* 34. because they are collateral to his grantor's interest in the land, and therefore do not run with it (*b*).

A court of equity refused on bill to compel an assignee of a term in mortgage to discover his assignment, the object of the lessor in requiring it, being to make him liable to the covenants of the mortgagor, although he had not taken actual possession of the premises The Court dismissed the bill, and left the party to his remedy at law (*c*)

But in a subsequent case, where one hundred pounds were lent by way of mortgage upon an assignment of a building lease, and the mortgagee never entered nor took possession, but lost the money lent, the defendant in equity having recovered against the mortgagee, as assignee, the rent reserved on the lease, the bill was to be relieved against the recovery at law, and the Court dismissed it, saying, the mortgagee was ill advised to take an assignment of the whole term (*d*).

Upon re-consideration of this question in the case of *Eaton* against *Jacques*, it was determined that a mortgagee, assignee of a term for years, should not be liable to the covenants in the lease, unless he had taken actual possession. But this doctrine no longer obtains (*e*).

Indeed that the assignee is liable only in respect of actual possession is entirely contradicted by a case which arose on a bill by the executor of a lessor against the depositary of a lease to secure to him a debt, for the specific performance of a covenant to rebuild houses upon the premises in the eleventh year of the term, which was a term of seventy-one years; to be held for the first ten years at a pecuniary rent, for the eleventh year at a pepper-corn rent, and for the rest of the term at a pecuniary rent. The defendant, by his answer, stated the fact of the disposal by way of mortgage, and insisted that having no title but as mortgagee, he was not bound to rebuild Lord *Thurlow* Chan. thought that there could not be a decree to rebuild, as he could no more undertake the conduct of a rebuilding than of a repair. But his lordship said, it was no matter whether the defendant took it as a pledge, or as a purchase, for he could not take the estate as a security, and refuse the burthen that was upon it, but having once taken it, he could not abandon it. that being then only an assignee in equity, no action could be brought, and that the only relief that he could give the plaintiff, as he could not give him damages, was to put him in a situation to recover

(*a*) [illegible] R 6,8 (*b*) [illegible] (*c*) Pow on Mort 233 (*d*) [illegible] (*e*) Doug 455.

them, his lordship therefore decreed, that the defendants should take an assignment of the lease and execute a counterpart, and that they should pay the costs (a)

Indeed, the principle, that a mortgagee is liable only in respect of his possession seems no longer to be recognized in either a court of law or equity (b) — Thus, where the plaintiff was the original lessee of a term, which he assigned to Kay, who assigned it by way of mortgage to the defendant as a security for the re-payment of a sum of money, the action was brought to recover the amount of ground-rent paid by the plaintiff during the interest of the defendant as mortgagee Lord *Kenyon* said, that the defendant was liable as assignee his liability was not limited by his possession, but as long as he had the legal estate, so long he continued liable to perform the covenants in the lease If he wished to avoid that liability, he should have taken an under-lease (c).

A mortgagee in possession is not obliged to lay out money any further than to keep the estate in necessary repair —If the estate lies at such a distance that he must employ a bailiff to collect the rents, what he paid to the bailiff shall be allowed, but not where he does or may receive the rents himself (d).

If *A*. mortgage land to *B*. upon condition to re-enter on payment of 10*l* ; and afterwards *A*. before the day of payment is come, being in possession, make a lease for years by indenture to *C* and then afterwards performs the condition, this shall make the lease to *C* good against himself by estoppel (e).

Section XVII. *Of Leases by Tenants by Elegit, Statute-Merchant, and Statute-Staple, &c.*

As tenants under these executions have only uncertain interests, determinable at any time on payment of the sum secured, they cannot enter into any contract for a lease, which will not be liable to be put an end to in the same event, but till such contingency occurs their demises are good It however very rarely happens that leases are granted by persons thus entitled, and we shall not therefore enter more at large into the subject.

Section XVIII. *Of Leases by Copyholders, wherein of Licence*

A copyholder cannot, unless by special custom or by licence from the lord, convey any common law interest in his lands to another, as

(a) 1 Pow on Mort. 241. (b) Stone v. Evans Sitt at Westm T T 37 G 3 T's M S S.

such an act is incompatible with his tenancy, so that if he make a lease for years without licence, though by parol only (*a*); or even if it be to commence *in futuro* (*b*), it will be a forfeiture of his tenement. But an interest must actually pass, for a promise or covenant to demise will not create a forfeiture, for it is no lease (*c*).

But a copyholder may make a lease for one year without a licence, and thereupon may maintain an ejectment (*d*).

By special custom a copyholder may make leases for three, nine, or twenty-one years, or for life and forty years after, without licence from the lord, upon which also he may maintain an ejectment (*e*).

But a custom that the lease shall be void if the lessor dies, is good, though not if the lessor alien (*f*).

Although a lease for a year, without licence, be good, yet a lease for one year *et sic de anno in annum* during ten years, being a good lease for ten years, is a forfeiture; but otherwise of a lease for one year, with a covenant for the holding it for a longer time at the will of the lessor. So a lease for a year *et sic de anno in annum* for the life of the lessee, being a lease for two years at least, is not good. So, if *de anno in annum*, excepting one day in every year, for it is a certain lease for two years, excepting two days, which is a lease in effect for more than one year, and although there be the intermission of a day, yet that is not material (*g*).

So, if a copyholder make three leases together, each to commence within two days after the expiration of the other it is a mere evasion of the custom, and therefore not good (*h*).

So if a copyholder, to secure a person who has become bound for him, covenant that such person shall hold and enjoy the copyhold estate for seven years, and so from seven years to seven years, for the term of forty-nine years, if the copyholder so long live, it is a forfeiture of the estate, though there is a clause that the deed should be void on the bond being paid, for this deed, though intended only as a collateral security, amounts to a present lease (*i*).

A copyholder, having licence to lease, ought to pursue his licence strictly, otherwise his lease is void (*k*).

As, if he has a licence to lease for twenty-one years from Michaelmas last, and he leases for twenty-one years from December next. So if he has a licence to lease for two years and he leases for three years. So if a copyholder in fee has a licence to lease for years, if he so long live, and he leases for years absolutely (*l*).

So, a copyholder having licence to make a lease for twenty-one years, cannot make two leases for that term, for he has satisfied his licence by one lease (*m*).

(*a*) [illegible] Cro. Eliz. 198. (*b*) [illegible] (*c*) [illegible] Keb. 638. 1 Bulst. [illegible]
(*d*) Cro. Jac. [illegible] Cro. [illegible] Cro. Eliz. 222, 53[illegible] 718.
(*e*) [illegible] Copyholds, [illegible] (*f*) Ibid. (*g*) Cro. Jac. [illegible]
(*h*) Cro. C[illegible] 2[illegible]3. (*i*) 2 M[illegible] (*k*) Com. Dig. [illegible]

If a copyholder makes a lease by licence, the lessee may assign with licence, or make an under-lease, for the lord by his licence has parted with his interest (*a*).

So if the lessor after a lease by licence dies without heir, the lessee shall have it for his term against the lord; for the licence is a confirmation of the lord (*b*).

If the lord license his copyholder to make a lease of lands in the tenure of *A* though they are in the tenure of *B* yet the licence is good (*c*).

A copyholder, having a licence to lease, may lease for fewer years than his licence allows, as a lease for three years, under a licence to let for twenty-one, which is good (*d*).

If the lord license his copyholder for life to make a lease for three years, if he so long live, a lease for three years absolutely is good: for a lease by a copyholder for life determines by his death, and therefore the condition annexed, being implied by law, is void (*e*).

If the lord license upon condition, the condition is void; for he gives nothing, but only dispenses with the forfeiture (*f*).

A licence may however be upon a condition precedent; for till the condition be performed it is no licence (*g*).

If a copyholder make a lease for years of land whereof a feme by custom is to have her widow's estate, she shall not avoid the lease, unless there be a special custom to avoid it, for he comes under the custom, and by the lord's licence, as well as the feme (*h*).

So if a copyholder, after a lease by licence, forfeits his copyhold, the lord shall not avoid the lease; or if he die, as before observed, without any heir (*i*).

If a copyholder by licence makes a lease for years, rendering rent, he cannot afterwards release the rent without a surrender of the reversion (*k*).

A lease for years by parol, made by the remainder man of a copyhold in fee, commences immediately, if the tenant for life join with him and surrender the estate to his use (*l*).

When the baron was seised of a manor in right of his feme, and let a copyhold parcel thereof for years by indenture and died, it was held that it should not destroy the custom to demise it by copy, but after the death of her baron, the feme might so demise it as before. The same law is, if tenant for life of a manor lets a copyhold parcel of the manor for years, and dies, it shall not destroy the custom as to him in reversion (*m*).

A lease for years by a copyholder, with the licence of the lord

(*a*) Com Dig *ut ant* (*b*) Ibid (*c*) Cro Eliz 160
(*d*) Ibid 535 Cro Jac 437. (*e*) Cro Eliz 462 (*f*) Ibid
(*g*) Com Dig *ut ant* (*h*) Cro Jac 36. (*i*) Com Dig *ut ante*
(*k*) Ibid (*l*) Cro. Eliz. 160. (*m*) Ibid 459.

where the widow by custom would be entitled to her freebench, if the copyholder had died seised, defeats the widow of her freebench (*a*).

A lease without licence, and contrary to the custom, in order to amount to a forfeiture must be a perfect lease, and must have a certain beginning and a certain end, for otherwise the lease is void, and carries but an estate at will at most, which is no forfeiture (*b*).

Therefore, where a copyholder had demised his copyhold for a year, and agreed to grant a further term of twenty-one years provided he could obtain of his lord a licence for that purpose, this was held to be a condition precedent, and that therefore no forfeiture was incurred.

So where a copyholder agreed to demise, and let certain premises, for a term of twenty-one years, and covenanted to procure a licence to let the same, and that the lessee should peaceably enjoy for the said term of twenty-one years; this was held to be an executory agreement, and not a lease, for if it were held to be a lease, a forfeiture would be incurred, whereas that would be contrary to the intent of the parties, who have cautiously guarded against it by the insertion of a covenant that a licence to lease should be procured from the lord (*c*).

A demise by a copyholder for one year, and at the end of that term from year to year for the term of thirteen years more, in all fourteen years, if the lord will give licence, and so as there shall be no forfeiture with the usual covenants in a farm lease, the licence is a condition precedent, and not being granted, there is no lease at law farther than from year to year, and there is no equity upon the circumstance, that the lord purchased his tenants interest with notice of demise, and an express exception of all subsisting leases or agreements for leases (*d*).

So an agreement by a copyholder to grant a lease for twenty-one years, if the licence of the lord could be obtained, and that he would use his best endeavours to obtain such licence, and that in the mean time it should be lawful for the lessee peaceably to enjoy and occupy the premises, does not amount to a lease for a longer time than a year, and is therefore not a forfeiture (*e*).

An infant copyholder without licence of the lord, made a lease for years by parol, rendering rent, and at full age was admitted, and accepted the rent, and then ousted the lessee, and in this case it was adjudged, that the lease was a good lease till avoided, and that a lease for years by a copyholder without licence is not a disseisin, and admitting that it should be a forfeiture in this case, yet if the lord enters for it, the infant may re-enter upon him, and so is no mischief, and therefore he, having accepted the rent at full age, hath made it good and unavoidable, and being at all events a good lease as to all strangers, for that reason principally it was adjudged that such acceptance had made it good (*f*).

(*a*) Co. Cop. [illegible] (*b*) Bac. Abr. tit. "Leases," (I. 6.) (*c*) 2 T. R. [illegible]
(*d*) 11 Ves. [illegible] (*e*) 2 [illegible] 54 (*f*) Bac. Abr. ubi supra.

A lease by a copyholder for a year, with a covenant to renew yearly we have before observed is not a forfeiture In such covenant it would perhaps be still better if it were worded "to permit and suffer" the lessee to have, hold, and enjoy the lands in such manner: for a covenant in that form, even of freehold lands, will not amount to an immediate lease, because the words "permit and suffer" prove that the estate is still to continue in him from whom the permission is to come; for if any estate thereby passed to the covenantee, he might hold and enjoy it without any permission from the covenantor, and therefore in such case the covenantee hath only the bare covenant for his security of enjoyment, without any actual estate made over to him (*a*).

A copyholder agreed to grant a lease for years, if a licence could be obtained, and also to procure the lessee a licence to dig fuller's earth, and that in the mean time the lessee might dig, filling up the holes. The lessee having dug, without filling them up, it was insisted that the omission was an act of waste, but it was held that the digging constituted the waste, and that as the under tenant dug by the lessor's own licence, he could not insist on the forfeiture (*b*).

The admittance of a copyholder, after a forfeiture is incurred, is clearly a waiver, and any act equally solemn will operate in the same manner Such acts as operate as a waiver do not operate as a new grant, but admit the tenant to be in of his old title (*c*)

Every one having a lawful interest in a manor, may make voluntary grants of copyholds escheated, or come to his hands, as well as admittances, rendering the ancient rents and services, which bind him who has the inheritance (*d*)

A grant therefore by any steward having colour of title, and granting not contrary to the command of the lord, is good. So of a clerk of a steward, if he holds a court and makes grants, for the tenants cannot examine his authority, nor need he give them an account of it So, of a deputy [illegible].

But a tenant at will of a manor cannot grant a copyholder licence to demise for years, and if tenant for life of a manor grants a licence to demise for years, it determines at his death (*f*).

Section XIX *Of Leases by Joint-Tenants, Coparceners, and Tenants in common.*

Joint-tenants, coparceners, and tenants in common, may either make leases of their undivided shares, or else may all join in a lease of the whole to a stranger One joint-tenant, or tenant in common, may also make a lease of his part to his companion, for this only gives him a

(*a*) Cro Jac. 312 Bac Abr [illegible]
(*b*) 2 Taunt 52
(*c*) 3 T R [illegible]
(*d*) Com Dig [illegible] "Copyhold," [illegible]
(*e*) Ibid. (C. 5)
(*f*) Ibid [illegible]

right of taking the whole profits, when before he had but a right to the moiety or share thereof, and he may contract with his companion for that purpose as well as with a stranger (*a*).

If there be two joint tenants, and they make a lease, by parol or deed-poll, reserving rent to one only, it shall enure to both; yet if the lease had been by deed indented, the reservation should have been good to him only to whom it was made, and the other should have taken nothing. The reason of the difference is this, where the lease is by deed poll or parol, the rent will follow the reversion, which is jointly in both lessors, and the rather, because the rent being something in retribution for the land given, the joint tenant to whom it is reserved ought to be seised of it in the same manner as he was of the land demised, which was equally for the benefit of his companion and himself, but where the lease is by deed indented, they are estopped to claim the rent in any other manner than is reserved by the deed, because the indenture is the deed of each party, and no man shall be allowed to recede from or vary his own solemn act (*b*).

If one joint tenant does a thing which gives to another an estate, or right in the land, it binds the survivor, as if a joint-tenant in fee or for life makes a lease for forty years (*c*).

Therefore, if two joint-tenants are in fee, and one lets his moiety for years, to begin after his death, this is good, and shall bind the other if he survive, because this is a present disposition, and binds the land from the time of the lease made, so that he cannot afterwards avoid it.

So if one joint-tenant grant the vesture or herbage of the land for years, and dies, this shall bind the survivor, or if two joint-tenants are of a water, and one grants a separate piscary for years and dies, this shall bind the survivor, because in these cases the grant of the one joint-tenant gives an immediate interest in the thing itself whereof they are joint-tenants (*d*).

If there are two joint-tenants for life, and one of them makes a lease for years of his moiety, either to begin presently or after his death, and dies, this lease is good and binding, against the survivor: the reason whereof is that notwithstanding the lease for years, the joint-tenancy in the freehold still continues, and in that they have a mutual interest in each other's life, so that the estate in the whole or any part is not to determine or revert to the lessor till both are dead, for the life of one as well as the other was at first made the measure of the estate granted out by the lessor, and therefore so long as either of them lives, if the joint-tenancy continues, he is not to come into possession (*e*). Now these joint-tenants having a reciprocal interest in

(*a*) 1 Inst. 186 a.

(*b*) Bac. Abr. tit. "Joint-tenants and Tenants in common," (H. 1.) Cro. Jac. 91.

(*c*) Com. Dig. tit. "Estates," (K. 7.) (*d*) Bac. Abr. ubi supra. (*e*) Bac. Abr. ubi supra. Cro. Jac. 91.

each other's life, when one of them makes a lease for years of his moiety, this does not depend on its continuance for his life only, but on his life, and the life of the other joint-tenant, whichsoever of them shall live longest, according to the nature and continuance of the estate whereout it was derived; and then so long as that continues, so long the lease holds good, and by consequence such lessee shall hold out the surviving joint-tenant and the reversioner, till the estate, whereout this lease was derived, be fully determined.

But if a rent were reserved on such lease, this is determined and gone by the death of the lessor for the survivor cannot have it, because he comes in by title paramount to the lease, and the heirs of the lessor have no title to it, because they have no reversion or interest in the land (*a*), but the executors or administrators may maintain an action of debt or covenant; this remedy being now given to the representatives of such a lessor, for by statute 11 *G.* 2 *c.* 19 *s.* 15 the executors or administrators of tenant for life shall, on his death, recover of the lessee a rateable proportion of the rent from the last day of payment to the death of such lessor.

A. and *B.* being joint-tenants for life, a lease made by *A* of the moiety to have and to hold after the death of *B.* for sixty years if *A.* so long live, and of the other moiety to have and to hold after the death of *A.* for sixty years if *B* so long live, and *A* dies, *B.* surviving, is bad for both moieties: for by the first words it was a good lease from *A.* of his part, upon the contingency surviving *B* but that never happened, and as to *B*'s part, *A* had no power to lease or contract for it during the life of *B* though he had happened after to survive him, for it was but a bare possibility, which could not be leased or contracted for, and therefore the lease was void in the whole (*b*).

So, if one joint-tenant make a lease for years, "if he and his companion live so long," and afterwards surrender his moiety, and take back another estate, the lease determines by the death of either of them: for it hath no continuance longer than the jointure continues, which is severed by the surrender, a new estate being taken (*c*).

If joint-tenants join in a lease, this shall be but one lease, for they have but one freehold, but if tenants in common join in a lease, this shall be the lease of each for their respective parts, and the cross confirmation of each for the part of the other, and no estoppel on either part, because an actual interest passes from each respectively, and that excludes the necessity of an estoppel, which is never admitted, if by any construction it can be avoided (*d*).

(*a*) Pr. Abr. *ut ante.* (*b*) Cro Jac 92 377. (*c*) Cro Jac 377.
(*d*) [illegible] Bac. Abr. tit. "Joint-Tenants, and Tenants in Common,"

SECTION XX. *Of Leases pursuant to Authority, wherein of Leases by Attornies, Agents, &c.*

If one hath power, by virtue of a letter of attorney, to make leases for years generally by indenture, the attorney ought to make them in the name and style of his principal, and not in his own name, for the letter of attorney gives him no interest or estate in the lands, but only an authority to supply the absence of his principal by standing in his stead, which he can no otherwise do than by using his name, and making them just in the same manner and style as his principal would do if he were present. If he should make them in his own name, though he added also "by virtue of the letter of attorney to him made for that purpose," yet such leases seem to be void, because the indenture being made in his name, must pass the interest and lease from him, or it can pass it from nobody. It cannot pass it from the principal immediately, because he is no party, and it cannot pass it from the attorney at all, because he has nothing in the lands; and then his adding, "by virtue of the letter of attorney," will not help it, because that letter of attorney made over no estate or interest in the land to him, and consequently he cannot, by virtue thereof, convey over any to another (a).

Neither can such interest pass from the principal immediately, or through the attorney (b), for then the same indenture must have this strange effect at one and the same instant, first to draw out the interest from the principal to the attorney, and from the attorney to the lessee, which it certainly cannot do, and therefore all such leases made in that manner, seem to be absolutely void, and not good, even by estoppel against the attorney, because they pretend to be made not in his own name absolutely, but in the name of another, by virtue of an authority which is not pursued (c).

This case therefore of making leases by a letter of attorney, seems to differ from that of a surrender of a copyhold, or of livery of seisin of a freehold by letter of attorney; for in those cases when they say, "we *A.* and *B.* as attornies of *C.*" or, "by virtue of a letter of attorney from *C.* of such a date, *&c.*" "do surrender, *&c.*" or "deliver to you seisin of such lands," these are good in this manner, because they are only ministerial ceremonies, or transitory acts *in pais*, the one to be done by holding the court rod, and the other by delivering a turf or twig; and when they do them as attornies, or by virtue of a letter of attorney from their principals, the law pronounces thereupon as if they were actually done by the principal himself, and carries the possession accordingly (d).

(a) [illegible] (b) Ibid. (c) 2 Lev. R. [illegible]
(d) Bacon, Lea. 142.

But in a lease for years it is quite otherwise, for the indenture or deed alone convey the interest, and are the very essence of the lease, both as to the passing it out of the lessor at first, and its subsistence in the lessee afterwards. The very indenture or deed itself is the conveyance, without any subsequent construction or operation of law thereupon; and therefore it must be made in the name and style of him who has such interest to convey, and not in the name and style of the attorney, who has nothing therein; but in the conclusion of such lease it is proper to say, "in witness whereof *A B* of such a place, &c. in pursuance of a letter of attorney hereunto annexed, bearing date such a day." or if the letter of attorney be general, and concern more lands than those comprised in the present lease, then to say, "in pursuance of a letter of attorney, bearing date such a day, &c. a true copy whereof is hereunto annexed, hath put the hand and seal of the principal," and so to write the principal's name, and deliver it as the act and deed of the principal, in which last ceremony of delivering it in the name of the principal of such attorney, this exactly agrees with the ceremony of surrendering by the rod, or making livery by a turf or twig, by the attorney in the name and as attorney of his principal; which proves that there is a great diversity between using the name of the attorney in the making of leases, and using his name in making a surrender of copyhold or livery of seisin of a freehold estate.

A special agent under a limited authority cannot bind his principal by an act beyond the scope of such limited authority (*a*).

The Court of Chancery will interfere, where an agent procures his principal to grant a lease on disadvantageous terms, it appearing that the agent took an interest in the lease (*b*).

If the defendant insist that the lease declared on is not the plaintiff's, the plaintiff may shew that it was made by *A.* who had authority from him to execute it in his name, and the authority need not be produced. But the lease must be made and executed in the name of the principal (*c*).

But in a recent case it was held, that where a party executes a deed under a power of attorney, the power ought to be produced (*d*).

Agreement for a lease, made with an agent who [illegible], under a power of attorney, and a lease executed by such agent in pursuance of the agreement, shall bind the principal (*e*).

Where a man does such an act [illegible] other means but by virtue of [illegible], it shall be [illegible] of his authority, but where [illegible], and does an act without [illegible] his authority [illegible] to be done by virtue of his interest (*f*).

A bailiff of a manor cannot, [illegible] of his office, make leases for

(*a*) 3 T. R. [illegible] (*c*) [illegible] R. [illegible]
[illegible]

years, for his business is only to collect rents, gather the fines, look after the forfeitures, and such like: but he hath no estate or interest in the manor itself, and therefore cannot contract for any certain interest thereout. But the lord of the manor may give him a special power to make leases for years, as he may do to any stranger, and then such leases, if they are pursuant to the power, and made in the name of the lord, will be as good as leases by the lord himself, for the bailiff, though he hath such power, cannot make them in his own name (*a*).

But a general bailiff of a manor may make leases at will, without any special authority, because, being to collect and answer the rents of the manor to his lord, if he could not let leases at will, the lord might sustain great prejudice by absence, sickness, or other incapacity to make leases when any of the former leases were expired, and such leases at will are for the benefit of the lord, and can be no ways prejudicial to him, because he may determine his will when he thinks fit (*b*).

Such, however, must be taken to be strict tenancies at will, otherwise, as general tenancies at will are construed to be tenancies from year to year, and half a year's notice to quit is required, before a tenant can be ousted, such tenancies might prove very prejudicial to the lord's interest.

But if the bailiff of a manor hath a special power to make leases for years, as he ought to make them in the name of his master, so they ought to be made in writing, that the authority may appear to be pursued, a parol lease such bailiff has no power to make (*c*).

(*a*) Bac. Abr. "Leases," (I. 8.) [illegible] (*b*) Ib. [illegible] (*c*) Bac. Abr. [illegible]

CHAPTER IV.

To whom Leases may be made.

EVERY person is capable of being a lessee, unless rendered incompetent by some legal disability, such as infancy, coverture, insanity, &c.

Spiritual persons.—By 43 G. 3. c. 84. (which recites the 21 H. 8. c. 13.) it is made lawful, from and after the passing of the act (*July* 7, 1803) for any spiritual person to take to farm to himself, or to any person or persons to his use, by lease, grant, words or otherwise, for term of life, years, or at will, any messuage, mansion, or dwelling-house, with or without orchards, gardens, or other appurtenances, although not in any city, borough, or town, and any spiritual person having or holding any [benefice, 46 G. 3. c. 109. s. 1.] donative, perpetual curacy, or parochial chapelry, not having sufficient or convenient glebe or demesne lands annexed to, or in right of, or by reason of his benefice, or cure, or chapelry, or any stipendiary curate, or unbeneficed spiritual person, with the consent in writing of the bishop of the diocese, may take to farm to himself, or to any person, to his use for a limited term of years, any farm or farms, lands, tenements, or hereditaments, that may, under all the circumstances, appear to such bishop proper to be taken or occupied by such spiritual person, for the convenience of his household and hospitality only, without being liable to any penalties, &c. under the recited Act, or any other Acts by reason thereof: provided that nothing herein shall authorize any non residence of any such spiritual person as aforesaid. s. 4.

And it shall be lawful for any spiritual person or persons, by himself or themselves, or any other, to his or their use, to have, hold, use, or occupy in ferm, any manors, lands, tenements, or hereditaments, demised, leased, or granted to him or them, or his or their property and estate, or to take, purchase, receive, or hold, as the property and estate of such spiritual person, any lease or leases for life or lives, or for term or terms of years, absolute or determinate on any life or lives, or to take any annual rent, or other annual advantage or profit by occasion of any lease or ferm of any manors, &c. the property or estate of any such spiritual person or persons belonging to him or them, either in his or their own right, or in right of any other person, or by reason of his or their holding any spiritual dignity or benefice, or so taken, purchased, &c. as aforesaid, as the property or estate of such spiritual person, notwithstanding the said recited or any other Act. Provided that nothing herein contained shall authorize any spiritual person holding any dignity, prebend, benefice, donative, perpetual curacy, or parochial chapelry, or serving a stipendiary curacy, to take, receive, or hold any manors, &c. after the passing of this act, for the purpose of occupying or to occupy the same, for the cultivation thereof, or procuring profit therefrom, by himself, or any bailiff or servant, to his use, unless the same shall have been taken, received, or holden under a lease granted to such person on or before the first day of *January* 1803, or unless by the consent in writing of the bishop as aforesaid. s. 5. And by s. 6 such spiritual persons are authorized to buy or sell cattle or corn for the occupation or profit of such farms, &c. so holden. Provided that they do not buy or sell any cattle or corn in person in any market, fair, or place of public sale.

And any spiritual person having any vicarage or perpetual curacy, or any stipendiary curate thereof may occupy by himself or any other to his use, the impropriate parsonage, rectory, or vicarage, or any part thereof, or take any profit or rent out of such farm, notwithstanding the said recited or any other act. But if such impropriate parsonage, rectory or vicarage, or such part thereof, shall not have been occupied, at any time before the passing of this Act, by the same or any other such spiritual person as aforesaid, such person shall remain liable to the penalties, &c. under the said recited or any other Act, unless he shall have obtained the licence of the bishop for such occupation. s. 8.

And any clergyman who shall be licensed or be exempted from residence under this or any other Act, may take to farm and occupy in the parish where he resides, or any adjoining parish, such lands for the convenience of his household and hospitality only, as the bishop may in writing allow. s. 9.

All contracts or agreements made after the passing of the Act for letting houses, in which any [illegible] persons shall be, by order of the archbishop or bishop, required to reside, shall be void, and persons holding possession after the day appointed by such order, shall forfeit 40s. for each day he shall so hold over, such penalty to be recoverable by action of debt, &c. in any court of record at *Westminster*, or the courts of great sessions in *Wales*, and to go to such person who shall inform and sue for the same, together with costs; [illegible] of such contracts or agreements made before the passing of this Act, no such penalty shall be incurred for three months from the service of the copy of such order as aforesaid upon such occupier of such house of residence, but after such period the person continuing to hold shall forfeit 40s. for each day [illegible] holding over as aforesaid. s. 34. 37.

No penalty for farming shall be [illegible] under this or any other statute, till the [illegible] day of *July*, 1803 [illegible] this Act deprive any spiritual persons of any [illegible] under the said [illegible] Act or otherwise. s. 43. 44.

Infant.—In default [illegible]

of the lease made, and upon demurrer, the Court held the lease *voidable* only at his election, for if it were for his benefit, it shall be no ways void, but the infant at his election may make it void, by refusing and waiving the land before the rent-day comes, in which case no action of debt would lie against him; but the defendant not having so done, and being of age before the rent-day due, and it not being shewn to the court that in this case the rent was of greater value, the plaintiff had judgment (*a*)

If a person jointly interested with an infant in a lease, obtain a renewal to himself only, and the lease prove beneficial, he shall be held to have acted as trustee, and the infant may claim his share of the benefit, but if it do not prove beneficial, he must take it upon himself. This is the peculiar privilege of the unprotected situation of an infant (*b*)

Where a lease to an infant however is not by deed, he will perhaps be liable at all events for use and occupation of the premises in which he resides; for he is liable for necessaries, under which description lodging must surely come wherefore such case would probably be held to fall within the fair liability which the law imposes on infants of being bound for necessaries, which is a relative term, according to their station in life (*c*).

Feme-Covert —A feme-covert cannot be a lessee, for her free agency is so suspended during coverture, that she may plead *non est factum* to an action on any covenant in the lease, for evidence that she was covert at the time of executing the lease, will prove it to be not her deed. For use and occupation of premises, her baron will be liable (*d*).

Aliens.—With respect to aliens, the statute of 32 *H* 8. *c.* 16 *s.* 13 makes all leases of any dwelling house or shop, within this realm or any of the king's dominions, made to any stranger, artificer, or handicraftsman born out of the king's obeisance, not being a denizen, void and of none effect (*e*) This statute may be pleaded in bar to an action of debt for rent, brought against an executor or administrator, but in pleading it, it seems necessary to aver that the messuage demised was a dwelling house or shop A place need not be alleged where he was an alien and an artificer (*f*)

The above mentioned statute is still in force, but though it makes *leases* of dwelling houses or shops granted to any stranger artificer void, yet if such artificer occupy a dwelling-house or shop under an *agreement* which does not amount to a lease, as if he be tenant from year to year, or for a shorter time, an action for use and occupation will lie against him notwithstanding the statute (*g*)

[illegible]

An alien therefore is incapable of being party to a lease; for being born in a foreign country out of allegiance to the king, the policy of the laws has placed every obstacle in his way to prevent him from acquiring possessions and the influence that accompanies them, in a country that does not claim his allegiance, and with the interest of which he is unconnected The exceptions to this wise principle of exclusion are created only by the consequences of commerce for the convenience of trade, therefore, an alien friend is now permitted to acquire a property in goods, money, and other personal (not real) estate, and he may hire a house for his habitation for the greater convenience of carrying on his trade, but he cannot assign or dispose of his interest in it, even to a natural-born subject.— The general naturalization act for all foreign protestants, however, which was carried into execution by stat 7 *Ann* c 5 it was found necessary to repeal, after three years' experience, by stat 10 *Ann* c. 5. except the clause for naturalizing the children of English parents born abroad, and the impolicy and injustice of putting foreigners upon the same footing as the subjects of the country, are probably sufficiently manifest to prevent any similar experiment in future.

An alien may indeed take by purchase; but then it is for the benefit of the crown: unless the crown however interpose, he may maintain an action for lands purchased by him (*a*).

But there is no instance where a woman alien is in possession of an estate, but that it must be for the benefit of the crown; and the husband by marrying her cannot be said to be seised of such estate (*b*)

But though an alien cannot, as such, take a lease of a dwelling-house or shop, by reason of the statute 32 *H* 8 *c*. 16. yet he may occupy a tenement of 10*l* a year, and carry on his trade there like any other person and as he may do so, he has that interest which enables him to gain a settlement by the provision of the legislature (*c*).

All children born out of the king's dominions, whose fathers, (or grandfathers by the father's side) were natural born subjects, though their mothers were aliens, are now by various statutes deemed to be natural born subjects themselves to all intents and purposes, unless their said ancestors were attainted, are banished beyond sea for high treason, or were at the birth of such children in the service of a prince at enmity with Great Britain But grandchildren of such ancestors shall not be privileged in respect of the father's duty, except they be protestants, and actually reside within the realm, nor shall be enabled to claim any estate or interest, unless the claim be made within five years after the same shall accrue

The issue of an English woman by an alien, born abroad, is an alien.

(*a*) [illegible] Pol. [illegible] 8 (*b*) 2 [illegible] 3 (*c*) [illegible] R 1[illegible]

The children of aliens born in England are, generally speaking, natural born subjects, and entitled to all the privileges of such (*a*).

Denizens.—A denizen is an alien born, but who has obtained, *ex donatione regis*, letters patent to make him an *English* subject, an high and incommunicable branch of the royal prerogative. A denizen is a kind of middle state, between an alien and a natural born subject, and partakes of both of them (*b*).

He may take lands by purchase or devise, which an alien may not, but cannot take by inheritance.

A denizen therefore may be a lessor or lessee, for the chief incapacity which he retains regards the defect of inheritable blood, so that in other respects his situation may, in a great degree, be assimilated to that of a bastard. He cannot however take any grant of lands, &c. from the crown; nor sit in the council, or in either house of parliament (*c*).

Naturalization cannot be performed but by act of parliament, for by this an alien is put in the same state as if he had been born in the king's ligeance, except only that by the stat. 12 *W.* 3 he is incapable, as well as a denizen, of being a member of the privy council, or of either house of parliament, holding offices, taking grants of the crown, &c.

(*a*) 1 Bl. Com. [illegible] (*b*) [illegible] (*c*) Stat. 12 W. 3, [illegible]

CHAPTER V.

Of the subject matter of Leases

SECTION I. *Of corporeal Hereditaments, wherein of Farms, Lands, Houses, and Lodgings.*

SECTION II. *Of incorporeal Hereditaments, wherein of Tithes, Tolls, Advowsons, Rent, &c.*

SECTION I. *Of corporeal Hereditaments*

AFTER such time as leases for years began to be looked upon as fixed and permanent interests, and that the lessees were sufficiently provided to defend themselves and their possessions against the acts and incroachments, as well of the lessor as of strangers, men found it their interest to improve and encourage this sort of property, and therefore extended it to all sorts of interests and possessions whatsoever, being led thereto by that known rule, that *whatsoever may be granted or parted with for ever, may be granted or parted with for a time* (*a*)

Not only lands and houses, therefore, have been let for years, but also goods and chattels, though the interest of the lessee therein differs from the interest he hath in lands or houses so let for years, for if one lease for years a stock of live cattle, such lease is good, and the lessee hath the use and profits of them during the term, but yet the lessor hath not any reversion in them to grant over to another either during the term or after, till the lessee hath re-delivered them to him, as he would have of lands in case of such lease for years; for the lessor hath only a possibility of property in case they all outlive the term, for if any of them die during the term, the lessor cannot have them again after the term, and during the term he hath nothing to do with them, and consequently of such as die, the property rests absolutely in the lessee (*b*).

So, whether they live or die, yet all the young ones coming of them, as lambs, calves, &c. belong absolutely to the lessee as profits arising and severed from the principal, since otherwise the lessee would pay his rent for nothing, and therefore this differs from a lease of other dead goods and chattels, for there, if any thing be added for the repairing, mending, or improving thereof, the lessor shall have the improvement

[illegible]

and additions together with the principal, after the lease ended, because they cannot be severed without destroying or spoiling the principal. neither is the succession of young ones, in case any of the old ones die, to be resembled to a corporation aggregate, whereof when any die, those that succeed shall be said to be part of the same corporation, for the corporation in its public capacity never dies, but this being a lease of such and such individual cattle, when any of them die, the possibility of reverting property, which was left in the lessor, is determined, and at an end But the lessee, in such case, cannot kill, destroy, sell, or give them away, during the term, without being subject to an action of trespass, as it should seem (*a*)

Touching the import of the word "hereditament," Lord *Kenyon* observed (*b*), that it was not so strong a word as tenement, but was merely a description of the thing itself, and not the quality of it or interest in it and this accords with the difference taken between the two words *hæreditas* and *hæreditamentum*, for the word *hæreditas* imports the estate which a man has in the land, *hæreditamentum* the land itself which may be inherited, and therefore cannot be applied to the estate in the land (*c*) *Holt*, C. J. however says the word "hereditament" implies a fee (*d*): which is consonant to Sir *E. Coke*'s exposition of the word, which he says is by much the largest and most comprehensive expression; for it includes not only lands and tenements, but whatsoever may be inherited, be it corporeal or incorporeal, real, personal, or mixed (*e*).

Corporeal hereditaments consist wholly of substantial and permanent objects, all which may be comprehended under the general denomination of land only, for *land* comprehends, in its legal signification, any ground, soil, or earth whatsoever, so the word "land" includes, not only the face of the earth, but every thing under it, or over it; and therefore, if a man grant all his lands, he grants thereby all his mines of metal and other fossils, his woods, his waters, and his houses, as well as his fields and meadows not but that the particular names of the things are equally sufficient to pass them, except in the instance of water, by a grant of which, nothing passes but a right of fishing, and to recover the land at the bottom of which, it must be called so many "acres of land covered with water" But the capital distinction is this, that by the name of a castle, messuage, toft, croft, or the like, nothing else will pass, except what falls with the utmost propriety under the term made use of, (though indeed, by the name of a castle, one or more manors may be conveyed, and *è converso*, by the name of the manor, a castle may pass); but by the name of land, which is *nomen generalissimum*, every thing terrestrial will pass (*f*).

(*a*) Bac Abr tit. "Leases." (A) (*b*) 8 T R 503. (*c*) 1 Com R 164.
(*d*) Holt. 236. (*e*) Co Litt 19, 20 2 Bl. Com 17 Shep. Touch 91
(*f*) 2 Bl. Com. 18.

Leases for life, or years, or at will (now construed to be from year to year), may be made of any thing corporeal or incorporeal that lieth in livery or grant (*a*).

A man therefore may demise his farm, which may comprehend a messuage and much land, meadow, pasture, wood, &c. thereunto belonging, or therewith used, for this word doth properly signify a capital or principal messuage, and a great quantity of demesnes thereunto appertaining (*b*).

So, by the name of a messuage, he may pass a house, a curtelage, a garden, an orchard, a dove-house, a shop or a mill, as parcel of the same, or a toft, or a cottage, a toft, a chamber, a cellar, &c. Yet these may pass by their own single names also, as, "of one messuage, one curtelage, &c. (*c*)."

If *A.* lets a garden ground for years, and the lessee demises part of the term to an under-tenant, who builds on it, by a grant of the garden ground the buildings thereon will pass (*d*).

So, a house, and in case of a lease of a house, together with goods, it is usual to make a schedule thereof and affix it to the lease, and to have a covenant from the lessee to re-deliver them at the end of the term, for without such covenant the lessor could have no other remedy, but trover or detinue for them after the lease ended (*e*).

The demise of a house "with the appurtenances," will, it seems, pass the house, with the orchards, yards, and curtelage, and garden, but not the land (*f*), especially if it be at a distance, though occupied with the house, but if the lessor had built a conduit, though in another part of the land, yet the conduit would pass with the house, because it is necessary, *et quasi*, appendant thereto (*g*) · yet if the lessee erect such a conduit, and afterwards the lessor, during the lease, sell the house to one, and the land wherein the conduit is to another, and afterwards the lease determines, he who has the land wherein the conduit is may disturb the other in the using thereof, and may break it, because it was not erected by one who had a permanent estate or inheritance, nor made one, by the occupation and usage of them together, by him who had the inheritance.- So, the demise of a house, "and the appurtenances," will not pass an adjoining building not accounted parcel of the house although held with it for thirty years (*h*). But in one case it was held that a grant from the crown, of a house *cum pertinentiis* would pass land that was occupied with the house . in this case however it should not be overlooked that the point arose on a special verdict, in which the house and land were found to be all one (*i*).

Whether the thing claimed as appurtenant be accounted parcel of

(*a*) Shep. Touch. 268. (*b*) Ibid. 9[illegible] (*c*) Ibid. 12[illegible]
(*d*) Cro. Jac. 648. (*e*) Bac. Abr. tit. "Leases" (A) (*f*) Co. Car. [illegible] Cro. Jac. 526
(*g*) [illegible] 121 (*h*) Cro. Car. [illegible] (*i*) [illegible] 169

not, and the intention of the parties, are the rules by which to judge in these cases (*a*)

Thus, where there is a conveyance in general terms of all that acre called *Black-acre*, every thing which belongs to *Black-acre* passes with it, but whether parcel or not of the thing demised is always matter of evidence (*b*).

It may be necessary, however, to put a different construction on leases made in populous cities from that on those made in the country. It is known, for example, that in the metropolis different persons have several freeholds over the same spot, (as in the case of the *Adelphi*), different parts of the same house are let out to different people, such is the case in the inns of court It would therefore be very extraordinary to contend that if a person purchased a set of chambers, then leased them, and afterwards purchased another set under them, the after-purchased chambers would pass under the lease (*c*).

So, the demise of premises in *Westminster* late in the occupation of *A.* (particularly describing them), part of which was a yard, was held not to pass a cellar situate under that yard, which was then occupied by *B* another tenant of the lessor, for though *primâ facie* indeed, the property in the cellar would pass by the demise, yet that might be regulated and explained by circumstances; and, as the construction of all deeds must be made with a reference to their subject matter, it is right in such cases to let in evidence to shew the state and condition of the property at the time when the lease was granted (*d*)

The respective apartments of a house may be, and frequently are, let to several and distinct individuals, which tenancies are termed lodgings, and the tenants thereof lodgers, respecting which see more at large hereafter.

Section II *Of incorporeal Hereditaments.*

An incorporeal hereditament is a right issuing out of a thing corporate, (whether real or personal) or concerning, or annexed to, or exercisable within the same Incorporeal hereditaments are principally these, *viz* advowsons, tithes, tolls, estovers, commons, ways, offices, franchises, corrodies or pensions, annuities, and rents (*e*)

Incorporeal hereditaments are generally speaking capable of being demised, and such demise must be by deed, for they lie in grant and not livery; so things incorporeal may be granted by copy of court-roll (*f*).

(*a*) Cro Car. 17 (*b*) 1 T. R 704 (*c*) Ibid 703
(*d*) Ibid (*e*) Co Litt. 19, 20. (*f*) 1 T. R [illegible]60. [illegible] 3-3 1 Str. 9.

Advowsons.—An advowson is a valuable right, and properly the object of sale; it is therefore real assets in the hands of the heir: but as the exercise of this right is a publick trust, it cannot, it ought not, to produce any profit.—Therefore, though an advowson may be granted, either by a grant by deed or will, of the manor, *&c.* to which it is appendant, without any exception of the advowson, in which case it will pass, (for it is parcel of the manor, except in the case of the king) or by grant of the advowson alone, and such grant may be either in fee, or for the right of one or more turns, or for as many as shall happen within a time limited; yet it cannot properly be the subject of a demise, for as no profit is permitted to accrue, no rent can be reserved, nor any services performed to the proprietor.

This, however, does not seem to be quite correct: for there is no doubt, (says Mr *Wooddeson*,) but that the lessee of tithes, an *advowson*, or any incorporeal hereditament, would be liable to an action of debt for the rent agreed upon (*a*). So where lessee for years of an advowson was presented to the advowson by the lessor, it was adjudged to be a surrender of his term (*b*).—Thus it seems clear that an advowson may be the subject of a demise: and though L. C. *Talbot* doubted (*c*) whether the word "tenements," which had been said to carry an advowson in a will, extended to incorporeal inheritances, yet it appears to be the better opinion, that as lands and houses are tenements, so is an advowson a tenement (*d*).

Tithes.—Tithes have been defined to be, a tenth part of the increase, yearly arising and renewing from the profits of lands, the stock upon lands, and the personal industry of the inhabitants; and are an ecclesiastical inheritance, collateral to the land, and properly due to an ecclesiastical person.

A parson of a church may grant his tithes for years, and yet they are not in him (*e*).

By the statute 5 *G.* 3. c. 17. entitled "An act to confirm all leases already made by archbishops and bishops, and other ecclesiastical persons, of tithes and other incorporeal hereditaments, for one, two, or three life or lives, or twenty-one years, and to enable them to grant such leases, and to bring actions of debt for the recovery of rents reserved and in arrear on leases for life or lives," any other person or persons, having any spiritual or ecclesiastical promotions, are enabled to grant such leases of tithes, tolls, or other incorporeal inheritances, "which shall be as good and effectual in law against such archbishop, bishop, masters and fellows, or other heads and members of colleges or halls, deans and chapters, precentors, prebendaries, masters and guardians of hospitals, and other persons so granting the same, and their successors, and every of them, to all intents and purposes, as any lease or leases

(*a*) 2 Wood. 69. (*b*) Cro. Jac. 81. (*c*) Ca. temp. Talbot, 141.
(*d*) Co. Litt. 19. 20. 2 Bl. Com. 17. 3 P. Wms. 61. (*e*) [illegible] 241.

already made, or to be made by any such archbishop, &c." by virtue of the stat. 32 *H* 8 *c* 28. or any other statute then in being, and action of debt may be brought by such lessors for rent in arrear, as in the case of any other landlord or lessor.

Tolls.—Tolls also, may be let or mortgaged (*a*).

Estovers.—So, estovers (of which more hereafter) may be leased the grantee, therefore, of house-bote, or hay bote, may let it to another (*b*).

Commons.—With respect to commons, the stat. 13 *G* 3. *c.* 81 *s.* 15. empowers the lord of any manor with the consent of three-fourths of the persons having right of common upon the wastes and commons within the manor, at any time to demise or lease, for any term or number of years, not exceeding four years, any part of such wastes and commons, not exceeding a twelfth part thereof, for the best and most improved yearly rent that can by public auction be got for the same; and directs that the clear net-rents shall be applied to drain, fence, and otherwise improve the residue of the wastes and commons.

A lessee for lives cannot acquire a fee by encroachment upon the waste adjoining the land demised, though accompanied by thirty years' uninterrupted possession, but it shall be intended that he incloses the waste in right of the demised premises, for the benefit of the lessor after the term expired, more especially, if his lessor be seized in fee of the waste. Acts exercised in assertion of right upon one part of a waste are admissible in evidence against occupiers of another part of the same waste (*c*).

Ways.—Ways are, or a right of way, are demiseable with the land, for the grantee or lessee shall have all the ways, casements, &c. which the grantor or lessor had (*d*)

Therefore, where one as trustee conveys land to another, to which there is no access but over the trustee's land, a right of way passes of necessity, as incidental to the grant (*e*)

If a man, upon a lease for years, reserve a way to himself through the house of the lessee to a back-house, he cannot use it but at seasonable times and upon request (*f*)

Offices.—An office may be granted by way of lease, provided no inconvenience or injury to the public is likely to ensue, and it may be granted in fee-tail, for life, or years, or at will (*g*)

But an office to which a trust is annexed, or which concerns the administration of justice, cannot be granted for years, for then it would go to the executor, or administrator, or ordinary, and might be seised upon outlawry, &c (*h*). Therefore the office of marshal of the King's Bench cannot be granted for years, because it is an office of trust and daily attendance, and such a termor for years may die intestate, and

(*a*) 2 T R 169. (*b*) Shep Touch 222. Bac Abr. tit. "Leases" (A)
(*c*) 1 Taunt 208 (*d*) 6 Mod. 3, 149 Cro. Jac 170, 190 (*e*) 8 T R. 50, 56
(*f*) 1 Vent. 48. (*g*) Com. Dig. tit. "Officer." (B. 7. &c) (*h*) Ibid.

then it would be in suspence until administration is committed, which is the act of another court (*a*)

It hath however been held, that a lease thereof for years during the life of the grantee is good, for hereby the danger of the office going to executors is avoided It appears also, that the dean and chapter of *Westminster* made a lease for years of the Gate-house prison [since pulled down] and the lessee had committed several offences which amounted to a forfeiture, for which the office was seised. but no objection was made to its being let for years. There seems to be a difference, however, between the two cases: the first, namely, that of the Marshal of the King's Bench, (since regulated by statute 13 *G.* 2. *c.* 17.) was a grant from the crown, in whom all offices, in relation to the administration of justice, are originally and inherently lodged, and therefore for the crown to grant out such office for years may be liable to the objections before-mentioned; but in the latter case, namely that of the Gate-house prison, the dean and chapter are the immediate grantees of the crown, and they have the office to them and their successors for ever in fee, and are perpetual gaolers themselves, and answerable to the crown, notwithstanding any lease over to another, and therefore they always take security of such under-lessee for their own indemnity (*b*).

Such offices as do not concern the administration of justice, but only require skill and diligence, may be granted for years, because they may be executed by deputies, without any inconvenience to the public.

Where one made a grant for years of the stewardship of a court-leet and court-baron, it was held void as to the court-leet, being a judicial office, but good as to the court baron, being only ministerial, and the suitors judges thereof; but the grant appearing afterwards to be for years determinable upon the death of the lessee, it was held good for both, because there was no danger of its coming to executors or administrators.

An office cannot be demised by parol (*c*)

Dignities and honours cannot be granted for years.

Franchises—Franchises may be demised, except indeed in some few particular cases, as where the franchise is a personal immunity, &c. Thus a fair or market, either with or without the right of taking toll, either there or at any other public places, as at bridges, wharfs, or the like, may be demised. Every fair is a market, but not *è contra* (*d*).

Corrodies and Pensions—Touching corrodies and pensions, the great endowments of lands, rents, and revenues, given to the churchmen by the laity, were for the maintenance of hospitality and works of charity: the founders and benefactors thereby obtained a right of corrody or entertainment at such places, in nature of free quarter (*e*) A corrody

(*a*) 3 Mod. 135. (*b*) 6 Mod. 57. Bac. Abr. tit. "Leases" (A)
(*c*) 2 Ld Raym. 855. Bac. Abr. tit. "Leases" (A) (*d*) 2 Inst. 220, 221.
(*e*) 2 El. Com. 41. Bac. Abr. tit. Gov. of the [illegible]

therefore is a right of sustenance, or to receive certain allotments of food for one's maintenance, in lieu of which, especially when due from ecclesiastical persons, a pension or sum of money is sometimes substituted, and these are chargeable on the person of the owner of the inheritance in respect thereof. It is said, that a corrody may be due to a common person by grant from one to another. A corrody is either certain or uncertain, and may be not only for life or years, but in fee. If one hath a corrody for life, he may let it to another, or to the grantor himself (*a*).

Annuities.—An annuity is an annual sum of money granted to another in fee, for life, or years, which charges the person of the grantor only; or it may be due by prescription, which always implies a grant (*b*). Such annuity may be demised by way of assignment (*c*).

Rents.—Rents form the last kind of incorporeal hereditaments, and may be the subject of a lease.

The word *rent*, or render, *reditus*, signifies a compensation or return, it being in the nature of an acknowledgment given for the possession of some corporeal inheritance (*d*).

There are at common law three manner of rents; rent-service, rent-charge, and rent-seck. *Rent-service* is so called because it hath some corporal service incident to it, as at the least fealty: for if a tenant hold his land by fealty, and ten shillings rent, or by service of ploughing the lord's land and five shillings rent, these pecuniary rents being connected with personal services, are therefore called rent-service, and for these, in case they be behind or in arrear at the day appointed, the lord may distrain of common right, without reserving any special power of distress; provided he hath in himself the reversion, or future estate of the lands and tenements, after the lease or particular estate of the lessee or grantee is expired. *A rent-charge* is where the owner of the rent hath no future interest, or reversion expectant in the land: as where a man by deed maketh over to others his whole estate in fee-simple, with a certain rent payable thereout, and adds to the deed a covenant or clause of distress, that if the rent be in arrear, or behind, it shall be lawful to distrain for the same: in this case the land is liable to the distress, not of common right, but by virtue of the clause in the deed, and therefore it is called a rent-charge, because in this manner the land is charged with a distress for the payment of it (*e*).—A clear rent-charge must be free from the land-tax (*f*).

If a rent charge be granted in fee with a clause of distress, and a fine be levied of the lands, to the use and intent that if the said *yearly rent* should be behind, and no sufficient distress, the grantee, his heirs or assigns, may enter till the rent be paid, on *half a year's rent* becoming

(*a*) New Terms of Law. B[illegible] Abr[illegible] Leases" ([illegible])
(*b*) Co. Litt. 144 b. Com. Dig. [illegible] "A[illegible]" ([illegible]) (*c*) Ibid. (E.)
(*d*) 2 Bl. Com. 41. (*e*) I[illegible]. (*f*) Doug. 628.

arrear, the grantee may enter; for this is not a condition, but a limitation to the use, and shall be construed according to the intent of the parties; and the yearly rent was arrear, when any of the half-year was arrear (*a*).

If a rent-charge be granted out of a lease for years, it hath been adjudged that the grantee may bring annuity when the lease is ended (*b*)

Rent-seck or barren rent, *idem est quod reditus siccus*, is in effect nothing more than a rent reserved by deed, but without any clause of distress (*c*).

There are also other species of rents, which are reducible to the following three. *Rents of assize*, which are the certain established rents of the freeholders and ancient copyholders of a manor, and which cannot be departed from: those of the freeholders are frequently called chief-rents, *reditus capitales*, and both sorts are indifferently denominated quit-rents, *quieti reditus*, because thereby the tenant goes quit and free of all other services.

Rack-rent is only a rent of the full value of the tenement or near it (*d*)

A fee-farm rent is a rent-charge or rent-service, which is reserved on a grant in fee, the name is founded on the perpetuity of the rent or service, not on the *quantum* (*e*)

This point however is questioned, though as Mr. *Hargrave*'s seems to us to be the better opinion, we have adopted it *Vide Doug.* 605.

A grant of lands therefore reserving so considerable a rent, was indeed only letting lands to farm in fee-simple instead of the usual terms for life or years (*f*). Since the statute of *quia emptores*, *Westm.* 18 *Ed* 1. *st.* 1 it seems such grants by any subject cannot be made, because the grantor parting with the fee is by operation of that statute without any reversion, and without a reversion there cannot be a rent-service (*g*).

If the reservation be of corn, as in the case of an hospital renewed lease, where the *reddendum* was "so many quarters of corn," it will be understood to mean legal quarters, reckoning the bushel at eight gallons, although the old leases before the statute 22 and 23 *Car* 2. *c* 12 contained the same *reddendum*, and although till lately the lessees paid by composition, reckoning the bushel at nine gallons (*h*).

These are the general divisions of rent, and the difference between them (in respect of the remedy for recovering them) is now totally abolished by stat 4 *G* 2. *c.* 28; as all persons may have the like remedy by distress for rents-seck, rents of assise, and chief-rents, that is for such as had been paid for three years, within twenty years before the passing that act, or for such as have been since created, as in case of rents reserved upon lease (*i*)

(*a*) Cro. Jac. 510. (*b*) Moore c. 450. (*c*) 2 Bl. Com. 41.
(*d*) Hargr. n. 5 Co. Litt. 141. (*e*) Bl. Com. *ut ante*. (*f*) 2 Bl. Com. 43.
(*g*) Hargr. ubi *supra*. (*h*) 6 T. R. 332. (*i*) 3 Bl. Com. 43.

Statute 12 *C.* 2 *c.* 24 *s.* 5. provides that nothing therein contained shall be construed to take away any rents certain, or other service, incident or belonging to tenure in common socage, or the fealty and distress incident thereunto, and that such relief shall be paid in respect of such rents as is paid in case of a death of a tenant in common socage

Occasionally also, acts of parliament empower the officers of government to grant leases of the duties thereby imposed; as the act 12 *C.* 2 *c.* 23. *s* 27. respecting the duties of excise upon ale, beer, &c. and also *c.* 25. *s.* 3. of the same reign, &c..

CHAPTER VI.

For what Term Leases may be made.

SECTION I. *Of Terms for Life, and how created.*

SECTION II. *Of Terms for Years, absolutely or on condition, wherein of the commencement, duration, and termination of them, and of the surrender and renewal of Leases.*

SECTION I. *Of Terms for Life, and how created.*

WHERE a lease is granted for life, it confers a freehold interest in land, the duration of which is confined to the life or lives of some particular person or persons, or to the happening, or not happening, of some uncertain event (*a*). But a demise for the term of a life or lives, requires to be perfected by livery of seisin; and the assignments of leases for lives are commonly made by lease and release.

If lands are demised or granted to a man generally, without denoting the quantity of estate intended to be given, and livery be made upon it, such demise or grant to another generally, by tenant in fee, shall be an estate to the lessee for his own life, for his life is greater in consideration of law than another's life, and therefore if he leases to him in remainder or reversion for his life, he shall have it after the death of the lessee, for it was not a surrender: but if it be by tenant in tail, it shall be for the life of the lessor, for that is all he can lawfully grant, unless he lease according to the stat. 32 *H.* 8. *c.* 28 (*b*).

So, a demise to another for a time indeterminate, passes for life, if livery be made (*c*).

Or a demise of things which lie in grant, without livery (*d*).

Estates for life granted absolutely, will, generally speaking, endure as long as the life for which they were granted (*e*).

But there are some estates for life which may determine upon future contingencies before the life for which they are granted expires, as where a lease is to a man *quamdiu se bene gesserit*, to a woman *durante viduitate* or *dum sola*, to husband and wife during coverture; to *A.* as long as he inhabits, or pays such rent, or till he be preferred to such a benefice, or till out of the profits he has paid 100*l* or other sum, or during his exile, if he be absent from his country voluntarily, and not

(*a*) Cruise Dig. Estate for Life.
(*b*) Co. Dig. tit. Estate (F 1) and Co. Lit. 42 a, [illegible]
(*c*) Ibid.
(*d*) Ibid.
(*e*) 2 Bl. Com. 121.

by edict In these and such like cases the duration of the estate depends merely upon the condition (*a*)

So, if the king grants an office at will, and a rent for it for his life, the grantee has an estate for life in the rent, though it determines with his office (*b*)

But if one make a lease for life, and say that if the lessee within one year pay not 20*s.* he shall have but a term for two years, by this if he do not pay the money he has only a lease for two years, even though livery of seisin be made upon it (*c*)

But where a person devises lands to his executors for payment of his debts and until his debts are paid, although the determination of such estate be uncertain, yet it is not an estate for life, for if it were, it must determine at the death of the executors, which would frustrate the intention of the testator, for all the debts might not be then paid. The law therefore gives the executors a chattel interest, which will go to their executors and continue until all the testator's debts are paid, and the freehold and inheritance will descend in the mean time to the heir But if a limitation of this kind were made by deed, it is a freehold conditional (*d*).

Of Livery of Seisin.—Livery by the common law, is necessary to be made upon every grant of an estate of freehold in hereditaments corporeal, whether of inheritance or for life only.

Livery of seisin is either in *deed* or in *law*

Livery in *deed* is thus performed the lessor, or his attorney, together with the lessee, or his attorney, (for this may as effectually be done by deputy or attorney, as by the principals themselves in person,) come to the land, or to the house, and there, in the presence of witnesses, declare the contents of the lease on which livery is to be made. Then the lessor, if it be of land, delivers to the lessee, all other persons being out of the ground, a clod, or turf, or a twig, or bough, there growing, with words to this effect, "I deliver these to you in the name of seisin of all the lands and tenements contained in this deed" But if it be of a house, the lessor must take the ring, or latch of the door, the house being quite empty, and deliver it to the lessee in the same form, as in the case of land and then the lessee must enter alone, and shut to the door, and then open it, and let in the others If the conveyance be of divers lands, lying scattered in one and the same county, and then in the lessor's possession, livery of seisin of any parcel in the name of the residue is sufficient for all, but if they be in several counties, there must be as many liveries as there are counties, for if the title to these lands comes to be disputed, there must be as many trials as there are counties, and the jury of one county are no judges of the notoriety of a fact in another. Also, if the lands be out on lease, though all

(*a*) Co Litt *ut ante* (*b*) Ibid (*c*) Co Litt 218

(*d*) Cruise's Dig [illegible] 3 s 8 1 Inst 42 a 3 Rep 81 b 96 a Co [illegible] 3.6 1 P Wms [illegible].

lie in the same county, there must be as many liveries as there are tenants, because no livery can be made in this case, but by the consent of the particular tenant, and the consent of one will not bind the rest.—In all these cases, it is prudent and usual to endorse the livery of seisin on the back of the deed, specifying the manner, place, and time of making it, together with the names of the witnesses (*a*).

Livery in *law* is where the same is not made on the land, but in sight of it only, the lessor saying to the lessee, "I demise, grant, and to farm let, such land unto you, enter and take possession (*b*)." Here if the lessee enter during the life of the lessor, it is a good livery, but not otherwise, unless indeed he dare not enter through fear of his life, or bodily harm; and then his continual claim made yearly in due form of law, as near as possible to the lands, will suffice without entry, and such continual claim by tenant for life is sufficient for him in reversion or remainder. This livery in law cannot however be given or received by attorney, but only by the parties themselves (*c*).

If a lease be to *A.* and *B.* livery to one of the lessees is sufficient (*d*).

A lease for life of any thing whatsoever, whether it lie in livery or in grant, if it be *in esse* before, cannot begin at a day to come, for an estate of freehold cannot commence *in futuro* (*e*).

Therefore if a lease be made *habendum* from *Michaelmas* next, or after the death of the lessor, or after the death of *J. S.* to the lessee for life, this lease would not be good (*f*).

So also where one doth make a lease of land to another for years, the remainder to a stranger for life, in this case livery of seisin must be had and made to the lessee for years, or else nothing will pass to him in remainder, and yet the lease for years will be good (*g*). For if a man leases to *A* for years, remainder to *B.* in fee, in tail, or for life, he must make livery to *A* (*h*).

But livery of seisin is not needful or requisite to be had and made in cases where such estate for life is made or granted of any lands by matter of record; nor where such estate is created by way of covenant and raising of use, or of exchange, or endowment; nor where such estate is passed or granted by way of surrender, devise, release, or confirmation; or by way of increase or executory grant, as when the fee-simple is granted to the lessee for life or years in possession (*i*).

Neither is it requisite, or can be made, where any incorporeal hereditaments are granted for life. Nor is it requisite in some cases, where an estate of freehold is made of a corporeal thing, as if a house or land belong to an office, and the office be granted by deed, the house or land passes as incident thereunto. So if a house or chamber belong to a corrody (*k*).

(*a*) 2 Bl. Com. 315. (*b*) Ibid. 316. (*c*) Gilb. L. of Ten.
(*d*) Com. Dig. tit. "Feoffment" (P. 1). (*e*) Shep. Touch. 272. 2 Bl. Com. [illegible] 314.
(*f*) Shep. Touch. 272. Cro. [illegible] 725. (*g*) Ibid. 212. (*h*) Com. Dig. tit. "Feoffment" (B 1).
(*i*) Shep. Touch. [illegible]. (*k*) Ibid.

Neither is it needful, where one doth grant to me and my heirs all the trees growing on his ground; for these will pass without livery of seisin at all (*a*).

Though, if a man make leases for three lives, there must be livery, yet if tenant for life with power to make leases for three lives, makes a lease accordingly, livery is not necessary (*b*).

Tenant for life or cestuique vie beyond sea, &c.—By the 19 *Car.* 2. *c.* 6. Whereas divers lords of manors and *others* have used to grant estates by copy of court-roll for one, two, or more lives, according to the custom of their several manors, and have also granted estates *by lease* for one or more life or lives, or else for years determinable upon one or more life or lives, and it hath often happened that such person or persons for whose life or lives such estates have been granted, have gone beyond the seas, or so absented themselves for many years, that the lessors and reversioners cannot find out whether they be alive or dead, by reason whereof such lessors and reversioners have been held out of possession for many years, after all the lives upon which such estates depended are dead, in regard that the lessors and reversioners, in actions for recovery of their tenements, have been put to prove the death of their tenants when it was almost impossible to discover the same; for remedy thereof it is enacted, that if such person or persons for whose life or lives such estates have been or shall be granted, shall remain beyond the seas, or elsewhere absent themselves in this realm for seven years together, and no sufficient proof be made of their lives in any action for recovery of such tenements by the lessors or reversioners, in such case they shall be accounted dead, and the judges shall direct the jury to give their verdict accordingly. *s.* 1, 2.

Provided, that if any shall be evicted out of any lands or tenements by virtue of this Act, and afterwards such person or persons upon whose life or lives such estate or estates depend, shall return again from beyond seas, or shall on proof in such action as aforesaid be made appear to be living or to have been living at the time of the eviction, that then and from thenceforth the tenant or lessee who was ousted of the same, his or their executors, administrators, or assigns, may re-enter, re-possess, have, hold and enjoy the said lands or tenements in his or their former estate, during the life or lives, or for so long term as the said person or persons upon whose life or lives the said estate or estates depend, shall be living, and shall, upon action brought by them against the lessors, reversioners, tenants in possession, or other persons respectively, which since the said eviction received the profits of the said lands or tenements, recover for damages the full profits thereof, with lawful interest from the time that they were ousted and kept out of the same lands or tenements, and this as well in the case where the said person or persons upon whose life or lives such estate or estates did

(*a*) Shep. Touch. 211. (*b*) 1 Ld. R[illegible]

depend are or shall be dead at the time of bringing such action; as if they were then living. *s* 5.

And by the 6 *Ann. c* 18. any person who hath or shall have any claim to any remainder, reversion or expectancy, in or to any estate after the death of any person within age, married woman, or other person whatsoever, upon affidavit in the court of Chancery by the claimants of their title, and that they have cause to believe that such party is dead, and that his or her death is concealed by such guardian, trustee, husband, or any other person, may once a year, if the party [illegible]d think fit, move the Lord Chancellor, Keeper, or Commissioners [illegible] Great Seal to order, and they shall order such guardian, [illegible] husband, or other person, suspected to conceal such person, at [illegible]e and place as the Court shall direct, on personal or other due ser[illegible]e of such order, to produce and shew to such person or persons (not exceeding two) in such order named by the parties prosecuting the same, such minor, married woman, or other persons aforesaid and if such guardian, *&c* shall neglect or refuse to produce and shew such infant, *&c* on whose life such estate doth depend, according to the said order, then the Court is required to order such guardian, *&c* to produce such minor, *&c* in Court or before commissioners by the Court appointed, at such time and place as the Court shall direct, two of which commissioners to be nominated by the party prosecuting such order at their costs and charges, and if such guardian, *&c* neglect or refuse to produce such infant, *&c.* in Court or before such commissioners, whereof return shall be made by such commissioners, and be filed in the petty bag office, in either of the said cases the said minor, *&c.* shall be taken to be dead, and it shall be lawful for any person claiming any right, title, or interest, in remainder, or reversion, or otherwise, after the death of such infant, *&c.* to enter upon such lands, *&c.* as if such infant, *&c.* were actually dead. *s* 1

And if it shall appear to the said Court by affidavit that such minor, *&c.* for whose life such estate is holden, is or lately was at some certain place beyond the seas in such affidavit to be mentioned, the party prosecuting such order may, at their costs and charges, send over one or both the persons appointed by the said order, to view such minor, *&c.* and in case such guardian, *&c* shall refuse or neglect to produce or procure to be produced to such person or persons, a personal view of such infant, *&c* then such person or persons are required to make a return thereof to the Court, to be filed in the petty bag office, and thereupon such minor, *&c* shall be taken to be dead and any person claiming any right, *&c* after the death of such infant, *&c.* may enter upon such lands, *&c* as if such infant were actually dead. *s* 2.

Provided, that if it shall afterwards appear, upon proof in any action brought, that such infant, *&c* for whose life any such estate is holden, were alive at the time of such order made, that then it shall be lawful for such infant, married woman, or other person having any estate or interest, determinable upon such life, to re-enter upon the said lands, *&c* and for such infant, married woman, or other person, having any estate or interest, determinable upon such life, their executors, administrators or assigns, to maintain an action against those who since the said order received the profits of such lands, *&c.* or their executors or administrators, and therein to recover full damages for the profits so received from the time that such infant, *&c* were ousted of possession. s 3

Provided always, that if such guardian, trustee, husband, or other person, holding or having any estate or interest determinable upon the life or lives of any other person or persons, shall by affidavit or otherwise to the satisfaction of the Court, make appear that they have used their utmost endeavours to procure such infant, *&c.* to appear in the said Court or elsewhere, according to the order of the said Court, and that they cannot procure or compel such infant, *&c* so to appear, and that such infant, *&c.* is, are, or were living at the time of such return made and filed as aforesaid, then it shall be lawful for such person or persons, to continue in possession of such estate and receive the rents and profits thereof during the infancy of such infant, and the life or lives of such married woman or other person or persons, on whose life or lives such estate or interest depends, as fully as they might have done if the Act had not been made s 4

And every person who, as guardian or trustee for any infant, and every husband seised in right of his wife only, and every other person having any estate determinable upon any life or lives, who after the determination of such particular interests, without the express consent of the next immediately entitled, shall hold over and continue in possession of any manors, messuages, lands, tenements, or hereditaments, shall be adjudged trespassers. and the party entitled and their executors and administrators, may recover in damages against every such person or persons so holding over and their executors and administrators, the full value of the profits received during such wrongful possession s. 5

SECTION II. *Of Terms for Years, absolutely, or on condition; and herein of the commencement, duration, and termination of them; and of the surrender and renewal of Leases.*

Tenant for term of years shall be, where a man lets lands, tenements, or hereditaments to another for a term of certain years, and every estate which must expire at a period certain and prefixed, by whatever words created, is an estate for years (*a*).

Therefore this estate is frequently called a term, *terminus*, because

(*a*) Com Dig. tit. "Estate" (G. 1) [illegible]

its duration or continuance is bounded, limited, and determined (*a*). It is properly called a term of years and the lease is made for ten, a hundred, a thousand years and the like, as the lessor and lessee agree; for the word "term" doth not only signify the limits and limitation of time, but also the estate and interest that doth pass for that time (*b*).

Such terms are frequently created for particular purposes, as to raise [illegible] and when the purpose is answered, they attend the inheritance [illegible] are created, as has been before mentioned, by way of [illegible] often created in the nature of a lease for long terms, as five hundred [illegible] portions, and for other purposes, in family settlements, and such as are not accounted leases, but terms to attend the inheritance: no man has a lease, for example, of two thousand years, as a lease, but as a term to attend the inheritance (*d*). Half the titles in the kingdom are so (*e*).

An estate for a thousand years is only a chattel, and reckoned part of the personal estate (*f*).

Therefore, if a lease be devised to one, and the heirs male of his body, yet his executors shall have it; for a term is but a chattel, which cannot be entailed, and such [illegible] may well alien the term to whom he pleases (*g*).

If, however, it be limited to attend the inheritance, it may be entailed, though the entail of the inheritance and of the term be by different clauses, or deeds executed at different times (*h*).

Commencement of a Lease for Years.—With respect to the commencement of a lease for years, as it is a mere chattel, it may be made to commence either *in præsenti*, or *in futuro*, according to the agreement of the parties; and the lease that is to commence *in futuro*, is called [illegible], or future interest (*i*).—A lease for years therefore, may begin at a day to come, as at *Michaelmas* next, or for three or ten years after, or after the death of the lessor, or of *J. S.* and is as good as where it doth begin presently (*k*).

So a lease to commence *ad festum Michaelis* [illegible], after the determination of a former lease, is as good as if it had been *in præsenti* (*l*).

A lease to commence after the determination of a prior lease, shall begin presently, if the prior lease was void at law (*m*).

So a lease intended to commence *in futuro*, which [illegible] the prior lease on which it depends in a material point, shall begin immediately (*n*).

This rule, that if the former lease be [illegible] in the [illegible], and a new lease made, to begin at the expiration of the said recited lease, that such new lease shall begin presently, holds as well in the lease it-

[illegible footnotes]

self, as where the jury find an indenture of lease, whereby it is recited, that the lessor made such former lease of such date and under such rent without finding it in fact, but only by way of recital in the deed, such second lease shall in construction of law be adjudged to begin presently, though in the deed it is limited to begin after the expiration of the first lease so recited, because the jury do not actually find the first lease, but only a recital of it in another deed, which recital may be false for aught that appears to the Court: and then the second lease shall begin presently, as if no such first lease were at all, since the not finding it effectually is as if there were none such made (a).

With regard to the date of a lease, it was formerly held that a lease to commence *a dato* included the day of the date, but that *a die datus* excluded the day (b).

But it has since been held, that the word "from" may mean either inclusive or exclusive, according to the context and subject matter (c), though this decision has been much questioned.

Therefore, where the plaintiff in ejectment declared upon a lease for years, *habendum* from the sealing and delivery, and declared that the sealing and delivery was 1 *May*, and that the ejectment was the same day: it was moved in arrest of judgment, that the ejectment could not be supposed the same day, for the lease did not begin till the next day ensuing the sealing and delivery. But the Court disallowed the exception, for where the lease is to begin from the time of the sealing and delivery, or generally to hold for twenty-one years next following, the ejectment may well be supposed to be the same day: for the beginning of the lease is presently upon the sealing and delivery, and therefore such lease shall end at the same time and hour (d).

A lease "from the day of the date," and "from henceforth," is the same thing (e).

Indeed, as to the date, this may be considered either as an impossible date, or an uncertain date, between which the general difference taken in the books is, that if a lease be made to begin from an impossible date, there the lease shall take effect from the delivery, because it could not be any part of the agreement between the parties, as from the 30th day of *February*, or the 32d day of *April* next (f): but where the limitation is uncertain, as a lease made the 10th day of *October*, *habendum* from the 20th day of *November*, without saying what *November* was meant, whether last past, or next ensuing, or what other *November*, the lease is thereby vitiated, because the limitation was part of the agreement, but the Court cannot determine it, not knowing how the contract was (g).

(a) Bac. Abr. tit. "Leases" (I. 1.)
(b) 2 Salk. 413. 1 Ld. R[illegible] 84.
(c) C[illegible]
(d) Bac. Abr. tit. "Leases" (I. 1.)
(e) Cro. Jac. 258.
(f) Bac. Ab[illegible]
(g) 1 Mod. 180.

So, where a lease is made to begin from the nativity of our Lord last past, without saying from the feast of the nativity, this lease shall begin presently, because it could be no part of the agreement between the parties that the lease should begin from the nativity itself, which is past so many hundred years ago, and therefore for this impossibility of relation, the lease shall begin presently (*a*); but if it were to begin from the nativity of our Lord generally, or next ensuing, omitting the word "feast," *Twisden* was of opinion that such a lease should be void for the uncertainty of the commencement; but *Siderfin* in reporting the case, makes a *quære*, if it shall not begin presently; and in truth, this seems the most reasonable opinion, for as to impossibility of relation, there is the same in this as there is in the other, and therefore by the same reason, it shall begin presently. The editor of *Bacon* asks what sound reason can be assigned why it should not commence from the *Christmas* intended by the parties? which well applies to the lease to begin from the nativity of our Lord next ensuing, if not to the former (*b*).

Where a lessee for an hundred years made a lease for forty years to *B* if he should so long live, and after leased the same lands to *C habendum* for twenty-one years from the end of the term of *B* to begin and be accounted from the date of these presents; and the question was, if the lease to be should be said to begin presently, or after the term of *B.*? the judges were clearly of opinion, that the lease to *C.* should not be accounted from the time of the date, but from the end of the term of *B* because by the first words it is a good lease in reversion in that manner, and then it shall not be made void by any subsequent words; for as *Coke* said, the last words ought to be construed to give an interest as a future interest presently, and the actual possession after the expiration of the first forty years is well granted by the first words (*c*).

In ejectment the plaintiff declared upon a lease made 14th *Jan.* 30 *Eliz.* from *Christmas* before for three years, and upon evidence the plaintiff shewed a lease bearing date 13th *Jan.* the same year, and proved to have been then executed, [illegible] was moved, for this variation between the declaration [illegible], that the jury might be discharged; but [illegible] that the [illegible] lease was sufficient to support the [illegible] the lease was sealed and delivered 13th [illegible] (*d*).

A term may commence [illegible] day, in point of computation, and at a [illegible] in point of interest (*e*).

Therefore, [illegible] to hold from a day past for fifty years then

(*e*) [illegible]

next ensuing, the said term to commence and begin immediately after the determination of an existing lease in the same premises," was not esteemed uncertain at its commencement (*a*).

So, a lease *habendum* to the lessee for his life, which term shall begin after the determination of a previous term for three lives, is good (*b*)

So, if an indenture of demise bear *teste* 25th *March*, 15 *Car.* and is delivered the day of the date, and the *habendum* is from and after the day of the date of these presents, for and during the time and term of seven years from henceforth next and immediately following, fully to be compleat and ended, this lease begins in computation from the delivery of the deed, which was the day of the date, and in interest the next day after the date, and so all the words will have an operation for it appears that he was not to have the possession till the next day after the date, by the words *habendum* from and *after* the day of the date, which excludes the day of the date. but that the seven years should commence by computation from the delivery, *viz.* from henceforth, which refers to the limitation of the seven years (*c*).

In ejectment the plaintiff declared, that *J S.* demised to him *per quoddam scriptum obligatorium* such lands *habend' a die datus indenturæ prædict'*, on not guilty pleaded, it was found and adjudged for the plaintiff in *Ireland* and it being assigned for error here, that there was no time specified when this lease should begin for it was *habend' a die datus indenturæ prædict'*, and no indenture was mentioned before, but only *scriptum obligatorium*, yet *per Curiam* it was resolved, that the writing should be intended an indenture, though improperly called *scriptum obligatorium*, for every deed obligeth, or if it should not be intended an indenture, then it begins presently, as if it had been from an impossible limitation, as the 40th of *Sept* or such like (*d*)

A lease of lands by deed, since the new stile, to hold from the feast of St Michael, must be taken to mean from new *Michaelmas*, and cannot be shewn by extrinsic evidence to refer to a holding from old *Michaelmas* [and therefore a notice to quit at old *Michaelmas*, though given half a year before new *Michaelmas*, is bad] (*e*)

But all leases for years, whether they begin *in præsenti*, or *in futuro*, must be certain, that is, they must have a certain beginning, and certain ending, and so, the continuance of the term must be certain, otherwise they are not good (*f*).

Yet if the years be certain, when the lease is to take effect in interest or possession, it is sufficient, for until that time it may depend upon an uncertainty, *viz* upon a possible contingent precedent before it

(*a*) 2 Barr. 1090 (*b*) Cro Eliz 269 (*c*) Bac. Abr *ut ante*
(*d*) Ibid. (*e*) 11 East 312 (*f*) Shep Touch 272

begin in possession or interest, or upon a limitation or condition subsequent; but in case it is to be reduced to a certainty upon a contingent precedent, the contingent must happen in the lives of the parties; and though there appear no certainty of years in the lease, yet if by reference to a certainty it may be made certain, it is sufficient (*a*).

As, if a lease be granted for twenty-one years after three lives in being, though it is uncertain at first when that term will commence, because those lives are in being, yet when they die it is reduced to a certainty (*b*).

So if *A.* seised of land in fee, grant to *B.* that when *B.* shall pay to *A.* twenty shillings, that from thenceforth he shall hold the land for twenty-one years; and after *B.* pays the twenty shillings; in this case, *B.* shall have a good lease for twenty-one years from thenceforth (*c*).

So if *A.* grant to *B.* that if his tenant for life shall die, that *B.* shall have the land for ten years, this is a good lease; and if one makes a lease for years after the death of *C.* if *C.* die within ten years, this is a good lease if *C.* die within the ten years, otherwise not (*d*).

So, if a lease for years be made of land in lease for life, to have and to hold from the death of the tenant for life,—or to have and to hold from *Michaelmas* next after the death of the tenant for life,—or from *Michaelmas* next after the determination of the estate of the tenant for life, these are good leases (*e*).

Even if one make a lease to begin after the death of *J. S.* and to continue until *Michaelmas*, which shall be *anno Domini* 1650, this is a good lease (*f*).

So, if a man make a lease to *B.* for ninety years, to begin after the death of *A.* on condition to be avoided upon the doing of divers acts by others, and afterwards makes another lease of the land, *habendum* after the determination or redemption of the former lease, it seems this is a good lease and certain enough (*g*).

So, if a man have a lease of land for an hundred years, and he make a lease of this land to another, to have and to hold to him for forty years, to begin after his death, this is a good lease for the whole forty years, if there shall be so many of the hundred years to come at the time of the death of the lessor. So if he grant all his estate, or all his term, or all his interest, in the premisses of the deed, and then say, to have and to hold the land, &c. to the grantee for all the residue of the term of an hundred years that shall be to come at the time of his death; by this the whole estate and interest of the grantor in the land doth pass presently, by these words in the deed; and if in this case the lessee for an hundred years make a lease of the land, to have and to hold after his death for an hundred years, this will be a good lease for as

(*a*) Shep. Touch. 272.
(*b*) 8 Co. R. 46.
(*c*) Shep. Touch. 273.
(*d*) Ibid.
(*e*) Ibid.
(*f*) Ibid.
(*g*) Ibid. 274.

many of the first hundred years as shall be to come at the time of his death (*a*).

So, if *A.* doth make a lease of land to *B.* for so many years as *B.* hath in the manor of *Dale*, and *B.* hath then a lease for ten years in such manor, this is a good lease for ten years (*b*).

So, if a lease be made during the minority of *J. S.* or until *J. S.* shall come to the age of twenty-one years, these are good leases, and if *J. S.* die before he come to his full age, the lease is ended. So, if a man make a lease for twenty-one years, if *J. S.* live so long; or if the coverture between *J. S.* and *D. S.* shall so long continue, or if *J. S.* shall continue to be parson of *Dale* so long, these and such like leases are good (*c*).

If one makes a lease to *A.* for twenty-one years, and after makes another lease to *B.* for years, to begin from the end and expiration of the aforesaid term of twenty-one years demised to *A.*, and then the lease to *A.* is determined, either by an express surrender, or by an implied surrender in law, as by *A.*'s acceptance of a new lease for life from the lessor, the lease to *B.* shall begin presently; but if the lease to *B.* had been to begin after the end and expiration of the aforesaid of twenty-one years, there the lease to *B.* should not begin upon the surrender, forfeiture, or other determination of the first term to *A.* till the twenty-one years actually run out by effluxion of time: the reason of which difference is, that in the first case the "word term" comprehends as well the estate or interest in the land, as the time for which it is demised; and therefore, the second lease being limited to begin *from* the end and expiration of the aforesaid term of twenty-one years, whenever the term is determined, the lease to *B.* shall begin; but in the other case the lease to *B.* is not to begin till *after* the end and expiration of the twenty-one years, which cannot be ended but by effluxion of time (*d*).

So, it was held that a proviso in a lease for years to *A.* to re-enter if lessee died within the term, is a mere condition, and not a limitation, and a second lease *habendum cum post mortem sive per mortem suam redditionem seu forisfacturam predict' A. vacari acciderit*, is good, and commences when the first term is determined by effluxion of time (*e*).

So, if one makes a lease to another for so many years as *J. S.* shall name, this at the beginning is uncertain, but when *J. S.* hath named the years, (in the life-time of the lessor), this ascertains the commencement or continuance of the lease accordingly.—But if the lease had been made for so many years as the executors of the lessor should name, this could not be made good by any nomination, because *to*

(*a*) Shep. Touch. 273. (*b*) Ibid. 274. (*c*) Ibid.
(*d*) Bac. Abr. tit. "Leases," (L. 1.) (*e*) Cro. Jac. 71.

every lease there ought to be a lessor and lessee, and here the nomination which ascertains the commencement not being appointed till after the death of the lessor, makes the lease defective in one of the main parts of it, *viz* a lessor, and therefore of consequence must be void, which is also the reason that in the first case the nomination ought to be made in the life-time of the lessor, and not by *J S.* after his death, for then it will be void (*a*).

A lease in reversion of several parcels of land, made to commence on the happening of several contingencies, shall take effect and commence respectively as those contingencies happen (*b*).

In a case where *B.* had a lease for twenty-one years of copyhold lands to commence after the determination of the estate which *A.* at that time had therein, and the widow of *A.* being entitled to her free-bench, happened to outlive her husband twenty-one years, it was held by the Lord Chancellor, that the estate of the wife was only an excrescence of her husband's estate, which did not determine till the wife's death, at which time the lease made to *B* should commence and continue for twenty one years (*c*).

A lease for years, reserving rent "after the rate" of 18*l* a year, is void for uncertainty (*d*)

As to leases void for uncertainty in respect to the time of their commencement, if *A* be seised of land in fee, and lease it to *B.* for ten years, and it is agreed between them that *B* shall pay to *A* 100*l* at the end of the said ten years, and that if he do so and shall pay the said 100*l.* and 100*l* at the end of every ten years, that then the said *B* shall have a perpetual demise and grant of the premises from ten years to ten years continually following *extra memoriam hominum, &c.*, this, although it be a good lease for the first ten years, yet it is void for all the rest for uncertainty (*e*).

So, if the lessor grant the land to another, to have and to hold to him for and during all the residue of the term of one hundred years that shall be to come at the time of the death of the grantor, this is void for uncertainty · had he granted all his estate, or term, or interest, it had been otherwise (*f*)

So, it is said, if a lease be made to *A* for eighty years, if he live so long, and if he die within the said term or alien the premises, that then his estate shall cease; and then he doth further by the same deed grant and let the premises for so many years as shall remain unexpired after the death of *A* or alienation, to *B* for the residue of the *said term* of eighty years, if he shall live so long in this case the lease to *B* is void, for after the death of *A.* the term is at an end, but if he say for the residue of the eighty years, it is otherwise (*g*)

(*a*) Bac Abr tit "Leases," (L 2) (*b*) Cro Eliz 199
(*c*) Bac Abr ut ante (*d*) 4 Mod 78 (*e*) Shep. Touch. 273
(*f*) Ibid 274 (*g*) Ibid

So, a lease made to another until a child in its mother's belly shall come to the age of twenty-one years, is not good (*a*).

So, if *A.* make a lease to *B.* for so many years as *A* and *B.* or either of them shall live, not naming any certain number of years, this cannot be a good lease for years (*b*).

So, if the parson of *Dale* make a lease of his glebe for so many years as he shall be parson there; this is not certain, neither can it be made so by any means, and yet if a parson shall make a lease from three years to three years so long as he shall be parson, this is a good lease for six years, if he continue parson so long, and for the residue void for uncertainty *Vide post* 172 (*c*)

So, if I make another a lease of land, until he be promoted to a benefice; this is no good lease for years, but void for uncertainty (*d*).

So, if I have a piece of land of the value of 20*l. per annum*, and I make a lease of it to another, until he shall levy out of the profits thereof 100*l* this is no good lease for years, but void for uncertainty.—But if I have a rent-charge of 20*l per annum*, and let it to another until he shall have levied 100*l* this is a good lease for five years (*e*).

Note In all these cases of uncertain leases made with limitations as aforesaid, as until such a thing be done, or so long as such a thing continue, &c. if livery of seisin be made upon them, they may be good leases for life, determinable upon these contingencies, albeit they be no good leases for years (*f*).

In leases for years, or other chattel interests, livery of seisin is not necessary, but instead thereof an actual entry is requisite, to vest the estate in the lessee for to many purposes he is not tenant for years until he enter (*g*).

Before entry the lessee hath but an *interesse termini*, an interest of a term, and no possession, and therefore a release, which enures by way of enlarging an estate, cannot work without a possession, for before possession there is no reversion. Such is the case of leases at common law, for if it be so framed as to be a bargain and sale under the statute, the possession is immediately executed in the lessee, so that no entry is necessary (*h*)

Yet if a tenant for twenty years in possession make a lease to *B.* for five years, and *B* enter, a release to the first lessee is good, for he had an actual possession, and the possession of the lessee is his possession So it is if a man make a lease for years, the remainder for years, and the first lessee doth enter, a release to him in the remainder for years is good to enlarge his estate A release therefore that enures by enlargement cannot work without a possession; but an actual estate in possession is not necessary, for a vested interest suffices for such a release

(*a*) Sheph. Touch. 27[illegible] (*d*) Ibid. 275 (*e*) Ibid
(*b*) Ibid (*g*) Ibid (*f*) Ibid
(*c*) 2 Le Con. 311 [illegible] C[illegible] 46 [illegible] (*h*) Ibid. 270 &c. [illegible]

to operate upon.—But lessee may release the rent reserved before entry, in respect of the privity (*a*).

Neither could the lessor grant away the reversion by the name of the reversion before entry, unless the lessee attorned, which is now unnecessary (*b*).

If a man make a lease for a thousand years, this lease is perfect by the delivery of the deed without any livery of seisin (*c*).

The interest, *interesse termini*, which the lessee hath before entry, is grantable to another; and although the lessor die before the lessee enter, yet the lessee may enter into the lands: so, if the lessee die before he enter, yet his executors or administrators may enter, because he presently by the lease hath an interest in him; and if it be made to two, and one die before entry, his interest shall survive (*d*).

This *interesse termini* is in the lessee, whether the lease be made to commence immediately, or at a future day (*e*).

This entry by the tenant himself serves the purpose of notoriety, as well as livery of seisin from the grantor could have done; which it would have been improper to have given in this case, because that solemnity is appropriated to the conveyance of a freehold (*f*).

When the lessee therefore has actually so entered, and thereby accepted the grant, the estate is then and not before vested in him, and he is possessed, not properly of the land, but of the term of years, the possession or seisin of the land remaining still in him who hath the freehold (*g*).

Duration of a Lease for Years.—As to the certainty of leases for years in respect of their continuance or duration, this ought to be ascertained either by the express limitation of the parties at the time of the lease made, or by a reference to some collateral act, which may with equal certainty measure the continuance thereof, otherwise it will be void (*h*).

If a man makes a lease for years, without saying how many, this shall be a good lease for two years certain, because for more there is no certainty, and for less there can be no sense in the words (*i*).

If a man leases lands for such a term as both parties shall please, this is but a lease at will, because what that term will be is utterly uncertain, and the pleasure of the parties seems to be limited to attend the continuance as well as the commencement and first fixation thereof (*k*).

So, if a parson makes a lease for a year, and so from year to year as long as he shall continue parson, or as long as he shall live, this is a lease for two years at least, if he lives and continues parson so long, and after the two years, or at most after three years, but an estate at will for the uncertainty, unless livery be made (*l*).

(*a*) Co. L. [illegible] (*b*) [illegible] 46 [illegible] 8 (*c*) Shep. Touch. [illegible]
(*d*) Co. Litt. [illegible] (*e*) Com. Dig. tit. "Estates," (G. 14) (*f*) 2 Bl. Com. [illegible]
(*g*) [illegible] 144 (*h*) Bac. Abr. tit. "Leases," (L. 3) (*i*) Ibid.
(*k*) Ibid. (*l*) Ibid.

A parson made a lease of his rectory to one for three years, and at the end of those three years, for other three years, and so from three years to three years, during the life of the lessor, the whole Court held it clearly a lease for twelve years; but by *Coddridge*, if the lease had been for three years, and so from three years to three years, and so from the said three years to three years, this had been but a lease for nine years, because the words "from the said three years" tie up the relation retrospectively to the three years last mentioned, which make in all but six years, and then there are but three years more added, which make the whole but nine years; and for the words "during the life of the lessor," they cannot enlarge it to any further certain number of years, by reason of the uncertainty of the lessor's life, and therefore beyond the twelve years, or nine years, it amounts only to a lease at will, unless livery were made, which must necessarily pass a freehold determinable upon the lessor's death (a).

Yet in one book, where a lease was made for three years, and after the end of those three years, for other three years, and so from three years to three years, during the life of the lessor, this was held to be only a lease for nine years; because the words "and so from three years" shall be referred to the three years last mentioned, for otherwise these words would exclude the three years next after the six years, and make the three last years to begin after nine years, and so make a chasm in the lease by shutting out the three years next after the six years, so as for the three last years it should be only a future interest: which case seems to be of a new stamp, and to thwart the preceding case as to the resolution of it being a lease for twelve years, and there *Jones* and *Wild* held, that a lease from three years to three years, was but a lease for three years to commence *in futuro* (b).

One made a lease for three years, and so from three years to three years until ten years be expired; this was resolved to be a lease but for nine years, and that the odd year should be rejected, because that cannot come to fall within any three entire years according to the limitation, which in this case are to be taken altogether as one year, or else so much of the limitation as cannot come within that description must be rejected; and this seems to agree with *Brook* [tit. *Lease*,] and *Plowden*, [*Reports*, 273, 522 a.] who in general hold a limitation in that manner, from year to year, for forty, fifty, or one hundred years, to be a good lease for the whole term, because there is no such break of an odd year at the latter end of the lease, as there is in the other case (c).

A parol demise to hold from year to year, and so on as long as it shall please both parties, is a lease for two years, and after every subsequent year begun, is not determinable till that year be ended (d).

If therefore *A.* demise lands to *B.* for a year, and so from year to

(a) Bac. Abr. tit. "Lease" [illegible] (b) [illegible] 3 Keb. 62, 63.
(c) Bac. Abr. [illegible] 2 [illegible] 1.
(d) 2 Salk. 414 [illegible]

year; this is not a lease for two years and afterwards will, but it is a lease for every particular year, and after the year is begun, the defendant cannot determine the lease before the year is ended. But in a lease at will, the lessee may determine his will after the payment of his rent at the end of a quarter, but not in the beginning, lest his lessor should lose his rent. In that case, therefore, the question seems to have been, whether after the third year commenced, the lessor was entitled to the whole year's rent, and *Holt* held that he was, because the tenant could not determine the estate in the middle of the year, and the expression "for every particular year does not mean that such a lease operates as a distinct demise for each year separately, but that when any year has commenced, it is good for the whole of that year (*a*)."

So, where *A* agreed by parol to sell an estate to *B.* on certain terms provided *B.* would continue *C.* his tenant, "not for one year only, but from year to year" (*C.* having just before been let into possession under a contract for the purchase of the estate, which he had failed to pay for in time, and had therefore forfeited his deposit,) and *A.* thereupon agreed to take *C.*'s forfeited deposit as part of the purchase-money. *A.* and *B.* afterwards reduced their agreement respecting the purchase into writing, in which no notice was taken of the stipulation concerning *C.*'s tenancy, yet it was held that this stipulation, being collateral to the written agreement, was binding upon *B.* and that the agreement operated as a tenancy for two years certain at least, though a rent was not then mentioned, but was to be settled afterwards, and that the tenancy could not be put an end to at the expiration of the first year by six months' notice to quit (*b*).

This point is well illustrated by the subsequent case, which was sent by the Lord Chancellor to the Court of *C. P.* for the opinion of that Court (*c*).

The defendant, *John Spurrier*, on the 14th *Oct.* 1791, entered into the following agreement with one *William Atkinson*.

"*London*, 14*th October*, 1791.

"Memorandum. I, *William Atkinson* of *Saint Olaves*, *Southwark*, have this day agreed to take on lease of *John Spurrier* the dwelling-house and premises now occupied by him in *Old Bread Street*, together with a bed room now in the possession of *Mr. Amory*, and which bed room is over the one now used by the said *John Spurrier* himself, to hold for seven, fourteen, or twenty-one years, at the yearly rent of one hundred and fifty pounds, payable half yearly, including all taxes which are to be paid by the said *John Spurrier*, the term and rent to commence from Christmas next, the usual fixtures, carpets and floor-cloths fitted to the floors, to be taken and paid for at a fair valuation by the said *William Atkinson*. An outside door to be put to the kitchen entrance of the house at the expence of the said *John Spurrier*." And on the back

(*a*) 1 L[illegible] 414. (*b*) 4 Term R. 31. (*c*) 3 Bos. and Pul. 399.

of the said agreement was the following memorandum: "I agree to let the premises mentioned on the other side hereof upon the terms and conditions expressed therein *John Spurrier*" The said *W Atkinson* accordingly took possession of the premises and afterwards disposed his interest therein to the plaintiff *Richard Daun*, who took possession thereof and paid the rent.—The defendant on the 20th of *June*, 1798, duly gave notice to the plaintiff to quit the premises at *Christmas* then next, which the plaintiff refused to do, alledging that the defendant had no right to determine the agreement at the expiration of the first seven years, but that the tenant only had that right, in consequence of which, the defendant, in *Hilary Term*, 1799, duly commenced an action of ejectment in *K B.* in order to obtain possession. upon which the plaintiff and *W Atkinson* in the same term filed a bill against the defendant for a specific performance of the said agreement, and that the defendant might be compelled to execute a lease of the premises to them, or one of them, for twenty one years

The question for the opinion of the court was, whether upon the legal construction of the said agreement, the defendant had a right to determine the term of twenty-one years, thereby agreed to be granted at the end of the first seven years?—The opinion of the Court was delivered by

Lord *Alvanley*, C. J. This question turns upon the legal construction of the agreement stated in the case. It is to be observed, that the agreement is not an offer on the part of the lessee to take a lease for seven, or a lease for fourteen, or a lease for twenty-one years, but it is an offer to take a lease with an *habendum*, as stated by the lessee in his proposals, *viz* to hold for seven, fourteen, or twenty-one years. The lessor having assented to let the premises upon the terms and conditions proposed, it must now be taken as if a lease had been actually granted containing such an *habendum* as that stated in the proposals It is for us, therefore, to determine what is the legal construction of such an *habendum* in a lease. It has been contended that where the terms are not defined, either positively or by any circumstance, but an alternative is stated which cannot be made certain without the option of one of the parties, the lease is determinable at the option of either. There seems to be great authority for such a proposition, for undoubtedly Lord *Kenyon* and Mr J. *Buller* both intimate in the case of *Goodright* v *Richardson and Hall*, [3 T R 462.] that the option would be in either party But it must not be forgotten (for I wish it to be understood that, had the judgment of the Court in that case proceeded upon the point alluded to, it would probably have guided our judgment in the construction of such doubtful words as those which occur in this case) that Lord *K.* and Mr J *B* only threw out their opinion *obiter*, had it been otherwise, there are no authorities, particularly that of Lord *Kenyon*, upon a point arising out of real property, to which I should be more disposed to defer. The lease in that case was for three, six, or nine years, determinable in the year 1788, 1791, and 1794, and the construction put upon that lease was that it gave an option to either party, but that such option must be exercised with reasonable notice previous to the expiration of any of the terms; and as reasonable notice had not been given, the Court held that the lease was not determined. With respect to the case of *Ferguson* v. *Cornish* there referred to [2 Bur. 1034] it is surprising that any doubt should have arisen, and indeed it does not appear that any doubt was entertained by the Court. A lease having been granted for seven, fourteen, or twenty-one years, and an action of covenant having been brought against the lessee during the first seven years, it was contended by the lessee that it was no lease at all according to the old doctrine, that a lease uncertain in its commencement or duration was void. Lord *Mansfield* held that, at all events, it was a good lease for seven years. These two cases decide nothing with respect to the point now before the Court. It remains, therefore, for us to consider, notwithstanding the opinions thrown out in these two cases, Whether, according to the construction which deeds between lessor and lessee have received, the power of determining the lease in this case must not be confined to the lessee? Much is to be found in the books relative to the construction of deeds which contain covenants in the alternative, from all which the rule appears to be perfectly clear, that if a doubt arise as to the construction of a lease between lessor and lessee, the lease must be construed most beneficially for the latter. It is laid down in the books that if a man covenant to do one of two things, and he does either, the covenant is not broken. Thus in 1 *Roll Abr.* tit. *Condition* XI *pl.* 3 *fo* 446. it is said that if a condition be that the obligor shall enfeoff a man of lands in *D* or *S* upon request, the obligor has his election of which of the two he shall enfeoff him. So, in *pl.* 4 it is laid down, that if the condition be that the obligor shall pay 20*l* or a pint of wine upon request, he has his election. This election, however, is said to depend upon which of the two parties to the contract is to do the first act. Therefore, if a man make a grant in the alternative, and the grantee enter into possession, the grantor is no longer at liberty to exercise an option. So, if *A.* says to *B.* I grant you a horse out of my stable, he puts it in the power of *B* to take which horse he shall think proper. In the bishop of *Bath's* case, 6 *Co.* 35 *b.* it was resolved, that the construction of law as to the commencement of leases should be taken strongest against the lessor and most beneficially for the lessee. Another strong authority to this effect is Sir *Richard Heyward's* case, 2 *Co.* 35 *a.* where one having demised, granted, bargained, and sold certain lands, and the question being, Whether the grantee should take by demise or by bargain and sale, it was held that the grantee had his election. In Dyer 261. *b.* the court of *C. P.* held, that where a lease of premises, which had been granted for thirty-one years, was granted to a new lessee *a die confectionis praesentium tenendum praedicto finito usque ad finem termini 31 annorum tunc immediate sequentium*, that the terms should commence in possession from the end of the former term, and not from the making of the deed, and the reason which they give for the opinion is, that every grant shall be expounded most favourably for the grantee, and if the lease were to commence from the making of the deed the lessee would have only four years It is true that *Brown* doubted upon this point and that the court of *K. B.* came to a different decision. But although the court of *K B* might not think proper to go so far in favour of the lessee as the court of *C P* did, yet it does not follow that they were disposed to deny the rule of construing leases favourably for the lessee, for where two periods are mentioned in a deed, from which the commencement of lease is to take place, the legal construction is that it shall commence from which of the two periods shall first happen, and so it was determined in *Dyer* 312. *b. in marg* This principle of exposition is sound, but it is not applicable to this case, which does not depend upon the priority of different periods, but upon the question, In whom the option of deciding upon the alternative is vested ? The lease agreed for in the present case was for seven, fourteen, or twenty-one years An option, therefore, was certainly intended. If then the principle be just, that a lease is to be construed most favourably for the lessee, why are we to determine in this instance that the option is in the lessor If indeed a provision had been inserted that the lease should be determinable at the option of either party, the lessor would have been entitled to take advantage of it · but where no such provision is inserted, the true construction seems to be that the lessee is entitled at his option, to take that term which is most beneficial to himself. Notwithstanding, therefore, the opinions which have been referred to of Lord *Kenyon*, and Mr. J. *Buller*, we think that where no custom of the country exists upon the subject, the principle of construing deeds between lessor and lessee requires us to hold, that where a grant is made in an alternative which cannot be determined by intrinsic circumstances, the option is left in the lessee · and we shall certify accordingly There is a case of *Kible* v *Hall*, *Latt.* 363 370 which bears very strongly upon this subject In that case, a lease having been granted to *A* and *B.* for forty years if they and three others, or any of them, should so long live, a second lease was granted "*habendum* from the administration [probably misprinted for annunciation,] which should be in the year 1568, or from and after the surrender, forfeiture, or other determination of the said lease to *A* and *B.*" and some of the persons for whose life the first lease was granted having survived the year 1568, a question arose when the second lease ought to commence. The case indeed does not appear by the report to have been finally determined, but the Court strongly inclined to think that the lessee should have his election, because that construction ought to be adopted which is most favourable for lessees:

A lease "for seven, fourteen, or twenty-one years, as the lessee shall think proper," upon which the lessee enters and continues in possession, is undoubtedly a good lease for seven years, whatever may be its validity as to the two other eventual terms of fourteen and twenty-one years (*a*).

So, a lease in 1785, for three, six, or nine years, determinable in 1788, 1791, and 1794, is a lease for nine years determinable at the end of three or six years, by either of the parties, on giving reasonable notice to quit (*b*).

An agreement to grant a lease for seven, fourteen, or twenty-one years, without saying at whose option, gives the option to the lessee alone (*c*).

One lets a stable for a week for 8*s.* and so from week to week at 8*s.* a week, as long as both parties pleased, this was held at most but a lease for three weeks certain, and for the residue at will, so that the lessee at the end of the three weeks was not punishable for negligently keeping his fire, that being only an involuntary waste, wherewith lessee at will is not chargeable (*d*).

Where a lease is to two for forty years, if they so long live, *Rolle* [in his reports, 309, 310] seems to think that this does not determine by the death of one of them, because it is an interest in both, which shall survive; but the other books are against it, because their life is but a collateral condition and limitation of the estate, which therefore is broken when one dies;—this differs therefore from a lease to two persons for their lives, for that gives an estate to both for their lives, and both have an estate of freehold therein in their own right; which consequently cannot determine by the death of one of them, for then the other could not be said to have an estate for his life, as the lessor at first gave it (*e*).

So, where one made a lease for forty years, "if his wife or any of their issue should so long live," it was adjudged that the lease was not determined by the death of one of them, but should continue till all were dead by reason of the disjunctive *or*, which goes to and governs the whole limitation: but if the words had been "if his wife *and* issue should so long live," there clearly, by the death of any of them within the forty years, the term had been at an end, by reason of the copulative *and*, which conjoins all together, and makes all their lives jointly the measure of the estate (*f*).

A lease was for twenty-one years, if the lessee lived so long and continued in the lessor's service; the lessor dies; and, Whether the term was determined? was the question. Three of the Justices held, that

[illegible]
[illegible]
[illegible]

the lease continued, for there is not any *laches* in the lessee that he did not serve, but it is the act of God that he did not serve any longer. but the fourth was strongly against it, because it is a limitation to the estate, that it shall not continue longer than he serves (*a*)

If a person, having an interest for three years only, make a lease for five years, it would be good for the three years for where an authority is given to any one to execute any act, and he executes it contrary to the effect of his authority, this is utterly void, but if he executes his authority and withal goes beyond the limits of his warrant, this is void for that part only wherein he exceeds his authority (*b*).

If a lease be made for life or years to *A* and afterwards the lessor makes a lease for years to *B* regularly, this concurrent lease to *B*. is a good lease at least for so many years of the second lease as shall be to come after the first lease is determined according to the agreement. as if the first lease to *A* be for twenty years, and the second lease to *B* be for thirty years, and both begin at one time, in this case the second lease is good for the last ten years (*c*

If the lord of a manor may by the custom grant copyhold estates "to three persons *habendum* to them successively, as they shall be named and not otherwise," a surrender to *A*. for his own life, and for the lives of *B* and *C* is warranted by the custom (*d*.

Although, as hath been said, a lease for years must have a certain beginning, and a certain end, yet the continuance thereof may be uncertain, for the same may cease and revive again in divers cases. As if tenant in tail make a lease for years reserving 20*s* and after take a wife and die without issue, now as to him in the reversion the lease is merely void. but if he endow the wife of tenant in tail of the land (as she may be though the estate tail be determined now is the lease as to tenant in dower who is in of the estate of her husband revived again as against her, for as to her the estate tail continues, for she shall be attendant for the third part of the rent-services, and yet they were extinct by act in law (*e* So it is, if tenant in tail make a lease for years as before, and die without issue, his wife ensient with a son, and he in the reversion enter, against whom the lease is void, but after the son be born the lease is good, if it be made according to the statute, and otherwise is voidable So, if tenant in fee-simple take a wife, and then make a lease for years, and die, and the wife is endowed, in this case she shall avoid the lease, but after her decease the lease shall be in force again (*f*)

So, a rent charge for life is suspended by the acceptance of a lease of the land, and by the surrender of such lease, revives again (*g*).

Termination of a Lease for Years.—With respect to the termination of

(*a*) Cro Eliz 643. (*b*) Bull N P 176 Comp. Cop. 93. (*c*) Shep Touch 275
(*d*) 6 Mod 73 (*e*) Co. Litt. 46 (*f*) 32 H 8 c 28 Shep Touch 27[illegible]
(*g*) Cro Car. 121.

a lease, a demise may be determined by either of these circumstances occurring, namely, by the period expiring during which the premises were leased, which may take place upon the contingency, if there be any, happening, by surrender to the lessor; by cancellation of the deed [*de quo quære?*]; by condition within the deed or indorsed thereon; or by forfeiture for the breach of some contract express or implied

1. *Termination by Efflux on of Time.*—The common means whereby a lease determines, is by the period expiring for which the lands, *&c.* were demised; or upon the contingency happening that was to create, as it were, such period, as where a lease is made during the minority of *J S.* when *J S.* comes to his full age the lease terminates; or if he die before, it is ended

Where a lease is expired, the tenant still continues liable, unless he deliver up complete possession of the premises, or the landlord accept of another in his room (*a*)

The circumstance of the landlord signing a notice, by which a tenant, whose lease is expired, orders his under-tenant to pay his rent to him in future, is not evidence of his agreement to accept him as his tenant, unless it be proved that he knew the contents of the notice (*b*)

2. *Termination by Merger.*—Another means, whereby a lease for years may be defeated, is by way of merger, that is, when there is an union of the freehold or fee and term of years in one person at the same time; in which case the greater estate merges or drowns the lesser because they are inconsistent and incompatible (*c*)

Thus, if a lease for years be made to commence after the death of *A* and the grantee of the inheritance afterward makes a lease for years to *B.* and then the lessee of the future interest assigns to the grantee of the inheritance, the future interest is drowned in the inheritance (*d*)

So, where a fee-farm rent is purchased in, by the person that is seised in fee of the lands out of which it issues, it is merged in the inheritance (*e*).

Lord *Coke* lays it down for a general rule, that one cannot have a term for years in his own right and a freehold *in auter droit*, but that his own term shall drown in the freehold, and puts these cases If a man, lessee for years, intermarries with the feme lessor, this shall merge and drown his own term for years, but if a feme lessee for years intermarries with the lessor, her term is not thereby drowned, because, says he, one may have a term of years *in auter droit*, and a freehold in his own right, as the husband in this case shall have. So if lessee for years make the lessor his executor, the term is not thereby drowned, because the lessor hath the term *in auter droit*.—So also, if the master

(*a*) [illegible] R [illegible] (*c*) [illegible] Bac Ab. [illegible]
(*b*) [illegible] 619 (*d*) 10 [illegible]

of an hospital, being a sole corporation, by the consent of his brethren makes a lease for years of the possession of the hospital, and afterwards the lessee for years is made master, the term is drowned *causa qua supra*, but if it had been a corporation aggregate, the making of the lessee master had not extinguished the term, no more than if the lessee had been made one of the brethren yet if a lessee for years of the glebe be made parson, the term is merged by reason of the union of the term and freehold in him to his own right and use, though he has them in several capacities (a).

But this rule seems to admit of divers exceptions: for if a husband be possessed of a term in his own right, and the inheritance descend to his wife, the term will not merge by his descent in *auter droit*, for it was by act and operation of law (b). So if a lease had been made upon trust, for the advancement of such a woman, and the lessee had after intermarried with that woman, and then the inheritance had descended to her, this, it was agreed, would not merge the term, but he might clearly dispose thereof to the purpose intended, because he had it *in auter droit* and to another use —So, it seems to be agreed, that if a man being possessed of a term for years in right of his wife purchases the inheritance, that by this the term for years, though in right of his wife, is merged and extinct, because the purchase was the express act of the husband, and therefore amounts in law to a disposition of the term, by reason of the merger consequent thereupon But a bare intermarriage of the feme termor with the reversioner will not work a merger of the term, because by the intermarriage the term is cast upon the husband by act of law, without any concurrence or immediate act done by him to obtain the same; and therefore, in such case, the law will preserve the term in the same plight as it gave it to the husband, till he by some express act destroys it, or gives it away (c).

Where however the husband himself is lessee for life, and intermarries with the lessor, this merges his own term, because he thereby draws to himself the immediate reversion, in nature of a purchase by his own voluntary act, and so undermines his own term, whereas, in the other case, the term existing in the feme till the intermarriage, is not thereby so drawn out of her or annexed to the freehold as to merge therein, because that attraction which is only by act of law consequent upon the marriage, would, by merging the term, do wrong to a feme-covert, and to take the term out of her, though the husband did no express act to that purpose, which the law will not allow But in such case, if the feme should survive, and have dower of these lands, this seems a merger of her term for a third part at least, because now she hath the term and freehold both in her own right, and then the access of of the freehold must *pro tanto* merge and drown the term (d).

(a) Bac Abr [illegible] Co I [illegible] (b) Cro Jac [illegible]
(c) Bac. Abr [illegible] [illegible]

But if a feme executrix takes husband, and the husband after purchases the reversion, and dies, yet the feme surviving shall not have the term to any other purpose but as assets to pay debts; for as to any right of her own therein, the term is extinct by such purchase of the husband, because that was his own express voluntary act, and therefore amounts to a disposition of the term by the merger wrought thereupon (a).

One lets lands to *A.* for life, and twenty years over, and after lets the same lands to *B.* for forty years, to commence after the death of *A.* and the end of the said twenty years; then *B.* intermarries with *A.* and *A.* dies, and *B.* the husband hath the term for twenty years, yet his term of forty years is not surrendered by it, because that was not begun, but was a future [illegible], to begin wholly after the first lease ended; so there was no union at all of the terms (b).

Land was given to the husband and wife, and to the heirs of the husband; the husband makes a lease for years, and dies, and the wife enters and intermarries with the lessee: it was holden that this term was not extinct, because the entry of the wife put a total interruption to the interest of the lessee, and avoided the term entirely as to herself, because she was in of the freehold by survivorship paramount the lease, and then the lease cannot take place again till after her death against the heirs of her husband, and whether she will outlive the term or not is uncertain; so that during her life, the lessee had no interest, but only a bare possibility, which cannot be touched or hurt, by the intermarriage, but continues just as it was before (c).

As more particular notice of cases touching this matter would tend little, if at all, to elucidate the subject of this work, we shall merely mention, that a court of law cannot merge estates unless it finds them in the same person, and required (subject to some exceptions) in the same right. But courts of equity look into the beneficial interests and views of parties, and do not regard whether the estates are strictly in the same person, or in different persons. Hence it is a general rule with these courts, that where the owner of an estate becomes entitled to a charge upon it secured by a term of years, such term shall sink for the benefit of the heir. Thus, though the owner were a lunatic, the term shall merge, for as between his mere absolute real and personal representatives, no equity can exist.—But exceptions to this rule are admitted in several instances.

3. *Termination by Surrender.*—A third mode by which a lease may be made to determine, is by surrender, which properly is a yielding up of an estate for life or years to him that hath the immediate estate in reversion or remainder, wherein the estate for life or years may drown by mutual agreement (d); and it differs from a release in this respect, that

(a) [illegible] Abr. [illegible]
(b) [illegible]
(c) Bac. Abr. tit. Leases (S 3)
(d) Co. Litt. 33[illegible].

the release operates by the greater estate descending upon the less; whereas a surrender is the falling of a less estate into a greater (*a*)

A surrender is made by these words, "hath surrendered, granted, and yielded up" The surrenderor must be in possession, and the surrenderee must have a higher estate, in which the estate surrendered may merge: therefore tenant for life cannot surrender to him in remainder for years. In a surrender there is no occasion for livery of seisin; for there is a privity of estate between the surrenderor and the surrenderee, the particular estate of the one and the remainder of the other being one and the same estate, livery therefore having been once made at the creation of it, there is no necessity for having it afterwards (*b*).

If an estate be surrendered, the whole estate is determined without other ceremony, and as to the parties themselves, it will be determined to all intents (*c*)

By the statute of frauds and perjuries (29 *Car.* 2 *c* 3) it is provided, that no leases, estates, or interests, either of freehold or term of years, shall be surrendered, unless it be by deed or note in writing, signed by the party so surrendering or their agents thereunto lawfully authorized by writing, or by act and operation of law. *s.* 3.

It was held, that a lease for years cannot be surrendered by cancelling the indenture without writing, because the intent of the statute was to take away the manner they formerly had of transferring interests in lands, by signs, symbols, and words only; and therefore, as a livery and seisin on a parol feoffment was a sign of passing the freehold, before the statute, but is now taken away by the statute, so the cancelling a lease was a sign of a surrender before the statute, but is now taken away, unless there be a writing under the hand of the party —It has also been held, that the statute does not make a deed absolutely necessary to a surrender, for it directs it to be made either by deed or note in writing, which note in writing, though not a deed, must, it is conceived, be stamped, according to stat 23 *G* 3 *c* 58. *s.* 1 which imposes a duty on "any conveyance, surrender of grants or offices, release," &c and the surrender of a lease is the surrender of a grant, and is, as it were, a re-demise (*d*)

As to what estate a surrender may operate upon, it was once doubted whether years could merge in years, but it seems to be now settled, that if a term in reversion be greater than a term in possession, the greater would merge the lesser, as ten years may be surrendered and merge in twelve or fourteen years (*e*)

Even though the reversion were for a less number of years, yet the surrender would be good, and the first term drowned, as if one were the lessee for twenty years, and the reversion expectant thereupon were

(*a*) Co Lit 337 n 1 (*b*) 2 Bl Com 326 Co Lit 337
(*c*) Com Dig tit. Surrender (L 1) Co Lit 338 *b*. (*d*) [illegible] to Co. Lit 338.
(*e*) Bac. Abr. tit. "Leases" (S 2) Cro. Eliz 302

granted to one for a year, who granted it over to the lessee for twenty years, this would work a surrender of the twenty years' term, as if he had taken a new lease for a year of his lessor, for the reversionary interest coming to the possession drowns it, and the number of years is not material, for as he may surrender to him who hath the reversion in fee, so he may to him who hath the reversion for any lesser term (*a*).

It was held therefore, that where lessee for twenty years makes a lease for ten years, and the lessee for ten years surrenders to his lessor, viz. to the lessee for twenty years, that this is good, and the lessor shall have so many of the years as were then to come of his former term of twenty years, that is, as it seems, so many years as were to come of his reversion shall be now changed into possession (*b*).

Whether a lease for years in possession may be surrendered so as to be merged in a lease in remainder, be the term in remainder greater or lesser than the term in possession, seems to be no where settled, an estate for life however cannot, it is conceived, be surrendered to or merge in a reversion if it be only for years, but this is held otherwise elsewhere (*c*).

Surrenders in law, or implied surrenders, are excepted in the statute of frauds, and remain as they did at common law, if the lease, which is to draw out such surrender, be in writing pursuant to that statute (*d*).

As to the surrender in law of leases in possession, this is wrought by acceptance of a new lease from the reversioner, either to begin presently, or at any distance of time during the continuance of the first lease, the reason why such acceptance of a new lease amounts to a surrender, and determination of the first is, because otherwise the lessee would not have the full advantage that he had contracted for by acceptance of the second lease, if the first should stand in the way and consume any of those years comprised in the second lease, for which reason and to enable the lessor to perfect and make good his second contract, the lessee must be supposed to waive and relinquish all benefit of the first (*e*).

If therefore lessee for life, or years, take a new lease of him in reversion, of the same thing in particular contained in the former lease for life or years, this is a surrender in law of the first lease. For this purpose, it is not necessary that the surrenderor be in possession, for if a lease be to commence at *Mich.* next, and the lessee take a new lease before *Mich.* this is a surrender in law of the first lease (*f*).

So, if lessee for years accept a new lease from the guardian in socage (*g*).

(*a*) Cro. Eliz. 302. 2 Ld. Raym. 402. (*b*) Ibid. Pop. [illegible] (*c*) [illegible]
(*d*) Shep. [illegible] 301 & Com. [illegible] Surrender (I. 2), Pow. (?) [illegible] 29. C. 2. c. [illegible]
(*e*) [illegible] Cro. [illegible] 522 [illegible] (*f*) Shep. [illegible] 301
(*g*) [illegible] Surrender [illegible]

So, if lessee for twenty years takes a lease for ten years, to begin at *Michaelmas*, there is no doubt but that the term of twenty years is surrendered or determined presently, for by the lessee's acceptance he allows the lessor able to let the land during the other lease, and indeed by such acceptance the lessor hath power to make a new lease during the former, and at the time of the lease making (*a*).

If there be two lessees for life, or years, and one of them take a new lease for years, this is a surrender of his moiety, whereby it appears that a surrender in law may be made of some estates which cannot be surrendered by a surrender by deed, for *potior est dispositio legis quam hominis* (*b*)

But the reversion of the surrenderee must be an immediate reversion (*c*)

If therefore *A* lets to *B* for ten years, who lets to *C* for five years, *C.* cannot surrender to *A.* by reason of the intermediate interest of *B* but in such a case *B.* may surrender to *A* and after so many years *C.* likewise, because then his lease for five years is become immediate to the reversion of *A* (*d*).

Where the lessee for years of a house accepts a grant of the custody of the same house, it is a surrender, and has been so adjudged, for the custody of the same thing which was let before, is another interest in the same thing leased, and cannot stand with the first lease (*e*).

If the first lease be of the land itself, and the second lease is of the vesture of the same land, this is held to be a surrender of the first lease.

So, if the lessee accepts a grant of common, or rent out of the same land, to commence at a certain day within the term (*f*)

So, if the grantee of an office accepts a new grant of the same office, it will be a surrender (*g*)

Lessee for years to begin presently cannot, till entry or waiver of the possession by the lessor, merge or drown the same by any express surrender, because till entry there is no reversion wherein the possession may drown. but if the lessee had entered, and assigned his estate to another, such assignee before entry might have surrendered his estate to the lessor, because by the entry of the lessee the possession was severed and divided from the reversion, which possession, being by assignment transferred to the assignee, may without other entry be surrendered, and drown in the reversion (*c*).

If there be two joint-tenants, and one of them have the particular estate, and the other the fee-simple, as where an estate is limited to two and the heirs of one of them, and he that hath the estate for life aliens his part to a stranger, in this case the alienee may surrender to

(*a*) Cro. Eliz. 522 (*b*) Shep Touch. 302 (*c*) Plowd. 541
(*d*) Bac. Abr. [illegible] (*e*) Cro. Jac. 177 (*f*) Com. Dig. tit. Surrender (I 2)
(*g*) Ibid. (*c*) Bac. [illegible] "Leases" ([illegible])

the other joint-tenant,—so, if there be three joint-tenants for life, and the fee-simple is limited to the heirs of one of them, and one of the joint-tenants for life releases to the other, and he to whom this release is made surrenders to him that hath the fee-simple, this is a good surrender of a third part.—But otherwise one joint-tenant cannot surrender to another joint-tenant although he who makes the surrender be tenant for life, and he to whom it is made be tenant in fee-simple (*a*).

One executor may surrender an estate or lease for years, which the executors have in the right of their testator (*b*).

But if one enter into land, and make a lease for the trial of the title only, and afterwards the lessor (he and the lessee being both out of possession) make another lease of the same thing to the lessee, it seems this is no surrender of the first lease; but if the lessor enter before he make the lease, *contra* (*c*).

If the husband have a lease or estate for years in the right of his wife, he alone, or he and his wife together, may surrender it; but if the husband have an estate for life in the right of his wife, being tenant in dower or otherwise, and he alone, or he and she together, surrender it, this surrender is good only during the life of the husband, except it be made by fine (*d*).

Lessee for twenty-one years took a lease of the same lands for forty years, to begin immediately after the death of *J. S.* it was held, that this was not any present surrender of the first term, because *J. S* might wholly outlive that term, and then there would be no union to work a surrender, and it being *in equilibrio* in the mean time, whether he will survive it or not, the first term shall not be hurt till that contingency happens, for if *J. S.* die within the first term, then what remains of it is surrendered and gone by the taking place of the second (*e*).

Although the statute of frauds directs that the deed or notice in writing shall be signed by the surrenderor, yet where an agreement was entered into between the lessor and lessee, at the instance of the former, for the surrender of a lease, an assignment actually prepared, the key delivered up and accepted, and a long acquiescence on the part of the lessor, without any claim or demand upon the lessee, it was decreed in equity that the lessee should be discharged of the rent from the time he had delivered up the key (*f*).

But (*g*) if in a lease determinable on three lives, it is covenanted that on the death of one, the lessee may if he please surrender, and that the lessor shall thereupon and upon payment of a fine, grant a new lease for three lives in the terms of the old lease, and in a new lease there is a covenant to surrender the same absolutely, as a life drops equity

(*a*) Shep. Touch. 302. (*b*) Ibid. (*c*) Ibid.
(*d*) Shep. Touch. [illegible] (*e*) Bac. Abr. tit. "Leases" (S 5.)
(*f*) Bac. on Leases, 211. (*g*) 9 Mod. 56.

will assist the lessee to retain possession as if the prior lease had continuance (*a*).

If lessee re-demise his whole term to his lessor, it is a surrender in law, and as fully as if it had been actually surrendered: and this notwithstanding a reservation of rent be made (*b*).

So, where a lease came into the hands of the original lessor, by an agreement entered into between him and the assignee of the original lessee, "that the lessor should have the premises as mentioned in the lease, and should pay a particular sum over and above the rent annually, towards the goodwill already paid by such assignee," it was adjudged that such agreement operated as a surrender of the whole term (*c*).

But if a lessee reserved to himself any interest in or part of the estate, it is no surrender. For if lessee for years makes a lease to his lessor for all but a day, this is clearly no surrender of his lease, because the day disjoins the union, and prevents the merger which would have followed if the lease had been for the whole term; for then the lessor would have had the whole estate entire in him, as he had before he made the lease, and consequently the lease would be merged and drowned in the reversion (*d*).

So, if he lease to his lessor for the lessor's life, for he has a possibility to have it again (*e*).

An agreement between the lessor and a stranger that the lessee shall have a new lease, is no surrender (*f*).

If lessee accepts a new lease in trust for another, it is no surrender (*g*).

So, if he accepts a grant of a thing consistent with the lease of the land, it is no surrender; as if the lessee of a manor accepts the grant of a bailiwick, or the stewardship of the same manor, for it is collateral; so if he accepts the office of parkkeeper of the same park for his life, that is no surrender, for the same reason (*h*).

But where lessee for years of an advowson was presented to the advowson by the lessor, it was adjudged to be a surrender of his term (*i*).

So, if a copyholder in fee take a lease for years of the same land, it is an extinguishment of his copyhold *in perpetuum*; but if he take a lease for years of the manor, that is but a suspension of his copyhold during the term (*k*).

It is said, that if a man hath lands in *A.* and other lands in *B.* and lets those in *A.* for twenty-one years, and the next day lets all his lands in *B.* for ten years, it is not any surrender of the lands in *A.* but shall be

(*a*) 4 Bro. R. 419. (*b*) 2 Mod. 175. (*c*) 1 T. 441.
(*d*) Com. Dig. tit. "Surrender" (H) (I. 2.) Bac. Abr. tit. "Leases" (S. 3.)
(*e*) Com. Dig. *ut ante*. (*f*) Cro. Eliz. 173. (*g*) Com. Dig. *ut ante*.
(*h*) Cro. Jac. 176. (*i*) Ibid. 84. (*k*) Ibid.

construed as a lease of all the other lands, which may well stand with the former lease (*a*).

So if a lessee take a grant of a rent-charge out of the same land for life, or if a lessee for life take a grant of a rent-charge for years, that is not any surrender, because he might have the benefit of that rent after the estate in the land is determined: but if a lessee for life take a grant of a rent-charge for life out of the same land, that is a surrender, for otherwise the rent-charge cannot take any effect.

So it is said, if the lessor grants a rent, common, *&c.* out of the land to his lessee, without saying at what time it shall commence, it is no surrender, but it shall be intended after his term (*b*). [But *quære* this? for if the delivery of the deed constitute the commencement, as it does in all cases where no date occurs or period is fixed, it seems it would be a surrender.]

So, if the king grant an office by patent, or make a demise for years, the acceptance of a new patent in the one case, or of a new lease in the other, is no surrender of the first grant (*c*).

A fine levied by a tenant for life to a reversioner in fee, to the use of the conusée and his heirs, upon condition broken to the use of the conusor for life, and one year over, is not a surrender (*d*).

No surrender, express or implied, in order to or in consideration of a new lease, will bind, if the new lease is absolutely void; for the cause, ground, and condition of the surrender, fails; it is not indeed reasonable in itself, nor can it be the intent of the parties, that an acceptance of a bad lease, should be an implied surrender of a good one. Indeed a void contract for a thing that a man cannot enjoy, cannot in common sense and reason imply an agreement to give up a former contract (*e*).

The mere cancelling in fact of a lease is not a surrender of the term thereby granted within the statute of Frauds, which requires such surrender to be by deed or note in writing, or by act or operation in law; nor is a recital in a second lease that it was granted in part consideration of the surrender of a prior lease of the same premises a surrender by deed or note in writing of such prior lease. Where tenant for life with a special power for leasing, reserving the best rent in consideration (as recited) of the surrender of a prior term of ninety-nine years (of which above fifty were unexpired) and certain charges to be incurred by the tenant for repairs and improvements, *&c.* granted to him a new lease of the premises for ninety-nine years, by virtue of the power reserved to her or any other power vested in or in any wise belonging to her, which new lease was void by the power for want of reserving the best rent. Held that the second lease being void under the power should not operate in law as a surrender of the prior term as passing an

(*a*) Cro. Jac. [illegible] (*b*) Com. Dig. *ut ante.* (*c*) Cro. Car. 197.
(*d*) [illegible] (*e*) [illegible] Bur. 18[illegible] [illegible] 1980.

interest out of the life estate of the grantor, contrary to the manifest intent of the parties, and consequently that the prior term, though the indenture of lease were in fact cancelled and delivered up when the new lease were granted, might be set up by the tenant of the premises in bar to an ejectment by the remainder man after the death of tenant for life (*a*).

So if a surrender is intended for a particular purpose, and that purpose (the only motive of it) fails, the surrender ought to fail too (*b*).

If therefore the new lease does not pass an interest according to the contract and intention of the parties, an acceptance of it is not an implied surrender of the old lease (*c*).

A lessee may surrender upon condition, and if the condition be broken, the particular estate shall be revested (*d*).

If lessee agrees to quit upon condition, and the condition be not performed, it does not amount to a surrender of his interest. as where a person being in possession of premises as tenant from year to year, under an agreement for a lease of fourteen years, and the rent being in arrear, executed a deed, which stated that he had agreed to quit the premises, and that a valuation was to be made of his effects, which were in the mean time to be assigned to a trustee for the landlord. The deed accordingly assigned the effects upon trust to have the valuation made, and out of the amount to retain the arrears of rent, and pay the residue to the tenant. The tenant, however, did not in fact quit possession, nor was any valuation made, and it was held that the agreement to quit being conditional, and the condition not having been performed, nor the agreement in any manner acted upon, it did not operate as a surrender of the tenant's legal term from year to year, and consequently that the landlord's right to distrain for the arrears of rent continued after six months from the making of the deed (*e*).

If lessee for years surrender his whole term to the original lessor upon condition, he may upon non-performance of the condition re-enter and revive the term (*f*).

Lessee for life made a lease for years, rendering rent, and after surrendered to the lessor upon condition, then the lessee for years takes a new lease for years of the lessor, and after the lessee for years performed the condition, and evicted the lessee for years who re-entered, and the lessee for life brought debt for the first rent reserved, and it was ruled, that it was not maintainable, for the lease out of which it was reserved is determined and gone, for though the surrender of the tenant for life, which made the lessee for years immediate tenant to the first lessor, and so enabled him to make such surrender, was conditional, yet the ce-

(*a*) 6 East 661. (*b*) 3 Burr. 1807. 4 Burr. 1980.
(*c*) Com. Dig. tit. "Estates," (G 13.) (*d*) Co. Litt. 218 b.
(*e*) 12 East 134. (*f*) 2 Mod. 176.

feasance of the estate for life by performance of the condition cannot defeat the estate of the lessee for years, which was absolute and well made, and then the rent reserved thereon is gone likewise (*a*).

If lessee for years of lands accepts a new lease by indenture of part of the same lands, this is a surrender for that part only, and not for the whole, because there is no inconsistency between the two leases for any more than that part only which is so doubly leased, and though a contract for years cannot be so divided or severed, as to be avoided for part of the years, and to subsist for the residue, either by act of the party or act in law, yet the land itself may be divided or severed, and he may surrender one or two acres, either expressly or by act of law, and the lease for the residue will stand good and untouched (*b*).

As to surrenders of leases *in futuro* or future interests, a lessee for years of a term to begin at a day to come cannot surrender it by an actual surrender before the day of the term begin. But he may by a surrender in law (*c*).

To make a good surrender in deed of lands, these things are requisite. 1. That the surrenderor be a person able to make, and the surrenderee a person capable and able to take and receive a surrender, and that they both have such estates as are capable of a surrender, and for this purpose, that the surrenderor have an estate in possession of the thing surrendered at the time of the surrender made, and not a bare right thereunto only. 2. That the surrender be to him that hath the next immediate estate in remainder or reversion, and that there be no intervening estate. 3. That there be a privity of estate between the surrenderor and surrenderee. 4. That the surrenderee have a higher and greater estate in the thing surrendered than the surrenderor hath, so that the estate of the surrenderor may be drowned therein. 5. That he have the estate in his own right, and not in the right of his wife, &c. 6. That he be sole-seised of this estate in remainder or reversion, and not in joint-tenancy (*d*).

Such persons, therefore, as are disabled to grant, are disabled to surrender (*e*), and such persons as are disabled to take by a grant, are disabled to take by a surrender; so such persons as may be grantees may be surrenderees, therefore a surrender to an infant is good, provided it be a surrender in law, by the acceptance of a new lease, and that such new lease increase his term or decrease his rent, a surrender by an infant-lessee by deed is absolutely void (*f*).

In respect to pleading a surrender, if a surrender be by acceptance of a new lease, it is not good to say, that the lessee being possessed of a former lease, the lessor demised to him, but that the lessee surren-

(*a*) Bac. Abr. tit. "Leases" (S. 3) (*b*) Bac. Abr. tit. "Leases" (D. 3)
(*c*) Shep. Touch. 304. Cro. Eliz. 522. 605. (*d*) Shep. Touch. 303.
(*e*) Ibid. (*f*) Cro. Car. 504.

dered and then the lessor demised, or that the lessor entered and demised (*a*).

So, regularly he ought to plead that he surrendered the estate and land, but if the party plead a surrender of a lease, it is sufficient to say, "the demise aforesaid."

So, regularly he ought to shew, that the lessor assented to the surrender, where the other party pleads or brings an action in disaffirmance of it, but it is not of necessity, and the omission will be aided after verdict (*b*) and when it is pleaded that the lessor agreed to the surrender, it shall be intended that he entered, and it is not usual to plead a re-entry upon a surrender, no more than when a feoffment is pleaded, to plead livery and seisin thereof, because it is admitted (*c*).

A surrender has in certain circumstances been presumed, where evidence of the fact was not to be had: indeed, the Court will not require positive proof of a surrender in any case where there is sufficient presumption of it (*d*).

But there must be presumption of the surrender from some facts or circumstances, for length of time alone is nothing, and though the Court in one case did lay it down that after a recovery of forty years standing, they would without any other circumstances, presume a conditional surrender to have been made by the tenant for life, yet there were other circumstances in the case to induce a supposition of a surrender having been made. So where possession had not gone with the recovery, the Court would not presume a surrender by the tenant for life.—Entry in an attorney's book was admitted in evidence on the subject (*e*).

A surrender of a lease was presumed in order to let in the statute of limitations (*f*).

Of the Renewal of Leases.—Concerning the renewal of leases, some nice points occur in the books, touching the construction of covenants for that purpose.

A. and *B.* covenant in a lease for sixty-one years, that at any time within one year after the expiration of twenty years of the said term of sixty-one years, upon the request of the lessee and his paying 6*l.* to the lessors, they would execute another lease of the premises unto the lessee for the further term of twenty years, to commence from and after the expiration of the said term of sixty-one years, &c. and so, in like manner, at the end and expiration of every twenty years, during the said term of sixty-one years, for the like consideration and upon the like request, would execute another lease for the further term of twenty years, &c. to commence at and from the expiration of the term then last before granted, &c. Under this covenant, the lessee cannot claim a further term at the end of the first and second twenty years in the

(*a*) Com. Dig. tit. Surrender, (*O*.) (*b*) Ib. (*c*) Cro. Car. 501.
(*d*) 2 Bur. 1072. (*e*) Ib. 1077. (*f*) 1 Bur. 126.

lease, for this is an agreement on the part of the lessors to grant a further lease on a precedent condition to be performed by the lessee, which in the principal case he had not done (a).

Under a devise of seven different estates, to a sister, brothers, and nephews respectively, one to each stock including as to six of the estates three several lives in succession, on each estate, and as to the seventh, which, in the first instance, was only limited to two persons for life in succession, giving those two a power to add another life or lives to make three, in like manner as after mentioned for other persons to do the same, and then giving this general power, that when and so often as the lives on either of the estates before given shall be by death reduced to two, that then it shall be in the power of the person, or persons, then enjoying the said estate or estates to renew the same with the person, or persons, to whom the revenue thereof shall belong, by adding a third life in such estate and paying such reversioner two years' purchase for such renewal, and also to exchange either of the said two lives on payment of one year's purchase Held that this power of renewal only authorized the addition of one life to the three on each estate, and of making one exchange of a life (b).

Where a lessor covenants that if a lessee surrender at any time during the term, he will grant him a new lease, and then accepts a fine of the premises, this is a breach of the condition, and in an action of debt on bond for the performance of covenants, the lessee need not shew that he offered to surrender (c)

If a lease for ninety-nine years, determinable on three lives be conveyed in trust for *A* for life, and *A* covenant to use his utmost endeavours as often as any of the persons on whose lives the premises are held shall die, to renew the same by purchasing of the lord of the fee a new life in the room of such [illegible] shall fail, it is no breach of the covenant if [illegible] of the lives failing he procure [illegible] upon his own life (d)

A lease was for [illegible] years [illegible], with covenant to tenants to renew [illegible] twenty-one years to twenty-one years, to make up ninety-nine years [illegible] expiration of the first term, an arrear of rent being due and no application being made for a renewal, the lessor brought an ejectment and obtained judgment [illegible] possession, on a bill filed in Chancery for a renewal on payment of the rent in arrear and interest, it was decreed, the delay being accounted for, and there being no neglect on the part of the lessee or prejudice to the lessor (e) But where it was covenanted that the lessor would renew whenever any life or lives dropped, provided that if the lessee, his executors or administrators, upon [illegible] the death of any of the life or lives, shall refuse or neglect to renew [illegible] application thereon, &c. or tender such

(a) 1 T. R. 225 [illegible] Lev. 249 (d) [illegible] Cro. Eliz. 450 479
(b) [illegible] 4 T. R. [illegible]

new lease, and pay or tender a certain fine, [illegible] the [illegible], &c. to be void: by such neglect the lessee forfeits his right of renewal, and may, it seems, be ejected for not applying when the first life dropped (*t*).

An agreement was in writing between landlord and tenant, signed by the landlord [illegible] conv[illegible] comp[illegible]tion of the rep[illegible] convenient [illegible], but blanks were left [illegible] the day of [illegible] the repairs being completed, the landlord [illegible] a lease to commence from [illegible], and on refusal [illegible] a bill in Chancery for [illegible] new lease was [illegible], and so was it [illegible] [illegible].

The lessee of [illegible] S[illegible] ment to [illegible] to the provision [illegible] 32 *H.* 8. c. 28. [illegible], the old lease must be [illegible] next after making the new lease [illegible] the surrender of the former lease [illegible] prebendary [illegible], the surrender should be void, [illegible] was not absolutely gone, but the lessee [illegible]. But the court held [illegible] the statute, [illegible] should not be [illegible] outstanding [illegible]. Here the new lease was made within [illegible] became an absolute surrender both in deed and in law [illegible] of the lessee, without further act to be done by him. In [illegible] there is the word *ended* as well as [illegible] the first lease is not [illegible] in the first lessee to keep [illegible] was ended [illegible] (*x*).

Where a lessor covenanted [illegible] the request of the lessee within the term, but [illegible] however did request [illegible] ought to have been made by [illegible] might be [illegible] losing his rent. But [illegible] The executors of every [illegible] naming, and the [illegible] the lessee might be [illegible] improvement of the premises, for [illegible] the testator or his executors requested [illegible] not be personal. As to the [illegible] vent, and such as the defendant would not care to trust, to this it may be answered, that a clause of re-entry is in the lease, and the value of the premises being doubled by the improvements of the original lessee, such clause will secure the landlord against any insolvency of the tenant. The usual term being for twenty-one years, let the defendant demise the premises to the plaintiff for twenty-one years, or for any lesser term, as the plaintiff shall elect; and though the lease is to be made on the same covenants, yet that shall not take in a covenant for the renewing this lease, forasmuch as the lease would never be at an end (*a*). [Lord *Hardwicke* said this case did not apply as an authority on the subject, being rather like an award and a compromise, than a decree (*b*). But see [illegible] *post*, 3 Ves. Jun. 298.]

Whether the Lord Chancellor's apprehension in the above case, of the perpetuity of the lease, had he permitted to be inserted "covenants for the remaining lease," be well or ill founded seems rather doubtful.

Indeed, where (*c*) *A.* demised to *B.* for the life of the said *B.* and also for the lives of *C.* and *D.* and covenanted that if *B.* his heirs, &c. should be minded at the decease of the said *B. C.* and *D.* or any of them, to surrender the said demise and take a new lease, and thereby add a new life to the then two in being in lieu of the life so dying, that then he the said *A.* his heirs, &c. upon payment of every life so to be added in lieu of the life of every of them so dying would grant a new lease for the lives of the two persons named in the former lease and of such other person, as the said *B.* his heirs, &c. should appoint in lieu of the person named in the preceding lease, as the same should respectively die, "under the same rents and covenants." There had been successive renewals from the time of a former lease granted by the ancestor of *A.* and in each a like covenant of renewal. Lord *Mansfield*.—The question in all these cases is "Whether under the same rents and covenants" shall be construed *inclusive* or *exclusive* of the clause of renewal. Arguments drawn from every part of the agreement are material: here the parties themselves have put the construction upon it, for there have been frequent renewals, and in all of them the covenant of renewal has been uniformly repeated. How then shall the Court say the contrary?—*Willes*, J. The act of the parties seems to differ in this case from all the cases cited; here there have been four or five renewals and in the same terms. I [illegible] not think otherwise than that *Furnival* and *Crew* (*d*) would be a sufficient authority alone to determine this case, because there, the additional words "and so to continue renewing from time to time" were inserted. But the case of *Bridges* v. *Hitchcock* is very much the same as this; for there the words were "under the same rents and covenants," and no other words. I cannot say that in this country this kind of

(*a*) 2 P. W. [illegible]
(*b*) Co[illegible] 819. 2 Eq. P. [illegible]
(*c*) 3 Atk. [illegible] Mo[illegible]
(*d*) 3 Atk. 83.

4

lease should be much favoured, though the inducement for granting them in *Ireland* may be a good one. *Ashurst*, J. I think this is a very hard case on the part of the lessor, and there does not seem any mutuality, as in the case of improvement of lands. But as there have been four successive renewals, the lessor himself has put his own construction upon the covenant: and therefore is bound by it. *Buller*, J. I think the case of *Bridges* v. *Hitchcock* (a) decides this. In that case, both the House of Lords and the Exchequer determined, that the words "under the same rents and covenants" in the *new lease*, contained a *perpetual covenant* to renew.

But the judgment of the Master of the Rolls (Lord *Alvanley*) in *Baynham* v. *Guy's Hospital* (b), (in which case a right of renewal was held to be forfeited by the laches of the tenant) seems to demolish a doctrine which goes to establish a perpetuity, which the law abhors. Master of the Rolls.—I strongly protest against the argument used by the learned judges in *Cooke* v. *Booth*, *Cowp.* 819, as to construing a legal instrument by the equivocal acts of the parties and their understanding upon it; which I will never allow to affect my mind. That case was sent to law by Lord *Bathurst*. The learned judges thought fit to return an answer to the Chancellor, that the legal effect was a perpetual renewal, upon the ground, that by voluntary acts, which the parties might or might not have done, the parties themselves had put a construction upon it. Mr. J. *Willes* stated, that as his only ground, Lord *Mansfield* made it his chief ground; but that ground was disapproved by Lord *Thurlow*; and is, I think, totally unfounded. I never will construe a covenant so. I never was more amazed, and Mr. J. *Wilson*, who argued it with me, was astonished at it. When it came back, Lord *Bathurst* not having retained the great seal long enough for it to come again before him, it came to Lord *Thurlow*, who said that, sitting as Chancellor, when he asked the opinion of a court of law, whatever his own opinion might be, he was bound by that of the court of law: therefore he decreed a renewal, but said he should be very glad if Mr. *Booth* would carry it to a superior tribunal. We had a consultation, and I wrote to Mr. *B.* upon it; but he, being only tenant for life, refused to appeal. There stands the case of *Cooke* v. *Booth*. I see I have put a note upon that case referring to *Tritton* v. *Foote* (c), (in which case it was holden that a covenant of renewal under the same covenants is exclusive of the covenant to renew, all) which is a positive determination against the claim. I collect, therefore, from these cases, this, that the courts in *England* at least, lean against construing a covenant to be for a perpetual renewal, unless it is perfectly clear that the covenant does mean it. *Furnival* v. *Crewe*, relied on in *Cooke* v. *Booth*, had clear words for a perpetual renewal, which made it impossible to construe it otherwise.

(a) 1 Br. P. C. 522. (b) 3 Ves. jun. 298. (c) 2 Br. P. 636.

One in consideration of 5*l.* 8*s.* in nature of a fine and of a yearly rent of 6*s.* 9*d.* demised certain grounds with the buildings, &c. for twenty-one years with a proviso for distress, if the rent were in arrear for fourteen days, and the lessor covenanted at the end of eighteen years of the term or before on request of the lessee to grant a new lease of the premises for the like fine for the like term of twenty-one years at the like yearly rents with all covenants, grants, and articles as in that indenture contained, held that this covenant was satisfied by the tender of a new lease for twenty-one years containing all the former covenants except the covenant for future renewal, and held that an averment that the covenant for renewal in the indenture declared on corresponded with various other leases before then successively made by the owners of the inheritance for the time being could not be taken in aid to construe the meaning of the indenture, for supposing such evidence admissible in any case where the renewals had been uniformly the same, yet *non constat* from this averment that all the former leases contained the same covenants for renewal (*a*).

Where a lease contained a covenant for perpetual renewal, a specific performance was refused under circumstances, as laches and alterations in the property, so that it could not be enjoyed according to the stipulations (*b*).

Tenant-right of renewal.—It has long been an established practice to consider those who are in the possession of lands under leases for lives or years, particularly from the crown, colleges, &c. as having an interest beyond the subsisting term, and this interest is usually denominated "the tenant right of renewal," which tenant though not [illegible] certain or even contingent estate, there being no means of compelling a renewal, yet it is so adverted to in all transactions relative to leasehold property, that it influences the price in sales, and is often an inducement to accept of it in mortgages and settlements ([illegible]).

For other cases on this subject we refer to the cases cited below ([illegible]), cautioning the reader at the same time against an implicit reliance, [illegible] on the authority [illegible] points applicable to [illegible], [illegible] the [illegible] case, which turned (as has been observed) on a [illegible]

By the statute 4 G. 2. c. 28. which recites that whereas many persons hold considerable estates by leases for lives or years, and lease out the same in parcels to several under-tenants, and whereas many of those leases cannot by law be renewed without a surrender of all the under-leases derived out of the same, so that it is in the power of any such under-tenant to prevent or delay the renewing of the principal lease, by refusing to surrender their under-leases, notwithstanding they have covenanted so to do, to the great prejudice of their immediate landlords, the principal lessees, for preventing such inconveniences, after reciting the

[illegible]

renewal of leases more easy for the future, it is enacted, that in case any lease shall be duly surrendered in order to be renewed, and a new lease made and executed by the chief landlord or landlords, the same new lease shall, without a surrender of all or any the under-leases, be as good and valid to all intents and purposes as if all the under-leases derived thereout had been likewise surrendered at or before the taking of such new lease; and every person, &c. in whom any estate for life or lives, or for years, shall be vested by virtue of such new lease, and his, &c. executors and administrators shall be intitled to the rents, covenants, and duties, and have like remedy for the recovery thereof, and the under-lessees shall hold and enjoy the messuages, lands, and tenements, in the respective under-leases comprised, as if the original leases, out of which the respective under-leases are derived, had been still kept on foot and continued, and the chief landlord and landlords shall have the same remedy by distress or entry in and upon the messuages, &c. for the rents, &c. reserved by such new lease, so far as the same exceed not the rents reserved in the lease out of which the under-lease was derived, as they would have had in case such former lease had been still continued, or the under-lease had been renewed under such new principal lease. s. 6.

(T) *The Determination of a Lease by cancelling the Deed.* — Another means whereby a lease may be, or rather might have been, determined, is by cancelling the deed by which it is granted.

Whatever doubts may have been formerly entertained as to the effect of cancelling or otherwise destroying a lease of lands, &c. now, since the statute of frauds and perjuries, 29 Car. 2. c. 3. which makes all leases for above three years to have only the force and effect of leases at will, unless they be in writing, and signed by the parties, &c. the deed or writing, whereby such lease is made, seems to be of the same essence as the lease itself, and therefore the cancelling or destruction of that seems to destroy and avoid the lease itself, because it destroys all evidence allowed for the support thereof: though in such case Chancery frequently sets up the lease again, or compels the party to execute a new one for the residue of the term, which is not against the prohibition of the act, because there was once a good and effectual lease made pursuant to the statute (a).

Though that statute excepts leases not exceeding the term of three years, yet even these are not absolutely excepted, for it goes on, not exceeding the term of three years from the making thereof, whereupon the rent reserved to the landlord during such term shall amount unto two-third parts at least of the full improved value of the thing demised; and that no leases, estates, or interests, either of freehold or terms for years, or any uncertain interest, not being copyhold or customary interest of, in, to, or out of any messuages, manors, lands, &c. shall be assigned, granted, or surrendered, unless it be by deed or note in

(a) B[illegible]

writing signed by the party so assigning, granting, or surrendering the same, or their agents thereunto lawfully authorized by writing, or by act and operation of law.

Since the above statute, therefore, it should seem that a deed cannot be determined by cancellation of the indenture, for that the surrender by deed or note in writing was especially prescribed in lieu thereof.

The mere cancelling, in fact, of a lease, is not a surrender of the term thereby granted, within the stat. of Frauds, which requires such surrender to be by deed or note in writing or by act or operation in law (*a*).

5 *Termination by condition indorsed.*—A lease may also be determined by force of a condition indorsed upon the back side thereof, if it be before the ensealing and delivery, as well as by force of a condition within the deed (*b*).

A proviso in a lease for twenty-one years, that if either of the parties shall be desirous of determining it in seven or fourteen years, it shall be lawful for either of them, his executors or administrators, so to do, upon twelve months' notice to the other of them, his heirs, executors or administrators, extends, by reasonable intendment, to the devisee of the lessor, who was entitled to the rent and reversion (*c*).

It is now clearly held, that to avoid the consequences of bankruptcy, a landlord may take a clause that the lease shall determine on the bankruptcy of the tenant; and many prudent men take such a clause (*d*).

6 *Termination by forfeiture of the Lease.*—The sixth and last mode by which a demise may be determined is by forfeiture of his lease.

Any act of the lessee, by which he disaffirms or impugns the title of his lessor, occasions a forfeiture of his lease; for to every lease the law tacitly annexes a condition, that if the lessee do any thing that may affect the interest of his lessor, the lease shall be void, and the lessee may re-enter; besides, every such act necessarily determines the relation of landlord and tenant; since to claim under another, and at the same time to controvert his title; to affect to hold under a lease, and at the same time to destroy that interest out of which the lease arises, would be the most palpable inconsistency (*e*).

A lessee may thus incur a forfeiture either by act *in pais*, or by matter of record. By matter of record, where he sues out a writ or resorts to a remedy which claims or supposes a right to the freehold; or where, in an action by his lessor, grounded upon the lease, he resists the demand under the grant of a higher interest in the land, or where he acknowledges the fee to be in a stranger: for having thus solemnly protested against the right of his lessor, he is estopped by the record from claiming an interest under him. By act *in pais*: as where he aliens the estate in fee, which however, (except the king be in remainder or

(*a*) 6 T. R. 661. (*b*) Cro. Jac. 456. (*c*) 12 East 464.
(*d*) 15 Ves. jun. 268. (*e*) Bac. on Leases 119.

reversion, in which case a feoffment in fee will effect it,) must be by feoffment with livery, for that only operates upon the possession, and affects a disunion, it cannot be by grant, or any conveyance operating only on the grantor's interest, and passing only what he may lawfully part with, nor consequently, can it be of things lying in grant a lease by the tenant for more years than he has in the land is still more venial; because it is only a contract between him and his under-lessee (or rather assignee) which cannot possibly prejudice the interest of the original lessor, and does not even pretend to usurp or touch the freehold or inheritance (*a*).

A forfeiture by tenant for years in levying a fine, not having been taken advantage of by the entry of the then reversioner to avoid the lease, cannot be taken advantage of after the reversion has been conveyed away, so as to recover the estate in ejectment from the tenant, upon the several demises of the grantor and grantee of such reversion (*b*)

A forfeiture is also incurred by the breach of express or conventionary conditions for the lessor, having the *jus disponendi*, may annex whatever conditions he pleases to his grant, provided they be not illegal, unreasonable, or repugnant to the grant itself, and upon the breach of these conditions may avoid the lease (*c*).

Therefore, though it has been held that a lessee might make a feoffment, and that notwithstanding the presence of the lessor, for that the lessee has the possession and may dispose of it, yet it was an extinguishment of the lease, and the lessor might enter for the forfeiture (*d*)

The law however will always lean against forfeitures, as courts of equity relieve against them and as courts adhere strictly to the precise words of the condition in order to prevent a forfeiture, so, where a forfeiture has manifestly been committed, they will not allow the lessor to take advantage of it, if they find that he has afterwards done any act that amounts to a waiver of it, as by acceptance of rent due after the forfeiture incurred, or action brought to recover the same (*e*)

Forfeitures of leases stand on the same ground with forfeitures of copyholds, and there are a great many cases in the old books, where it is held, that a mere knowledge and acquiescence in an act constituting a forfeiture, does not amount to a waiver, but there must be some act affirming the tenancy (*f*)

The forfeiture must be known to the lessor at the time, in order to render his acceptance of rent or any other act a waiver (*g*); for it has been established in many cases, that acceptance of rent shall not operate as a waiver of the forfeiture, or as a confirmation of the tenancy,

(*a*) Bac. on Leases 119 (*b*) 12 Mod. 444 (*c*) 2 T. R. 13? Co. Litt. 2?5
(*d*) Co. Litt. 222 (*e*) Bull. N. P. 96 Bac. on Leases 226 3 T. R. 17? 2 Comp. 247.
(*f*) 3 T. R. 8? (*g*) Co. Cop. [illegible]

unless the landlord had notice that a forfeiture was incurred at the time (a).

So, when it is said that a forfeiture may be waived, it must be understood to apply to those cases in which, by the terms of the contract, the estate, upon the tenant's doing or [illegible] the act which he has stipulated either to refrain from or to perform, is determinable, and not where it absolutely determines, for, it is to be observed, that where the estate of lessee is *ipso facto* void by the condition or limitation, no acceptance of rent after can make it to have a continuance, otherwise it is of an estate only voidable by entry (b).

A tenant for life, having power to grant building leases for sixty-one years, reserving the best improved ground rent, granted a lease for that term, which was not expressed to be a building lease but which contained a covenant by the lessee to [illegible] the premises demised (old houses) "or such other houses as [illegible] during the term." Held that this was not [illegible] (c). Such a lease being granted by tenant for life, who had [illegible] power whereout the legal interest, is void, and [illegible] capable of being confirmed by the remainder-man accepting rent (d).

Indeed it is understood law, that though an acceptance of rent may make a voidable lease good, it cannot make valid a lease which was actually void at first (e).

If *A* tenant for life subject to forfeiture, [illegible] *B* [illegible] to *C* for a term, and afterwards, apprehending that it has forfeited, acquiesce in *D*'s claim to and receipt of the rent from *C*, his executor may, on showing that he acquiesced under a false apprehension, recover from *C* the amount of the rent erroneously paid to *D*; for in order to constitute a confirmation of the payment, some act must appear to have been done by *A* with knowledge of his own situation. "Suppose," said Mr. J. *Buller*, "that one disseises another of an estate, and continues in possession of the rents and profits with the knowledge of the disseissee, will any body say that the disseisee shall not recover against the tenant (f)."

A lessee under a lease which contained a proviso against exercising certain trades, underlet the premises to one, who partitioned off the shop into two apartments, in one of which he carried on the business of a fishmonger, and the other he underlet to a butcher. The landlord lived next door, and was privy to the conversion of the premises to those uses; but though the [illegible] rent to the lessee, no payment of rent was proved to have been made to the landlord subsequently to the alteration. After a lapse of six years the landlord brought an ejectment, and it was held, that his long forbearance was not a waiver of the for-

(a) [illegible] (c) [illegible] 169.
(b) [illegible] (d) [illegible] 176. (f) 1 Bos. & Pul. 326.

tenance, but that some positive act of waiver, as receipt of rent, is necessary; but it was said, that if the landlord had lain by and seen money laid out in improvements, that would have been a circumstance from which a jury might imply consent to the alteration (a).

Under a proviso of re-entry upon under-letting, an advertisement inserted by the tenant in a public paper, stating that a lease of the premises would be granted, does not amount to a forfeiture (b).

Of Leases in reversion.—With respect to leases in reversion, it is to be observed that "all leases where there is a precedent estate out, are leases in reversion" (c).

Thus if one lets a manor for thirty years, and the next day lets it to another for forty years to commence from *Lady-day* next after the date, this passes a reversionary interest; for the lease being for years is a chattel which may well expect or wait; and if I have a rent in fee I may grant it for years to commence at *Michaelmas*, for an estate doth not pass, but an interest.

So, a husband may make a lease of lands held in joint-tenancy with his wife, to commence after his death, and it will be good though the wife survive; for the husband having an interest to dispose of in his life, he might dispose of all the term, and it should bind the wife; so where he hath disposed by an act executed in his life of the interest of the term, which hath created a term in interest, this is as good as if he had granted all the term (d).

As to the manner of making such leases for years where there is a prior lease or estate then in being, they cannot be made by parol lease; for besides that by the statute of Frauds, 29 Car. 2, c. 3 (e), no parol lease for above three years is to have any other effect than only as a lease at will, a deed is of the very essence of the grant of a reversion, or reversionary interest, and without it no reversion or reversionary interest can pass out of the lessor. Such leases therefore must be made by either deed-poll, or indenture (f).

If one makes a lease for life, and afterwards grants that the lands or reversion shall remain to another for twenty-one years after the death of the tenant for life, these words are sufficient to pass a reversionary interest by way of future lease, though there is not the word "demise," or any other word usual or proper to describe a lease for years by; for here, being a deed is sufficient to prove a present contract for the reversionary interest of these lands, after the estate for life determined, these in case of leases for years, which is but a contract, are in themselves sufficient without respect to any other form (g).

A lease in reversion of several parcels of land, made to commence on the happening of several contingencies, shall (as has been ob-

(a) [illegible] (b) [illegible] (c) Doug. [illegible]
(d) [illegible] (e) [illegible] (f) Bac. Abr. [illegible] "Lease" (N).
(g) [illegible]

[illegible]ven) take effect and commence respectively as those contingencies happen (*a*).

If one had made a lease for life, or for eighty years, if the lessee should so long live, and after by indenture let the same lands to another for years to begin presently, and then the first lease determined by death, surrender, or forfeiture, the second lessee should have the lands in possession presently for the residue of the years, because such second lease, by reason of the estoppel, took effect between the parties presently, and therefore shall come in possession whenever the first lease is out of the way. But if such second lease had been only by deed-poll, there must have been an attornment to have made it good as a grant of the reversion, as there must likewise in the other case, where it was made by indenture; and without such attornment the second lease could only have taken effect in possession upon the determination of the first lease by the death of the lessee according to the express limitation; and not upon any sooner or other determination by surrender, forfeiture, or otherwise (*b*).

The nature of a lease in reversion we have more particularly explained in Ch. III. Sect. VII.

Of Attornment.—Touching the subject of attornment, (which now exists scarcely in any case) it may be as well to observe, that after the statute *quia emptores terrarum* (*c*) was passed, by which subinfeudation was prohibited, it became necessary that when the reversioner or remainder-man after an estate for years, for life, or in tail, granted his reversion or remainder, the particular tenant should attorn, or consent to pay his rent, &c. to the grantee. This necessity of attornment was in some degree diminished by the statute of uses (*d*), as by that statute the possession was immediately executed to the use, and by the statute of wills, by which the legal estate is immediately vested in the devisee: attornments however are now rendered almost unnecessary in any case, by the statute of *Anne*, which enacts that all grants and conveyances of manors, lands, rents, reversions, &c. by fine or otherwise, shall be good without the attornment of the tenant; but notice must be given of the grant to the tenant, before which he shall not be prejudiced by payment of any rent to the grantor, or of breach of the condition for non-payment (*e*). Also, by an act (*f*) in the last reign, attornments of lessees, &c. made by tenants to strangers claiming title to the estate of their landlords shall be null and void, and their landlord's possession not affected thereby: the statute, however, does not extend to vacate any attornment made pursuant to a judgment at law, or with the consent of the landlord, or to a mortgagee on a forfeited mortgage.

(*a*) [illegible] 199 (*b*) [illegible] (N) (*c*) 18 E. 1 St. 1.
(*d*) [illegible] (*e*) 4 Ann. c. 16. [illegible] (*f*) 11 G. 2. c. 19. [illegible]
[illegible]

Of Estoppel.—*Leases for years sometimes enure by way of estoppel*, which word signifies an impediment or bar to a man's invalidating his own solemn act.

Therefore, if one makes a lease for years, by indenture, of lands wherein he hath nothing at the time of such lease made, and afterwards purchases those very lands, this shall make his lease as good and unavoidable as if he had been in the actual possession and seisin thereof at the time of such lease made; because he having by indenture expressly demised those lands, is by his own act estopped and concluded to say that he did not demise them, and if he cannot aver that he did not demise them, then there is nothing to impeach the validity of the indenture, which expressly affirms that he did demise them, and consequently the lessee may take advantage thereof, whenever the lessor comes to such an estate in those lands as is capable to sustain and support that lease, *for an estoppel that affects the interest of the land shall run with it into whose hands soever the land comes* (a)

But if it appear, by recitals in the lease, that he had nothing at the time of the demise, and afterwards he purchases the lands as aforesaid, that will not enure by estoppel (*b*).

This estoppel by indenture is so mutual and reciprocal, that if a man takes a lease for years by indenture of his own lands, whereof he himself is in actual seisin and possession, this estops him during the term to say that the lessor has nothing in the lands at the time of the lease made but that he himself or such other person was then in actual seisin and possession thereof, for by acceptance thereof by indenture, he is for the time as perfect a lessee for years, as if the lessor had at the time of making thereof the absolute fee and inheritance in him. But if such lessee of his own lands, being ejected by the lessor, should bring an ejectment, and the lessor should plead not guilty, and give the lease and some matter of forfeiture thereof in evidence to support his plea, without pleading, and relying on the estoppel, and the jury should find the special matter, viz. that the defendant had nothing in the lands at the time of such lease made, but that the plaintiff himself was then in actual seisin and possession thereof, whether the Court, upon this verdict, are bound to adjudge according to the truth of the case, namely, that such lease by one who had then nothing in the lands was void; or if they are to adjudge according to the law, working by way of estoppel upon such lease by indenture, seems to be a doubt upon the books, but Lord *Coke* lays it down for a rule, that the jury do well to find the truth, viz. that the lessor had then nothing in the land, but then upon such finding, the Court is to adjudge, according to the operation of law upon the estoppel wrought to both parties by

(a) Bac. Abr. tit. "Leases," (O) 6 Mod. 258. 2 Ld Raym. 1048. s. c. 1 Salk. [illegible] s. c. 3 L. R. 371.

(b) 1 Ld Raym. 729.

the indenture, that they are bound; and this seems to be the better opinion (*a*).

Thus, if one brings debt for rent upon an indenture, if the defendant plead *nil debet*, he cannot give in evidence that the plaintiff had nothing in the tenements, because if he had pleaded this specially, the plaintiff might have replied the indenture, and estopped him, or might demur, for the declaration being on the indenture, the estoppel appears on record. But if defendant plead *nil habuit*, &c. and the plaintiff will not rely on the estoppel, but reply *habuit*, the jury shall find the truth (*b*).

But if such lease for years were made by deed-poll of lands, wherein the lessor had nothing, this would not estop the lessee to aver that the lessor had nothing in those lands at the time of the lease made, because the deed poll is only the deed of the lessor, and made in the first or third person; whereas the indenture is the deed of both parties, and both are, as it were, put in and shut up by the indenture. This however is where both parties seal and execute the indenture, as they may and ought; for otherwise, if the lessor only seals and executes it, the lessee seems to be no more concluded than if the lease were by deed-poll; for it is only the sealing and delivery of the indenture as his deed that binds the lessee, and not his being barely named therein, for so he is in the deed-poll; but that being only sealed and delivered by the lessor, can only bind him, and not the lessee, who is not to seal and execute it: yet it should seem that such lease by deed-poll binds the lessor himself as much as if it were by indenture, because it is executed on his part with the very same solemnity, and therefore it should seem he is bound by such lease by way of estoppel (*c*).

Estoppels ought to be mutual, otherwise neither party is bound by them; therefore, if a man take a lease for years of his own lands from an infant or feme-covert by indenture, this works no estoppel on either part, because the infant or feme, by reason of their inability to contract, are not estopped; therefore neither shall the lessee be estopped (*d*).

So, if a man take a lease for years of his *own* lands by patent from the king, rendering rent, this shall not estop the lessee, as an indenture between common persons in such case would do, because the king cannot be estopped; and if he be not estopped, neither shall the lessee (*e*).

If one lets lands to me by deed enrolled, unknown to me, and brings debt upon the lease, I may say *non lessa pas*, it seems; but he who made such lease is concluded to say the contrary, which is in point to establish, that in case of a deed poll (as this which is called a deed enrolled

(*a*) Bro. [illegible] (*b*) Bull. N. P. 170. Salk. 277 cited 2 Ld Raym. 1154, 1550. (*c*) Bac. [illegible] (O). (*d*) 1 Co. Lit. 352. (*e*) Bro. [illegible]

must be intended to be) the lessor himself is estopped, though the lessee be at large; and this cannot be intended an indenture, because then the lessee would have been estopped likewise, if he had sealed it, which in this case it appears he did not, because it was unknown to him, and therefore was not estopped, whether it were by indenture or deed-poll.

These estoppels continue no longer on either part than during the lease; for as they began at first by making the lease, so by determination of the lease, they are then end likewise; for then both parts of the indenture belong to the lessor [illegible]).

When an interest actually passes by the lease, there shall be no estoppel, though the interest purported to be granted be really greater than the lessor at that time had power to grant. As if *A* lessee for the life of *B* makes a lease for years by indenture, and after purchases the reversion in fee, and then *B* dieth, *A* shall avoid his own lease, though several of the years expressed in it be still to come; for he may confess and avoid the lease which took effect in point of interest, and determined by the death of *B* ([illegible]).

If a man takes a lease for years of the herbage of his own land by indenture, this is no conclusion to say that the lessor had nothing in the lands at the time of the lease made, because it was not made of the lands themselves (*c*).

If *A.* seised of ten acres, and *B.* of other ten acres, join in a lease for years by indenture, they are several leases according to their several estates, and no estoppel is wrought by the indenture to either party, because each has an estate whereout such lease for years or interest may be derived; and the reason why estoppels are at any time allowed is, because otherwise, when the party had nothing in the lands, the indenture must be absolutely void, which would be hard to say, when the party hath under his hand and seal done all in his power to make it good; and since it can be good no otherwise, it shall be good by estoppel, rather than be absolutely void; but when an interest passes from each lessor, the indenture works upon such interests to carry that, and therefore leaves no room for its operating by way of estoppel; but yet, since both equally joined in the lease, without distinguishing the several interests they had therein, the indenture works by way of confirmation, with respect to each from whom the whole interest did not pass, that is *A.*'s confirmation for *B.*'s part, and *B.*'s confirmation for *A.*'s part (*d*).

So, if two tenants in common of lands join in a lease for years by indenture of their several lands, this shall be the lease of each for their respective parts, and the cross confirmation of each for the part of the other, and no estoppel on either part, because an actual interest pass

(*b*) Co. Litt. 47. Co. [illegible] (*c*) Co. Litt. 47. [illegible]
(*d*) Ibid. 45 a. Br. Abr. [illegible]

from each respectively, and excludes the necessity of an estoppel, which is never admitted, if by any construction it can be avoided, as being one of those things which the law looks upon as odious, because it clokes and disguises the truth (*a*).

But if two joint-tenants for life or in fee, join in a lease for years by indenture, reserving the rent to one of them only, this shall give him the rent exclusive of the other: and here the estoppel turns not upon the interest passed by the lease, for that is several according to their several rights as in the other cases, which excludes any estoppel, but it turns upon the reservation of the rent, which being made in this manner, to one exclusive of the other by indenture, works an estoppel against all the parties to say the contrary, and though the rent issues out of one part as well as the other, yet it not being part of the thing demised, but moving, as it were, rather by way of grant from the lessee after the lease made, the lessors are considered as accepting it in this manner by indenture, which concludes them as well as it doth the lessee (*b*).

But if the lease had been by parol or deed-poll, reserving rent to the one joint-tenant only, this would not have excluded the other joint-tenant from an equal share therein, because this reservation coming, as it were, by way of grant from the lessee, and being only by parol or deed-poll, could not conclude the lessors, who, with respect to the rent, were as it were, grantees, and only passive, and the rent shall follow the reversion in proportion to their several estates, and so let in both parties to an equal participation thereof (*c*).

If two coparceners join in a lease for years, by indenture, of their several parts, this is said in one book to be but as one lease: because they have not several freeholds therein, but only one, as both making but one heir, and therefore shall join in an assize, but where in ejectment the plaintiff declared of a lease by two coparceners *quod dimiserunt*, exception being taken to it, the exception was allowed, because the lease was several as to each coparcener for their own respective moiety: and this seems to be the better law, because though they have but one freehold with regard to their ancestor, and therefore if disseised, shall join in an assize, yet as to their disposing power thereof they have several rights and interests, so that neither of them can lease or give away the whole (*d*).

But where the declaration in ejectment was of the joint-demise of *A* and *B* and on evidence it appeared that they were tenants in common, the plaintiff failed (*e*).

A lease for years may operate as to part by estoppel, and as to the residue by passing an interest (*f*).

(*a*) Co. Litt. 45. a. Bac. Abr. tit. "Leases" (O).
(*b*) Ibid. Co. Litt. 47. a. Gilb. on Rents, 63. (*c*) Ibid.
(*d*) Bac. Abr. tit. "Leases" (O). (*e*) Co. Litt. 45. a. (*f*) Salk. 275.

Debt on bond conditioned for the performance by *R. G.* of all the covenants on his part mentioned in a certain indenture, bearing even date with the bond, made or expressed to be made between the plaintiff and the said *R. G.* Plea, that before the execution of the bond it was agreed that the plaintiff should grant to *R. G.* a lease under certain covenants, and that the defendant should enter into a bond as surety for the performance of those covenants; that the defendant did accordingly enter into the bond on which the action was brought, and that the indenture mentioned in the condition thereof is the lease so agreed upon and no other, but that the said lease never was executed. On demurrer, it was held that the defendant was estopped by the condition of the bond from pleading this plea. Lord *Eldon*, C. J. observed, that the condition of the bond was for the performance of covenants comprised in a certain indenture "made or expressed to be made" between the trustees and the defendant; and that the object of introducing those words seemed to have been, that whether the execution of the indenture could be proved or not, the covenants contained in the paper writing which purported to be an indenture between the trustees and the defendant should be considered as the covenants of the defendant (*a*).

As to estoppels, though the reason why they are allowed seems to be, that no man ought to allege any thing but the truth for his defence, and what he has alleged once is to be presumed true, and therefore he ought not to contradict it, for *allegans contraria non est audiendus* (*b*), yet, estoppels in general are not to be favoured; they are to be extended only as far as positive rules have gone, because the tendency of them is to prevent the investigation of the truth of the case (*c*).

Of future Interests being barred.—Respecting future interests, as to their being barred or destroyed, it has already appeared, that all leases for years at common law when they come *in esse*, are to be executed by the entry of the lessee; but as to future interests, it has been clearly held, that if one make a lease to commence two years after, when the two years shall have expired, the lessee before any entry may grant his term, although the lessor continues in possession, because such lessee's *interesse termini*, was not divested or turned to a right, but continued in him in the same manner as it was at first granted, and in the same manner he transfers it over to another, who by his entry may reduce it into possession whenever he thinks fit (*d*).

One made a lease for years, to begin after the end of a former lease for years then in being; the first lease determined, and before entry of the second lessee, he in reversion entered and made a feoffment in fee, and levied a fine with proclamations, and five years passed without entry or claim of the second lessee, and if his term were barred? was the question

(*a*) 2 Bos. & Pul. 29[illegible].
(*b*) 4 T. R. 254; 8 Mod. 313.
(*c*) Co. Litt. 352. a.
(*d*) Bac. Abr. tit. "Leases" (P); Co. Litt. 57.

It was adjudged, that by this fine and non-claim his term was barred, because after the first lease expired, the second lease was actually then come *in esse*, and reducible into possession by an entry presently, and then his not entering, which was his own fault and laches, could not stop the operation of the fine from running against him (*a*)

But if such fine had been levied during the continuance of the first lease, it was agreed, that in such case the operation thereof should not begin to run out against the second lessee till the first lease were determined, because till then the second lease was only in *interesse termini*, which the second lessee could not reduce into possession by any entry till the first lease determined, and therefore was not obliged to take notice of the acts of strangers, or of the ter-tenant in possession, for if such future interest might be divested before it came *in esse*, the lessee or grantee thereof, having never entered, would have no means to revest it, and therefore till it comes *in esse*, the law takes care to secure it to the lessee or grantee in the same manner as it was at first granted, but when the first lease is at an end, then the second lessee is to take care of it himself, and if he suffer five years to elapse after that time without entry or claim, this will bar such interest, because his right then commences in possession, and from thenceforth the operation of the fine begins to run against him. The case in *Noy* 123 has been denied by *Treby* [illegible] to be law (*b*).

As the lessee must enter when his lease comes into possession, so, if he enters before, it will be a disseisin, and no continuance of possession, though after the term actually begins, will purge the disseisin, or alter the estate of the lessee (*c*)

Yet debt lies for the rent in respect of the privity of contract upon the lease made (*d*)

Where one declared of a lease 16 *April* [illegible] from the annunciation last past for ten years, "by virtue of which he entered and held the tenements aforesaid from the said annunciation" this was held good, and that the lessee was no disseisor, for it shall be intended that he entered and occupied before by agreement, and a diversity was taken between this case, where the commencement of the lease is limited from a time past, and that where it is limited to begin at a time to come, in which case the entry of the lessee before that period is a disseisin (*e*).

Of Terms in trust.—As to terms or leases for years in trust, the relation of landlord and tenant is little, if at all, elucidated by a consideration of them, but as they have occasionally been mentioned in the course of the work, it may not perhaps be superfluous shortly to notice them

These terms are either vested in trustees for the use of particular persons, or for particular purposes, or else upon trust to attend the inheritance. In the first case they are called *terms in gross*, and the per-

(e) [illegible] 3 Mod. 198 [illegible]

sons entitled to the beneficial interest, have a right in equity to call on the trustees, or persons who have the legal interest in the term, for the rents and profits of the lands, and also for an absolute assignment of the term (*a*).

It has been held, that if a man be *cestuique trust* of a term, it is not assets within the statute of frauds (*b*).

It has been held by the court, that a fine levied in pursuance of a trust cannot destroy any lease made by *cestuique trust*, but though a fine by *cestuique trust* does not destroy or extinguish the trust, yet it is not safe to do it, by reason of the danger of not being able to prove an agreement to the contrary.

Upon trial of an issue out of Chancery, it was upon evidence agreed, that if one made a lease for an hundred years in trust for himself and his wife, and afterwards they both join in levying a fine to a purchaser for a valuable consideration who had no notice of this lease in trust, though the fine does not convey the term itself to the conuzee, the estate in law being in the trustee, yet this destroys the trust, so that the lease shall not hurt the purchaser.

Terms attendant on the inheritance owe their existence to the following circumstances. When terms for years became fully established, and the interest of the term was secured against the effect of fictitious recoveries, long terms became common: in all cases of this kind, though the purposes for which the term was raised were fully satisfied, yet it did not determine, so that the legal interest continued in the trustee; but as the owner of the inheritance was entitled to all the benefit and advantage of it, the term became, in fact, consolidated with the inheritance, and is usually called a term attendant on the inheritance (*c*).

Of Leases by way of Mortgage.—Tenant for years may also be created by way of mortgage, the nature of which is explained in *Chap.* III. *Sect.* XIV. We shall therefore merely again observe, that

As to mortgages, by way of creating terms, this was formerly by way of demise and re-demise, as for example, *A* borrowed money of *B* whereupon *A* would demise the land to *B*. for a term of 500 &c. years absolutely, with common covenants, against incumbrances and for further assurance, and then *B* would the day after re-demise to *A* for 499 years, with condition to be void on non-payment of the money at the day to come. This manner of mortgaging came in after the 21 *H.* 8. c. 15 for falsifying recoveries, when a fixed interest was settled in terms for years: it was esteemed best for the mortgagor, because it avoided all manner of pretention from the incumbrances and dower of the feoffee in mortgage, and it was reputed best for mortgagee, inasmuch as it avoided the wardship and feudal duties of the tenure, and was

(*a*) Cruise Dig. Tit. XII c. 3. (*b*) [illegible] 2 V[illegible] (*c*) Cruise Dig. Tit. XII c. [illegible]

only inconvenient in this—that if the second deed were lost, there appeared to be an absolute term in the mortgagee (*a*).

The common method of mortgaging however, is by a demise of the land for a term, under a condition to be void on payment of the mortgage-money and interest, and a covenant is inserted at the end of the deed, that till default shall be made in the payment of the money borrowed, the mortgagor shall receive the rents and profits, without account (*b*).

A mortgage in the form of a lease was granted of a feme covert's estate, by the husband and wife. After the husband's death, the deed being in the hands of the mortgagee, the widow had directed the tenants in possession to attorn to the mortgagee, had settled with him for the balance of the rents, styling him mortgagee, and had not questioned his possession for many years. In delivering the judgment of the Court, Lord *Mansfield* said, that they were all of opinion that the conveyance in this case, though in the form of a lease, was in substance a mortgage, and not being within the reason for which leases by a feme-covert are held to be only voidable, was absolutely void on the death of the husband: but that the acts done by the widow, the deed being in possession of the mortgagee, were tantamount to a re-delivery, which, without a re-execution, is equivalent to a new grant (*c*).

Where the lease is not a beneficial lease, it is for the interest of the mortgagee to continue the tenant, and where it is, the tenant may put himself in the place of the mortgagor, and either redeem himself or get a friend to do it (*d*).

Upon a refusal of the money by the mortgagor, a tender being made at the place and at some time of the day specified in the condition, the condition is saved for ever, and the land is discharged, because upon the tender the demise is void (*e*).

But if one mortgage his reversion in fee to the lessee for years, whereby his term is surrendered, and afterwards pays the money pursuant to the condition, yet his term shall be extinguished and not revived (*f*).

(*a*) [illegible]
(*b*) [illegible]
(*c*) [illegible]
(*d*) [illegible]

CHAPTER VII.

For what Term Leases may be made.

SECTION I. *Of Tenants from Year to Year, wherein of Notice to quit.*

THAT which was formerly considered as a tenancy at will has been since properly construed to enure as a tenancy from year to year (*a*), which, therefore, may now be said to be when a man lets lands or tenements to another, without limiting any certain or determinate estate, especially if an annual rent be reserved (*b*).

A general parol demise, therefore, at an annual rent, where the bulk of the farm is enclosed and a small part of it in the open common fields, is only a lease from year to year, and not for such time as the round of husbandry continues (*c*). But where the crop, as of liquorice, madder, &c. does not come to perfection in less than two years, it might be otherwise (*d*).

Averment in a declaration that plaintiff was possessed of premises for the remainder of a certain term of years then unexpired therein, which he agreed to assign to the defendant, is supported by evidence of a tenancy from year to year (*e*).

The distinction taken between a tenant from year to year and a tenant for a term of years, is rather a distinction in words, than in substance. A tenant from year to year is entitled to estovers, and the same advantages as a tenant for a term of years; in truth, he is a tenant from year to year as long as both parties please; and considering how many large estates are held by this tenure, it would be dangerous to say that the term ceased at the end of the year (*f*).

It would be extremely unjust, that a tenant who occupies land, should, after he has sown it, be turned out of possession without reasonable

(*a*) 8 T. R. [illegible] T. R. 16.
(*b*) 2 Bl. R. 1171.
(*c*) 1 Campb. 317.
(*d*) Com. Dig. tit. "Estates" (H. 1.)
(*e*) Ibid.
(*f*) 6 T. R. 297.

notice to quit; and it was in order to avoid so unjust a measure, that so long ago as in the time of the Year-Books it was held that a general occupation was an occupation from year to year, and that the tenant could not be turned out of possession without reasonable notice to quit, and that rule has always prevailed since (*a*). The doctrine, in truth, respecting notice to quit was laid down as early as the reign of *Henry* VIII (*b*)

Touching the distinction between six months' and half a year's notice, the case in the Year-Books requires half a year's notice, for the moment the year began the tenant had a right to hold to the end of that year (*c*) The six months' notice, therefore, means half a year, and not merely the space of six months at any time of the year; for such half year's notice must expire at the end of the year, or it will not be a good notice (*d*)

Premises are let from year to year upon an agreement that either party may determine the tenancy by a quarter's notice, this notice must expire at that period of the year when the tenancy commenced (*e*)

Where a tenant by lease continues to hold after the expiration of it, as [illegible], and assigns to another, the tenancy of the assignee shall be held to commence at the day on which it commenced under the lease, and a notice to quit on that day only is good, notwithstanding the assignee came in on a different day

In tenancies from year to year, there must be six months' notice on either side to quit, according to the ancient law, except where any special agreement, or the custom of particular places, intervenes (*f*).

Where rent is reserved quarterly, it does not dispense with the regular six months' notice to quit required by law; but is merely a collateral matter (*g*)

So, though a lease be void by the statute of frauds as to the duration of the term, the tenant holds under the terms of the lease in other respects, and therefore the landlord can only put an end to the tenancy at the expiration of the year (*h*)

If there be a lease for a year, and by consent of both parties the tenant continue in possession afterwards, the law implies a tacit renovation of the contract; for where a tenant holds over after the expiration of his term, without having entered into any new contract, he holds upon the former terms they are therefore supposed to have renewed the old agreement, which was to hold for a year. But then it is necessary, for the sake of convenience, that if either party should be inclined to change his mind, he should give the other half a year's notice before the expiration of the next or any following year (*i*).

(*a*) [illegible] T R 85 (*b*) 1 T R 163 13 H 8 15 b (*c*) Ibid
(*d*) [illegible] 3 Wils 25 1 H Bl 97 1 T R 163 1 Esp R 266
(*e*) 2 [illegible] 678. (*f*) 2 Bl R. 1225 3 T R [illegible]
(*g*) 1 Esp. R. 266. (*h*) 5 T. R. 471. (*i*) 1 T R. 162.

So, where tenant for life grants a lease for years which is void against the remainder-man, and the latter, before he elects to avoid it, receives rent from the tenant, whereby a tenancy from year to year is created, yet this is with reference to the old term, and therefore a half year's notice to quit from the remainder-man ending with the old year, is good (*a*)

So, where tenant for life makes a lease for years, to commence on a certain day, and dies before the expiration of the lease, in the middle of the year, the remainder-man receives rent from the lessee, (who continues in possession, but not under a fresh lease) for two years together on the days of payment mentioned in the lease. this was held to be evidence from which an agreement will be presumed to subsist between the remainder man and the lessee, that the lessee should continue to hold from the day, and according to the terms of the lease, so that notice to quit ending on that day is proper (*b*)

Tenant in tail having received an ancient rent of 1*l* 16*s* 6*d* from the lessee in the possession under a void lease granted by tenant for life under a power, the rack rent value of which was 30*l* a year, cannot maintain an ejectment laying his demise, at least, on a prior day without giving the lessee some notice to quit, so as to make him a trespasser after such recognition of a lawful possession either in relation of tenant, or at least as continuing by sufferance till notice (*c*)

It once was doubted, whether if the landlord or tenant died, the same notice to his executors or administrators was necessary as would have been requisite had he lived, and it was even suggested that a month's notice in such case would suffice (*d*).

It is now settled, however, that in the case of a tenancy from year to year as long as both parties please, if the tenant die intestate, his administrator, as his legal representative, has the same interest in the land which his intestate had, for such tenancy is a chattel interest, and whatever chattel the intestate had must vest in his administrator as his legal representative (*e*).

So half a year's notice to quit must be given to a tenant at will (that is to say a yearly tenant) or his executor, or an ejectment will not lie (*f*)

This principle is so settled that it has been adjudged (*g*) that the executor of a tenant from year to year of an estate under 10*l* a year, may gain a settlement by residing on it forty days on the ground (*inter alia*) that he resided on an estate of his own and continued there forty days irremovable, and that he had a permanent interest [illegible] whether beneficial or not, was immaterial for the purpose [illegible], while the office of executor continued. *Lawrence*, J [illegible] that it was settled in *D.* [illegible]

(*a*) 1 T R 85 7 T. R [illegible] (*b*) [illegible] (*c*) [illegible]
(*d*) 1 Bl. R 596. (*e*) [illegible] R 16. (*f*) [illegible] (*g*) [illegible]

Shore v. *Porter*, (3 *T. R.* 13.) that if a tenant who held from year to year died intestate, his administrator has the same interest in the land that the intestate had. Then what was the interest of the pauper's testator? He had a right to continue on the estate another year, unless six months' notice to quit were given; and of course the pauper, his executor, had the same right. In regard to an objection taken in respect to the want of a probate, the learned Judge cited a case (*a*) that gave a decided answer to that: a termor devised his term to another, whom he made his executor, and died; the devisee entered and without any probate; and it was held that the term was legally in the executor by his entry and an execution of the devise without any probate. So that if there had been no probate of the will in this case, still the term was vested in the pauper, the executor.

In this respect the right and the remedy must be reciprocal; as the representative capacity of executor or administrator is not affected by the testator or intestate having been in the situation of either landlord or tenant.

But although, if the testator die in the possession of a term for years, it shall vest in the executor, and although if it be worth nothing, he cannot waive it, for he must renounce the executorship *in toto* or not at all; yet this is to be understood only where the executor has assets: for he may relinquish the lease, if the property be insufficient to pay the rent; but in case there are assets, to be at the loss for some years, though not during the whole term, it seems the executor is bound to continue tenant till the fund is exhausted, when on giving notice thereof to the lessor, he may waive the possession (*b*).

So in the case of an infant. Therefore, where an infant becomes entitled to the reversion of an estate leased from year to year, he cannot eject the tenant without giving the same notice as the original lessor must have given (*c*). Also if a tenant hold under an agreement for a lease at a yearly rent, wherein it is stipulated that the agreement shall continue for the life of the lessor, and that a clause shall be inserted in the lease, giving the lessor's son power to take the house for himself when he came of age, the son must make his election in a reasonable time, as for example, [illegible] or forming it, after he comes of age, the delay of a year is unreasonable, and the tenant cannot be ejected upon half a year's notice to quit served after such a delay (*d*).

So, where an ejectment has been brought on the demise of an infant, which [illegible] compromised, and the tenant in possession [illegible] to the defendant, though the infant, on coming of age, does not accept rent or do any act to confirm the tenancy, yet, as the former ejectment was brought [illegible] for his benefit, he shall not be allowed [illegible] consider the tenant as a trespasser, and bring a new ejectment without giving notice to quit (*a*).

Tenant from year to year also before a mortgage or grant of the reversion, is entitled to six months notice to quit before the end of the year from the mortgagee or grantee (*b*).

Thus where a tenant held from the 22d of *November* as a yearly tenant, and a mortgagee who became such in *July* was desirous of ousting him, it was too late to give notice then for the tenant to quit at the end of the current year, for the tenant, at the time that the mortgagee's title accrued had as permanent an interest in the estate till the 22d of *November*, as if it had been leased to him by deed till that period (*c*).

There is no distinction in reason between houses and lands, as to the time of giving notice to quit: it is necessary that both should be governed by one rule. There may be cases where the hardship would be felt in determining that the rule did not extend to houses as well as lands; as in the case of a lodging-house in *London* being let to a tenant at *Lady-day*, to hold from year to year, if the landlord should give notice to quit at *Michaelmas*, he would by that means deprive the lessee of the most beneficial part of the term, since it is notorious that the winter is by far the most profitable season of the year for those who let lodgings. The notice should be half a year preceding the expiration of the year (*d*).

Tithes in this respect are assimilated to land. If, therefore, a composition for tithes be made by *A.* as proprietor, and he lease them to *B.* whose interest is afterwards put an end to by *A* before any alteration is made in the composition, *A.* cannot determine it without six months' notice (*e*).

The notice to quit has reference, in all cases, to the letting; therefore, where a house was taken by the month, it was held that a month's notice was sufficient to entitle the plaintiff to recover (*f*).

Though reasonable notice must be given before the end of the year by landlord or tenant, and such notice is generally required to be half a year's, yet it varies according to the custom of different countries (*g*).

Therefore, where the arable part of a farm was to be entered on, and quitted on the 13th of *February*, it was considered to be no more than what the custom of most countries would have directed without any special words, on a taking from *Lady-day* to *Lady-day*, that being the time when the land is to be prepared for *Lent*-corn, and as the tenant outgoing has the benefit of the way-going crop, any inconvenience to him is obviated, whereas great mischief might happen to landlords if compelled to give notice so early as *August*, as it would enable the tenant to harrass the land (*h*).

(*a*) 5 Esp. R. [illegible] (*b*) [illegible] (*c*) [illegible] (*d*) [illegible]
(*e*) 1 Pul & Pos [illegible] (*f*) [illegible] R 94 (*g*) [illegible]
(*h*) [illegible]

The preceding case, however, is said to have been much questioned, if not over-ruled, by Lord *K[illegible]*, at *Nisi Prius*, in the case of *Doe on the demise of Lord Grey de Wilton* at *Stafford Summer Assizes* [illegible], which was an ejectment brought by a landlord on a notice to quit. The defendant held a farm, as to the arable lands from *Candlemas*, [illegible] to the buildings and pastures from *Lady-day*, the rent [illegible] and *Lady-day*. The notice to quit was given six months before *Lady-day*, but not six months before *Candlemas*. His Lordship [illegible] the plaintiff, and is stated to have said that the notice must be given half a year before *Candlemas* (*a*). But it does not appear whether the notice to quit was given half a year before *Lady-day* or not, so as to bring it within the rule laid down in *Doe* v. *Snowdon*. *Quære* whether the case of *Doe* v. *Snowdon*, [2 *Bl. R.* 1224] [illegible] not turn upon the construction of a notice to quit given to a tenant from year to year, which not being upon a contract under seal, might be governed by the custom of the country, in relation to which the parties might be supposed to have contracted; for which purpose the entry on the arable land was not considered as a general taking possession of it at that period, but only for a special purpose, *viz.* to plough and prepare for the *Lent*-corn (*b*).

Under an agreement by a tenant of a farm to enter on the tillage land at *Candlemas*, and on the house and all other the premises at *Lady-day* following, and that when he left the farm he should quit the same according to the times of entry as aforesaid, and the rent was reserved half yearly at *Michaelmas* and *Lady-day*, held that a notice to quit delivered half a year before *Lady-day*, but less than half a year before *Candlemas* was good, the taking being in substance from *Lady-day*, with a privilege for the incoming tenant to enter on the arable land at *Candlemas*, for the sake of ploughing, &c. (*c*)

Under an agreement of demise dated in *January* of a dwelling house and other buildings for the purpose of carrying on a manufacture, together with certain meadow, pasture, and bleaching grounds, water-courses, &c. for a term of thirty-five years to commence, as to the meadow ground from the 25th of *December* last, as to the pasture from the 25th of *March* next, and as to the housing mills and all the rest of the premises from the 1st of *May*, reserving the first half year's rent on the Day of Pentecost, and the other half year's rent at *Martinmas*, held that the substantial subject of demise being the house and buildings for the purpose of the manufacture which were to be entered on the 1st of *May*, that was the substantial time of entry to which a notice to quit ought to refer, and not to the 25th of *December* when the incoming tenant had liberty of entering on the meadow, which was merely accessory to the other and principal subject of demise. Notice to quit [illegible] of two tenants on the premises, who held under a

(*a*) 2 [illegible] (*b*) [illegible] 382. (*c*) 6 East 120.

joint demise, is evidence that the notice reached the other who [illegible] elsewhere (*a*).

So, by special custom, three months' notice, or twelve [illegible], [illegible] be the proper notice (*b*).

As by the custom of *London*, where a tenant under the yearly [illegible] of 40*s.* is entitled to a quarter's notice to quit; but a tenant above [illegible] rent must have half a year's notice (*c*).

The custom of the country is also admissible evidence to explain the nature of the holding, as whether a general holding from *Michaelmas* means old or new *Michaelmas* (*d*).

Difficulties frequently arise in respect to ascertaining the commencement of the term, and cases occur in the books wherein reasonable notice has been held to be sufficient, whereas in other instances it has been decided that the half year's notice that the law requires is indispensable.

Thus, where the lessor of the plaintiff in an ejectment could not prove the time when the term commenced, and the tenant proved it to be different from the time to quit mentioned in the notice, the plaintiff was nonsuited (*e*).

But notwithstanding, where the notice was given on the 29th of *September*, being the day after *Michaelmas*, to quit at *Lady-day* following, Mr. J. *Heath* ruled the notice [illegible] this was probably on the principle of its being reasonable notice, and what is reasonable is matter of circumstance (*f*).

So, it is said to have been ruled at *Nisi Prius*, that where notice to quit has been served on the tenant, and the landlord being ignorant of the time when the tenancy commenced, has given the notice to quit at the wrong time, that is, not at the end of the year, that the tenant when the notice is served ought to inform the landlord of his error and mention the true time (*g*).

The rule however is otherwise, for if notice to quit at *Midsummer* be given to a tenant holding from *Michaelmas*, he may insist on the insufficiency of the notice at the trial in ejectment though he did not make any objection at the time that it was served, but said "I pay [illegible], and it is hard to [illegible] me thus;" for the expression is [illegible] (*h*).

But a notice to quit at [illegible] personally on the tenant, who made no objection at the time, [illegible] evidence from whence it may be inferred that the tenancy [illegible] period (*i*).

So if [illegible] at the same time of the year at which [illegible] does not, on receiving it, object to the [illegible] the year of his tenancy determines [illegible] (*k*).

(*a*) [illegible] 531. (*b*) [illegible] (*c*) 1 [illegible] (*d*) [illegible] R. 276.
(*e*) [illegible] [illegible] N. P. 461.
(*f*) 1 [illegible] (*k*) 2 [illegible] 159.

But a notice to quit if not served personally upon the tenant in possession, is no evidence to prove the commencement of the tenancy (*a*).

A notice was given on the 22d of *March*, by a landlord to his tenant to quit at the expiration of the current year. A declaration in ejectment, laying the demise on the first of *November*, was on the 16th of *January* following served upon the tenant, who at the time made no objection to the notice to quit, but said he should go out as soon as he could fit himself. This was held to be *primâ facie* evidence, that the tenancy commenced at *Michaelmas*, and was determined before the day of the demise (*b*).

Where a house and land are let together, to be entered upon at different times, and it does not appear from the terms of the demise from what time the whole is to be taken as being let together, it is a question of fact for the jury which is the principal, and which the accessorial subject of demise, in order that the judge may decide whether a notice to quit the whole was given in time (*c*).

In an ejectment cause, a point was raised, whether a notice to quit was sufficient? The taking was proved to be from *old* Michaelmas to *old* Michaelmas, and the notice was general to quit at *Michaelmas*. *Heath* J., on an objection to the notice as not being sufficiently certain, cited a *MS.* case from his note-book, in which a similar notice was held good, and overruled the objection (*d*).

A lease of lands by deed since the new stile, to hold from the feast of *St. Michael* must be taken to mean from *new Michaelmas*, and cannot be shewn by extrinsic evidence to refer to a holding from *old Michaelmas*, and a notice to quit at *old Michaelmas*, though given half a year before *new Michaelmas*, is bad (*e*).

It has been holden, that a notice to quit at *Lady-day* was *primâ facie* evidence of a holding from *Lady-day* to *Lady-day*, till the contrary were shewn (*f*).

So, a notice delivered to a tenant at *Michaelmas*, 1795, to quit "at *Lady-day* which will be in the year 1795," was holden to be a good notice to quit at *Lady-day*, 1796, for the intention was clear, and 1795 shall be rejected as an impossible year (*g*).

Indeed where the notice was to "quit possession of the rooms or apartments which you now hold of me, on the 25th of *March*, or the 8th day of *April* next ensuing," Lord *Kenyon* held that it was sufficient notice to the tenant to quit if he received it six months before the end of the tenancy, the notice here was intended to meet an holding commencing either at *old* or *new Lady-day*, and at whichsoever day it actually commenced, the notice was calculated to meet it, being given on *new Michaelmas-day*, and the demise laid after the 8th of *April* (*h*).

(*a*) 3 Camp. [illegible]   (*b*) 2 Campb. 559.   (*c*) 11 East, 498.
(*d*) Glouc. Sum. Ass. 1800. [illegible] MSS.   (*e*) 11 East, 312.
[illegible]

So, where the premises in question were part of a considerable estate which the plaintiff had demised, and the defendant not having taken them of him, but of his tenant, the time at which the tenancy commenced was unknown to the plaintiff, who gave the following notice to quit.

"William Butler,

"Take notice, that I hereby require you to quit and deliver up to me the possession of the house and premises you hold of me, situate in *Rose and Crown Court, Moorfields*, in the parish of *St. Leonard, Shoreditch*, in the county of *Middlesex*, at the end and expiration of the current year of your tenancy thereof, which shall expire next after the end of one half year from the date hereof. Dated this 20th day of *June*, 1796. *J. Phillips.*"

Lord *Kenyon* held this notice to be sufficient to entitle the plaintiff to recover possession, notwithstanding that no particular day was mentioned, and the plaintiff had a verdict (*a*).

Although the tenant may insist on the insufficiency of the notice at the trial of an ejectment, and if he prove another commencement of his term than that which it mentions, may defeat the plaintiff of his right to recover, yet if he disputes the time when his tenancy commenced, that the notice to quit does not correspond with it, it is incumbent on *him* to shew the true commencement of his tenancy (*b*), for it is sufficient for the plaintiff to prove his having given six months' [half a year's] notice to quit, and that the ejectment has been brought after that time was expired (*c*).

So, where a tenant being applied to respecting the commencement of his holding, informs the party that it begins on a certain day, and notice to quit on that day is given at a subsequent time, the tenant shall be bound by the information which he so gave, and not be permitted to shew that in fact it began at another period; and in such case, it makes no difference, whether the information so given proceeded from mistake or design, as it has equally the mischief of leading the landlord into error, and inducing him to proceed to recover the possession of the term, the commencement of which he had taken from the defendant's own information (*d*).

Demise from *A* to *B* for twenty-one years, if both should so long live; but if either should die before the end of the said term, then the heirs, executors, &c. of the person so dying should give twelve months' notice to quit, &c. Held that the lease could only be determined by twelve months' notice given "by the representatives of the party dying before the end of the term," and consequently that such notice given by the lessor to the representatives of the lessee (who died during the term) did not determine it (*e*).

If premises are taken "for twelve months certain and six months

(*a*) 2 Esp. R. 589. [illegible] R. 362. ( ) 4 Esp. R. [illegible]
[illegible] R. 6[illegible] ( ) [illegible]

notice to quit afterwards," the tenancy may be determined by a six months' notice to quit expiring at the end of the first year (*a*

Where a power is given to a party to [illegible] a lease on [illegible] notice in [illegible], he cannot [illegible] by giving a [illegible] notice ([illegible].

A parol [illegible], it should seem, would be sufficient [illegible] to determine [illegible], [illegible] other cases it should be in writing ([illegible]

Although [illegible] of tythes cannot be without deed, yet a [illegible] agreement for [illegible] tythes must be determined by a notice, [illegible] to the notice given in a holding of land (*e*)

Where there are three joint-trustees of an estate, notice to quit or discontinue the possession given by two is bad, even though given in the name of the third, and the third trustee afterwards adopts it and joins in the demise in ejectment (*f*)

But where there are two tenants of premises held in common, notice to one is sufficient (*g*).

Such notice should be clear and certain in its terms, and not ambiguous or optional.

A farm was leased for twenty-one years at a rent of 180*l* per annum, consisting, as described in the lease, of the Town Barton, and its several parcels described by name, at the rent of 83*l*., other closes named, at other rents, and the Shippen Barton and its several parcels described by name at another rent, with a power reserved to either party to determine the lease at the end of fourteen years, on giving two years' previous notice. It was held that a notice by the landlord to his tenant to quit "Town Barton, &c." agreeably to the terms of the covenant between them at the end of the fourteenth year of the term, given in due time, was sufficient; for *the Town Barton* meant Town Barton *cum sociis*,—otherwise, as there was no power to determine the lease as to part only, the notice could have no operation at all [illegible].

Where a house, lands, and tythes are held under a parol demise at a joint rent, a notice to quit "the house lands and premises with the appurtenances," includes the tythes, and is sufficient to put an end to the tenancy ([illegible]

If a notice to quit be in these words, "I desire you to quit, or else that you agree to pay double rent," the tenant having an option, the notice would not be sufficient (*k*).

But where notice in writing was served on a tenant and was in the following words, "I desire you to quit possession on *Lady-day* next, or I shall insist upon double rent," the Court held it to be sufficiently positive, the latter words were added only by way of threat of the consequence of holding over the possession (*l*),

[illegible] Comp. [illegible] (*e*) Willes, 43 ([illegible]) 3 Bur. 1603 [illegible]
[illegible] 125 [illegible] ([illegible]) 1 Pea. & Pal. 465 2 Bro. C. C. [illegible]
([illegible]) ([illegible]) 5 [illegible] 196 ([illegible]) [illegible] 247
[illegible] [illegible], Doug. 176. ([illegible]) [illegible]

It is not necessary that a notice to quit should be directed to the tenant in possession, if proved to be delivered to him at the proper time. Therefore, where notice was given on the 29th of *September*, and was in the following words

"Take notice that you quit possession of the rooms and apartments which you now hold of me, on the 25th day of *March* or the 8th day of *April* next ensuing

(Signed) "*J. Mattheurson*"

This notice was not directed to the defendant, but it was proved to have been served on him on the 29th of *September*.

Lord *Kenyon* said, that the notice to quit was, in point of form, good, and that it was sufficient to shew that the defendant was the tenant to the lessor of the plaintiff, which was necessary in all cases of ejectment by a landlord against his tenant, and had been done here, and that the service was on him in that character (*a*).

The delivery of the notice to quit to the servant of the tenant at his dwelling-house, to whom the nature of it was explained, though such dwelling-house was not situated on the premises and it did not appear to have come to the tenant's hands, is strong presumptive evidence that it reached him, which may be rebutted by the evidence of the servant (*b*).

But the mere leaving of a notice to quit at the tenant's house, without further proof of its being delivered to a servant, and explained, or that it came to the tenant's hands is not sufficient to support an ejectment (*c*).

If a landlord receive rent due, after the expiration of a notice to quit, it is a waiver of that notice. But if the money had not been received as rent, but as a satisfaction for the injury done by the tenant in continuing on his late landlord's premises as a trespasser, then the late landlord might have recovered in ejectment (*d*).

A landlord of premises about to sell them, gave his tenant notice to quit on the 11th of *October*, 1806, but promised not to turn him out unless they were sold, and not being sold till *February*, 1807, the tenant refused on demand to deliver up possession, and on ejectment brought, it was held that the promise which was performed was no waiver of the notice, nor operated as a license to be on the premises, otherwise than subject to the landlord's right of acting on such notice if necessary, and therefore that the tenant not having delivered up possession on demand after a sale, was a trespasser from the expiration of the notice to quit (*e*).

Though notice to quit is in general waived by the receipt of rent due subsequent to such notice, yet the mere acceptance of rent by a landlord subsequent to the time when the tenant ought to have quitted according to the notice given him for that purpose is not itself a waiver,

(*a*) 1 Esp. R. 5. (*c*) 4 T. R. 464. (*d*) 5 Esp. 153.
(*b*) 6 T. R. 220. 1 Bl. R. 311. (*e*) 10 East, 13.

on the part of the landlord, of such notice; but matter of evidence only to be left to the jury, under the circumstances of the case: for the landlord might possibly have accepted the rent under terms or made an express declaration that he did not mean to waive the notice, and that notwithstanding his acceptance or receipt of the rent, he should still insist upon the possession, or fraud or contrivance might have been practised on the part of the tenant in paying it.—The question therefore, in such cases, is in *quo animo* the rent was received, and what the real intention of both parties was (*a*).

Where rent is usually paid at a banker's, if the banker, without any special authority, receives rent accruing after the expiration of a notice to quit, the notice is not thereby waived (*b*).

Where a landlord gave notice to quit different parts of a farm at different times, which the tenant neglected to do in part, in consequence of which the landlord commenced an ejectment, and before the last period mentioned in the notice was expired, the landlord, apprehending that the witness by whom he was to prove the notice would die, gave another notice to quit at the respective times in the following year, but continued to proceed with his ejectment, it was held that the second notice was not a waiver of the first (*c*).

So if a landlord gives notice to his tenant to quit at the expiration of the lease, and the tenant hold over, the landlord is entitled to double rent; and a second notice delivered to the tenant after the expiration of such notice "to quit on a subsequent day or to pay double rent," is no waiver of the first notice, or of the double rent which has accrued under it (*d*). [The circumstance of the double rent having accrued under the first notice, differs in this case from that cited *ante* from *Doug.* 176, where an option was clearly given.] (*e*).

Where a second notice was given to a tenant to quit at *Michaelmas*, 1811, it was held a waiver as to him of a former notice given to the original lessee (from whom he claimed by assignment) to quit at *Michaelmas* 1810 (*f*).

Where one in remainder, after the expiration of an estate for life, gave notice to the tenant to quit on a certain day, and afterwards accepted of half a year's rent, such acceptance being only evidence of holding from year to year, is rebutted by the previous notice to quit, and therefore the notice remains good (*g*).

But when three months' notice was given where the rent was reserved quarterly, and the landlord expressed neither his assent nor dissent to admit it, and took the rent up to the time when his tenant quitted, it was construed to be such an acquiescence as amounted to presumptive evidence that the parties intended to dispense with the notice, and was therefore deemed a waiver of it (*h*).

(*a*) [illegible] 2[illegible] [illegible] 386. (*c*) 2 East R. 23[illegible]. (*d*) 3 Campb. 117.
(*b*) [illegible] 1 [illegible] R. [illegible] (*f*) 1[illegible] (*g*) [illegible] 161. (*h*) [illegible] R. 2[illegible]6.

So, if at the end of the year (where there has been a tenancy from year to year) the landlord accepts another as his tenant, without any surrender in writing, such acceptance shall be a dispensation of the notice to quit (*a*).

Notice to quit, however, is not necessary in every case. Thus when a lease is determinable on a certain event, or at a particular period, no notice to quit is necessary, because both parties are equally apprized of the determination of the term (*b*).

So, if the tenant have attorned to some other person, or done some other act disclaiming to hold as tenant to the landlord, in that case no notice is necessary (*c*). Indeed if a tenant put his landlord at defiance, his landlord may consider him either as his tenant or a trespasser, and in the latter case need not give him a notice to quit before he brings his ejectment (*d*).

But a refusal to pay rent to a devisee in a will which was contested is not such a disavowal of the title as to empower such devisee to maintain an ejectment without giving a previous notice (*e*).

A mortgagee may recover possession against the mortgagor, or a tenant under a lease from the mortgagor posterior to the mortgage, without notice to quit, for when the mortgagor is left in possession, the true inference to be drawn is an agreement that he shall possess the premises at will in the strictest sense and therefore no notice is ever given him to quit (*f*).

So, a mortgagee need not give notice to a tenant to quit before bringing his ejectment, if he means only to get into the receipt of the rents and profits of the estate, though the mortgage be made subsequent to the tenant's lease. But in such case he shall not be suffered to turn the tenant out of possession by the execution. In the present case the lease was only from year to year, and with respect to the last year, might be considered as a lease subsequent to the mortgage, but the Court held that it would have been the same if the lease were for a long term (*g*).

Wherever the lessee holds under a void demise, no notice is necessary, as in the case just mentioned of a lease by a mortgagor after the mortgage (*h*).

So (*i*), where an ejectment for lands in *Surry*, the case was that *Elizabeth Compton* being entitled to a copyhold of inheritance held of the manor of *Kennington*, was admitted to it in 1767; in 1780 Mr. *C.* her husband granted a lease to *M.* for forty years, (under whom the defendant claimed) without the consent or the joining of his wife and therefore contrary to stat. 32 *H.* 8. *c.* 28 *s.* 3. In 1782 Mrs. *C.* died, leaving her husband and an only daughter (now the lessor of the plaintiff)

(*a*) 2 Esp. R. 505. (*b*) 1 T. R. 54, 162. (*c*) Bull. N. P. 96. Esp. N. P. 463. (*d*) Peake's R. 197. (*e*) Ibid. (*f*) Doug. 22. (*g*) Bull. N. P. 96. (*h*) 1 T. R. 95. Esp. N. P. 463. (*i*) Ibid. 464. 7. T. R. 85.

her heir at law. Mr *C.* received the rent till the time of his death in 178[illegible], and Mrs *A.* the lessor of the plaintiff, also received it after his death, as reserved by the lease, till 1789, when on discovery that the lease was void under stat. 32 *H.* 8 and also not warranted by the custom of the manor, the present ejectment was brought without giving notice to quit. For the defendant it was insisted that the lease was good, or at most only voidable, and confirmed by acceptance of rent by Mrs *A.* the plaintiff, but that even if she had not confirmed the lease, she had made the holding a tenancy from year to year, and therefore he should have given notice to quit, but both points were over-ruled by Mr J. *C*[illegible], who tried the cause, and the plaintiff recovered (*a*).

[illegible] *P*[illegible], however, was objected to by [illegible] *F*[illegible], who [illegible] [illegible] without much consideration, [illegible] put in the balance against all the other [illegible] (*b*).

It [illegible] where the estate or lease is *ipso facto* void [illegible] no acceptance of the rent after can make it [illegible] a continuance, otherwise it is of an estate or lease voidable [illegible] the distinction is, because the acceptance of rent [illegible] make a new lease, and the old one was determined [illegible] acceptance of the rent in the other, is a sufficient [illegible] it is the lessor's will to continue the lease, for he is not entitled to the rent but by the lease (*d*).

It [illegible] be again observed that where the relation of landlord and [illegible] does not subsist, notice to quit is out of the question.

[illegible] the receipt from the *cottager* of a quit-rent reserved on the grant of [illegible] does not constitute a tenancy from year to year, so as to [illegible] notice to quit, the rent not being received [illegible] [illegible], but attributable to another consideration [illegible] the question of tenancy from year to year, the payment of rent [illegible] a holding from year to year if, as in the case of [illegible], it be not a payment of rent as between landlord and tenant (*e*).

In the case of [illegible] v. *Shaley*, *Dorch.* [illegible] *Summer Assizes*, 1806, where the [illegible] plaintiff claimed thirty acres of leasehold, on a lease [illegible] long since extinct, on which a rent of 13*s.* 4*d.* was reserved, it appeared that after the lease had run out, the steward not knowing that, had continued regularly to receive the 13*s.* 4*d.* on the day on which it was reserved by the lease, wherefore it was objected that the payment of rent created a tenancy from year to year, and that there ought to have been a notice to quit. But, however, *Thompson B.* [illegible] not necessary, that no contract as of a tenancy from year to year could be presumed, that the payment was made *also intuit*[illegible],

[illegible] 175[illegible] (*b*) [illegible] T. R. 85 (*d*) Co. Lit. 215. Willes, 169
[illegible] (*e*) 3 East's R. 260.

and that the case fell within the principle of that determined in 3 East, 260,—(cited 10 East, 165.)

Tenant from year to year underlet part of the premises, and then gave up to his landlord the part remaining in his own possession, without either receiving a regular notice to quit the whole, or giving notice to quit to his sub lessee, or even surrendering that part in the name of the whole. The landlord cannot entitle himself to recover against the sub-lessee, (there being no privity of contract between them) upon giving half year's notice to quit in his own name, and not in the name of the first lessee, for as to the part so underlet, the original tenancy still continued undetermined (*a*).

SECTION II. *Of Tenants for a less Term than from Year to Year, and herein of Lodgings.*

We have had occasion before to observe, that any one possessed of a certain quantity of interest may alienate the whole or any part of it, unless restricted from so doing by agreement of the party from whom he derives that interest or estate or by the terms upon which he takes it.

Upon the same principle he may demise it or any part of it for any term shorter than that of which he is possessed, and when part of a messuage or tenement is let to another, it is called a lodging or lodgings.

Of Lodgings.—Lodgings may be let in the same manner as lands and tenements in general, however, they are let either by agreement in writing between the landlord and tenant, or by parol agreement.

It is a general rule in the case of a yearly tenancy, that notice to quit must be half a year before the expiration of the year; the case of lodgings depends upon a particular contract, and is an exception to the general rule. The agreement between the parties may be for a month or less time, and there much shorter notice would be sufficient where the tenant has held over the time agreed upon, than in the other case (*b*).

The whole question depends upon the nature of the first contract: so that if the parties have agreed that the tenant shall hold for a term certain, no notice of course can be necessary (*c*), but if the tenant hold for no particular period, reasonable notice must be given, which is regulated generally, if not always, by the local custom of the particular place or district, which for the most part requires the same space of time for notice as the period for which the lodgings are taken, as a

(*a*) 14 East. 234. (*b*) 1 T. R. 16[illegible]. (*c*) Ibid.

week's notice, where taken for a week; a month's where taken for a month, and so forth, but this is not always the case, for it is not always necessary (it is presumed) that a quarter's notice should be given where the rent is paid quarterly, and it is understood to be a quarterly taking, for a month's notice is sometimes customary, and which probably a court and jury would think generally reasonable (*a*).

If a house, originally entire, be divided into several apartments, with an outer door to each apartment, and no communication with each other subsists, in such case the several apartments are considered in law as distinct mansion houses But if the owner live in the house, all the untenanted apartments shall be considered as parts of his house. Yet, if there be two several tenements originally and they become inhabited by several families, who make but one avenue for both, and use it promiscuously, the original severalty is so far recognized and regarded, that they continue to be severally rateable to the poor (*b*).

These lodgings constitute such an interest according to the duration of the term, that to many purposes the lodgers are considered in law in the light of householders, and enjoy the same protection and greater immunities, for they are not compellable to serve parish offices.

As to the question, what shall be deemed the house of the party within the meaning of *domus mansionalis*, it turns upon the fact of there being an outer door or not, for every house certainly must have an outer door.

Thus chambers in inns of court and in colleges, which have each of them an outer door that opens upon the common staircase, have been held, in cases of burglary, to be the houses of the respective occupiers. From the nature of these buildings, they are all as several houses, and have separate outer doors which are at the extremity of the obstruction; because the staircase is no outer door: again, they are enjoyed as separate property; in *Lincolns Inn* they have separate estates of inheritance, in the others they have estates for life, and in colleges as long as they reside So, if that which was one house originally comes to be divided into separate tenements, and there is a distinct outer door to each, they will be separate houses, as *Newcastle House*. The distinction therefore can only be between several outer doors, and one outer door (*c*).

Therefore if one hire a part of a house to lodge in, which is actually divided from the rest, and have a door of his own to the street, a burglary committed therein may be alledged *in domo mansionali* of such person (*d*); and even if the owner occupy a shop or cellar in the house, unless he sleep therein, it is the mansion of each lodger, although there be but one outer door; but it is otherwise, if the owner sleep therein (*e*).

(*a*) 1 Esp R 94 (*b*) 6 Mod 214 (*c*) Cowp 8.
(*d*) 1 Haw P.C. 164. s 15. (*e*) Ibid. n. 9

A house, in fact, wherein a man dwells for only part of the year, or which he has actually hired, but not moved into; or a chamber in an inn of court, or a house hired by a man's wife, for her separate residence without his knowledge, "for it is the husband's house," are all of them sufficient to satisfy the words *domus mansionalis* (*a*).

But if the person had taken an apartment as a shop or workhouse, for his use in the day-time only, it seems that a felony therein cannot be alledged to have been committed in the mansion-house: not of him that lets it, because it is severed by the lease from that part of the house which belongs to him, nor of him to whom it is let, because he does not take it to lodge in. But if he sleep in any part of the building, however distant from the shop, it may be alledged to be his mansion-house, provided the owner does not sleep under the same roof also (*b*).

So where a burglary is committed in the apartments of one who lodges in a house, the circumstance of the owner living in it, or occupying only a shop or cellar, in which he does not sleep, makes a very material difference as to the form of the indictment: for in the latter case, the lodger has the outer door entirely to himself, and the burglary in such case must be laid in the house of the lodger; but it is otherwise in the former case, for there it must be laid in the house of the owner (*c*).

If with intent to rob a house, a person takes lodgings in it, and then fall on the landlord and rob him, such person is guilty of burglary (*d*).

As to the stat. 39 *Eliz.* c. 15. making it a capital felony to commit a larceny of goods to the value of 5s. in a dwelling-house in the day-time, it seems agreed that a chamber in one of the inns of court wherein a person usually lodges, is properly a dwelling-house within the statute; but a lodging in *Whitehall* or *Somerset House* is not (*e*).

But this privilege of a lodger's tenement being regarded as his mansion-house, extends only to the purposes of protection to a man and his family, and is to be taken strictly (*f*). A bailiff, therefore, in the execution of mesne process may break open the door of a lodger, having first gained peaceable entrance at the outer door of the house; for the rule, that every man's house is his castle, must be confined to the breach of windows and of outer doors intended for the security of the house against persons from without endeavouring to break in (*g*).

For the protection of landlords against a species of pillage to which persons letting ready furnished lodgings are much exposed, it being doubted whether the taking things in a lodging-room was more than a breach of trust at common law, because of their being lent to a person and lawfully in their possession, therefore the taking away from such

(*a*) 1 Haw. P. C. 165; (*b*) Ibid. 164. s. 16. (*c*) Cowp. 8.
(*d*) Haw. P. C. 161. s. 5. (*e*) 2 Haw. P. C. 520. s. 9? Cro. Car. 47.
(*f*) Cowp. 1. (*g*) Fost. C. L. 319. Homicide c. 8. s. 20.

lodgings, with an intent to steal, embezzle, or purloin any chattel, bedding or furniture, which by contract or agreement they are to use, or shall be let to them with the said lodgings, is made larceny and felony (*a*).—A man and his wife cannot both be guilty of the same larceny in robbing their lodgings, for if they both had committed it together, the woman must be acquitted, for she is under his coercion. If the lodgings be let jointly, it is the taking of the husband only (*b*).

In respect to letting houses, though, as has been before observed (*c*), there is no distinction in reason between houses and land, as to the time of giving notice to quit in yearly tenancies, it being necessary that both should be governed by one rule, and that where rent is reserved quarterly, it does not dispense with the regular six months notice to quit required by law, but is merely a collateral matter (*d*): yet in the case of a house being let for a shorter term than a year, the holding assimilates itself to that of a lodging: therefore where a house was taken by the month, it was held that a month's notice was sufficient: for a notice to quit has reference in all cases to the letting (*e*).

A tenant from week to week, continuing in possession after the expiration of a notice to quit and demand made, is not liable to an action on the stat. 4 *Geo.* 3d. c. 28. for double value (*f*).

If the lodgings be furnished, it may be as well to have a schedule of the goods they contain affixed to the agreement, if there be one in writing, in the same manner as in the case of a lease of a house with goods (*g*).

Section III. *Of strict Tenants at Will.*

Although courts of law have of late years leaned as much as possible against construing demises (*h*), where no certain term is mentioned, to be tenancies at will, but (as we have just seen) have rather held them to be tenancies from year to year so long as both parties please, especially where an annual rent is reserved (*i*), and although it is said, that in the country, leases at will in the strict legal notion of a lease at will, being found extremely inconvenient, exist only notionally, the observation, Mr *Hargrave* thinks, means, not that estates at will may not arise now as well as formerly, but only that it is no longer usual to create such estates by express words, and that the Judges incline strongly against implying them (*k*).

Tenant at will is where lands or tenements are let by one man to another, to have and to hold to him at the will of the lessor, by force of which lease the lessee is in possession. In this case, the lessee is called tenant at will, because he hath no certain nor sure estate, for the

(*a*) 3 W. & M. c. 9. s. 5. (*b*) 1 Hale P. C. 513. n. 3. (*c*) 1 T. R. 162. (*d*) Esp. 166. (*e*) Ibid. 94. (*f*) 2 Campb. 453. (*g*) [illegible]art, 142. (*h*) 2 Bl. Com. 147. (*i*) [illegible] Lev. R. 160. (*k*) 1 Co. Litt. 55.

lessor may put him out at what time it pleaseth him. But every lease at will must be at the will of both parties (*a*).

If a termor grants the land generally, the grantee is but tenant at will; for it does not appear that the grantor meant to pass his whole interest, and this is enough to satisfy the grant. But if a termor devises the land, all his term passes, for the devisee cannot be tenant at will, because the devisor must die before the devise can take effect, and one cannot be tenant at will to a dead man (*b*).

If one lease for years, with a proviso, that lessor may enter at his will, it is a lease at will (*c*).

So, if one demises a tenement to another excepting the new house for his habitation, when he pleases to stay there, and at other times for the use of the lessee; the lessee has the new house as tenant at will (*d*).

So, if one give to another licence to take the profits of his land without mentioning for how long a period, or reserving an annual rent, it shall be a lease at will (*e*).

A man who enters and enjoys under a void lease, and pays rent, is a tenant at will, and not a disseisor (*f*).

But if a man enter by colour of a grant or conveyance which was void and did not stand with the rule of law, he shall be disseisor, and not a tenant at will (*g*).

A mortgagor is in some respects strictly tenant at will, and in many cases is like a tenant at will (*h*).

Therefore if a mortgagee covenants that the mortgagor shall take the profits till default of payment; or that the mortgagor and his heirs shall take the profits, in the one case the mortgagor, and in the other his heir after his death, shall be tenant at will (*i*).

But if mortgagee covenants that he will not take the profits till default of payment, and the mortgagor enters immediately; he shall not be tenant at will, but only at sufferance, for it was not agreed that he should take, but that the mortgagee should not take (*k*).

A mortgagor however is not properly a tenant at will to the mortgagee, for he is not to pay him rent: he is indeed as much if not more like a receiver than a tenant at will, though in truth he is not either (*l*). He is only a tenant at will, because he is not entitled to the growing crops after the will is determined, for the mortgagee may bring his ejectment at any moment that he will, and he is entitled to the estate as it is with all the crops growing on it (*m*).

If tenant for years continues after his term, and his rent is paid and accepted as before, it is said that he shall be tenant at will, but that

(*a*) Co. Lit. 55. (*b*) 1 Salk. 436. (*c*) Co. Lit. 55. a. (*d*) 4 Mod. 9.
(*e*) 3 Salk. 223. (*f*) 1 Wils. 176. (*g*) Com. Dig. tit. "Estates" (H. 2.)
(*h*) 1 T.R. 382. (*i*) Com. Dig. ut ante (H. 1.) Cro. Jac. 660.
(*k*) Com. Dig. tit. "Estates" (H. 2.) (*l*) Doug. 282, 3. (*m*) 1 T.R. 382.

while he so continues, till his rent is paid and accepted, he is tenant at sufferance or rather at will. This however would be now construed to be a tenancy from year to year (*a*).

When tenancy at will was more known than it is now, the relation might be determined at any time, not as to those matters which during the tenancy remained a common interest between the parties, but as to any new contract the will might be instantly determined. When that interest was converted into the tenancy from year to year, the law fixed one positive rule for six months' notice, a rule that may in many cases [illegible] convenient; in others, as for instance, that of nursery-grounds, most inconvenient (*b*).

If a tenant whose lease is expired is permitted to continue in possession, pending a treaty for a further lease, he is not a tenant from year to year, but so strictly at will, that he may be turned out of possession without notice (*c*).

A lessee at will may take a release of the inheritance, and thereby his estate is enlarged; or a confirmation for his life, upon which a remainder may be dependant (*d*)

Where a lease is made at will, rent being payable quarterly, the lessee, after a quarter of a year is commenced, may determine his will, but then he must pay that quarter's rent (*e*); and if the lessor determine his will after the commencement of a quarter, he shall lose his rent for that quarter. So, if half yearly (*f*).

Tenant at will may be ousted also by express words, or by implication. as if lessor come upon the land, and say that lessee shall not continue over, he may determine his will, though in the absence of the lessee. But words off the land will not, till notice to the lessee (*g*)

Any act of desertion, or which is inconsistent with an estate [illegible] will, done by the tenant, operates as a determination of the estate as assignment over to another, or commission of an act of waste (*h*).

If therefore tenant at will take upon him to make a lease for years, which is a greater estate than he may make, that act is a disseisin [and a determination of the will.] (*i*)

But though lessee at will make a lease to commence at a future day, it does not amount to a determination, till the lease commences in point of interest So of an extent, till the [illegible], and of outlawry, till seizure (*k*)

Though a person let into possession under an agreement to purchase, may be considered as tenant at will, yet his admission of a fictitious lease

(*a*) [illegible] "Estate" (H [illegible]) (*b*) 16 Ves [illegible]
(*c*) 2 [illegible] R [illegible] (*d*) Com Dig [illegible] (H [illegible])
(*e*) 3 [illegible] 79 1 Ld Raym 702 2 Ibid 1008
(*f*) Com D[illegible] (H 9) (*g*) Ibid (H. 6)
(*h*) [illegible] Dig [illegible] 17 1 Ju[illegible] a 55. b. n. 12. (*i*) Co. Co. [illegible]
(*k*) Com Dig [illegible]

by entering into the common consent rule is not a constructive determination of the will whereon an ejectment is maintainable (*a*).

But, though a tenant at will is at the will of both parties, the will shall not be determined by every act (*b*).

Thus, where a feme lessee at will takes husband, or a feme makes a lease at will and takes husband, although the feme hath put her will in her husband, yet it shall not be said to be a determination without the election of the lessor or the husband (*c*).

In tenancies at will the rent becomes due in consideration of the occupation; which, it is said, must therefore be averred (*d*).

Tenant at will has an estate that he cannot forfeit for treason (*e*).

SECTION IV. *Of Tenants at sufferance.*

Tenant at sufferance is he who enters by lawful demise or title, and afterwards wrongfully continues in possession: as if tenant *pur auter vie* continues in possession after the death of the *cestui que vie* (*f*).

So, any one, who continues in possession without agreement, after a particular estate is ended (*g*).

There is a great diversity therefore between a tenant at will and a tenant at sufferance, for tenant at will is always by right, whereas tenant by sufferance entereth by a lawful lease, and holdeth over by wrong (*h*).

But against the king there is no tenant at sufferance, for the king not being capable of committing laches, such person will be an intruder (*i*).

So, if a guardian continue in possession after the full age of the heir: he is not a tenant by sufferance, but an abator (*k*)

Mortgagee covenants that mortgagor shall quietly enjoy till default of payment, and assigns: after assignment, mortgagor is only tenant at sufferance; for his continuing in possession does not turn the term to a right (*l*)

(*a*) 13 East, 210 (*b*) Cro Car. 303 (*c*) Ibid. 304.
(*d*) 1 Ld Raym 171. Salk 209 (*e*) 1 Wills. 176 (*f*) Co Lit 57
(*g*) Com. Dig *ut ante.* (*h*) Co. Lit. 57 b. (*i*) Ibid. (*k*) Ibid. an 271.
(*l*) Salk 245

CHAPTER VIII.

Of the general Incidents to Leases.

SECTION I. Rent, when and how payable.

Of Public Impositions, parochial and parliamentary.

SECTION II. Taxes.

SECTION III. Poor's Rate.

SECTION I. Rent, when and how payable, &c.

IN a preceding part of this work we have had occasion to explain the nature of rent, and the different kinds thereof.

It must be remembered, that a rent cannot at law issue out of a term of years, but must come out of the reversion; therefore, if a lessee assign his term, he cannot distrain for the rent without expressly reserving a power for that purpose (a).

The reservation of rent ought to be certain, for if a man demise, rendering "after the rate of" 18*l*. *per ann.* while the lease continues, it will be void; for it does not appear what rent he shall pay in certain, or at what time: wherein it differs from a contract for goods, for in such case the jury may judge of the value (b).

Reservation of Rent.—As to what is deemed a good reservation of rent, if a man makes a lease of *Blackacre*, to commence *in futuro*, and of *Whiteacre*, to begin *in præsenti*, rendering rent payable at *Michaelmas* before the commencement of the term in *Blackacre*, this is a reservation immediately, for it is but one entire rent, and as such is payable according to the reservation (c).

So it is, if a man grants a future interest in land; as if it be a lease for years to commence five years after the making of the lease, the lessor may reserve a rent immediately, because this is a good contract to oblige the lessee to pay, and the lessor may have an action of debt on the contract, and may likewise have his remedy by distress for the arrears when the lessor comes into possession (d).

A lease of the vesture or herbage of the land, reserving rent, is

(a) 2 Wils. 375. (b) 1 Salk. 2[?]2. 4 Mod. 79. (c) Gilb. on Rents, 75.
(d) Ibid.

good; because the lessor may come upon the land to distrain the lessee's beasts feeding thereon (*a*).—But a reservation of grass, herbage, or other vesture of the land would be bad, because they are part of the thing demised (*b*).

So, where by articles of agreement indented between *A.* and *B.* it is covenanted and agreed, that *A.* doth let *Blackacre* to *B.* for five years, provided always that *B.* shall pay at *Michaelmas* and *Lady-day* 10*l.* by even portions yearly, this proviso is a good reservation of the rent, for as the words amount to an immediate demise of the land, the rent, which is but a retribution for the land, ought to be paid immediately, and it cannot be construed to be a sum in gross, because by the words of the articles, (which being indented are the words of both parties,) it is to be paid yearly (*c*).

A difference is here to be noted between a rent reserved entire in the *reddendum* upon a demise of several things in the same lease, (for the reservation shall be taken as one and entire) and where the rent is not at first reserved entire, but upon the reservation is several and apportioned to the several things demised. – For instance, if a lease be made of several houses, rendering the annual rent of 5*l.* at the two usual feasts, *viz.* for one house 3*l.*, for another 10*s.* and for the rest of the houses the residue of the said rent of 5*l.* with a clause of re-entry into all the houses for non-payment of any parcel of the rent, this is but one reservation of one entire rent, because all the houses were leased, and the 5*l.* was reserved as one entire rent for them all, and the "*viz.*" afterwards does not alter the nature of the reservation, but only declares the value of each house (*d*).

But if the lease had been of three houses, rendering for one house 3*l.*, for another 20*s.* and for the third 20*s.* with a condition to re-enter into all for the non-payment of any parcel, these are three several reservations, and in the nature of three distinct demises, for which the avowries must likewise be several; for each house in this case is only chargeable with its own rent, the entire sum being not at first reserved out of all the houses demised, and afterwards apportioned to the several houses according to their respective value, as in the former case, but the particular sums are at first reserved out of the several houses, and therefore the non-payment of the rent of one house, can be no cause of entry into another (*e*).

So, if one demises the scite and demesnes of a manor, and also the manor itself, and all other lands and tenements thereunto belonging, reserving for the said scite and demesnes and premises therewith letten 9*l.* this is not a joint, but a several lease, *viz.* one lease for the scite and demesnes, and another for the residue of the manor, and the reservations also are several and distinct (*f*).

(*a*) Gilb. on Rents, 26. (*b*) Co. Litt. 47. (*c*) Gilb. on Rents, 32. (*d*) Ibid. 34.
(*e*) Ibid. (*f*) Ibid. 36. Cro. Eliz. 341.

So, if a lease be made of two manors *habendum*, one manor for 20*s.* and the other manor for 10*s* these are several reservations: and each manor is charged with its respective rent (*a*).

If the respective rents were equal sums, it would make no difference it seems; so as the words in the *habendum* make it as several leases

But where one made a lease of a cellar for a year, and if at the end of the year the parties should agree that the demise should continue, then to have and to hold the same for three years, "rendering from that time annually during the said term 40*s.*" this is one entire reservation, as well for the first year as for the three years, for the words *dictis terminis* extend to both terms indifferently (*b*)

As there may be several reservations in the same lease, by the words of the parties, so there may by act of law: as where a lease is made to a bishop in his public capacity, and *J. S.* reserving a rent, the lessees are not joint-tenants, but tenants in common, and therefore the reservation must be several, and the reversion to which the rent is incident must follow the nature of the particular estates on which it depends, and therefore must be several also (*c*)

So, if there be two tenants in common, and they make a lease for life, rendering rent, this reservation though made by joint words, shall follow the nature of the reversion, which is several in the lessors, and therefore they shall be put to their several assises, if they be disseised, as if they had been distinct reservations.—But if the reservation had been of a horse, or hawk, or any other thing not in its own nature severable, then, for the necessity of the case, the law admits them to join in one assise (*d*).

Upon a surrender reserving rent, though the rent is not good by way of reservation, yet it shall be so by way of contract

If a lessee, however, simply covenant to pay such a sum yearly, without mentioning it as a consideration of the demise of the premises, it has been held to be not a rent, but a sum in gross (*e*)

In an action of debt on an agreement, it appeared that the plaintiff covenanted by the agreement to grant a lease of certain premises upon certain conditions therein specified and at a certain rent. The defendant covenanted to pay a certain rent, and perform certain conditions on which the lease was to be granted. The declaration averred that the defendant had entered, upon a breach for non-payment of rent A former lease to one *Edmunds* had subsisted, at the expiration of which that mentioned in the agreement as to be granted to the defendant, was to commence, the declaration averred that *Edmunds's* lease had expired, and that the defendant had entered, but not that any lease had been made. There was also a count for use and occupation.—Upon demurrer to the first special counts, Lord *Kenyon*, C. J said, "I have

(*a*) [illegible] 35 (*b*) Ib. [illegible] (*c*) Ib. [illegible]
(*d*) Ib. [illegible] (*e*) 1 T. R. 441.

always admired an expression of Lord *Hardwicke* 'that there is no magic in words.' It appears that a rent was to become due on a certain day mentioned: perhaps this money to be paid is not strictly to be called rent, the relation of landlord and tenant not having then commenced: but still the parties intended that this money should be paid, according to the best construction I can give of the agreement. Collecting therefore the meaning of the parties, without encumbering myself with the technical meaning of the word *rent*, I think the case is with the plaintiff. The other Judges agreed in opinion with Lord *Kenyon*. They observed that the conditions mentioned in the lease were the conditions of sale at the auction at which it was bargained for. The intent seemed to be that the defendant should after the determination of *Edmunds's* lease, take possession and proceed to cover in the house. On the house being covered in, the plaintiffs were to grant a lease; but in order to instigate the defendant to do this, he was to pay annually a certain sum before the granting of the lease, equal to what he was to pay afterwards, the whole being denominated "rent." If that were not meant, the covenant to pay rent was useless, for the lease, when made, would certainly contain such a covenant.—The deed and conditions of sale were very obscurely worded, though it appeared that the city of *London* had used that form for upwards of a century (*a*).

Note also, a diversity between a reservation, which is always of a thing not *in esse*, but newly created or reserved out of the land or tenement demised, and an exception, which is ever of part of the thing granted, and of a thing *in esse* (*b*).

Rent reserved upon a lease issuing out of copyholds and freeholds (the lease of the copyhold being made with licence) was held good (*c*). But the rent shall be considered as issuing out of the freehold only, as in the case of rent issuing out of land and goods.

In a lease of lands, for which the lessor is bound to reserve the best rent that can be gotten, he must reserve the best rent that can be gotten at the time the lease is made, without any regard to a former lease in which the rent might have been fairly reserved on account of money to have been expended in improvements (*d*).

If there be an order, confirmed by parliament, that an indenture of demise, upon which a rent was reserved, should be vacated and cancelled, and that a stranger should enter into the lands demised and receive the profits, yet the same rent in value granted by the lessee for the better securing the rent reserved, is not discharged, although the intention appears that there should be but one rent paid (*e*).

The rent must be reserved to the lessor himself, and not to a stranger (*f*); for it ought to be made to him from whom the land

(*a*) City of London v. Dews, T. T. 41 G. 3. T.'s MSS.
(*b*) Co. Litt. 47. [illegible]
(*c*) Cro. Eliz. 622.
(*d*) Esp. R. 80.
(*e*) 1 Saund. 195.
(*f*) Co. Litt. 47, 143. b.

passes, and where one reserves rent to a stranger, neither the heir nor stranger shall have it (*a*).

Therefore, if a man, and *B.* his son, reciting that *B* is his heir apparent, let for years, to commence after the death of the father, (who was sole seised) and rendering rent to the said *B* it will be void; for a reservation to him by his proper name, and not to him as heir, is the same as if it were to a stranger—But the king may make a reservation of rent to a stranger (*b*).

So, if a lease for years be made, rendering rent to the heirs of the lessor, the reservation, it is said, is bad, because not to the lessor first (*c*).

The clearest and safest way is, to reserve the rent generally during the term, without saying to whom and leave it to be distributed by the law For if the reservation of rent be general, the law generally directs it according to the interest and the nature of the thing demised (*d*).

This has always been taken most in advantage of the lessee and against the lessor, and yet so as the rent be paid during the time (*e*); for if no person be mentioned, the reservation shall be extended by implication of law, to the lessor and his heirs (*f*)

But if the reservation be only to the lessor, and the deed do not say also "to his heirs, executors, &c" this reservation shall continue only for the life-time of the lessor, and shall determine with his death: for *expressum facit cessare tacitum* (*g*).

So, if a man reserved rent to him or his heir, it will be good to him for his life and void to the heir (*h*). So also if the lessor be seised in fee, and make a lease for life or years, rendering rent to the lessor, or his executors or assigns, in this case the rent shall continue only for the life of the lessor (*i*).

But if the reservation be to the lessor, his heirs and assigns, in the copulative, or in the disjunctive to him or his heirs, or to him or his successors, (if it be the lease of a corporation,) during the term, then all the assignees of the reversion shall enjoy it (*k*).

So, if the reservation be thus "yielding and paying so much rent," without any more words, this shall be taken for all the time of the estate, and shall go to him in reversion accordingly (*l*)

For, if the rent be made payable yearly, without saying during the term, the payment must be made during the term (*m*)

Therefore if a man seised of land in fee makes a lease for years, reserving rent to him and his assigns during the term, this reservation shall not determine by the death of the lessor as was once wrongly

[illegible]

ruled, but the rent shall go to his heir (*a*), for though there be no mention of his heirs in the reservation, yet there are words which evidently declare the intention of the lessor to be that the payment of the rent shall be of equal duration with the lease, the lessor having expressly provided that it shall be paid during the term, consequently the rent must be carried over to the heir, who comes into the inheritance after the death of the lessor and would have succeeded in possession of the estate if no lease had been made and if the lessor assigns over his reversion, the assignee shall have the rent as incident to it, because the rent is to continue during the term, therefore it must follow the reversion, since the lessor made no particular disposition of it separate from the reversion (*b*)

If tenant in tail demise for years rendering rent to him and his heirs, this goes to the heir in tail (*c*).

If tenant for life, with power to make leases, demises, rendering rent to him, his heirs and assigns, it shall be adjudged to him in remainder (*d*).

One seised in fee lets for years reserving rent "during the term" to the lessor, his executors, administrators and assigns, and lessee covenants to pay it accordingly, and the lessor devises the reversion and dies, the reservation is good to continue the rent during the whole term, and the devisee shall have an action of covenant for non-payment (*e*).

If a copyholder by licence leases, rendering rent to him and his wife, and his heirs, where by the custom the wife has her free-bench, the wife shall have the rent as incident to the reversion (*f*).

If a lease be made by a husband, reserving rent to him for life, and to his wife for life, it will be a reservation during the life of the survivor (*g*).

A posthumous child, born after the next rent day had incurred, after the death of his father, is under the stat. 10 & 11 *W.* 3. c. 16 intitled to the intermediate profits of the lands settled, as well as the lands themselves, for that act of parliament was made to enable posthumous children to take estates as if born in their father's life time, though there should be no estate limited to trustees to preserve the contingent remainders (*h*).—Indeed it is now laid down as a fixed principle, that wherever such consideration would be for his benefit, a child *in ventre sa mere* shall be considered as absolutely born, for all the cases establish this point, that there is no distinction between a child *in ventre sa mere* and one actually born (*i*).

It may be observed that "heir" is the only word of privity in law

(*a*) Gilb. on Rents, 66; Shep. Touch. 113. (*b*) Com. Dig. tit. Rent. B. [illegible] (*c*) 2 Saund. [illegible] 219, 83[illegible], &c. [illegible]

(*d*) Cro. Eliz. 2[illegible] (*e*) Com. Dig. tit. Rent. B. [illegible] (*f*) [illegible] (*g*) [illegible] (*h*) [illegible] (*i*) [illegible] requisite to the reservation of rents, and in conditions; the heir being, in representation, in point of taking by inheritance, the same person with the ancestor (*a*).

A man may reserve a rent to himself for his life and a different rent to his heir (*b*).

If there be two joint-tenants, and they make a lease for years by parol, or deed-poll, reserving rent to one only, yet it shall enure to both. But if the lease had been indented, the reservation should have been good to him only to whom it was made, and the other should have taken nothing.—The reason of the difference is this: where the lease is by deed-poll, or by parol, the rent shall follow the reversion, which is jointly in both lessors, and the rather, because the rent being something given to the joint-tenant to whom it is reserved in retribution for the land, he ought to be seised of the rent in the same manner as he is of the land demised, which is equally for the benefit of his companion and himself; but where the lease is by deed indented, they are estopped to claim the rent in any other manner than it is reserved by the deed, because the indenture is the deed of each party, and no man shall be allowed to recede from his own solemn act Co. Litt. 47. A Gilb on Rents, 63

So, if two joint-tenants let by deed to *A* rendering to them 10*s. per ann* and only one seals the deed, the demise shall be but of a moiety, rendering only 5*s. per ann* (*c*).

If a rent be payable yearly without saying "during the said term," yet the payment must be made every year during the continuance of the lease (*d*).

If therefore a lease be made for years, provided that the lessor shall pay for it at *Michaelmas* and *Lady Day* 10*l.* by equal portions "during the term," though this rent is not made payable yearly, yet the law construes it to be so, because it is payable at the two feasts during the term, and then consequently it must be paid yearly; for if there be any omission of the payments in any one year during the lease, it is not paid at the two feasts during the term (*e*).

So, if a man demise for five years, rendering 100*l.* to be paid by equal portions during the term, it shall be paid yearly though that word was omitted (*f*).

If a lease be made rendering rent at two usual feasts of the year, without specifying what feasts, the law construes such payments to be made at *Michaelmas* and *Lady-day*, because those are the usual days appointed in contracts of this nature for payments (*g*)

So, if a man grants a rent of 10*l* to another payable at the two usual feasts of the year, this shall be intended by equal portions, though not so mentioned in the deed; because where there are two several

(*a*) Hob. 1[illegible] (*b*) Com Dig [illegible] Co Litt. 213 b 214 a
(*c*) Com Dig tit Rent (B 6) (*d*) Gilb on Rents, 51 (*e*) [illegible]
(*f*) Com. Dig tit Rent (B 3) (*g*) Gilb. on Rents, 61

days appointed for payment, it is the most equal construction, that a moiety of the rent shall be paid at each day (*a*).

If a man make a lease to another the 6th day of *August*, rendering yearly the rent of 40*s* at two terms of the year, *viz* at *Lady-day* and *Michaelmas*, by equal portions, though in this case by the appointment of the parties, *Lady day* be the first term mentioned, yet the first payment shall be made at *Michaelmas* ensuing the date of the lease; for without such transposition of the words of the deed, the intention of the parties could never be fulfilled, because the rent is reserved annually, and the lessor would lose the profits of one half year if the rent was not payable the first *Michaelmas*, and the lessee must enjoy the land from the date of the lease to the first *Michaelmas* without paying any thing, and so likewise from the last *Lady-day* of the term to the expiration of it; because though the rent ended in *August*, yet the payment was not to be made till the *Michaelmas* following, before which time the lease expired (*b*).

So, if a man makes a lease the 1st of *May*, reserving rent payable quarterly: this shall be intended quarterly from the making of the lease, for if the beginning of the quarter should be construed to be any other day than the date of the lease, the lessor would lose the profits of his land for some time, and consequently not have quarterly payment made during the continuance of the lease (*c*).

A rent was reserved half yearly from *Michaelmas*; an action brought for half a year's rent ending the 25th day of *March*, which was not half a year from *Michaelmas*; and the rent being reserved half yearly without mentioning any day, there must be a full half year before it is due; but otherwise, where it is made payable at such and such feasts, quarterly or half yearly, there though the quarter or half year in reality be not then expired, yet, as to the reservation and payment, it is (*d*).

If rent be reserved quarterly or half yearly, each apportionment of rent is a distinct debt (*e*).

Where there are special days of payment limited upon the *reddendum*, the rent ought to be computed according to the *reddendum*, and not according to the *habendum* but where the reservation is general, as half yearly or quarterly, and no special days are mentioned, there the half year or quarter must be computed according to the *habendum* (*f*).

If tenant in fee makes a lease for years to begin at *Michaelmas*, rendering 100*l.* *per annum* at *Michaelmas* and *Lady-day*, or within ten days after every feast; it seems to be the better opinion that the rent is due the last *Michaelmas-day* of the term, without any regard to the ten days; for the reservation being annual, at the two feasts, or within ten days, it shall be construed to be at the end of every ten days *during the term*, as most agreeable to the design of the contract; and therefore

(*a*) Gilb. on Rents, 51. (*b*) Ibid 49 (*c*) Ibid 50 (*d*) 7 Mod 97
(*e*) 2 Vent 129 (*f*) 2 Ld Raym 820 1 Salk 141 [illegible]

the law rejects the ten days after the last feast, because the term ending at *Michaelmas*, there cannot be ten days after it during the term, for payment of the rent This construction is the more reasonable, because to give the lessee his election to make the last payment either at *Michaelmas* or ten days after, were to put it in his power to avoid payment of the last half year's rent for if it could be construed not to be due till the end of the ten days, the lessor could never oblige him to pay it, because then the term would be ended before the rent became due; for the addition of the ten days was only to enlarge the time of payment, but not to prevent the payment, or to remit any part of the rent (*a*).

If a man, possessed of a term of one hundred years, make a lease for fifty, reserving rent to himself and his heirs, this rent determines at his death, for his heir cannot have it, because he cannot succeed to the estate, it being but a chattel interest, to which the rent, if it continues after the life of the lessor, must belong, and the executors cannot have it, because there are no words to carry it to them (*b*). [It would however form a part of the residuary estate, it is conceived, and be assets in the hands of the executor or administrator: and this construction is warranted by Lord *Hale* expressly in the case cited. For a term of years, being but a chattel real, is assets in the hands of the executor or administrator, and if such be the nature of the thing demised, the rent reserved upon it will of course accompany its principal, and not go to the heir (*c*)]

Where, however, an inheritor reserves rents, upon a lease for years, this shall not go to the executor, but to the heir, with the reversion, other than arrearages of it behind at the death of the testator (*d*)

Therefore where the lessor died upon *Michaelmas-day* between three and four o'clock in the afternoon, before sun-set, the rent being reserved payable on *Michaelmas-day*, the question was, whether the executor or the heir, or, which is the same, the jointress of the lessor, should have the rent? It was decreed that the rent should go to the heir or jointress, because at the time of the death of the lessor, there was no remedy nor means to compel the payment thereof (*e*)

Apportionment of rent.—At common law, rent cannot be apportioned, neither can a rent-charge, or rent-seck (*f*), but the reversioner becomes entitled to the accruing rent from the rent-day, antecedent to the decease of the tenant for life, whose representative was entitled only to the arrearages due at some rent-day before the death of the testator or intestate for the law does not apportion rent in point of time, neither does equity (*g*)

If, therefore, a tenant for life made a lease for years, and died th[illegible]

(*a*) 2 [illegible] Rep. 822 1 S[illegible] [illegible] Cro Jac 227, 233 (*b*) [illegible]
(*c*) 1 [illegible] 162 [illegible] Dig. tit. Rent (B 5) (*e*) Went. Off. [illegible]
(*d*) 2 S[illegible] 578 [illegible] 287 (*f*) C[illegible] p 14[illegible]
(*g*) 1 Salk 65 Ca. [illegible] 256 1 P Wms 392 2 P Wms 176

day before the rent was due, (which is not payable till the last moment of the day on which it is expressly reserved in the lease,) the rent was lost both to the executor and the reversioner, and the law being so, equity would not relieve (*a*).

The strict adherence to this rule of law was productive therefore of a very manifest and grievous injustice. This however has been in a great degree remedied by the statute 11 *G.* 2. *c.* 19. *s.* 15. which after reciting, that Whereas where any lessor or landlord, having only an estate for life, in the lands, tenements or hereditaments, demised, happens to die before, or on the day, on which any rent is reserved or made payable, such rent or any part thereof, is not by law recoverable by the executors or administrators of such lessor or landlord, nor is the person in reversion intitled thereto, any other than for the use and occupation of such lands, tenements, or hereditaments, from the death of the tenant for life, of which advantage hath often been taken by the under tenants, who thereby avoid paying any thing for the same; *enacts*, that Where any tenant for life shall happen to die before or on the day on which any rent was reserved or made payable upon any demise or lease of any lands, tenements, or hereditaments which determined on the death of such tenant for life, the executors or administrators of such tenant for life shall and may, in an action on the case, recover of and from such under-tenant or under-tenants of such lands, &c. if such tenant for life die on the day on which the same was made payable, the whole, or if before such day, then a proportion of such rent according to the time such tenant for life lived, of the last year or quarter of a year, or other time in which the said rent was growing due as aforesaid, making all just allowances or a proportionable part thereof respectively.

In a leading case on the above statute, (in which Lord *Hardwicke* inclined to extend the remedy to the representatives of a tenant in tail whose lease determined with his life,) the facts were these. Tenant in tail, remainder to the defendant in fee, leased for years, and died without issue a week before the day of payment of the half year's rent. The lessee at the day paid all the half year's rent to the defendant. The executor of the tenant in tail brought this bill for apportionment of the rent. By the L. C. *Hardwicke*, this point has never been determined, but this is so strong a case that I shall make it a precedent. There are here two grounds for relief in equity; the first arises on the statute of the 11 *G.* 2. the second arises on the tenant's having submitted to pay the rent to the defendant. The relief arising upon this statute, is either from the strict legal construction, or equity formed upon the reason of it. And here it is proper to consider, what the mischief was before the act, and what remedy is provided at common law. If tenant

(*a*) 2 P. Wms. 502.

for life, or any who had a determinable estate, died but a day before the rent reserved on a lease of his became due, the rent was lost: for no one was entitled to recover it. His representatives could not, because they could only bring an action for the use and occupation; and that would not lie where there was a lease, but debt or covenant. nor could the remainder-man, because it did not accrue in his time. Now this act appoints the apportioning the rent, and gives the remedy. But there are two descriptions of persons to whose executors the remedy is given: in the preamble, it is one having only an estate for life, in the enacting part it is, tenant for life. Now tenant in tail comes expressly within the mischief. I do not know how the judges at common law construe it, but I should be inclined in this court to extend it to them. I should make no doubt, were this the case of tenant in tail after possibility of issue extinct, for he is considered in many respects as tenant for life only he cannot suffer a recovery, he may be enjoined from committing waste, such as hurts the inheritance, as felling timber, though not for committing common waste, being considered as to that as tenant in tail Were it the case of tenant for years determinable on lives, he certainly must be included within the Act, though it says only tenant for life, it would be playing with the words to say otherwise. These cases shew the necessity of construing this Act beyond the words. Tenant in tail has certainly a larger estate than a mere tenant for life, for he has the inheritance in him, and may, when he pleases, turn it into a fee, but if he does not, at the instant of his death he has but an interest for life. Such too is the case of a wife tenant in tail *ex provisione mariti*. Upon this point I give no absolute opinion As to the equity arising from the statute, I know no better rule than this, *equitas sequitur legem*. Where equity finds a rule of law agreeable to conscience, it pursues the sense of it to analogous cases If it does so as to maxims of the common law, why not as to the reasons of Acts of Parliament? nay, it has actually done so, on the statute of forcible entry, upon which this court grounds bills, not only to remove the force, but to quiet the possession That Act requires a legal estate in possession. this court extends the reason to equitable interest. But I ground my opinion in this case upon the tenant's having submitted to pay the rent. He has held himself bound in conscience to pay it for the use and occupation of the land the last half year. He paid it to the defendant, which he was not bound to do in law. and in such case, the person he pays it to shall be accountable, and considered as receiving it for those who are in equity entitled to it. The division must be that prescribed by the statute, and then the plaintiff is entitled to such a proportion of the rent as accrued during the testator's life-time. And accordingly it was decreed (*a*).

(*a*) 1 [illegible] Ambl. 198. [illegible]

So, rent paid to receivers by tenants holding under demises determinable upon the decease of tenant in tail, who died without issue, was afterwards apportioned between the representative and the remainder-man. But in this case the Lord Chancellor *Thurlow* observed that the case of *Paget* and *Gee* (above cited from *Burn* and *Ambler*) seemed rather to be a decision what the statute ought to have done, than what it had done: but that the question here seemed to turn on another ground, that the tenant holding from year to year, or from period to period, from a guardian without lease or covenant, cannot be allowed to raise an implication in his own favour that he should hold without paying any rent to any body (*a*).

Thus, by the statute 11 *G.* 2. rent is apportionable where it has accrued on a lease determinable on the life of the tenant for life. Still however the rigid rule of law obtains as before the statute, where the estate does not so terminate, but continues notwithstanding the death of tenant for life, as where it is under a power, or by licence of the lord (if a copyhold), or not pursuant to the enabling statute 32 *H.* 8. in case of a tenant in tail; so that in either of these cases if the party die at any time before the accruing rent has become payable, his representatives, and his creditors, lose every benefit which they would have derived from his estate and the rent goes to the reversioner. Such being the case, we would recommend the parties concerned to attend to the suggestion of Lord Chancellor *Cowper*, who observed that the gift in law of the rent which the lessee of tenant for life obtained previous to the statute, by the death of tenant for life in the middle of a half year, might be guarded against by reserving the rent weekly (*b*).

Quit-rent will not be apportioned as between tenant for life and remainder-man (*c*).

If lessee for years of land, rendering rent, accepts a new lease from the lessor, of part of the land, which is a surrender of this part, the rent shall be apportioned, for this comes by the act of the parties (*d*).

If a man leases three acres for life or years rendering rent and after grants the reversion of one acre, the rent shall be apportioned (*e*).

A lease was made of land and a flock of sheep, rendering rent. All the sheep died. Several justices and serjeants were of opinion that the rent was apportionable and many others that it was not; but all thought that it was equitable and reasonable to apportion it and afterwards the case was argued in the reading of *Moore* the *Lent* follow-

(*a*) 2 Br. R. 6[illegible]. (*b*) 1 P. Wms. 392. (*c*) 10 Ves. 66.
(*d*) Vin. Abr. [illegible] (*e*) Ibid. 7.

ing, and it seemed to him and to four justices, that the rent should be apportioned, inasmuch as no default was in the lessee (*a*).

If a man being seised in fee of *Blackacre*, and possessed for twenty years of *Whiteacre*, leases both for ten years, rendering rent, and dies, by which the reversion of one acre comes to his heir, and the other acre to his executor, the rent, it seems, shall be apportioned, because it happens by act of law (*b*).

A lessee who grants or assigns part of his estate is, notwithstanding, liable on his covenant to pay the entire rent, for he cannot apportion it; the action as between lessor and lessee being personal and upon a mere privity of contract, and on that account transitory, as any other personal contract is (*c*).

But covenant lies against the assignee of the lessee of an estate for a part of the rent, as in such cases it is properly a real contract in respect of the land, and is local in its nature, and not transitory; and in case of eviction, the rent may be apportioned as in debt or replevin (*d*).

Where a man seised in fee of a manor holden in moieties by socage, and knight's service, (since abolished) and of a parsonage appropriate, leased them for an entire rent, and on his death, devised the manor for life, remainder in tail, it was held that the remainder-man, on a surrender to him of the estate for life, might distrain on the lessee for an apportionment of the rent, and that a bar to his avowry must shew the value of all the premises, and answer the rate of the apportionment. So, on an avowry for an entire rent, if the plaintiff plead eviction of part of the land by elder title, he must shew how much in value was evicted and how the rent ought to be apportioned (*e*).

But a lessee, who is evicted in consequence of a statute acknowledged by a former owner of the estate, cannot be sued by his lessor for an apportionment of the rent (*f*).

So, if I lease lands, reserving 20*l* rent yearly, and at the end of three quarters be evicted, the lessor shall have no rent, for rent shall never be apportioned in respect of time, for being one contract and one debt it cannot be divided and *annua nec debitum judex non separat* (*g*). Where there are two parceners, and one will take advantage of a forfeiture, and the other not, there must be an apportionment (*h*).

For by entry into any part of the premises demised, the rent is suspended. But if the lessor enter by virtue of a power reserved, or even as a mere trespasser, if the lessee be not evicted, it will be no suspension of the rent (*i*).

(*a*) Vin. Abr. tit. "Apportionment" (C 10). (*b*) Ibid. (B 3). (*c*) Cro. Eliz. 633, 637. Dyer [illegible]. 2 Lut's R 575. (*d*) Ibid. 581. (*e*) Cro. Eliz. 771. Cro. Jac. 160. (*f*) Cro. Eliz. 255. (*g*) 1 Salk. 65. (*h*) Vin. Abr. tit. "Apportionment" (A 28). 1 Salk. 186. (*i*) Bull. N. P. 165. 177. Cowp. 243.

Rent when due.—By the old law, it was demandable and payable before the time of sun-set of the day whereon it was reserved; for anciently the day was accounted to begin only from sun-rising, and to end immediately upon sun-set (*a*).

But Lord *Hale* held, that although the time of sun-set was the time appointed by the law to demand rent in order to take advantage of a condition of re-entry, and to tender it in order to save a forfeiture, yet the rent is not due until midnight: for if a man seised in fee, makes a lease for years, rendering rent at the feast of St *John the Baptist*, upon condition of re-entry for non-payment; now the lessor, if he will take advantage of the condition, must demand it at sun-set; yet if he dies after sun-set, and before midnight, his heir shall have this rent and not his executors, which proves that the rent is not due until the last minute of the natural day (*b*).

A difference, it seems, subsists between the case of a lease made by tenant in fee, or under a power, and that of one made by a bare tenant for life: in the latter case, if the lessor lives to the beginning of the rent-day, at which time a voluntary payment of rent may be made, that is sufficient to entitle the executor to the rent, rather than it should be lost; but in the former case, by the death of the lessor before the last instant, the rent will go along with the land to him in the reversion or remainder, because being payable on those days during the term, the lessee has till the last instant to pay his rent, and consequently the lessor dying before it was completely due, his representatives can make no title to it (*c*).

As to the time for the payment of rent, where a time certain is appointed for that purpose, neither agent nor principal is bound to attend at any other time; and if the thing be to be done on a day certain, but no hour of the day is set down wherein the same shall be done, in this case, they must attend such a distance of time before sun-set, that the money may be counted, and the demand should be made on the most notorious part of the premises (*d*).

[See also "Condition to re-enter on non-payment of rent" *post Chap.* X. *Sect.* II.]

Section II. *Of Taxes.*

It is a general principle that the occupier of the premises is liable to pay all parliamentary taxes and parochial rates, as respects the rights of the public

(*a*) Co. Litt. 302 a. 2 Pl. Com. 42. (*b*) 1 Saund. 287. (*c*) 1 Saund. 287, n. 17. (*d*) 4 Rep. 73. [illegible] 31.

Thus the land-tax is not the landlord's tax with respect to the public, though it is, as between landlord and tenant. In fact, the land itself, in the hands of the occupier, is the debtor to the public (*a*): the land-tax, therefore, is *primâ facie* the tenant's tax, because all the remedies are against him (*b*).

The land-tax differs from the poor's-tax. The landholder who receives the rent is to pay the land-tax, but the poor's-tax is payable by the occupiers. The occupier ought to be rated regularly by name: therefore as some particular person cannot be fixed upon who may be properly rated as occupier, it follows as a necessary consequence, that no rate can at all be made upon the premises (*c*).

The land tax acts, from the 4th of *W.* & *M.* c. 1. s. 13. and the 28th *G.* 3. *c.* 2. *s.* 17. & 35. to the present time, direct the tenant to pay the land tax in the first instance, and to deduct out of the rent so much of the rate as in respect of the said rent the landlord should and ought to pay and bear, and the landlords both mediate and immediate, according to their respective interests, are required to allow such deductions.

Under a covenant, therefore, in a building lease, by the tenant, to pay all the taxes, except the land-tax, the landlord is to pay only the *old* land-tax, and not the additional land-tax occasioned by the improvement of the estate; for the legislature did not mean that the whole of the land-tax in respect of *all* the rent should be borne by the original landlord, but each was to make that allowance in proportion to the rent that came to him (*d*).

Upon the same principle *A.* having granted a building lease to *B.* at the yearly rent of 7*l.* which estate *B.* improved and afterwards underlet at 54*l.* *per annum*, *A.* was held liable only to pay the land-tax in proportion to the old rent (*e*).

So, on a lease in which rent was reserved, to be paid "without any deduction or abatement whatsoever," it was resolved that as the land-tax act enables the tenant to deduct that tax out of his rent, he has in all cases a right to stop it, unless there is an express agreement to the contrary.

The owner of a quit-rent shall pay taxes only in proportion to what the land pays: but if the matter has been examined by the commissioners of the land-tax, the court of Chancery will not re-examine it (*f*).

A house within the limits of an hospital, appropriated to an officer of the hospital for the time being, is not assessable to the land-tax (*g*).

But a bill in equity will not lie for a tenant to be relieved out of the

(*a*) Dou[illegible] 226 [illegible]
(*b*) C[illegible] 2 Bu[illegible] 1053.
(*c*) 3 T. R. [illegible]
(*d*) 2 C[illegible] Bott. P. L. [illegible] 281.
(*e*) [illegible] T. R. [illegible] 2 Str. 1197.
(*f*) 1 P. Wms. 328.
(*g*) 1 H. Bl. P. 6[illegible]

arrears of rent, for taxes which he has actually paid on account of rent reserved to a charity, which appears to be exempted from taxes (*a*).

The act of the 7th *G.* 3. *c.* 37. exempting the owner of certain lands embanked from the river *Thames* from all taxes and assessments whatsoever, does not exempt the occupiers of houses built on such lands from the payment of the house and window duties imposed by stat. 38 *G.* 3. *c.* 40 (*b*).

Houses built on lands embanked from the *Thames*, pursuant to stat. 7 *G.* 3. *c.* 37. which vests those lands in the hands of the owners "free from taxes," are not liable to the general land-tax imposed by stat. 27 *G.* 3. though such act is conceived in general terms, and was passed subsequently to the act creating the exemption. Nor are such houses liable to the rates imposed by stat. 11 *G.* 3. *c.* 29 (*c*).

Of Party Walls.—The statute 14 *G.* 3. *c.* 78. is "An Act for the further and better regulation of buildings and party-walls;" but being very voluminous, we refer the reader to the Act itself. In the construction of that statute *Eyre*, C. J. observed, that it was easy to see that it was an ill penned law, and that its meaning was left uncertain (*d*).

The lessor of a house at a rack-rent, (there being no other person entitled to *any* kind of rent) is liable to contribute to the expences of a party-wall under the statute, though the lessee has improved the house demised (*e*).

So, if a lessee of a house at a rack-rent underlet it at an advanced rent, he is liable to contribute to the expences of a party-wall built under the statute, nor is the operation of the Act at all varied by any covenants to repair, entered into between the landlord and his tenant. In this case, *Eyre* C. J. said, I think that it was intended by the legislature that the tenant should pay a moiety of the expence to the person building the wall, and reimburse himself by deducting the amount out of the rent of his immediate landlord, leaving it to him to make his claim on such other persons as he may think liable: that appears to me to be the best construction for putting the business in a practicable shape. I should incline to that opinion, even if it were made out that the covenant on the part of the tenant [among the covenants on the part of the lessee was one to make "all needful and necessary reparations and amendments whatsoever,"] included this case, for though the conduct of the tenant might be a breach of covenant, it would be fitter that the damages should be settled in an action of covenant, than to break in on the rules established by the statute. I know of no way of executing this law, if we enter into all the derivative claims of different landlords. If the tenant pays the money, let him reimburse himself,

(*a*) 1 P. Wms. 12[illegible] (*b*) 8 T. R. 463. (*c*) 4 T. R. [illegible]
(*d*) 1 Bos. & Pul. [illegible] (*e*) [illegible] T. R. 21[illegible]. [illegible] T. R. 461.

and leave the other parties to dispute among themselves. And *Buller* J. (who entirely agreed with the C. J.) said, There are three parties in this business, the man who built the wall, the tenant, and the tenant's immediate landlord. The owner of the adjoining house pursued the directions of 14 G. 3. c. 78. which gave him a right to call on the plaintiff (the tenant) for a moiety of the expence, that being settled, how does the case stand between the tenant and his landlord? I agree that we must not consider whether the landlord be the owner of an improved rent, but [illegible] he has an improved rent, since he receives more than the person of whom he took the premises; and if the landlord has the improved rent, he certainly is liable, though there be only one year of the term to come. As to the question, whether the expence can be [illegible], that does not arise here, but if any thing could be found to warrant the opinion thrown out by Lord *Mansfield* in *Stone* v. *Greenwell* (cited in 3 *T. R.* 46.) that the parties might be liable to a rateable proportion in some cases, it would tend much to the advancement of justice. The building a party wall is certainly a great improvement to the premises, and every person interested in the fee and receiving a benefit from it, ought to contribute (*a*).

It is [illegible] clear that the owner of the improved rent, not of the ground rent, is liable to pay the expences of a party-wall built under the statute (*b*).

But where the tenant of a house covenanted in his lease to pay a reasonable share and proportion of supporting, repairing, and amending all party-walls, &c. and to pay all taxes, duties, assessments, and impositions parliamentary and parochial, "it being the intention of the parties that the landlord should receive the clear yearly rent of 60*l.* in net money without any deduction whatever;" during the lease the proprietor of the adjoining house built a party wall between that house and the house demised, under stat. 14 *G.* 3. c. 78. held that it was the tenant, not the landlord, who was bound to pay the moiety of the expence of the party-wall. [illegible], said Lord *Kenyon*, the covenants in the lease render it necessary to consider which of the parties would have been liable under the Act of Parliament [illegible]. We collect the intention from the whole of the instrument. If this had rested itself merely upon a covenant to pay taxes, &c. I should not have thought a tenant liable, but here is a covenant that the landlord should have the rent clear and net. A covenant is always taken most strongly against the covenantor. I cannot bring my mind to doubt from the whole but that the tenant should pay the whole. *Grose* J. This is as if the landlord had reserved a clear rent charge to himself. *Lawrence* J. The intention of the parties was that the landlord should have his rent free from any charge. It is not necessary to decide which party is the

(*a*) 1 B. & P. 30. (*b*) 5 T. R. 150.

owner of the improved rent. *Le Blanc* J. I ground myself on the covenant that the tenants should pay a reasonable proportion of the party-wall (*a*).

A lessee for twenty-one years at a pepper-corn rent for the first half-year and a rack rent for the rest of the term, who by agreement was to put the premises in repair, and covenanted to pay the land-tax and all other taxes, rates, assessments, and impositions, having assigned his term for a small sum in gross, was held not to be liable to pay the expence of a party-wall, either by the provisions of the stat. 14 *G.* 3. c. 78. or the covenant; for where the parties contract for a lease at rack-rent, the landlord is the person who ought to bear the expence of such party-wall (*b*). So, where the parties stand, as in the principal case, in the relation of landlord and tenant, the former is liable under the Act of Parliament to pay the expence; for the legislature intended to throw the burden on the lessees of building leases, by whom the value of the estates is considerably improved, and who afterwards made under-leases reserving improved rents (*c*).

If however a large sum were paid for the purchase of a lease, the original lessee, though no improved rent were reserved to him, would, it seems, be liable to pay this expence within the Act of Parliament (*d*).

The three months' notice required by s. 38. of the 14 *G.* 3. c. 78. is necessary only where the person who at the time when it is necessary to build, &c. is liable to pay, cannot agree with the owner of the adjoining house (*e*).

The penalty of 10*l.* inflicted by s. 67. of the statute, for not having the new building surveyed, is recoverable against the master builder, where the regulations of the Act are not complied with, and not against the proprietor of the premises (*f*).

SECTION III. *Of the Poors-Rates.*

The foundation of the Poor Laws was laid by the stat. 43 *Eliz.* c. 2. which was passed for the best of purposes, namely, to compel the idle to be industrious, and to relieve the wants of the unfortunate, and afford them those comforts which they are disabled to procure from infirmity or age: from neglect and abuse however, its provisions, and those of many other Acts passed for the same wise and benevolent purposes, are in a great measure frustrated.

By sect. 1. of the stat. of *Eliz.* it is enacted, "that the churchwardens of every parish, and four, three, or two substantial house-holders

(*a*) 8 T. R. 602. (*b*) 5 T. R. 158. (*c*) Ibid. (*d*) Ibid.
(*e*) 5 T. R. 130. (*f*) 3 Esp. R. 223.

there, as shall be thought meet, having respect to the proportion and greatness of the same parish and parishes, to be nominated yearly in *Easter* week, or within one month after *Easter*, under the hand and seal of two or more Justices of the Peace in the same county, whereof one to be of the *Quorum*, dwelling in or near the same parish or division where the same parish doth lie, shall be called overseers of the poor of the same parish. And they, or the greater part of them, shall take order from time to time, by and with the consent of two or more such Justices of the Peace as is aforesaid, for setting to work the children of all such whose parents shall not, by the said churchwardens and overseers, or the greater part of them, be thought able to keep and maintain them, and use no ordinary and daily trade of life to get their living by. And also to raise weekly or otherwise (*by taxation of every inhabitant*, parson, vicar, and other, *and of every occupier* of lands, houses, tithes, impropriate, propriations of tithes, coal-mines, or saleable under-woods, in the said parish, in such competent sum and sums of money as they shall think fit) a convenient stock of flax, hemp, wool, thread, iron, and other necessary ware and stuff, to set the poor on work. And also competent sums of money for and towards the necessary relief of the lame, impotent, old, blind, and such other among them, being poor, and not able to work, and also for the putting out such children to be apprentices, to be gathered out of the same parish, according to the ability of the same parish, and to do and execute all other things as well for the disposing of the said stock, as otherwise concerning the premises, as to them shall seem convenient."

Sect. 4. "It shall be lawful, as well for the present as subsequent churchwardens and overseers, or any of them, by warrant from any two such Justices of Peace as is aforesaid, to levy as well the said sums of money and all arrearages, of every one that shall refuse to contribute according as they shall be assessed, by distress and sale of the offender's goods, as the sums of money or stock which shall be behind upon any account to be made as aforesaid, rendering to the parties the overplus; and in defect of such distress, it shall be lawful for any two such Justices of the Peace to commit him or them to the common gaol of the county, there to remain without bail or mainprise, until payment of the said sum, arrearages, and stock. And the said Justices of the Peace, or any of them, to send to the house of correction or common gaol such as shall not employ themselves to work, being appointed thereunto as aforesaid; and also any such two Justices of Peace to commit to the said prison every one of the said churchwardens and overseers who shall refuse to account, there to remain without bail or mainprise, until he have made a true account, and satisfied and paid so much as upon the said account shall be remaining in his hands."

Sect. 19 enacts "That if any action of trespass or other suit shall happen to be attempted and brought against any person or persons, for taking of any distress, making of any sale, or any other thing done, by authority of this present Act, the defendant or defendants, in any such action or suit, shall and may either plead not guilty, or otherwise make avowry, cognisance, or justification for the taking of the said distresses, making of sale, or other thing done by virtue of this Act, alledging in such avowry, *&c.* that the said distress, sale, trespass, or other thing, whereof the plaintiff or plaintiffs complained, was done by authority of this Act, and according to the tenor, purport, and effect of this Act, without any expressing or rehearsal of any other matter or circumstance contained in this present Act, to which avowry, cognisance, or justification, the plaintiff shall be admitted to reply, That the defendant did take the said distress, made the said sale, or did any other act or trespass supposed in his declaration, of his own wrong, without any such cause alledged by the said defendant whereupon the issue in every such action shall be joined, to be tried by verdict of twelve men, and not otherwise, as is accustomed in other personal actions: And upon the trial of that issue the whole matter to be given on both parties in evidence, according to the very truth of the same, and after such issue tried for the defendant, or nonsuit of the plaintiff after appearance, the same defendant to recover treble damages, by reason of his wrongful vexation in that behalf, with his costs also in that part sustained, and that to be assessed by the same jury, or writ to enquire of the damages, as the same shall require."

By stat. 17 *G.* 2. *c.* 37. waste lands improved and drained shall be rated to the relief of the poor within such parish and place which lies nearest to such lands and the Justices in general quarter sessions may hear and determine disputes concerning the same, and cause the land to be fairly assessed in such parish as they shall think proper *s.* 1, 2.— But the allotments of the sessions shall not affect the boundaries of parishes, other than for the purposes of rating such laws (*a*)

On inclosure of waste in the parish of *A* on which the land-holders of the parish of *B* have right of common appurtenant, the allotments given in lieu of that right shall be assessed to the poor of the parish of *A*. The common itself *quasi* common was certainly not rateable, not being the subject of occupation, but if at all it must have been assessed as an accessory to the principal at *B* (*b*).

So, where the inhabitants of one parish had common appendant in certain waste grounds which lay in another parish, and the question was whether the commoner should pay taxes for this and should be assessed in the parish where the waste lay, or in that wherein his farm lay? it was held, that he ought to be assessed where his farm lay, for

(*a*) 1 Const's Lett. 81 [illegible]

(*b*) Ibid pl. 128. 2 Bl. R. 1245

that the common is incident, and could pass by grant of the farm, &c. So that it should be considered as part of the farm, and the farm to be taxed the higher (*a*)

But a farmer, it seems, is not rateable for the stock on his farm necessary for its manurance, though for superabundant riches and stock he ought to be rated (*b*)

The poors rate is not a tax on the land, but a personal charge in respect of the land.—In general, the farmer or occupier, and not the landlord, is liable to this tax, for the poors-rate is a charge upon the occupier in regard to his possession, and not on the lessor in regard to the rent received (*c*)

The occupier of land is rateable to the poor, and it is immaterial by what tenure he holds it, or whether he has any title, or not (*d*) for if a disseisor obtain possession of land, he is rateable as the occupier of it. If a man does not live within a parish, he is to be assessed according to his land; but if he live within the parish, he is to be rated as dwelling there (*e*)

The Act 20 *G.* 3 *c* 17. *s.* 19 for regulating the right of voting does not, in the form of assessment that it gives, prevent parishes from rating landlords or other persons by name, or they may still declare their intention to rate the landlord (*f*).

But payment of a poors rate assessed on the occupier of a house is not in itself evidence of occupation by the party so paying (*g*)

Every inhabitant ought to be rated according to the present value of his estate, whether it continue of the same value as when he purchased it, or be rendered more valuable by the improvements which he has made on it. If a person choose to keep his property in money, and the fact of his possessing it be clearly proved, he is rateable for that. but if he prefer using it in the melioration of an estate or other property, he is rateable for the same in another shape. Suppose a person has a small piece of land in the heart of a town, which is only of small value, and he afterwards build on it, he must be rated to the poor according to its improved value with the building upon the land.—In short, in whatever way the owner makes his estate more valuable, he is liable to contribute to the relief of the poor in proportion to that improved estate (*h*).

So personal property, if visible, and yielding a certain annual permanent profit, is rateable

It may be stated, therefore, as a general proposition, that the imme-

(*a*) 1 Salk 169

(*b*) 1 Const's Bott 115 pl 150, 151 2 Ld Raym 1281 4 Burr 2297 Cowp 452

(*c*) 2 Const's Bott 92 pl 122

(*d*) 1 T R 341 7 ibid. 593, 6[illegible]3

(*e*) 1 Const's Bott 93 pl 125

(*f*) 2 Ibid 268 pl 280

(*g*) R v P[illegible], Sitt at Westm after E T 1800 T's MSS

(*h*) 6 T R 155 7 T R 549

6

diate profits of land (some mines excepted) are a proper subject of assessment, or, to speak more correctly, that the person who is in possession of the immediate profits of land may be taxed to the relief of the poor in respect of those profits (*a*).

The court is not precluded, by the Sessions stating in the case "that the party rated is the occupier," from examining into the propriety of that conclusion, if Sessions also state all the circumstances of the case, and desire to have the opinion of the superior Court upon the whole (*b*). Where, however, the Sessions found that the master gunner at *Seaford* was the "occupier" of the battery-house there, which was the property of the Crown, and from whence he was removeable at pleasure, it was held that the *fact* found, of his being "the occupier," precluded any other question, and fixed his liability to be rated (*c*).

Where the aftermath of a meadow was vested in Trustees with power to let the same in pastures for cattle, and they let it out to various persons, but not for any certain term, or in any certain proportions, at so much a head for horses, &c., it was held that the Trustees must themselves be taken to be the occupiers of the land, and were consequently rateable for the same (*d*).

In the case of St *Luke's* Hospital, and of *Chelsea* Hospital, the officers are rateable as occupiers. The corporation of *London* are not *de facto* the occupiers of *St Bartholomew's* Hospital, the poor are occupiers; but they are not rateable.

The general rule of law must be followed, which is, "That you must find an occupier to be rated." The poor people cannot be rated at all; the servants cannot be rated as occupiers; nor can the corporation be charged as occupiers (*e*).

For property is not rateable to the poor, unless there be some person in the beneficial occupation of it (*f*).

Therefore, the trustees of a Quaker's meeting-house, of which no profit is made by pews, &c. are not rateable. So, a person employed by the Philanthropic Society to superintend the children at annual wages, under an agreement that he shall have a "dwelling-house free from taxes, &c." with certain other perquisites, and who may be dismissed at a minute's warning on receiving three months' wages, is not rateable as the occupier of the house provided by the Society, she having no distinct apartment in the house but a bed-chamber, and her family not being allowed to live there (*g*).

But the occupiers of a charitable foundation in the actual occupation of the alms house and lands for their own benefit, in the manner prescribed by the rules of the constitution, and liable to be dismissed

(*a*) 2 H. Bl. 260. (*b*) 5 T. R. 587. (*c*) 3 T. R. 497.
(*d*) 13 East R. 155. (*e*) 4 Bur. 2439. 2 Bur. 1053. 1063. 1 Bl. R. 250. (*f*) 4 T. R. 730. (*g*) 5 T. R. 79. Ibid. 587.

for any breach of such rules, are rateable in respect of such occupation (*a*)

Therefore the master of a free-school, appointed by the minister and inhabitants of the parish under a charitable trust, whereby a house, garden, &c. were assigned "for the habitation and use of the master and his family, freely without payment of any rent, income, gift, sum of money, or other allowance, whatsoever," for teaching ten poor boys of the inhabitants, is rateable for his occupation of the same. for it is not like the case of an exemption by Act of Parliament, by which the legislature had a right to bind every person, for here the party was appointed by deed, and only those who are parties to a deed are bound by it (*b*).

A corporation seised of lands in fee for their own profit are within the meaning of stat. 43 *Eliz* c 2 inhabitants and occupiers of such lands, and in respect thereof liable in their corporate capacity to be rated to the poor (*c*).

But the possessions of the Crown or of the public are not rateable to the relief of the poor and as to public buildings, those are such as are applied to public purposes (*d*)

A warehouse may be rated to the proprietor or occupier according to the use to which it is applied If it be left for instance to the excise or custom-house for public purposes, the burthen must be borne by the proprietor: but if it be afterwards converted to a private use, the occupier of it will be liable to the rates (*e*).

Therefore, stables rented by the Colonel of a regiment, by order of the Crown, for the use of the regiment, are not liable to be rated (*f*)

But persons holding houses or lands under the Crown, or under any hospital, if for their own separate benefit, are liable to be rated (*g*)

The ranger of a royal park, therefore, is rateable, as for inclosed lands in the park yielding certain profits —But he is not rateable for the herbage and pannage, which yield no profit (*h*)

Tolls directed by Act of Parliament to be applied to public purposes were held not to be rateable (*i*).

But lands purchased by a company, and converted into a dock, according to Act of Parliament, which declares that the shares of the proprietors shall be considered as personal property, are rateable in proportion to the annual profits (*k*).

An exemption in a private statute in 12 *Car* 2. of lands given to charitable uses "from all public taxes, charges and assessments whatsoever, civil or military," extends to the poors-rate (*l*).

(*a*) 1 East's R 584 (*b*) 6 T R. [illegible] (*c*) Cowp 79 83, 84
(*d*) 2 T R 375 2 Bos & Pul 129 (*e*) 4 T R 8 (*f*) 2 T R 375
(*g*) 3 T R [illegible] (*h*) 1 T R 358 2 H. Bl R 26[illegible] (*i*) 4 T R 75[illegible]
(*k*) 1 T R 21[illegible] (*l*) 5 T R 622

The masters in chancery are not rateable as occupiers of their respective apartments in *Southampton Buildings* under the Paving Act 11 G 3. c. 22., for they are for public purposes, and the masters have no individual benefit in them (a)

If the owner of a house occupy part of it, he is liable to be rated for the whole, unless there be a distinct occupation of the rest by some other person (b)

Houses, shops and sheds which render an annual revenue, are rateable to the poor (c).

A house and engine for carding cotton, which are rented as one entire subject, and described by the general name of "an engine-house," may be rated. So may the profits of a weighing machine-house (d)

A person entitled to toll tin and farm dues (which are certain portions of the tin raised by the adventurers in the tin-mines) is liable to be rated in respect thereof (e)

Lead-mines, it has been held, are not rateable to the poor. But a lessee (under the Crown) of lead mines, is rateable for the profits arising from lot and cope, which are duties paid him by the adventurer without risk on his part (f).

The lessee of a coal-mine has even been held to be rateable, though he derived no property from the mine; the mine being rateable property. If the property be rateable, and the party rated be in the occupation of it, the Court cannot examine any farther and enquire whether or not the tenant has made an unprofitable bargain. Suppose a landlord makes so hard a bargain with his tenant, that the latter derives no benefit from the farm, must not the tenant be rated to the poor? The landlord certainly is not liable (g).

So, a slate-work, (or as it is improperly called a slate mine) is rateable to the poor (h).

Linen works are rateable in the hands of the occupier, though there be risk and expence in the working, and the profits be uncertain (i).

The objects of a charitable foundation in the actual occupation of the alms house and lands for their own benefit in the manner prescribed by the rules of the constitution, and liable to be discharged for any breach of such rules, are rateable in respect of such occupation (k)

Where *A* having granted to *B* a lease for years of way-leaves (for the purpose of carrying coals,) and the liberty of erecting bridges, and levelling hills over certain lands, *B.* made the waggon ways, inclosed

(a) 2 Bos & Pull 1[illegible]9 (b) 4 T R 477 (c) 1 Const's Bott 11[illegible] pl 144
(d) 1 T R 727 (e) 3 T P 48[illegible] (f) 1 B R 2[illegible]9 Cowp 451
(g) 5 T R 596 (h) 2 East's R [illegible] (i) 1 East's R 5[illegible]
(k) Ibid 584.

them, thereby excluding all other persons, erected bridges, and built two houses on the lane for his servants. [illegible] was held to be liable to be rated to the poor for "the ground called the waggon-way (*a*)."

But a mere easement is not rateable. Therefore, a party who has an exclusive right to use a way leave, paying so much *per* [illegible] for the goods carried over it, is not liable. *Quære*, Whether the owner of the land who receives a profit for such way-leave, is not liable to be rated for such an increase of value: for it is not a grant of the profits of the land (*b*).

The proprietors of tithes are liable to be rated; therefore fish being titheable by custom, such tithe is rateable: for the legislature intended that, when rates are made for the relief of the poor, every person should contribute according to the benefit which he receives within the parish. Here the parties receive a certain benefit arising from the tithe of fish in this parish, and run no risk whatever. To say that only property which is visible should be rated, is carrying the rule of exemption too far; for oblations and other offerings, which constitute the rectorial or vicarial dues, are rateable (*c*).—If a rector makes a verbal lease of his tithes for a year, and the lessee let the tithes to the respective landholders for sixpence *per* acre more than he is to pay the rector, the lessee is the occupier of the tithes, he having them in such a manner as to make a profit of them (*d*).

A sum of money made payable by the owners of lands in lieu of tithes by Act of Parliament, with a clause of [illegible], is liable to the poors rate: for it is a mere composition for tithes, which were before subject to the poors rate; and the superadding a power of distress does not turn it into a rent, but rather proves the contrary; for if it were a rent, the distress would be incident to it, without any special provision in the Act (*e*).

So payments in lieu of tithes settled under a compromise between a parson and a parish, and confirmed by Act of Parliament, are rateable (*f*).

A parson is rateable for his tithes as the occupier of a tenement; so is a vicar; and the liability is not removed, though he lets his tithes to the parishioners; and the tax must be upon the parson and not upon the lessee of his tithes (*g*).

Quit-rents, and other casual profits of a manor, are not rateable.—But ground rents are rateable (*h*).

If *A* rent a quantity of land together with a mineral spring arising therefrom, at a gross yearly rent, he is rateable to the poor for the whole

(*a*) [illegible] R. [illegible] 3 T. R. 9[illegible] (*b*) 3 T. R. [illegible]
[illegible] (*d*) C[illegible] P. [illegible]
(*e*) [illegible]
(*f*) 3 P. [illegible] R. [illegible] 113 [illegible]

of such rent, though the annual value of the mere land is only in proportion of two to eight of the reserved rent.

Whether or not chambers in an Inn of Court are rateable is undetermined: the fact of their being extra-parochial does not seem to be a sufficient ground of exemption, for if it were, the poor of extra-parochial places would be deprived of the benefit of the statute of *Elizabeth*, which has been construed to extend to them.—However, most of the old colleges being extra-parochial, are upon that ground not rateable (*a*).

The overseers and churchwardens may make a poors-rate, without the concurrence of the parishioners: and if a rate be necessary, they may be compelled by *mandamus* to make it. But such rate is not binding till allowed by two Justices out of sessions, for the sessions cannot order an original rate to be made, and the allowance by the Justices is compellable by *mandamus* (*b*).

How to be made and raised.—A rate being made by the churchwardens and overseers, it is proclaimed in the church, when it becomes formal and public. If any one feel aggrieved by the making of the rate (he need not be damnified by the rate), he must appeal to the next sessions, and if any point of law arise on hearing the appeal, it may be removed into the Court of King's Bench, by *certiorari*, in order to be determined.

The stat. 17 *G.* 2. *c.* 3. *s.* 1. after reciting that, Whereas great inconveniences do often arise in cities, towns corporate, parishes, townships, and places, by reason of the unlimited power of the churchwardens and overseers of the poor, who frequently on frivolous pretences, and for private ends, make unjust and illegal rates in a secret and clandestine manner, contrary to the true intent and meaning of a statute made in the forty and third year of the reign of Queen *Elizabeth*, intituled, "An Act for the Relief of the Poor," enacts, That the churchwardens and overseers, or other persons authorized to take care of the poor in every parish, township, or place, shall give or cause to be given public notice in the church, of every rate for the relief of the poor, allowed by the Justices of the peace, the next Sunday after the same shall have been so allowed, and that no rate shall be esteemed or reputed valid or sufficient, so as to collect and raise the same, unless such notice shall have been given.

If a poors-rate be not published in the church on the *Sunday next* after it is allowed, it is a nullity, and payment under it cannot be enforced, though there be no appeal to the sessions. Supposing the parish officers were to give notice of the rate at some other public place in the parish, it would not be sufficient, though it may be equally notorious.

(*a*) 2 Com. R. 534.
(*b*) 2 Ld Raym. [illegible] 1 Ibid. 798. 1 Barnard. [illegible] 1 Bl. R. 63[illegible]

The omission is a radical defect in the rate itself which nothing can cure (*a*).

In an action of trespass by a person whose goods were distrained for non-payment of the rate, the publication of the rate under the stat. 17 *G.* 2. *c.* 3. must be proved (*b*).

The superior court cannot enter into the inequality of the rate, unless it appear to them to be self evidently, necessarily, and unavoidably unequal: they cannot presume it to be so (*c*). The Justices at the sessions are the proper judges respecting the equality or inequality of the rate (*d*). The distinction between orders of Justices, and special verdicts has been long established: in the latter, where it concludes generally, the whole case must appear upon record; but the very reverse is the rule which obtains in the case of orders of Justices, for the Court will intend every thing to be right which does not appear to be otherwise, and they will not entertain any doubt upon a subject upon which the Justices did not (*e*).

By stat. 17 *G.* 2. *c.* 3. the overseers shall permit the inhabitants to inspect every rate at all seasonable times, on payment of 1*s.* and shall on demand give copies thereof to any inhabitant at the rate of 6*d.* for twenty-four names: on penalty of 20*l.* for refusal. And true copies of all rates for the relief of the poor shall be entered in a book within fourteen days after any appeal from any such rate is determined, which the overseers shall attest by their names thereto, which book shall be kept for public perusal. *s.* 2, 3, 13.

And overseers neglecting to execute this Act, shall, if no other penalty is provided, forfeit to the poor not exceeding 5*l.* nor less than 20*s.* *s.* 14. And where there are no churchwardens, overseers may perform all matters relating to the poor. *s.* 15.

Where a statute says that a company shall not be liable to any rate which had not *usually* been assessed, it only means, that they shall not have any other *kind* of rate imposed on them than those which were then levied, but does not fix the proportion of the rate (*f*).

Where to be collected.—A person shall be rated for profits, where they become due, not where they happen to be received (*g*).

Where a navigation ran from *A.* to *B.* through several intervening parishes, and the tolls for the whole navigation were collected in those two parishes, it was holden that they might be assessed in the two parishes for the whole amount according to the proportion collected in each (*h*).

A barge way and toll gate in the hamlet of *Hamptonwick*, purchased by the city of *London*, by virtue of stat. 17 *G.* 3. *c.* 18. (for completing the navigation of the *Thames*, and empowering the city to levy tolls and

(*a*) 4 T. R. [illegible] (*b*) 8 T. R. 661. (*c*) 4 T. R. 291. (*d*) 6 T. R. 635. 6.
(*e*) 2 [illegible] 294, 575. (*f*) 2 [illegible] 662. (*g*) Ibid. (*h*) Ibid.

duties towards the charges of navigation,) was held to be rateable for such tolls as became due there, notwithstanding the tolls were collected in a different parish (*a*)

The grantee of the navigation of the river *Ouse*, is rateable to the poor of *Cardington* in respect to the tolls arising there, though he himself resides, and the tolls are collected, elsewhere (*b*)

So, where a Navigation Act empowered the proprietors to take so much *per* mile *per* ton for all goods carried along the canal, it was holden, that they were rateable to the poor for the tolls in the different parishes where the tolls became due, that is, where the respective voyages finished, though for their own convenience they were authorized to *collect* the tolls where they pleased, and did in fact collect them in other parishes (*c*)

So, where by a Navigation Act the proprietor was entitled to a toll of 4*s. per* ton for goods carried from *A.* to *B.* or from *B.* to *A.* and to a proportionable sum for any less distance, and was also enabled to appoint any place of collection; it was holden that the tolls for goods carried the whole voyage from *A.* to *B.* were rateable in *B.* though in fact they were collected in a parish between *A.* and *B.* because the tolls become due where the voyage is completed (*d*).

County Justices cannot rate a parish within their jurisdiction, *in aid* of another parish, lying within a borough which has an exclusive jurisdiction, though within the same hundred and county (*e*)

By stat. 17 *G.* 2. *c.* 38. *s.* 12. it is enacted, That where any person or persons shall come into or occupy any house, land, tenement, or hereditament, or other premises, out of, or from which any other person assessed shall be removed, or which at the time of making such rate was empty or unoccupied, that then every person so removing from, and every person so coming into, or occupying the same, shall be liable to pay such rate in proportion to the time that such person occupied the same, respectively in the same manner, and under the like penalty of distress, as if such person so removing had not removed, or such person so coming in or occupying had been originally rated and assessed in such rate, which said proportions, in case of dispute, shall be ascertained by two justices of the peace.

By stat. 43 *Eliz.* *c.* 2. *s.* 4. (*ante*) the present as well as subsequent overseers are empowered to levy the poor-rate and arrears thereof by distress, as therein directed. And the warrant may be granted as well by city Magistrates as by country Justices, (r. 6 [illegible]) though the distress has relation to taxes to which they are liable. 16 *G.* 2. [illegible]

Distress for Poors-Rate.—By stat. 17 *G.* 2. *c.* 38. *s.* 7. "for the more effectual levying money assessed for the relief of the poor," it is enacted,

[illegible]

That the goods of any person assessed and refusing to pay, may be levied by warrant of distress, not only in the place for which such assessment was made, but in any other place within the same county or precinct; and if sufficient distress cannot be found within the said county or precinct, on oath made thereof before some Justice of any other county or precinct, (which oath shall be certified under the hand of such Justice on the said warrant,) such goods may be levied in such other county or precinct by virtue of such warrant and certificate; and if any person shall find him or herself aggrieved by such distress as aforesaid, it shall and may be lawful for such person to appeal to the next General or Quarter Session of the Peace for the county or precinct where such assessment was made; and the Justices there are hereby required to hear and fully determine the same. And in case any person refuse to pay the present overseers, the succeeding overseers may levy the arrears and reimburse their predecessors. [See also 11 *G.* 3. c. 23. s. 9.]

By stat. 27 *G.* 2. c. 20. the Justices granting such warrant of distress shall therein order the goods so to be distrained to be sold within a certain time to be limited in such warrant, so as it be not less than four days, nor more than eight days; unless the sum for which such distress shall be made, together with the reasonable charges of taking and keeping such distress, be sooner paid. And the officer may deduct the charges of taking, keeping, and selling such distress, out of the money arising from the sale, and also the sum distrained for. But he shall, if required, shew the warrant to the party distrained upon, and shall permit a copy thereof to be taken. s. 1, 2.

A distress and sale, indeed, given by statute, is in the nature of an execution.

By stat. 28 *G.* 3. c. 49. s. 12. Justices acting for adjoining counties and personally resident in one of them, may grant warrants of distress; and the acts of any officer in obedience thereto shall be as valid as if they had been granted by Justices acting for the proper county; but such warrants must be directed and given in the first instance to the constable or other officer of the county to which they relate, and such constable, &c. may take persons apprehended, &c. before Justices in the adjoining county. And by stat. 33 *G.* 3. c. 55. where sufficient distress cannot be found within the jurisdiction of the Justice who granted the warrant, it may, on being backed by a Justice of another county, be executed therein. Also by 28 *G.* 3. c. 49. s. 4. Justices for counties at large may act as such within any city being a county of itself situate therein or adjoining to such county, provided they are Justices for such city.

By 17 *G.* 2. c. 38. s. 8. to prevent all vexatious actions against overseers of the poor, it is enacted, that where any distress shall be made for any sum of money *justly due* for the relief of the poor, the distress itself shall not be deemed to be unlawful, nor the party making it be deemed a trespasser, on account of any defect, or want of form in the warrant for the appointment of such overseers, or in the rate or assessment, or in the warrant of distress thereupon; nor shall the party distraining be deemed a trespasser *ab initio*, on account of any irregularity, which shall be afterwards done by the party distraining, but the party aggrieved by such irregularity, shall or may recover full satisfaction for the special damage sustained thereby, and no more, in an action of trespass, or on the case, at the election of the plaintiff or plaintiffs.

Note. A warrant may be made to distrain before the time for which the rate is made is expired (*a*). The practice in those cases has been to grant a conditional warrant to distrain, and by *Holt*, C. J. *communis error facit jus* (*b*).

A constable may levy a poors-rate on goods in another parish, for though he cannot execute out of his own district a warrant directed generally to all constables, yet he may execute any where within the limits of the Justice's jurisdiction, a warrant directed particularly to him (*c*).

A distress for a poors rate for lands not in the occupation of the plaintiff may be replevied notwithstanding the Sessions on appeal had confirmed the rate, the determining that a man may be assessed for what he does not occupy being an excess of jurisdiction (*d*).

The granting of a warrant of distress by magistrates to enforce payment of a poors-rate, is a judicial, not a ministerial act (*e*). Before a distress for the rate be levied, a summons should go to the party, that he may have an opportunity to shew that he has paid for it, or otherwise to exonerate himself: for a poors rate cannot be distrained for before it be demanded and the payment thereof refused (*f*).

If a landlord tender the poors rate for his tenant, the overseers must receive it, and a warrant ought not to be granted to distrain upon the tenant (*g*).

If a landlord direct a tenant, who is overseer of the poor, to pay on the landlord's account, rates irregularly assessed on him, and promises that the levies shall eat out the rent, the tenant may set them off, or prove them as payment in an action for use and occupation (*h*).

If personal property be rateable, it is not to be done at random, and to leave the party rated to get off as he can, but the officer making the rate must be able to support what he has done by evidence (*i*).

Where a person is overcharged in a poors rate, the Sessions may re-

(*a*) Bull. N. P. 82. (*d*) 1 Const's Bott. 242 pl. 230. (*g*) 1 Ld. Raym. 545.
(*b*) 2 Bl. R. 1330. (*e*) 7 T. R. 270. (*f*) 1 Const's Bott. 242 pl. 230.
(*c*) [illegible] 212 pl. 239. Doug. [illegible] (*h*) 3 Taunt. 76. (*i*) 4 T. R. [illegible]

have him on appeal, and amend the rate, by lessening the sum assessed on him, under the 17 *G.* 2. *c.* 38 (*a*).

The stat. 21 *J.* 1. *c.* 12. enacts, That Justices of the peace, mayors, bailiffs, churchwardens, and overseers of the poor, constables, and other peace officers, may plead the general issue, and give the special matter in evidence. It also enacts, That any action brought against them shall be laid in the proper county, and if upon the general issue pleaded the fact shall appear to be done in another county, the jury shall find the defendant not guilty.

By stat. 7 *J.* 1. *c.* 5. If case, trespass, battery or false imprisonment shall be brought against any Justice of the peace, mayor, bailiff, constable, &c. concerning any thing by them done by virtue of their office, they may plead the general issue, &c. and if the verdict shall pass with the defendant, or the plaintiff shall be nonsuited, or suffer any discontinuance thereof, the defendant shall have his double costs allowed by the Judge before whom the matter is tried.

This act has been construed to extend to under-sheriffs and deputy-constables, though they are not particularly mentioned (*b*).

Now stat. 21 *J.* 1. *c.* 12 extends this Act to churchwardens and overseers of the poor (*c*).

The officers must get a certificate from the Judge, that the action was brought against him for something done in the execution of his office, in order to entitle himself to double costs (*d*).

Likewise the stat. 24 *G.* 2. *c.* 44. enacts, that no writ shall be sued out against a Justice for what he shall do in the execution of his office, till notice in writing of such intended writ shall have been delivered to him, or left at the usual place of his abode a month before, and the Justice may tender amends, and in case the same is not accepted, plead such tender in bar to the action, together with the plea of not guilty, and any other plea with leave of the Court, and if upon issue joined thereon the jury shall find the amends so tendered to have been sufficient, then they shall give a verdict for the defendant. It likewise enacts, That no action shall be brought against any constable or other officer, or any other person acting by his order, for any thing done in obedience to a Justice's warrant, until demand be made of the perusal and copy of such warrant, and the same has been refused for the space of six days, and in case the warrant be shewed and a copy taken, and afterwards an action be brought against the constable, without making the Justice who signed or sealed the warrant, a defendant, the jury shall, on producing the warrant, find a verdict for the defendant, notwithstanding any defect of jurisdiction in the Justice, and if such action be brought jointly against the Justice and him, upon producing the warrant, the jury shall

(*a*) 2 T. R. 6[illegible] (*b*) Bul. N. P. 332 (*c*) Ib. (*d*) Ib.

find for him and if they find against the Justice, the plaintiff shall recover the costs he is to pay to such defendant against the Justice, with a proviso, that if the Judge certify that if the injury was wilfully and maliciously committed, the plaintiff shall be entitled to double costs: and a proviso likewise, that such action shall be commenced within six calendar months after the act committed.

The above Act extends only to actions of tort.

The officer must prove that he acted in obedience to the warrant, and where the Justice cannot be liable, the officer is not within the protection of the Act (*a*)

If a man be imprisoned on a Justice's warrant on the first day of *January*, and kept in prison till the first day of *February*, he will be in time if he brings his action within six months after the first of *February*, for the whole imprisonment is one entire trespass The Justice having pleaded tender of amends, the plaintiff obtained a rule for the defendant to bring the money into Court for the plaintiff to take the same, upon discontinuing his action (*b*).

An overseer of the poor, who distrains for a poors-rate under a Justice's warrant, is an officer within the protection of the Act (*c*).

But a churchwarden taking a distress for a poors-rate under a warrant of magistrates, is intitled to the protection of 24 *G* 2. *c*. 44. in having the magistrates made defendants with him in an action of trespass (*d*)

Upon a distress for a poors-rate being replevied, the Justices who granted the warrant need not be joined, according to the directions of the 24 *G* 2. *c* 44., for replevin is an action *in rem*, to which the statute has never been held to extend and so (it was said) with respect to an action of trespass, if an excess of jurisdiction has been, and the assessment was *coram non judice*, for such is not like the case where the Justice hath a general jurisdiction, and whose warrant the officer is implicitly bound to obey (*e*)

Overseers cannot be guilty of trespass in levying a poors-rate by distress, although the rate is objectionable, if the party has not appealed to the Sessions: neither does any defect in the rate unappealed from, avoid the warrant (*f*).

No action of debt will lie for a poors-rate (*g*)

Whether the representative of a party assessed to the poors rate be liable to distress for the rate, seems doubtful. It seems clear, however, that the representative is entitled to notice, before his testator's or intestate's goods are distrained: in order that he may have the same opportunity of exempting them from the distress, as his testator or intestate would have had (*h*).

(*a*) 2 Bur 1766 (*b*) Bull N P 24. (*c*) Ibid I cited 24[illegible] (*d*) 2 Bl R 1,31 [illegible] 7 T R. 270 (*f*) 1 Cowp's Bott 256 pl 242. 1 Bur. 587. (*g*) 2 Bur 11_7 (*h*) Ibid 1 Bl R. 284, s. c.

As to what is distrainable for a poors rate, the principle of a distress being a pledge, does not in this case obtain as it does in respect of rents and amerciaments. In this instance the duty is personal, and the thing distrained is in satisfaction of the non-performance of it, and not as in the old common law distresses, in the nature of a *nomine pœnæ*, to compel payment (*a*). The solid distinction is, that the seizing under the 43 *Eliz.* and such like Acts of Parliament, is but partly analogous to the common law distress (as being replevisable, *&c.*), but is much more analogous to the common law execution, like a *fieri facias*, where the surplus, after sale, shall be returned (*b*).

Therefore money, it seems, may be distrained for a poors rate. So the tools of a man's trade, his wearing apparel, and all other articles necessary to enable him to earn the money for which the goods are taken (*c*). So, beasts of the plough are distrainable for the poors-rate, even although there were other distrainable goods on the premises; on the principle of analogy to an execution (*d*).

The Appeal.—With respect to the particular grounds and the course of appeal, the reader is referred to stats. 5 *G.* 2. *c.* 19. 17 *G.* 2. *c.* 38. & 41 *G.* 3. *c.* 23. and to the cases thereon in 1 *Const's Bott's Poor Laws.*

(*a*) 1 Bur. 588. (*b*) 1 Willes, 169. (*c*) 1 Const's Bott. 242. pl. 230. p. 229. (*d*) 1 Bur. 588.

CHAPTER IX.

Of the general Incidents to Leases (continued.)

SECTION I. *Of Waste; wherein of Fixtures.*

SECTION II. *Of Common of Estovers.*

SECTION III. *Of Emblements.*

SECTION I. *Of Waste.*

WASTE, *vastum*, is a spoil or destruction in houses, gardens, trees, or other corporeal hereditaments, to the disherison of him that hath the remainder or reversion in fee-simple or fee-tail (*a*) — Waste, is either *voluntary*, which is a crime of commission, as by pulling down a house, or it is *permissive*, which is a matter of omission only, as by suffering it to fall for want of necessary reparations, both of which are equally injurious to him that hath the inheritance (*b*) Voluntary waste chiefly consists in 1st felling timber-trees; 2dly, pulling down houses, 3dly, opening mines, or pits, 4thly, changing the course of husbandry, 5thly, destroying heirlooms (*c*).

Whatever does a lasting damage to the freehold or inheritance is waste, therefore, removing wainscot, floors, or other things once fixed to the freehold of a house, is waste With respect however to what shall be deemed fixtures of such a nature, or under such circumstances as that they can or cannot be removed by an out-going tenant, or taken by his executor, or by the heir, the law is much less strict at this day, than it used to be. The old and general rule of law was, that whatever was fixed to the freehold became part of it, and could not be taken away. But of late years there have been exceptions to this rule (*d*). The first is between landlord and tenant, the latter of whom may now take away during the term all chimney-pieces, and even wainscot put up by himself, so of beds fastened to

(*a*) Co. Litt. 53
(*b*) 1 Cruise's Dig tit 3 s 14.
(*c*) Wood's Inst 521
(*d*) 3 Atk 16 n. 1.

the ceiling with ropes, nay even though nailed, and all such things necessary for trade, as brewing utensils, furnaces, coppers, fire-engines, cyder-mills, &c. as he has himself put up or erected (*a*).

But such removal must be *within the term*, otherwise he will be deemed a trespasser. Thus, where tenant for years made an under-lease of a house to *J. S.* who was by trade a soap-boiler: *J. S.* for the convenience of his trade, put up vats, coppers, tables and partitions, and paved the back-side, &c. and now upon a *fieri facias* against *J. S.* which issued on a judgment in debt, the Sheriff took up all these things, and left the house stripped and in a ruinous condition, so that the first lessee was liable to make it good, and therefore brought a special action on the case against the Sheriff and those that bought the goods, for the damage done to the house. *Et per Holt* C. J. it was held, 1st. that during the term, the soap-boiler might well remove the vats he set up in relation to trade, and that he might do it by the common law, (and not by virtue of any special custom) in favour of trade and to encourage industry: but after the term, they became a gift in law to him in reversion, and are not removeable, 2dly. that there was a difference between what the soap-boiler did to carry on his trade, and what he did to complete the house, as hearths and chimney-pieces, which he held not removeable, [the latter however at least, are now removeable,] 3dly, that the Sheriff might take them in execution, as well as *the under-lessee might remove them*, and so this was not like tenant for years without impeachment of waste: in that case he allowed the Sheriff could not cut down and sell, though the tenant might, and the reason is, because in that case, the tenant hath only a bare power without an interest, but here the under-lessee hath an interest as well as a power, as tenant for years hath in standing corn, in which case the Sheriff can cut down and sell (*b*).

Where the tenant, however, has by law a right to carry away any erections or other things, on the premises which he has quitted, the inclination of Lord *Kenyon's* mind was that he had a right to come on the premises, for the purpose of taking them away: but as to that point, the defendant in the principal case had let judgment go by default (*c*).

In trover for ten load of timber, the case was, that the defendant had been tenant to the plaintiff, and erected a barn upon the premises, and put it upon pattens and blocks of timber lying upon the ground, but not fixed in or to the ground: and upon proof that it was usual in that country to erect barns so, in order to carry them away at the end of the term, a verdict was given for the defendant (*d*). But though Lord Chief Justice *Treby* thought proper in that case, to take

(*a*) 1 Atk. 477, 8.
(*b*) 1 Atk. 477. 1 Salk. 368.
(*c*) 4 Esp. R. 33.
(*d*) Bull. N. P. 34.

advantage of the custom of the country, yet it is apprehended that it would now be determined in favour of the tenant without any difficulty.—But when a purchaser of lands had brought an ejectment against the tenant from year to year, and the parties had entered into an agreement that judgment should be entered for the plaintiff, with a stay of execution till a given period, though in such agreement no mention was made of any buildings or fixtures, it was held that the tenant could not in the mean time remove buildings (a wooden stable standing upon rollers) or fixtures (posts or rails) from the premises, which he had himself erected before action brought; because the fair interpretation of such agreement was, that the defendant should in the mean time do no act to alter the premises, but should deliver them up in the same condition, as when the agreement was made, and judgment signed. For though he would clearly have been entitled to take away the articles, if he had done it during the continuance of his term from year to year, yet by the agreement the parties had made a new contract, which put an end to the term (s).

If however, a man sells a house where there is a copper, or a brewhouse where there are utensils, unless there was some consideration given for them, and a valuation set upon them, they would not pass (t).

In an action of covenant brought by the plaintiff against the defendant who had been his lessee, under a lease containing a covenant that the lessee should leave all the buildings which then were, or should be erected on the premises during the term, in repair, &c. the breach assigned was, that the defendant took down and carried away two sheds, which had been erected during the term. The defendant pleaded performance of the covenants and issue was taken on the breach as above assigned. The buildings in question were two sheds, called *Dutch* barns, which had been erected by the defendant during his term, and which his counsel contended he had a right to remove. Lord *Kenyon.*—If a tenant will build upon premises demised to him a substantial addition to the house, or add to its magnificence, he must leave such additions at the expiration of the term, for the benefit of his landlord. But the law will make the most favourable construction for the tenant, where he has made necessary and useful erections for the benefit of his trade or manufacture, and which enable him to carry it on with more advantage. It has been held so in the case of cyder-mills, and in other cases, and I shall not narrow the law, but hold erections of this sort, made for the benefit of trade, or constructed as the present, to be removeable at the end of the term. It was then contended, that by the express words of the covenant the tenant was

(s) 1 H. B. 258. (t) 1 Atk. 175.

to leave all erections on the premises at the end of the term Lord *Kenyon.*—I am aware of the full extent of that, and not quite sure that it concludes the question. It means that the tenant should leave all those buildings which are annexed to and become part of the reversionary estate (*a*) [See Lord *Ellenborough's* Notice of this *Nisi Prius* Case, in *Elwes* v. *Maw*, 1 East's R 38]

A covenant by a tenant to yield up in repair at the expiration of his lease all buildings which should be erected during the term upon the demised premises includes buildings erected and used by the tenant for the purpose of trade and manufacture, if such buildings be let into the soil, or otherwise fixed to the freehold, but not where they merely rest upon blocks or pattens (*b*)

Fixtures.—Hangings, pier-glasses, &c though forming part of the wainscot and fixed with nails and screws to the freehold, are not to be taken as part of the freehold, but are removeable by the lessee of the house (*c*).—So marble chimney-pieces may be removed by the tenant (*d*).

To trespass for breaking and entering, &c and pulling down and taking away certain buildings, &c the defendant, as to the breaking and entering, suffered judgment by default, and pleaded not guilty as to the rest It was held, that such plea was sustained by shewing that the building taken away, which was of wood, was erected by him as tenant of the premises, on a foundation of brick, for the purpose of carrying on his trade, and that he still continued in possession of the premises at the time when, &c. though the term was then expired.—At the trial, Lord *Kenyon* observed, that the mere erection of a chimney would not prevent the right of taking away the rest of the building, which surrounded it, where the trade was carried on In *Dudley* and *Dudley*, a steam-engine, to which a chimney necessarily belonged, was held to be removeable. Modern determinations have, for the benefit of trade, allowed many things to be removed, which the rigour of former determinations, considering them as fixed to the freehold, prohibited. The case of cyder-mills is familiar to us all. The construction ought to be favourable to the tenant, and my opinion is, that he was warranted in removing the building in question; but I will reserve the point (*e*) And upon the case being argued afterwards, his Lordship said, That the old cases upon this subject leant to consider as realty whatever was annexed to the freehold by the occupier, but in modern times the leaning has always been the other way in favour of the tenant, in support of the interests of trade, which is become the pillar of the state. What tenant will lay out his money

(*a*) [illegible] Esp. R. 11 (*b*) 1 Taunt. 1[illegible] (*c*) 1 P. Wms. [illegible]
(*d*) [illegible] (*e*) [illegible] Esp. R. [illegible]

in costly improvement of the land, if he must leave every thing behind him which can be said to be annexed to it? Shall it be said, that the great gardeners and nurserymen in the neighbourhood of this metropolis, who expend thousands of pounds in the erection of greenhouses, hot-houses, &c. are obliged to leave all these things upon the premises, when it is notorious that they are even permitted to remove trees, or such as are likely to become such, by the thousand, in the necessary course of their trade? If it were otherwise, the very object of their holding would be defeated. This is a description of property divided from the realty; and some of the cases have even gone further in favour of the executor of tenant for life against the remainder-man, between whom the rule has been holden stricter, for it has been determined that the executor of tenant for life was entitled to take away the fire-engine of a colliery. The case of *Fitzherbert* v. *Shaw* (1 *H. Bl. R.* 258. *vide ante.*) turned upon the construction of an agreement that such things should be left on the premises, and decided nothing against the general principle. Here the defendant did no more than he had a right to do: he was in fact still in possession of the premises at the time the things were taken away, and therefore there is no pretence to say that he had abandoned them. And by *Lawrence* J. it is admitted that the defendant has a right to take these things away during the term; and all that he admits upon this record against himself by suffering judgment to go by default as to the breaking and entering is, that he was a trespasser in coming upon the land, but not a trespasser *de bonis asportatis*; as to so much therefore he is entitled to judgment (*a*).

Another exception is between tenant for life or in tail, and the reversioner or remainder-man. The former also, may remove brewing utensils, furnaces, coppers, fire-engines, cyder-mills, &c. which he has erected, and by which he not only enjoys the profit of the estate, but carries on a species of trade; and if he does not remove them in his lifetime, they go to his executor (*b*). Reasons of public benefit and convenience have tended to establish this principle; and indeed it is but consonant to common ideas of justice: as for instance, in the case of a fire-engine, it is very well known that little profit could be made of coal mines without such an engine, and tenants for life would be discouraged in erecting them, if they must go from their representatives to a remote remainder-man, when the tenant for life might possibly die the next day after the engine was set up (*c*). So, emblements go to the executor, and not to the remainder-man, the public being interested in the produce of corn and other grain. But corn growing belongs, it is said, to a devisee of land, and not to the

(*a*) 2 La. R. [illegible] (*b*) [illegible] (*c*) [illegible] Atk. [illegible] executor. Though a devisee of goods, stock and moveables shall take it from both (*a*). Hangings, chimney-glasses, or pier glasses, being matters of ornament and furniture, do not go with the house, but to the executor (*b*)

The rule however still holds as between heir and executor: the freehold descending on the heir, the executor cannot enter to take away fixtures without being a trespasser (*c*). Indeed, in questions between the heir or devisee and the executor, cupboards, presses, lockers and other fixtures of the like kind, may with propriety enough be considered as annexed to and parts of the freehold. The law will presume, that it was the intention of the owner under whose bounty the executor claimeth, that they should be so considered, to the end that the house might remain to those, who by operation of law or by bequest should become intitled to it, in the same plight he put it, or should leave it, entire and undefaced But in capital cases Mr. Justice *Foster* (*d*) was of opinion, that such fixtures which merely supply the place of chests and other ordinary utensils of household, should be considered in no other light than as mere moveables, partaking of the nature of those utensils, and adapted to the same use. Therefore in favour of life, a distinction is to be taken between cases relative to mere property and such wherein life is considered ---An action of trover (*e*) was brought by the plaintiffs as administrators of *Robert Lawton* against the defendant for certain salt-pans which were put into wyche houses in *Cheshire*. The pans were brought in pieces The wyche houses are of no use without the pans, nor is the brine of any use without them. There was room for the workmen to walk round them within the building. The pans were fixed by brick and mortar to the floor of the building, and there was a furnace under it. The building and lodging rooms at the end of it; which building, with the pans, let for 8*l* a week. The question was, whether these pans were to go to the executor or to the heir. The ancestor was seized in fee Lord *Mansfield* delivered the opinion of the Court. All the old cases (and there are some to be found in the year-books, see *Shep. Touch*. 469, 470.) lean in favour of the heir, and so rigidly, that if a tenant was to put up a wainscot or pictures let into the wainscot, *&c.* he could not take them away. There has been a relaxation of two species of property, the one between landlord and tenant, as marble chimney-pieces, and things which are necessary for trade, *&c.* and in the removal of these there is no hurt to the landlord. The tenant says, I leave the premises just as I found them The other species in which there has been a relaxation is, between tenant for life and the remainder-man. If the former has been at any expence for the benefit of the estate, as by erecting a fire-

(*a*) Bull. N. P. 34 (*b*) 1 P. Wms. 94 (*c*) 1 Atk. 477 (*d*) Fost. 139
(*e*) Lawton v. Lawton, B. R. East 22 G. 3. cited [illegible] 3 Atk. 16 & 1 H. Bl. R. 259 [illegible]

engine, or any thing else by which it may be improved, in such case it has been determined that the fire-engine should go to the executor, on a principle of public convenience, being an encouragement to lay out money in improving the estate, which the tenant would not otherwise be disposed to do. The same argument may be applied to the case of tenant for life and remainder-man, as to that of landlord and tenant, namely, that the remainder man is not injured, but takes the estate in the same condition as if the thing in question had never been raised. The tenant for life will not erect such things unless they can go to his executor. But I cannot find any case (except that about the cyder-mill) where there has been any relaxation between the heir and executor. That case is not printed at large, but it most probably turned upon a custom. Now consider the present case, which is very strong. A salt brine in the county of *Cheshire* is a most valuable inheritance. But there is no enjoying the inheritance without the buildings and salt-pans: they are of no use but for that purpose and the inheritance is of no value without them. To the executors they can be worth no more than old iron and old bricks, if taken away: he could never mean therefore, to give them to the executor, and put him to the expence of taking them away without any advantage to him, who could only have the old materials, or a contribution from the heir in lieu of them. Here the ancestor erected them at his own expence on his fee simple. It is impossible that he should mean them to be severed at his death, for they are worth nothing to an executor, and very valuable to the heir, who gains 8*l per* week by them. On the reason of the thing therefore, and the intention of the testator, they must go to the heir. It would have been a very different consideration, if this salt brine had been let to a tenant who had erected these pans. There he might have said, I was at the expence of erecting them, and therefore my executor should have them, and I leave the estate as I received it: that as I stated before, would be for the encouragement and convenience of trade, and the benefit of the estate. Therefore we are of opinion they go to the heir. Judgment for the defendant.

This subject, so important to every one in the situation of landlord or tenant, is treated in a manner so elaborate and perspicuous by the present learned and noble Chief Justice of the Court of *King's Bench*, in the judgment delivered by him in the case of *Elwes* v. *Maw* (*a*), that the information which we are desirous to convey to our readers would be incomplete were we to forbear to insert any part thereof.

The immediate point decided was, that a tenant in agriculture, who erected at his own expence and for the mere necessary and convenient occupation of his farm, a beast-house, carpenter's shop, fuel house, cart-house, pump-house, and fold-yard wall, which buildings were of

(*a*) 3 East R. [illegible]

brick and mortar, and tiled, and let into the ground, cannot remove the same, though during his term, and though he thereby left the premises in the same state as when he entered.

In delivering the judgment of the Court, Lord *Ellenborough*, having stated the above facts of the case, said, The question for the opinion of the Court was, Whether the defendant had a right to take away these erections? Upon a full consideration of all the cases, we are all of opinion that the defendant had not a right to take away these erections.

Questions respecting the right to what are ordinarily called fixtures, principally arise between three classes of persons. 1st. Between different descriptions of representatives of the same owner of the inheritance, viz. between his heir and executor. In this first case, *i. e.* as between heir and executor the rule obtains with the most rigour in favour of the inheritance, and against the right to disannex therefrom, and to consider as a personal chattel any thing, which has been affixed thereto. 2dly. Between the executors of tenant for life or in tail, and the remainder man or reversioner, in which case the right of fixtures is considered more favourably for executors, than in the preceding case between heir and executor. The 3d case, and that in which the greatest latitude and indulgence have always been allowed in favour of the claim to having any particular articles considered as personal chattels, as against the claim in respect of freehold or inheritance, is the case between landlord and tenant.

But the *general rule* on this subject is that which obtains in the first mentioned case, *i. e.* between heir and executor, and that rule was found in the year-book 17 *E.* 2. *p.* 518. and laid down at the close of *Herlakenden's* case, (4 *Co.* 64. and *Co. Litt.* 53. in *Cooke* v. *Humphrey*, *Moore*, 177. and in Lord *Darcy* v. *Askwith*, *Hob.* 234. and in other cases) is that where a lessee, having *annexed* any thing to the freehold during the term, afterwards takes it away, it is waste. But this rule at a very early period had several exceptions attempted to be engrafted upon it, and which were at last effectually engrafted upon it, in favour of trade and of those vessels and utensils which are immediately subservient to the purposes of trade. In the year book 42 *E.* 3. 6. the right of the tenant to remove a furnace erected by him during his term is doubted and adjourned. In the year-book of the 20 *H.* 7. 13 *a.* & *b.* which was the case of trespass against executors for removing a furnace fixed with mortar by their testator and annexed to the freehold, and which was holden to be wrongfully done, it is laid down, that "If a lessee for years make a furnace for his advantage, or a dyer make his vats or vessels *to occupy his occupation during the term*, he may remove them; but if he suffer them to be fixed to the *earth after the term*, *they then belong to the lessor*. And so of a baker. And it is at his will to remove such things within the term by some, and this shall be against the opinions aforesaid." But the rule in this extent in favour of tenants is doubted afterwards in 21 *H.* 7. 27. and narrowed there, by allowing that the lessee for years could only remove, within the term, things fixed to the ground, and not to the walls of the principal building. However in process of time the rule in favour of the right in the tenant to remove utensils set up in relation to trade became fully established: and accordingly we find Lord *Holt* in *Poole's* case, *Salk.* 368. laying down, (in the instance of a soap boiler, an under tenant whose vats, coppers, &c. fixed had been taken in execution, and on which account the first lessee had brought an action against the sheriff,) that "during the term the soap-boiler might well remove the vats he set up in relation to trade;" and that he might do it by common law, and not by virtue of any special custom, "in favour of trade, and to encourage industry," but that after the term they became a gift in law to him in reversion, and were not removeable. He adds, that there was a difference between what the soap-boiler did to carry on "his trade" and what he did to complete "his house" as "hearths and chimney-pieces," which were held not removeable. The indulgence in favour of the tenant for years during the term has been since carried further, and he has been allowed to carry away matters of ornament, as ornamental marble chimney-pieces, pier-glasses, hangings, wainscot fixed only by screws, and the like. *Beck* v. *Rebow*, 1 *P. Wms* 94. *ex parte Quincy*, 1 *Atk.* 477 and *Lawton* v. *Lawton*, 3 *Atk.* 13. [see also *ante.*] But no adjudged case has yet gone the length of establishing that buildings subservient to purposes of agriculture, as distinguished from those of trade, have been removeable by an executor of tenant for life, nor by the tenant himself who built them during his term. In deciding whether a particular fixed instrument, machine, or even building, should be considered as removeable by the executor, as between him and heir, the Court in the three principal cases on this subject (*viz.* 3 *Atk.* 13 *Ambler* 113. and 1 *H. Black.* 259 in *n.* [and *Atk. s. c.*] may be considered as having been decided mainly on the ground, that where the fixed instrument, engine, or utensil, (and the building covering the same falls within the same principle,) was an accessory to a matter of a personal nature, that it should be itself considered as personalty. The fire-engine in 3 *Atk.* and *Ambler*, was an accessory to the carrying on the trade of getting and vending coals, a matter of a personal nature. Lord *Hardwicke* says, in the case in *Ambler*, "A colliery is not only an enjoyment of the estate, but *in part carrying on a trade.*" And in the case in 3 *Atk.* he says, "One reason that weighs with me is its being a *mixed* case, between enjoying the profits of the lands, and carrying on a *species of trade*, and considering it in this light, it comes very near the instances in brewhouses, &c. of furnaces and coppers." Upon the same principle, Lord C. B. Comyns may be considered as having decided the case of the cyder-mill, [illegible] between enjoying the profits of the land and carrying on a species of trade; and as considering the cyder-mill as properly an accessory to the trade of making cyder (a). In the case of the salt-pans, Lord Mansfield does not seem to have considered them as accessory to carrying on a trade, but as merely the means of enjoying the benefit of the inheritance. He says, "The salt-spring is a valuable inheritance, but no profit arises from it unless there be a salt-work, which consists of a building, &c. for the purpose of containing the pans, &c. which are fixed to the ground. The inheritance cannot be enjoyed without them. They are accessories necessary to the enjoyment of the principal. The owner erected them for the benefit of the inheritance." Upon this principle he considered them as belonging to the heir, as parcel of the inheritance for the enjoyment of which they were made, and not as belonging to the executor, as the means or instruments of carrying on a trade. If however, he had even considered them as belonging to the executor, as utensils of trade, or as being removeable by the tenant, on the ground of their being such utensils of trade, still it would not have affected the question now before the Court, which is the right of a tenant for agricultural purposes to remove buildings fixed to the freehold, which were constructed by him for the ordinary purposes of husbandry, and connected with no description of trade whatsoever; and to which description of buildings no case (except the Nisi Prius case of Dean and Allalley, Esp. R.) before Lord Kenyon, and which did not undergo the subsequent review of himself and the rest of the Court, has yet extended the indulgence allowed to tenants in respect to buildings for the purposes of trade. In the case in Bull. N. P. 34. of *Culling* v. *Tuffnal*, before Lord C. J. *Treby*, at *Nisi Prius*, he is stated to have holden that the tenant who had erected a barn upon the premises, and put it upon pattens and blocks of timber lying upon the ground, but not fixed in or to the ground, might by the custom of the country take them away at the end of his term. To be sure he might, and that without any custom, for the terms of the statement exclude them from being considered as *fixtures*; "they were not fixed in or to the ground." In the case of *Fitzherbert* v. *Shaw*, 1 H. Bl. 258. we have only the opinion of a very learned Judge indeed, Mr. J. *Gould*, on what would have been the right of the tenant, as to [illegible] shed built on brick-work, and some posts and rails which he had erected, if the tenant had done so during the term; but [illegible] tenant was [illegible] to his new contract, the question, what the tenant might have done in virtue of his right under the old term, if [illegible], could never have come judicially before him. No.

Prius; and when that question was offered to be argued in the Court above, the counsel were stopped, as the question was excluded by the new agreement. As to the case of *Penton* v. *Robart*, 2 *East's R.* 88, it was the case of a varnish-house, with a brick foundation let into the ground, of which the wood-work had been removed from another place, where the defendant had carried on his trade with it. It was *a building for the purpose of trade*, and the tenant was entitled to the same indulgence in that case, which, in the cases already considered, had been allowed to other buildings for the purposes of trade, as furnaces, vats, coppers, engines, and the like. And though Lord *Kenyon*, after putting the case upon the ground of leaning, which obtains in modern times, in favour of the *interests of trade*, upon which ground it might be properly supported, goes further, and extends the indulgence of the law to the erection of green-houses and hot-houses by nurserymen, and indeed by implication to buildings by all other tenants of lands; there certainly exists no decided case, and, I believe, no recognized opinion or practice on either side of *Westminster Hall*, to warrant such an extension. The *Nisi Prius* case of *Dean* v. *Allaley* (reported in Mr. *Woodfall's* book, and Mr. *Espinasse*, 3, 2 vol. 11.) is a case of the erection and removal by the tenant of two *sheds* called *Dutch barns*, which were, I will assume, unquestionable fixtures. Lord *Kenyon* says, "The law will make the most favourable construction for the tenant, where he has made necessary and useful *erections* for the *benefit of his trade* and *manufacture*, and which enable him to carry it on with more advantage. It has been so holden in the case of cyder-mills and other cases; and I shall not narrow the law, but hold erections of this sort made for the benefit of trade, or constructed as the present." Lord *Kenyon* here uniformly mentions the *benefit of trade*, as if it were a building subservient to some purpose of trade, and never mentions agriculture, for the purposes of which it was erected. He certainly seems, however, to have thought that buildings erected by tenants for the purposes of farming, were, or rather *ought to be* governed by the same rules which had been so long judicially holden to apply to buildings for the purposes of trade. But the case of buildings for trade has been always put and recognized as *a known allowed exception* from the general rule, which obtains as to other buildings, and the circumstance of its being so treated and considered, establishes the existence of the general rule to which it is considered as an exception. To hold otherwise, and to extend the rule in favour of tenants in the latitude contended for by the defendant, would be, as it appears to me, to introduce a dangerous innovation into the relative state of rights and interests holden to subsist between landlords and tenants. But its danger or probable mischief is not so properly a consideration for a court of law, as whether the adoption of such a doctrine would be an *innovation at all*; and being of opinion that it would be so, and contrary to the uniform current of legal authorities on the subject, we feel ourselves, in conformity to and in support of those authorities, obliged to pronounce that the defendant had no right to take away the erections stated and described in this case.

If a house be destroyed by tempest, lightning, or the like, which is the act of Providence, it is no waste and the stat. 6 *Ann* c 31 enacts, that no action shall be prosecuted against any person in whose house any fire shall accidentally begin; with a proviso that the Act shall not defeat any agreement between landlord and tenant (*a*). It seems to be somewhat doubtful whether tenant by the curtesy is within this statute. So, of tenants in dower (*b*).

Waste may be done in houses, by pulling them down, or suffering them to be uncovered, whereby the rafters or other timber of the house are rotten: but the bare suffering them to be uncovered, without rotting the timber, is not waste. So, if a house be uncovered when the tenant cometh in, it is no waste in the tenant to suffer the same to fall down. But though the house be ruinous at the tenant's coming in, yet if he pull it down it is waste, unless he re-edify it again yet if a house built *de novo* was never covered in, it is no waste to abate it. Also, if glass-windows (though glazed by the tenant himself) be broken down or carried away, it is waste, for the glass is part of his house. If the house be uncovered by tempest, the tenant must in convenient time repair it and though there be no timber growing upon the ground, yet the tenant must at his peril keep the house from wasting (*c*).

The law favours the support and maintenance of houses for the habitation of mankind therefore if two or more joint-tenants or tenants in common be of a house of habitation, and the one will not repair the house, the other shall have by the law a writ of *de reparatione faciendâ*, and the writ saith *ad sustentationem ejusdem domûs teneantur* So it is, if the lessor, by his covenant, undertake to repair the houses, yet the lessee (if the lessor doth it not) may with the timber growing upon the ground repair it, though he be not compellable thereunto (*d*).

But if the tenant do or suffer waste to be done in houses, yet if he repair them before any action brought, there hath no action of waste against him, but he cannot plead *quod non fecit vastum*, but the special matter (*e*). For the tenant may cut trees to mend houses, &c. and to do reparation but if houses decay by the default of the tenant, to cut trees to amend them is waste (*f*). Not so, however, if they were ruinous at the time of the lease made but if a frame was once covered in in the time of the lessor, and the lessee erase it after his death, the heir shall have waste (*g*)

(*a*) 2 Bl Com 281 (*b*) 1 [illegible] 57 [illegible] 1 Cr[illegible] [illegible]
(*c*) Co 1[illegible] [illegible], and notes. (*d*) Co. 1[illegible] [illegible]
[illegible] [illegible] Q. B. [illegible]

The tenant cuts down trees for reparations, and sells them, and afterwards buys them again and employs them about necessary reparations; yet it is waste by the vendition: he cannot sell trees and with the money cover the house (*a*).

If the tenant of a dove-house, warren, park, vivary [a fishpond], estangues, or the like, do take so many that such sufficient store be not left as he found when he came in, this is waste, and to suffer the paling to decay, whereby the deer is dispersed, is waste (*b*).

If tenant cut down or destroy any fruit-trees, growing in the garden or orchard, it is waste, but if such trees grow upon any of the ground which the tenant holdeth out of the garden or orchard, it is no waste (*c*).

To suffer the germins [*à germina*, the young roots of trees] upon the roots of the trees to be again newly destroyed, (having before felled the trees) it is new waste, and treble damages shall be recovered for both (*d*.)

Waste may also be committed in respect of timber trees, (*viz.* oak, ash, and elm, and these be timber trees in all places) either by cutting them down or topping them, or doing any act whereby the timber may decay; for timber is part of the inheritance. Also, in countries where timber is scant, and beech or the like are converted to building for the habitation of man, or the like, they are all accounted timber. Cutting down of willows, beech, birch, asp, maple, or the like, standing in the defence and safeguard of the house, is destruction: so, if there be a quickset fence of whitethorn, if the tenant stub it up, or suffer it to be destroyed, this is destruction, and for all these and the like destructions, an action of waste lieth. But cutting up of quicksets is not waste, if it preserves the spring, nor is cutting of ash under the growth of twenty years waste (*e*).

With respect to what wood shall be deemed timber (by which is meant such trees only as are fit to be used in building and repairing houses) it is the custom of the country which makes some trees timber, which in their nature, generally speaking, are not so, as horse-chesnut and lime-trees, so of birch, beech, and asp; and as to pollards, notwithstanding what is said in *Plowd* 470. that these are not timber, and that tithes are to be paid of their loppings, (which could not be if pollards were timber,) yet if the bodies of them be sound and good, I incline to think them timber, *secus* if not sound, they being in such case fit for nothing but fuel. *Per* Lord Chancellor *King*. So walnut-trees, where of considerable value, are to be estimated as timber (*f*).

As to pollards, where an action was brought to recover the value of certain pollard trees, on an estate purchased by the defendant of the

(*a*) Co. Lit. [illegible] (*b*) Ibid. 53. (*c*) Ibid. (*d*) F. N. B. 59. M. f.
(*e*) Co. Lit. [illegible] 2 P. Wms. 601. (*f*) 2 P. Wms. 601.

plaintiff, in the particular of which it was expressed, that all timber and timber-like trees should be taken at a fair valuation, the defendant resisted payment for the pollards, not deeming them to come under the general description of timber-like trees: but, after a long hearing, a verdict was given for the plaintiff, for the value of the said pollards (a).—Where trees are of value, and the parties cannot agree in the valuation of them as timber, the Court of Chancery will send it to be tried, whether by the custom of the country, any and which of them are timber (b). It was determined in the county of *York*, that birch-trees were timber, because they were used in that county for building sheep-houses, cottages, and such mean buildings: and all the Justices on a conference were of opinion, that in that county they were timber and belonged to the inheritance, and therefore could not be taken by the tenant for life (c).

Windfalls are the property of the lord; for the timber while standing is part of the inheritance: but whenever it is severed, either by the act of God, as by a tempest, or by a trespasser and by wrong, it belongs to him who has the first vested estate of inheritance, whether in fee or in tail, who may bring trover for it (d). So, where there are intermediate contingent estates of inheritance, and the timber is cut down by combination between the tenant for life and the person who has the next vested estate of inheritance; or if the tenant for life himself has such estate and fells timber; in these cases, the Court of Chancery will order it to be preserved for him who has the first contingent estate of inheritance under the settlement (e). A tenant for life without impeachment of waste has as full power to cut down trees and open new mines, for his own use, as if he had an estate of inheritance; and is in the same manner entitled to the timber, if severed by others. This privilege, given by words, *without impeachment of waste*, is annexed to the privity of estate, so that if the person to whom that privilege is given change his estate, he loses the privilege. It has been held that the intent of this clause is only to enable the tenant to cut down timber and open new mines, and that it does not extend to allow destructive or malicious waste; such as cutting down timber which serves for shelter or ornament of the estate (f).

If the tenant suffer the houses to be wasted and then fell down timber to repair the same, this is a double waste (g).

Digging for gravel, lime, clay, brick, earth, stone, or the like, or for mines of metal, coal, or the like, hidden in the earth, and not open when the tenant came in, is waste (h), but the tenant may dig for gravel or clay for the reparation of the house, (though no pit

(a) [illegible] 1803, [illegible] Mich. [illegible] C. B.
(b) 2 P. Wms. 606. (c) [illegible], 813. (d) 3 P. Wms. 26[illegible]. (e) 1 [illegible] R. 5[illegible].
(f) Co. Lit. 220 a. [illegible] 3 Wood. [illegible]. (g) Co. Lit. 53. (h) Ibid.

were open at the time of the lease,) as well as he may take convenient timber trees (*a*). But if the pits or mines were open before, it is no waste in the tenant continuing to dig them for his own use, for it is now become the mere annual profit of the land. Though mines be open at the time, one cannot take timber to use in them (*b*).

It is waste to suffer a wall of the sea to be in decay, so as by the flowing and reflowing of the sea the meadow or marsh is surrounded, whereby the same becomes unprofitable; but if it be surrounded suddenly by the rage or violence of the sea, as by tempest, without any default of the tenant, it is no waste punishable. So it is, if the tenant [illegible] not the banks or walls against rivers, or other waters, whereby the meadows or marshes be so overflowed [illegible] become rushy and unprofitable (*c*).

It is a general principle, that the law will not allow that to be waste, which is not in any way prejudicial to the inheritance. Nevertheless it has been held, that a tenant or lessee cannot change the nature of the thing demised.—Therefore if the tenant convert arable into wood, or [illegible], or meadow into arable, it is waste, for [illegible] not only the course of husbandry, but the proof of his evidence. The same rule is to be observed with regard to converting one species of edifice into another, even though it be thereby improved in its value (*d*). Thus if a lessee convert a corn-mill into a fulling-mill, it is waste, though the conversion be to the lessor's advantage. So, the conversion of a brewhouse of 120*l.* *per annum* into other houses let for 200*l.* *per annum* is waste, because of the alteration of the nature of the thing, and of the evidence (*e*). So, if the tenant pull down a malt-mill and build a corn-mill it is waste.—Waste in the house is waste in the curtilage, and waste in the hall is waste in the whole house (*f*).

An injunction was granted against proceeding with alterations in a house under an agreement for a lease, upon circumstances that would probably prevent a specific performance, viz. surprise, the effect of fraudulent misrepresentation and concealment, and the particular nature of the alteration, for the conversion of a private house to the purpose of a coachmaker's business, wholly changing the nature of the subject (*g*).

A tenant was restrained from cutting turf for sale, his lease giving a right of estovers only, notwithstanding an uninterrupted practice of eighty years (*h*).

A tenant from year to year having received notice to quit, a motion was made for an injunction to restrain him from taking away the crops

(*a*) 1 Wood's Inst. [illegible]; 1 El. C. [illegible] (*c*) Co. Lit. 53 [illegible]
(*b*) Cro. J. 1[illegible] [illegible] (*g*) [illegible]
[illegible]

&c. contrary to the usual course of husbandry, and from cutting and damaging the hedge-rows, &c. The Court observed that though there was no case of this sort upon a tenancy from year to year, yet the principle applies equally to such a tenancy as to a lease for a longer term. The Judges have uniformly said in modern times that a tenant from year to year must treat the farm in a husband-like manner, according to the custom of the country; and the Court must give its aid equally in that case, with the qualification that he is not to remove any thing except according to the custom of the country (*a*).

[See also with respect to timber the following Section.]

Section II. *Of Common of Estovers; allowance of Wood.*

Common of estovers, or *estouviers*, that is necessaries, or materials, (from *estoffer* to furnish,) is a liberty of taking necessary wood for the use and furniture of a house or farm from off another's estate. Estovers are three kinds in law, and are incident to the estate of every tenant, whether for life or years, but not at will, for such estate is too mean (*b*).

The Saxon word bote (*c*), which signifies allowance or compensation, is used by us as synonymous to the French *estovers*, and therefore house-bote is a sufficient allowance of wood to build or repair the house, or to burn in it, which latter is sometimes called fire-bote; plough-bote and cart-bote are wood to be employed in making and repairing all instruments of husbandry, as ploughs, carts, harrows, rakes, forks, &c. (*d*), and hay-bote or hedge-bote is wood for repairing hedges or fences, as pales, stiles, and gates, to secure inclosures. These botes or estovers must be reasonable ones, and such any tenant or lessee may take off the land let or demised to him, without waiting for any leave, assignment, or appointment of the lessor, unless he be restrained by special covenant to the contrary, (which is usually the case;(*e*), for house-bote, hay-bote, and fire-bote, do appertain unto a termor of common right, and he may take wood for the same but if the tenant take more house-bote than needful, he may be punished for waste (*f*).

Common of estovers cannot be appendant to land, unless it be by prescription: but to a house to be spent there. Therefore, though it be said, that a custom that if the house fall, the materials shall be the tenant's, would not be good, yet when a house, having estovers appendant or appurtenant is blown down by wind, if the owner rebuild it in the same place and manner as before, his estovers shall continue

(*a*) 16 Ves. Jun. 173. (*b*) Co. Lit. 122 a; 2 Bl. Com. 35. (*c*) Ibid.
(*d*) Wood. Ins. 324. (*e*) F. N. B. 59 M. (*f*) Termes de Le.

So, if he alter the rooms and chambers, without making new chimnies, but if he erect any new chimnies he will not be allowed to spend any estovers in such new chimnies (*a*). But a prescription to have estovers not only for repairing but building new houses on the land is good, yet it seems, if a man have common of estovers by grant, he cannot build new houses to have common of estovers for those houses (*b*).

It may not here be superfluous to explain the meaning of the terms *appendant* and *appurtenant* (*c*).—A thing *appendant* is that which beyond memory has belonged to another thing more worthy, which it agrees with in its nature and quality. Therefore a common of turbary may be appendant to a house (*d*); for a thing incorporeal may be appendant or appurtenant to a thing corporeal, but a thing corporeal cannot be appendant to a thing corporeal, as land cannot be appendant to land; and common appendant must be by prescription, for it cannot begin at this day (*e*). A thing *appurtenant* is that which commences at this day, as if a man at this day grant to one common of estovers, or of turbary, in fee-simple, to burn in his manor, and if he make a feoffment of the manor the common shall pass to the feoffee (*f*). Common appurtenant therefore is claimable by an existing grant, as well as by prescription, which always implies a grant, and a right of common by prescription may be regulated by custom (*g*).

The lord may have the land of his tenant common appendant to his own demesnes: and occupiers of land may, by custom, claim a right *in alieno solo* (*h*); though inhabitants cannot, for inhabitancy is too vague a description, and extends to many others, besides the actual occupiers of houses or land (*i*).

If a man have common of estovers in the woods of another, and he who is tenant and owner of the wood cut down all the wood, he who ought to have the estovers shall not have an action of waste but shall have assise of his estovers (*k*). Trespass also would lie and be a better remedy (*l*).

If the tenant who hath common of estovers shall use them to any other purpose than he ought, he that owns the wood may bring trespass against him, as where one grant twenty loads of wood to be taken yearly in such a wood, ten loads to burn, and ten to repair pales, here he may cut and take the wood for the pales, though they need no amending, but then he must keep it for that use (*m*).

So, where two elms were cut down for the purpose of repairs, one

(*a*) Co. Lit. 121 b. [illegible] N. [illegible] 180 C. b. 12 Mod. 95. 4 Rep. 87. 4 Leon. 383.
(*b*) Cro. Jac. 256. 1 N. R. 180 H. (*c*) Co. Lit. 121 b. (*d*) 1 Rol. 230 l. 36. [illegible] l. 50 [illegible]
(*e*) Co. Lit. 121 b. 1 Vent. 407. 1 N. B. 181 N.
(*f*) Cro. Car. 482. (*g*) 2 T. R. [illegible] (*h*) F. N. B. 180 D. c. (*i*) 2 Bl. R. 928.
(*k*) F. N. B. 59 [illegible] (*l*) 12 Mod. 579. (*m*) 9 Rep. 113.

of which only was used, it was said that although that tree which was not employed (and which had been felled five years) was more than sufficient to repair the house, yet seeing that the tenant cut it down for that purpose, and peradventure did not know what would serve for that purpose, it was not any forfeiture, for it had been judged, that where one cut down wood to make hedges, and used the greater part thereof in hedging, yet for the rest that was cut down for that purpose, no tithes shall be paid (*a*).

Though the tenant may cut down and take sufficient wood to repair walls, pales, fences, hedges, &c. as he found them, yet he may not do so to make new ones (*b*).

The tenant may cut down dead wood, and it is not waste to fell seasonable wood which is used to be felled every twenty years, or within that time (*c*), but oaks cannot be said to be seasonable wood, which are passed the age of twenty years, but by a custom in any place where is plenty of wood (timber), oaks under twenty years may be seasonable wood, and such custom may be alledged in the wood itself (*d*).

A termor may cut the underwood growing under the great woods and tall woods (*e*); but if there be not any tall wood, then he cannot cut the underwood (*f*), for where waste was brought for topping and lopping twenty ashes and twenty elms, on demurrer it was adjudged for the plaintiff (*g*). It has however, notwithstanding, been held to be a good custom, that copyholders in fee shall have the loppings of pollengers, and the lord cannot, in such case, cut the trees down, for that would deprive the copyholder of the future loppings. [Pollengers or pollards are such trees as have been usually cropped, therefore distinguished from timber-trees (*h*).] And it has been resolved that by the common law, a copyholder may cut off the under boughs, for such lopping cannot cause any waste (*i*).

Though the termor hath of common right oaks, elm, ash, &c. for repair of the house, and underwood, &c. for inclosures and firing, yet it is said he cannot cut either oaks or ash for fire-wood, but the cutting at the age of seven years is not waste (*k*).

If a man cut wood to burn, where he hath sufficient dead wood, it is waste (*l*).

A rector may cut down timber for the repairs of the parsonage house, or of the chancel, but not for any common purpose, and if it is the custom of the country, he may cut down underwood for any purpose, but if he grubs it up it is waste. He may cut down [illegible]

[illegible]

likewise for repairing any old pews that belong to the rectory; and he is also entitled to botes for repairing barns and outhouses belonging to the parsonage (*c*). And a parson or prebendary shall have a writ of waste upon their lease (*d*).

It is true, that the first owner of the inheritance *in esse* shall have timber blown down, but as an estate in contingency is no estate, and the trees must become the property of somebody, therefore the first remainder-man an or the inheritance in being takes them (*e*).

So, with respect to the case of a copyholder, who has only a possessory property in the timber trees of which if severed from the freehold by tempest or otherwise, the property will be in the lord; and a custom for the tenant to claim such trees would be a hard one, and so likewise of the materials of the house (*d*). In either case, being things annexed to the inheritance, the severance shall not transfer the property, this therefore is to be understood as of a copyholder not of inheritance (*e*).

For, as to a right to cut down timber by custom, where a copyholder hath the inheritance, and where his successor comes in by his nomination, there such a custom may be good (*f*); but a custom for a copyholder for life to cut down and fell trees was held not to be good, unless it be to build new houses on the land (*g*).

A custom that every copyhold tenant may cut down trees at their will and pleasure, is unreasonable and void, for then a tenant at will might do it, so it is for a copyholder for life to do it, and one of the reasons given is, that the succeeding copyholder would not have wherewithall to maintain the house and plough, which plainly intimates, that a copyholder may cut timber to make reparations, and the rather, because permissive waste is a forfeiture in him (*h*).

The lord may cut down timber trees, leaving sufficient, and the custom to cut makes no alteration, for it has been resolved, that every copyholder may take trees for house-bote of common right, so that the laying the custom seems to be only by way of caution (*i*).

The right of the lord to take trees on a copyhold, perhaps, is rendered somewhat doubtful by the reversal on error brought in parliament of the judgment in the case of *Ashmead* against *Ranger* (*k*).

It is clear that a copyholder may take the necessary estovers or botes on his copyhold without a special custom (*l*).

But to enable him to make them on *other lands*, a special custom must be shewn (*m*).

(*a*) 2 Atk. 217. (*b*) F. N. B. 60 K. (*c*) 2 Atk. 755. (*d*) 11 Mod. 68. (*e*) Ld. [illegible] 95. (*f*) [illegible] (*g*) Cro. Jac. 25. (*h*) Gilbert's Tenures, 237. Cro. Jac. [illegible] (*i*) Gilbert's Tenures, 237. (*k*) 11 Mod. 1[illegible] 12 Mod. [illegible] Salk. [illegible] H. [illegible], 162. [illegible] Rep. 71. 1 Ld. Raym. 551. (*l*) 1 Ld. R[illegible]. (*m*) [illegible] 11 Mod. 68. (*n*) [illegible] 31 b.

As a tenant for life has a right to what may be sufficient for repairs and botes, care must be taken in felling timber to leave enough upon the estate for that purpose, and whatever damage is done to the tenant for life on the premises by him held for life, the same ought to be made good to him (*a*).

Estovers may be granted in fee, and in a grant of estovers the grantor may take the trees with the grantee. But underwood is a thing of inheritance and perpetuity, and may be granted in fee by copy of court-roll, and will support trespass *quare clausum fregit*; for in such case, the grantor cannot meddle with the woods, nor can his lessee; for he hath only granted the underwood, and not estovers or so many loads of wood. A grant may be made to a person by a deed to which he is no party (*b*).

If the lord of a manor cut down so many trees as not to leave sufficient estovers, his copyholder may bring trespass against him, and recover the value of the trees in damages; and even if the lord leave sufficient estovers, yet he shall recover special damages, *viz.* for the loss of his umbrage, breaking his close, treading down his grass, &c. for the tenant had the same customary or possessory interest in the trees that he has in the land; and if the lord has a mind to cut trees, his business is to compound with the tenant (*c*). [But see *Ashmead* v. *Ranger*, *ante*.]

The lord of a manor, as such, has no right without a custom to enter upon the copyholds within his manor, under which there are mines and veins of coal, in order to bore for and work the same, and the copyholder may maintain trespass against him in so doing (*d*).

But an enclosure of the common by the lord may be no interruption of the tenants' enjoyment of their common of estovers; nay, probably it may be better for such enclosure. If indeed, by such enclosure, their common of estovers were affected, or they were interrupted in the enjoyment of it, they might certainly bring their action, and the lord, in such case, could not justify such enclosure in prejudice to those rights (*e*).

If the lord of a manor plant trees on a common, the commoner has no right to abate them, though there be not a sufficiency left; his remedy is by action. But if the lord so plant as to destroy the common, such an act would be considered as a nuisance, and the commoner might abate it (*f*).

The distinction seems to be this: if the lord of the manor make a hedge round the common, or do any other act that entirely excludes the commoner from exercising his right, the latter may do whatever is necessary to let himself into the common; but if the commoner can

(*a*) [illegible] 263. (*b*) Cro. Eliz. 413. (*c*) 12 Mod. 379. Bull. N. P. 85 [illegible]
(*d*) [illegible] (*e*) 6 T. R. 478. (*f*) 2 [illegible] Pul. R. 23.

get at the common, and enjoy it to a certain extent, and his right be merely abridged by the act of the lord, in that case his remedy is by an action on the case, or by an assise, and he cannot assert his right by any act of his own (*a*).

Section III. *Of Emblements.*

The word emblements is derived from the French *emblavence de bled*, corn sprung or put above ground, and strictly signifies the profits of sown land, but the doctrine of emblements extends not only to corn sown, but to roots planted or other annual artificial profits (*b*).—Hops growing out of antient roots have been held to be like emblements, which shall go to the husband or executor of the tenant for life, and not to him in remainder, and are not to be compared to apples or fruits, which grow of themselves (*c*).

But it is otherwise of fruit-trees, grass, and the like, which are not planted annually at the expence and labour of the tenant, but are either a permanent or a natural profit of the earth: for when a man plants a tree, he cannot be presumed to plant it in contemplation of any present profit, but merely with a prospect of its being useful to himself in future, and to future successions of tenants (*d*).

It shall be intended *primâ facie*, that the property of the corn is in the owner of the soil. But, the public being interested in the produce of corn and grain, (among other reasons for the rule) emblements go to the executor, and not to the remainder-man (*e*).

In some cases, indeed, he who sows the corn shall have the emblements, in others not.

If tenant in fee, or in tail, or in dower, die after sowing the corn, and before severance, his executor, or administrator generally shall have the emblements (*f*).

Tenant for life, or his representatives, shall not be prejudiced by any sudden determination of his estate; because such a determination is contingent and uncertain.—Therefore, if a tenant for his own life sows the land, and dies before harvest, his executors shall have the emblements or profits of the crop, for the estate was determined by the act of God, and it is a maxim in the law, that *actus Dei nemini facit injuriam*. The representatives therefore of the tenant for life shall have the emblements, to compensate for the labour and expence of tilling, manuring, and sowing the lands, and also for the encouragement of

(*a*) Willes 157. 6 T. R. 485. (*b*) 2 Bl. Com. 12[illegible]. (*c*) Cro. Car. [illegible]
(*d*) 2 Bl. Com. 123. (*e*) 2 Saund. 401. 1 P. Wms 94. (*f*) Com. Dig. tit. Biens [illegible]

husbandry, which being a public benefit, tending to the increase and plenty of provisions, ought to have the utmost security and privilege that the law can give it (*a*).

Therefore if a man sows land and lets it for life, and the lessee for life die before the corn be severed, his executor shall not have the emblements, but he in reversion; but if he himself had sowed the land and died, it were otherwise (*b*).

So, if tenant for life sows the land, and grants over his estate, the grantee dies before the corn severed, such grantee's executor shall not have the corn (*c*).

So, if the lessee of a tenant for life be disseised, and the lessee of the disseisor sows the land, and then the tenant for life dies, and he in remainder enters, yet he shall not have the emblements, but the lessee of the tenant for life (*d*).

So it is also, if a man be tenant for the life of another, and *cestui que vie*, or he on whose life the land is held, dies after the corn sown, the tenant *pur auter vie* shall have the emblements (*e*).

The same is also the rule, if a life estate be determined by the act of law (*f*).

Therefore if a lease be made to husband and wife during coverture (which gives them a determinable estate for life) and the husband sows the land, and afterwards they are divorced *a vinculo matrimonii*, the husband shall have the emblements in this case; for the sentence of divorce is the act of law.

So if tenant in tail give or grant his emblements of corn growing on the ground, the donee may cut and take them after the death of the tenant in tail (*g*).

So every one who has an uncertain estate or interest, if before severance of the corn, his estate determine either by the act of God or of the law, he shall have the emblements, or they shall go to his executor or administrator (*h*); for, so it is in all cases regularly, where a man sows land whereon he hath such an estate as may perhaps continue until the corn be ripe (*i*).

But if the estate be determined by the tenant's own act, as by forfeiture by tenant for life for waste committed, or if a tenant during widowhood marries, in these and similar cases the tenants having thus determined their estates by their own acts, shall not be entitled to take the emblements (*k*).

The under-tenants or lessees of tenants for life, have the same, nay greater, indulgences, than their lessors, the original tenants for life. The same, for the law of estovers and emblements, with regard to

(*a*) 2 [illegible] 122. [illegible] (*b*) [illegible]
(*c*) [illegible] (*f*) [illegible] (*g*) [illegible] 231 [illegible]
(*d*) [illegible] 2 Bl. Com. 122.

the tenant for life, is also law with regard to his under-tenant, who represents him and stands in his place. Greater, for in those cases where tenant for life shall not have the emblements because the estate determines by his own act, the exception shall not reach his lessee who is a third person (*a*) thus, in the case of a woman who holds *durante viduitate*, her taking husband is her own act, and therefore deprives her of the emblements, which, if she be a feme copyholder, the lord shall have, but if she leases her estate to an under-tenant who sows the land, and she then marries, this her act shall not deprive the tenant of his emblements, who is a stranger and could not prevent her (*b*).

With regard to emblements or the profits of lands sowed by tenant for years, there is this difference between him and tenant for life: that where the term of tenant for years depends upon a certainty, (as if he holds from *Midsummer* for ten years,) and in the last year he sows a crop of corn, and it is not ripe, and cut before *Midsummer*, the end of the term, his landlord shall have it (*c*), for the tenant knew the expiration of his term, and therefore it was his own folly to sow that of which he never could reap the profits. In such case the landlord, it is said, must enter on the lands to take the emblements (*d*).

But where the lease for years depends upon an uncertainty, as upon the death of the lessor, being himself only tenant for life, or being a husband seised in right of his wife, or if the term of years be determinable upon a life or lives, in all cases of this kind, the estate for years not being certainly to expire at a time foreknown, but merely by the act of God, the tenant, or his executors, shall have the emblements in the same manner that a tenant for life would be entitled thereto (*e*).

Not so, however, if it determine by the act of the party himself as if tenant for years surrenders before severance, or does any thing that amounts to a forfeiture, in which case the emblements shall go to the lessor, and not to the lessee, who hath determined his estate by his own default (*f*).

If, however, lessor covenants that lessee for years shall have the emblements which are growing at the end of the term, there the property of the corn is well transferred to the lessee, though it be not severed during the term (*g*).

If tenant at will sows his land, and the landlord before the corn is ripe, or before it is reaped, put him out, yet the tenant shall have the emblements, and free ingress, egress, and regress, to cut and carry away the profits and this for the same reason upon which all the cases of emblements turn, namely, the point of uncertainty since the te-

(*a*) 2 Bl Com 123; (*b*) 1 Bac. Abr. 51[illegible]. (*c*) Co. [illegible] 450 (*d*) 2 Bl Com. 145. (*e*) 2 Bl Com 145 (*f*) [illegible] (*g*) Co Litt 55. a

ment could not possibly know when his landlord would determine his will, and therefore could make no provision against it, and having sown the land, which is for the good of the public, upon a reasonable presumption, the law will not suffer him to be a loser by it (*a*).

So, if the estate of a tenant at will be determined either by his death or by the act of the landlord, he or his executors may reap the corn sown by him.—Wherefore the corn sown by a tenant at will (who dies before harvest) and purchased by another person, cannot be distrained by the landlord for rent due to him from a subsequent tenant (*b*).

But it is otherwise, and upon reason equally good, where the tenant himself determines his will; for in this case the landlord shall have the profits of the land (*c*).

So in the case of entry of the lessor before sowing, the lessee at will shall not have the costs of ploughing and manuring (*d*).

A lets lands to *B* for ninety-nine years determinable on his life, with a proviso of re-entry if let to tillage without licence; *C*, under-tenant ploughs and sows in the life-time of *B*, who dies, no re-entry being made; the proviso was gone, for it could only operate during the continuance of the lease; and *A* having never been in possession by right of re-entry for the condition broken, can have no advantage thereof; and he who ploughed and sowed the land, has, in law and justice, a right to reap and take the emblements (*e*).

If a husband holds lands for life, in right of his wife, and sows the land, and afterwards she dies before severance, he shall have the emblements (*f*).

So where the wife has an estate for years, life, or in fee, and the husband sows the land and dies, his executors shall have the corn (*g*).

But if the husband and wife are joint-tenants, though the husband sow the land with corn and die before it be ripe, the wife, and not his executors, shall have the corn, she being the surviving joint-tenant (*h*).

If a widow is endowed with lands sown, she shall have the emblements, and not the heir; and a tenant in dower may dispose of corn sown on the ground, or it may go to her executors, if she die before severance (*i*). Indeed it is provided by the stat. of *Merton*, 20 *H.* 3. c. 2. that a doweress may dispose by will of the growing corn, otherwise it goes to her executors (*k*).

But where lands are limited to a woman during life for her jointure, she has the same rights with respect to estovers and emblements, and is under the same restrictions respecting waste, (unless there is a deficiency in her jointure,) as other tenants for life. A jointress is not, however, entitled to the crop sown at the time of her husband's

[illegible]

death; because a jointure is not a continuance of the estate of the husband, like dower: on the death of a jointress, therefore, her representatives are not entitled to emblements (*a*).

If tenant by statute-merchant sows the land, and before severance a sudden and casual profit happens, by which he is satisfied, yet he shall have the emblements (*b*).

Where lands sown are delivered in execution upon an extent, the person to whom they are so delivered shall have the corn on the ground (*c*).

So, where judgment was given against a person, and then he sowed the land, and brought a writ of error to reverse the judgment, but it was affirmed; it was adjudged that the recoveror should have the corn (*d*).

If a man enter by title paramount, he shall have the emblements, as if a disseisor sow and the disseisee enter before severance (*e*).

The advantages also of emblements are particularly extended to the parochial clergy by the stat. 28 *H.* 8. *c.* 11., which considers all persons who are presented to any ecclesiastical benefice, or to any civil office, as tenants for their own lives, unless the contrary be expressed in the form of the donation. By this statute, if a parson sows his glebe and dies, his executors shall have the corn, and such parson may by will dispose thereof *s.* 6. (*f*).

A. grants to *B.* that he may sow *A.'s* land, which is done accordingly; yet *A.* shall have the emblements, because *B.* hath not an interest (*g*).

If the lessee for a tenant for life be disseised, and the lessee of the disseisor sow the land, and then the tenant for life dies, and he in remainder enters, yet he shall not have the emblements, but the lessee of the tenant for life, for *quicquid plantatur solo, solo cedit* (*h*).

Where there is a right to emblements, ingress, egress, and regress are allowed by law, in order to enter, cut, and carry them away when the estate is determined (*i*).

Emblements are distinct from the real estate in the land, and subject to many, though not all, the incidents attending personal chattels: they are deviseable, and at the death of the owner, shall vest in his executor, and not his heir, they are forfeitable by outlawry in a personal action, and by the stat. 11 *G.* 2. *c.* 19. (though not by the common law) they may be distrained for rent arrear (*k*).

But though emblements are assets in the hands of the executor, are forfeitable upon outlawry, and distrainable for rent, they are not in

(*a*) 9 V[illegible] 274 [illegible] 221 C[illegible] D[illegible] VII [illegible] s. 34, 35, 36
(*b*) C[illegible] 54 (*d*) 2 Buls. 213 (*e*) Co. Lit. 55 b.
(*f*) 2 B. Com. [illegible] (*g*) Co. Lit. 5[illegible] 1 (*h*) Cro. Eliz. (463)
(*i*) [illegible] 6 [illegible] 24

other respects considered as personal chattels, and particularly they are not the object of larceny before they are severed from the ground (*a*).

Of Gleaning.—It may perhaps be as well to introduce here a word respecting gleaning or leasing. An idea very universally prevails among the lower classes of the community that they have a right to glean, that is, to take from off the land the corn that remains thereon after the harvest has been gotten in, than which notion nothing can be more erroneous. By custom, indeed, such a right may possibly in some particular places exist; and the laudable kindness of tenants generally induces them to permit the poor to collect the corn they have left upon the land, and to appropriate it to their own use. As a right, however, it has no more existence than a right to take the tenant's furniture from out of his messuage, and the pillage in the one case is as much felony as the plunder would be in the other: for the act is not simply a trespass, but a felony, and the compiler well remembers a conviction at the Old Bailey on an indictment found for the exercise of this supposed right. The parties were tried before Mr. Justice *Rooke*, (if he mistake not) about six years ago. Indeed, it has been determined, after two solemn arguments, that no such right exists at common law; whatever may possibly be the case on the ground of custom in particular places (*b*).

For though it is no larceny, but a bare trespass, to steal corn or grass growing, it is larceny to take them being severed from the freehold, whether by the owner or by the thief himself, if he steals them at one time and then come again at another time and take them (*c*).

(*a*) 2 Bl. Com. 404. (*b*) 1 H. Bl. R. 53. 4 Burr. 1926. (*c*) 1 Haw. P. C. c. 33. s. 21.

CHAPTER X.

Of the general Incidents to Leases (continued).

SECTION I. *Of implied Covenants and Agreements.*
SECTION II. *Of express Covenants and Agreements.*

SECTION I. *Of implied Covenants and Agreements.*

COVENANT, contract, and agreement, are often used as synonymous words, signifying an engagement entered into, by which one person lays himself under an obligation to do something beneficial to, or to abstain from an act which, if done, would be prejudicial to another (*a*).

A covenant is either implied or expressed, it subsists either in law or in fact.

An implied covenant, or a covenant in law, is that which the law intends and implies, though it be not expressed by words in the deed.

For quiet enjoyment.—Thus, when one makes a lease for years by the words "demise and grant," without any express covenant for quiet enjoyment, in this case, the law intends and makes such a covenant on the part of the lessor, which is, that the lessee shall quietly hold and enjoy the thing demised against all persons, at least, having title under the lessor, and at least during the lessor's life, and (as some think, 1 *Inst.* 384.) during the whole term (*b*), and hereupon an action of covenant may be brought against him in the reversion, so that if the heir that is in by descent put out the termor of his father, the termor may have this action against him.—If the party ousting the covenantee has no title, the covenantee it is said cannot, where the covenant is created by law, bring an action of covenant against the lessor (*c*).

But though such covenant in law is general against all persons that have title during the term, and extends to the heir after the death of the lessor, as against himself only, and shall charge the executors or administrators for any disturbance in the life of the covenantor, yet

(*a*) Bac. Abr. tit. "Covenant."
(*b*) Shep. Touch. 160.
(*c*) 2 Brownl. 167. Cro. Eliz. 214.

(it is said) it shall not charge them for any disturbance afterwards. [But see 1 *Inst.* 384.] He that sues, therefore, upon this covenant must shew that he was molested or evicted by one that had an elder title (*a*).

An implied covenant for quiet enjoyment, comprehends a covenant by implication that the lease shall be valid and not void or voidable, for of such there could of course be no enjoyment at all and this principle is the same as that which respects any conveyance; for where a man undertakes to convey, he undertakes to convey by a good title (*b*).

To cultivate the Land.—A covenant is implied also, on the part of the lessee that he will use the land demised to him in a husbandman like manner and not unnecessarily exhaust the soil by neglectful or improper tillage for the bare relation of landlord and tenant is a sufficient consideration for the tenant's promise to manage a farm in a husband-like manner (*c*).

It is likewise so notoriously the duty of the actual occupier to repair the fences, and so little the duty of the landlord, that without an agreement to that effect, the landlord may maintain an action against his tenant for not so doing, upon the ground of the injury done to his inheritance (*d*).

To keep Messuage, &c. in Repair.—So, in case of a house or other tenement, a covenant is implied that the tenant will keep it in repair: a tenant for life therefore shall be obliged to keep the tenant's houses on the estate in repair, even though he be such without impeachment of waste. and such is the case even with respect to a tenant at will; for the tenant ought in justice to restore the premises in as good plight as they can be, consistent with such deterioration as is unavoidable (*e*).

A mortgagee in possession need only keep the estate in necessary repair (*f*).

A yearly tenant however is bound only to tenantable, and not to lasting repairs.

Thus where an action was brought to recover damages for suffering the plaintiff's house to be out of repair. The case was that the defendant had rented a house of the plaintiff as tenant at will at 31*l per ann.* which he had quitted after the defendant had given up possession, the house being found to be much out of repair, the plaintiff had an estimate made of the sum necessary to put it into complete and tenantable repair, for which sum this action was brought. But Lord *Kenyon* said, it was not to be permitted to the plaintiff to go for the damages so claimed. A tenant from year to year was bound to commit no waste,

(*a*) Shep. Touch. 167. (*b*) 1 H. Bl. 280. 2 Ibid. 123. (*c*) 5 T. R. 373.
(*d*) 4 T. R. 319. (*e*) 2 Atk. 183. (*f*) 1 Atk. [illegible]

and to make fair and tenantable repairs, such as putting in windows or doors that have been broken by him, so as to prevent waste and decay of the premises; but that in the present case the plaintiff had claimed a sum for putting on a new roof on an old worn out house; this his Lordship thought the tenant not to be bound to do, and that the plaintiff had no right to recover it (*a*).

But a strict tenant at will, it is said, is not bound to repair or sustain houses, like tenant for years (*b*).

It has been held that if a man has an upper room in a house, an action would lie against him to compel him to repair his roof (*c*), and so where a man has a ground-room, that they over him might have an action to compel him to keep up and maintain his foundation: but this seems to be erroneous. there is, indeed, a writ in *Nat Brev.* 127. to a mayor, to command him that has the lower rooms to repair the foundation, and him that has a garret to repair the roof; but that was grounded on a custom (*d*).

Payment of Rent.—As in every contract, there must be a legal consideration to make it valid, so where the relation of landlord and tenant subsists, some *quid pro quo* must subsist also. Therefore, unless the lease be granted in consideration of a fine or a sum in gross, an implied contract is raised on the part of the tenant that he shall pay an annual rent.

These implied covenants are said to be inherent, that is, such as appurtain especially to the land; as that the thing itself shall be quietly enjoyed, shall be kept in reparation, and shall not be aliened; or to pay rent, not to cut down timber trees, or to do waste, to fence the coppices, when they be new cut and the like (*e*).

An implied covenant is in all cases controuled within the limits of an express covenant, for *expressum facit cessare tacitum* (*f*).

Thus for example, with respect to the covenant for quiet enjoyment; if a man leases for years by the words "I have demised, *&c.*" and the lessor covenants that the lessee shall enjoy during the term without eviction by the lessor, or any claiming under him (*g*), this express covenant qualifies the generality of the covenant in law and restrains it by the mutual consent of both parties, that it shall not extend farther than the express covenant: and this is consonant to the principle, that where there is an express promise, another promise cannot be implied (*h*).

Caution, therefore, is to be used in introducing into a lease express covenants in certain cases; as the evil intended to be guarded against,

(*a*) 2 Esp R 590 (*b*) 1 Cruise's Dig tit IX s 14, 15. (*c*) 11 Mod 8
(*d*) 6 Mod. 314 (*e*) Shep Touch. 161.
(*f*) 4 Co. 80 1 Saund 60 Cro Eliz 674 1 Mod. 113. 2 Ld. Raym 14, 19.
(*g*) Bac Abr. tit. "Covenant" (B) Cro. Eliz. 674. (*h*) 7 T. R. 304.

may frequently be prevented or recompensed in a more limited degree, by an express, than an implied covenant.

The distinction between implied covenants by operation of law, and express covenants, is that express covenants, are to be taken more strictly (*a*).

If a bond is for performance of covenants, it is forfeited by a breach of a covenant in law; as if the lessee be evicted out of the premises demised (*b*).

Where the plaintiff paid money to the defendant, on the defendant's promise to make him a lease of land, and before the lease made the defendant was evicted, the plaintiff recovered the money in this action, the consideration not having been performed (*c*).

Section II. *Of express Covenants.*

Covenants.—An express covenant is the agreement or consent of two or more by deed in writing, sealed and delivered, whereby either of the parties promises the other that something is done already, or shall be done afterwards. He that makes the covenant is called the covenantor, and he to whom it is made the covenantee (*d*).

The general principle is clear, that the landlord having the *jus disponendi*, may annex whatever conditions he pleases to his grant, provided they be not illegal or unreasonable (*e*).

No particular technical words are requisite towards making a covenant; for any words, it seems, which shew the parties' concurrence to the performance of a future act will suffice for that purpose, as "yielding and paying, *&c.*" (*f*).

Thus if lessee covenants to repair, "provided always and it is agreed, that the lessor shall find great timber, *&c.*" this makes a covenant on the part of the lessor to find great timber by the word "agreed," and it shall not be a qualification of the covenant of the lessee; but without this word, it would have been only a qualification of the covenant of the lessee (*g*).

Covenants are either real or personal (*h*).—Covenants real, or such as are annexed to estates, shall descend to the heirs of the covenantee, and he alone shall take advantage of them, and such covenants are said to run with the land, so that he that hath the one, is subject to the other; for which reason warranties were called real covenants.—Cove-

(*a*) 3 Burr. 1639 (*b*) 1 Esp. N. P. 281. 4 Co. 80.
(*c*) Palm. 364. 1 Esp. N. P. 3. Vide ante C. II. S. II. (*d*) Shep. Touch. 160.
(*e*) 2 T. R. 137. (*f*) 1 Bur. 290. 2 Mod. 92.
(*g*) Bac. Abr. tit. "Covenant" (A) & [illegible] (*h*) [illegible]

nants personal, are such whereof some person in particular shall have the benefit, or whereby he shall be charged; as when a man covenants to do any personal thing, as to build, or repair a house, &c. or the like (*a*).

In a lease of ground with liberty to make a watercourse, and erect a mill, the lessee covenanted for himself, his executors, *and assigns*, not to hire persons to work in the mill, who were settled in other parishes without a parish certificate; held that this covenant did not run with the land, or bind the assignee of the lessee (*b*).

As to the construction of covenants, all contracts are to be taken according to the intent of the parties expressed by their own words, and if there be any doubt in the sense of the words, such construction shall be made as is most strong against the covenantor; lest by the obscure wording of his contract, he should find means to evade and elude it (*c*).

Under a lease for fourteen or seven years, the lessee only has the option of determining it at the end of the first seven years, every doubtful grant being construed in favour of the grantee (*d*).

So tenant by the curtesy, in tail after possibility of issue extinct, in dower, for life, for years, by statute or *elegit*, guardian, &c. hold their estates subject to a condition in law, so that if either of them alien his land in fee, or claim a greater estate in a court of record than his own, he forfeits his estate, and he in remainder or reversion may enter, and if such tenant do waste, he in reversion shall recover the place wasted (*e*).

Of Conditions.—A condition signifies some quality annexed to a real estate by virtue of which it may be defeated, enlarged, or created upon an uncertain event. Also qualities annexed to personal contracts and agreements are frequently called conditions, and these, as well as covenants, must likewise be interpreted according to the real intention of the parties, &c. (*f*).

Conditions are either precedent or subsequent. Where a condition must be performed before the estate can commence, it is called "a condition precedent," but where the effect of the condition is either to enlarge or defeat an estate already created, it is then called "a condition subsequent" (*g*).

Conditions are most properly created by inserting the very word "condition" or the words "on condition," but the word commonly and as effectually made use of is that of "provided," wherefore a condition, and a proviso, are synonymous terms (*h*).

But if a proviso, or condition have dependance upon another clause

(*a*) Shep. Touch. 161. (*b*) 10 East 130. (*c*) Bac. Abr. t.t. "Covenant" (F.)
(*d*) 9 East 15. (*e*) Shep. Touch. 125. (*f*) Ibid. t.t. "Conditions."
(*g*) Cru. Dig. XIII. t.t. 1. s. 6. 1 Inst. 216 a. 237 a. n. 1. (*h*) Shep. Touch. 160.

of the deed, or be the words of the lessee, to compel the lessor to do something, then it is not a condition, but a covenant only; as if there be in the deed a covenant that the lessee shall scour the ditches, and then these words follow, "provided that the lessor shall carry away the earth" (*a*).

If the words run thus. "provided always, and the lessee, *&c.* doth covenant, *&c* that neither he nor his heirs shall do such an act," this is both a condition and a covenant (*b*).

If a man make a lease for years by indenture "provided always and it is covenanted and agreed between the parties, that the lessee shall not alien," this is both a condition and a covenant; for it was adjudged that this was a condition by force of the proviso, and a covenant by force of the other words (*c*)

If a man leases for years, rendering rent, and the lessee covenants to repair, *&c.* and afterwards the lessor devises to the lessee for more years, yielding the like rent, and under such covenants as were in the first lease, yet this makes no condition, for though after the first lease is ended, the lessee shall not be bound by the covenants, yet the will expressing that the lessee should have the lands, observing the first covenants, it shall not be taken to be a condition by any intent to be collected out of the will; for covenants and conditions differ much (*d*).

With respect to what shall be deemed a condition, it is a rule in provisoes, that where a proviso is that the lessee shall perform or not perform a thing, and no penalty is annexed to it, that is a condition, otherwise it would be void, but if a penalty is annexed, it is a covenant (*e*).

A condition may be annexed to an estate of inheritance, freehold, or for years, or to a grant of tithes by the clergy (*f*).

So, estates made by deed to infants, and feme coverts, upon condition, shall bind them, because the charge is on the land (*g*).

The heir, though not named, may take advantage of a condition annexed to a real estate (*h*). and where the condition of an obligation was to make a lease, or pay 100*l* the obligee dying, though the election was taken away, it was held that the executor should have the 100*l.* agreeably to the rule in cases of heirs (*i*)

But a condition shall not be construed to extend to things of common right, as if the condition be that one shall enjoy such land immediately upon the grantor's death, though the executor take the emblements, the condition does not extend to it (*k*).

A lease for life on condition, being a freehold, cannot cease without

(*a*) Shep Touch 122 (*b*) Ibid (*c*) Co Lit 203 b.
(*d*) Bac Abr tit. "Conditions" (G) (*e*) Cro Eliz. 242.
(*f*) Com Dig. tit. "Conditions." (A 7) (*g*) 2 Danv. 30. (*h*) 1 Ves. 47.
(*i*) 1 Salk. 172 (*k*) Com Dig tit. "Condition" (F.)

entry; but if it be a lease for years, the lease is void *ipso facto* on breach of the condition, without any entry (*a*).

As to what shall be a suspension of a condition, if lessee for years hath execution by *elegit* of a moiety of the rent and reversion against the lessor, where the lease is upon condition, this is a suspension of all the condition during the time of the extent, and though but a moiety of the rent is extended, yet the entire condition is suspended. So it is if a stranger hath execution by *elegit* (*b*).

A condition may be contained in the same deed; or indorsed upon the deed, or may be contained in another deed executed the same day. So a condition to defeat a deed may be annexed to the reservation of the rent, explaining the manner of payment (*c*).

A proviso or condition differs also from a covenant in this, that a proviso is in the words of, and binding upon both parties, whereas a covenant is in the words of the covenantor only

Under a power to tenant for life to lease for years, reserving the usual covenants, &c a lease made by him, containing a proviso, that in case the premises were blown down, or burned, the lessor should rebuild, otherwise the rent should cease, is void, the jury finding that such covenant is unusual (*d*)

So, under a power to a tenant in possession to let all or any part of the premises, so as the usual rents be reserved, a lease of tithes, which had never been let before, was held void (*e*).

So, a covenant not to assign without licence, was held by *Thurlow*, L. C J not to come within a contract to grant a lease with common and usual covenants "Common and usual" covenants, his Lordship observed, must mean covenants incidental to the lease. and that though the covenant not to assign without licence might be a very useful one where a brewer or vintner let a public house (as was the case here), that would not make it a common covenant (*f*).

Covenant for quiet enjoyment —An express covenant, usual on the part of the lessor, is for quiet enjoyment of the premises demised, or to save harmless the lessee from all persons claiming title

A covenant for quiet enjoyment implies, of course, that the lease shall be a good and valid demise, as a bad lease would be a breach of such covenant for the reasons assigned before. This being the case, the old covenant, for farther assurance, becomes unnecessary, and has therefore fallen into disuse (*g*).

Indeed, according to the ancient mode of conveyance, deeds were confined to a very narrow compass. The words "grant and enfeoff," amount to a general warranty in law, and have the same force and effect.

(*a*) 1 Inst 214. (*b*) Bac Abr tit "Conditions" (O 3)
(*c*) Com. Dig *ut ante* (A. 9) (*d*) 1 T. R. 705 (*e*) 3 T R. 665
(*f*) 3 Br. R. 632. (*g*) Shep Touch 170

The covenants therefore, which have been introduced in more modern times, if they have any use besides that of swallowing a quantity of parchment, are intended for the protection of the party conveying, and are introduced for the purpose of gratifying the general warranty, which the old common law implied (*a*).

If one make a lease of land to another, and covenant that he shall quietly enjoy it without the let or molestation of any person whatsoever, or without the let of any person whatsoever claiming by or under the lessor; in both these cases, the covenant, it is said, shall be taken to extend to such persons as have title, or claim some estate under the lessor, for if, in the first case, the lessee shall be disturbed by any claim, entry, or otherwise by any person that hath no title; or in the second case, by any person who shall claim under another and hath title, or that shall claim under the lessor, this is held to be no breach of the covenant. *Sed quaere* as to the first case, for herein some conceive a difference between a covenant in deed, and a covenant in law, and howsoever the latter is extended only to evictions by title, yet that the covenant in deed shall be extended further; therefore that if *A.* make a lease to *B.* and covenant that *B* shall quietly enjoy it during the term without the interruption of any person or persons, in such case, if a stranger, having no right, interrupt *B.* he may have an action of covenant, as, when such a promise is by word, an action on the case will lie upon it (*b*).

A covenant for quiet enjoyment does not extend to oblige the lessor to rebuild (*c*).

A covenant that the lessee shall quietly enjoy against all claiming, or pretending to claim, a right in the premises, was held to extend to all interruptions, be the claim legal or not, provided it appear that the disturber do not claim under the lessee himself (*d*).

It seems indeed to have been at one time held, that if the lessor undertook expressly that the lessee should enjoy during the term "quietly, peaceably, and without interruption," it would extend as a covenant against all tortious ejectments whatsoever; but this doctrine is now overruled (*e*)

For, where a covenant was inserted in a conveyance of lands in *America*, during the *American* war, that the grantor had a legal title, and that the grantee might peaceably enjoy, *&c* without let, interruption, *&c* of the grantor and his heirs, "and of and from all and every other person or persons whomsoever," it was held not to be broken by the States of *America* seizing the lands as forfeited for an act done previous to the conveyance, notwithstanding the subsequent acknowledgment of

(*a*) 2 Bos. & Pul. 26. (*b*) Shep. Touch. 166. Lofft's R. 460. (*c*) Ambl. 620.
(*d*) 10 Mod. 384. 1 Com. R. 230. 1 L. R. 673. (*e*) 1 Esp. N. P. 273. Hob. [illegible]

her independence by this country for such a covenant does not extend to the acts of wrong doers, but only to persons claiming title (*a*), and even a general warranty, which is conceived in terms more general than the present covenant, has been restrained to *lawful* interruptions (*b*).

So, if a lease be made for a term of years by deed, so that the lessor is chargeable by writ of covenant, if a stranger who has no right oust that termor, yet he shall not have a writ of covenant against his lessor; for a covenant for quiet enjoyment shall not be construed to extend to a wrongful ejectment by a stranger, unless so expressed; because for this wrong, the lessee may have his remedy by action against the stranger himself (*c*).

But if he to whom the right belongs oust the termor, then he shall have covenant against the lessor, so if the lessee be ejected by the lessor himself (*d*).

So, if the lessor covenants against the acts of a particular person or particular persons, covenant will lie (*e*).

If a man covenant that he will not interrupt the covenantee in the enjoyment of a close, the erection of a gate which intercepts it, is a breach of the covenant, although he had a right to erect it (*f*).

If the lessor covenants with the lessee that he hath not done any act to prejudice the lease, but that the lessee shall enjoy it "against all persons," in this case, these words "against all persons" shall refer to the first, and be limited and restrained to any acts done by him, and no breach shall be allowed but in such an act (*g*).

In a covenant that the lessee shall quietly enjoy, &c. with an exception of the king, his heirs, and successors, an interruption by the king's patentee is a breach of the covenant; for such patentee is not excepted (*h*).

If a lessee holds his estate on condition of paying an annuity, non-payment is a breach of covenant for quiet enjoyment, although no demand of it was made, and the lessee himself might have paid it (*i*).

But if a covenant be to save the lessee harmless from a rent charge, if the lessee pay it without compulsion, he pays it in his own wrong (*l*).

The lessor after a demise of certain premises with a portion of an adjoining yard, covenanted that the lessee should have "the use of the pump in the yard jointly with himself, whilst the same should remain there, paying half the expences of repair." The words,

(*a*) 3 T. R. 584. (*b*) Ibid. 587.
(*c*) Ibid. 1 a. 22 H. 6. 52. b. pl. 26. Cro. Eliz. 914. Cro. Jac. 425. Bull. N. P. 161.
(*d*) 3 T. R. 387. n. a. Cro. Eliz. 213; [illegible] Cro. Eliz. 213; 1 Str. 400.
(*f*) 8 Mod. 318. (*g*) [illegible] (*h*) [illegible] 518. (*i*) Ibid. 683.
(*l*) 3 Salk. 108.

"*whilst* &c." reserve to the lessor a power of removing the pump at his pleasure, and it is no breach of the covenant, though he remove it without reasonable cause, and in order to injure the lessee; but without those words, it would have been a breach of covenant to have removed the pump (*a*)

In cases wherein the lease being avoided, becomes in fact a nullity, a covenant for quiet enjoyment is completely broken.

For payment of Rent.—A covenant for the payment of the rent is also generally inserted in the lease.

The tenant's liability to pay rent subsists during the continuance of the lease, notwithstanding he may become a bankrupt, and be deprived of all his property (*b*).

So, where the lessee covenants generally to pay rent, he is bound to pay it though the house be burned down (*c*).

So, a lessee who covenants to pay rent and to repair, with express exception of casualties by fire, or tempest, is liable upon the covenant for rent though the premises are burned down, and not rebuilt by the lessor after notice; for whatever was the default of the lessor in not repairing, and though it is a hard case, yet the lessee must at all events perform his covenant, by which he was expressly bound to pay rent during the term (*d*).

The rule is, that when the law creates a duty, and the party is disabled to perform it without any default in him, and he has no remedy over, the law will excuse him but when the party by his own contract creates a duty or charge upon himself, he is bound to make it good if he may, notwithstanding any accident by inevitable necessity; because he might have provided against it by his contract (*e*).

Where plaintiff was lessee of a colliery, at the rate of so much *per* wey, and the colliery became not worth working, upon the plaintiff offering to pay for all the coal that could be got, he was relieved by the Court of Chancery against the future rent, and the covenant in the lease to work the colliery (*f*).

Of forehand Rents or Fines.—Another species of rent occurs, payment of which is generally stipulated by a covenant in the lease: and this is sometimes called a fore-hand rent, and sometimes a foregift or income, but more commonly a fine, which is a premium given by the lessee on the renewal of his lease, and has been considered as an improved rent (*g*)

In the case of renewal of a lease, by an ecclesiastical corporation, though a dean and chapter are reasonable in the fines they demand, if an accident delays the lease, which has not happened from their fault

(*a*) 7 T. R. 116 (*b*) 7 T. R. 616. 8 T. R. 61 (*c*) 2 Str. 763. 1 Ld Raym. 1477 S. C.
(*d*) 1 T. R. 31[illegible] 3 Bur. 164[illegible] 6 T. R. [illegible] (*e*) 6 T. R. 751. (*f*) 2 Br. R. 3[illegible]
(*g*) 1 T. R. [illegible] 3 T. R. [illegible]

or that of the tenant, yet if it is not completed till a new member comes in, he shall have his proportion (*a*).

Nomine Poenæ.—A farther security for the payment of rent is sometimes agreed upon, by the insertion of a covenant by the terms of which the lessee forfeits a certain sum upon non-payment of such rent This *nomine poenæ*, as it is called, is incident to the rent, and shall descend to the heir. If an annual rent, therefore, be devised, the *nomine poenæ* passes as incident thereto and the grantee may have an action of debt for the arrearages thereof (*b*)

By accepting the rent, however, the party it should seem waives the penalty (*c*).

Though forfeiture is mentioned to be *nomine poenæ*, or for not paying a collateral sum, it is no *nomine poenæ* if it be not of a rent.

A penalty of a similar kind is also inserted sometimes in case the lessee dig for bricks, or lessen the quantity or value of the soil by similar means. But a covenant of this nature (unless the penalty be sufficiently great) is perhaps less expedient than the implied one, or an express one to use the land in an husband-like manner, or not to dig, &c. for a *nomine poenæ* in leases to prevent the tenant from plowing (*ex gr.*) is the stated damages (*d*); so that damages &c could not be recovered beyond the amount of the penalty in the one case, whereas in the other cases, the landlord would have a prospect of being recompensed to the extent of the injury done (*e*).

If there be a *nomine poenæ* given to the lessor for non-payment, the lessor must demand the rent before he can be entitled to the penalty, or if the clause be, that if the rent were behind, the estate of the lessee should cease and be void, in these cases there must be an actual demand made, because the presumption is, that the lessee is attendant on the land to save his penalty and preserve his estate, and therefore shall not be punished without a wilful default, and that cannot be made to appear without a demand be proved, and that it was not answered, and such demand must be made at the day prefixed for the payment, and alledged expressly to have been made in the pleading.—The action of ejectment is now the usual mode adopted for taking advantage of the tenant's default, in which he can only plead the general issue; but the lessor of the plaintiff must be prepared to prove a demand, where a demand is absolutely necessary (*f*) [See also *post* "Condition to re-enter on non-payment of rent"]

Bond for performance of Covenants. If a man covenants to enter into a bond to the lessee for the enjoyment of certain lands demised,

(*a*) 3 Atk 473
(*c*) Cowp 247
(*e*) Doug 49, 50

(*b*) Co Litt 61 b Cro Eliz 895 Lutw 1156
(*d*) 3 [illegible] 296
(*f*) [illegible] "Conditions" (O 2) *Vide post*

and does not express what the sum shall be, he shall be bound in such a sum as is equal to the value of the land (*a*).

A bond for the performance of covenants or agreements has been held to be only a security (under stat. 8 & 9 *W.* 3. *c.* 11.) to the extent of the penalty (*b*). Yet, it has also been held that the penalty is merely a security, and that where it is not sufficient, the plaintiff may recover damages as well as the penalty, and that nothing can prove the principle stronger than the constant practice, where an action is brought on a bond, of giving damages (*c*).

A bond for non performance of covenants is forfeited by a breach of covenant in law, as if the lessee be evicted out of the premises demised (*d*).

Covenant to pay Taxes.—With respect to taxes, the tenant commonly covenants to pay all public impositions, except the land-tax.

When one covenants with another that he shall have lands discharged of all rents, the covenantee ought to be discharged of a quit-rent (*e*).

So, a grantee of a fee-farm-rent, "without any deduction, defalcation, or abatement whatsoever," is entitled to the full rent without deducting the land-tax (*f*).

So, if a tenant covenant to pay a rent without deducting taxes, a statute authorizing the tenants to deduct, will not repeal the covenant (*g*).

A covenant to pay taxes generally, includes parliamentary taxes, and, as a consequence, the land-tax: for when "taxes" are generally spoken of, if the subject-matter will bear it, they shall be intended parliamentary taxes given by the crown (*h*).

So, if a lease be made for years, rendering rent free and clear from all manner of taxes, charges and impositions whatsoever, the lessee is bound to pay the whole rent without any manner of deduction for any old or new tax, charge or imposition whatsoever (*i*).

If a tenant covenant to pay "all taxes," this binds him to the payment of such taxes only as were in being when the lease was made, and not to taxes or charges afterwards imposed (*k*).

So, a covenant to discharge from taxes extends to subsequent taxes of the same nature, but not to those of a different nature (*l*).

A covenant to pay taxes on the land does not extend to the rates to church and poor, for they are personal charges (*m*).

Covenants relative to this subject are generally inserted in leases, and are authorized by the land-tax acts, which provide "that nothing

(*a*) 3 Co. 78. [illegible] (*b*) Dc[illegible] (*c*) 2 [illegible] R. 389.
(*d*) 4 Co. 80. 2 Keb. [illegible] 1 Com. R. 1[illegible] (*f*) Doug. 624.
(*g*) 1 Ld. Raym. 323. (*h*) D[illegible] 14, 615. 12 M[illegible] 268. 11 M[illegible] 2[illegible]
(*i*) Bac. Abr. tit. "Co[illegible]" [illegible] 13[illegible] D[illegible] (*l*) 1 [illegible] 223.
(*k*) 1 [illegible] 192. 3 L. R. [illegible] (*m*) [illegible] 314.

" therein contained shall be construed to alter, change, determine, or " make void any contracts, covenants or agreements whatsoever, be- " tween landlord and tenant, or any other persons, touching the pay- " ment of taxes and assessments."

A distinct covenant in a lease whereby the tenant bound himself to pay the property tax and all other taxes imposed on the premises or on the landlord in respect thereof (though void and illegal by the statute 46 *Geo.* 3. c. 65. s. 115) will not avoid a separate covenant in the lease for payment of rent clear of all parliamentary taxes or generally; for such general words will be understood of such taxes as the tenant might lawfully engage to defray (*a*).

Under a covenant by a tenant for the payment of 80*l.* yearly rent, all taxes thereon being to him allowed, and also that he would pay all further or additional rates on the premises, or on any additional buildings or improvements made by him, and a covenant by the landlord to pay all rates on the premises, or on the tenant in respect of the said yearly rent of 80*l.*, except such further or additional taxes as may be assessed on the premises, the tenant is bound to defray all increase of the old, as well as any new rates, beyond the proportion at which the premises were rated at the time of the lease, which was 20*l.* in respect of the 80*l.* rent (*b*).

Where land was mortgaged to secure an annual payment of 20*l.* to a widow, in satisfaction of her dower, this annual payment being secured out of land ought to answer taxes as the land does, but if the tenant in the payment of the annuity to the widow omits to deduct for taxes, he shall not make her refund in equity, [but it may be recovered at law in an action of *assumpsit*, being money paid to her use, *&c.*] (*c*).

Covenant to cultivate the Land.—In husbandry leases, it is usual to insert a special covenant, as to the mode of cultivation, for without such a covenant, the lessee would be left to his choice as to the treatment of the land; provided he breaks not the implied covenant to treat it in a husbandman-like manner.

Respecting a covenant to use the land in a husbandman-like manner and to deliver it up in like condition, it was held to be matter of law to determine what was using the land in an husbandman-like manner, and *Buller* J. gave it as his opinion, that under such a covenant the tenant ought to use on the land all the manure made there, except that when his time was out, he might carry away such corn and straw as had not been used there, and was not obliged to bring back the manure arising from it (*d*). [This is a covenant which we conceive would be governed in its construction by the mode in which the land

(*a*) 11 East, 165. (*b*) 14 East, [illegible] (*c*) 3 P. Wms. 128 [illegible] (*d*) 1 Esp. N. P. C. [illegible]

demised had been usually cultivated, by the nature of the soil, and by the custom of the country.]

Indeed, in a recent case, it was observed by Lord *Ellenborough*, that evidence that an estate had been managed according to the custom of the country, would be always a medium of proof that it had been treated in a good and husbandman-like manner (*a*).

Lessee covenants to leave sufficient compost on the so[illegible] of the landlord at the end of the term, he the lessee having the [illegible]d, barn, and a room to lodge in and dress diet. This was hol[illegible]o be a mutual covenant and not a condition. It differs from a case where the tenant covenants to repair, if the lessor finds sufficient timber, for t[illegible]re the proviso restrains the covenant. but in this case, said Lord *Mansfield*, there is not the least foundation for such construction (*b*).

To repair and deliver up in good condition, &c.—As to an express covenant to repair, if a lessee covenants to keep a house in repair, and leave it in as good plight as it was at the time of making the lease (*c*): in this case, the ordinary and natural decay is no breach of the covenant, but the lessor is bound to do his best to keep it in the same plight. and therefore should keep it covered (*d*).

An agreement by the tenant to leave a farm as he found it, is an agreement to leave it in tenantable repair. and will maintain a declaration so laid (*e*).

A covenant in a lease to deliver up at the end of the term, all the trees standing in an orchard at the time of the demise, "reasonable use and wear only excepted," is not broken by removing trees decayed and past bearing, from a part of the orchard which was too crowded (*f*).

A general covenant to repair, and to deliver up in repair, extends it seems, to all buildings erected during the term (*g*).

Therefore were a lease was made of three messuages for forty-one years, in which the lessee covenanted "to pull them down and erect "three others in their place, and also to leave the said premises and "houses thereafter to be erected at the end of the term in good "repair" and afterwards the lessee pulls down the three houses and builds five, he must leave them all in good repair at the end of the term for though in the first covenant he is bound only to repair the messuages agreed to be erected, yet by the last covenant he is obliged to leave in good repair the houses thereafter to be erected indefinitely which extends to all houses that shall be built upon the premises during the term (*h*).

(*a*) 4 East's R 154 *post* C XV s 1

(*b*) Lofft's R. 57

(*c*) Fitz Abr tit "Covenant," fol 4.

(*d*) *Et vid* 2 Esp R 590 *ante*

(*e*) 2 Bl Rep 842 *et vid* 1 N B 145. K *post.* C XV. s 1

(*f*) 2 Campb 449

(*g*) 1 [illegible] N R 277

(*h*) Bac Abr tit "Covenant" (F)

So, if a man takes a lease of a house and land, and covenants to leave the demised premises in good repair at the end of the term, and he erects a messuage upon part of the land, besides what was before; he must keep, or leave this in good repair also (*a*).

But in a building and repairing lease, a covenant "to leave the "demised premises, with all new erections, well repaired," was construed to extend to the new erections only, a sum of money being agreed to be laid out in new erections and rebuilding, and the covenant "to keep in repair" extending only to new erections (*b*).

Where in a lease with a clause of re-entry, there is a general covenant on the part of the tenant to keep the premises in repair; and it is further stipulated by an independent covenant, that the tenant within three months after notice, shall repair all defects specified in the notice, the landlord after serving him with a notice may within the three months bring an ejectment against him, for a breach of the general covenant to repair (*c*).

A court of equity cannot decree a specific performance of a covenant to repair; and where an ejectment is brought by a landlord for breach of a covenant to repair, it would seem that equity cannot relieve (*d*).

Accidental Fire.—A lessee of a house, who covenants generally to repair, is bound to rebuild it, if it be burned by accidental fire. So, if the premises be consumed by lightning or the King's enemies, he is still liable (*e*).

Touching the progress of the law as to the accidental burning of houses, so far as regards landlord and tenant at common law lessees were not answerable to landlords for accidental or negligent burning: then came the statute of *Gloucester*, which by making tenants for life and years liable to waste without any exception, consequently rendered them answerable for destruction by fire. thus stood the law in Lord *Coke's* time.

But now by the statute 6 *Anne*, c. 31 the antient law is restored, and the distinction introduced by the statute of *Gloucester* between tenants at will and other lessees is taken away. for by the 6th section of that statute it is enacted, That no action, suit, or process whatsoever shall be had, maintained, or prosecuted against any person in whose house or chamber any fire shall accidentally begin, or any recompence be made by such person for any damage suffered or occasioned thereby and if any action shall be brought, the defendant may plead the general issue and give the Act in evidence and in case the plaintiff become nonsuit, or discontinue his action or suit, or if a verdict pass against him, the defendant shall recover treble costs.

(*a*) Bac. Abr. tit. Covenant (F). (*b*) 1 B. R. 290, 291. (*c*) 2 Campb. 520.
(*d*) 16 Ves. J. 402. (*e*) [illegible] Rep. 627; 6 T. R. 650. Dyer, 33. 2 Show. [illegible]
Jun. 34. Co. Litt. 57 a. [illegible]

Section 7. provides, That nothing in the Act contained shall extend to defeat or make void any contract or agreement between landlord and tenant.

An exception of accidents by fire is now in many cases introduced into leases to protect the lessee, who would (as we have seen) be liable to rebuild under his covenant to repair (*a*), and where lessee of a house and wharf covenanted to repair, accidents by fire excepted, the house was burned down, and the lessor having insured received the insurance money, but neglected to rebuild, and brought an action at law for the rent, a bill for an injunction till the house was rebuilt was held proper (*b*).

But though such exception will protect the lessee from his covenant to repair, yet he is liable (as we have also seen) to payment under a covenant to pay rent, though the premises be burnt down and not rebuilt by the lessor, by which he is deprived of all use and enjoyment of them (*c*).

There is no equity in favour of a lessee of a house, liable to repair, with the exception of damage by fire, for an injunction against an action for payment of rent upon the destruction of the house by fire (*d*).

When there is a covenant to repair on the part of the lessee, if he pull down houses, no action will lie against him till the end of the term, for before that period he may repair them. But if he cut down timber or trees, covenant lies immediately, for such cannot be replaced in the same plight at the end of the term (*e*).

If the covenant be, "it is agreed that the lessee shall keep the "house demised in good repair, the lessor putting it in good repair," covenant lies against the lessor on these words, if he do not put it into repair (*f*).

It has been held, that if the lessor covenant to repair during the term, if he will not do it, the lessee may repair and pay himself by way of retainer (*g*); but *Holt*, C. J. doubted of this, unless there was a covenant to deduct the expences of the repairs from the rent; and though cases occur in the books, wherein it has been thought by some of the judges that a lessee might expend part of the rent in repairs of the premises if they required repair, and might set off such expenditure in an action either of debt or covenant for rent, yet such an opinion is erroneous, for the lessor and lessee have their respective remedies on the covenants contained in the lease; and the maxim of law, "so to judge of contracts as to prevent a multiplicity of suits," does not apply (*h*).

So that the point seems to be now settled, for upon a plea of [illegible]

(*a*) 6 T. R. [illegible] (*b*) [illegible] Atk. [illegible] (*c*) 1 H. [illegible] 321. (*d*) [illegible]
(*e*) [illegible] (*f*) [illegible] (*g*) 1 Lev. 297. [illegible] 222.
[illegible] (*h*) 1 T. R. [illegible]

debet in an action of debt for rent, the defendant cannot give in evidence disbursements for necessary repairs, for he might have had covenant against him (*a*)

Where notice of pulling down and rebuilding a party-wall was given under the Building Act 14 *G* 3. c. 7, 8, and the tenant of the adjoining, who was under covenant to repair, finding it necessary in consequence to shore up his house, and to pull down and replace the wainscot and partitions of it, instead of leaving such expences to be incurred, and paid by the owner of the house, giving notice in the manner prescribed by the Act, employed workmen of his own to do the necessary works and paid them for the same held, that he could not recover over against his landlord such expences incurred by his own orders, and paid for by him in the first instance, the landlord being made to reimburse his tenant only in those cases, where money has been paid by the tenant to the owner of the adjoining house, for works done by him (*b*)

A covenant to repair is a covenant that must run with the land, for it affects the estate of the term, and the reversion in the hands of any person that has it (*c*)

Covenant to reside on the Premises.—A covenant in a lease that the lessee, his executors and administrators, shall constantly "reside upon "the demised premises" during the demise, is binding on the assignee of the lessee, though he be not named Indeed, the 1st and 6th resolutions in Spencer's case are directly in point· which resolutions are 1st That when the covenant extends to a thing *in esse*, parcel of the demise, the thing to be done by force of the covenant is *quodam modo* annexed and appurtenant to the thing demised and shall go with the land, and shall bind the assignee, although he be not bound by express words 6th. That if lessee for years covenants to repair the houses during the term, it shall bind all others as a thing which is appurtenant, and goeth with the land, in whose hands soever the term shall come, as well those who came to it by act of law, as by the act of the party; for all is one, having regard to the lessee And if the law should not be such, great prejudice might accrue to him, and reason requires that they who shall have the benefit of such covenant when the lessor makes it with the lessee, should on the other side be bound by the like covenant, when the lessee makes it with the lessor (*d*).

So where *A* gave by will his tenant-right, which he held by lease, to *B* but not to dispose of, nor sell it, and if he refused "to dwell 'there or keep it in his own possession," then that C. should have his "tenant-right of the farm" *B* having borrowed money, left the

(*a*) Bull N P 176 (*c*) 12 East, 237. (*d*) 1 Salk. 21[illegible]
(*b*) 2 H Bl 1[illegible]

title deeds with his creditor as a security, and confessed a judgment to secure the money, and having also given a judgment to another creditor who issued an execution against him, the sheriff sold the lease to the creditor with whom the deeds were deposited, he paying the debt of the plaintiff in the execution: and *B.* having left the premises and ceased to dwell there on the day of the execution, before the sheriff entered, it was holden that *C.* the remainder-man was entitled to enter, for that the acts of *B.* amounted to a voluntary departing with the estate (*a*).

Not to permit particular Trades to be carried on.—In leases of tenements, especially in towns, a covenant is frequently inserted to restrain the lessee from carrying on, or assigning the houses to persons carrying on obnoxious trades, and also from having or permitting any sale of furniture in the house: a precaution which becomes very necessary, not merely from the injury which may otherwise be done to the premises, but likewise from the respectability being lessened, and the good-will of them being thereby diminished (*b*).

If the lessee of a house covenants not to lease the shop, yard, or other thing belonging to the house, to one who sells coals, nor that he himself will sell coals there, and afterwards he leases all the house to one who sells coals, he has broken the condition (*c*).

Where the lessee of a house and garden for a term of years, covenanted not to use or exercise any trade or business whatever, and afterwards assigned the lease to a *Schoolmaster*, who carried on his business in the house; the assignment was held to be a breach of the covenant (*d*).

Schedule of the Goods.—In case of the lease of a house, together with the goods, it is usual (as we have before mentioned) to make a schedule thereof and affix it to the lease, and to have a covenant from the lessee to re-deliver them at the end of the term, for without such covenant the lessor can have no remedy but trover or detinue for them after the lease is ended: for as the law does not create any covenant upon such personal things, an express covenant becomes necessary (*e*).

Covenant not to assign.—A covenant not to assign, and a proviso of re-entry in case the lessee do assign, are generally contained in leases. The landlord relies perhaps on the tenant's honesty, or he approves of his skill in farming, and thinks that he will take more care of the farm than another, and therefore he has a right to guard against the event of the estate's falling into the hands of any other person, who may not manage it so well as the original tenant: indeed it is but reasonable that a landlord should exercise his judgment with respect to the person

(*a*) 2 T. R. 421 [illegible] 8 T. R. 300 [illegible]
(*b*) 2 T. R. 1[illegible]
(*c*) Bac. Abr. tit. "Condition" (O).
(*d*) Bac. Abr. tit. "Covenant" (B), *ante* 142, [illegible]
(*e*) 1 Mod. [illegible]

to whom he trusts the management of his estate; a covenant, therefore, not to assign is legal, and covenants to that effect are frequently inserted in leases (*a*).

But under an agreement for a lease the lessor is not without express stipulation entitled to a covenant restraining alienation without licence; as a proper and usual covenant (*b*).

The power of assignment is incident to the estate of a lessee without the word "assigns" unless expressly restrained, and such restraints on alienation are construed with jealousy (*c*).

If a lessee for years covenant, that if he, his executors, or assigns alien, it shall be lawful for the lessor to re-enter, it seems this is a good condition, and not a covenant only, and the lessor may take it as either a covenant or a condition, but not as both (*d*).

A clause in the lease in these words, Provided always and it is further covenanted, that the lessee shall not assign his term to any other, except to the lessor, paying as much as another, and that if the lessor will not have it, then the lessee may alien it to none except his mother or his son, was held to be a good condition to defeat the estate, for "provided always" implies a condition, if there be not words subsequent which may peradventure change it into a covenant, as where there is another penalty annexed to it for non performance (*e*).

If a lease contain a condition that the lessee shall not assign without licence, and the lessor, after notice of the assignment without licence, accept of rent from the assignee, he dispenses with the condition (*f*).

For it is to be observed, that where the lease is *ipso facto* void by the condition, no acceptance of rent after can make it have a continuance (*g*); otherwise it is of a lease voidable by entry, because the acceptance of rent cannot make a new lease and the old one was determined; but the acceptance of rent in the latter case is a sufficient declaration that it is the lessor's will to continue the lease, for he is not entitled to the rent but by the lease (*h*). But the acceptance of rent after a condition broken, without notice of the breach, is not a continuance of the estate; except the condition be of such a nature as to be equally within the conusance of both lessor and lessee (*i*).

If a man lease a house and land, upon condition that the lessee shall not parcel out the land, nor any part thereof from the house, and afterwards the lessee leases the house and part of the land to one, and leases the residue of the land to another, this is a breach of the condition, for by the word "parcelling" is intended a division or

(*a*) 2 T R 138. (*b*) 15 Ves J 258. (*c*) 15 Ves 264 5.
(*d*) Shep. Touch 124. and 1 2. (*e*) Cro Eliz 242.
(*f*) Cro Car. 511 Cro Eliz. 572 2 T R 425. (*g*) Co Lit 215 1. Saund. 157.
(*h*) Doug 50 Cowp. 182. (*i*) Cro. Eliz. 553. 2 T. R. 425.

separation of the land from the house: it was therefore adjudged that the first grant was a breach of the condition, because every division and severance of the house and land is within the words and intent of the condition (*a*). But if the lessor afterwards accept of rent, it will bar his entry for the condition broken. For where a lease for years was made, upon condition to be void if the lessee assigned over the term [illegible] he afterwards made an assignment, and the lessor, knowing it, accepted the rent [illegible] adjudged, that this would not make the lease good, because it was absolutely void before the acceptance (*b*).

Where the covenant was not to assign the whole or any part of the lands demised without the lessor's consent, and the lessor entered into part thereof, and then the lessee assigned, this was held to be a breach of the covenant, notwithstanding the lessor's entry (*c*).

If the lessee reserves the rent to himself on granting over, it is an under-lease and not an assignment, though he parts with the whole term for what cannot be supported as an assignment, shall be good as an under-lease against the party granting it (*d*).

So where the covenant was "That the lessee should not assign over "his term without the lessor's consent first had in writing," and the lessee devised the term without any such consent obtained, this was held not to be such an assignment as was a breach of the covenant (*e*).

But whether it would be so held at this day, may well be doubted (*f*).

If a lessee for years covenant not to alien without licence of the lessor, under penalty of forfeiting the lease, and he afterwards aliens without licence, equity will not relieve him (*g*).

But if a condition be to do such an act, and the lessor discharges him of part, the whole condition is destroyed, as if a condition be to plough his land, or build his house, and he discharges him of part (*h*).

So where the lessor license his lessee to alien part, he may alien the residue without licence; for the lessor cannot enter, because if he should enter for the condition, he should enter upon the entire, as it was limited, and if he should enter upon the entire, he would destroy that which he had licensed to be aliened, which he cannot do (*i*).

Indeed, on a proviso that the lessee and his assigns shall not alien without licence, if the lessor give licence, the condition is entirely destroyed, and the assignee may afterwards assign or demise the whole or any part of the term without licence. But it is otherwise

(*a*) [illegible] "Condition" (O) (*b*) Cro. Eliz. 528. 1 Salk. 4. (*c*) [illegible]
(*d*) [illegible] Dow. 18- (*e*) Sty. 483. (*f*) Cro. Eliz. 816. [illegible]
(*g*) 9 Mod. 112. (*h*) [illegible] "Condition" (Q) 1 R[illegible]
(*i*) [illegible] Cro. Eliz. 816. [illegible] 12 Ves. 1/1.

of a devise of the term, for that would have been a breach of the condition (*a*).

So, if a lease be upon condition, that the lessee or his assigns shall not alien, unless to his brother: if the lessee assigns his term to his brother, it seems *he* shall not be restrained by the condition (*b*).

A proviso in a lease for re-entry upon assignment by the lessee, his executors, administrators, or assigns without licence ceases by assignment with licence though to a particular individual (*c*).

But if a lease be upon condition to husband and wife, that if it comes to any other hand than their own, and their issues, the lessor shall re-enter if the husband dies, and the wife takes another husband, the lessor shall re-enter (*d*).

So, also, if the lease contain a proviso, that the lessee, his executors, or administrators, shall not set, let, or assign over the whole or any part of the demised premises without licence in writing on pain of forfeiting the lease, the administratrix of the lessee cannot under-let without incurring a forfeiture. A parol licence to let part of the premises does not discharge the lessee from the restriction of such a proviso: for as the party is charged by a sufficient writing, so must he be discharged by a sufficient writing, or something of as high an authority, agreeable to the maxim *unum quodque dissolvitur eo ligamine quo ligatur* (*e*).

If a lease be made to a man and his assigns for twenty-one years provided that he shall not assign, the proviso being repugnant to the premises is void, but it would have been good, if the word "assigns" had been omitted (*f*).

A proviso against assignment without licence in a lease to a lessee, his executors, administrators, and assigns, is not repugnant, the construction being such assigns as he may lawfully have, viz. by licence, or by law, as assignees in bankruptcy (*g*).

Where a lessee covenanted that neither he nor his executors or administrators would assign the term without the lessor's consent, with a power of re-entry to the lessor in such case, and that the lease should be void, the lessee died, his executor entered and afterwards became a bankrupt, and the lease was assigned over by the assignees under his commission for a valuable consideration to the plaintiff, who brought his bill in equity to be relieved against the proviso, and to stay proceedings in an ejectment brought against him upon it. Lord *Macclesfield* held clearly that the assignment, being done by the authority of a statute, would supersede any private agreement between

(*a*) Com Dig tit "Condition" (Q) 1 Rol [illegible] ... 2 Ves 191 (*b*) Com Dig tit "Condition" (Q) 1 Rol [illegible] 422 [illegible]
(*d*) Com Dig ubi sup (Q) (*e*) 2 L. R. 425 (*f*) [illegible]

the parties, and that the assignment by the assignees was no breach of the condition (*a*)

But though bankruptcy supersedes an agreement not to assign without licence, that has been held only in favour of general creditors; and where there is no actual lease, but it rests upon agreement to grant a lease, an individual cannot have a specific performance in opposition to such proviso, and it is very doubtful whether the general assignees could obtain it, even if there was no such provision (*b*)

Although conditions in restraint of alienation are legal and usual, courts of law have always held a strict hand over such methods of defeating leases, and have countenanced very easy modes of putting an end to them (*c*).

Therefore where the words of the condition were "That the "lessee, his executors or administrators, shall not at any time or "times during this demise, assign, transfer, or set over, or other-"wise do or put away this present indenture of demise, or the pre-"mises hereby demised, or any part thereof," it was held that this condition was not broken by an under-lease; for that "assign, "transfer, and set over," were mere words of assignment, whereas the present was an under-lease, [the words, "demise over" were omitted in the proviso;] and that devising a term, [see *Bac. Abr.* tit. *Conditions*, O.] or the lessee becoming a bankrupt, or dying intestate, would be "a doing and putting away the lease," so being in debt, by confessing a judgment and having the term taken in execution, was the like. but that none of these amounted to a breach of this condition (*d*)

So, upon the principle of one of the grounds of adjudication in the preceding case, it has been held, that a lease taken in execution on a warrant of attorney to confess a judgment given by the lessee is not a forfeiture of the lease, under a covenant by such lessee "not to let, set, assign, transfer, make over, barter, exchange, or otherwise part with the indenture, &c," for a distinction is to be taken between those acts which a party does voluntarily, and those that pass *in invitum* of which latter class is the one in question (*e*).

But where it appears that the warrant was executed for the express purpose of getting possession of the lease, the maxim applies, that that which cannot be done *per directum*, shall not be done *per obliquum:* in such case, therefore, it being in fraud of the covenant, the landlord may, under a clause of re-entry for breach of the condition, recover the premises in an action of ejectment from a purchaser under the sheriff's sale (*f*).

(*a*) 2 T. R 136.
(*b*) 12 Ves 504.
(*c*) 2 Bl Rep. 767. 3 Wils. 235. s. c.
(*d*) Ibid
(*e*) 8 T. R. 61
(*f*) 8 T. R. 300.

Where one leased for twenty-one years if the tenant, his executors, *&c.* should so continue to inhabit and dwell in the farm-house, and actually occupy the land, *&c.* and not let or assign over the lease: held that the tenant having become bankrupt, and his assignees having possessed themselves of the premises and sold the lease, and the bankrupt being out of the actual possession and occupation of the farm, the lessor might maintain an ejectment without previous entry (*a*).

An assignment by operation of law is not, it should seem, a breach of a general covenant of this nature: the landlord, therefore, does well to protect himself as far as he can by the particularity of the words contained in his covenant (*b*).

Thus a proviso in a lease that the landlord shall re-enter on the tenant's committing an act of bankruptcy whereon a commission shall issue, is good, for it is a proviso not contrary to any express law, or to reason, or public policy; and the landlord in such case parts with his term on account of his personal confidence in his tenant, which is manifestly the case in all leases where clauses against alienation are inserted (*c*)

Where there is a right of entry given for assigning or under-letting, if a person is found in the premises, appearing as the tenant, it is *prima facie* evidence of an under-letting sufficient to call upon the defendant to shew in what character such person was in possession, as tenant, or as servant to the lessee (*d*).

Covenant to insure.—A covenant in the lease of a house, to insure during the term to a given amount in some sufficient insurance office, is not void for uncertainty, but means that the premises shall be insured against fire in some office where such insurances are usually effected (*e*).

Construction of covenants, &c.—A covenant in an indenture of lease for twenty one years from Michaelmas, that the tenant should not, during the term, cut down any of the coppice of less than ten years' growth, or at any unseasonable time of the year but at the end of the term the landlord agreed to pay to the tenant, the value of all such growth of coppice as should be then standing and growing, was held according to its grammatical construction (uncontrolled by any other part of the instrument shewing a different intent) to bind the landlord, to whom the words of the covenant were to be attributed, to pay the tenant for the value of all the coppice of less than ten years' growth left standing on the demised premises at the end of the term; though no special consideration appeared on the face of the deed for the landlord's agreeing to make a compensation to the tenant for the value of such part of the coppice, which the tenant was not entitled

(*a*) 8 East, 185. (*b*) 2 T R 134 (*c*) Ibid 138, 140.
(*d*) 5 Esp 4. (*e*) 3 Campb. 134.

to cut. One Judge, who dissented, thought that the words "such growth" referred to a growth of ten years, though inaccurately expressed; founded on a strong presumption of the meaning of the parties, as gathered from the restriction on the tenant not to cut coppice of less than ten years' growth, and to the period of the year when the tenancy would end, which was before the cutting season, but after a portion of the coppice would be of ten years' growth (*a*).

The assignor in a deed of assignment of a lease, after reciting the original lease granted to another for the term of ten years, which by mesne assignments had vested in him, and that the plaintiff had contracted for the absolute purchase of the premises; bargained, sold, assigned, transferred, and set over the same to the plaintiff, for and during all the rest, &c. of the said term of ten years, in as ample manner as the assignor might have held the same, subject to the payment of rent and performance of covenants, and then covenanted that it was a good and subsisting lease, valid in law, in and for the said premises thereby assigned, and not forfeited, &c. or otherwise determined, or become void or voidable. It was held that the generality of this covenant for title, which was supported by recital of the bargain for an absolute term of ten years, was not restrained by other covenants which went only to provide for or against the acts of the assignor himself or those who claimed under him; such as, 1st, a covenant against incumbrances, except an under-lease of part by the assignor for three years, 2dly, for quiet enjoyment 3dly, for further assurance: and therefore where it appeared that this original lease was for ten years, determinable on a life in being, which dropped before the ten years expired, though not till after the covenant of the assignor, it was held that the assignee might assign a breach upon the absolute covenant for title (*b*).

In the execution of an agreement for a lease with proper covenants, the party has a right to such covenants as arise out of the general well known practice as to such leases, and not contradicting the incidents of the estate belonging to a lessee; one of which is the right to have the estate without restraint, beyond what is imposed upon it by operation of law, unless there is an express covenant for more.—Where there is an agreement of this kind, the law implies what are proper covenants, as connected with the character and title of the lessor (*c*).

Where a man entitled to an estate of inheritance agrees to make leases with a covenant for perpetual renewal, each lease to contain the same covenant for ever, the agreement must be carried into execution (*d*).—But an agreement for a lease with a covenant for perpetual

(*a*) 13 East, 80. (*b*) 15 East, 530. (*c*) Ibid.
(*d*) 16 Ves. J. 84.

renewal at a fixed rent, of church lands, renewable upon fines continually increasing, was decreed to be delivered up on the ground of surprise, neither party understanding the effect of it (*a*).

Condition to re-enter on non-payment of Rent.—A condition that, if the rent be behind by the space of any given time after the day prescribed for payment, the lessor shall re-enter, is good; and such condition is not saved by the attendance of the lessee with the rent merely on the first day of payment, for if the lessor be not then there to receive it, the lessee must equally attend on the last day (*b*).

If a lease be made rendering rent, on condition, that if the rent be not paid within twenty days, the lessor shall re-enter, and the rent is not paid, in this case the condition is broken (*c*), but the lessor cannot enter until he has made a legal demand, and if he die before he do it, his heir shall never take advantage of that breach, but is discharged for ever (*d*).

Nobody can have the re-entry but he who should have the rent were there no lease, and so is the very text of *Littleton*, *Co. Lit.* 213. *s.* 346, 347. by construction therefore it must be so. As to demand, a clause of re-entry is required (in the principal case, which was a lease under a power) as a security for rent, demand is requisite both by common law and statute, a clause of re-entry will never be allowed to operate further than as a security for rent (*e*).

As to demand of rent before re-entering for non-payment, on an objection being taken for the omission thereof, (respecting which it became unnecessary for the court to give any opinion) these authorities were mentioned (*f*).. *Co. Lit.* 201. *b.* 1. *Rol. Abr.* 459. *pl.* 1, 2, 6, 5 *Co.* 40. 7 *Co.* 28 *b.* *Freem.* 242. 2 *Ld. Raym.* 750. and 1 *Salk.* 259.

A material difference subsists between a remedy by re-entry and a remedy by distress, for the non-payment of rent. Where the remedy is by way of re-entry for non-payment, an actual demand must be made previous to the entry, otherwise it is tortious, and trespass would lie, because a condition of re-entry is in derogation of the grant, and the estate at law, being once defeated, is not to be restored by any subsequent payment; but a notice of distress is of itself a demand (*g*).

But where the power of re-entry is given to the lessor for non-payment without any farther demand, there it seems, that the lessee has undertaken to pay it, whether it be demanded or not, and no presumption in his favour can arise in this case, because, by dispensing with the demand, he has put himself under the necessity of making an actual proof that he was ready to tender and pay the rent. It

(*a*) 16 Ves. J. 72. (*b*) Bac. on Leases, 220. (*c*) Ibid. (*d*) 6 T. R. 458.
(*e*) Lofft's R. 319. (*f*) 6 T. R. 459. (*g*) Shep. Touch. 148. n. 1.

would, however, be adviseable for the lessor even in this case to demand the rent, as the payment should be on the land, provided no place is fixed for the purpose, and a tenant may be prepared to prove that he was on the land the day the rent became due, ready to pay (*a*)

Also as to the necessity of a demand of the rent, there is a difference between a condition and a limitation; for instance, if a tenant for life, (as the case was by marriage settlement, with power to make leases for twenty-one years, so long as the lessee, his executors, or assigns shall duly pay the rent reserved) makes a lease pursuant to the power, the tenant is at his peril obliged to pay the rent without any demand of the lessor; because the estate is limited to continue only so long as the rent is paid, and therefore, for the non-performance according to the limitation, the estate must determine: a demand however had better be made, for the reason before stated (*b*).

If a place be limited and agreed on by the parties where the condition is to be performed, the party who is to perform it is not obliged to seek the party to whom it is payable elsewhere, nor is he to whom it is to be performed obliged to accept of the performance elsewhere, but he may accept it at another place, and it will be good (*c*).

Rent reserved payable yearly is to be paid on the land; because the land is the debtor, and that is the place of demand appointed by law. So if a man leases rendering rent, and the lessee binds himself in a sum to perform the covenants, this does not alter the place of payment of the rent; for it may be tendered on the land without seeking the obligee: except where the condition is for the performance of homage or other corporeal service to the person of the lord (*d*)

The lessee of the King must pay his rent, without demand, at the Exchequer, wherever it may be; but if the King grant the land in reversion, the rent must be demanded on the land, before the patentee can enter as for a forfeiture on non-payment (*e*).

As to the landlord's right of re-entry being waived, if a lessor receive rent-arrear by an act affirming the lessee's possession, it bars his right of re-entry for non-payment on the day it was due (*f*)

Thus, in an action of ejectment, the case was, a prebend let land for years rendering rent, and a re-entry for non-payment. The rent was demanded and was not paid, and two days afterwards the lessor received the rent of him and made him an acquittance by the name of his fermor. Whether this receipt barred him or not of his re-entry? was the question. It was clearly resolved that the bare receipt of the

(*a*) Bac. Abr. tit "Conditions." (O 2) (*b*) Ibid. (*c*) Ibid (O. 4)
(*d*) Ibid Co. Lit. 201 b. (*e*) Cro. Eliz. 462. (*f*) Ibid. 3.

rent after the day was no bar, for it was a duty due to him. but a distress for the rent, or the receipt of rent due at another day, was a bar, for those acts affirm the lessee to have lawful possession: so if he makes him an acquittance with a recital that he is his tenant. In the principal case, the lessor calling him his fermor, was a full declaration of his meaning to continue him his tenant, and it was adjudged that the entry was not lawful (*a*).

So, where a lease was made to one for life rendering rent at *Michaelmas*, with a clause of re-entry for non-payment, the rent was in arrear, and afterwards the lessor brought an action for the rent: adjudged, that notwithstanding this action, he (the lessor) might still enter for a breach of the condition · for the action for the rent did not affirm the lease, because it shall be intended to be brought as for a duty due upon a contract, but if he had distrained for the rent not being paid at the day, then he can never afterwards enter for a breach of the condition, because the distress affirms the continuance of the lease (*b*).

So, a gift was made to the husband and wife, and to the heirs of their bodies; they afterwards made a lease of the lands, reserving rent on such a day, with a clause of re-entry: then the husband died, and the rent being in arrear, the issue in tail accepted it: adjudged that this was no affirmance of the lease as to himself, because the rent was not due to him whilst his mother was living, but it had been otherwise, if he had accepted it after her death (*c*).

It is indeed a rule, that the mere acceptance of rent shall not operate as a waiver of a forfeiture, or as a confirmation of the tenancy, unless the landlord had notice that a forfeiture was incurred at the time or did some other act indicating his intention to continue the lessee in his term (*d*) and such acceptance is matter of evidence only as to the *quo animo*, to be left to the jury under the circumstances of the case (*e*).

Touching conditions of re-entry for non-payment of rent or the breach of any other covenant, the law upon that subject is so well digested in Mr. Serjeant *Williams's* excellent edition of *Saunders's Reports*, that his note containing it may well be here introduced.

Where a condition of re-entry is reserved for non-payment of rent, several things are required by the common law to be previously done by the reversioner, to entitle him to re-enter (*f*) 1. A demand must be made of the rent · [and where there are several demises at distinct rents, separate demands must be made for each, though they be both reserved in the same lease. *Vaugh* 71.] 2. The demand must be of the precise rent due; for if a penny more or less be demanded, it will be ill.

(*a*) Cro Eliz. 462. (*b*) 3 Salk 3 (*c*) Ibid (*d*) 2 T R. 431
(*e*) Cowp 243. (*f*) 1 Saund 287. n 16

[And what remains payable, after the land-tax, or a ground-rent demanded of and paid by the tenant, or any other part of the rent agreed upon, has been lawfully deducted by the tenant, will of course constitute the rent due, 4 *T. R.* 511.] 3. It must be made precisely upon the day on which the rent is due and payable by the lease to save the forfeiture: as where the proviso is, "that if the rent shall be behind and unpaid by the space of thirty or any other number of days, after the days of payment, it shall be lawful for the lessor to re-enter," a demand must be made on the thirtieth or other last day. 4. It must be made a convenient time before sun-set. 5. It must be made upon the land, and at the most notorious place of it. Therefore if there be a dwelling-house upon the land, the demand must be at the front or fore-door, though it is not necessary to enter the house, notwithstanding the door be open. But if the tenant meet the lessor either on or off the land at any time of the last day of payment, and tender the rent, it is sufficient to save a forfeiture, for the law leans against forfeitures. 6. Unless a place be appointed where the rent is payable; in which case a demand must be made at such place. 7. A demand of rent must be made in fact, and so averred in pleading, although there should be no person on the land ready to pay it. 8. If after these requisites have been performed by the reversioner, the tenant neglects or refuses to pay the rent, then the reversioner is entitled to re-enter. [for if the lessor or his sufficient attorney remain upon the land the last day on which the rent ought to be paid, until it be so dark that he cannot see to tell the money, and the money thus demanded be not paid, this is a denial in law, though there be no words of denial, upon which a re-entry may be made. 1 *Inst.* 201. 4 *Rep.* 73.] However, it is to be observed, that no *actual* entry is necessary to be made by him into the land, but it is sufficient to bring an ejectment only: though it was held otherwise until Lord *Hale's* time, when it was decided that the entry confessed by the defendant in the ejectment, was sufficient without any actual entry: which decision has been adhered to ever since.—It follows, as a necessary inference from what has been premised, that a demand made after or before the last day on which the lessee has to pay the rent, in order to prevent a forfeiture, or off the land, will not be sufficient to defeat the estate. But now to obviate these niceties in some cases, the stat. 4 *G.* 2. *c.* 28. (of which hereafter,) prescribes a particular mode of proceeding in cases of premises left vacant and a half year's rent being due, but no sufficient distress being thereon (*a*).

The same requisites which are deemed necessary in order to entitle the lessor to re-enter, are also necessary in order to entitle him to recover a *nomine pœnæ*, as it is called, which is not considered so much as

(*a*) 1 Saund. 287. n. 16.

a remedy for the recovery of the rent, as a penalty to oblige the tenant to a punctual payment of it; and being so immediately connected with the subject of this chapter, we have thought proper to notice it in this part of the work. A *nomine pœnæ* being so considered, therefore where a proviso is, that if the rent be in arrear for the space of thirty days next after the days of payment, the lessee shall forfeit ten shillings a day by way of penalty, in that case in order to entitle the lessor to recover the penalty, there must be a demand of the rent in like manner in every respect, as we have before seen is required in cases of re-entry for non-payment of rent.—A distinction is taken between a power to re-enter, or a *nomine pœnæ*, and a power of distrain as where a rent is granted payable, &c. and in default of payment if it be demanded, the grantee may distrain in this case, it is held not to be necessary to make a demand on the day, as in the case of re-entry, or a *nomine pœnæ*, but he may demand the rent at any time after (*a*).

In cases of conditions of re-entry there is a difference between leases for *lives* and leases for *years*, and with respect to the latter, there is also a difference between *them*, which arises entirely from the manner in which the condition of re-entry is expressed in the lease (*b*).

As to leases for lives, it is held that if the tenant neglect or refuse to pay his rent after a regular demand, or is guilty of any other breach of the condition of re-entry, the lease is only voidable, and therefore not determined until the lessor re-enters, that is, brings an ejectment for the forfeiture and this, though the clause of the condition should be, that for non-payment of the rent, or the like, the lease shall cease and be void (*c*) for it is a rule, that where an estate commences by livery, it cannot be determined before entry, therefore if the lessor, after notice of the forfeiture, which is a material and issuable fact, accept rent which accrued due after, or does any other act which amounts to a dispensation of the forfeiture (as bringing covenant for half a year's rent, subsequent to the time of the demise laid in an ejectment for the forfeiture) the lease which was before voidable, is thereby affirmed (*d*)

But if there be a lease for years, with a condition, that for non-payment of the rent or the like, the lease shall be null and void, in such case if the lessor makes a legal demand of the rent, and the lessee neglects or refuses to pay, or if the lessee is guilty of any other breach of the condition of re-entry, the lease is absolutely determined, and cannot be set up again by acceptance of rent due after the breach of the condition, or by any other act.—Yet if in such lease the clause be, that for non-payment of the rent it should be lawful for the lessor to re-enter, the lease is only voidable, and may be affirmed by acceptance of rent

[illegible] 26. [illegible] Ball. N. P. 96.

accrued after, or other act, if the lessor had notice of the breach of the condition at the time (a).

Regularly, when any man will take advantage of a condition, if he may enter, he must enter, and when he cannot enter he must make a claim, and the reason is, that a freehold and inheritance shall not cease without entry or claim (b), and also the grantor may waive the condition at his pleasure.—It is also to be observed that an entry upon an estate generally, is an entry for the whole, and if it be for less, it should be so defined at the time (c).

It is laid down for a rule, generally, that he who enters for a condition broken shall be seised in his first estate, or of that estate which he had at the time of the estate made upon condition, and therefore shall avoid all mesne charges and incumbrances (d).

Generally as to covenants, touching the operation of an Act of Parliament in respect to them, where the question is, whether a covenant be repealed by an Act of Parliament, this is the difference, viz. where one covenants not to do an act or thing which it was lawful to do, and an Act of Parliament comes afterwards and compels him to do it, the statute repeals the covenant so, if one covenants to do a thing which is lawful, and an Act of Parliament comes in and hinders him from doing it, the covenant is repealed but if a man covenants not to do a thing which at the time was unlawful, and an Act comes and makes it lawful to do it, such Act of Parliament does not repeal the covenant (e).

Though all the rent of the lessee is assigned by Act of Parliament, if there are no words of discharge the lessee's executor is still liable to covenant for the rent (f)

Where by an order, confirmed by Act of Parliament, that an indenture of lease, upon which rent was reserved, should be vacated and cancelled, and that a stranger should enter into the demised lands, and receive the profits: the same rent in value, granted by the lessee for the better securing of the rent reserved, is not discharged, though the intention appears that they should be but one rent paid (g).

It has however been held that if a man covenant to do a thing, and it is afterwards prohibited, yet the covenant is binding, for that a penal statute cannot have a retrospective operation (h).

There is a difference between covenants in general and covenants, secured by a penalty or forfeiture (i) In the latter case, the obligee has his election, he may either bring an action of debt for the penalty,

(a) Shep. ut ante. (b) [illegible] 2.? (c) 3 [illegible] R. [illegible]
(d) Co. Lit. 202 Bac. [illegible] O 4.
(e) 1 Salk. 198 [illegible] (f) Bac. [illegible] Co[illegible]
(g) 1 Sid. [illegible] (i) 3 Mod. 39
(h) 4 Burr. 2225 [illegible]

after the recovery of which he cannot resort to the covenant, because the penalty is to go in satisfaction for the whole or if he does not choose to go for the penalty, he may proceed upon the covenant, and recover more or less than the penalty, *toties quoties* (*a*).

Upon this distinction they proceed in courts of equity; they will relieve against a penalty, upon a compensation, but where the covenant is "to pay a particular liquidated sum," a court of equity cannot make a new covenant for a man, nor is there any room for compensation or relief (*b*)

Thus in leases containing a covenant against ploughing up meadow; if the covenant be "not to plough," and there be a penalty, a court of equity will relieve against the penalty; and will even go further than that to preserve the substance of the agreement (*c*). But if it is worded "to pay 5*l* an acre for every acre ploughed up," there is no alternative, no room for any relief against it, no compensation, it is the substance of the agreement, it is the particular liquidated sum fixed and agreed upon between the parties, and is therefore the proper *quantum* of the damages (*d*).

Indeed, nothing can be more obvious, than that a person may set an extraordinary value upon a particular piece of land or wood, on account of the amusement which it may afford him. In this country a man has a right to secure to himself a property in his amusements and if he choose to stipulate for 5*l*. or 50*l*. additional rent upon every acre of furze broken up, or for any given sum of money upon every load of wood cut and stubbed up, there seems nothing irrational in such a contract (*e*).

The court of chancery will relieve against forfeiture under a covenant for non-payment of rent but not where the recovery in ejectment was also upon breach of other covenants (*f*).

Equity will likewise relieve against a forfeiture incurred by breach of a covenant to lay out a specific sum in repairs in a given time (*g*)

Where articles contain covenants for the performance of several things, and then one large sum is stated at the end to be paid upon breach of performance, that must be considered as a penalty. But where it is agreed that if a party do such a particular thing such a sum shall be paid by him, there the sum stated may be treated as liquidated damages

It is therefore clear, that where the precise sum is not the essence of the agreement, the *quantum* of the damages may be assessed by the jury. but where the precise sum is fixed and agreed upon between

(*a*) 2 Bl. R. 1190 6 T. R. 303 (*b*) 9 Mod. 113. 4 Burr. 2228
(*c*) Ibid (*d*) [illegible] Atk. 396 [illegible] 2 Bro. P. C. 436 (*e*) 2 Bos. & Pul. [illegible]
(*f*) 15 Ves. 6[illegible]. 18 Ves. [illegible] (*g*) 12 Ves. 2[illegible] [illegible] 16 Ves. [illegible]

the parties, that very sum is the ascertained damage and the jury are confined to it (*a*).

Thus, where there is a clause of *nomine pœnæ* in a lease to a tenant to prevent his breaking up and ploughing old pasture ground, the intention thereof being to give the landlord some compensation for the damage he has sustained from the nature of his land being altered, the whole *nomine pœnæ* shall be paid, and not at the rate of 5*l* *per cent* only for the rent reserved (*b*)

Where a conveyance of land is void, so as no estate passes, all dependent covenants are void also, otherwise of covenants independent (*c*).

For a lease must either be good or bad in its creation. Therefore, where it was expressly found, that a covenant in a lease, under a power requiring the insertion of "usual covenants," was unusual, the question was, Whether that circumstance avoided the lease itself, or only that particular covenant and it was observed that the party had no power to lease at all, unless in the form prescribed, which became a condition precedent. It being manifest that the lease was not made pursuant to the power, it was void in his creation, and the reversioner had a right to take advantage (*d*).

If tenant for a term of years lease for a less term and assign his reversion, and the assignee take a conveyance of the fee, by which his former reversionary interest is merged, the covenants incident to that reversionary interest are thereby extinguished (*e*).

(*a*) 4 Bur 2229 (*b*) 2 Atk. 289 (*c*) 1 Salk. 199. (*d*) 1 T. R 70. (*e*) 3 T. R 393

CHAPTER XI.

Of Assignments and Under-Leases,

And in what cases Assignees are bound by Covenants, or may make advantage of them, whether the Assignment or Under-Lease be absolute, or by way of Mortgage.

AN assignment is the transferring and setting over to another some right, title, or interest in things, in which a third person, not a party to the assignment, has a concern and interest (*a*)

Every one therefore who has an estate or interest in lands and tenements, may assign it (*b*) as tenant for life, for years, *&c* [But a tenant at will, or sufferance, cannot assign, it is conceived, for reasons before mentioned (*c*).]

So the interest or estate that a man hath by extent, is assignable from man to man at pleasure (*d*) So, an annuity may be demised by way of assignment and an office in certain cases may be assigned (*e*). And every one who has a present and certain estate or interest in things which lie in grant, may assign; as in a rent, common, advowson, &c. (*f*). Though the interest be future, As a term for years to commence *in futuro*, for the interest is vested *in presenti*, though it does not take effect till a future time (*g*).

So a possibility of a term is assignable in equity for a good consideration, though not so at law and though the assignment of a contingent interest, which a husband has in right of his wife, or the possibility of a term, is not strictly good by way of assignment, yet it will operate as an agreement where there is a valuable consideration; but it must be an assignment of that particular thing, and not rest only in intention and construction of words in a covenant (*h*)

So, a lessee for years of the crown may assign his term, though he is ousted by a stranger (*i*) for the reversion being in the crown he cannot be out of possession but at his pleasure; but ordinarily a lessee cannot assign his term if an actual ouster had taken place, till he re-enter (*k*)

A power, where it is coupled with an interest, may be assigned,

(*a*) Bac. Abr. tit. "Assignment." (*b*) Com. Dig. tit. "Assignment" (A)
(*c*) *Ante* p. 82, 236 (*d*) Shep. Touch. 242 (*e*) *Ante* 148, 150
(*f*) Com. Dig. *ut ante* (*g*) Ibid (*h*) 9 Mod. 102. 2 P. Wms. 608
(*i*) Cro. Eliz. 275. (*k*) Ibid. 15.

though a bare power is not assignable therefore if a lease be made with an exception of the trees, and a power be reserved to the lessor to enter and cut them down, he may assign this power to another person; but if it be not properly pursued, the lessee may maintain trespass both against the lessor and his assignee (*a*)

A lease was made for years of lands excepting the woods the lessor grants the trees to the lessee, and he assigns the land over to another, the trees do not pass by this assignment to the assignee (*b*)

But generally a chose in action, bare right, or possibility cannot be assigned, and where it is otherwise it arises from the enactment of some statute, or the construction of a court of equity.

As a right is not assignable, if the conusee of a statute sue an extent, and a *liberate* is returned, yet if he suffer the conusor to keep possession, he cannot assign the lands, for his possession under the *liberate* is by his own entry turned to a right (*c*)

But the king by virtue of his prerogative may assign a chose in action, and the assignee may sue either in his own name or in the king's (*d*).

Yet if the king grant a chose in action to another, as he may, his grantee cannot assign it to another (*e*).

A. a copyholder covenants to assign and surrender to *B.* which covenant is presented to the homage, but before any surrender *B* assigns his interest to *C* to whom *A* surrenders, *C.* has a right to be admitted on payment of a fine for his own admittance only for all the lord has a right to require is to have a tenant, and a private agreement like this, not followed up by a surrender of the estate, cannot give the lord of the manor a right to any fine (*f*).

If a termor for years make a lease for a time exceeding his interest, it shall operate as an assignment (*g*).

An assignment, as contradistinguished from an under-lease, signifies a parting with the whole term (*h*); and when the whole term is made over by the lessee, although in the deed by which that is done, the rent, and a power of re-entry for non-payment, are reserved to him, and not to the original lessor, yet this is an assignment and not an under-lease, and in such case, the original lessor or his assignee of the reversion, may sue or be sued on the respective covenants in the original lease, even though new covenants are introduced in the assignment (*i*)

So, if a lessee for three years assign his term for four years, or demises the premises for four years, he does not thereby gain any tortious reversion, but it amounts to an assignment of his interest (*k*)

[illegible] the words "grant, assign, and set

[illegible] (*c*) Goldsb. [illegible] (*d*) 4 Mod. [illegible] (*e*) Cro. Jac. [illegible]
[illegible] (*f*) 2 [illegible] 84 (*g*) 1 [illegible] 99 (*i*) 1 Str. [illegible]
[illegible] 1 [illegible] 53 (*k*) 1 [illegible] 99

over;" but no particular expressions are necessary for the purpose, provided the intention of the parties is sufficiently explained.

No consideration need be expressed in an assignment, for the assignees being subject to the payment of the rent reserved by the lease, is held to be a sufficient consideration (*a*).

An assignment must, by the statute (*b*) of Frauds, be in writing; the statute enacts, that no leases, estates, or interests, either of freehold or terms of years, or any uncertain interest, (not being copyhold or customary interest,) of, in, to, or out of any messuages, manors, lands, tenements, or hereditaments, shall be assigned, granted, or surrendered, unless it be by deed or note in writing, signed by the party so assigning, granting, or surrendering the same, or their agents thereunto lawfully authorized by writing, or by act and operation of law.

A parol assignment of a lease from year to year, granted by parol, is void under the Stat. of Frauds (*c*).

An assignee of lease, to shew his interest in the premises is bound to prove the execution of the lease, and all mesne assignments (*d*).

If a trader before bankruptcy deposits a lease as a security for money, but no mortgage or assignment of it then takes place, the assignees may recover it, it conferring no legal title (*e*).

The party assigning is called the assignor and he to whom the assignment is made, the assignee.

The proper covenants on the part of the assignor are, that the indenture of lease is good in law, that he has power to assign; for quiet enjoyment; and for further assurance.

The proper covenants on the part of the assignee are that he will pay the rent, or perform the services, as the case may be, and also perform the covenants contained in the indenture of lease, or save harmless the assignor therefrom.

Assignees are in fact, or in law.—Under the word "assigns," the assignee of an assignee *in infinitum*, the heir of an assignee, or assignee of an heir shall take. So, if a man covenant with another, "his executors and assigns," the assignee of an assignee, and his executors, and the assignee of an executor or administrator of every assignee, are included and shall have covenant (*f*).

It seems that an action will not lie by an assignor against an assignee, for he has no reversionary interest (*g*).

In leases, the lessee being a party to the original contract, continues always liable, notwithstanding any assignment (*h*).

Therefore covenant will lie against a lessee for years on an express

(*a*) Nov. Mo. 92. 1 Mod. 263. 2 Mod. [illegible] (*b*) 29 Car. 2. c. 3.
(*c*) 1 Camp. [illegible] (*d*) Ibid. [illegible] (*e*) 5 Esp. 105.
(*f*) Com. Dig. tit. "Assignment," (F.) Co. Lit. 384. b.
(*g*) [illegible] 2 Saund. [illegible] (*h*) Doug. 462.

covenant, as to repair, pay rent, *&c.* notwithstanding he has assigned his term and the lessor has accepted rent from the assignee.—But an action of debt will not lie after acceptance of rent (*a*)

So, the executor of a lessee is liable to the grantee of the reversion on such covenants, though the lessee may have assigned his term and the grantee have accepted rent of the assignee (*b*)

For no assignment nor acceptance of the rent by the hands of the assignee shall take from him the advantage of suing him or his executors upon an express covenant, no more than if a lessee had obliged himself in an obligation to pay his rent, his assignment over of his term, and the acceptance of the rent by the lessor of the assignee, shall not take from him the advantage of the obligation (*c*)

For the personal representative of a lessee for years is his assignee, and a covenant to repair runs with the land, as it is to be performed on it, and therefore binds the assignee (*d*). So with respect to a covenant to make further assurance (*e*).

So, if there is a covenant which runs with the land, and the lessee assigns over, and the assignee dies intestate, the lessor may have covenant against the administrator of the assignee and declare against him as assignee, for such covenants bind those who come in by act of law, as well as by act of the parties (*f*)

Though all the estate of the lessee is assigned by Act of Parliament, if there are no words of discharge the lessee's executor is still liable to covenant for the rent (*g*)

Where there is a bond for the performance of the covenants in a lease, if the lessee assigns the lease, he may likewise assign the bond but this must be before any of the covenants are broken, for if any of the covenants are broken, and the lessee afterwards assigns the lease and bond, and the assignee puts the bond in suit for those breaches, it has been held to be maintenance (*h*)

An assignee must take the thing assigned, subject to all the equity to which the original party was subject (*i*).

The assignee of a term is bound, therefore, to perform all the covenants which are annexed to the estate, for when a covenant relates to and is to operate on a thing in being, parcel of the demise, the thing to be done by force of the covenant is, as it were, annexed to the thing demised, and shall go with the land, and bind the assignee in the performance, though not named for the assignee, by the acceptance of the possession of the land, makes himself subject to all the covenants that run with the land, of which repairing is one, building another, to pay

(*a*) Cro. Jac. [illegible] Cro. Car. [illegible] 4 Mod. 81 3 Salk. 48 Cro. Jac. 334
(*b*) [illegible] Cro. Jac. 522 3 Salk. [illegible] (*c*) Cro. Car. 188
(*d*) [illegible] (*e*) Cro. Car. 553 (*f*) Esp. N. P. [illegible]
(*g*) [illegible] Covenant [illegible] (*i*) Godb. 81 (*h*) [illegible]

rent a third, *&c.* and to such he is bound without being named by the special word "assigns" (*a*).

So, where there was a covenant to use the land in a husbandman-like manner, and leave it in like condition, it was held to be such a covenant as ran with the land, and that the executor of the landlord might sue on it (*b*).

The assignee, however, is liable only in respect of his possession of the thing: he bears the burthen while he enjoys the benefit, and no longer; and if the whole is not passed, if a day only is reserved, he is not liable (*c*).

But under an absolute assignment of a term the assignee may be sued on the covenants before he has taken actual possession: for by the assignment the title and possessory right might pass and the assignee become possessed in law; and as to the actual possession, that must depend on the nature of the property whether it can take place; thus the premises might be waste or unprofitable ground, or ground intended to build upon (*d*).

So, a mortgagee, though not in possession, is liable to perform the covenants in the lease; for a mortgagee is liable not on the score of possession, but as assignee; and his liability is not limited by his possession, but continues as long as he has the legal estate. He should have taken an under-lease (*e*).

As to the extent to which the lessee or assignee is liable in covenant, there is a considerable difference.

1. The lessee has, from his covenant, both a privity of contract and of estate; and though he assigns, and thereby destroys the privity of estate, yet the privity of contract continues, and he is liable in covenant notwithstanding the assignment (*f*).

2. But the assignee comes in only in privity of estate, and therefore is liable only while he continues to be legal assignee; that is, while in possession under the assignment: except, indeed, in the case of rent, for which, though he assign over, he is notwithstanding liable as to the arrears incurred before, as well as during his enjoyment; and such assignee was made liable in equity, though the privity of estate was destroyed at common law (*g*).

If a lessee covenants that he and his assigns will repair the house demised, and the lessor grants over the term, and the assignee does not repair it, an action of covenant lies either against the assignee at common law, because this covenant runs with the land; or it lies against the lessee, at the election of the lessor, who may charge both; but ex-

(*a*) Bull. N. P. 159. Esp. N. P. 289. 3 Salk. 4. (*b*) Esp. N. P. 2[illegible]

(*c*) Doug. 184. 460. (*d*) Ibid. 462. n. [1.]

(*e*) Stone *v.* Evans, *ante* 113. (*f*) Doug. 458. 764.

(*g*) Bac. Abr. tit. "Covenant" E. 4. 1 Bos. & Pul. 2[illegible]. 2 East's R. 580.

ecution shall be against one of them only, for if he take both in execution, he that is last taken shall have an *audita querela* (*a*).

So, covenant lies against an assignee on a covenant not to plough, although assigns are not named in the deed, for it is for the benefit of the estate, and runs with the land (*b*)

So, if *A.* leases lands to *B* and *B* covenants to pay the rent, repair houses, &c during the said term, and afterwards assigns to *C* the assignee is bound to perform the covenants during the term of the first lessee, though the assignee be not named; because the covenant runs with the land made for the maintenance of a thing *in esse* at the time of the lease made (*c*)

A covenant may be dividable and follow the land therefore an action of covenant will lie against an assignee of part of the thing demised (*d*).

Therefore, where one demised two houses, with covenant on the part of the lessee for himself and assigns to repair, the lessee assigned one of them, and for not repairing the lessor brought covenant against the assignee, which action was held well to lie (*e*) So, in case of eviction, the rent may be apportioned as in debt or replevin (*f*)

So, it seems, it lies by an assignee of part of the estate demised. or the assignees of several parts may join (*g*).

The assignee of part of an estate is not liable for rent for the whole (*h*).

But if a lessee grant or assign part of his estate, yet the entire privity of contract is not at an end, and the lessee would, it seems, remain liable on his covenant to pay the entire rent, for he cannot apportion it (*i*).

Lessee of tithes covenants for him and his "assigns," that he will not let any of the farmers in the parish have any part of the tithes this covenant runs with the tithes, and binds the assignee (*k*)

Where a covenant is for the benefit of the estate demised, it will extend to the assignee, though not named.

Therefore, a covenant that a lessee should reside on the demised premises during the term, was held to extend to his assignee, though not named in the covenant (*l*)

The assignee may assign, and thereby get rid of his subsequent rent, and of the covenants which run with the land and as he may do so at law, so *a fortiori* may he do so in equity, for though the tenant's liability

(*a*) Cro Jac 523 (*b*) Ibid 125 (*c*) Bac Abr tit "Covenant" (E. 3)
(*d*) 1 Roll 522 1 5 Jones 245 Cro Car 222 (*e*) Ibid
(*f*) 2 Lut's R 575 (*g*) Com Dig tit "Covenant" (B 3) 1 Leon 252.
(*h*) Ibid 109 Doug 186 (*i*) Ibid Cro Eliz 633 637. 2 Lut's R. 579
(*k*) 3 Wils 25 (*l*) 2 H. Bl. R. 133

on his covenant to pay rent subsists during the continuance of the lease, notwithstanding he may become a bankrupt and be deprived of all his property, there is no personal confidence in the assignee of the lessee, and when he parts with the lease, he also gets rid of his liability (*a*).

But an assignee, who assigns over, is liable to covenant for the rent incurred during his enjoyment, and if covenant be brought, he may plead that before any rent was due he granted all his term to *J. S.* who by virtue thereof entered and was possessed (*b*), and this will be a good discharge without alledging notice of the assignment, and the assignment will be good though made to a beggar, or to a person leaving the kingdom, provided the assignment be executed before his departure; or therefore made a day before the rent due to a prisoner in the *Fleet*, nor can the plaintiff take advantage of it by replying *per fraudem*, unless he can prove a trust. It was the lessor's own fault and folly to take the first assignee for his tenant; nor is he without remedy, for he may bring covenant against the lessee, or may distrain upon the land. In truth, if you have no remedy against the assignee, you must lose your rent, and get possession of the premises as soon as you can. The only case, Lord *Eldon* thought, in which a question of fraud could arise, was, where the assignor had kept possession of the premises of which he made a profit, and had made an assignment to prevent responsibility. but even there, if the possession were profitable, there would always be something on the premises for the landlord to distrain: for which reason his Lordship doubted whether there ever could be such a thing as a fraudulent assignment, and whether an issue on such a point could ever be well taken. The defendants in the principal case, had a right to devest themselves of the interest, by the mere form of an assignment, which drives the plaintiff to take possession. *Buller*, J. also thought, that the only case, where the replication *per fraudem* could be good, was where the assignor continued in possession (*c*).

As therefore by the assignment the title and possessory right pass and the assignee becomes possessed in law, and is only liable while in actual possession (*d*), so, if he assign over before a breach, though *his* assignee have not taken actual possession, yet he (the first assignee) is not liable to an action of covenant (*e*).

It is not necessary that notice should be given to the reversioner of an assignment over. In an action against the assignee of a term, the plea of an assignment over ought to shew that such assignment over was made after the assignment stated in the declaration. but if it does not, no

(*a*) 2 Atk. 546. 12 Mod. 23. 2 Str. 1221. 4 T. R. 99. 8 T. R. 61. Doug. 461 n. r. 1 Bos & Pull. 23. (*b*) Bull. N. P. 159. 4 Mod. 72.
(*c*) Salk. 81. 4 Mod. 71. 12 Mod. 23. Doug. 764. 1 Bos. & Pull. 23.
(*d*) Doug. 444. (*e*) 1 B. & P. 21.

objection can be made against it after replication that such assignment over was fraudulent (*a*).

Where there is an exception in a lease of an entry, and liberty to wash in the kitchen, and a passage for that purpose, an action will lie against an assignee for hindering the lessor; for a covenant relating to a way or other profit *apprendre* goes with the tenement and binds the assignee (*b*)

If a man leases for years, and the lessee covenants for him and his assigns to pay the rent, so long as he and they shall have the possession of the thing let, and the lessee assigns, the term expires, and the assignee continues the possession afterwards. an action of covenant will lie against him for rent behind after the expiration of the term; for though he is not an assignee strictly according to the rules of law, yet he shall be accounted such an assignee as is to perform the covenants (*c*).

Touching the difference of debt and covenant against an assignee, it is extremely clear that a person who enters into an express covenant in a lease, continues liable on his covenant, notwithstanding the lease be assigned over The distinction between the actions of debt and covenant, which was taken in early times, is equally clear. if the lessee assign over the lease, and the lessor accept the assignee as his lessee, either tacitly or expressly, it appears by the authorities that an action of debt will not lie against the original lessee. but all those cases with one voice declare, that if there be an *express covenant*, the obligation on such covenant still continues. and this is founded not on precedents only, but on reason, for when a landlord grants his lease, he selects his tenant, he trusts to the skill and responsibility of that tenant; and it cannot be endured that he should afterwards be deprived of his action on the covenant to which he trusted, by an act to which he cannot object (as the assignment of a bankrupt's interest) as in the case of execution In such a case the lessor has no choice of the under-tenant. so, in the principal case, the assignees of the bankrupt were bound to sell the term, and perhaps they might assign to a person in whom the lessor had no confidence, wherefore the lessee was held liable, notwithstanding his bankruptcy. Where a disposition of the lease has been made by virtue of a *fieri facias*, or an *elegit*, the lessee continues liable on his covenant, notwithstanding the estate be taken from him against his consent (*d*).

An assignee is not liable on a covenant that relates to something not in being at the time of the demise, or merely personal or collateral to the thing demised; as to pay a sum of money in gross, to build *de novo*,

(*a*) 1 Ld Raym 367 3 Salk 48.

(*b*) 1 Show 388. 1 Salk 196

(*c*) Bac. Abr. : "Covenant" (E. 3) Sale, 477.

(*d*) 4 T R. 98. Noy. Max 91

or the like, for it does not run with the land, and therefore assignees are not bound even though they be expressly named.

Thus, if a man leases sheep or any thing personal, and the lessee covenants for himself and "his assigns" at the end of the term to deliver up the sheep or things so let, or such a price for them; if the lessee assign, this covenant shall not bind the assignee, for it is but a personal contract, and wants such privity as is between the lessor and the lessee and his assigns, by reason of the reversion (*a*)

Tithes, however, are so far assimilated to land, being the profits thereof, as to form an exception (*b*)

As the assignee of a term is not liable on a mere collateral covenant, therefore where the lessee of certain premises covenanted to pay annually, during the term of twenty-one years, twenty shillings, to the churchwardens of the parish, his assignee was held to be not liable (*c*)

But though generally a personal or collateral covenant affects not an assignee, yet if the covenant regard something to be done upon the land, and the assignee be named, though it were not in being at the time of the demise, and be in some measure collateral, as to build a wall, or new house upon the land, &c. it shall bind the assignee, because he will receive the benefit of it (*d*)

Yet, though the assignee be named in the original covenant, if it has been broken before assignment, no action will lie against him, for he shall not be answerable for a breach which he never committed

Thus, where the lessee covenanted to pull down certain old houses, and rebuild others within seven years, but did not perform the covenant, and at the end of seven years assigned, an action was brought against the assignee and held not to lie, the breach being complete before the assignment (*e*) had the covenant, however, been broken before the assignment, as if the lessee had assigned before the time expired, the assignee would have been liable (*f*).

Neither is an assignee liable for the breach of any covenant, as for rent due, after he has assigned over his term, because the privity of estate is gone and this though the assignment over be made without notice to the lessor and though such assignment goes to the *feme covert*, for she may purchase (*g*)

The assignee therefore of a term, declared against as such, is not liable for rent accruing after he has assigned over, though it be stated that the lessor was a party executing the assignment, and agreed there-

(*a*) 5 Co 17 3 Rep [illegible] (*c*) 3 Wils 25 (*b*) Cro Jac 438
(*d*) 5 Co 16 b Com Dig tit "Covenant" (C 3) Bull N P 159
(*e*) 1 Bl R 351 3 Bur 1272 [illegible] (*f*) Salk 199 1 Ld Raym 388
(*g*) 1 Free 3 6 [illegible] Mod 91. 1 Stra 340, Doug 452 Co Lit 3 a 356 b.

by that the term, which was determinable at his option, shall be absolute (*a*).

Yet where a breach is continuing it shall be otherwise: as if a covenant be to repair within such time after notice, if the lessee does not repair upon notice by the assignee, covenant lies, though it was out of repair before the assignment (*b*).

A rent shall not be decreed against the assignee of a wine-licence lease, who purchased without notice of the rent; for the rent does not run with the licence, but is due upon the contract only (*c*).

A covenant not to assign generally, must be personal and collateral, and can only bind the lessee himself; for there never can be any assignee (*d*).

As an assignee shall be bound by a covenant real annexed to the estate, and which runs along with it, so shall he take advantage of such (*e*).

Therefore, if the lessor covenants to repair, or if he grants to the lessee so many estovers as will repair, or that he shall burn within his house during the term: these, as things appurtenant, shall go with it into whose hands soever it comes (*f*).

So, if a man leases land to another by indenture, the covenant in law created by the word "demise," shall go to the assignee of the term, and he shall have advantage of it (*g*).

But though generally an assignee of a term who comes in by act of law, as well by deed as by statute-merchant, shall have the benefit of covenants; an assignee of a lease by estoppel is an exception to the rule: for there is a difference where a covenant is annexed to a thing which of its nature cannot pass at the first without deed, and where not: for in the first case, the assignee ought to be in by deed, otherwise he shall not have advantage of the covenant (*h*).

If one by indenture lease a house for forty years, and the lessee covenants with the lessor that he will sufficiently repair the house during the term, and that the lessor may enter every year, to see if the repairs are done: and if upon view of the lessor it was repaired according to the agreement, that then the lessee should hold the house for forty years after the first term ended, and the lessee grants to another all the interest in the term and terms which he had in the tenements, and after the first term ended; the assignee shall not take the benefit of this agreement.

But if *A.* leases a house to *B.* for years, who covenants to repair, and that *A.* his heirs, executors, and administrators, may at all times enter, and see in what plight the same is, and if upon such view any default

(*a*) Doug. 764. (*b*) Com. Dig. tit. "Covenant" (B.) (*c*) [illegible]
(*d*) 3 Wils. [illegible] (*e*) Bac. Abr. tit. "Covenant" (E. 5.) (*f*) [illegible]
(*g*) Ibid. (*h*) Cro. Eliz. 373. 457.

4

shall be found in the not repairing, and thereof warning shall be given to *B.* his executors, *&c.* then within four months after such warning such default shall be amended; and afterwards, the house in default of *B.* becomes ruinous, and *A.* grants the reversion to *C.* who upon view of the house gives warning to *B.* of the default, *&c.* if it be not repaired *C.* may have an action as assignee of *A.* against *B.* though the house became ruinous before *C.* was entitled to the reversion, for the action is not founded upon the ruinous state of the house, and the time when it first happened, but for not repairing within the time appointed by the covenant after the warning (*a*).

But an assignee shall not have an action upon a breach of covenant before his own time (*b*).

The assignee of a term may take advantage of a covenant against the assignee of the reversion, and he may have this remedy by way of retainer against such assignee.

Therefore where *A.* leased lands to *B.* for two hundred years, and by the same deed covenanted for himself, his heirs, and assigns, with *B.* his executors, and assigns, that if *B.* were disturbed for respite of homage, or enforced to pay any charge or issues lost, he should withhold so much of his rent as he should be enforced to pay, and *A.* grants his reversion to *C.* and *B.* assigns the term to *D.* *D.* may take the benefit of this covenant against *C.* for it runs with the land (*c*).

An assignee shall not be prevented of a benefit allowed by law, for the avoidance of a rent (*d*).

At common law, no grantee or assignee of a reversion could take the benefit or advantage of a condition for re-entry. It was therefore enacted by stat. 32 *H.* 8. c. 34. that all persons grantees of the reversion of any lands from the king, or grantees or assignees of any common person, their heirs, executors, successors, and assigns, shall have like advantage against the lessees, *&c.* by entry for non-payment of rent, or for doing waste or other forfeiture, and the same remedy by action only for not performing other conditions, covenants, and agreements contained in the said leases, as the lessors or grantors themselves had.

On this statute it is to be observed,

1. That as the words of the statute are against lessees, it does not extend to covenants upon estates in fee or in tail, but only upon leases made for life or years (*e*).

2. That an assignee of part of the estate of the reversion may take

(*a*) Bac. Abr. ut ante. (*b*) Cro. Eliz. 863. (*c*) Ib. [illegible] (*d*) 2 Vern. [illegible]
(*e*) Esp. N. P. 293. Co. Litt. 21[illegible] Cro. Eliz. 863.

advantage of the condition; as if lessee for life be, *&c.* and the reversion is granted for life, so if lessee for years, *&c.* be, and the reversion is granted for years, the grantee for years shall take advantage of the condition in respect of the word "executors" in the Act (*a*).

3. But a grantee of part of the reversion shall not take advantage of the condition: as, if the lease be of three acres, reserving a rent upon condition, and the reversion is granted of two acres, the rent shall be apportioned by the act of the parties, but the condition is destroyed, for that it is entire and against common right: except indeed in the case of the king (*b*).

4. Whoever comes in by the act of the party, as by bargain and sale of the reversion, or by grant of the reversion in fee to the use of *A.* is an assignee within the statute, as the bargainee in the one case, and *A.* in the other (*c*).

But such as come in merely by act of law, as the lord by escheat, or are in of another estate, shall not take benefit of the statute (*d*).

5. The grantee shall not take advantage of a condition before he has given notice to the lessee, but he may of a covenant (*e*).

6. The grantee or assignee shall take advantage of such conditions only as are incident to and for the benefit of the reversion, as rent, waste, repairs, making fences, scouring ditches, preserving woods, and such like, and not for the payment of any sum in gross, the delivery of corn, wood, or the like. So, "other forfeiture" relates to such things as are incident to the reversion and run with the land (*f*).

7. The assignee of the lessor may maintain covenant against the lessee after the lessee had assigned, and he had accepted rent from the assignee, for such is within the statute (*g*).

So, an assignee of a reversion, who hath accepted rent from the assignee, of the term, may maintain covenant against the executor of the lessee, or the assignee of the term for a breach of covenant running with the land, though it be committed after the assignment of the reversion (*h*).

But otherwise it is of a covenant in land, which is only created by the law, or of a rent, which is created by reason of the contract, and is by reason of the profits of the land, wherein none is longer chargeable with them than while the privity of estate continue with them (*i*).

8. The surrenderee of a copyhold reversion may bring debt or cove-

(*a*) Co. Lit. 215 a.
(*b*) Ibid.
(*c*) 2 [illegible]
(*d*) Ibid.
(*e*) Cro. Jac. 476.
(*h*) Cro. Jac. 522.
(*g*) Ibid.
(*f*) Co. Lit. 215 b.
(*i*) Ibid. 5[illegible]

nant against the lessee within the equity of this statute, for it is a remedial law, and no prejudice can arise to the lord (*a*).

Assignment by way of Mortgage.—With respect to assignments by way of mortgage, being merely conditional, they are not considered as an actual transfer of property, but as a security only for money.

So, if a lessee for years, with covenants to repair, assigns to *J. S.* by way of mortgage, and *J S* never enters, equity will not compel him to repair, though he had the whole interest in him and though it was his own folly to take an assignment of the old term, when he should have taken a derivative lease, by which means he would not be liable at law (*b*)

But a case occurs, where such an assignee, though he never entered, and had lost his mortgage money, was by law compelled to pay the rent, and having sued in equity could have no relief (*c*). And it is now held that the mortgagee having the legal estate shall be liable as assignee, whether in possession or not (*d*)

If mortgagor and mortgagee make a lease in which the covenants for the rent and repairs are only with the mortgagor and his assigns, the assignee of the mortgagee cannot maintain an action for the breach of these covenants, because they are collateral to his grantor's interest in the land, and therefore do not run with it (*e*)

But if the tenant for a term convey the term by way of mortgage, and then join with the mortgagee in a lease for a shorter term, in which the covenants for the rent and repairs are only with the mortgagor and his assigns, and the interests of the mortgagor and mortgagee become extinguished during the lease by the reversioner acquiring their estates, still the mortgagor may maintain an action of covenant against the lessee, the covenants being in gross (*f*)

That which cannot be supported as an assignment shall be good as an under-lease against the party granting it (*g*)

Under a proviso that all assignments of lease shall be void, if not enrolled, under-leases are not included (*h*)

An under-lease is not an assignment to the effect of working a forfeiture under a proviso not to assign

It has therefore become usual to insert a proviso in leases, that the lessee, &c. shall not let, set, transfer, or assign over or otherwise part with the whole or *any part* of the premises (*i*)

An under-lease, made by a lessee for years, determinable on a future day certain, and to commence immediately on his death, is good, he dying within the time (*k*)

Therefore a man possessed of a term for twenty years, may grant

(*a*) [illegible] 185 (*b*) Doug 462 n 1 2 Vern 275 (*c*) Ibid 374
[illegible] 113 (*d*) 3 T R 393 (*f*) Ibid 678 (*g*) Doug 188 n
[illegible] 96 3 Wils 234 2 Bl. R. 767. Ibid [illegible] 184. (*i*) 2 T. R 425. (*k*) Cro. Jac 459

the lands for nineteen years, to commence after his death, and it will be good for so many of the twenty years as shall be unexpired at the time of his death (*a*).

It was formerly held that an action on the case would lie by a lessee for years against his under-tenants for so negligently keeping his fire that the premises were burned down: though not against a tenant at will (*b*).

But by stat. 14 *G.* 3. *c.* 78. *s.* 86. it is enacted, that no action, suit, or process whatever, shall be had, maintained, or prosecuted, against any person in whose house, chamber, stable, barn, or other building, or on whose estate any fire shall accidentally begin, nor shall any recompence be made by such person for any damage suffered thereby, any law, usage, or custom to the contrary notwithstanding.

The landlord or original lessor cannot sue an under-tenant on a covenant for rent contained in the original lease (*c*).

An under-tenant, whose goods were distrained and sold by the original landlord for rent due from his immediate tenant, cannot maintain an action for money paid to the use of the latter: for immediately on the sale under the distress, the money paid by the purchaser vested in the landlord, in satisfaction of the rent, and never was the money of the under tenant (*d*).

An under-lease of the whole term amounts to an assignment (*e*).

But if the lessor reserves the rent to himself on granting over, it is an under-lease and not an assignment, though he parts with the whole term (*f*).

An action will lie by the assignee of a reversion for years against an under-lessee on a covenant to leave the premises in repair (*g*).

(*a*) 2 Str 737. (*b*) 4 Mod 9 12 Mod 15 (*c*) Doug 183 (*d*) 11 East, 52
(*e*) 1 Ld Raym 99 (*f*) 1 Str 404 [illegible] (*g*) Cro Eliz 596

CHAPTER XII.

Of Changes happening by Marriage, Bankruptcy, Insolvency, or Death wherein of Assignees, Devisees, Executors, and Administrators, and in what Cases they are bound by, and may take advantage of Covenants.

CHANGES *by Marriage.*—The marriage is a gift in law to the husband of all the wife's chattels real, as a term for years in right of his wife, so of estates by statute-merchant, statute-staple, elegit, *&c.* and of these he may alone dispose, or forfeit, or they may be extended for his debts (*a*).

But if he makes no disposition of them in his lifetime, they survive to his wife, and therefore he cannot devise them. For the husband is only possessed of a term in her right, and the term or legal interest continues in her (*b*). for the law does not love that rights should be destroyed; but, on the contrary, for the supporting of them invents notions and fictions, as abeyance, *&c.* (*c*).

So a feme covert is of capacity to purchase of others without the consent of her husband, and though he may disagree and divest the estate, yet if he neither agree nor disagree, the purchase is good (*d*).

If a woman, lessee for years, takes husband, who afterwards purchases a new lease to them both for their lives of the same lands, this is a surrender in law of the first term, and shall bind the wife, because it amounts to an actual disposition thereof, which the husband had power to make (*e*).

So, if a man marries a woman who is *cestui que trust* of a term, the husband may as well dispose of this trust as if the legal interest was in her (*f*). But not if the trust was created with his privity and consent (*g*).

Even where the husband was possessed of a term in right of his wife from whom he was divorced *à mensâ & thoro*, he was restrained from selling it (*h*).

(*a*) Bro. Abr. tit. "Baron et Feme" (C 2). [illegible] (*b*) [illegible] (*c*) 1 Ld Raym 515. Co. Litt. 342. [illegible] Ibid. 3 [illegible] 6 b. (*d*) Ba. Ab. [illegible] (*f*) [illegible] 18. 3 Atk. 45[illegible] [illegible] (*h*) 9 Mod. 44.

But such term, whereof the husband is possessed in right of his wife, may be extended for the debts, or forfeited for the crimes of the husband, for these are legal dispositions thereof, which shall bind the wife (*a*).

But if a husband should grant a rent, common, &c. out of such term and die, this would not bind the wife surviving, because the term or possession itself being left to come entire to the wife, all intermediate charges or grants thereout by the husband determine with his death, for the title of the wife to such term has relation to the time of their intermarriage, and so is paramount to all collateral charges or grants made thereout by the husband after.

So, a grant by the husband of the herbage or vesture of such land which he held in right of his wife for years, will be void after his death, because they are part of the land itself, and not collateral to it (*b*).

If the husband and wife be evicted of a term which he hath in right of his wife, and the husband brings an ejectment in his own name, and hath judgment to recover, this makes an alteration in the term and vests it in the husband, because, not making his wife a party to the recovery, he takes the whole wrong to be done to himself, and consequently if he recovers, it must be by virtue of that right whereof he was disseised.

An estate by the curtesy is subject to the charges of the wife; so that if a woman, tenant in-tail, acknowledges a statute and afterwards marries, has issue, and dies, the lands may be extended in the hands of the husband holding as tenant by the curtesy (*c*). So, where a husband is but tenant by the curtesy, and has only an interest for life in the wife's estate, he cannot affect that estate without her joining (*d*).

Husband and wife make a lease for years by indenture of the wife's lands reserving rent, the lessee enters, the husband before any day of payment dies, the wife takes a second husband, and he at the day accepts the rent and dies: it was holden, that the wife could not now avoid the lease, for by her second marriage she transferred her power of avoiding it to her husband, and his acceptance of the rent binds her, as her own before such marriage would have done; for he, by the marriage, succeeded into the power and place of his wife, and what she might have done, either as to affirming or avoiding such lease before marriage, the same may the husband do after the marriage (*e*).

So the wife's acceptance of rent or fealty, &c. will make good and unavoidable leases for years, made by her and her husband at common

(*a*) [illegible] (*b*) Ibid. (*c*) [illegible] (*d*) [illegible]
(*e*) [illegible] Bro. [illegible]

law, or by her husband solely, if they be by indenture or deed-poll; so, if the wife die before her husband, the same election and power of affirming or avoiding such leases descends to her issue or heir for such leases are good, till those who succeed to the estate defeat and avoid them by their disagreement thereto (*a*).

Therefore where a woman tenant in-tail, having issue by a former husband, after his death married a second husband, and they by indenture joined in a lease for years of the wife's lands rendering rent, and then the wife died without issue by the second husband, so that he was not entitled to be tenant by the curtesy, it was holden, that till the issue by the first husband entered, this lease remained good (*b*).

So, where a man seised of land in right of his wife, makes a lease for years, rendering rent, and then his wife dies without issue by him, whereby he is not tenant by the curtesy, but his estate is determined: yet he may avow for the rent till the heir hath made his actual entry, because the lease was at first good, and drawn out of the seisin of the wife, and therefore, till the entry of the heir, remains good between the lessor and the lessee, so that the lessee may maintain an action of covenant, and the lessor distrain and avow for the rent, till the heir hath entered (*c*).

If a term of years be granted to a feme covert and another, or if a feme sole and another are joint-tenants of a term of years and the feme takes husband, yet in both cases the joint tenancy still continues, for the marriage makes no severance or alteration of it, but gives the husband the same power his wife had before, by an actual disposition of her moiety to break the joint tenancy, and bind his wife's interest therein; but without such disposition, the joint-tenancy continues, and if the husband dies, the whole shall go accordingly (*d*).

So, if such joint-tenants are ousted of the term, the wife shall join with the husband and the other joint-tenant in ejectment, and the wife shall have judgment to recover as well as the husband; and if in such case before any actual disposition made by the husband, his wife die, the whole term shall go to the surviving joint-tenant and no part thereof to the husband; because, though the husband, if he survives, is by law to have all chattels real and personal of his wife's, and this term was a chattel real, yet the title of the other joint-tenant to have the whole by survivorship, coming at the same instant and being the elder title, shall prevail against the husband (*e*).

Although by the marriage, the husband and wife become one person in law, and therefore such an union works an extinguishment or revocation of several acts done by her before the marriage, yet in things

(*a*) Bac. Abr. [illegible] (*c*) [illegible] (*e*) [illegible]
(*b*) Bac. Abr. [illegible] (*d*) [illegible]

which would be manifestly to the prejudice of both husband and wife, the law does not make her acts void (*a*).

Therefore, if a feme sole makes a lease at will, or is lessee at will, and afterwards marries, the marriage is no determination of her will, so as to make the lease void, nor can she herself without the consent of her husband determine the lease in either case (*b*).

The husband, as head or governor of the family, has an absolute power over the chattels real and personal of which he is possessed in right of his wife, to dispose of them as he thinks proper, and no act or concurrence of her's is of any avail, either in confirming or controuling such disposition (*c*)

Therefore, if an express condition (as to pay rent) be annexed to the estate of a woman, who takes husband, the laches of the husband to perform the condition, loses the estate for ever (*d*)

But the laches of the husband to perform a condition in law, which does not require skill or confidence, (as not to alien in fee, does not prejudice his wife (*e*)

The real estate however of the feme is under a different regulation from that by which her chattels real and personal are governed, for it is under the power of the husband no longer than during the coverture, and therefore any disposition of it made by him alone may be defeated, also, all charges laid on it by him, fall off with his death (*f*)

But the husband during coverture may take the rents and profits of the whole estate of his wife and as he has the sole disposition of all interests of his wife, he may, for an interest which vests in the wife, or accrues to her during coverture, either sue alone, or with his wife (*g*)

If a feme sole hath right to have common for life, and she takes husband, and he is hindered in taking the common, he may have an action alone without his wife, it being only to recover damages (*h*).

But if baron and feme are disseised of the land of the feme, they must join in an action for the recovery of the land (*i*).

If *A* demise a house to *B* for years, and *B* covenants to repair the said house during the term, and afterwards *A* grants the reversion to baron and feme, ... the baron may have an action alone upon this covenant (*k*).

But if lands be conveyed with a covenant for further assurance to husband and wife, she must be joined with him in an action for the breach of such covenant (*l*).

In those cases where the debt or cause of action will survive to the

[illegible]

wife, the husband and wife are regularly to join in the action; as in recovering debts due to the wife before marriage, in actions relating to her freehold or inheritance, or injuries done to her person (*a*)

In other cases, as in actions for a profit accrued during the coverture to the husband in right of his wife, in which the husband may sue alone or join with his wife, it is the more sure mode to join (*b*)

If there be a lease by the wife *dum sola*, payment of the rent ought to be to the husband, and payment to the wife without the husband's order, though there be no notice of the marriage, shall not discharge the lessee (*c*) [For other matter relative to this subject see *ante* C. III. s. 12]

Of Dower.—A woman is entitled to dower of a reversion expectant on a term for years Thus if a man, either before or after marriage, make a lease for years reserving rent, his wife will be entitled to a third of the land for her dowry, and also to a third of the rent, as incident to the reversion (*d*).

The widow holds her dower discharged from all judgments, leases, mortgages, or other incumbrances, made or created by her husband after the marriage (*e*)

Dower is even protected from distress for a debt due to the crown, contracted during the marriage, and if the lands are distrained upon, the doweress may have a writ to the sheriff commanding him not to distrain, or to restore the distress, if any be taken (*f*)

A rent issuing out of land whereof a woman is dowable may be assigned in lieu of dower and if a tenant in tail assign a rent out of the land intailed to a woman entitled to dower out of such estate tail, not exceeding the yearly value of her dower, it will bind the issue (*g*) But rent assigned in lieu of dower, as it comes in lieu of land, ought to be absolute as the assignment of the land itself (*h*).

A jointress is not so favoured in law as a doweress. But the Court of Chancery will set aside a term of years in favour of a jointress, though it will not do so in favour of a woman entitled at law to dower, because a jointress has a fixed interest by the agreement of the party (*i*).

Of Changes by Bankruptcy.—The legal right that the landlord has to distrain the goods of his tenant for rent in arrear, is not affected by the tenant's bankruptcy while the goods remain on the premises

For a landlord is considered in a higher degree than a common creditor, and it would be hard to preclude him from distraining, where there are goods on the premises (*k*)

(*a*) Bac. Abr. [illegible] (*b*) Com. Dig. tit. Baron and Feme (X) (*c*) Ibid (O)
(*d*) 1 Leo. 32 1 Cruise's Dig. tit. 6 c. 3 s. 10, 11 (*e*) 1 Inst. 46 a. 4 Rep. 65. Cruise's Dig. tit. 6 [illegible] (*f*) 1 Inst. 31 a. F. N. B. 150 [illegible] 5 41
(*g*) 1 Roll. Abr. 682. (*h*) Cro. Eliz. 425. (*i*) Prec. in Ch. 5 1 Cruise's Dig. tit. 7 s. 12
(*k*) 1 Atk. 105.

The issuing a commission of bankrupt therefore against a tenant, and the messenger's possession of his goods, does not hinder the landlord from distraining for rent; but while upon the premises, they are still liable (*a*).

Money paid for rent to a landlord who was about to distrain, by a trader after an act of bankruptcy committed, is not recoverable back by the assignees (*b*).

The landlord may distrain the goods for his entire debt, even after assignment or sale by the assignees, if the goods are not removed: the reason is, because no provision is made in the case of bankruptcy by the statute (8 *Ann.* c. 14.) which gives the landlord a year's rent on executions (*c*).

But it is a principle that a landlord has no lien in such case after the goods are removed from the premises (*d*).

Therefore if the landlord neglects to distrain, and suffers the goods to be sold by the assignees and removed from off the premises, he can only come in on an average with the rest of the creditors (*e*).

Also, if landlord prove his debt for rent under the commission and swear that he has no security, he thereby waives, it should seem, his right to distrain, and the vendee of such goods under the assignee will be entitled to the goods (*f*).

So, a landlord who petitions to be paid the rent in arrear at the time of the commission being taken out, seven years after the effects had been sold by the assignees, was considered only as a common creditor, and compelled to come in *pro rata*, his demand being a stale one (*g*).

A mortgagee who has paid the arrears of rent on a bankrupt's estate, unless he has an order of the Court of Chancery to stand in the landlord's place, shall not be preferred to the creditors under the commission (*h*).

Where on goods being sold under a distress for rent, a balance remained in the hands of the constable, the tenant or his representative could only come in for his proportion with the other creditors: if any thing had remained in specie it might have been different, but in this case the money was embezzled.

Assignees are not entitled to the benefit of a covenant for the renewal of a lease (*i*).

The commissioners cannot assign a lease wherein a condition is contained, making the lease void on the tenant committing an act of bankruptcy whereon a commission shall issue: for such a proviso is legal, and the landlord may re-enter by virtue thereof (*k*).

It has been determined, however, that the commissioners may assign

(*a*) 1 Atk. 104. (*b*) 5 Esp. 200. (*c*) Ibid. 103. (*d*) Cooke's B. L. 22. (*e*) 1 Bro. 427. 1 Atk. 102, 103. (*f*) Ibid. 104. (*g*) Ibid. 103. (*h*) Ibid. (*i*) 2 Vern. 97. (*k*) 2 T. R. 133. 15 Ves. J. 268.

a lease granted to a bankrupt, in which there is a proviso that the lessee, his executors, or administrators shall not assign without the lessor's consent in writing (*a*).

An assignee of a bankrupt, a devisee, and a personal representative, and one who purchases a term from the sheriff under an execution, are assignees in law to the purpose of being liable to actions on a covenant for rent in a lease to the bankrupt's devisor or intestate (*b*).

But the assignees of a bankrupt are not liable for the rent of premises assigned to them by the commissioners, unless they take possession (*c*).

Neither are the assignees liable to an action of covenant for rent in arrear, accrued subsequent to the bankruptcy of premises which had been the bankrupt's (*d*).

Debt on the reddendum in a lease, will not lie against the lessee for rent accrued after his bankruptcy, when he had ceased to occupy the premises, and the assignee is in possession under the commissioners' assignment (*e*). But the bankrupt's lessee, though out of possession, is still liable upon his *covenant* to pay the rent (*f*).

Whatever doubt may have been at one time entertained, as to the bankruptcy of the lessee being a bar to an action of covenant brought against him (*g*), it is now settled that the bankruptcy of the defendant cannot be pleaded in bar to an action of covenant for rent: for the 34 *H.* 8. c. 4. s. 1. only assigns the interest of the bankrupt in the land, but does not destroy the privity of contract between the lessor and lessee, wherefore an action of *covenant* remains after the estate is gone, though generally speaking it is otherwise of the action of *debt*. Covenant is founded on a privity collateral to the land (*h*). A covenant of this kind is mixed; it is partly personal and partly dependant on the land; it binds both the person and the land; and this brings the case within the principle of *Mayor* v. *Steward* (*i*), (in which case the *dictum* of Mr. J. *Yates*, that as the bankrupt was divested of his whole estate, and rendered incapable of performing the covenants, it would be a hardship upon him if he should still remain liable to it, when he is disabled from performing it, was clearly extra-judicial, though as proceeding from that excellent lawyer, it was deserving of great weight.)

A right of action therefore, on a breach of covenant, not secured by a penalty, and where the damages are to be recovered are uncertain, is not barred by the certificate of the defendant, who became a bankrupt after the covenant was broken (*k*).

Indeed, it is extremely clear, that where a bankrupt has taken a lease and entered into covenants for payment of rent and for repairing, &c.

(*a*) Cooke's B. L. 370. Ambler, 480. (*b*) Doug. 184. (*c*) 1 Esp. R. 233. Peak's N. C. 238. 2 H. Bl. 319. (*d*) 1 Esp. R. 283. (*e*) 8 East, 314. in note. (*f*) 1 Hen. Black. 433. 4 T. R. 94. (*g*) 1 T. R. 86. (*h*) 1 H. Bl. 433. 4 T. R. 94. 5 ... (*i*) 2 Bur. 2439. (*k*) C T. R. 187.

though the lease is taken from him and blended with the general mass of his property and divided amongst his creditors, yet his certificate will not deliver him from his liability to perform the covenants contained in that lease (*a*).

Changes by Insolvency.—Respecting the change made in the situation of landlord or tenant by the insolvency of either of them, it is to be observed that all interests in lands, and chattels real, must be inserted in the schedule which is to contain an enumeration of the insolvent debtor's estate and effects.

A conveyance to a creditor of an insolvent debtor's estate by the clerk of the peace does not vest the estate in such creditor by relation either to the date of the order or of the conveyance, but only from the actual execution of such conveyance by the clerk of the peace. Therefore, such creditor cannot recover in ejectment upon a demise laid before the execution, though after the estate was out of the insolvent debtor, and the order was made to convey the same to the lessor. Had another demise by the clerk of the peace been laid, it would have obviated any inconvenience which could have arisen in this case from the lessor's ignorance of the time at which the assignment was actually executed (*b*).

Where there is a bond with a penalty, and also a deed of covenant, and the tenant takes the benefit of an Insolvent Act, whereby the bond is discharged, he is still liable on any future breach of his covenant, unless specially saved by the statute (*c*).

Changes by Death.—The alteration that is effected by the death of the landlord or tenant has reference to a devisee, or an executor or administrator; for as to the heir, he is out of question, as such, with respect to a chattel interest.

By the statutes 32 and 34 *H.* 8. *c.* 1. *s.* 5. a man may devise all his lands, tenements, and hereditaments, reversions and remainders.

Therefore, if one devise a reversion after an estate for life, or in tail, and that comes to his possession, the land passes: and a general residuary clause in a will carries a reversion.

So, by a devise of ground-rent on leases for years, the reversion passes. So, a bequest of "leasehold ground-rents in *S*" passes the reversionary leasehold interest as well as the reserved rent (*d*).

If one bequeath his indenture of lease, his whole estate in the lease passeth. So, if a termor of a house or land bequeath the same to *B.* without expressing how long he should have it, he shall have the whole term and number of years (*e*).

Under a bequest of the testator's interest in leaseholds, a renewed lease obtained by his executrix was held to pass (*f*). But a renewed lease does not pass under the words "lease or premises" (*g*).

(*a*) [illegible] 380. (*b*) 2 Lord R. 277. (*c*) D[illegible] 393. (*d*) 2 [illegible] 1 [illegible] 1 B. R. 76.
(*e*) [illegible] 224. (*f*) 12 Ves. J. 256. (*g*) 16 Ves. J. 197, 199.

Of Devisees.—A devisee of the lands is entitled to all those chattel interests which belong to the heir and in one respect he has an advantage to which the heir is not entitled.

Thus it has been holden, that if *A.* seised in fee of lands sow, and devise it to *B.* for life, remainder to *C.* in fee, and die before severance, *B.* shall have the emblements, and not the executor of *A.* Or that if *B.* die before severance, his executor shall not have them, but they shall go to him in remainder. Or that if the devise be only to *B.* and *B.* die before severance, there his executor shall have them (*a*).

A devisee of the goods, stock, and moveables, is entitled to growing corn in preference both to the devisee of the land and the executor (*b*).

A devisee is an assignee in law, and as such is liable to an action on a covenant in a lease to pay rent, or on any other covenant that runs with the land (*c*).

As he is liable to covenants that regard the reversion, so it is presumed he is capable of maintaining an action for the breach of such covenants, for by the common law, upon a covenant in law, the assignee of the estate shall have an action (*d*).

A devisee therefore, is in the predicament of an ordinary assignee, by whom an action lies upon every covenant that concerns the land; as to pay rent, not to do waste, &c.

The devisee of the equity of redemption, (the legal estate being in a mortgagee) is not liable on covenant as assignee of all the estate, right, title, and interest of the original covenantor (*e*).

An action of covenant does not lie upon the stat. of 3 *W.* & *M.* c. 14 against a devisee of land to recover damages for a breach of covenant made by the devisor, but the remedy thereby given, is confined to cases where debt lies (*f*).

Executors and Administrators.—With respect to executors and administrators, the executor or administrator shall have by virtue of his executorship or administration, all the chattels real and personal of the testator, as well those that are in possession, as leases for years of land, rent, common, or the like, corn growing or cut, trees, and grass cut and severed, as also those that are in action, as right and interest of execution upon judgment, statutes, &c. (*g*).

So, the executor or administrator of the lord shall have the fines assessed upon the tenants upon their admittances in the lord's time (*h*).

So, if I [illegible] for life rendering rent, and the rent is behind, and then I die, [illegible] the arrearages of rent due to me in my life-time shall go to my executor or administrator in the nature of a chattel (*i*).

(*a*) [illegible] 15, [illegible] (*b*) [illegible] (*c*) Doug. 184 (*d*) Com. Dig. tit. "Covenant" [illegible] (*g*) Shep. Touch. 468
(*h*) Ibid. [illegible]

So, if a rent be granted out of land to me in fee-simple, fee-tail, for life or years, and it be not paid to me in my lifetime, these arrearages shall go to my executor or administrator, and not to any other (*a*).

So, also, if a parson have an annuity in fee in right of his church, and it be behind and the parson die in this case the executor or administrator, not the successor of the parson, shall have the arrearages (*b*)

If I be seised of land and possessed of a flock of cattle, and let it to another for years, and he covenant by the lease to pay me and my wife, our heirs and assigns 100*l* *per ann.* during the term, in this case, after my death, and my wife surviving me, her executor or administrator, and not my heir, shall have this payment (*c*).

So, if one make me a lease of land first for years, and then grant me the trees for a number of years, to begin after the end of the term of the land, I have the trees in the nature of a chattel, and if I die, my executor or administrator shall have them (*d*)

So, if a lease for years of land be granted to me and my heirs, or to me and my successors, and I die: my executor or administrator, and not my heir, shall have the term (*e*).

The same law is, if a covenant or an obligation be made to me and my heirs for in these cases, this is still a chattel in me that shall go to my executor or administrator, and he only shall take advantage of it · and if my heir or successor happen to get the deed, the executor or administrator may recover it from him (*f*).

If a lease be made to me for twenty years, without naming my executors or administrators or assigns, in this case, if I die, my executor and administrator, notwithstanding, shall have it during the term (*g*).

So, if a lease for years be made to a bishop and his successors, and he die, his executor or administrator, not his successor, shall have it (*h*).

If the lessee for life make a lease for years absolutely, this in law is a lease for so many years if the life so long live, and shall go to the executor or administrator after his death (*i*).

In the case of a tenancy from year to year as long as both parties please, if the tenant die intestate, his administrator has the same interest in the land which his intestate had for whatever chattel the intestate had must vest in his administrator as his legal representative (*k*).

The charters and evidences that concern any of my chattels which my executor or administrator is to have, shall go with the same chattels — So also any charters whatsoever, if they be pledged to me for money, shall go to my executor or administrator until the money be paid (*l*

[illegible]

Those deeds and evidences, that belong to the heir as incident to the inheritance, shall not go to executor or administrator (*a*).

The executor or administrator shall not have the grass and trees growing on the ground, no more than the soil or ground itself whereon they grow (*b*).

Neither is an administrator or executor entitled to pales, walls, stalks, fish in ponds, deer, or conies in parks, pigeons in pigeon-houses, or the like (*c*).

If a lease be made for life or years, of land, whereon a house is standing, or timber is growing, and the house is prostrate or the timber is cut or fallen down (by whomsoever, or by what means soever it be,) the materials of this house and this timber are now become a chattel: and therefore, if the lease be without impeachment of waste, it shall go to the lessee, and after his death to his executor or administrator; but if the lease be otherwise, it shall go to the lessor, and after his death to his executor or administrator.—But, if the timber be cut for reparation only, or the lessee will employ the materials of the house to build it again, and the lease continue, it may be so employed, and then the executor or administrator of the lesser may not take it (*d*).

An executor or administrator regularly shall charge others for any debt or duty due to the deceased, as the deceased himself might have done, and the same actions which the deceased might have had, the same actions for the most part the executor or administrator may have also (*e*).

Therefore he may have an action of account, upon the case, or *assumpsit*, for use and occupation of his testator's or the intestate's premises (*f*).

So, an action of ejectment will lie by the executor or administrator for an ejectment of the testator out of a term (*g*).

An action of debt also, for rent behind in the lifetime of the deceased, may be brought by his executor or administrator (*h*) for if any rent or arrearages of rent be due to me upon a grant of rent out of my land to me, or reservation of rent upon any estate made by me of land, in these cases, my executor or administrator may have an action of debt for this rent, or he may distrain for it, so long as the land that is chargeable with the rent, and out of which it issues, is in his possession that ought to pay it, or in the possession of any one that claims by or under him (*i*).

As an executor or administrator shall regularly charge others for any debt or duty due to the deceased, so shall he be charged by others for

(*a*) 8 T. R. 592. & 2 Bl. Com. 428. 3 Ves. J. 222. (*b*) Shep. Touch. 469. (*c*) Ibid.
(*d*) Ibid. 471. (*e*) Ibid. 481. (*f*) Ibid. (*g*) Shep. Touch. 481.
(*h*) Ibid. (*i*) Shep. Touch. 482.

any debt or duty due from the deceased, as the deceased himself might have been charged in his lifetime, so far forth as he hath any of the estate of the deceased to discharge the same (*a*).

Therefore, if a lease for years be made rendering rent, and the rent is behind, and the lessee die, in this case the executor or administrator of the lessee shall be charged for this rent (*b*)

So, also, if a lessee for years assign over his interest and die, his executor or administrator shall be charged with the arrearages before the assignment, but not with any of the arrearages due after the assignment (*c*).

For if the testator die in possession of a term for years, it shall vest, as before mentioned, in the executor, and although it be worth nothing he cannot waive it, for he must renounce the executorship *in toto*, or not at all (*d*). But this is to be understood only where the executor has assets, for he may relinquish the lease, if the property be insufficient to pay the rent, but in case there are assets to bear the loss for some years, though not during the whole term, it seems the executor is bound to continue tenant till the fund is exhausted, when, on giving notice to the lessor, he may waive the possession. If, however, he enter on the demised premises, as by his office he is bound to do, the lessor may charge him by action of debt as assignee in the *debet* and *detinet* for the rent incurred subsequent to his entry (*e*).

If the profits of the land exceed the amount of the rent, as the law *primâ facie* supposes, such of the profits as are sufficient to make up the rent shall be appropriated to the payment of the lessor, and cannot be applied to any other purpose. Therefore, if in such case the lessor bring an action against the executor for the rent, he cannot plead *plene administravit*, for that plea would confess a misapplication of the profits, since no other payment out of them can be justified till the rent be answered (*f*)

On the other hand the profits of the land may be inadequate to the rent In a variety of cases, they may be easily supposed insufficient for a given period, although the lease may on the whole be beneficial: as in respect to rent for the occupation of premises from *Michaelmas* to *Lady Day* especially, where almost the whole profit is taken in the summer; as in the case of a lease of tithes, or of meadow grounds, which are usually flooded in the winter. So, the profits for a series of years may be less than the amount of the rent, although the lease for the whole term may be of no small value; as in the case of a lease of woods, which are fellable only once in eight or nine years, and the felling has been very recent (*g*)

(*a*) Shep. Touch. 482 (*b*) Ibid. 483 (*c*) Ibid. (*d*) Toll. L. of Ex. & Ad. 109
(*e*) Went. Off. of Ex. 122 (*f*) Toll. L. of Ex. & Ad. 220 (*g*) Ibid.

In these and the like instances, the executor is personally liable only to the extent of the profits, and for such proportion of the rent as shall exceed the profits, is chargeable merely in the capacity of executor, or, in other words, as far only as he has assets and in such case, to an action brought by the lessor against him in the *debet* and *detinet*, he must disclose the matter by special pleading, and pray judgment whether he shall be charged otherwise than in the *detinet* only, for more than the actual profits (*a*).

Thus the profits of the land are to be applied by the executor, in the first place, to the discharge of the rent, and if that fund prove insufficient, the residue of the rent is payable out of the general assets, and stands on the same footing with other debts by specialty and this whether the rent reserved be by lease, in writing, or by parol (*b*).

But an executor or administrator shall not charge another, or have any action against him for a personal wrong done to the testator, when the wrong done to his person or that which is his, is of that nature as for which damages only are to be recovered, therefore, an executor or administrator cannot sue another for a trespass done to him in his cattle, grass, or corn, or for waste done by his tenant in his lands, for these are said to be personal actions which die with the person, according to the rule, *actio personalis moritur cum personâ* (*c*)

So, an executor or administrator shall not be charged for any personal wrong done by the deceased, and therefore no action may be brought against him for any such cause, as for cutting down trees, or for suffering his cattle to eat up the plaintiff's grass (*d*).

An action for use and occupation by the deceased, however, may perhaps be maintained against his executor or administrator.

Touching the cases in which executors or administrators are affected by the covenants made by or in favour of their testators and intestates. An action for the breach of a covenant made to the deceased lies for an executor or administrator, so, for a covenant broken in the lifetime of the testator, the executor, and not the heir or assignee, shall have the action of covenant (*e*), although (it is said) it were a covenant real, (as to use the land in an husbandman-like manner), which runs with the land, and the damages shall be recovered by the executor, though not named, as he personally represents the testator (*f*)

Yet where the lessee covenanted to repair, and to leave the premises in repair, it was held (in a case long prior to that last quoted from *Esp N. P.*) that the heir should have an action of covenant on this,

(*a*) Toll. L. of Ex. & Ad. 220 (*b*) Ibid (*c*) Shep. Touch. 483 (*d*) Ibid. 484
(*e*) Shep. Touch. 481. 2 Lev. 26 [illegible] (*f*) Esp. N. P. [illegible]

though not named for it was a covenant which runs with the estate, and so should go with the reversion to the heir (*a*).

The distinction taken (if any subsists) is perhaps by reason of the one injury not savouring of waste, and the other savouring of waste; for remedies for waste regard the reversion, and therefore lie with the heir; or it may be that the remedy for breach of covenant to repair is given to the heir, because his personal comfort and convenience are abridged by such a breach, which cannot occur to one deceased, whereas a covenant to use land in a husbandman-like manner, and to leave it in such condition, regards rather the temporal interest than the personal comfort of the covenantee.

Executors shall also have a writ of covenant of a covenant made to their ancestors for a personal thing. Yet according to *The Touchstone* where the covenant is but personal, as where one makes a lease for years, and the lessor covenants to pay the quit-rents, but he does not say during the term, by this it seems the executor or administrator of the lessor shall not be charged (*b*).

If the lessor covenants with the lessee to make him a new lease at the end of his term, and the lessee dies, his executor may have covenant on this, though not named (*c*).

Executors or administrators who come to any term of lands or tenements, as such, are bound by the covenants which run with the estate, as belonging to the personal property of the testator or intestate (*d*).

Where lands come to an executor or administrator, he may be charged for a breach in his own time, as for non-payment of rent, or with an action of covenant, either in that right or as assignee, but there is this difference (*e*). If declared against as assignee, he is chargeable as ter-tenant, or one who hath the actual possession of the land, and the judgment is *de bonis propriis* (*f*). But if the action be brought against him as executor or administrator, the judgment shall be *de bonis testatoris*, even where the breach has been committed in his own time, as for repairs, &c. for it is the testator's covenant which binds the executor, as representing him, and he therefore must be sued by that name (*g*).

Covenant lies by the lessor against the administrator of the assignee of the lessee, against whom he may declare as assignee, for breach of a covenant that runs with the land (*h*).

If a covenant by two lessees be joint and several, it shall bind the executors of the deceased lessee, even though he died before the

(*a*) [illegible] 92 [illegible] Salk. [illegible]
(*b*) [illegible] 145. (*c*) Bro. [illegible] Covenant 12. Shep. Touch. 482.
(*c*) Plowd. Com. 286. (*d*) Hob. 148. [illegible] 12. 1 Salk. 37 [illegible] 4.
(*e*) [illegible] (*g*) [illegible] Hob. 188. [illegible] (*h*) Bull. N. P. [illegible] N. P. 290.

term commenced, and the whole term, interest and benefit survive to the other lessee (*a*)

If a man covenant for himself only to pay money, build a house for quiet enjoying, or the like, and he doth not say in the covenant "his executors and administrators," yet hereby his executors and administrators are bound and shall be charged (*b*)

Yet if a lessee for years covenant for himself to repair the houses demised, omitting other words, it seems in this case he is bound to repair only during his life, and the executors and administrators are not bound (*c*).

But upon a covenant implied, an action of covenant (it is said) will not lie against an executor (*d*).

[illegible]

CHAPTER XIII.

Of the Remedies for and against Landlord and Tenant.

Part I. Of Remedies for Landlord for Recovery of Rent.

Section I. Landlord's Remedy for Rent by Distress.

OF the various remedies which the law affords to the landlord for the recovery of rent from his tenant, that by distress, as being the most ancient, and one most summary in its nature, and therefore most commonly resorted to, first claims our consideration.—It is recommended, in preference to others, by Lord Coke, as the most plain and certain; and the statute 2 W. & M. sess. 1. c. 5. recognizes it as "the most ordinary and ready way for recovery of arrears of rent (a)."

Distress [illegible], is the taking of a personal chattel out of the possession of the wrong-doer into the custody of the party injured, to procure a satisfaction for the wrong committed. The thing itself taken by this process is also frequently called a distress (b).

[illegible]—A distress is not an action, but a remedy without suit, and was a remedy given to the lord, to recover the rent or services which the tenant had obliged himself by his feudal contract to

(a) Co. Litt. 162. [illegible]

pay by way of retribution for his farm, for rent is considered as a retribution for the land, and is therefore payable to those who would otherwise have had the land (*a*)

For all services a distress may be made of common right for distresses were incident by the common law to every rent-service, and by particular reservation to rent charges also, but not to rent-seck, till the stat 4 *G.* 2 *c.* 28 extended the same remedy to all rents alike, and thereby in effect abolished all material distinction between them (*b*)

So that now we may lay it down as an universal principle, that a distress may be taken for any kind of rent in arrear, the detention whereof beyond the day of payment is an injury to him that is entitled to receive it (*c*)

By whom Distress may be made—Therefore, if a person seised in fee grants out a lesser estate, saving the reversion of rent, or other services, the law gives him, without any express provision, remedy for such rent or services by distress (*d*).

But for a rent which issues out of an incorporeal inheritance, the reversioner cannot distrain, as if I have a right of common in another man's soil, and I grant it to *A* reserving rent, if the rent be behind, I cannot distrain the beasts of *A*. because that the right of common, which every man has, runs through the whole common.—The king however is an exception to this rule, for he by his prerogative can distrain upon all the lands of his lessee.

So, a man cannot distrain for rent issuing out of tithes, because there is no place where the distress can be taken

A person who has not the reversion cannot distrain of common right, but he may reserve to himself a power of distraining, or the reservation may be good to bind the lessee by way of contract, for the performance whereof the lessor may have an action of debt (*e*)

Thus if the assignee of a term surrenders to the original lessor, though he reserves a sum in gross to be paid annually, he cannot distrain for that or the original rent, but he may have an action of *assumpsit* for such sum in gross (*f*).

So, if a lessee for years assign his term rendering rent, he cannot distrain for it without a particular clause for that purpose, because he has no reversionary interest, the only remedy that the assignor has, is by an action on his contract

If under an agreement for a lease at a certain rent the tenant is let into possession before the lease is executed, the lessor cannot during

(*a*) Gilb. L. of Dist. [illegible] Co. Litt. [illegible]
(*b*) 3 Bl. Com. 6
(*c*) Gilb. L. of Dist.
(*d*) [illegible]
(*e*) [illegible]
(*f*) [illegible]

the first year distrain for rent, for there is no demise express or implied (*a*)

A devisee may distrain for rent devised to him out of the lands, if the land is charged with distress, and not otherwise

For a rent granted for equality of partition by one coparcener to another, or for a rent granted to a widow out of lands whereof she is dowable in lieu of dower, or for a rent granted in fee of lands upon an exchange, the grantee may distrain without any provision of the parties, though he has no reversion, the law giving him a distress in these cases, lest the grantee should be without remedy.

But if a man grants rent over to another, after arrearages incurred, he cannot distrain for such arrearages, because they are by the grant divided from the freehold of the rent.

If a person enter upon certain premises subject to the approbation of the landlord, who afterwards [illegible] approve, but upon an agreement that the tenant will pay an [illegible] rent as well for the time he had been in possession, as for the future, the landlord was willing to let him continue in possession [illegible] such case, the landlord may distrain for the advanced rent accrued before the agreement as well as for what accrues afterwards, such agreement giving him the same power by relation to his tenant's first entry into possession, as it did to recover his rent in future

So, a mortgagee, after giving notice of the mortgage to the tenant in possession, under a lease prior to the mortgage, may distrain for the rent in arrear at the time of the notice, (although he was not in the actual seisin of the premises or in the receipt of the rents and profits at the time it became due) as well as for rent which may accrue after such notice, the legal title to the rent being in the mortgagee

A receiver appointed by the Court of Chancery may distrain for rent, [illegible] need not apply first to that court for a particular order for the purpose, because, as that court never makes an [illegible] order, but [illegible] day for a tenant to pay, it might be an injury to the estate to wait till that time, as it would give the tenant an opportunity to convey his goods off the premises in the mean time.—If, however, there is any doubt who has the legal right to the rent, then the receiver should make an application to the court for an order [illegible] in the name of the person who has that right

One joint-tenant may distrain alone, but then he must avow in his own right and as bailiff to the other (*b*).

[illegible] tenant in common may distrain for his share of the [illegible]

[illegible]

the terre-tenant holding under him and another tenant in common, where such terre-tenant has paid the whole rent to the other tenant in common after notice not so to pay it (*a*)

A man may distrain cattle without any express authority, and if he obtain the assent of the person in whose right he did distrain, his assent will be as effectual as his command could have been, for such assent shall have relation to the time of the distress taken (*b*).

By the common law the executors or administrators of a man seised of a rent-service, rent-charge, rent-seck, or a fee-farm, in fee-simple, or fee-tail, could not distrain for the arrearages incurred in the lifetime of the owner of such rents.

It was, therefore, enacted by stat. 32 *H.* 8. c. 37. s. 1. That the executors and administrators of tenants in fee, fee-tail, or for term of life, for rent-services, rent-charges, rent-seck, and fee-farms, may distrain upon the lands chargeable with the payment thereof, so long as such lands remain in the possession of the tenant who ought to have paid such rent or fee-farm, or of any other person claiming under him by purchase, gift, or descent.

By section 3 of the same statute it is enacted, that if a man hath [illegible] right of his wife any estate in fee-simple, fee-tail, or for term of life, [illegible] rents or fee-farms, and the same rents or fee-farms [illegible] due and unpaid at the death of his wife, such husband may distrain for the said arrearages in the same manner as if his wife had [illegible] living.

By section 4 it is enacted, That if any person have such rents or fee farms for term of life or lives of other persons, he, his executors or administrators, may distrain for arrearages of such rent incurred at the death of the *cestui que vie*, in the same manner as if such *cestui que vie* had been still living.

This statute is a remedial law, and extends to the executors of all tenants for life, as well to those executors who before the statute were entitled to an action of debt, as to those who had no remedy whatever (*c*) so that Lord *Coke's* idea that the preamble concerning the executors and administrators of tenant for life is to be intended of tenant *pur autre vie* so long as *cestui que vie* lives, seems to be too narrow (*d*)

But where a tenant for life of a rent-charge confessed a judgment which was extended by *elegit*, and the tenant for life dying, the [illegible] distrained, and in replevin avowed for the arrears incurred in the lifetime of the tenant for life, upon demurrer the distress was holden to be bad and not warranted by the statute, first, because in case of the conusee

(*a*) 5 T. R. [illegible] [illegible]
[illegible] (*d*) C[illegible]

is not enumerated in it; secondly, because he comes in in the *post*, and not under the tenant for life (a).

Neither is the executor of a grantee of a rent-charge for divers years, if he so long live, within the statute (b).

Lord [illegible], if a man makes a lease for life, or a gift in tail reser[illegible] this is a rent-service within the statute; from whence it may [illegible] that he thought that a rent reserved upon a lease for [illegible] and I apprehend that it is not, for the [illegible] of such a rent, and it is [illegible] of such tenants only who are mentioned in the Act. [illegible], in trespass, where it appeared that the defendant had dis[illegible] the plaintiff's goods for rent due to his testator upon a lease for [illegible] L[illegible] C. J. [illegible] held it to be within the statute, and the de[illegible] a verdict (c).

The statute does not extend to copyhold rents, but only to rents out of free-land (d).

What things are distrainable.—With respect to the things which may be taken under this process, a distress being anciently considered merely as a pledge in the hands of the lord to compel the tenant to pay the service, or perform the duty, could not at common law be sold, but was to be restored in the same plight to the owner when such service or duty was performed, and nothing could be distrained unless it could be returned *in specie* and undamaged. It follows, that money cannot be distrained unless it be in a bag, for then it may be identified perhaps; so milk, fruit, &c. cannot be distrained, nor, till made distrainable by statute, could hay or sheaves of corn be the subject of a distress, unless they were in a cart (e).

As to the things, however, which may be distrained or taken in distress, we may lay it down as a general rule, that all chattels personal are liable to be distrained, unless particularly protected or exempted (f).

By stat. 2 *W.* [illegible] it is enacted, That it shall be lawful for any, having arrear of rent, to [illegible] of corn, or corn loose or in the [illegible] or granary, or upon any [illegible] of the land or ground [illegible] the same in the place where the same shall be found, [illegible] shall be replevied, or [illegible].

By stat. 11 *G.* 2. c. 19, [illegible] the [illegible] take and [illegible] a distress for arrears of rent, all sorts of corn and grass, [illegible], roots, fruits, pulse, or other product whatsoever, grow[illegible]

[illegible]

any part of the estate demised, and the same may cut, gather, make, cure, carry and lay up, when ripe, in the barns, or other proper place on the premises, and if there should be no barn or other place on the premises, then in any other barn or proper place which he shall procure, as near as may be to the premises, and in convenient time appraise, sell, or otherwise dispose of the same towards satisfaction of the rent and of the charges of such distress, appraisement, and sale, the appraisement thereof to be taken when cut, gathered, cured, and made, and not before. provided always, (sec. 9) that notice of the place where such distress shall be lodged, shall, in one week after the lodging thereof, be given to the tenant, or left at the last place of his abode and that if the tenant shall pay or tender the arrears of rent and costs of the distress before the corn, &c. be cut, the distress shall cease, and the corn, &c. be delivered up.

The tools and utensils of a man's trade cannot be distrained while there is any other distress on the premises, or even while they are in actual use therefore the axe of a carpenter, the books of a scholar, and the like, are not distrainable while any other distress can be had, or while they are in actual use (*a*)

Thus, in trover for a stocking loom which had been distrained for rent, where it appeared that an apprentice was using the loom at the time it was taken, the Court held that it could not legally be taken while the apprentice was using it

But in trover for three tape-looms, where it appeared that they had been distrained for rent, because there was no other sufficient distress upon the premises, the Court held the distress good, as it did not appear that the looms were in actual use at the time they were taken

Lest this rule, however, should be carried so far as to privilege the sheep of the tenant, and the beasts of the plough, (these being the materials of husbandry, to plough and manure the land), and by that means the landlord be totally disappointed of the rents, this matter has been settled by the statute *de distrinctione scaccarii*, 51 *H* 3 [illegible] which is in affirmance of the common law, and enacts that no man shall be distrained by the beasts of his plough or his sheep, either by the king or any other, while there is another sufficient distress, unless a deed for damage feasant, in which case the thing that does the trespass must make compensation

Note In an action on the above-mentioned statute, it is not necessary to show that there was a sufficient distress, *praeter*, &c. but it must come on the other part, *viz.* to plead that there was not [illegible]

(*a*) Gilb. L. of Dist. 36, [illegible]

sufficient distress, *prater*, &c It must be intended that there was [illegible] sufficient at the time of the distress, and it is not material what was before [illegible]

The rule [illegible] which exempts utensils, tools, instruments [illegible], &c [illegible] distress, has been adjudged to hold as to [illegible], &c not for poor's rates, &c [illegible] of present consideration, and are noticed in *Chap.* VII [illegible]

[illegible] that all things upon the premises are liable [illegible] the landlord's distress for rent, whether they be the effects of [illegible] because of the lien which the landlord has on them in respect of the place where the goods are found, and not in respect of the person to whom they belong

But this rule has many exceptions in favour of trade, to protect the goods of third persons which happen to be upon the tenant's premises in the way of his trade, therefore things sent to public places of trade, as cloth in a taylor's shop, yarn in a weaver's, a horse in a smith's, and the like, are not distrainable.

A gentleman's chariot standing in a coach-house belonging to a livery-stable keeper, is, it seems, liable to a distress, for that there is not a shadow of legal claim to the exemption

But if a horse goes with yarn, &c to a weaver, &c or fetches yarn from thence and carries it to a private house to be weighed, and it is hung there till the yarn be weighed, neither the horse nor yarn can be distrained

So, a horse that brings corn to market, and is put into a private yard while the corn is selling, cannot be distrained, because the bringing of the corn there is in the way of trade, and consequently of public benefit.

So, goods in the possession of a common carrier are protected from distress for the benefit of trade, as if they be delivered to him to put into a waggon in a private barn.

Neither can the horse on which I am riding be distrained, for it is in use

Nor can wearing apparel if in use be distrained, but wearing apparel not in use is distrainable for rent (a).

The goods of a tenant are liable for a year's rent notwithstanding outlawry in a civil suit.

Therefore, where a sheriff's officer, being in possession of the tenant's effects under an outlawry, made a distress for rent, sold the goods distrained, and afterwards the outlawry was reversed the officer was held liable to pay the produce of the goods in an action

(a) 1 T. R. 226

for money had and received, for they were not *in custodiâ legis*, the judgment being mere waste paper. If during the time that he was in possession under the outlawry, he was put to any expence in reaping and getting in the crops, he may maintain an action against the tenant to recover those expences.—Even if the outlawry had not been reversed, the landlord would have been entitled to a year's rent, because *capias utlagatum* at the suit of the party is to be considered only as a private execution ([illegible]).

But sect. 8. of the stat. 11 G. 2. c. 19. every landlord may take and seize, as a distress for arrears of rent, any cattle or stock of his tenant feeding or depasturing upon any common appendant or appurtenant, or any ways belonging to any part of the premises demised.

It seems to be now settled, that where beasts escape, and come upon land by the negligence or default of their owner, and are trespassers there, they may be distrained immediately by the landlord for rent arrear (*h*).

But where they come upon land by the insufficiency of fences, which the tenant, being a lessee, ought to repair, the lessor cannot distrain such beasts, till they have been *levant* and *couchant*, and after that actual notice has been given to the owner that they are there, and he has afterwards neglected to remove them. But such notice, it is said, is not necessary where the distress is by the lord of the fee for an ancient rent, or by the grantee of a rent-charge.

Therefore, where a stranger puts in his beasts to graze for a night by the consent of the lessor and licence of the lessee, yet the lessor may distrain them for rent due out of those lands which he consented that the beasts should graze on, because such consent was no waiver of his right to distrain, unless it had been expressly agreed so, for being but a parol agreement, it could not alter the original contract between the lessor and lessee, from which the power to distrain arises. The circumstance of the beasts being on the road to market does not privilege them from the distress.

As to cattle, therefore, the safest way is to drive them to a public inn, for an inn being *publica domus*, and every man having a right to put up at it, the cattle and goods of a guest are not distrainable there.

The privilege which exempts cattle and goods from being distrained at an inn, arises from the circumstance of their being there by authority of law, for common inns are so much devoted to the public service that their owners are obliged to receive all guests and horses that come to them for reception.

(*g*) 7 T. R. [illegible] (*h*) [illegible] Ld. Raym. [illegible] [illegible]

But the cattle or goods must be actually within the premises of the inn itself, to be exempted from distress, and not in any place to which the tenant may have removed them for his convenience: for where a race-horse was distrained for rent at a stable half a mile distant from the inn, the distress was determined to be a good one, and that the plaintiff had no remedy but against the innkeeper.

But if fraud be used to obtain this remedy, a court of equity will afford relief.

Thus, where the servants of a grazier driving a flock of sheep to London were encouraged by an innkeeper to put the sheep into pasture grounds belonging to the inn, and the landlord seeing the sheep, consented that they should stay there for one night, and then distrained them for rent, the grazier was relieved against the distress (a).

It has been thought by the Court of Chancery, that the grounds used with an inn ought to have the same privilege as the inn itself, and therefore that the cattle of strangers or passengers ought not to be distrained there.

This privilege also extends, it seems, only to temporary guests; for a person who hires an unfurnished room in an inn, by such hiring, becomes an under-tenant, and any furniture that he may have brought into such room must be liable to the landlord's distress. A landlord may distrain for the rent of ready furnished lodgings (b).

In a case where a rent-charge had been in arrear for twenty years, and cattle escaping out of the adjoining grounds, had been distrained for the arrears, the distress was relieved against in equity. For a rent-charge the grantee cannot distrain a stranger's beasts until they are *levant* and *couchant*: for this rent does not stand upon a feudal title, as rent-service does, but is said to be against common right; wherefore the stranger's beasts must be so long resident on the lands out of which the rent-charge issues, that notice may be presumed to the owner of them; that is, they must be lying down and rising up on the premises for a night and a day without pursuit made by the owner of them.

Whatever is part of the freehold is exempted from distress, for that which is part of the freehold cannot be severed from it without detriment to the thing itself in the removal; consequently it cannot be such a pledge as may be restored in the same condition to the owner: besides that which is fixed to the freehold is part of the thing demised; those things therefore that favour of the reality are not distrainable.

This privilege extends to such things as the tenant will not be permitted on any consideration to remove with him from the premises by reason of their being annexed to and considered as part of the freehold, and not because they are absolutely affixed to the freehold and cannot

(a) Prec. Ch. [illegible]

(b) 2 Bos. Pul. N. R. 224

be moved therefrom, for a temporary removal of them for purposes of necessity is not sufficient to destroy the privilege

Thus, a smith's anvil on which he works is not distrainable, for it is accounted part of the forge, though it be not actually fixed by nails to the shop.

So, a millstone is not distrainable, though it be removed out of its proper place in order to be picked; because such removal is of necessity, and the stone still continues to be part of the mill.

That which is in the hands and actual occupation of another cannot be distrained, for that cannot be a pledge to me of which another has the actual use (*a*).

So, wearing apparel cannot be distrained whilst on the person of the owner, but if taken off, though merely for the purpose of natural repose, it may be distrained, upon the principle of not being in actual use

Goods in the custody of the law are not distrainable, for it is *ex* [illegible] repugnant that it should be lawful to take goods out of the custody of the law, and that cannot be a pledge to me which I cannot reduce into my actual possession.

Therefore goods distrained for damage feasant cannot be taken for rent, nor goods in a bailiff's hands under an execution; nor goods seized by process at the suit of the king, or taken under an attachment; nor while a replevin lie for them

Neither can goods be distrained which have been sold under execution of a writ of *fieri facias*, but so circumstanced that it has not been proper to remove them from the premises Thus, where a tenant's corn while growing was seized and sold under a *f. fa* and the vendee permitted it to remain till it was ripe and then cut it, after which, and before it was fit to be carried, the landlord distrained it for rent, both the Courts of K B and C [illegible] held that it was not distrainable. But where corn was taken in execution and sold by the sheriff under the stat 2 *W.* & *M.* c. 5 s. 3 and the vendee permitted it after severance to lie on the ground, the Court held it to be distrainable for rent

A landlord having a legal right to distrain goods while they remain on the premises, the issuing a commission of bankrupt against the tenant, and the messenger's possession of the goods of the tenant, will not hinder him from distraining for rent, and the assignment by the commissioners of the bankrupt's estate and effects is only changing the property of the goods, which while on the premises remain liable to be distrained

But if the landlord neglects to distrain, and suffers the goods to be sold by the assignees, he can only come in *pro ratâ* with the rest of the creditors.

(*a*) [illegible] 386.

In some cases the distress itself is not protected even from a subsequent process: thus where the question was, whether goods were not liable to be seized on an immediate extent for the king's own debt, after a distress had been taken of the same goods by a landlord for rent justly due to him, before an actual sale of the goods? the Court of the Exchequer determined that the extent took place of the landlord's claim for rent, upon the authority of a much stronger case which had been before determined in that Court, in which the time for the sale had expired, and an attachment had been moved for against the sheriff, for not having executed the writ of *venditioni exponas*.

But if a replevin come after goods are sold on the execution, the defendant must claim property; for then they are out of the custody of the law, and in the hands of a private person.

Lastly, as every thing which is distrained is presumed to be the property of the wrong doer, it follows that such things wherein no man can have an absolute and valuable property, as dogs, cats, rabbits, and all animals *feræ naturæ*, cannot be distrained.

Yet if deer, which are *feræ naturæ*, are kept in a private enclosure for the purpose of sale or profit, this so far changes their nature, by reducing them to a kind of stock or merchandise, that they may be distrained for rent.

When we speak of chattels not distrainable, it must be understood with reference to the subject of this chapter, namely, as a remedy for the recovery of rent, for all chattels whatever are distrainable damage feasant, it being but natural justice that whatever doth the injury should be a pledge to make compensation for it.

Where a wrongful distress is made, and the party whose goods are so distrained pays money in order to redeem them, he may maintain trover against the wrong doer (a).

Distress, when, where, and how made.—With respect to the time, place, and manner of making a distress, it is to be observed, that, a distress for rent cannot be made in the night, [which season is said to be from after sun-set till sun-rise,] because the tenant hath not thereby notice to make a tender of his rent, which possibly he might do in order to prevent the impounding of his cattle (b).

The distress for rent must be for rent in *arrear*, therefore it may not be made the same day on which the rent becomes due, for if the rent be paid at any time during that day, whilst a man can see to count it, the payment is good. Strictly indeed the rent is demandable and payable before the time of sun-set of the day whereon it is reserved; yet it is not due till the last minute of the natural day, for if the lessor die after sun-set, and before midnight, the rent shall go to the heir, and not to the executor.

(a) 6 T. R. 29[illegible]. (b) Gilb. L. of Dist. 56, &c.

But the custom of a place, or an agreement between the landlord and tenant, if there be no objection to it in point of law, may empower the landlord to distrain for it earlier, for *conventio vincit legem*.

Therefore if a trader, after committing an act of bankruptcy, take a shop, and agree to pay a year's rent in advance, where by the custom of the country half a year's rent becomes due on the day on which the tenant enters, the landlord after an assignment under the commission, and before the year be expired, may distrain goods on the premises for half a year's rent, or if he buy the tenant's goods, he may retain the amount of the half year's rent.

A distress must not be after tender of payment, for if the landlord come to distrain the goods of his tenant for rent, the tenant may, before the distress, tender the arrearages, and if the distress be afterwards taken, it is illegal. So, if the landlord have distrained, and the tenant make a tender of the arrearages before the impounding of the distress, the landlord ought to deliver up the distress, and if he does not, the detainer is unlawful.

But tender of rent after distress is impounded, is insufficient, for then it is in the custody of the law (*a*).

An action on the case will not lie for detaining cattle distrained and impounded, where a tender of amends was not made till after the impounding, and *semble* such an action could not be supported, even if the tender of amends had been made before the impounding; as the proper mode of trying the validity of distress is by action of replevin or trespass (*b*).

A tender of rent at the proper time and place will save a distress, or entry, or other condition in the lease, though the landlord refuse to take it, the tenant having done all that he was bound to do: the landlord may, however, maintain an action of debt, or covenant for his rent, but shall not recover damages or costs for non-payment (*c*).

A distress may be made for rent accrued after the expiration of a notice to quit, but it is a waiver of the notice, the taking of the distress being a proof of the landlord's intention to confirm the tenancy.

At common law, and before any innovation was made by statute, the landlord could not have distrained for his rent after the determination of his lease; but now a distress for rent may be made though the lease be determined (*d*).

For by stat. 8 *Ann.* c. 14. s. 6, 7, it is enacted, That it shall be lawful to distrain after the determination of the lease, in the same manner as if it had not been determined, provided the distress be made within six calendar months after the determination of the lease, and

(*a*) 5 T. R. 432. (*b*) 1 Camb. [illegible] (*c*) 1 Vent. 21. 1 Saund. 130. 3 Salk. [illegible]
(*d*) 6 T. R. 665.

during the continuance of the landlord's title or interest, and also during the possession of the tenant

But where, by the custom of the country, the off-going tenant is allowed any advantages respecting the premises which he has quitted, as for example, a certain period within which to get in and dispose of, or to thresh and keep, his corn, &c. the interest and connection between the landlord and tenant is so continued by the operation of such customary right, that the former is entitled to distrain for rent in arrear after six months have expired since the determination of the lease.

So, if a tenant dies, and his representative enters upon the premises, and continues therein until the end of the term, and afterwards, the landlord may at any time within the six months after the end of the term, under the restrictions prescribed by the Act, distrain for the arrears which were due at the time the original tenant died, as well as for what accrued afterwards

No private person can distrain beasts of his own land, or on the high road, which is privileged for the convenience of passengers and the encouragement of commerce.

But though chattels or pledges on the land only are to answer the lord's rent, yet if the lord comes to distrain, and the tenant, seeing him, drives the cattle off the land, the lord may follow the beasts and distrain out of his fee, if he had once a view of his cattle on his land. But if the beasts go off the land of themselves before the lord observes them, he cannot distrain them afterwards, as he might, where the tenant drives them off.

Where there are separate demises, there ought to be separate distresses on the several premises subject to the distinct rents, for no distress on one part can be good for both rents.

But where lands lying in different counties, are held under one demise at one entire rent, a distress may be lawfully taken in either county for the whole rent in arrear, and chasing a distress over is a continuance of the taking But where the counties do not adjoin, a distress cannot be chased out of one county into the other.

By statute 11 *G.* 2 *c.* 19. [of which more particularly hereafter,] if any tenant for life, years, at will, sufferance, or otherwise shall fraudulently or clandestinely convey his goods off the premises, to prevent his landlord from distraining the same, such person, or any person by him lawfully empowered, may, in thirty days next after such conveyance, seize the same wherever they shall be found, and dispose of them in such manner as if they had been distrained on the premises

But, by sect 2. of the same statute, the landlord shall not distrain any goods which shall have been previously sold, *bonâ fide*, and for a valuable consideration, to any person not privy to such fraud

By sect. 3. every tenant who shall convey away his goods, and every person who shall knowingly aid or assist him therein, or in concealing the same, shall forfeit to the landlord double the value of such goods.

By sect. 7 of the same statute, it is enacted, That where any goods or chattels, fraudulently or clandestinely conveyed off the premises to prevent the landlord from distraining them for rent, shall be put, placed, or kept in any house, barn, stable, out-house, yard, close or place, locked up, fastened or otherwise secured, it shall be lawful for the landlord, his steward, or other person impowered by him for that purpose, to take and seize as a distress for rent, such goods and chattels (first calling to his assistance, the constable, headborough, borsholder, or other peace-officer of the hundred, district, or place where the same shall be suspected to be concealed; and, in case of a dwelling-house, (oath being also first made before a justice of the peace, of a reasonable ground to suspect that such goods or chattels are therein,) in the day-time to break open and enter into such house, barn, stable, out-house, yard, close and place; and to take and seize such goods and chattels for the arrears of rent, as he might have done, if they had been in an open place.

If a landlord comes into a house and seizes upon some goods as a distress in the name of all the goods in the house, it will be a good seizure of all.

Distresses ought not to be excessive; but in proportion to the sum distrained for, according to the statute of *Marlbridge*, 52 *H*. 3. *c*. 4.

Thus, if the lord distrain two or three oxen for 12*d*. this is unreasonable: so if he distrain a horse or an ox for a small sum, where a sheep or a swine may be had, this is an excessive distress.—But if there be no other distress on the land, then the taking of one entire thing, though of never so great value, is not unreasonable.

As these distresses cannot be sold, the owner upon making satisfaction, may have his chattels again.

By stat. 17 *C*. 2. *c*. 7. in all cases, where the value of the cattle distrained shall not be found to be of the full value of the arrears distrained for, the party to whom such arrears are due, his executors or administrators, may distrain again for the said arrears.

But a second distress cannot, it seems, be at all justified, where there is enough which might have been taken upon the first, if the distrainer had then thought proper. For in a case where this question occurred, it was resolved, that a man who has an entire duty (as a rent for example) shall not split the entire sum, and distrain for one part of it at one time, and for the other part of it at another time, and so *toties quoties* for several times; for that is great oppression.

But if a man seize for the whole sum that is due to him, and only mistakes the value of the goods seized, which may be of uncertain or imaginary value, as pictures, jewels, race horses, &c. there is no reason why he should not afterwards complete his execution by making a further seizure.

For taking an excessive distress, a man is not liable to a criminal prosecution.

Neither can a general action of trespass be maintained for an excessive distress.

But the remedy is by a special action founded upon the statute of *Marlbridge*. On this statute even there can be no remedy where there is a remedy at the common law, nor if the plaintiff has recovered in replevin; for the action on the statute is founded upon there being a cause of distress, of which the recovery in replevin shews there was none; moreover, in replevin, damages were recoverable for the taking, and a man shall not be permitted to say that there was a cause of distress, after he has recovered upon the ground of its being unlawful.

The Court of Chancery made an order specifically to restore to a tenant the stock on the farm seized by the landlord under a distress and bill of sale, the landlord not stating whether the sum under which by the terms of the contract he was not to enforce his remedies, was due (*a*).

If any distress and sale be made, as for rent in arrear and due, when in truth not any is due, in such case the owner may recover double the value, with full costs of suit, in an action of trespass, or upon the case, on the stat. 2 *W.* & *M. sess.* 1. *c.* 5. *s.* 5.

If the distress be made without cause the owner may make *rescous*, that is, rescue it; but if it be impounded, he cannot break the pound and retake it, because then it is in the custody of the law.

Distress how to be used.—Notice of the distress, with the cause of such taking, must be given to the owner by the stat. 2 *W.* & *M. sess.* 1. *c.* 5. *s.* 1.

As to the manner in which the distress is to be used and disposed of, a distress is to be kept in a pound, which is nothing more than a public prison for goods and chattels, and is either *overt*, or open, or *covert*, or shut. All living chattels are regularly to be put into the pound *overt*, because the owner at his peril is to sustain them, wherefore they ought to be put in such an open place as he can resort to for the purpose.

By the stat. 1 & 2 *Ph.* & *M. c.* 12. *s.* 1. no distress of cattle is to be driven out of the hundred, rape, wapentake, or lathe, where the same is taken, except it be to a pound *overt* within the same shire, not above three miles from the place where the same is taken; nor impounded in several places, whereby the owner may be constrained to sue several replevins, on pain of forfeiting to the party grieved one hundred shillings, and treble damages.

(*a*) 2 Ves. 177.

By sect 2. of the same statute, no person shall take for keeping in pound or impounding any distress, above fourpence for any one whole distress and where less hath been used, there to take less ; on pain of forfeiting 5*l.* to the party grieved, besides what he should take above four-pence.

But where lands lying in two adjoining counties were held under one demise at one entire rent, and the landlord distrained cattle in both counties for rent arrear, it was holden, that he might chase them all into one county if the counties had not adjoined, it would have been otherwise

The offence created by this statute for impounding a distress in a wrong place, is but a single offence, and shall be satisfied with one forfeiture, though three or four are concerned in doing the act, as the offence cannot be severed so as to make each offender separately liable to the penalty, the meaning of the statute being that the penalty shall be referred to the offence, not to the person

As, where three persons distrained a flock of sheep, and severally impounded them in three several pounds, whereby, &c. it was held, that they should forfeit but one 5*l* and one treble damages

Trespass will not lie against the poundkeeper merely for receiving a distress, though the original taking be *tortious* for the pound is the custody of the law, and the poundkeeper is bound to take and keep whatever is brought to him at the peril of the person who brings it. and if wrongfully taken they are answerable, not he, for when cattle are once impounded, he cannot let them go without a replevin or the consent of the party. If however the poundkeeper goes one jot beyond his duty and assents to the trespass, that may be a different case

Neither can a poundkeeper bring an action if the pound be broken, but it must be brought by the party interested.

Beasts, as is said, ought to be put in a public pound, for if they are placed in a private pound, the distrainer must keep them at his peril with provision, for which he shall have no satisfaction, and if they die for want of sustenance, the distrainer shall answer for them

Dead chattels however, as household goods, &c. which may receive damage by the weather, must be put into a pound *covert*, otherwise the distrainer is answerable for them if they be damaged or stolen away, and this pound covert must be within three miles, and in the same county.

Now, by stat 11 G. 2. c 19. s. 10. any person distraining may impound or otherwise secure the distress of what kind soever it be, in such place or on such part of the premises as shall be most convenient, and may appraise and sell the same, as any person before might have done off the premises

The distrainer cannot work or use the thing distrained, whether lie in a pound *overt* or *covert* because the distrainer has only the custody of the thing as a pledge, but the owner may make profit of it at his pleasure.

An exception to this rule exists in respect to milch kine, which may be milked by the distrainer because it may be necessary to their preservation, and consequently of benefit to the owner [Cases in the books cast some degree of doubt on the legality of this *dictum* in Cro. *Jac* 148. (see *Hunt's Gilbert's Law of Distress*, 74.) but the reason of the thing is so forcible, that we incline to think that the *dictum* of that day respecting this point, would be recognized as law at this period.]

The distrainer cannot tie or bind a beast in the pound, though it be to prevent its escape, for any act of the distrainer that tends to the injury of it is done at his peril

But if cattle distrained die in the pound, without any fault of the distrainer; in such case he who made the distress shall have an action of trespass, or may distrain again, if the distress was for rent

If a distress be taken without cause, before it be impounded, the party may make a *rescous* But if it be impounded, he cannot justify the breach of the pound to take it out of the pound, because the distress is then in the custody of the law, if however the pound be unlocked, it seems he may take them.

By the common law, if a man break the pound, or the lock of it, or any part of it, he greatly offends against the peace, and commits a trespass against the king, and to the lord of the fee, the sheriffs, and hundredors in breach of the peace, and to the party in delay of justice wherefore hue and cry is to be levied against him as against those who break the peace, and the party who distrained may take the goods [illegible] wheresoever he finds them, and again impound them

Besides which, by stat. 2 *W.* & *M.* [illegible] 5 [illegible] for any pound-breach or *rescous* of goods distrained for rent, the person grieved thereby shall, in a special action upon the case, recover treble damages and costs, against the offender, or against the owner of the goods if they be afterwards found to have come to his use or possession.

In an action on this statute, it has been adjudged, that the word "treble" shall be referred as well to the word "costs," as to the word "damages," and consequently that the costs shall be trebled as well as the damages (*a*). Indeed it is determined in general, that where a statute gives treble damages the costs shall be trebled [illegible] (*b*).

As to what shall be a [illegible], if the [illegible] while being driven to the pound go into the house of the owner, who [illegible] them not, upon demand of them by the distrainer, this is a [illegible] in law

With respect to the disposition of the distress, which being cons-

(*a*) 1 Ld. Raym. [illegible] (*b*) 1 [illegible]

dered as a pledge could not at the common law be sold. By the stat. 2 *W. & M. sess.* 1. *c.* 5. *s.* 2. it is enacted, That where any goods shall be distrained for rent reserved and due upon any demise, lease or contract whatever, and the tenant or owner of the goods distrained, shall not within five days next after such distress taken and notice thereof, with the cause of such taking, left at the chief mansion-house or other most notorious place on the premises, replevy the same; in such case the person distraining shall, with the sheriff or under-sheriff of the county, or with the constable of the hundred, parish, or place where such distress shall be taken, cause the goods so distrained to be appraised by two sworn appraisers, (whom such sheriff, under-sheriff, or constable shall swear to appraise the same truly, according to the best of their understandings,) and after such appraisement may sell the same for the best price that can be gotten for them, for satisfaction of the rent, and charges of the distress, appraisement and sale, leaving the overplus, if any, with the sheriff, under-sheriff, or constable, for the owner's use.

In the notice for the sale of a distress under this statute, it is not necessary to set forth at what time the rent became due for which the distress has been made.

If the person distraining is sworn one of the appraisers, it is illegal, for he is interested in the business; and the statute says that *he*, with the sheriff, &c. shall cause the goods to be appraised by two sworn appraisers.

The landlord must remove the goods at the end of five days, and will be deemed a trespasser for any time beyond it that he keeps them. The five days allowed before a distress can be sold, are inclusive of the day of sale, wherefore it seems the distress may be removed on the sixth day.

Thus where a distress was made and a regular notice of sale given on the 12th day of *May*, and on the afternoon of the 17th day of the same month the goods were removed and sold, it was held that on the evening of the 17th five days from the time of the distress had completely expired, and that the removal and sale were regular according to the time allowed by the statute.

Where one, who entered under a warrant of distress for rent in arrear, continued in possession of the goods upon the premises for fifteen days, during the four last of which he was removing the goods, which were afterwards sold under the distress: held that at any rate he was liable to trespass *quare clausum fregit*, for continuing on the premises and disturbing the plaintiff in possession of his house, after the time allowed by law (*a*).

(*Vol. I.*) Y

Notice to the owner is sufficient as against him unless a replevin had been sued by the tenant, in which case, personal notice to the tenant is sufficient to warrant a sale under the stat 2 *W. & M. sess.* 1. *c* 5. *s.* 2 and is preferable indeed to notice left at the mansion-house

Upon the sale of such distress the appraisers need be sworn by the constable only of the hundred in which the distress is impounded

An irregularity in this process does not now render the distrainer, as he was at the common law, a trespasser *ab initio* for by stat 11 *G* 2. *c.* 19. *s.* 19. it is provided, that where any distress shall be made for any kind of rent justly due, and any irregularity shall be afterwards done by the party distraining or his agent, the distress shall not be deemed unlawful, nor the distrainer a trespasser, *ab initio*, but the party grieved may recover satisfaction for the special damage in an action of trespass, or on the case at his election.

Therefore trespass will not lie for an irregular distress, where the irregularity complained of is not in itself an act of trespass, but consists merely in the omission of some of the forms required in conducting the distress, such as procuring goods to be appraised before they are sold. The true construction of the provision in 11 *G* 2. *c* 19. *s.* 19 that the party may recover a compensation for the special damage he sustains by an irregular distress "in an action of trespass or on the case," is that he must bring trespass, if the irregularity be in the nature of an act of trespass, and case, if it be in itself the subject matter of an action on the case (*a*)

But, by sect. 20, no tenant shall recover in such action, if tender of amends had been made before the action brought · and by sect 21 the defendant in such action may plead the general issue and give the special matter in evidence.

Under the plea of the general issue, given by this Act, a landlord cannot justify, except for acts done as landlord therefore, although he may justify as far as the distress goes, he cannot under this issue justify expulsion So also if the goods remain on the premises beyond the five days, he cannot justify, under this issue, entering the house to remove them afterwards, but must plead a licence to justify the asportation, or *liberum tenementum* to justify the expulsion.

For goods sold therefore before five days have expired next after the distress and notice, an action of trover will not lie, that being a remedy which cannot be pursued since the stat. 11 *G* 2 *c* 19 as it tends to place the landlord in the same situation as he was before the passing of that Act the action ought to be brought specially for the particular irregularity.

But though the tenant shall make satisfaction for the real damage

(*a*) 2 Camp. 115

only sustained, by any irregularity in taking or disposing of the distress; yet by the stat. 2 *W. & M. sess* 1 *c* 5. *s* 3. if any distress and sale shall be made for rent pretended to be due to the person distraining, where in truth no such rent is due, the tenant shall recover double the value of the goods distrained, together with full costs of suit.

Goods distrained by the plaintiff were delivered by him to the defendant on his promising to pay the rent, an action for money had and received would not lie for the value of the goods, though defendant do not pay the rent (*a*).

Where there are three joint lessees, two of whom assign their interest to the third, whose sole liability the landlord has not consented to accept, the goods of the plaintiff being put on the premises by permission of such third lessee and distrained by the landlord for rent and he having paid it, the three lessees are liable to him for money paid to their use (*b*).

Section II. *Of the Action of Debt, where the Lease is by Deed.*

Another remedy for the recovery of rent is by action of debt, or covenant, where the premises are demised by deed.

An action of debt or covenant lies for non-payment of the rent on the word "yielding" in a lease for years, for it is an agreement to pay the rent, which will make a covenant.

The action of debt is founded upon a contract, either express or implied, in which the certainty of the sum or duty appears, and the plaintiff is to recover the sum *in numero*, and not in damages (*c*).

Debt, being an action founded on an express contract, rents reserved on leases for years were at all times recoverable by this species of remedy (*d*)

So, debt lies for rent upon a lease, though the defendant entered before his title began for though clearly he is a disseisor by his entry, and the accruing of his term shall not alter his estate, yet debt lieth for privity of contract, and whether the entry be tortious or not, it cannot discharge the contract for payment of the rent (*e*)

At common law, debt did not lie for rent reserved upon a freehold lease during the continuance of the lease (*f*).

But the stat. 8 *Ann.* c. 14. *s.* 4. enacts, That any persons entitled to [illegible] rent on a lease for life or lives, may have an action of debt

(*a*) [illegible] 3 Esp. R. 8. [illegible] 8 T. R. [illegible] (*c*) Bull. N. P. 16[illegible]
[illegible] (*f*) Cro. Eliz. 169. [illegible] 550

during the existence of the life, as on a lease for years during the term.

By the stat. 32 *H.* 8. *c.* 37. *s.* 1. the executors and administrators of tenants in fee, fee-tail, or for life, of rent-services rent-charges, rents-seck and fee-farms, may bring debt for the arrearages against the tenant who ought to have paid the same. This statute extends to all tenants for life.

Though it be not necessary in general to set out the indenture in the declaration in debt for rent, yet it seems necessary where the action is brought on a lease of tithes, which being an incorporeal hereditament lying in grant, could not be granted without deed (*a*).

If one of two lessees assign his interest, and the other die before the rent becomes due, an action of debt in the *debet et detinet* will lie against the assignee and executrix of the deceased lessee for the whole rent (*b*).

So, if the lessee for years will assign all his term in part of the land, the lessor shall have a joint action against the lessee and assignee (*c*).

If there is a lessee for years, and he assigns all his interest to another, yet may the lessor still have an action of debt against him for rent in arrear after the assignment: first, because the lessee shall not prevent by his own act such remedy as the lessor hath against him on his contract; 2dly, that the lessee might grant the term to a poor man, who would not be able to manure the land, and so for need or malice the land would lie untilled, and the lessor be without remedy, either by distress or action of debt (*d*).

But the lessor may either tacitly or expressly accept the assignee for his tenant, and so discharge the original lessee; and if he once accepts rent from the assignee, (who is bound however no longer than while in possession) he can never resort back again to the first lessee (*e*).

The executor or administrator of a lessee for years, may, like any other assignee, assign the term, and shall not be chargeable for rent after the assignment (*f*).

In a plea of assignment in a lease of tithes, it is necessary for the defendant to allege that he assigned the term by indenture, for that was always required by the common law, and the statute of frauds 29 *C.* 2. *c.* 3. does not apply to cases of incorporeal hereditaments, for they are not within the mischief intended to be remedied by the statute (*g*).

If the lessor assign his rent, without the reversion, the assignee (if the tenant agrees) may maintain an action of debt for the rent, because the privity of contract is transferred (*h*).

(*a*) 2 Saund. 297 [illegible] (*d*) Cro. Jac. 311 [illegible]
(*b*) 1 Lev. Raym. 1[illegible] 4 T. R. 98 (*e*) Bul. N. P. 271 [illegible] 1 R. 95
(*c*) [illegible] (*f*) 2 Saund. 108 [illegible] (*h*) 3 Salk. 11[illegible]

If the lessor grant away his reversion, he cannot have an action of debt for the rent, which being incident to the reversion, passes with it.—The grantee of the reversion, therefore, can alone have the action (*a*).

But the grantee even cannot have debt against the lessee if he has assigned over; for there was no privity between them but by reason of the privity of estate, and that being gone by the assignment, this action will not lie (*b*). Such is the case, whether the person claiming the rent comes in by succession or grant: thus the successor of a prebend cannot bring debt against the executor of a lessee of the prebendary, where such executor had assigned (*c*).

But if a lessee assign part of the land demised, a grantee of the reversion shall have debt against him for the whole rent: for the entire estate remaining in one part of the land, the privity remained entire and would support the action (*d*).

A devisee may maintain debt for his share of the rent, and if there be a devise of a rent to be equally divided between three, each may have his action for his share (*e*).

An agreement between the lessor and the assignee of the original lessee, "that the lessor should have the premises as mentioned in the lease, and should pay a particular sum over and above the rent annually towards the good-will already paid by such assignee," operates as a surrender of the whole term, and the sum reserved for good-will being to be paid annually in gross and not as rent, the assignee cannot distrain either for that, or for the original rent, but he has a remedy by assumpsit for the sum reserved for the good-will (*f*).

If a lessee for years re-demise his whole term to the lessor with a reservation of rent, it operates as a surrender of the original lease, and therefore he cannot maintain debt for rent against the executor of the original lessor; but must seek relief in equity (*g*).

If a lessee assign his whole term to a stranger, he may bring debt for the rent reserved on the contract against him or his personal representatives.

So, if the lessee for years assigns all his term to another, reserving the rent to himself, he shall have an action of debt for the arrears during the term; so though not properly a rent for want of a reversion, yet it partakes of its nature, being a return for the profits which are annual (*h*).

Debt does not lie for rent upon an expired lease. Therefore where lessee for life made a lease for years, rendering rent, and afterwards surrendered to the lessor upon condition, the lessee for years took a new lease for years of the lessor; the lessee for life performed the

(*a*) Esp N P 222 (*b*) Cro Eliz. 328 (*c*) Ibid 555
(*d*) Ibid 633 (*e*) Ibid 657 (*f*) 1 T R. 441.
(*g*) 2 Mod. 171 (*h*) 1 Sid 475

condition, and put out the lessee for years, who re-enters, and the lessee for life brought debt for the first rent received; and it was ruled that it was not maintainable, for the lease out of which it was reserved was gone and determined; for though the surrender of the tenant for life, which made the lessee for years immediate tenant to the first lessor and so enabled him to make such surrender, was conditional, yet the defeisance of the estate for life, by performance of the condition, cannot defeat the estate of the lessee for years, which was absolute and well made, and then the rent reserved thereon is gone likewise (*a*).

Yet, if a lease be made to a woman *dum sola*, and she marries, the term expires and she dies, debt lies against the husband for rent accruing during her lifetime, for he is chargeable by reason of the perception of the profits (*b*).

So, in the case of a lease for years, rendering rent, and for non-payment the lease to be void, although the lease become void, yet for rent due before, debt lies (*c*).

The Declaration.—In declaring in debt for rent on a lease for years, the plaintiff need not set forth any entry or occupation, for though the defendant neither enters nor occupies, he must pay the rent, it being due by the lease or contract, and not by the occupation; therefore though it is usual in the declaration to say "by virtue of which the lessee entered," yet it is not necessary (*d*).

If rent is reserved quarterly and half yearly, each gale is a distinct debt for which the lessor may have his action, and may declare for an entire gale at the end of any quarter or half year without shewing how the former quarter or half year has been satisfied. But if he declares only for part of the gale due at the end of any half year or quarter, it is bad, unless he shews how the remaining part was satisfied, for otherwise the lessee may be exposed to many actions for the same demand (*e*).

Whenever rent or any other duty is reserved quarterly or half yearly, the declaration should always state when it was due and owing, or it will be bad (*f*).

So, if the plaintiff declares for less rent than a year without shewing how the rest was satisfied, it is bad, and no action will lie for half a year's rent if the rent be reserved annually (*g*).

In debt for rent against the devisee of the lessee, the plaintiff must shew that the defendant entered by assent of the executor, or *virtute legationis* and a demand must be made of the rent.

(*a*) Cro. Eliz. 264. [illegible] Abr. tit. "Lease." [illegible] (*b*) 1 Lev. 25
(*c*) Cro. Eliz. 78 (*d*) [illegible] 229. 1 Ld. Raym. 171
(*e*) 1 [illegible] 129. 3 [illegible] 118. 2 Saund. 303 [illegible] (*f*) [illegible] 3
(*g*) Cro. Eliz. 325, 6

Where the plaintiff in his declaration undertakes to recite a lease, any mis-recital is fatal, if the action be founded on such lease.

Thus, if a lease, upon which a gross sum and three fowls are reserved by way of rent, is represented in pleading to have reserved the gross sum without mentioning the fowls, the variance is fatal (*a*)

In debt by a remainder-man for rent reserved upon a lease by tenant for life, the plaintiff must shew what authority the tenant for life had to make the lease (*b*).

The *venue* may be laid either where the land lies or where the deed was executed, or it should seem in any place, if the action is against the original lessee (*c*)

But if the action is against the assignee of the lessee, it must be laid where the land lies, for he is chargeable only on the privity of estate (*d*)

So, against the executor of the lessee, the action must be brought where the land lies, for he is chargeable as assignee on the privity of estate only (*e*)

So also debt for rent by the assignee of the lessor against the lessee, must be brought where the land lies. but it is otherwise in the case of covenant which is transitory (*f*)

In debt for rent against an executor or administrator, if the whole rent has incurred in the lifetime of the lessee, the action against his executor must be in the *detinet* only and the executor, though he do not enter, is still chargeable in the *detinet*, because he cannot so waive the term as not to be liable for the rent as far he has assets (*g*).

But for the rent incurred after the death of the lessee, the action may be brought either in the *debet* or *detinet*, if the executor enters; for he is charged as assignee in respect of the perception of the profits, and it is not material whether he has assets or not Therefore he cannot in such case plead *plene administravit* and if judgment be given against him, it is *de bonis propriis*.—But if the land be of less value than the rent, he may plead the special matter, *viz.* that he has no assets, and the land is of less value than the rent, and may pray judgment whether he shall be charged otherwise than in the *detinet* only The lessor has his election to charge him either in the *debet* and *detinet*, or the *detinet* only, in which latter case the judgment is *de bonis testatoris* (*h*)

It seems sufficient to declare against the defendant as executor, without naming him so in the beginning of the declaration (*i*)

But after a judgment obtained against an executor, one may have debt in the *debet* and *detinet* suggesting a *devastavit*, and thereby charge

(*a*) 2 Ld Raym 792 Doug 668 (*b*) 2 Ld Raym 792 (*c*) 2 Salk 651 2 Str [illegible]
(*d*) Ibid Carth 177 1 Bos. and Pul 23 (*e*) Esp N P. 21[illegible] (*f*) 1 Wils [illegible]
(*g*) 1 Saund 1. n. 1 (*h*) Ibid (*i*) Ibid 112 n. 2

him *de bonis propriis* for it is then properly his own debt, and a judgment against an executor or administrator by default, confession, or after verdict, is an admission of assets to satisfy the judgment, and if no assets are to be found, it is evidence of a *devastavit* (*a*)

An executor may bring an action before probate; but he cannot declare till probate be granted, for when he comes to declare he must produce his letters testamentary If, however, the probate has been lost, an exemplification from the ordinary will be sufficient (*b*)

But an administrator cannot bring an action till administration be granted. for the power of an administrator is derived from the ordinary, as that of an executor is from the will (*c*)

Declarations by executors or administrators must be in the *debet* only, for a person can only be said to be the party to whom the money when received would belong, that is, to the testator's or intestate's estates, not to his executor or administrator Such is the case, though the rent be reserved on a demise which commenced on the death of the testator, so that he never received any rent (*d*).

In actions by an executor, the declaration should state "that the "testator was dead and the plaintiff complete executor" But if the executor has recovered and had judgment, and afterwards brings a *sci. fa.* on it, such averment is not necessary, though it would be otherwise, had the *scire facias* been on a judgment obtained by the testator himself, for by the first judgment the testator's right was established, but where the first judgment has been by the testator, the executor's right does not appear without such averment (*e*).

So, a declaration by an administrator is good, stating in general "that administration was granted to him by the bishop of, &c." without saying that he was ordinary, or to whom the right to grant administration belonged, unless it be a peculiar jurisdiction, in which case it should be set out The reason is, that the defendant might contest the right of the person granting administration, or shew that administration was granted to another, or that there were *bona notabilia.* But a verdict would cure the fault (*f*).

In a declaration by an executor of an executor, he should set out "that the first executor proved the will" for otherwise the plaintiff has no title, for if there had been no probate granted to the first executor an administration *cum testamento annexo* should be granted of the effects of the first testator to the next of kin But this also would be cured by a verdict (*g*).

If the action is brought by the assignee of the reversion against the lessee for rent, he must set forth the seisin in fee in the first tenant,

(*a*) 1 Saund. 216, 219 & 237. in n (*b*) [illegible] 302 1 Str. 412 (*c*) Esp. N. P. 218
(*d*) [illegible] Cro. [illegible] 840 (*e*) 1 Str. 651 (*f*) Cro. Eliz. 879.
(*g*) [illegible]

and the several mesne assignments, down to himself: for these are necessary to make out his title, and the validity of these assignments being matter of law, ought to be set forth for the court to judge of (*a*).

For it is a general rule, that estates in fee-simple may be alleged generally, but the commencement of estates-tail, and other particular estates must be shewn, where they go to the ground of the action; but not so where they are only inducement: the life therefore of the tenant in tail or for life ought to be averred (*b*).

But where the action is by the lessor or his heir against the assignee of the lessee, the plaintiff need not set out the several mesne assignments to the defendant, for they do not lie within his knowledge: but it is sufficient for the plaintiff to set forth the original demise to the first lessee, whose estate and interest have by several mesne assignments come to the defendant; and proof of possession and occupation shall be sufficient to charge him (*c*).

An assignee of a lease, assigned to him by an administrator, is not obliged, it should seem, to make a *profert in curiam* of the letters of administration (*d*).

Respecting the *venue*, it may in addition be observed that, in debt for rent upon a lease, founded on the privity of estate, as when brought by the assignee or devisee of the lessor against the lessee; or by the lessor or his personal representatives, against the assignee of the lessee; or against the executor of the lessee, in the *debet* and *detinet*, the action is local, and the *venue* must be laid in the county where the estate lies.—But in debt by the lessor against the lessee, or his executor in the *detinet* only, the action is transitory, and the *venue* may be laid in any county (*e*).

The Pleas.—The pleas to an action of debt for rent reserved on a lease by deed are, 1. *Nil debet;* 2. *Non est factum;* 3. *Riens in arrear;* 4. Entry and eviction; 5. Infancy.

Wherever the debt is founded on the deed, the plea cannot contradict it: but there is a difference where the specialty is but an inducement to the action and matter of fact is the foundation of it, for there *nil debet* is a good plea: as in debt for rent by indenture for the plaintiff need not set out the indenture. Therefore the defendant may plead *nil debet* to debt for rent reserved by indenture, which he could not do in the case of a bond; because an indenture of lease does not acknowledge an absolute debt as a bond does, for the debt arises from the enjoyment of the thing demised, and so is but inducement (*f*).

Nil debet is a good plea in debt for rent on a lease by indenture, for

(*a*) Esp. N. P. 220 (*b*) Ibid. (*c*) Ibid.
(*d*) 3 Wils. 3 (*e*) Tidd's Pract.
(*f*) 2 Ld Raym. 1503; Esp. N. P. 233; 4 Tidd's Pract.

the foundation of the action is a mere fact, namely, the arrears of rent, and the indenture is held to be only inducement, which the plaintiff need not set out in his declaration (*a*)

But, though the defendant may plead *nil debet*, he cannot give in evidence under it, that the plaintiff had nothing in the tenements (*b*).

Though in debt for rent on a demise by indenture, it is not necessary to declare that it was by indenture, but "*quod cum dimisisset*" generally is sufficient, yet if the defendant pleads *nil habuit in tenementis*, it is said to be *primâ facie* a good plea, because no estoppel appears upon the record (*c*), and if the plaintiff replies that he had a sufficient estate to make the demise, he loses the benefit of the estoppel, and as he will not rely thereon, but will reply *habuit*, the jury shall find the truth, but if he replies (as he ought to do) that the demise was by indenture, and concludes *unde petit judicium*, if the defendant shall be admitted to plead the plea against his own acceptance of the lease by indenture, the defendant shall be stopped (*d*).

But where the declaration states the lease to be by indenture, the plaintiff need not reply the estoppel, but may demur, because the estoppel appears on the record otherwise, as is before mentioned, if the declaration be "*quod cum dimisisset*," without saying that it was by indenture (*e*)

In debt on bond conditioned for the payment of rent reserved upon a demise according to certain articles, the defendant is estopped to say, that he had not any thing in the land demised by the articles (*f*)

Nil habuit in tenementis has been held to be a good plea on demise by deed poll, because, as to the lessee, it is no estoppel It seems indeed settled that it is not admitted to be pleaded by a lessee in any case where occupation is enjoyed for the Court will not permit a tenant to impeach his landlord's title nor indeed will an action for rent lie where the title is in dispute. So, a tenant cannot set up the title of the mortgagee against the mortgagor. because he holds under the mortgagor and has admitted his title (*g*).

But a tenant is not at all events estopped to deny his landlord's title, the estoppel exists only during the continuance of his occupation, and if he be ousted by a title paramount, he may plead it (*h*).

If in a lease special days of payment are limited by the *reddendum*, the rent must be computed according to that, and not the *habendum* (*i*)

In debt for rent, where the plaintiff had declared for more than was due upon his own shewing, upon *nil debet* pleaded, he had judgment and damages and costs, notwithstanding, and it being moved in arrest

(*a*) 2 [illegible] 297 [illegible] (*c*) 2 Lev. R[illegible] 2[illegible] 6 T. R. 62 [illegible] 7 T. R. [illegible] 6 T. R. 62 6 Mod. 248 2 Ld. Raym. 1551, 4 [illegible] 276 [illegible] (*e*) [illegible]
(*b*) Bull N. P. 170 2 Ld. Raym. 1551 (*d*) 1 Saund. 277 1 Saund. 2[illegible]
(*f*) Cro. Eliz. 362 (*g*) 3 Lev. 146 Bull. N. P. 22[illegible] 5 T. R. 5 M[illegible] T. R. [illegible]
(*h*) [illegible] R. [illegible] (*i*) [illegible] 131

of judgment that the plaintiff had made an entire demand for rent to a certain sum when it appeared that he could not have an action for so much, yet the Court held that he might release the surplus and damages, and take judgment for the residue (*a*).

If the lessor accepts rent due at the last day of payment, and gives a discharge thereof and acquittance, this shall discharge all preceding arrears, and this would be good evidence on *nil debet*, for it is not presumable that a man would give a receipt for the last gale of rent, when the former gales were unpaid (*b*).

So, if the defendant pleads "levied by distress" and so *nil debet*, he may give a release or payment in evidence and even though there never was any distress made, yet is the evidence of payment or the release good, for the issue is on the debt, and the defendant proving it discharged, by any means, supports this issue (*c*)

If the lessor has covenanted to repair, and bring debt for his rent, it seems that the lessee may plead that he expended the rent in necessary repairs, and so owes nothing (*d*). but he must plead this specially, and cannot give it in evidence on the general issue, for he might have covenant on it against the lessor, wherefore also, if the lessor had brought covenant for rent instead of debt, the lessee could not plead expenditure in reparations at all, the remedy being reciprocal (*e*).

However, where there is an express covenant in the same indenture, that the lessee may deduct for charges and repairs, there clearly the defendant may plead it in bar to debt for rent (*f*)

So, the defendant may plead *non est factum*, for, denying the existence of the deed, there can be no estoppel (*g*)

If the defendant plead *non est factum*, the plaintiff must prove the execution of the deed, and proof that one who called himself *B* executed it, is not sufficient, if the witness did not know it to be the defendant (*h*).

Under this plea, the defendant may give in evidence any thing that proves the deed to be avoided, though it were delivered as his deed, for the plea is in the present tense, and if it be avoided, it is not now his deed (*i*)

But if the defendant plead rasure & sic *non est factum*, nothing else is evidence but rasure (*k*)

Riens in arrere is a good plea in debt for rent, though it would be bad in covenant for rent. for in covenant such plea confesses the covenant broken, and goes only in mitigation of damages (*l*). Therefore, where the defendant pleaded "that nothing of the rent is in arrear

(*a*) Mod. 214. (*c*) Esp. N. P. 234. Co. Litt. 373 a. 3 Co. 65 b. 1 Sid. 44.
(*b*) Salk. 284. Cro. Eliz. 14[illegible]. (*d*) Ibid. 222. (*e*) Bull. N. P. 176. 9 Mod. 60. 1 Ld Raym. 42[illegible]
[illegible] R. 650. (*f*) 1 Lev. 152. Esp. N. P. 234. (*g*) Ibid. Bull. N. P. 17[illegible].
(*h*) [illegible] 171. (*i*) Ibid. (*k*) Salk. 284. (*l*) Esp. N. P. 235.

" and unpaid as by the declarations is above supposed," it was held to be the same as if he had said *nil debet*, and that it related to the time of the action brought, as well as that of the plea pleaded, for if the rent was due and is not at the time of the plea, it could not have ceased to be due, but by the plaintiff's accepting it, and if so, he waives the action, though it was well brought at the time (*a*).

Under this plea, the defendant may deny the validity of the lease (*b*).

The defendant may also plead payment at or after the day, for acceptance of rent may be pleaded in bar to debt for rent, though not to a recovery in covenant (*c*).

If the defendant plead a tender on the land at the day, he must make a *profert* of the money (*d*)

Where the plaintiff gave a note of hand for rent in arrear, and took a receipt for it when paid, the defendant afterward distrained for the rent, and the plaintiff brought trespass it was holden, that notwithstanding this note, the defendant might distrain; for it is no alteration of the debt till payment (*e*)

So, if a landlord accept a bond for rent, this does not extinguish it, for the rent is higher, and the acceptance of a security of an unequal degree is no extinguishment of a debt. But a judgment obtained upon a bond would be an extinguishment of it (*f*).

Entry and eviction of the whole or any part of the premises demised, is a good plea in bar to an action of debt for the rent.

It must be a tortious entry and eviction, or expulsion, to occasion a suspension of the rent, a plea that states a mere trespass will not be sufficient (*g*) for if the lessor enter by virtue of a power reserved, or as a mere trespasser, yet if the lessee be not evicted, it will be no suspension of the rent (*h*).

Therefore, where the lessee pleaded in bar that the lessor entered on the premises and broke and pulled down the ceiling of a summer-house and tore up the benches, whereby the lessee was deprived of the use thereof, without any eviction being stated, it was held to be bad (*i*).

Debt was brought upon a lease for years of land in *D* for rent arrear for a year and a half at the *Annunciation*, 19 *J.* 1 The defendant pleaded, and confessed the lease and reservation; but further pleaded, that the lessor and all those whose estate, &c. had common in ten acres in *E* always for their beasts *levant et couchant* upon the said tenements, every year after corn sown, from *August* 7, until the corn reaped and carried away, and that before any rent was due, the

(*a*) Cowp. 590. (*b*) Cro. Eliz. 398. (*c*) 1 Tidd's Pract. 7 Mod. 198.
(*d*) 1 Ld Raym. 83. (*e*) Bull. N. P. 182. (*f*) Ibid. (*g*) Cowp. 242.
(*h*) Bull. N. P. 177. (*i*) Cowp. 242.

lessor inclosed the said ten acres, wherein he ought to have had his common, with hedges and ditches, and ejected him, so as he might not use his common, and thereby his rent was extinct: whereupon it was demurred, (among other objections) that the land inclosed is not alleged to be sown with corn; otherwise, by his prescription, he is not to have common, and the Court held that the plea was ill (*a*).

The plea must state an eviction or expulsion of the lessee by the lessor, and a keeping him out of possession until after the rent became due, otherwise it will be bad (*b*).

In debt for rent, it is optional for the defendant to plead the entry and expulsion by the plaintiff, or to give it in evidence upon *nil debet* (*c*).

Infancy is another good plea in debt for rent: but a lease made to an infant is not void, but voidable only; and if it be beneficial to him, he is liable to an action for the rent reserved (*d*).

Therefore, where to debt for rent, the defendant pleaded infancy at the time of the lease made: on demurrer, the Court held that the lease was voidable only at the election of the infant, manifested by waiving the land before the rent-day came; but he not having done so, and being of age before the rent-day came, it was deemed an election, and the plaintiff had judgment (*e*).

A set-off may also be pleaded to a general issue in this action.

Touching this plea, it was first given by stat. *G.* 2. *c.* 22. which enacts, That where there are mutual debts between the plaintiff and defendant, or if either party sue or are sued as executors or administrators, where there are mutual debts between the testator or the intestate and the other party, one debt may be set off against the other, and such matter given in evidence on the general issue, or pleaded in bar; but if intended to be given in evidence on the general issue, notice must be given of the particular sum intended to be set off, and on what account it has become due.

The stat. 8 *G.* 2. *c.* 4. further enacts, That mutual debts may be set off against each other, notwithstanding such debts were of different natures, unless in cases where either of the debts accrued by reason of a penalty contained in any bond or specialty, in which case, the debt intended to be set off must be pleaded in bar, and in which plea shall be shewn how much is truly due on either side; and in case the plaintiff shall recover, judgment shall be entered for no more than appears to be due after one debt set against another.

The general issue mentioned in the statute must be understood to mean any general issue.

(*a*) Cro. Jac. 680.
(*b*) 1 Saund. 204. n. 2.
(*c*) 1 Mod. 35. 118.
(*d*) Cro. Jac. 320.
(*e*) Ibid.

With respect to the statute of limitations, although the words of that statute are general as to the limitation of all actions of debt for arrearages of rent, yet it has been adjudged that an action of debt for the arrearages of rent reserved by indenture was not within the meaning of the said statute (*a*)

With respect to a release, it is said that it cannot be given in evidence without pleading, for it being a discharge by deed, all legal solemnities must be shewn to the Court. But this seems to be erroneous, for we have seen that under the plea of *nil debet*, a release may be given in evidence; and a release may be given in evidence under any general issue (*b*).

A release of all demands will not operate to release rent before it becomes due, for then there is no demand, but it will release rent then due (*c*).

Therefore if a man lets land to another for a year, yielding the rent at *Michaelmas*, and before *Michaelmas* the lessor releases to the lessee all actions, yet after the Feast the lessor may have his action for rent, for the release does not discharge it, for the rent is no debt till the day on which it is payable, as it is payable out of the profits of the land, and if the lessee is evicted before the day, no rent is due; but the lessor may discharge the lessee of the rent before the day by a special release (*d*).

If the defendant insists that the lease declared on is not the plaintiff's, the plaintiff must shew that it was made by one who had authority from him to execute it in his name, and the authority need not be produced But the lease must be made and executed in the name of the principal (*e*).

In debt for rent by husband and wife, upon a lease by her and her first husband, it is a good plea that her first husband was sole seised, and that she had nothing in the land (*f*).

As to the evidence on the part of the defendant, if he plead *nil debet*, he may give the statute of limitations in evidence, for the statute is in the present tense, and so makes it no debt at the time of pleading (*g*)

So, upon the same issue, he may give entry and expulsion in evidence (*h*).

The jury, besides finding the debt, ought to give damages for the detention of it, which are usually one shilling, though under particular circumstances they may be more.

In debt for rent money may be brought into Court (*i*).

Though the debt is by specialty, yet if it depends upon something

(*a*) [illegible] (*d*) Dyer 28 [illegible] 1 Salk 284 Cro Eliz 140 (*g*) Salk 578
(*b*) [illegible] (*e*) Bull N P 177 (*f*) Cro Eliz 700 (*g*) Salk 278
(*c*) [illegible] (*i*) [illegible] 582 Salk 659

extrinsic, as rent for example, the plaintiff may have a verdict for what is really due, though more is demanded.

Therefore in an action of debt on a lease for rent, at 2*l* 13*s* a year, if the plaintiff declare for 100*l* due for so many years' arrear, and it appears that a mistake has been made, and that he has declared for 8*l.* too much, yet after verdict if he release the 8*l.* he shall have judgment for the residue. So, if he demand more than upon his own shewing is due, he may, after demurrer, remit the overplus, and enter judgment for the rest (*a*).

But where a sum certain is always claimed, the verdict must go to the whole of it, that is, if the jury find part to be due, they must find *nil debet* as to the rest (*b*).

If there be judgment against two, and one of them dies, the plaintiff may have execution against the survivor (*c*).

Of Debt on Bond for, &c.—In an action for debt on bond for performance of covenants, the breach must be as particular as the covenant (*d*).

So, it was held, that the defendant in pleading to such action covenants performed, must shew the indenture from the counterpart. However, as to such particularity being requisite *vide postea* (*e*).

In a debt on bond to perform all covenants, &c. a breach cannot be assigned for non-payment of rent, without shewing a demand, except performance be pleaded (*f*).

A demurrer to a breach of covenant after plea of covenants performed confesses the breach, and contradicts the plea (*g*).

Yet to a plea of performance to debt on bond for breach of covenants, a replication of non-payment of rent, without stating a demand, is good, for a denial of such demand would have been a departure from the plea (*h*).

Where performance is pleaded, and matter of excuse is afterwards set forth in the rejoinder, it is a departure, it should have been pleaded in bar (*i*).

Section III. *Of the Action of Covenant, where the Lease is by Deed.*

An action of covenant also lies by the landlord for the recovery of his rent, if the demise be by deed, for covenant is an action that lies for the recovery of damages for the breach of any agreement entered into by deed between the parties (*k*), but the agreement must always

(*a*) 8 Mod. 213. 1 [illegible] 227. a. (*e*) Sir T. Raym. 26.
(*b*) 11 Mod. 312. [illegible] 667, &c. Co. Litt. 828. (*g*) Ib. 829.
(*c*) Cro. Car. 7. Esp. N. P. 266.

be by deed, though whether it be by indenture or deed-poll it equally lies (*a*).

If the agreement be by indenture, it is sufficient in order to maintain this action against the covenantor that he has sealed it and delivered it to the covenantee, though the covenantee never sealed it (*b*)

Neither the word "covenant," nor any particular form of words, is necessary to constitute a covenant in deed; for any form of expression under the hand and seal of the parties, importing an agreement, will support this action, as amounting to a covenant (*c*).

Thus in the case of a lease of lands, in which are the words "yield-"ing and paying" so much rent, this is an agreement for the payment of rent, which amounts to a covenant, and this action lies for the non-payment (*d*) So, if the lease be, yielding such a rent, free and clear of all manner of taxes, charges, and impositions whatsoever, covenant lies if the lessee do not pay the whole rent discharged of all taxes, before or afterwards imposed (*e*).

The covenant to pay rent is absolute, and if the tenant sustains any injury, he may have his remedy, but cannot set it off against the demand for rent (*f*).

As where in covenant for a year's rent, from *Michaelmas* 1725 to 1726, the defendant shewed upon oyer of the lease, that he as lessee by covenant was bound to repair in all cases except fire, and then pleaded that before *Michaelmas* 1725 the premises had been burned down, and not rebuilt by the plaintiff during the whole year, so that he had no enjoyment for the whole time claimed on demurrer, the plaintiff had judgment notwithstanding (*g*).

Respecting executors and administrators, as in debt so in covenant for rent incurred after the death of the lessee, the lessor has his election to charge the executor either as executor, in which case the judgment must be *de bonis testatoris*, or as assignee without naming him executor, but stating generally in the declaration, that the estate of the lessee in the premises lawfully came to the defendant, in which case the judgment shall be *de bonis propriis* (*h*).

The assignee of a term is bound to perform all the covenants annexed to the estate, as if *A.* leases to *B* and *B* covenants to pay rent during the said term, and *B* assigns to *C*, *C.* is bound to perform the covenants during the term though the assignee be not named: because the covenants run with the land, being made for the maintenance of a thing *in esse* at the time of the lease made (*i*).

An assignee, however, is liable only in respect of his possession, and not for a breach before assignment (*k*).

(*a*) F N B 145 L. (*b*) Cro Eliz 212 (*c*) Esp N P 267 Doug 766
(*d*) [illegible] (*e*) Carth. 135 (*f*) 2 Str 763 1 T. R 319 (*g*) 2 Str 763. 6 T R 62
[illegible] R [illegible] (*i*) Bac. Abr. tit "Covenant" (E 3) (*k*) Doug 184 S. P. 19[illegible]

So, if a tenant who is chargeable with the rent assign over his interest in the land, the assignee is chargeable with the penalty for arrears incurred in his own time (*a*).

Also, if a man leases for years, and the lessee covenants for him and assigns, to pay the rent so long as he and they shall have possession of the thing let, and the lessee assigns, the term expires, and the assignee continues the possession afterwards, an action of covenant will lie against him for rent behind after the expiration of the term, for though he is not an assignee strictly according to the rules of law, yet he shall be accounted such an assignee as is to perform the covenants (*b*).

As to the question how far actual possession is necessary in order to enable the lessor to maintain covenant against the assignee, it has been decided that by the assignment the title and possessory right pass, and the assignee becomes possessed in law; and it is immaterial whether it be an assignment of the usual kind, or by way of mortgage, for the principle upon which the assignee is liable is in respect of his having the legal estate. Therefore, a mortgagee though out of possession was held liable as assignee, notwithstanding, and Lord *Kenyon* declared that he would overrule the case of *Eaton* and *Jacques* (*Dougl.* 455.) without the least reluctance (*c*).

But an assignee is only liable while in possession if he assign over before a breach, therefore though his assignee has not taken possession, yet he, (the first assignee) is not liable to any action of covenant (*d*).

Thus, where the defendant was the assignee of the original lessee, and covenant being brought against him for rent reserved on the lease, he pleaded, That before the rent became due he had assigned all his interest in the premises to one *Rigg*, who by virtue of such assignment, entered and was possessed; the plaintiff replied, that at the time when the rent became due, the defendant remained and continued in possession *absq. hoc* That *Rigg* had entered, *&c.* and on demurrer it was held, that the assignment being admitted, the actual possession was not sufficient to charge the first assignee, the possession in law being in the second assignee by virtue of the assignment (*e*).

So also, the assignee of a term declared against as such, is not liable for rent accruing after he has assigned over, though it be stated that the lessor was a party executing the assignment, and who agreed thereby, that the term, which was determinable at his option, should be absolute (*f*).

But an action of covenant cannot be maintained against an under-

(*a*) Cro. Eliz. 583.

(*b*) Bac. Abr. tit. "Covenant" (E 3.)

(*c*) Stone v. Evans, *ante* 113.

(*d*) 1 B. & P. 21.

(*e*) Doug. 461 n. 1.

(*f*) Ibid. 764.

lessee; for it is clearly settled, and is agreeable to the text of *Lyttleton*, that the action cannot be maintained, unless against an assignee of the whole term (*a*).

But the lessee being a party to the original contract, continues always liable, notwithstanding any assignment (*b*); for it is extremely clear, that a person who enters into an express covenant in a lease continues liable on his covenant notwithstanding the lease be assigned over (*c*).

For the lessee has from his covenant both a privity of contract and of estate, and though he assigns, and thereby destroys the privity of estate, yet the privity of contract continues, and he is liable in covenant notwithstanding the assignment (*d*). But the assignee comes in only in privity of estate, and is therefore liable only while in possession; that is, whilst he has the legal estate, except in the case of rent, for which though he assign over he is liable as to the arrears incurred before (it is said), as well as during his enjoyment; and such assignee was made liable in equity, though the privity of estate was destroyed at common law (*e*).

Covenant lies against the assignee of a lessee of an estate for a part of the rent, as in such case the action is brought on a real contract in respect of the land, and not on a personal contract; and in case of eviction, the rent may be apportioned, as in debt or replevin.—But it is otherwise in covenant against the lessee himself, who is liable on his personal contract (*f*).

The Declaration.—With respect to the pleadings on the part of the plaintiff, the declaration in an action of covenant should set out expressly that the covenant was made by deed. *Per scriptum factum suum W. concessit*, does not import a deed; neither does an allegation that the party covenanted *per quoddam scriptum*; and if the instrument is set out upon error brought, and concludes with "in witness whereof, I have hereunto set my hand and seal," it will not make good this defect (*g*).

This action being founded on a deed, the plaintiff need not set forth more than that part which is necessary to entitle him to recover; if he states what is impertinent, it is an injury to the other party, and may be struck out and costs allowed, upon motion. When it is said that the plaintiff need only set forth that part of the deed on which his action is founded, it is not meant that even that is necessary; for he is not bound to set forth the material part in letters and words; it will be sufficient to state the substance and legal effect, that is shorter, and not liable to misrecitals and literal mistakes. But what is alleged should be proved (*h*).

The proper mode, therefore, of declaring in covenant, is to set out

(*a*) Doug. 187. 459. Stone v. Evans, *supra*. (*b*) Doug. 460. (*c*) 4 T. R. 98.
(*d*) Doug. 460. (*e*) Bac. Abr. tit. "Covenant" (E. 4.) (*f*) 2 Ventr.'s R. 57.
(*g*) 2 Str. 814. (*h*) 1 Str. 230. Doug. 667.

that, by indenture, certain premises therein mentioned were demised, without stating them particularly, subject among other things to a proviso, setting out the substance of the covenant, and the breach (*a*)

In an action for mismanagement of a farm, it is enough to state that part of the instrument truly which applies to the breach complained of, if that which is omitted do not qualify that which is stated (*b*)

In declaring against an assignee, the plaintiff may declare against him generally as assignee, without setting out the intermediate assignments; for he may not know them perhaps and such is the case, though the plaintiff himself is an assignee (*c*).

So, where the action is against the original lessee, the breach need not extend to assigns, for the Court will not presume an assignment (*d*)

The distinction proceeds from the difference that subsists between the case where a thing is to be done *by* a person or his assigns, and that in which it is to be done *to* a person or his assigns. In the first place, the breach must be assigned in the disjunctive, that it was not done "either by the one or the other," but in the last case, it will be intended *primâ facie* to be done *to* the person himself, but if he assign his interest, then it may be done to the assignee, and if he did assign over his interest, it ought to be shewn on the other side.

Where the action therefore is brought *by* the assignee of a term, the plaintiff must set forth in his declaration all the mesne assignments of the term down to himself, for he is privy to them, and therefore shall not be allowed to plead generally that the lessee's estate of and in the demised premises came to him, or to some other person under whom he claims, by assignment (*e*)

But where an action is brought *against* an assignee of a term, such general form of pleading is sufficient, for the plaintiff is a stranger to the defendant's title, and therefore cannot set it out particularly. It is not sufficient, however, to say that the tenements came to the defendant by assignment, but it must be shewn that he is assignee of the term; for otherwise it might be an assignment of another estate than the term of the lessee. The usual form is "all the estate, right, title, and interest of the said *A* (the lessee) of, in, and to the said demised premises, afterwards, to wit, on, &c. in the year of our Lord, &c. at, "&c. aforesaid, by assignment came to the said defendant" (*f*).

So, in an action of covenant by an assignee, the declaration need not shew the deed of assignment; provided the subject in dispute may be assigned without deed, although the covenant on which the action is brought ought to be by deed (*g*).

(*a*) Cowp 665 (*b*) 13 East 1[illegible] (*c*) 8 Mod 72

(*d*) 5 Mod 133 11 Mod [illegible] 1 Salk 139 1 Str 228 s. c. Bull N P 164. 5 Mod [illegible] 12 Mod 86 s c Salk 139 s c. (*e*) [illegible] R. 112, [illegible] (*f*) [illegible]

(*g*) Cro. Eliz. 373. 4[illegible]6.

But all declarations against assignees state entry and possession; and this has been the case both before and since Lord *Coke's dictum* in *Cooke and Harris*, which was extrajudicial (*a*).

On an assignment of land by husband and wife, where they are seised to them and the heirs of the husband, it is sufficient to declare as assignee of the husband (*b*).

The assignee of a lease which appears to be good only by estoppel, cannot maintain an action on the covenants (*c*).

Tenants in common ought to join in the action of covenant for rent (*d*).

Where there is a joint-covenant by several, all should join in the action, or on craving oyer and demurring generally, it will be bad (*e*).

But if any named in the indenture have not sealed it, they should be excluded by an averment to that effect. But advantage must be taken by pleading in abatement, if the action be brought *against* part only of the covenantors (*f*).

Where the plaintiff cannot sue on a breach of covenant, without some previous circumstances being by him performed, the declaration should aver the performance of them (*g*).

Covenant for the non-payment of rent must be brought where the lands lie, though the rent be made payable in another place: as where the lands lay in *Ireland*, and the rent was reserved to be paid in *London*, it was adjudged, that the action should be brought in *Ireland* (*h*).

The distinction respecting the venue in this action, is this in covenant by the grantee of the reversion against the assignee of the lessee the action is local, and the venue must be laid in the county where the estate lies — But in covenant by the lessor or grantee of the reversion against the lessee, the action is transitory, and the venue may be laid in any county at the option of the plaintiff (*i*)

In covenant upon a lease a view being proper to be had, the venue was changed to the county where the premises lay, though most of the plaintiff's witnesses resided in the county where the venue was laid (*k*).

Where the covenant was "to pay or cause to be paid," the breach was sufficiently assigned by stating that the defendant had not paid, without saying "or caused to be paid," for had the defendant caused to be paid, he had paid, for *qui facit per alium facit per se* (*l*) · and in such case it might be pleaded in discharge (*m*).

Breach that 3*l*. for a year at *Lady-day* last was arrear and unpaid, is well on a general demurrer wherein it was objected that it did not appear where the money became due (*n*).

(*a*) [illegible] 453 (*b*) Cro. C. [illegible] 285 (*c*) [illegible] 373 457 (*d*) Bull. N P 158
(*e*) [illegible] N P 354 [illegible] 1146 (*f*) Ibid (*g*) Esp N P 301 Hob 217
(*h*) [illegible] R 575 [illegible] (*i*) Ibid (*k*) 8 East 268 (*l*) 1 Str 228
(*m*) [illegible] (*n*) [illegible] 139

The Pleas.—Touching the pleas to this action, in covenant there is, properly speaking, no general issue. for though the defendant may plead *non est factum*, as in debt in specialty, yet that only puts the deed in issue and not the breach of covenant. and *non infregit conventionem*, to a negative covenant, has been holden to be a bad plea In this action therefore, the defendant must specially controvert the deed, or shew that he has *performed* the covenant or is legally *excused* from the performance of it, or, admitting the breach, that he is *discharged* by matter *ex post facto* as a release, &c. (*a*).

The pleas therefore to this action for breach of covenant for payment of rent, are 1. Performance. 2. Other covenants in bar. 3. *Non est factum*. 4. Entry and eviction. 5. A release. 6 Accord and satisfaction. 7 Tender and refusal. 8. *Riens in arrere*, or payment at the day 9 Infancy.

A defendant cannot plead performance generally to negative and affirmative covenants (*b*).

Another covenant may be pleaded in bar, when they are both in the same deed. for the meaning of the parties is to be collected from the whole of the deed. Thus, in covenant for rent, the defendant was permitted to plead another covenant in the same indenture, that he, as lessee, might retain as much of the rent for repairs and charges (*c*)

But generally, reciprocal covenants cannot be pleaded one in bar of another, especially if they do not go to the whole consideration (*d*), for the damages might be unequal and in assigning a breach of covenant it is not necessary to aver performance on the plaintiff's side unless there be a condition precedent (*e*).

Therefore, if *A* covenant with *B*. to pay so much money for tithes, and to be accountable for all arrears of rent, and *B* covenant to allow him certain disbursements upon the account, *A* cannot plead in an action of covenant, that he was ready to account if *B* would allow him the disbursements; for the covenants being mutual, each of them has a remedy against the other for non-performance (*f*).

So, unliquidated damages, arising from the breach of other covenants to be performed by the plaintiff, cannot be pleaded by way of set-off (*g*).

A set-off is allowable, however, by the statutes of set-off, in an action of covenant for non-payment of money, as for rent, but the demand intended to be set-off, must be such as might have been the subject of an action either of debt, covenant, or *assumpsit* (*h*)

In covenant upon an indenture for non-payment of rent, the defendant pleaded *non est factum*, and gave a notice of set off, Mr. *J*

(*a*) Tidd's Pract. 593 (*b*) Cro. Eliz. 691 (*c*) 1 Lev. 152
(*d*) 2 Mod. 309. 1 H. Bl. 279 (*e*) 6 T. R. 571 (*f*) 2 Mod. [illegible]
(*g*) Cowp. 56. 6 T. R. 488 (*h*) Tidd's Pract. 62[illegible]

Denton at the assizes was of opinion, that he could not do so upon this issue, but upon a motion for a new trial the Court held, that the evidence ought to have been received, for the general issue mentioned in the Act must be understood to be any general issue, and accordingly ordered a new trial (*a*)

On the plea of *non est factum*, the issue is that there is no such deed as that stated in the declaration The lessor's title therefore, cannot on such plea be controverted (*b*)

The defendant may, under this plea, shew that some of the covenants in the deed have been altered or erased, or he may plead it, for if any covenant be altered or erased, the whole deed is discharged for the deed is a complication of all the covenants, so that by changing any, it remains no longer the same deed (*c*)

A deed may be pleaded as lost by time and accident, without *profert* thereof being made But if *profert* of the deed be made, the Court cannot dispense with oyer (*d*) So if it appear by the record that the defendant had oyer of a copy only, it is error but the Court will in certain cases dispense with oyer, as where an original lease is lost, and an application is made that a copy of the counterpart may be good oyer; and if it be once ordered that a copy be deemed a compliance with the rule demanding oyer, no error can appear on the record, because it does not there appear whether the oyer was given from an original deed or a copy. Much less is it necessary to make a *profert* of a deed which is pleaded only by way of inducement to the action (*e*)

As to the plea of *nil habuit in tenementis*, the general rule is, that a tenant cannot be permitted to controvert the title of his landlord (*f*): and it is founded on good sense, for so long as the lessee continues to enjoy the land demised, it would be unjust that he should be permitted to deny the title under which he holds possession But when he is evicted, he has a right to shew that he does not enjoy that which was the consideration for his covenant to pay the rent, notwithstanding he has bound himself by the covenant (*g*). If, therefore, the defendant hath been evicted, to be sure he cannot be compelled to pay rent, and he may plead that fact in answer to the plaintiff's demand. However, that generally speaking, an indenture operates by way of estoppel against the tenant, and precludes him from controverting the title of his landlord, is proved by *Lit. s* 58 *Co Lit.* 47. *b.* and by a variety of other cases (*h*).

Entry and eviction therefore is a good plea to an action of covenant, for rent is suspended by entry into any part. The eviction must be tortious, and such as ousts the defendant of his possession, for a mere

(*a*) Bull N P 182 (*b*) 2 Bl Rep 1153 Lep N P 306 (*c*) Phil Co 28
(*d*) 3 T R 151. (*e*) 8 T R 573 (*f*) 7 T. R 539 (*g*) 3 T R. 442
(*h*) 7 T. R 538

trespass will not suffice.—Entry and eviction must in covenant be pleaded, for it cannot, as in debt for rent, be given in evidence and to a plea of eviction the plaintiff may reply an entry by virtue of a power, and traverse the eviction (*a*).

Therefore, where in covenant for non payment of rent the plaintiff declared that he was seised of tithes, and by indenture demised them to the defendant rendering rent, and that the defendant covenanted to pay it, and assigned the breach in non-payment of so much, the defendant pleaded eviction, the plaintiff demurred, and judgment was given for the defendant; because it is a rent, and the eviction is a suspension of it, and therefore a good plea (*b*)

A release of all covenants is a good discharge of the covenant before it is broken; but a release of all actions, suits, and quarrels, would not be so; for at the time of the release no debt, duty, or cause of action existed (*c*).

Wherever a discharge is pleaded in the nature of a release, the defendant must plead it to be by deed, or it will be bad, for as the covenant is by deed, by deed only shall it be discharged (*d*).

It has been said, that where a covenant runs with the land, and the lease has been assigned, if the covenantee had released before a breach or action brought, it had barred the assignee even for a breach in his own time (*e*) [But this cannot, it is conceived, apply to a covenant for payment of rent for as an assignee shall be bound by covenants that run with the land, so he shall take advantage of them, and were it otherwise, in the case of rent the covenantee might in fact defraud his assignee by defeating the estate that he assigned to him] (*f*).

Accord and satisfaction is a good plea where there has been an actual breach, for not till then are damages claimable and this plea goes in discharge of damages, not of the covenant itself, for that remains (*g*).

Therefore, where the plaintiff declared that in consideration that he would permit *S P* to enjoy a farm at *C* for one year, the defendant covenanted to pay the rent of 72*l*. *per ann.* and also 200*l* then in arrear, and the breach assigned was the non payment of the rent, the defendant pleaded that "before any cause of action did arise on the covenant, that it had been agreed between him and the plaintiff, that the plaintiff should take 30*l* in discharge of all covenants, which the plaintiff had accepted," on demurrer this plea was held to be a bad one, for at the time there was no covenant broken or damages sustained (*h*).

Tender and refusal is also a plea to this action. The damages, not the debt, being for the most part the thing in demand by this action,

(*a*) 1 Saund R 204 n 2 (*b*) 2 ibid 304 n. 7 1 Ld Raym 77. (*c*) Esp N.P 207
(*d*) Ibid (*e*) Ibid 308 Cro Car 503. (*f*) Bull. N. P. 159
(*g*) Esp N. P 308 (*h*) Ibid

tender and refusal need not in general be pleaded with an *uncore prist* (a)

But where it is brought for rent, it being a debt ascertainable and certain, it is best to plead this plea with an *uncore prist.*

Riens en arrere, or payment at the day, is a good plea to covenant for non-payment of rent But "levied by distress," cannot be pleaded; for that is a confession that it was not paid at the day, to which time the breach refers (b).

Infancy is another plea in this action, which may or may not be good, according to circumstances.

If the defendant has leave to plead double under the stat 4 & 5 *Ann* c 16 he shall not be allowed to plead inconsistent pleas, as *non est factum*, and a condition precedent (c)

Bankruptcy is no plea to a covenant to pay rent (d), for besides that the rent was not a debt due at the time of the bankruptcy, and so could not be proved under it, it is a settled principle, that the tenant's liability on his covenant to pay rent, subsists during the continuance of the lease, notwithstanding he may become a bankrupt and be deprived of all his property but of the assignee of the tenant, otherwise (e).

In an action of covenant for rent, or for 5*l.* an acre for ploughing meadow, the count being for a liquidated sum, money may be paid into Court (f).

Where an action of covenant was brought upon a lease for non-payment of rent, and not repairing, &c. the court made a rule, that upon payment of what should appear to be due for rent, the proceedings as to that should be stayed, and as to the other breaches, that the plaintiff might proceed as he should think fit (g).

So the Court have referred it to the master to compute what is due in covenant for non-payment of rent (h).

Respecting the verdict and judgment in this action, in covenant for non-payment of rent at divers days which amounts to so much, if in the declaration the sum is miscast, it is not error, but the plaintiff shall have a verdict for so much as is really in arrear (i)

Judgment cannot be given on two covenants where one is bad; therefore where a general verdict was given, and entire damages were assessed, judgment was arrested (k).

So if covenant be brought against two, and there be judgment by default against one, and the other pleads performance, which is found for him, the plaintiff shall not have judgment against the other, for on the whole the plaintiff has no cause of action (l).

(a) Bull N P 308 (b) Ibid 330 (c) Ibid Gilb R 123
(d) 4 Burr 2444. 1 H Bl. 433 (e) 7 T R 616 8 T R. 61 (f) Ibid N P. 310
(g) 1 Barnes Pract 565 (h) 1 Wils 75 8 T R 410. (i) 5 Mod 213.
(k) Cro Eliz 685 (l) 1 Lev 63

In covenant for rent upon a lease by *A* to *B.* the point in issue was whether *C* (whose title both admitted) demised first to *A* or to another person *C.* is a competent witness to prove the point in issue, for the verdict cannot be given in evidence in any action which may afterwards be brought either by or against him (*a*)

A bill in equity may be brought for rent, where the remedy at law is lost or become very difficult, and such the Court will relieve on the foundation of length of time (*b*)

SECTION IV. *Action of Debt, for Use and Occupation.*

An action of debt will also lie, or of assumpsit for use and occupation, where rent is in arrear by a tenant who holds under a lease not by deed as under a writing without deed or a parol demise.

Of Debt —First with respect to the action of debt.

This action, we have before observed, is founded upon a contract, either express or implied, in which the certainty of the sum or duty appears, and the plaintiff is to recover the sum *in numero* and not in damages (*c*).

Where there was a tenant at will, with a rent reserved, the lessor might always have an action of debt for arrears of rent (*d*).

But in declaring on a lease at will for rent arrear, the plaintiff must shew an occupation; for the rent being only due in respect thereof, it should appear to the Court when the lessee entered and how he occupied (*e*)

Against tenants at sufferance, it seems that an action of debt lay not for rent arrear, for the contract was determined, and they are in by wrong but in such cases there is now a special provision.

Where a tenant holds over, for double value. —For by stat 4 *G* 2. *c.* 28. *s.* 1. it is enacted, That if any tenant or tenants for life, or lives, or years, or persons coming in under or by collusion with them, hold over any lands, tenements, &c. after the determination of their estates, after demand made and notice in writing given for delivering the possession thereof by the landlord, or the person having the reversion or remainder therein, or his agent thereunto lawfully authorized, such tenant or tenants so holding over, shall pay to the person so kept out of possession at the rate of double the yearly value of the lands, tenements, &c. so detained, for so long a time as the same are detained; to be recovered by action of debt, whereunto the defendant or defendants shall be obliged to give special bail.

(*a*) 3 T. R 308. (*b*) 1 Atk 598 (*c*) Bull N P. 167. (*d*) Esp. N P. 188
(*e*) 1 Salk. 209 Doug 457.

Debt for double value on the above statute does not lie against a weekly tenant (*a*).

For double rent. Also, by stat. 11 G. 2. c. 19. s. 18. it is enacted, That in case any tenant or tenants shall give notice of his, her, or their intention to quit the premises, and shall not accordingly deliver up the possession thereof, at the time in such notice contained, the said tenant or tenants, his, her, or their executors or administrators, shall from thenceforth pay to the landlord double the rent or sum which he, she, or they should otherwise have paid.

Upon these statutes it has been held, that

With respect to the 4 G. 2 it is a remedial law, the penalty being given to the party aggrieved (*b*)

The action under this statute stands in place of an ejectment (*c*), but is more beneficial and effectual (*d*)

The notice to quit may be before the expiration of the lease or time of demise or after (*e*)

The notice in writing is of itself a sufficient demand, within the words of the statute "after demand made and notice in writing given (*f*)"

In debt for double value under the stat. 4 G 2 the plaintiff after stating a demise to the defendant's wife and her subsequent intermarriage with the defendant, alleged in the first count a notice to quit and demand of possession delivered to the defendant and his wife, and in the second count alleged a notice to quit and demand of possession delivered to the wife, previous to her intermarriage with the defendant; held that to support the second count the husband need not be joined in conformity, and that to sustain the action, it was not necessary to aver to have given notice to the husband subsequent to the intermarriage (*g*).

A receiver appointed under an order of the Court of Chancery is "an agent lawfully authorized" within the words of the statute (*h*).

One tenant in common may maintain this action for double value of his moiety, for where the injury is separate, tenants in common may have several actions (*i*)

The administrator of an executor cannot sue for double the value of lands held over after notice to quit under a demise from the testator, according to 4 G 2. c 28. without taking out administration *de bonis non*, even though the tenant has attorned to her: for most certainly, in any case in which the plaintiff means to make title, she must take out administration *de bonis non* (*k*).

With respect to the stat. 11 G 2. a parol demise from year to year is a sufficient holding within the statute so as to subject the tenant to the

(*a*) 2 Camp. 453 (*b*) 5 Burr. 2698. (*c*) 3 East, 358 (*d*) 2 Bl. R. 1075.
(*e*) 2 Bl. R. 1076. (*f*) 5 Burr. 2694. (*g*) 1 Bos. & Pull. N. R. 172
(*h*) Ibid (*i*) 2 Bl. R. 1077. (*k*) 1 Bos. & Pul. 312.

penalty of double rent, if he hold over after he has given notice to quit (*a*)

The notice by the tenant to quit, need not be in writing. a parol notice to quit is sufficient (*b*).

The acceptance of (single) rent accrued since the notice, is, it seems, a waiver of the landlord's right to double rent, but does not necessarily imply that the tenancy should continue (*c*).

By stat 11 *G.* 2. *c.* 19 *s* 12. it is enacted, That every tenant to whom any declaration in ejectment shall be delivered for any lands, &c. shall forthwith give notice to his or her landlord, or his bailiff or receiver, under the penalty of forfeiting the value of three years improved or rack-rent of the premises to the person of whom he or she holds, to be recovered by action of debt.

Debt will lie for use and occupation generally, without setting forth the particulars of the demise, or where the premises lie (*d*).

Therefore, in a case, where to a count for use and occupation generally, the defendant demurred and assigned for causes that it did not set forth any demise of the premises, nor for what term they were demised nor what rent was payable, nor for what length of time the defendant held and occupied the premises, nor when the sum of 5*l.* thereby supposed to be due became due, nor for what space of time; after argument, the Court of Common Pleas gave judgment for the plaintiff on that count (*e*).

But if the particulars of a demise be alleged, they must be proved.

Therefore in an action for double rent on the stat. 11 *G* 2. *c.* 19. *s.* 18. where the declaration stated a lease for three years, but on the evidence it appeared, that the lease for three years was void under the statute of Frauds, and that the defendant was only tenant from year to year· though this was sufficient for the action, yet a lease for three years having been laid, and not proved, the plaintiff was nonsuited (*f*).

After a landlord has recovered in ejectment against his tenant, he may maintain debt upon the stat 4 *G.* 2. for double yearly value of the premises during the term the tenant held over after the expiration of the landlord's notice to quit (*g*).

A landlord declared in debt, first, for the double value, secondly, for use and occupation, the tenant pleaded *nil debet* to the first, and a tender of the single rent before action brought to the second count, and paid the money into Court, which the plaintiff took out before trial, and still proceeded held that this was no cause of nonsuit as upon the ground of such acceptance of the single rent being a waiver of the plaintiff's right to proceed for the double value, but that the case ought to have gone to the jury, and that the plaintiff's going on with the ac-

(*a*) 3 Burr 1603 1 Bl R 533. [illegible] (*b*) Ibid (*c*) Cowp 246
(*d*) 6 T R 62 6 Esp [illegible] (*e*) Ibid (*f*) Doug 668 (*g*) 9 East, 310

tion after taking the single rent out of Court, was evidence to shew that he did not mean to waive his claim for the whole value, but to take it *pro tanto* it seems that though the single rent were paid into Court on the second count, yet that if the plaintiff had not accepted it, but had recovered on the first count, the defendant would not have been entitled to have the money so paid in, deducted out of the larger sum recovered (*a*)

Debt against an executor shall be in the *detinet* only, for he is chargeable no farther than he has assets (*b*).

An administrator may be declared against as assignee in debt for rent, for the time that he enjoyed the land and was in possession, and must be in the *debet* and *detinet* (*c*).

An executor must bring debt in the *detinet* only, though this would be aided after verdict by the statute of Jeofails (*d*)

The Plea.—In debt for rent on a demise in writing without deed or by parol, the proper plea is *non demisit* (*e*).

Entry and eviction is a good plea to this action, so as it be such a tortious entry and expulsion as to prevent an enjoyment of the premises. For if there was no beneficial occupation, there can be no ground for the action.

The statute of Limitations, 21 *J.* 1 *c.* 16 which enacts, That all actions for rent arrear, or grounded on any lending or contract without specialty, must be brought within six years, is another good plea, and such plea must conclude with a verification, as when pleaded to an action of *assumpsit* (*f*)

As to the plea of infancy, see *ante* C IV.

So a plea of set-off is allowed, and also a tender and refusal. So a release.

Where to debt for rent on a demise of three rooms, the plea was, that the plaintiff demised the said three rooms and another room, and that he entered into the other room, but did not traverse the demise of the three rooms only, it was held to be bad for want of such a traverse (*g*).

It is now settled that in an action of debt on a simple contract, as this is, the plaintiff may prove and recover a less sum than he demanded by his writ (*h*).

Section V. *Of Assumpsit for Use and Occupation.*

Another remedy for the recovery of rent, where the demise is not by deed, lies by action of *assumpsit* for use and occupation

(*a*) 10 East, 48 (*b*) Bull N P 169 (*c*) Esp N P 217 Bull N P 169. (*d*) Ibid (*e*) Bull N P 170 Hind 332. (*f*) 1 Saund. 283 n. 2. (*g*) 1 Saund 206 (*h*) 1 H Bl. R 249.

In an action for use and occupation, the property tax will not be deducted at *nisi prius* from the rent due (*a*).

At common law it was holden, that *assumpsit* would lie for rent on an express promise, but not on an implied promise, and that such express promise must have been made at the same time with the lease (*b*). But now,

The stat 11 *G.* 2 *c* 19 *s* 14 in order to obviate some difficulties that many times occur in the recovery of rent, where the demises are not by deed, enacts, That it shall be lawful for the landlord, where the agreement is not by deed, to recover a reasonable satisfaction for the lands, tenements, or hereditaments, held or occupied by the defendant, in an action on the case, for the use and occupation of what was so held or enjoyed, and if in evidence on the trial of such action any parol demise or any agreement (not being by deed,) whereon a certain rent was reserved, shall appear, the plaintiff in such action shall not therefore be nonsuited, but may make use thereof as an evidence of the *quantum* of the damages to be recovered.

The action for use and occupation is founded on a contract, and unless there were a contract express or implied, the action cannot be maintained (*c*).

If there be an agreement by deed to demise, but the words do not amount to an actual demise, an action for use and occupation is maintainable (*d*).

But a written agreement, though coming out of the possession of the opposite party, cannot be given in evidence in any action unless it be legally stamped.

Therefore where counsel were about to ask a party as to his occupation and payment of rent to the defendant in an ejectment, he was stopped by Lord *Kenyon*, who observed, that the occupation had been under an agreement in writing, and the rent had been paid in pursuance of it; if, said his Lordship, the agreement cannot be given in evidence, you cannot enquire as to the occupation, the party might have been in possession by licence and permission of the defendant, and not as tenant (*e*).

A agreed in writing to pay the rent of certain tolls, which he had hired, "to the treasurer of the commissioners." held that no action for the rent could be maintained in the name of the treasurer, for the contract is to pay the commissioners through the medium of their officer (*f*).

Where there is a note in writing expressing the *quantum* of rent or the duration of the term, evidence of a parol agreement to annul or sub-

(*a*) 2 Camp. 181 (*b*) 2 Lev 152 Bull N P 138. (*c*) 1 T R 387.
(*d*) 4 Esp. R 59 (*e*) 2 Esp R 724 (*f*) 3 Bos & Pul. R. 147.

stantially to vary the written contract, is inadmissible; else the statute of Frauds would be eluded, and the same uncertainty introduced by suppletory or explanatory evidence, which that statute has suppressed in respect to the principal object (*a*).

Thus, where there was a written agreement that a lease should be let of a house at 26*l* *per ann.* on which an action was brought for use and occupation, the defendant paid 26*l* into Court. At the trial, the plaintiff offered to give parol evidence, that beside the 26*l* *per ann* the defendant was to pay the ground landlord 2*l.* 12*s.* 6*d.* but this evidence was rejected; particularly as no evidence was offered of the actual payment of such rent (*b*).

Parol evidence, indeed, of a verbal agreement cannot be received where it appears that it was reduced to writing: and this even where the written agreement, for want of being stamped, or for other informality or defect, was inadmissible (*c*) for parol evidence cannot be admitted to vary the substance of a written agreement (*d*). With respect to collateral matters, however, it is otherwise; for a person may shew by parol proof who is to put a house in repair, or the like, concerning which nothing is said in the written agreement. So, it may be admitted to explain a deed or other instrument; or to prove other considerations than those expressed in a deed (*e*).

This action being founded on a contract either expressed or implied, it is a general rule, that wherever the defendant uses or enjoys the premises by permission of the plaintiff [as his tenant,] he shall be liable in this action (*f*).

So, this action may be maintained by a grantee of an annuity, after a recovery in ejectment against a tenant who was in possession under a demise from year to year, for all rent in his hands at the time of the notice by the grantee, and down to the day of the demise: but not afterwards (*g*).

So after a recovery of possession of the premises, the plaintiff is entitled to the profits for use and occupation, to the time of the demise, but not after, if he thinks fit to sue for them (*h*).

But an action for use and occupation and an ejectment, when applied *at the same time*, are totally inconsistent for in one, the plaintiff says that the defendant is his tenant, and therefore he must pay him rent; in the other he says, that he is no longer his tenant, and therefore must deliver up the possession. He cannot do both (*i*).

This action therefore being founded on a contract express or implied, will not lie where the possession of the tenant is adverse and tortious;

(*a*) 2 Bl R 1250 3 W. l. 276 (*b*) 2 Bl R 1249
(*c*) 3 T R. 528 6 T. R 464 (*d*) 2 Bl. R 1250
(*e*) 2 Str 794 *in not.* 8 T R 379 (*f*) 8 T. R 327. (*g*) 1 T. R 378.
(*h*) Cowp 246 1 T R 387 (*i*) Ibid

unless indeed the plaintiff ceases to consider it as such, by waiving the tort, and recurring to his remedy by this action on the contract (*a*)

The defendant in this action, as in all actions for rent, is not admitted to call in question the plaintiff's title to the premises; or in any way to impeach it.

Therefore, in an action for use and occupation by an incumbent against a tenant of the glebe lands, the defendant cannot give evidence of a simoniacal presentation of the plaintiff, in order to avoid his title (*b*).

So, in an action for use and occupation, the plaintiff having given evidence of payment of rent by the defendant for nineteen years, the defendant would have gone into evidence to prove a title in another. *Per Wilmot J* Payment of rent and holding under a person for so long a time, is conclusive evidence against the defendant, and he cannot set up a title in another: and as to the objection that has been made, that the defendant may be liable to two actions for the rent, by persons having different titles, that cannot be the case, for though another has title, yet he cannot bring an action for the rent till he has made an entry, and recovered in ejectment, [which entry need not now be actually made in such case, but is supposed, 3 *Bur.* 1895. *Run. Eject* 199] and then it must be trespass for the mesne profits (*c*).

But it was agreed, that though a defendant cannot controvert the title of the plaintiff, yet he may give evidence to explain the holding under him, as that he was executor during the minority of *A. B.* and that his interest was then determined; for that admits the plaintiff's title, during the time the defendant held under him (*d*).

An action for use and occupation is maintainable without attainment upon the stat. 4 & 5 *Ann* c. 16. s 9, & 10. by the trustees of one, whose title the tenant had notice of before he paid over his rent to his original landlord; though the tenant had no notice of the legal estate being in the plaintiffs on the record (*e*).

In an action for use and occupation, where the defendant has come in under the plaintiff, he cannot shew that the plaintiff's title has expired, unless he solemnly renounced the plaintiff's title at the time, and commenced a fresh holding under another person (*f*).

In an action for use and occupation, where the defendant did not come in under the plaintiff, the plaintiff can only recover rent from the time he has had the legal estate in him, although he may have had the equitable estate long before (*g*).

The rule that a tenant cannot compel his landlord to interplead, does not prevail, where the claim of a third person arises by the act of the

(*a*) Cowp 246 1 T R. 387 (*b*) 5 T R 5 (*c*) Esp N P. 21.
(*d*) Ibid s c (*e*) 16 East, 99. (*f*) 2 Campb. 11.
(*g*) 2 Campb. 13. note.

landlord subsequent to the commencement of the relation of landlord and tenant (*a*)

By the abovementioned statute (11 *G.* 2 *c.* 19. *s.* 15.) it is enacted, That where any tenant for life shall happen to die before or on the day on which any rent was reserved or made payable upon any demise or lease of any lands, &c. which determined on the death of such tenant for life, that the executors or administrators of such tenant for life shall and may, in an action on the case, recover of and from such under-tenant, if such tenant for life die on the day on which the same was payable, the whole, or if before such day then a proportion of such rent, according to the time such tenant for life lived, of the last year, or quarter of a year, or other time in which the said rent was growing due.

[Respecting the above statute, see *ante* C. VIII. S. I. tit. *Rent, apportionment of.*]

An executor brought an action for rent due to his testator in his lifetime, and for other rent due in his own time, and there was another count on a *quantum meruit* for the rent of another messuage, in which he had not declared as executor. After judgment by default, and a writ of enquiry executed, upon error brought, judgment was reversed, because the demands were incompatible —but perhaps it would have been helped by a verdict, because for rent due in his own time, he need not declare as executor, and therefore, if it had been tried, the Judge ought not to have permitted him to prove rent due to himself in his own right (*b*).

The rule as to joinder in actions is, that only those causes of action can be joined, that admit of the same plea, and the same judgment (*c*)

An action for use and occupation will not lie, where the premises are let for a purpose illegal, or *contra bonos mores*, as to a prostitute (*d*).

An action for rent will not lie where the title is in dispute. the Court therefore will not try a title by the action for use and occupation; an ejectment is the proper remedy This was decided in a case before the Court of King's Bench, by Lord *Kenyon* C. J. wherein the action was brought against the tenant for rent, while the heir at law and a devisee were contesting their right to the premises (*e*).

The Pleas —In *assumpsit* under the statute for use and occupation of a house by permission of the plaintiff, *nil habuit in tenementis* is a bad plea for the action is founded on the promise, and therefore if the plaintiff had an equitable title or no title at all, yet if the defendant enjoyed by his permission, it is sufficient. for it is no more necessary

(*a*) 12 Ves. 333 (*b*) 2 Str 1271 [illegible]
(*c*) 12 Mod 180 1 Ld Raym 272 Wilks, 120 (*d*) 1 [illegible] R 1[illegible]
(*e*) MSS. Hil [illegible] 37 G III

for the plaintiff to say that it was his house, than in *assumpsit* for goods it is necessary to say that they were his goods (*a*).

But the plea would be good at common law, for there an interest is supposed to have passed from the lessor (*b*).

Yet *qu.?* whether at this day such plea would be admitted, even in an action for rent at common law, for if it would, the supposition of an interest having passed would be a fiction, not in furtherance of the ends of justice, but in destruction of them; and the rule laid down by Lord *Kenyon*, that "in an action for use and occupation it ought not "to be permitted to a tenant, who occupies by the licence of another, "to call upon that other to shew the title under which he let the "land or premises," is not a mere technical rule, but is founded on public convenience and policy, and as it was adopted by the Court, in conformity to the recognition of it in cases prior to the one then before them, as well as on the grounds of reason and equity, it may now be considered as a general rule, applicable to all cases of a similar kind.

The defendant may in this action, upon the plea of *non assumpsit*, which is the general issue, give in evidence any thing which proves nothing due, as the delivery of corn or any other thing in satisfaction; or a release, so he may give in evidence, performance (*c*). In short, the question in *assumpsit* upon the general issue is, whether there was a subsisting debt (*d*), or cause of action, at the time of commencing the suit: therefore though a distinction has been taken that payment or any other legal discharge must be pleaded, yet that distinction is not law, but in both cases, the defendant is allowed to give in evidence any thing that will discharge the debt (*e*).

But matters of law, in avoidance of the contract, or in discharge of the action, are usually pleaded, and it is necessary to plead a tender, set-off, or the statute of Limitations (*f*).

Assumpsit lies against a lessee from year to year upon his agreement to pay rent during his tenancy, notwithstanding his bankruptcy, and the occupation of his assignees during part of the time for which the rent accrued, which were pleaded in bar. *Quære?* whether a special plea in bar, stating no facts but what might have been proved under the general issue, but leaving other facts unanswered, which the general plea would have put in issue, be good (*g*).

(*a*) 1 Wils. 314. Bull. N. P. 139. Esp. N. P. 165. (*b*) Ibid. (*c*) Bull. N. P. 151.
(*d*) 1 Tidd's Pract. 592. (*e*) Bull. N. P. 152. (*f*) 1 Tidd's Pract. 593.
(*g*) 8 East, 311.

CHAPTER XIV.

Of the Remedies for and against Landlord and Tenant; wherein Of the Actions of Ejectment and Trespass for Mesne Profits for Recovery of Rent and Possession.

SECTION I. *When an Ejectment lies, and the Proceedings therein at Common Law.*

OF the various remedies which the law affords for the breach of a contract or the reparation of a wrong, none perhaps so intimately concerns the respective relations of landlord and tenant, as that admirable fiction of the courts of common law, called the action of ejectment.

Besides the remedy given to a landlord, where the lease contains a clause of re-entry on non-payment of rent, by the stat. 4 *G.* 2. *c* 28. *s.* 2. (of which hereafter) the action of ejectment lies at common law to recover possession, on

The expiration of the lease by effluxion of time; or
The determination of the lease by
Non-payment of rent, or
Non-performance of covenants.
Where the possession is vacant, or
Where the tenant is in possession.

In order however, to explain the action as applicable to these particular cases, we must go into a general account of the nature of the remedy by ejectment

History of the Action —By the antient common law, the only method of recovering the possession of land was by real action by writ of entry or assize, and this in no case where the estate was less than freehold · for a mere leasehold interest or term for years was in the early period of our constitution, when feudal principles more strictly prevailed, deemed of such little import, that no remedy was provided, whereby the tenant could regain his possession in case he was ousted by his landlord or by a stranger against the former he could proceed only upon his breach of covenant or agreement, against the latter indeed he might have his writ of ejectment, by which however he could recover damages only, and not the possession (*a*). In those times the ejectment was a mere personal action of trespass, and the proceedings were by *pone*, or by *capias* and distress infinite (*b*).

In process of time,—some say so early as the reign of *Ed* 4 (3 *Bl. Com.* 201.) but certainly about the time of *H.* 7. when long leases began to obtain,—the remedy by ejectment was extended and rendered more efficacious by the object of the action being completely changed, and the term itself recovered This was effected by the Courts of Law resolving to give judgment in ejectment that the lessee in ejectment should recover possession of the land itself by the process of a writ called an *habere facias possessionem* (*c*)

From this period, the practice in ejectment became wholly subject to the controul of the Court, and a new method of trial, unknown to the common law, was introduced (*d*)

Antient Practice.—It now became usual for a man that had a right of entry into any lands, to enter thereon and seal leases, and then the person that next came on the freehold *animo possidendi* was accounted an ejector of the lessee, by which means any man might be turned out of possession, because the lessee in ejectment would recover his term without any notice to tenant in possession, so that the Courts of Law made it a standing rule, that no plaintiff should proceed in ejectment to recover his lands against such a feigned ejector, without delivering to the tenant in possession a declaration, and making him an ejector and proper defendant if he chose it (*e*).—This rule of Court became absolutely necessary upon the alteration of the object of the action of ejectment, which was now *in rem*, for otherwise the Court might have been instrumental in doing an injury to a third person, because a declaration might otherwise be delivered to a stranger, a feigned defence be made, and a verdict, judgment, and execution

(*a*) 2 Sell. Pract. 162. (*b*) Ibid 162. (*c*) Ibid (*d*) Ibid (*e*) Ibid.

thereon obtained, whereby the tenant would have been ousted, without notice of any proceedings against him (*a*).—Upon this notice to the tenant in possession, and affidavit thereof made, it was usual for the tenant in possession to move the Court, that, as the title of the land belonged to him, he might defend the suit in the casual ejector's name, which the Court, upon affidavit of that matter, used to grant, and that the suit should be carried on in the casual ejector's name, the tenant in possession saving him harmless, and then the casual ejector was not permitted to release errors in prejudice of the tenant in possession, as the suit was carried on in his name by rule of Court and the process for costs was taken out against the casual ejector who was obliged to resort to the tenant in possession to recover back the same, and put his bond of indemnification in suit upon his refusal to pay them.

Such leases were to be actually sealed and delivered, otherwise the plaintiff could maintain no title to the term; they were also obliged to be sealed on the land itself, otherwise it amounted to maintenance by the old law to convey a title to any one, when the grantor himself was not in possession (*b*).

Such was the original method of proceeding in ejectment when the term was first begun to be recovered; but one alteration by degrees begat another, and fiction was heaped upon fiction. During the exile of King *Charles* the Second, an entirely new mode of proceeding was invented and introduced by Lord C. J. *Rolle*, which method has been followed ever since by the Courts, and is therefore called the modern practice in contradistinction from the antient one just described (*c*).

Modern Practice.—The new method of proceeding in ejectment depends entirely upon a string of legal fictions; neither actual lease, nor actual entry, is made by the plaintiff nor actual ouster by the defendant, but all are merely ideal, for the sole purpose of trying the title To this end, in the proceedings, a lease for a term of years is stated to have been made by him who claims title, to the plaintiff, who is generally an ideal, fictitious person, who has no existence. In this proceeding, which is the declaration, (for there is no other process in this action,) it is also stated, that the lessee, in consequence of the demise to him made, entered into the premises, and that the defendant, who is also now another ideal, fictitious person, and who is called the casual ejector, afterwards entered thereon and ousted the plaintiff, for which ouster the plaintiff brings the action. Under this declaration is written a notice, supposed to be written by the casual ejector, directed to the tenant in possession of the premises, in which

(*a*) 2 Sell Pr. 163 (*b*) Ibid (*c*) Ibid

notice the casual ejector informs the tenant of the action brought by the lessee, and assures him, that as he, the casual ejector, has no title at all to the premises, he shall make no defence, and therefore he advises the tenant to appear in Court at a certain time and defend his own title, otherwise he, the casual ejector, will suffer judgment to be had against him, by which the actual tenant will inevitably be turned out of possession (a)

The declaration is then served on the tenant in possession, with this friendly caution annexed to it, who has thus an opportunity to defend his title, which if he omits to do in a limited time, he is supposed to have no right at all, and upon judgment being had against the casual ejector, the real tenant will be turned out of possession by the sheriff (b)

But if the tenant applies to be made defendant, it is allowed him upon this condition, That he enter into a rule of Court to confess at the trial of the cause three of the four requisites to maintain the plaintiff's action, *viz.* the lease of the lessor, the entry of the plaintiff, and the ouster by the tenant himself, who is now made defendant instead of the casual ejector, which requisites, as they are wholly fictitious, should the defendant put the plaintiff to prove, he must of course be nonsuited at the trial for want of evidence; but by such stipulated confessions the trial will stand solely upon the merits of the title (c)

Upon this rule being entered into, the declaration is now altered by inserting the name of the tenant instead of the fictitious name of the casual ejector; and the cause goes to trial under the name of the fictitious lessee on the demise of *A. B.* (the lessor or person claiming title,) against *C. D.* (the now defendant,) and therein the lessor is bound to make out his title to the premises, otherwise his nominal lessee cannot obtain judgment to have possession of the land for the term supposed to be granted. But if he makes out his title in a satisfactory manner, the judgment is given for the nominal plaintiff, and a writ of possession goes in his name to the sheriff to deliver possession. But if the now defendant fails to appear at the trial, and to confess lease, entry and ouster, the nominal plaintiff must then indeed be nonsuited for want of proving these requisites, but judgment will nevertheless in the end be entered for him against the casual ejector; for the condition on which the tenant was admitted defendant is broken, and therefore the plaintiff is put again in the same situation as if he had never appeared at all. The same process, therefore, as would have been had, provided no conditional rule had been made, must now be pursued as soon as it is broken; but execution will be stayed, if any

(a) 2 Sell. Pract. 164. (b) Ibid. (c) Ibid.

landlord, after the default of his tenant, applies to be made a defendant, and enters into the usual rule to confess lease, entry, and ouster (*a*)

Thus the practice of sealing leases upon the premises (except in the case of vacant possession), and making an actual entry and ouster (unless to avoid a fine), are now dispensed with, and a more easy and expeditious method is adopted, while the same substantial justice is done to the tenant in possession, by proper notice being given him of the service of the declaration, nor is there any hardship in compelling him to confess lease, entry, and ouster, for they are mere formalities, and have nothing to do with the merits of the case —The great advantage, indeed, which has resulted from this fictitious mode is, that being wholly regulated by the Court, it has, from time to time, been so modelled, as to answer in the best manner every end of justice and convenience (*b*).

An ejectment, therefore, may be defined a mixed action by which a lessee for years, when ousted of his term, may recover possession, and damages, and costs. It is real in respect of the lands, but personal in respect of the damages and costs (*c*).

Who may have this Action

Possession gives the person enjoying it a right against every man who cannot shew a better title, the party therefore who would change the possession, must first establish a legal title to it for the proceedings in ejectment were instituted in order to try who is entitled to the possession of an estate on title (*d*)

In order to establish such legal title, the party must have a right of entry, or he cannot bring the ejectment, for it will not lie in such cases, where the entry of him that hath right is taken away by descent, discontinuance, twenty years' possession, or otherwise, and on those things whereon an entry cannot in fact be made, no entry shall be supposed by the fiction of the parties (*e*).

Therefore, where the assignee of a bankrupt brought an ejectment for part of the bankrupt's estate before the enrollment of the bankrupt's estate made to him by the commissioners, he was nonsuited, for the assignment is by bargain and sale, which, under stat 27 *H* 8 *c* 16. is ordered to be enrolled within six months and it is enacted by the stat 13 *Eliz* *c*. 7. and 28 *J* 1 *c* 19. that all the bankrupt's lands, tenements, &c shall be sold by deed indented and enrolled, so that before enrollment, the assignees have no legal title (*f*).

But in the case of a common bargain and sale it is otherwise, for

(*a*) 2 Sell Pract 165 (*b*) Ibid (*c*) Run Eject 1

(*d*) 7 T R 333. (*e*) Run Eject 15 3 Bl. Com. 206 2 Esp N. P. 430

(*f*) Ibid 431.

there the estate passes by the contract, and is executed by the statute of Uses; whereas the commissioners of bankrupt have a power expressly regulated by statute (*a*).

So, where tenant in tail works a discontinuance, as by a feoffment in fee and dies, the issue in tail cannot maintain this action, for they cannot enter Such also is the case as to other descents which toll entries (*b*

The stat. 32 *H* 8. *c* 28 alters the common law, by giving a right of entry to the wife or her heirs, after the death of the husband, who had aliened lands and tenements of the inheritance of the wife. so that she or her heirs may now support this action

So, by stat 11 *H* 7 *c* 20 it is enacted, That if any woman having an estate in dower, or for life, or in tail, jointly with her husband, or solely to her own use, but coming from him, shall alien, discontinue, &c. or suffer a recovery, such shall be void; and the husband's heir, or he who is entitled to the lands after her death may enter, and so may maintain this action.—Under this statute to enable the husband's heir to enter upon the lands of the gift of the husband and aliened by the wife against the statute, the remainder must have been limited to the heirs of the husband, not to a stranger, for the statute was intended for the benefit of the husband and his heirs (*c*).

Though a good and lawful title may subsist in the plaintiff, yet he may be barred of his right of entry, and therefore of his power to recover in this action, under the stat. 21 *J* 1. *c*. 16. which enacts, That no person shall make an entry into lands, &c but within twenty years after his right and title shall first accrue, with the usual savings for infants, feme coverts, and persons insane, &c

Therefore, if the lessor of the plaintiff is not able to prove himself or his ancestors to have been in possession within twenty years before the action brought, he shall be nonsuited

This possession must be an actual possession, not an implied or presumptive possession merely.

Therefore, in ejectment for mines, the possession of the manor is no evidence to avoid the statute, there being no entry within twenty years upon the mines, which are a distinct possession, and may be a different inheritance (*d*).

So also, a verdict in trover for lead dug out of the mine is no evidence, for trover may be brought on property without possession (*e*).

So, the possession of a manor is not the possession of a cottage built thereon, for if it were, the lord would have a better title to that than to any other part of his estate (*f*).

(*a*) R on Eject. 15 3 E Com 206 2 Esp N P 431 Sir T Jones, 196
(*b*) Lit Sect 595
(*c*) Cro Eliz 2.
(*d*) 2 Str 1142.
(*e*) Bull N. P. 102 s. c.
(*f*) Ibid. 103.

Receipt for rent by a stranger is no evidence of possession, so as to take it out of him in whom the right is, for it is no disseisin without the admission of him who right has, not even though he made a lease to the tenant by indenture reserving rent, unless he make an actual entry. So, though the tenant declare that he is in possession for the stranger, though it may be proper to be left to a jury, especially if the stranger have any colour of title (*a*).

If a declaration in ejectment has been delivered within twenty years, and a trial had, whereby lease, entry, and ouster has been confessed, if the plaintiff has been nonsuited in that action, and brings another ejectment after the twenty years expired, the former confession of lease, entry, and ouster, shall not be sufficient to save the running of the statute against the plaintiff, for there must be an actual entry within twenty years (*b*). But

Possession for twenty years without interruption shall be a good title in itself to enable the party to recover in ejectment, without any other title; for an uninterrupted possession for twenty years is like a descent which tolls an entry, and gives a possessory right that is sufficient to support this action (*c*). So that though the defendant be the person who has lawful right to the premises, yet he cannot justify ejecting the plaintiff who has had twenty years' previous peaceable possession: the possession, however, must be peaceable and uninterrupted, for repeated trespasses from time to time will not gain a possession (*d*).

This action therefore, will not lie by the landlord for encroachments by the tenant on the waste.

In such a case, Lord *Kenyon* revolted at the idea that the tenant could make the landlord a trespasser, which, he said, would unavoidably be the case, if the landlord could recover in this action. His lordship clearly held, that if a tenant inclose part of a waste, and is in possession thereof so long as to acquire a possessory right to it, such inclosure does not belong to the landlord; but, if the tenant has acknowledged that he held such inclosed part of his landlord, this would make a difference (*e*).

The twenty years' possession in order to give a title and so bar an ejectment, must be an adverse possession: for where it appears not to be adverse, the statute of limitations does not run.

Therefore where a man made a mortgage as a collateral security, the interest having been paid for twenty years and more, the mortgagee was held not to be barred of bringing his ejectment, though the mortgagor had continued for that time in possession: for their titles being the same, there was no adverse possession (*f*).

So also in ejectments by joint-tenants, the possession of one joint-

(*a*) Bull. N. P. 104. (*b*) Ibid. 102. (*c*) Esp. N. P. 432. 1 Ld. Raym. 741.
(*d*) 1 Ves. [illegible] (*e*) 1 Esp. R. 460. (*f*) 1 Ld. Raym. 740.

tenant or coparcener is the possession of the other, so as to prevent the statute of limitations from running against the title of either: so one joint-tenant levy a fine, though it sever the jointure, [illegible] amount to an ouster of his companion (*a*).

So, with respect to tenants in common, if one of them bring an ejectment against the other, there must be an actual ouster and adverse possession proved, in order to bar the defendant, for though one tenant in common may disseise another, it must be done by actual disseisin, and not by bare perception of the profits only, for generally speaking, the possession of the one is held to be the possession of the other (*b*).

Also, where two are in possession the law will adjudge it in him that hath the right for the statute never runs against a man but where he is actually ousted or disseised.

Where a right of entry is given in three months after notice of premises being out of repair, acceptance of rent after three months expired, does not prevent plaintiff from maintaining ejectment; particularly if the premises are not repaired at the time of the action being brought (*c*).

What shall be deemed an actual ouster, so as to constitute an adverse possession in one tenant in common against another, is matter for the consideration of the jury.

Thus, thirty-six years' sole and uninterrupted possession by one tenant in common, without any account to, demand made, or claim set up by his companion, was held to be sufficient ground for the jury to presume an actual ouster of the co-tenant, and they did so presume (*d*).

So, if upon demand by the co-tenant of his moiety, the other refuses to pay, and denies his title, saying he claims the whole and will not pay, and continues in possession, such possession is adverse and ouster enough (*e*).

In ejectments by tenants in common, an entry by one shall be good for all, for he shall be supposed to enter according to his estate.—A man cannot be disseised of an undivided moiety, and if a man be seised of the whole, and makes a lease to another of a moiety undivided, and a stranger ousts the lessee, he must bring his ejectment of a moiety, and so if they be both ousted, they must bring several ejectments (*f*).

For, where two persons claim by the same title, there shall not in general be an adverse possession presumed, so as to toll an entry of the one, but the entry of the other being deemed always lawful, shall preserve the unity of the title (*g*).

Thus, where the defendant made title under the sister of the lessor of the plaintiff, and proved that she had enjoyed the estate above twenty

(*a*) Salk. 285. Salk. 285. (*b*) Co. Lit. 199 b. 2. Ld Raym. 829. 2 Salk. 422 s. c. 2 Esp. N. P. 431.
(*c*) 1 Esp. R. 393. (*d*) Cowp. 217. (*e*) Ibid. 218. (*f*) Hob. 120. Esp. N. P. 434.
(*g*) Co. Lit. 242. Esp. N. P. 434.

years, and that he had entered as heir to her, the Court did not regard it, because her possession was construed to be by curtesy, and not to make a disherison, but by licence to preserve the possession of the brother, and therefore was held not to be within the intent of the statute But had the brother ever been in actual possession and ousted by his sister, it would have been otherwise, for then her entry could not possibly be construed to be to preserve his possession (*a*)

So, the possession of one co-heir in gavelkind is not the possession of the other, where he enters with an adverse intent to oust the other (*b*).

Where lights had been put out and enjoyed without interruption for above twenty years during the occupation of the opposite premises by a tenant, that will not conclude the landlord of such opposite premises, without evidence of his knowledge of the fact which is the foundation of presuming a grant against him, and consequently will not conclude a succeeding tenant who was in possession under such landlord from building up against such encroaching lights (*c*).

If there be several lessors and you lay the declaration *quod demiserunt*, you must shew in them such a title that they might demise the whole; and therefore if any of the lessors have not a legal interest in the whole premises, he cannot in law be said to demise them, for it is only his confirmation, where he is not concerned in interest (*d*).

But, where one claims under or through the other, there shall be no adverse possession.

Therefore, though if a cottage be built in defiance of the lord of a manor, and quiet possession of it has been had for twenty years, it seems it is within the statute, and the lord shall not recover, yet if it were built at first by the lord's permission, or any acknowledgment had been since made (though it were a hundred years since), the statute will not run against the lord; for the possession of a tenant at will for ever so many years is no disseisin; there must be a tortious ouster (*e*).

A lessor of a plaintiff may recover in an ejectment a reversionary interest subject to a lease and a right of present possession in another (*f*).

Husband and wife may join in a lease, without saying that it was by deed, though formerly held to be necessary (*g*).

A mortgagee may maintain an ejectment in order to obtain possession of the mortgaged premises or estate —But a distinction is to be observed where the ejectment is against the tenant holding under a lease prior to the mortgage, and where against the mortgagor himself, or against a tenant in possession under a lease or demise made subsequent to the mortgage (*h*)

For where lands are let for years and afterwards mortgaged, the te-

(*a*) Bull N P 102 Co Litt. 242 b (*b*) 1 Bl R 675. (*c*) 11 E[illegible], 372.
(*d*) Bull. N P 10[illegible] (*e*) Ibid. 104 (*f*) 1 T. R [illegible]61. in n.
(*g*) 2 Co 61. Esp N P 449. (*h*) Ibid 435

nant's possession is protected, and he cannot be turned out by the mortgagee. The Courts however now permit the mortgagee to proceed by ejectment against such tenant, if he has given notice to him before the action that he does not mean to disturb his possession, but only requires him to pay the rent to him, and not to the mortgagor (*a*).

But a mortgagee may recover in this action against a tenant who claims under a lease from the mortgagor granted after the mortgage, without the privity of the mortgagee, without giving such notice, for the mortgagor has no power, express or implied, to let leases not subject to every circumstance of the mortgage, and therefore such lessee is a trespasser, disseisor, and wrong-doer, and may be turned out by the mortgagee without notice to quit (*b*).

So, if the mortgagee assign the mortgage, and the assignee assigns to another, this last assignee may maintain this action for the mortgaged premises (*c*).

A second mortgagee who takes an assignment of a term to attend the inheritance, and has all the title deeds, and had no notice of the first mortgage, may recover in ejectment against the first mortgagee (*d*).

The devisee of a term of years may maintain ejectment to recover the term devised, but he must shew the assent of the executor; which will be sufficiently done by proof of the executor having paid a certain sum, where the term was devised to him for life, he paying to a particular party such sum (*e*).

But, in the case of the devise of a freehold, the devisee may immediately, and without any possession, maintain an ejectment for the lands devised, for after the testator's decease, the law casts the freehold on the devisee: and even should the heir enter and die seised, and a descent be cast, yet, it is said, the devisee may enter (unless he be barred by a fine levied by the heir and five years' non-claim) and maintain an ejectment (*f*).

Tenant by *elegit* may maintain this action in order to be put into possession under the *elegit*, of the lands returned by the inquisition before the sheriff (*g*).

The conusee of a statute-merchant also may bring this action.

The assignees of a bankrupt may maintain an ejectment for a term of years or lands which belonged to the bankrupt, for by the assignment, all the bankrupt's property, real and personal, is vested in the assignees, under stat. 13 *Eliz.* 7. s. 2. and therefore they must be invested with all the power necessary to get into possession.

But the assignment only operates on lands in the bankrupt's possession at the time of the assignment made, for as to future real estates, there must be a new bargain and sale (*h*).

(*a*) Doug. 282. Ibid. 23. in n. (*b*) Ibid. 21, 22. (*c*) Salk. 245. (*d*) 1 T. R. 755. (*e*) 1 T. R. 7?. (*f*) Co. Litt. 240. b. (*g*) Doug. 473. Bull. N. P. 104. (*h*) 1 Atk. 252.

A sale by the commissioners of lands of which the bankrupt is seised in tail by deed inrolled, shall have the same effect to bar the intail as if a recovery had been suffered of them by stat. 21 *J.* 1. *c.* 19. *s.* 12.

So, an award under a submission to arbitration, will give a good title, on which to maintain this action.

Thus, where ejectment was brought for certain lands, on several demises of *Greville*, *Morris*, and others, to support the title of the lessors of the plaintiff, a submission to arbitration by bond from *Morris*, and another, respecting these lands, was given in evidence, and an award by *R. Sh[illegible]*, and *R. M. Phillips*, Esqrs. the arbitrators, that the lands were the property of *Morris*, and this was relied on as conclusive evidence of the title of *Morris*. The counsel for the defendants objected that this was not sufficient, for that the award could convey no title. It might have been enforced by rule of Court, or action on the bond, if the possession was refused by the defendant; but that it did not avail there. *Lawrence*, J. "I am of a different opinion. The parties chose these gentlemen as judges to determine the right between them. They have determined that right, and their decision is binding on the parties, and I think is conclusive evidence of the right between them here." Verdict for the plaintiff. The learned Judge's opinion was confirmed by the Court of K. B. on a motion for a new trial in *Mich. T.* 1802 (*a*).

If a rent-charge be granted to any one, with a proviso that if the rent be in arrear it shall be lawful for the grantee, his heirs and assigns, to enter and hold the lands out of which the rent-charge is granted till he shall be satisfied out of the arrears; this shall give to the grantee such an interest that he may make a lease of the land by which he may maintain his ejectment (*b*).

The committee of a lunatic may bring an ejectment; but it must be in the name of the lunatic; for the committee is but as bailiff, and cannot make leases of the land (*c*).

An infant may maintain this action; but he must name a good plaintiff, who may be answerable for the costs (*d*).

Executors may maintain ejectment for land let to their testator for years, if the testator is ousted; for by stat. 4 *E.* 3. *c.* 6. an action is given to executors for goods taken out of their testator's possession, and the act extends to this case, because the term itself is recovered.—So, if the executors themselves of the lessee for years are ousted, they may have either a special writ on the case, or an action of ejectment (*e*).

(*a*) Doe dem. Greville and others *v.* Roper. At Hereford, Oxford Summer Assizes, 1802. MS. (*b*) 1 Saund. 112. 1 Lev. 170.
(*c*) Hob. 215. Hut. 16. 2 Wils. 130. (*d*) 1 Sid. 694.
(*e*) Bul. N. P. 102. 3 T. R. 13. 2 Atk. 286. Co. Litt. 129.

The administrator also of a yearly tenant as long as the lessor and lessee pleased, may maintain an ejectment; for the administrator has the same interest in the chattel as the intestate had.—So if the spiritual court grant administration *pendente lite*, such an administrator may bring this action.

An alien cannot maintain an ejectment, for he cannot take lands by descent

As to the issue of aliens, and to children born out of the realm, it is settled by stat. 25 *E.* 3. *s* 2. that children whose fathers and mothers, at the time of their birth, should be liege subjects of *England*, shall be inheritable to lands within the kingdom, though such children were born out of the kingdom, and by stat 7 *Ann.* 5. and 4 *G.* 2. *s.* 4 all children born out of the ligeance of the crown of *Great Britain*, whose fathers are natural-born subjects, shall be deemed natural-born subjects and so may inherit lands.

When a corporation aggregate is lessor of the plaintiff, it is said, they must give a letter of attorney to some person to enter and seal a lease upon the land, and therefore the plaintiff ought in such case to declare upon a demise by deed, (for they cannot enter and demise upon the land as natural persons can) though this will be aided after verdict (*a*). however, this seems to be unnecessary now, for this being a fictitious action, the demise need not now be set out to be by deed (*b*).

So, a corporation sole may bring ejectment · as a bishop against the copyholders of a manor belonging to the bishoprick, for a forfeiture committed while the see was vacant, and the lord of a manor may bring this action in the like case (*c*).

But where a pauper had been put in possession of a cottage forty years ago, by the then existing overseers of the poor, and had continued in the parish pay, and the cottage had been from time to time repaired by different overseers, till two years ago, when the pauper disposed of it to the defendant and went away yet it was held, that the existing overseers could not maintain ejectment for it, having no derivative title as a corporation from their predecessors, so as to connect themselves in interest with the overseers by whom the pauper was put in possession, and the pauper having done no act to recognize his holding under the demising sets of overseers (*d*).

But trespass cannot be maintained against a corporation as such; yet the lessor is not without remedy; for at any rate the tenancy may be determined by notice to the corporation served on its officers, and if after such determination, the cattle of any other person be found upon the premises they may be distrained (*e*).

(*a*) Bull N P 98
(*b*) Bull N P. 107 Esp N. P 440.
(*c*) 1 Ld Raym 136 Run Eject 149.
(*d*) 14 East R. 482
(*e*) 8 East, 230

A copyholder, if ejected by his lord, may maintain ejectment against him (*a*); for though he is called a tenant at will, yet it is according to the custom of the manor, and he cannot be put out while he performs his services (*b*).—But in such cases it seems to be necessary that he should be empowered either by the custom of the manor or the licence of the lord, to make a lease: but even without such a power the copyholder can maintain ejectment against all persons but the lord (*c*).

If the heir apparent of a copyholder in fee, surrender in the lifetime of his ancestor and survive him, the heir of such surrenderor is not estopped, by that surrender of his ancestor, from claiming against the surrenderee (*d*). For, in order to pass an estate by surrender, the estate must pass into the hands of the lord, through which it must be taken; and a fine differs from the case of a surrender, for that will be good against the heir by estoppel, although it passes no estate at all: but if a surrender be not good, there will be no estoppel (*e*).

So the party claiming by descent has as complete a title without admittance as with it, against all the world but the lord (*f*): wherefore the court will not grant a *mandamus* to compel the lord to admit such a copyholder: though generally the lord is compellable by *mandamus* or decree, to admit, as in case of a surrender (*g*).

So, a widow entitled to her free-bench may maintain this action before admittance, for it comes out of the estate of the husband: and is a customary right, *nomine dotis*, and so declared by *Bracton* (*h*).

But in the case of surrender, no complete title vests in the surrenderee till admittance, for till then it remains in the surrenderer: and if he dies, it is so much in him that his heir may maintain ejectment (*i*).

If, however, a surrender be made, the admittance shall relate to that time, so that the surrenderee may recover on a demise laid between the time of surrender and admittance (*k*).

For there is no rule better founded in law, reason and convenience than this, That all the several parts and ceremonies necessary to complete a conveyance shall be taken together, as one act, and operate from the substantial part by relation: thus, livery relates to the feoffment; inrollment to the bargain and sale, a recovery to the deed that leads to the use, so admittance shall relate to the surrender, especially when it is a sale for a valuable consideration (*l*).

(*a*) 8 East, 230. (*b*) Cro. Eliz. 535. (*c*) Ibid. 676.
(*d*) 3 T. R. 365. (*e*) 1 Ve. 270. (*f*) 2 T. R. 197. 1 Wils. 28.
(*g*) 5 Burr. 2787. (*h*) Hutt. 18. Hob. 181. 2 Danv. Abr. 184. And. 29.
(*i*) Yelv. 144. Bull. N. P. 108. 2 Wils. 13. 1 East's R. 632. 3 T. R. 169.
(*k*) 1 T. R. 600. (*l*) 5 Burr. 2787.

For what this Action will lie.

An ejectment will lie for nothing of which the sheriff cannot deliver possession under an execution: therefore it will not lie for incorporeal hereditaments, as a rent, common *per cause de vicinage*, which is a mere permission, or other thing lying in grant, *quæ neque tangi, nec videri possunt* (*a*).

But it will lie for common appendant or appurtenant, for the sheriff by giving possession of the land gives possession of the common (*b*)

The stat. 32 *H.* 8. *c.* 57. enacts, That where any person shall have an estate of inheritance in tithes or other spiritual profits which shall be in lay lands, he may maintain an ejectment or other action for them. —This action is now allowed where the tithes are in the hands of the clergy (*c*)

An ejectment lies for small tithes. therefore the action has been adjudged to lie for wool, being tithe; and by the same reason for an egg (*d*)

An ejectment will lie by the owner of the soil for land subject to a passage over it, as the king's highway: for the king has nothing but the passage for himself and his people, but the freehold and all profits belong to the owner of the soil, so do all trees upon it, and mines under it. therefore the owner may carry water-pipes under it (*e*)

But it shall be recovered subject to the easement; which the owner may get discharged by a writ *ad quod damnum* (*f*).

An ejectment for a manor, generally, is bad, without expressing the number of acres for services belonging to the manor (*g*).

An ejectment will lie for a church; but it must be demanded by the name of a messuage. In this case, it was said, that the curate may have a rule to defend *quoad* a right of entry to perform divine service; but that case has been over-ruled (*h*).

So an ejectment for "a certain place called the vestry in *D.*' was held well enough (*i*)

This action lies for an orchard, which may be demanded in the *præcipe* either by that name, or by the name of a garden (*k*).

So, it lies for a stable, and a cottage (*l*)

It seems to be the better opinion, that an ejectment will not lie for a close, and that giving it a particular name will not make it sufficiently certain for the sheriff to be able to deliver it: So it will not lie for "a piece of land (*m*)."

(*a*) Bull N P 99 (*b*) Ibid (*c*) Esp N P 428. (*d*) 2 Ld Raym 789 (*e*) Bur. 143. (*f*) Ibid. (*g*) Esp. N. P 428 Hetl 80. (*h*) Esp N. P 428. Salk 256. (*i*) 3 Lev 96 (*k*) Cro Eliz. 854 Cro. Jac 654. (*l*) Run. Eject. 122. (*m*) Ibid, Salk. 254. Cro. Jac 435 654

Nor for the third part of a close, or fourth part of a meadow, without setting forth the particular contents or number of acres; and such number should be stated with certainty, and not by estimation, also the nature of the land, as whether meadow, pasture, arable, &c. should be mentioned (*a*).

But for a close called *D* containing three acres of land, was held well enough for "land" signifies arable land, therefore both quantity and quality were specified. The cases, however, on this point are contradictory (*b*)

Ejectment for "a messuage *or* tenement" is too uncertain, the word "tenement" being of more extensive signification than the word "messuage" consequently it is uncertain what is demanded by the ejectment For the same reason it has been held that it will not lie for a tenement only (*c*).

Therefore, where in ejectment, the plaintiff declared of "one messuage or tenement" and had a verdict; it was moved in arrest of judgment, because an ejectment will not lie of a tenement; and "messuage *or* tenement" is so uncertain that the sheriff cannot tell of what he shall give possession; for a tenement may be of an advowson, a house or land of any kind. *Wilmot* C. J.—To be sure there are many old cases, where judgments in ejectment have been arrested for this supposed uncertainty, but I do not recollect any very modern case: There was a late case in B R. where the declaration was of a messuage *and* tenements, and that Court gave leave to strike out the words "and tenements," and to proceed for the messuage. I think "a messuage or tenement," in common parlance, means a messuage; and at this time of day, no mortal imagines that a tenement means any thing but a dwelling-house, for by long use it has acquired that definite signification.—*Hesitante curiâ*, a rule was made to shew cause why judgment should not be arrested (*d*)

This matter came on again, and was debated by counsel on both sides: when the Court seemed inclined to get over this objection if possible, and took further time to consider, until the last day of the term. [*Note.* It was first before the Court on the second day of Term.] but at last they thought themselves bound by the cases cited, and (against their inclination) arrested the judgment.

But it is questionable, whether the reason on which the objection is founded, ought at present to prevail; inasmuch as the sheriff now delivers possession of the premises recovered, according to the direction of the plaintiff himself (*e*).

(*a*) Run. Eject. 123 (*b*) Ibid. Cro. Jac. 435
(*c*) Run. Eject. 124. Cro. Eliz. 186. 1 East's R. 441 (*d*) 3 Wils. 13
(*e*) Run. Eject. 124

An ejectment for a messuage *and* tenement has been held good after verdict (*n*

So, a messuage or tenement, with other words expressing its meaning, is good, as "a messuage or tenement called the *Black Swan*," for the addition reduces it to the certainty of a dwelling-house (*o*)

So, for a messuage or burgage in *H* is good because they signify the same thing in a borough —So, for a messuage or dwelling-house for they are synonymous terms (*c*).

So, ejectment for a house is good but it is said that in the *præcipe* it ought to be demanded by the name of "a messuage (*d*)"

So, ejectment lies for part of a house, as of a chamber in a house, or of one room in a house (*e*).

But an ejectment of a kitchen was determined to be bad, for though the word be well understood in common parlance, yet because any chamber in a house may be applied to that use, the sheriff hath not certainty enough to direct him in the execution, and the kitchen may be changed between judgment and execution (*f*)

The courts have long discontinued the rules which govern the *præcipe*, and allow many things to be recovered in this action, which cannot be demanded in that writ. Indeed it has repeatedly been determined that such precise certainty is not requisite in ejectment, as in a *præcipe quod reddat*, in which it is necessary to describe the lands demanded once, at least, with certainty and precision, that the defendant may know what he is to defend Even in that proceeding, whenever the term used, either in respect to quantity or quality, was sufficiently certain and notorious to answer that purpose, it was good, though not particularly named in the Register —Of late years many things have been improved by art, which having required new appellations, are now not only perfectly understood by the law, but familiar to common understanding, though not to be found in antient law-books Words and names are arbitrary and as men contracted by such new appellations, it was but reasonable to permit the remedy to follow the nature of the contract. Indeed, whilst ejectments were compared to real actions, and arguments were drawn by analogy from them, they were of course fettered and this was very much the case, till after the reign of *James* the First But in later times, an ejectment has been considered with more latitude and greater liberality, as a fictitious action to try titles with more ease and dispatch, and with less expence to the parties (*g*).

Even formerly an ejectment would lie for a hop-yard —So, for aldercarr, a provincial term well known in *Norfolk*, where it signifies land covered with alders.—In *Yorkshire*, it is common to bring this action

(*o*) 1 L R [illegible] (*c*), 1 L R [illegible] 33[illegible] Run Eject 125.
(*d*) Ibid [illegible] 122. [illegible] 2 Wils 47
(*f*) Run Eject 122 [illegible] 12[illegible]

for cattle-gates, agreeable to which, it has been held, that an ejectment will lie for a beast-gate, a term used in *Suffolk* to denote land and common for one beast. A cattle gate is a distinct thing from a right of common; it passes by lease and release, cannot be devised but according to the statute of Frauds, and has been decided to be a tenement, within stat. 13 & 14 *C.* 2. c. 12. for the purpose of gaining a settlement (*a*).

Where an ejectment was brought for a croft and an acre of meadow, the plaintiff had a verdict, and a special judgment for his acre of meadow, releasing the costs and damages for all, for he was allowed his costs, because by the judgment he had a just cause of suit against the defendant.

So, this action will lie for fifty acres of furze and heath, and fifty acres of moor and marsh (*b*).

It lies, also, for so many acres of bog in *Ireland*, where that word has but one signification and comprehends only one sort of land.—So, it will lie for mountain in *Ireland*, because the word mountain is rather a description of quality than the situation of the land.—So, for "a quarter of land," in *Ireland*, for it may be a term as well known there as mountain is, and that the Courts here will intend (*c*).

An ejectment may be brought for ten acres of wood and ten of underwood, for they are of different natures, and even if otherwise *bis petitum* is no objection in an ejectment (*d*).

Whether it will lie for a fishery seems rather doubtful; the old cases are against it, but the more modern opinion inclines to support the action (*e*). For though an ejectment *de piscariâ* in such a river has been holden ill, and the action will not lie *pro quodam rivulo, sive aquæ cursu* called *D.* because it is impossible to give execution of a thing that is transient and always running; the doubt however seems to apply merely to the name by which it is recoverable, for an assize will certainly lie for a piscary, and there is no doubt that a fishery is a tenement, trespass will lie for an injury to it, and it may be recovered in an ejectment, and where a fishery is demised, it will be presumed that the soil passed along with it (*f*).

But it lies for a boilary of salt, for that is not, like a piscary, transient and running, but the water is fixed within a certain space and may be taken to be part of the soil; and by the grant generally of a boilary of the soil itself, passes (*g*).

An ejectment however for a water-course or stream of water is ill, for possession of it cannot be delivered; it should be of so much "land covered with water (*h*)."

(*a*) Run. Eject. 126. (*b*) 5 Burr. 2672. (*c*) Run. Eject. 128.
(*d*) Ibid. 129. (*e*) Ibid. 131. (*f*) 1 T. R. 361. (*g*) Run. Eject. 131.
(*h*) Run. Eject. 128. Yel. 143.

This action lies for the first crop, for the first grass, *primâ tonsurâ*, is the best profit of the property, wherefore he who has it is esteemed the proprietor of the land itself, till the contrary be proved (*a*).

So an ejectment lies for herbage, herbage being the most signal profit of the soil, and the grantee having at all times a right to enter and take it (*b*).

So, it should seem, this action would lie for the hay-grass and aftermath of a meadow, for the same reason (*c*).

So, it will lie for a sheep-walk; as *pro pastura centum ovium*, that is, as much land as will feed one hundred sheep (*d*).

But it will not lie for pannage, that not being the immediate produce of the soil itself, but merely the masts that fall from the trees, on which the swine feed (*e*).

An ejectment lay at common law for a rectory, which consisting of a church, glebe lands and tithes, has been said to resemble a manor; the church being compared to the mansion-house, the glebe lands to the demesnes, and the tithes to the services.

Chapels having become lay inheritances, are recoverable in ejectment like other lay estates: a chapel should however be demanded by the name of a messuage.

Ejectment will not lie for encroachments on the waste, made by the tenant.

On a lease of ground to build on, if the building corresponds with the abuttals, though they do not with the measured distance, as set out in the lease, if the lessor has seen the progress of the building without objection made, he shall not be allowed to claim the part inclosed upon, but his acquiescence shall be presumed (*f*).

So, where a man suffers another to build on his ground without setting up a right title till afterwards, a court of equity will oblige the owner to permit the person building to enjoy it quietly (*g*).

Of the Action of Ejectment, where the Tenant is in Possession.

As the old mode of proceeding must be adhered to in very few cases, we have noticed those cases under a separate head, conceiving that plan to be more perspicuous, than introducing them incidentally in treating of that part of the subject which regards the modern method of carrying on the action.

Having, therefore, concisely stated the general principle and practice of this action, and enumerated the cases in which, and the things for

(*a*) Cro. Car. 362. (*b*) Hard. 332. (*c*) 2 T. R. 452.
(*d*) Run. Eject. 137. (*e*) Ibid. (*f*) Run. Eject. 249.
(*g*) 2 Atk. 83. 3 Ibid. 99.

what, it lies, we proceed more particularly to consider the present practice in common, and indeed with the exception mentioned, in all cases.

The cases that more immediately apply to the subject of this work, are those in which a landlord is compelled to have recourse to this remedy in consequence of

1st, His tenant holding over without his permission and against his consent after the term has expired by effluxion of time for a man may come in by rightful possession and yet hold over adversely without a title, and if he does, such holding over, under circumstances, will be equivalent to an actual ouster (*a*)

2dly, His tenant determining the lease by non-payment of rent, or non-performance of covenants, where a right of re-entry and forfeiture are conditioned on the breach of them.

In these cases the modern method of proceeding prevails, for the nature of which we refer the reader to the introductory part of this title.

The proceedings in the Court of King's Bench may be either by bill or original, but the latter mode is preferable, as no writ of error can be brought thereon except in Parliament.—In the Common Pleas they are always by original (*b*)

The declaration and notice are the first process, no writ being sued out (*c*).

Ejectment being a local action, the venue must be laid in the county in which the premises are situate Proceedings being *in rem*, the effect of the judgment cannot be had, if the venue be laid in a wrong place. Possession is to be delivered by the sheriff of the county, and as trials in England are in particular counties, the officers are county officers the judgment therefore could not operate, if the action was not laid in the proper county (*d*).

But the premises being laid to be in *Farnham*, and proved to be in *Farnham Royal*, is not a fatal variance, unless it be shewn that there are two *Farnhams* (*e*)

As the plaintiff must recover by the strength of his own title, he must shew a good and subsisting one at the time of the ejectment brought, and therefore though the plaintiff by the new method of proceeding is not obliged to make an actual entry, or a real lease, yet he must lay the commencement of the supposed lease in his declaration preceding the ouster and ejectment of the defendant, because the wrong complained of by the plaintiff is, that the defendant entered upon his possession, which he hath title to by virtue of the demise

(*a*) Cowp 218 (*b*) 2 Sel. Pract 168 (*c*) Ibid.
(*d*) 6 Mod. 222. Cowp 176. (*e*) 13 East's R 9

mentioned in the declaration; therefore if the ejectment and ouster should be laid before the commencement of the lease, though such ouster be wrong: yet the plaintiff ought not to complain of it, for it was no wrong to him, inasmuch as by his own shewing it was done before his title commenced (*a*).

Where a demise was laid on the 24th of *June*, to hold from the said 24th of *June*, by virtue of which on the day and year last mentioned he (the plaintiff) had entered, and the defendant afterwards (to wit) on the 24th of *June*, had evicted him, it was held to be bad, for *from* being exclusive, the lease did not commence till the 25th of *June* (*b*).

The word "from" however has since received a more liberal construction, and "from the day of the date" are now held to import either inclusively or exclusively, so as to give effect to the deed, and to support the intention of the parties (*c*).

But where possession had been demanded on the 5th of *October* of the defendant, who had been tenant at will to the lessor of the plaintiff, and an ejectment was brought, and the demise was laid on the 1st of *October*, it was adjudged that the plaintiff could not recover, the tenancy not having been determined until after the day of the demise in the declaration (*d*).

In ejectment on the demise of an heir by descent, the demise was laid on the day the ancestor died, and held well enough after verdict; for as to the fraction of a day, a fiction of law may heal, but shall not hurt (*e*).

So, where the ejectment was brought by a posthumous son, and the demise laid from the time of his father's death, Lord *Hardwicke* inclined to think that it was good, and that the defendant would be estopped to say he was not born at the time of the demise laid, by stat. 10 & 11 *W.* 3. *c.* 16 (*f*).

But it is not necessary to lay any day certain upon which the plaintiff entered: it is sufficient to lay a demise after the title accrues, and then say in general "that he afterwards entered," &c. for so are the precedents (*g*).

The declaration should state the ejectment by the defendant to have been done subsequent to the date of the supposed lease made to him by the lessor of the plaintiff; for otherwise the ejectment, which is the injury complained of, would precede the time at which the plaintiff's title accrued, so that there could be no cause of action.

But though such be the proper form of declaring, yet this being a fictitious action, it is not fatal if laid otherwise: for in cases that have

(*a*) Esp. N. P. 441. Run. Eject. 214. 1 Bur. 177. (*b*) Esp. N. P. 414. 1 S[illegible]
(*c*) Run. Eject. 215. Cowp. 714. (*d*) 4 T. R. 681. (*e*) 3 Wils. 27[illegible]
(*f*) Bul. N. P. 105. (*g*) Bul. N. P. 10[illegible]

occurred where the ejectment was laid prior in point of time to the demise, yet the Court held it good (*a*).

Thus, in ejectment the plaintiff declared upon a lease, dated 1st *February* 1742, to hold from the 8th of *January* before, that afterwards, *viz.* 28th *January* 1752, the defendants ejected him.—It was insisted for the defendants, that the ejectment was laid to be before the plaintiff's title under the lease, which was not made till 1st *February*, and 1 *Sid.* 7. was cited; but it was holden, that the day of the ejectment being laid under a *viz.* was surplusage, and that "afterwards" should relate to the time of making the lease, and then all would be well enough, and the plaintiff had a verdict (*b*).

For the plaintiff need not mention in his declaration any particular day of the ouster, provided it appears to be subsequent to the term commenced, and before the action be brought; though in the precedents a day certain is always laid (*c*).

In the case of an ejectment to avoid a fine, however, an actual entry is necessary; and the plaintiff cannot lay his demise, or recover the mesne profits before such entry (*d*).

The declaration should also state, as has been before observed, both the quantity and the nature of the land to be recovered.

In like manner, where the ejectment was for five closes of arable and meadow, called —— containing twenty acres in *D.* upon not guilty pleaded, and verdict for the plaintiff, judgment was arrested, because it was not shewn how much there was of one, and how much of the other (*e*).

But the plaintiff need not declare for the exact quantity which he has a right to recover, for he may declare for any indeterminate quantity, and the form now used is to *viz.* one thousand acres of pasture, one thousand acres of arable, *&c.* for he shall recover according to the quantity to which he proves title.

Therefore where the plaintiff declared in ejectment of one hundred acres of land, and shewed his lease in evidence only for forty acres, and it was said that he had failed of his lease, for there was none such as that of which he counted, yet it was ruled to be good for so much as was comprised in the lease, and that for the residue, the jury might find the defendant not guilty (*f*).

So, if the plaintiff proves a title to but a moiety of that for which he declares, he shall only recover such half: as where he declared for a house, and proof went to shew that only part of it was built on the plaintiff's land by encroachment, he recovered so much as was built on his land (*g*).

(*a*) Cro. Jac. 96. (*b*) Bull. N. P. 106. (*c*) Cro. Jac. 311.
(*d*) 7 T. R. 727. (*e*) Salk. 254. (*f*) Cro. Eliz. 12.
(*g*) 1 Lev. 354.

But though part may be recovered on a demand for the whole, the reverse will not hold; for if the plaintiff prove more than he has declared for he shall not recover it, for he can recover no more than he goes for in his declaration (*a*).

But as to the plaintiff's title, he shall recover according to what it really is, though he declare for a longer term than he has a right to recover.

Therefore, where the lease declared upon was from the 25th of *March* 1765 for seven years, the plaintiff proved that *J S* was seised, and that by indenture in 1763 he demised the premises in question to *D* for seven years, to commence at *Midsummer* 1763, and that in 1647 *D.* assigned the residue of the term then unexpired to *Carruthers.* It was insisted for the defendant, that though in ejectment the lease is fictitious, yet the plaintiff must declare on such a lease as suits with the title of his lessor, here if he recover at all, he must recover a term which is of two years longer duration than his title. But *per* Lord *Mansfield* there is nothing in the objection, for if the lessor have a title, though but for a week, he ought to recover. In the ejectment the question in ejectment is, who has the possessory right.—Suppose a person has an interest for three years only, and should make a lease for five years, it would be good for the three years (*b*).

A declaration in ejectment contained two demises by two different lessors of two distinct undivided thirds, judgment was given against the plaintiff to recover his said terms. On error it appeared from the facts stated on a bill of exceptions to the judge's directions on a point of law, that the ejectment respected only one undivided third. Held well enough on this record, where the point was only raised by bill of exceptions. *Semble* that it would have been well even in a special verdict (*c*).

Where the title is in several persons, who are severally concerned in interest, it is usual to declare by several distinct counts, upon several demises, therefore when a term is limited to trustees for securing the payment of an annuity, or portions, &c. though the trustees seldom act, yet it is usual to declare upon their demise, and also upon the demise of the *cestui que trust.* By this means in such and similar cases, the plaintiff is not confined to one demise, but may resort to any other which he has stated, and under which he may be able to prove a title. and where several demises are apparently inconsistent, the Court, to assist the title of the lessor of the plaintiff, would perhaps permit him to enter a *non-pros.*, as to all the demises but that which he can legally sustain. and after verdict, if by any means the plaintiff can

(*a*) 1 Bur 330. (*b*) Beato d. (Lessee of Carruther,) v. Dendam Sit. at Middlesex after T. T. 5 G. 3. Bull. N. P. 106. (*c*) 2 Bos. & P. N. R. 2.

be supposed to have title, as stated in the declaration, the Court will support it (*a*).

If the declaration states the demise to the plaintiff to be of more lessors than one, it must appear that each lessor had a title to the whole of the land or premises demised, or it will be bad, for if one of them has not an interest in the whole, he cannot be said to demise it (*b*).

Therefore, where the plaintiff declared in ejectment on a lease made by *A.* and *B.* and on not guilty pleaded, the jury found a special verdict, That *A.* was tenant for life of the lands in question, and that *B.* had the remainder in fee, and that *A.* was living: on this finding, it was adjudged against the plaintiff, for it was not the lease of *A.* and *B.* but the lease of *A.* during his life, and the confirmation of *B.* (*c*).

So, an ejectment cannot be maintained on a joint-lease by tenants in common, for, as they are in by several titles, the freehold is several, and consequently each cannot demise the whole. There should therefore be a distinct count on the demise of each, or they may join in a lease to a third person, and such person may make a lease to try the title (*d*).

But joint-tenants may join in a lease to try the title: for being seised *per my et per tout*, each has title to the whole, wherefore the demise of each is good (*e*).

For the same reason, coparceners, it has been held, may join in a lease to the plaintiff in ejectment, *tamen quære de hoc* (*f*), for where in ejectment the plaintiff declared of a lease, by two coparceners, *quod demiserunt*, exception being taken to it, the exception was allowed, because the lease was several as to each coparcener for her respective moiety, for though they have but one freehold with regard to their ancestor, and therefore if they are disseised shall join in an assise, yet as to their disposing power thereof they have several rights and interests, so that neither of them can lease or give away the whole.—The usual mode, however, is to join in a lease to a third person who demises to the plaintiff, for a demise of all the parts is a demise of the whole (*g*).

In ejectment on the several demises of two persons, although the evidence shews the title to be exclusively in one of them, the other cannot be compelled to be examined as a witness for the defendant (*h*).

In ejectment on the several demises of three persons, each demise being of the whole, the lessors of the plaintiff are entitled to a verdict,

(*a*) [illegible] 211. 1 Wils. [illegible] 2 Burr. 988. 1180. 5 T. R. 15. (*b*) Esp. N. P. [illegible]
(*c*) [illegible] 6 Co. [illegible] (*d*) Cro. Jac. 166. Co. Litt. 200. 1 Wils. 232. (*e*) 2 Str. 1181.
(*f*) 1 Ld. Raym. 726. (*g*) Bac. on Lea. 194. (*h*) 3 Campb. [illegible]

upon evidence that they jointly granted a lease to the defendant, which has expired (*a*).

If four tenants in common jointly demise from year to year, such of them as give notice to quit may recover their several moieties in ejectment, on their several demises (*b*).

The plaintiff in ejectment, under the several demises of two, may, after notice to quit, recover the possession of premises held by the defendant as tenant from year to year, upon evidence that the common agent of the two had received the rent from the tenant, which was stated in the receipts to be due to the two lessors, even assuming such receipts to be evidence of a joint-tenancy, for a several demise severs a joint-tenancy: and supposing the contract with the tenant to have been entire, no objection lies on that account to the plaintiff's recovery in this case, as he had the whole title in him (*c*).

In ejectment brought upon the joint demise of several trustees of a charity, it is not enough for the defendant, who had paid one entire rent to the common clerk of the trustees, to shew that the trustees were appointed at different times, as evidence that they were tenants in common. for as against their tenant, his payment of the entire rent to the common agent of all, is at all events sufficient to support the joint demise, without making it necessary for them to shew their title more precisely (*d*).

Where the lessor of the plaintiff claims by lease, under a copyholder, he must shew that by the custom of the manor, [or by licence of the lord, *com. semb.*] the copyholder may let such leases for years; for if this be not set out in the declaration, and the count be general, it shall be esteemed a lease at common law, which a copyholder cannot make (*e*).

A lease by a copyholder for three years under a licence to let for twenty-one years is good; and the lessee may bring ejectment on it at the common law (*f*).

Indeed, a copyholder may declare on a lease for any number of years, without forfeiture; and the lessee of a copyholder, for a year, may sustain an ejectment for his estate is warranted by law, and it is the most speedy way for him to recover the possession (*g*)

Of amending the Declaration.

It is a rule both in the Court of King's Bench and that of the Common Pleas, that no declaration in ejectment can be amended before

(*a*) 3 Camp. 190. (*b*) 3 Durnf. R. 120. (*c*) 12 East's R. 57.
(*d*) 12 East's R. 221. (*e*) Cro. Eliz. 469. (*f*) Ibid. 535.
(*g*) Run. Eject. 226.

appearance, and that after appearance it can only be amended in form, not in matter of substance (*a*).

But amendments are now carried further than formerly, and that which used to be deemed substance, as the demise, *&c.* is now held matter of form, and amendable (*b*).

Thus where the ejectment was to avoid a fine, and the demise was laid before the plaintiff had made the entry, instead of after, it was, on motion, ordered to be amended, Lord *Mansfield* observing that demise is mere matter of form, it did not exist (*c*).

So, if the term demised to the plaintiff is expired, or likely to expire, before trial, the Court will now upon motion to amend, enlarge it upon payment of costs. So, the term was ordered to be enlarged, after it had expired twelve years; though the cause was at issue, and special jury struck, and the parties gone down to trial, before the mistake was discovered. For an ejectment is the creature of the Court, and open to every equitable regulation for expediting the true justice of the case (*d*).

But if the fault go to the title, or is in the process, it is not amendable (*e*).

As where in the declaration delivered to the tenant in possession, the said "*James*," instead of "*John*," was said to enter by virtue of the demise, the Court refused to amend it, for they considered it as process: and Justice *Wright* cited a case, where the premises were laid to lie, "*Twickenham* or *Isleworth*, or one of them," and the Court refused to let the plaintiff amend, by striking out the disjunctive words.

Yet in a latter case, an amendment has been made in the parcels and in the name of the plaintiff for the defendant (*f*).

Of service of the Declaration, Affidavits thereof, &c.

The declaration being considered as process to bring in the tenant, must therefore be personally served upon him, if it be known where he lives, and his residence be not on the premises for which the ejectment is brought (*g*). For service on the *person* in possession will not suffice, if it do not appear that he is tenant (*h*).

But where there are more tenants in possession than one, service on the wife of one of them will not be good service upon all. Thus, where upon cause being shewn against a rule to set aside proceedings, on the ground that *J. G.* had not been served with a declaration, an affidavit was produced, shewing that a declaration had been

(*a*) 2 Sell. Pract. 228 (*d*) Ibid. (*e*) 4 Burr. 2447
(*b*) 2 Bl. R. 940 Cowp. 841 (*e*) 2 Str. 1211 (*f*) 2 Sell. Pract. 218
(*c*) 2 Str. 1064 (*g*) 3 Tidd's Pract. 443

served on the premises on *Elizabeth* the wife of *H. G.*, and it was contended that such service was sufficient, though both *J.* and *H. G.* were tenants in possession, particularly as it appeared that *J. G.* was in the house at the time: the Court said, that the service was certainly good against *H.* but that it was defective against *J.* as those steps had not been taken which were necessary to supply a personal service on *J.* and that the judgment, therefore, as far as it affected *J.* must be set aside. The counsel against the rule then said, the plaintiffs must continue in possession of one moiety, and recover against *H. G.* *quod fuit concessum* by the Court, the counsel on the opposite side observing that the other defendant *J.* must be restored to the possession of the moiety taken from him (*a*).

A motion was made, that service on *A.* might be deemed good service of the declaration on the tenant under these circumstances. The premises consisted of a mansion and four small houses in a yard, surrounded by a wall, through which was a door to them, forming the only means of access, in one of which small houses resided *A.* who was permitted to live there merely to take care of them and of the mansion house, the rest of the messuages were vacant. The Court refused the present motion, and recommended the plaintiff to affix a declaration on the empty houses, and then to move that it be deemed good service (*b*).

Service of a declaration in ejectment by nailing it on the barn door of the premises, in which barn the tenant had occasionally slept, there being no dwelling-house, and the tenant not being to be found at his last place of abode, was allowed to be good service (*c*).

If the tenant himself cannot be found, service on his wife or child, or on his servant, on the premises, will be held good services. If, however, it be on the servant, some acknowledgment by the tenant or his wife should be made to render it sufficient, and that though it may not clearly appear that the declaration came to hand before the essoign day of the term (*d*).—But perhaps delivery to a servant at the tenant's dwelling-house, and explaining the meaning of it, would be now strong presumptive evidence for the jury to conclude that it reached the tenant (*e*).

Service of a copy of the declaration, *&c.* in ejectment, before the essoign day of the term, on the daughter of the tenant in possession, in the absence of him and his wife, is not sufficient, even though the tenant had since declared that he had received the same, if it did not appear that he had received it before the essoign day (*f*).

The Court held service of the declaration in ejectment on the wife of

(*a*) Doe v. J. C. H. G. &c., East. T. 40 G. 3 K. B. T.'s MSS.
(*b*) Anon. 1 Tidd's Pract. 443. (*e*) 1 Bos. & Pull. N. R. 297.
(*c*) 2 Bl. R. 800 Salk. 255 Run. Eject. 126. (*d*) 4 T. R. 464. (*f*) 14 East's R. 431.

the tenant in possession sufficient, provided it could be shewn, that the wife lived with her husband (*a*).

If the tenant abscond, it is usual to serve the declaration on some person residing at his house, and if that cannot be done, to affix the same upon the door, and then, on an affidavit of the circumstances, to move the Court for a rule upon the tenant to shew cause why such service should not be deemed good service, upon which the Court will prescribe the mode of serving the rule, which is generally made absolute upon affidavit of its service.

Thus, in such case, upon service on the tenant's niece, who was the only manager of his house and resident in it, and fixing up another copy on the premises, the Court made a rule to shew cause why judgment should not be entered up against the casual ejector, and further ordered, that notice of such rule to any person in the house should be sufficient, and that if no person were in the house, it should then be affixed to the door of the house (*b*).

So, where the tenant in possession was personated at the time of the service by another who accepted the service in her name, the Court made a rule to shew cause, why this should not be deemed good service upon the tenant herself, and why judgment should not be signed against the casual ejector, on default of her appearing; and that leaving a copy of this rule at her house with some person there, or, if no one was to be met with, affixing it on the door, should be good service of it. This rule was made absolute upon an affidavit "that the tenant was either not at home, or, if at home, was denied, and that her servant maid was at home, but could not be served, whereupon a copy of the rule was affixed on the door of the house;" and moreover "that on a subsequent day," upon a doubt whether what had been already done was sufficient, "the maid being at home and opening the window, but refusing to open the door, and denying that her mistress was at home, another copy was affixed to the door, and the maid was told the effect of it, and another copy was thrown in at the window, and the original rule was shewn to the maid (*c*)."

Such rules will be granted with a retrospect: for a like rule to shew cause why a preceding service of an ejectment upon a servant in the house of one *Hawkins*, tenant in possession, should not be deemed good service of it, was made on the second day of the term, on its appearing that *Hawkins* and his wife both kept out of the way to prevent their being personally served. The rule was made with a retrospect, in order that the plaintiff might not lose the assizes (*d*).

So, in another case, a rule was granted and afterwards made absolute, that service of a declaration in ejectment at the house of a tenant

(*a*) 1 Bos. & Pul. N. R. 368. (*b*) Barn. 192. 2 Burr. 1116. (*c*) [illegible] 1182.
(*d*) Ibid. [illegible] 1 Bl. R. 290. S. C.

in possession, on a day past, might be good service; and that service of the first rule at the house of the said tenant, should be good service (*a*).

But where cause being shewn against a rule for good service of the declaration in ejectment, it appeared that the declaration was tendered on the 18th, but that the defendant's servant said that he had orders not to receive any such thing, whereupon it was not served on that day, but was left at the house on the day following, notwithstanding that the defendant knew of the intention to serve him, the Court said, "You should have left the declaration on the 18th. We sometimes by rule make that service, under particular circumstances, good, which otherwise would have been imperfect, but here there was no service on the proper day, and we cannot antedate the service" Rule discharged (*b*).

Leaving the ejectment at the house, was ruled to be sufficient service, it appearing that the servant had refused to receive it, having been ordered by his master not to take in any papers (*c*).—But where it appeared that service was made upon the defendant's son, who accepted it, and said that he knew what it was for, and would deliver it over to his father, and both father and son were attornies; the Court notwithstanding held the service insufficient and said, it had been often ruled so (*d*)

But tender of the declaration, and reading the notice aloud, though the tenant refused to receive it, or runs away and shuts the door, or threatens with a gun to shoot the person serving it if he came near, have been held good service upon application to the Court, who act discretionally in this matter, according to the exigency of the case (*e*).

A declaration served on the churchwardens and overseers of a parish, who rented a house for harbouring some of the parish poor, and did not otherwise occupy the house than by placing the poor in it, was deemed sufficient service, and a rule made for judgment (*f*)

So, in ejectment for a chapel, if service of the declaration be made on the chapel wardens, or on the person entrusted with the keys of the chapel, it will be sufficient.

On affidavit that one of the tenants is a lunatic, and that one *C* lives with her, transacts her business, and has the sole conduct thereof, and of her person, but would not permit the deponent to have access to her, in order to serve her with the declaration whereupon he delivered it to the said *C.* a rule was made for the lunatic and *C.* both to shew cause, why such service should not be good, and service of the rule on the said *C.* be good (*g*).

If there be several tenants in possession, the plaintiff, it has been

(*a*) 1 Bl. R 317 (*b*) T 's MSS H T. 41 G 3 (*c*) 1 Str 575
(*d*) T 's MSS H.T 41 G 3 (*e*) Sell Pract 173 (*f*) Ib.d. 174. Barnes, 181
(*g*) Sell Pra. 174 Ba. 192.

said, must deliver a declaration to each of them but where the name of each was prefixed to the notice served on him, it was held that one rule only was necessary on motion for judgment against the casual ejector (*a*). However, in a latter case, it seems that service of one of two tenants in possession has been good service on both (*b*).

Affidavit of Service.—The declaration having been delivered, the person who delivered it must make affidavit (except in the case of vacant possession) that he delivered to the tenant or his wife, *&c.* a true copy of the declaration, and read or explained to him the notice annexed thereto. If a declaration was served on the child or servant of the tenant, the affidavit must state further, "that the service was afterwards acknowledged by the tenant."—The affidavit must be positive, namely, that *A B* was tenant in possession, or that he acknowledged himself to be so because no one should be evicted from possession without a positive affidavit, on which, if it be false, the person who made it may be legally and effectually subjected to the penalties of perjury (*c*).

Affidavit of service on *A B.* tenant in possession, or *C* his wife, is not sufficiently certain as to either (*d*).

So, service on the wives of *A.* and *B.* who, or one of them are tenants, was held not good (*e*).

The reason why it is necessary to state in the affidavit that the service was on the wife at the husband's house, is to shew that they were living together as man and wife, and that by such service, the husband may have notice of the proceedings. but the declaration may be served on the wife either on the premises or at the husband's house (*f*).

When several tenants have been served with copies of the declaration, if it is meant but as one ejectment and to be followed by one judgment, one affidavit of the service of all is sufficient, annexed to the copy of one declaration. But if the ejectments are made several, so as to have separate judgments, writs of possession, *&c.* then an affidavit must be annexed to separate copies of the ejectment of the service separately (*g*).

Moving for Judgment.—Upon the affidavit of service (which affidavit may be made by the party who served the declaration, or by any one who was present and saw it served), the plaintiff moves for judgment against the casual ejector, which is always granted, unless the tenant in due time, enter into the common rule to confess lease, entry, and ouster (*h*). This motion for judgment is a side bar, but where there is any thing in the service of the declaration out of the common way, it should be mentioned to the Court, and where the affidavit of service

(*a*) Bull. N. P. 98. (*b*) 1 Bos. & Pul. [illegible] (*c*) 7 T. R. [illegible] 1 Tidd Pr. [illegible] Run. Eject. [illegible] (*d*) Ibid. 173. (*e*) Ibid. 174. (*f*) 1 Tidd's Pract. [illegible] (*g*) 2 Sel. Pract. 178. (*h*) Bos. & Pull. [illegible]

is defective, the Court of King's Bench will give leave to file a supplemental affidavit (*a*).

Although judgment against the casual ejector be signed, yet if no possession is given, or trial lost, it may, on an affidavit of merits and payment of costs, be set aside (*b*).

In the King's Bench, if the premises are situate in *London* or *Middlesex*, and the notice requires the tenant to appear on the first day, or within the first four days of the next term, the plaintiff should regularly move for judgment against the casual ejector in the beginning of that term and then the tenant must appear within four days inclusive after the motion, or the plaintiff will be entitled to judgment. If however the motion be deferred till the latter end of the term, the Court will order the tenant to appear in two or three days, and sometimes immediately, that the plaintiff may proceed to trial at the sittings after term; though if the motion be not made before the last four days of the term, the tenant need not appear until two days before the essoign day of the subsequent term; and should the notice in such case require the tenant to appear in the next term generally, the tenant has the whole of that term to appear in (*c*).

In the Common Pleas, if the premises are situate in *London* or *Middlesex*, and the tenant has notice to appear in the beginning of the term, the plaintiff cannot take any thing by his motion for judgment against the casual ejector for default of appearance, unless such motion be made within one week next after the first day of every *Michaelmas* and *Easter* terms, and within four days next after the first day of every *Hilary* and *Trinity* terms.—But it has been holden that this rule does not extend to the case of a vacant possession, under the stat 4 *G.* 2 (*d*).

In country causes, though the declaration be delivered before the essoign day of *Easter* or *Michaelmas* term, yet the tenant, in both Courts, is allowed till four days after the next issuable (that is, *Hilary* or *Trinity*) term to appear, and if the cause arise in *Cumberland*, or any other county where the assizes are held but once a year, the tenant need not appear till four days after the term preceding the assizes.—But in the King's Bench the plaintiff must move for judgment the same term in which the tenant has notice to appear: though the practice is different in the Common Pleas, for there he may move for judgment at any time during the next issuable term (*e*)

By a late rule of the Court of King's Bench, the clerk of the rules is to keep a book, in which is to be entered all the rules which shall be delivered out in ejectments, instead of that formerly kept which contained a list of the ejectments moved. The entry is to specify the num-

(*a*) 3 Tidd's Pract. 414. (*b*) Sell Pract 178 (*c*) Run. Eject. 165.
(*d*) Ibid. (*e*) Ibid. 166

ber of the entry; the county in which the premises lie; the name of the nominal plaintiff, the first lessor of the plaintiff, (with the words "and others," if more than one), and also the name of the casual ejector: and unless the rule for judgment be drawn up and taken away from the office of such clerk within two days after the end of the term in which the ejectment shall be moved, no rule is to be drawn up or entered, nor any proceedings had in such ejectment.

By stat 11 *G.* 2. *c.* 19 the tenant must give notice to his landlord of any declaration in ejectment being delivered, under pain of forfeiting three years improved or rack-rent of the premises so had and enjoyed by the tenant

A tenant to a mortgagor who does not give him notice of an ejectment brought by the mortgagee, to enforce an attornment, is not liable to the penalties of this statute. for the Act expressly permits an ejectment to be brought for such purpose, and extends only to cases where ejectments are brought which are inconsistent with the landlord's title (*a*)

But where the tenant had not given notice to his landlord of the ejectment, and there was judgment against the casual ejector, the Court set aside the judgment and ordered the tenant to pay all the costs to the lessor of the plaintiff on the landlord's entering into the usual rule to try the title (*b*). Or the landlord may bring a writ of error, which operates as a *supersedeas* of the proceedings under the statute, and thereby stay execution (*c*).

Section II. *Who may defend the Action of Ejectment, &c.*

The Tenant —The tenant in possession must apply to the Court to be made defendant in the room of the casual ejector. This is done on condition that he confesses lease, entry, and ouster.

By the common law, no person is permitted to defend in ejectment, unless he be tenant, and is or hath been in possession, or receipt of the rent: for, besides that it was champerty for any person to interpose and cover the possession with his title if the party would make any person defendant with another, who was not concerned in the possession of the tenements, it was a mischief at the common law, because if the plaintiff recover against one of the defendants, the stranger had no remedy for his costs, but this is remedied by 8 & 9 *W* 3 *c.* 10 whereby costs are given to such strangers, unless the Judge certifies, immediately on the trial, that the party had probable cause for making him defendant

Moreover, as the tenant in possession could not be compelled to appear and enter into the common rule to become defendant instead of the

(*a*) 1 T R 467 (*b*) 4 Bur 1996 (*c*) 2 Str 1221.

casual ejector: so neither could the landlord alone, without joining with the tenant, enter into such rule, and be made sole defendant.

The Landlord.—To remedy this inconvenience, by stat. 11 *G.* 2. *c.* 19. *s.* 13 it is enacted, That it may be lawful for the Court, where such ejectment shall be brought, to suffer the landlord to make himself defendant, by joining with the tenant, in case he should appear; but in case such tenant shall neglect or refuse to appear, judgment shall be signed against the casual ejector, for want of such appearance: but if the landlord, *&c.* of any part of the lands, *&c.* for which such ejectment was brought, shall desire to appear by himself, and consent to enter into the like rule, that by the course of the Court, the tenant in possession in case he or she had appeared, ought to have done: then the Court, where such ejectment shall be brought, shall and may permit such landlord so to do, and order a stay of execution upon such judgment against the casual ejector, until they shall make further order therein.

The landlord's right to be joined in defending the premises is affirmed by this statute, for he had such right before. and it is optional in him to be made defendant or not, for the Court cannot compel him (*a*).

The Court, however, has no jurisdiction, it seems, to admit any person to defend instead of the tenant, but the landlord. In the construction, however, of the statute, the word "landlord" is extended to all claiming title consistent with the possession of the occupier, for it need not be the actual landlord, but it is sufficient if he have an interest only in the land. A purchaser, therefore, of a reversion, which appeared to be a pretended title, and where no rent had ever been paid, was held to be admissible as a defendant. So, it should seem, a mortgagee out of possession may now be admitted to defend, on the tenant's refusal. But a devisee (*cestui que trust*) out of possession is not deemed a landlord within the meaning of the act: for upon a motion to permit certain devisees to defend instead of the tenant, it was opposed on the ground that the devisees had never been in possession, and could not, therefore, be considered as landlords under 11 *G.* 2 *c.* 19 *s.* 13. and Lord *Kenyon* said, If the person requiring to be made defendant under the act, had stood in the situation of immediate heir to the person last seised, or had been in the relation of remainder-man under the same title as the original landlord, I am of opinion that he might have been permitted to defend as a landlord by virtue of the directions of the statute; but here, the very question in dispute, between the adverse party and himself, is, Whether he is entitled to be landlord or not. we, therefore, are not authorized to extend the provision of the statute to such a case as this (*b*). As to the case mentioned, it appears to have been by consent.—A devisee in trust, however, may

(*a*) Salk. 257. (*b*) 3 T R 783.

defend as landlord. So, an heir who had never been in possession. So, the heir at law or remainder man under the same title (*a*).

So, if an ejectment be brought by one claiming as heir of a copyhold, and the lord of a manor, who claims by escheat *pro defectu hæredis*, applies to be admitted defendant either with the tenant or alone, the Court will direct the lord to bring this action against the heir, and the heir will be admitted to defend. If the lord refuses, they will discharge the rule to be admitted; if the heir refuses, they will admit the lord to defend (*b*).

On the landlord being made a defendant under 11 *G.* 2. *c.* 19. on non-appearance of the tenant, the Court will stay execution against the casual ejector.

But where the landlord is permitted to defend without the tenant, judgment is always first signed against the casual ejector; the reason of which is that, under it, the plaintiff if he obtain a verdict, may get possession of the premises sued for, which he could not do by virtue of a judgment against a person out of possession (*c*).

As to the time when the landlord may be admitted defendant, a case occurred, in which judgment had been regularly obtained against the casual ejector by default — the landlord of the premises moved to set it aside, because his tenant had not given him any notice of his having been served with the declaration in ejectment. The plaintiff insisted that his judgment was perfectly regular, and that the tenant's omitting to give his landlord notice of the declaration being delivered was merely a matter between the landlord and his tenant, which could not affect the plaintiff's regular judgment, which had been fairly and duly obtained. The Court, however, were clearly of opinion that the possession ought not to be changed by a judgment in ejectment where there had been no trial or opportunity of trying; for the obtaining judgment might be owing to the default, or even treachery of the defendant's own tenant. But if the plaintiff had not been guilty of any collusion with the tenant, they thought it reasonable that the tenant, who was the person guilty of the default, should pay the costs: for the rule of the Court, which requires service upon the tenant in possession, is calculated with a view that the tenant should give notice to his landlord, in order that the ejectment cause might be tried between the proper parties interested in the question (*d*).

If judgment be signed, it is too late for the landlord to be made defendant. But the landlord may be let in after judgment when signed in consequence of the tenant's not giving notice (*e*).

But in no event will the Court endure that a lessee defend alone

(*a*) 3 Burr. 1297. 4 T. R. 122. (*b*) 3 Burr. 1290. (*c*) 2 Sell. Prac. 126. (*d*) 2 Burr. [illegible]. (*e*) 2 Sell. Prac. 187.

against his landlord, or those who claim under him, on a supposed defect of title (*a*).

A third Person.—In all cases, if the person who wishes to defend be neither tenant nor actual landlord, but has some interest to sustain, he must move the Court, on an affidavit of the fact, to be made a defendant, instead of, or with, the casual ejector; and the tenant's consent is not now necessary (*b*).

If a material witness for the defendant be also made a defendant, the right way is for him to let judgment go by default, but if he plead and by that means admit himself to be tenant in possession, the Court will not afterwards upon motion strike out his name. In such cases, however, if he consent to let a verdict be given against him for as much as he is proved to be in possession of, no reason appears why he should not be a witness for another defendant (*c*).

Consolidation Rule.—Where there are several defendants, to whom the plaintiff delivers declarations, who are severally concerned in interest, and the plaintiff moves to join them all in one declaration, yet the Court will not do it, but the plaintiff must deliver several declarations to each of them: because each defendant must have a remedy for his costs, which he could not have if they were joined in one declaration, and the plaintiff prevailed only against one of them and by this means the plaintiff might have a tenant of his own defendant with others, in order to save the costs (*d*).

But where several ejectments are brought for the same premises, upon the same demise, the Court on motion, or a Judge at his chambers, will order them to be consolidated the motion is for rule to shew cause (*e*)

Appearance.—The appearance, therefore, may be either by the tenant himself (as when he is in possession of his own estate, or agrees with his landlord to defend the action, or it is an ejectment by the landlord against his tenant or the like), or it may be by the tenant and the landlord jointly, or if the tenant refuses, it may be by the landlord alone

The appearance in all the above cases is effected in the same manner, except only that in the two last, counsel's signature must be got to a motion, which is of course to admit the landlord to defend, either with the tenant, or by himself if he refuses to appear, and a rule got from the clerk of the rules accordingly (*f*). Also, if the tenant refuse to appear, an affidavit of such refusal should be made, for the tenant is not obliged to appear in ejectment though the landlord is ready to indemnify him. Nor can an attorney, by order of the landlord, appear

(*a*) 2 Bl R. 1259 (*b*) Ibid 185 (*c*) Bull. N P 98. (*d*) Run. Eject 187
(*e*) Ibid. (*f*) 2 Sell Pract. 179

for the tenant such appearance and plea would be irregular, and ordered to be withdrawn (a).

The appearance in this action should be entered of the term mentioned in the notice, and where the notice to appear was in *Hilary*, and the tenant entered an appearance in *Michaelmas* following, and did nothing farther, and the plaintiff, finding no appearance of *Hilary*, and no common rule entered into or pleaded, signed judgment against the casual ejector, the Court held it regular; but afterwards set it aside to try the merits (b).

Touching the common or consent rule, it should be remembered that judgment against the casual ejector is always granted, unless the tenant in due time (that is, within the time allowed for his appearance) enters into the common rule to confess lease, entry, and ouster But if the tenant or his landlord wishes to defend the action, he must, within that time, constitute an attorney, who will make out the common rule, and leave it, with the general issue, at a Judge's chambers in the King's Bench, or at the Prothonotary's office in the Common Pleas. This rule is in substance nearly the same in both Courts, and the purport of it is, that the tenant or other defendant shall immediately appear, receive a declaration, plead not guilty in a plea of trespass and ejectment for the tenements in question; and that upon trial of the issue, he shall confess lease, entry, and ouster, and insist upon the title only: the effect of the rule being to bring the matter to the mere question of the plaintiff's possessory title (c).

In all cases, except that of ejectment brought to avoid a fine, (where there must be an actual entry,) the confession of lease, entry, and ouster, is sufficient to bar a nonsuit for want of proof of actual ouster. It is sufficient therefore in an ejectment brought for a condition broken, or by one tenant in common against another

The common rule, being made by assent of both parties, an attachment lies for the non-performance of it, as of all other rules of Court that are disobeyed, and this is all the remedy which the parties on both sides have for their costs (d)

If there be several persons who claim title, the rule may be drawn either generally or specially generally, as that *A.* who claims title to the premises in question in his possession, be admitted defendant for those premises, which puts a necessity upon the plaintiff to distinguish, by proof at the trial, what tenements are in each defendant's possession because by the rule, he is only to confess for the premises in his own possession; and if the plaintiff cannot distinguish, by proof what tenements are in each defendant's possession, he can have

(a) 2 Sell. Pract. 187. (b) Ibid. (c) Run Eject. 190 (d) Ibid. 202

no verdict, consequently no judgment. Or the rule may be drawn specially at the discretion of the defendant: as that *A* who claims title to such and such premises, (expressing them particularly,) be admitted defendant; which supersedes the necessity of proof that the premises are in his possession.—If the tenant enters into the common rule for so much of the premises as are in his possession, his attorney must, by rule of Court, immediately deliver to the plaintiff's attorney a note in writing thereof, and if the defendant's attorney will not give a note of the particulars of the land for which he was admitted defendant, the plaintiff may summon him before a Judge, who will order the rule thus specially to be drawn up, in case the party in possession will himself be defendant: but because the defendant's attorney is to draw up the rule, it being entered into by his consent, it is often drawn up in general terms, which puts the plaintiff to proof at the trial (*a*).

The lessor of the plaintiff is bound at the trial to prove the defendant in possession of the premises which he seeks to recover, notwithstanding that the defendant has entered into the general consent rule to confess lease, entry, and ouster, if the defendant contest his possession (*b*).

But now the practice is to insert in the margin of the consent rule, the premises to be defended, stating that they are part of the premises mentioned in the declaration, which makes the rule special, and thereby supersedes the necessity, as we have before observed, of the plaintiff proving in whose possession the premises are (*c*).

When the appearance is for part, the plaintiff may sign his judgment against the casual ejector.

That the lessor of the plaintiff, however, may the better know what exact part of the premises are defended, the defendant's attorney should give notice to the plaintiff's attorney what the premises are.

Proceedings when stayed.—In certain cases, the Court will stay the proceedings in ejectment, on a motion for a rule to shew cause.

Thus, where the lessor of the plaintiff is unknown to the defendant, the latter may call for an account of his residence or place of abode, from the opposite attorney, and if he refuse to give it, or give in a fictitious account, of a person who cannot be found, the Court will stay the proceedings until security be given for the payment of costs (*d*).

Also an ejectment on a clause of re-entry for non-payment of rent, under the stat. 4 *G.* 2. *c.* 28. (of which hereafter), proceedings will be stayed at any time after judgment and before execution executed, on the tenant bringing into Court all the rent in arrear and costs (*e*).

But the Court will not stay proceedings if a writ of possession i…

(*a*) Run. [illegible] 203. (*c*) [illegible] (*e*) [illegible] Prac. 181.
(*b*) 1 Lil's Prac. [illegible] (*d*) [illegible]

been executed. The application in such case is too late, no action pending; it cannot be granted without consent (*a*).

In ejectment by a mortgagee, for the recovery of the possession of the mortgaged premises, or in debt on bond conditioned for the payment of the mortgage-money, or performance of covenants in the mortgage where no suit in equity is depending for a foreclosure or redemption, by stat 7 *G.* 2. *c.* 20 if the person having a right to redeem shall at any time, pending the action, pay to the mortgagee, or in case of his refusal bring into Court all the principal monies and interests due on the mortgage, and also costs to be computed by the Court, or proper officer appointed for that purpose, the same shall be deemed and taken to be in full satisfaction and discharge of the mortgage, and the Court shall discharge the mortgagor of and from the same accordingly (*b*).

Upon this statute the Court stayed proceedings, although it was objected that the defendant had agreed to convey the equity of redemption to the plaintiff and if there be any doubt as to the amount of what is due, the Court of King's Bench will refer it to the Master, and that of Common Pleas to the Prothonotary, whose respective duty it is to tax the costs, and if the debt and costs are not paid, the plaintiff must proceed in the action, and cannot have an attachment (*c*)

The Court however would not stay proceedings in an ejectment brought by a mortgagee against a mortgagor, on the latter paying principal, interest, and costs, where the latter had agreed to convey the equity of redemption to the mortgagee (*d*).

A motion was to stay proceedings in ejectment on payment of mortgage money and costs, pursuant to this act, on shewing cause, the plaintiff produced an affidavit that the mortgagee had been at great expence in necessary repairs of part of the premises in his possession, (the ejectment was brought for the residue,) and therefore prayed that the Prothonotary might be directed to make allowance for such repairs. *Per Cur*—The rule must follow the words of the statute, the prothonotary will make just allowances and deductions (*e*).

But where there were two mortgages, the Court will not stay proceedings and compel a redemption of one mortgage only, upon payment of the principal, interest, and costs, on that mortgage, without paying the rest (*f*).

A judge made an order pursuant to this Act, to stay the mortgagee's proceeding in ejectment, upon bringing principal, interest, and costs into Court; and a rule was made to make the order a rule of Court (*g*) but it afterwards appearing to the Court, that notice had been

(*a*) [illegible] (*b*) [illegible] (*c*) [illegible]
(*d*) [illegible] (*e*) [illegible] (*f*) 2 B. P. 726

given by the mortgagee to the mortgagor that he insisted upon payment of two bonds, which were a lien upon the estate, the case was adjudged to be out of this act, and the rule *nisi* was discharged (*a*).

But where a rule, on the statute, to shew cause why proceedings should not be stayed on payment of the mortgage-money and costs, was made absolute, upon the lessors of the plaintiff, who were assignees of the mortgagee, insisting to be paid a bond and a simple contract debt due to themselves in their own right [illegible] *Cu.* —A bond is no lien in equity, unless where the heir comes to redeem.

The practice now is, to stay proceedings by summons before a Judge (*b*).

Proceedings also will be stayed, in the case of an infant lessor of the plaintiff, that of the death of plaintiff's lessor, perhaps, that of the defendant residing abroad, and where a former ejectment has been brought (*c*)

By the practice of making a rule to stay proceedings in this action, on the demise of an infant, until a responsible plaintiff be named, or security be given for the payment of costs, if an infant deliver a declaration to a defendant, some friend or guardian may set up as plaintiff, to be responsible to the defendant for his costs. But if such person die insolvent, so that the defendant cannot derive any benefit from the rule, the infant himself must answer for the costs the rule was made for his benefit, and an infant must not disturb the possession of others by unlawful entries, without being liable to costs.—Previous however to any motion in Court, enquiry should be made, whether there be a real and substantial plaintiff, or not for on enquiry, the guardian may undertake to pay the costs and in case he should, the Court would probably decline to interpose (*d*).

It has likewise been holden, that upon the death of the plaintiff's lessor, the proceedings may be stayed, till the plaintiff shall have given the defendant security for his costs (*e*)

So where an ejectment was brought on the demise of a person residing at *Antigua*, and in another case, where the lessor of the plaintiff resided in *Ireland*, the plaintiff was compelled to give the defendant a similar security in the latter case he was compelled to do it, although it was an ejectment brought under the direction of the Court of Chancery, where the bill was retained till after the trial of the ejectment and security had already been given there, which security however was only for 40*l* (*f*)

Proceedings were stayed till the costs of a former ejectment brought by the father of the lessor of the plaintiff against the defendant's father on the same title, were paid (*g*).

(*a*) 2 [illegible] Pr. [illegible] [illegible] (*f*) 1 Tidd's Prac. [illegible]
[illegible] R. [illegible] Eje. [illegible] [illegible] (*g*) 2 T R 64

But, excepting such instances, and that of a former ejectment, the Court will not compel the lessor of the plaintiff to give security for the costs.

Therefore, a rule was refused, for the lessor of the plaintiff to give security for the costs of an ejectment depending. *Buller* J said—The application is not warranted by any authority. There are only three instances in which the Court will interfere on behalf of a defendant, to oblige the plaintiff to give security for his costs. The first is when an infant sues, then the Court will oblige the *prochein amy*, or guardian, or attorney, to give security for the costs: secondly, where the plaintiff resides abroad, in which case the Court will stay proceedings till security be given for the costs: and thirdly, where there has been a former ejectment, but there the rule is to stay the proceedings in the second ejectment till the costs of the former are paid, and not till security be given for the costs of the second (*a*).

Though a Court may stay proceedings in a new ejectment until the costs of a former ejectment between the same parties, and also the costs of an action for mesne profits dependant thereon, are paid; yet they will not extend the rule to include the damages in the action for the mesne profits, however vexatious the proceedings of the present lessor of the plaintiff may have been (*b*).

Particulars of the Breaches.—In ejectment brought on the forfeiture of a lease, the Court will compel the plaintiff to deliver a particular of the breaches of covenant on which he intends to rely.

So, if the plaintiff declare generally, and the defendant have any doubt what lands the plaintiff means to proceed for, he may call upon him by a judge's order to specify them (*c*).

On the other hand, the plaintiff may call upon the defendant to specify for what he defends, when that is not ascertained by the consent rule.—But, in general, the injury complained in actions for wrongs is stated in the declaration, and therefore in such actions, it is not usual to make an order for the particulars: circumstances may, however, occur, which render it necessary (*d*).

Of the Plea and Issue, &c.

The general rule in the issue of this action is, that whatever bars the right of entry is a bar to the plaintiff's title. The plaintiff must, therefore, prove seisin within twenty years in himself or his ancestors, or must prove seisin in a third person, of a particular estate in the land, and that he claimed within twenty years after the reversion accrued, or that he or [illegible] was an infant, feme covert, *non compos*, imprisoned, [illegible]

(*a*) [illegible] 235. [illegible]
(*b*) [illegible]

beyond the sea, at the time when the title accrued, and that he claimed within twenty years after he came of age, &c or otherwise became a free agent by such disability ceasing. for every plaintiff in ejectment must shew a right of possession as well as of property, and therefore the defendant need not plead the statute of limitations, as in other actions (*a*)

A fine and non-claim, or a discent cast, which takes away the entry, are good pleas in this action, in bar of the plaintiff's right of entry (*b*)

So, an accord with satisfaction is a good plea, for it is an action of trespass in its nature (*c*).

So, by permission of the Court, the defendant may plead to its jurisdiction which permission the Court will grant before judgment *nisi* against the casual ejector (*d*).

Antient demesne, therefore, may be pleaded · but application to plead it must be made within the first four days; and there must be an affidavit, stating that the lands are holden of a manor, which is antient demesne; that there is a Court of Antient Demesne regularly holden; and that the lessor of the plaintiff has a freehold interest (*e*).

The opinion of the Court, touching this plea, was pretty clearly manifested in a motion for leave to plead, it being denied by reason of sufficient ground not being shewn to support it: on which occasion Mr. J. *Foster* observed, that as it was agreed to be necessary to ask the leave of the Court to plead this plea to a declaration in ejectment, it followed of course that it must be in the discretion of the Court either to grant or refuse their leave; and he thought that the affidavit in the principal case was not sufficient to oust that Court of its jurisdiction. He spoke of these Courts of Antient Demesne as putting people out of the protection of the law, and fitter to be totally destroyed than to be favoured and assisted. Mr J. *Wilson* said, it was a strange, wild jurisdiction, where the jurors are judges both of law and of fact, and ignorant country fellows are to determine the nicest points of law, and therefore he was not for granting such leave unless compelled by authority. Indeed, if the case is brought strictly within the rule, then the leave *must* be granted we cannot help it. The authorities down from *Alden's* case [5 *Co.* 105.] to this time, it is true, are "That antient demesne is a good plea in ejectment" But if you would oust this court of jurisdiction, you must shew "that another court has jurisdiction." Now this affidavit does not shew "that there are suitors in the other court," nor "that these lands are holden of a manor, which manor is holden in antient demesne:" whereas, if the lands only, and not the manor, are antient demesne, the matter cannot be tried in the

(*a*) Run Eject 234. (*b*) [illegible] 2[illegible] (*c*) Ibid (*d*) [illegible] B. R. 197 2 Sell Pract 18[illegible]
(*e*) [illegible]'s Pract 573 8 T R 47[illegible]

court of that manor. The affidavit ought to have shewn "That the lands are holden of a manor, which manor is antient demesne." It cannot be tried "Whether the lands themselves are antient demesne." Doomsday will not shew this. Doomsday will only shew whether the manor is so or not. The form of the plea makes this as clear as the sun. It ought also to be shewn that the lessor of the plaintiff has a freehold. How can he sue there in ejectment as a lessee of a term? Upon such a strange, wild jurisdiction as this, and upon such an affidavit, I am not for giving the defendant leave to plead this plea. Rule discharged (*a*).

In every such plea, therefore, the defendant must state another jurisdiction: as, if an action be brought here for a matter arising in *Wales*, to bar the remedy sought here, the jurisdiction in the Court in *Wales* must be shewn, and in every case to repel jurisdiction here, the party must shew a more proper and sufficient jurisdiction elsewhere (*b*).

Pleas either in bar or in abatement of the action are now, however, seldom, if ever, pleaded: for, according to the modern practice, the defendant, if he appear, is generally bound by the consent rule, to plead the general issue of not guilty: but where an ejectment was intended to try the right to a rectory, the defendant was admitted to plead that he himself was rector, and to traverse the rectorship of the plaintiff's lessor, in order by that means to bring the right in question (*c*).

For the most part, however, the defendant can plead the general issue only: which is therefore usually left, with the consent-rule, at the Judge's chamber, or the Prothonotary's to plead, and then judgment may be entered for want of a plea, as in other actions, without a special motion in Court for the purpose (*d*).

The present practice of delivering a declaration to the casual ejector before the Term, forces the defendant to issue the same Term (*e*).

In making up the issue, the first declaration must not be varied from, except in the defendant's name (*f*).

According to the words of the rule for judgment against the casual ejector, unless the tenant appears, a new declaration against him should in strictness be delivered before a plea in form can be required (*g*).

Where the name of the plaintiff's lessor was inserted in the body of the plea (as the person complaining) instead of that of the nominal plaintiff, judgment signed against the casual ejector under the idea that the plea was null and void was set aside, with costs, as irregular (*h*).

(*a*) 2 Bl. [illegible] 8 T. R. [illegible] Rep. [illegible] 2[illegible]8 [illegible]
(*c*) [illegible] (*e*) [illegible] (*f*) 2 L[illegible] 1411. (*g*) 2 [illegible] Pr. 18[illegible]
(*h*) [illegible]

A new defendant in ejectment may give a rule to reply and *non-pros* the plaintiff, who being nominal, can have no costs (*a*).

If the plaintiff after issue and before trial enters into part of the premises, the defendant at the assizes may plead it as a plea *puis darrien continuance*: nor is it in the discretion of the judge to reject it or not; but he is bound to receive it, it is made part of the record, and the trial is stopped, for the plaintiff cannot reply to it at the assizes (*b*).

Death of the Plaintiff.—The death of the plaintiff in ejectment shall not abate the action, especially if another person of the same name reside on the lands; for the Court will take notice that it is the lessor of the plaintiff that is concerned in interest (*c*).

As the plaintiff has a right to proceed both for the possession and the trespass, the death of the lessor, though he be only tenant for life, is no abatement; nor can it be pleaded *puis darrien continuance*, because the right is supposed in the lessee: and though the possession cannot be obtained, yet the plaintiff has a right to proceed for damages and costs; all that the Court can do, is to oblige him to give security for costs, when the lessor is dead (*d*). But if in such case the plaintiff is nonsuited for want of defendant's appearing and confessing, the executor of the lessor shall have no costs taxed on the common rule (*e*).

Of Defendant.—If one of several defendants die after issue joined and before verdict, the death should be suggested on the roll before trial, and a *venire* awarded to try the issues between the survivors.—Yet when the *venire* was awarded against both, and the verdict was against both, upon suggesting the death of the one upon the roll after verdict, the plaintiff had judgment for the whole against the other (*f*).

Of either Party.—If either party die after the commencement of the assizes, though before trial, it is within the stat. 17 *C.* 2. *c.* 28. made perpetual by 1 *J.* 2. *c.* 17. *s.* 5. whereby it is enacted, That in all actions personal, real or mixed, the death of either party between the verdict and judgment shall not be alleged for error, so as such judgment be entered within two terms after verdict.—If judgment be signed, though it be not entered on the roll within two terms after verdict, it is sufficient (*g*).

Of the Evidence.

In this action the legal title must prevail: nor is there any difference in this respect between the case of an ejectment brought by a trustee against his *cestui que trust* and any other person (*h*): the plaintiff cannot recover, but upon the strength of his own title; he cannot found his

(*a*) 2 Bl. R. 763. [illegible] 1 M. [illegible] 272.
(*d*) 2 S[illegible] 1769. (*e*) 2 [illegible] 193.
(*f*) Bu[illegible]
(*g*) 7 T. R. [illegible]

claim upon the weakness of the defendant's title, for possession gives the defendant a right against every man who cannot shew a good title. Therefore though the defendant have no title in himself, if he prove a title out of the lessor, it will be sufficient and any person in possession of an estate as tenant, or devisee, may it seems bring in a bill in equity to discover the title of a person bringing an ejectment against him, to have it set out and seen whether that title be not in some other (*a*).

Thus, in ejectment by landlord against tenant whose lease is expired, the latter is not barred from shewing that his landlord's title is extinct (*b*).

But when defendant would prove a title out of the lessor, it must be a subsisting one; for the mere production of an antient lease, though for a thousand years, will not be sufficient, unless he likewise prove possession under it within twenty years (*c*)

So, if the defendant produce a mortgage deed, the interest upon which has not been paid and the mortgagee never entered, it will not be sufficient to defeat the plaintiff, claiming under the mortgagor: because it will be presumed that the money was paid at the day, consequently it is no subsisting title. But if the defendant prove interest paid upon such mortgage, after the time of redemption, and within twenty years, it will be sufficient to nonsuit the plaintiff (*d*).

The true question in an ejectment is who has the possessory right.

Thus, where the tenant's title accrues prior to that of the lessor of the plaintiff, the latter cannot succeed in this action, and this, even though, (where he claims under an *elegit* subsequent to a lease granted to the tenant in possession,) he gives the tenant notice that he does not mean to disturb his possession, only wishing to get into the receipt of the rents and profits of the estate (*e*)

So, a satisfied term may be presumed to be surrendered; but an unsatisfied term, raised for the purpose of securing an annuity, during the life of the annuitant, cannot, but it may be set up as a bar to the heir at law, even though he claim only subject to the charge (*f*)

It has however been resolved by Lord *Mansfield* and many of the Judges, never to suffer a plaintiff in ejectment to be nonsuited by a term standing out in his own trustee, or a satisfied term set up by a mortgagor against a mortgagee; but to direct the jury to presume it surrendered The rule is to be understood thus that the trust estate shall not be set up in an ejectment to defeat the *cestui que trust* in a clear case, in such case, where the trust is perfectly clear and manifest, the rule stands upon strong and beneficial principles, because an ejectment

(*a*) Bull. N. P. 110. 1 Ves. 249. (*b*) 4 T. R. 682. (*c*) Bull. N. P. 110.
(*d*) Ibid. (*e*) 5 T. R. 2. (*f*) 2 T. R. 68[illegible]

the question is, who is entitled to the possession (*a*). But if the trust be doubtful, a Court of law will not decide upon it in an ejectment (*b*).

So where a legal term was created for a particular purpose, if that purpose were satisfied, or if it were unsatisfied and not connected with the litigating parties, it shall never be set up between them in ejectment, but shall be considered as if it had never been created (*c*).—In laying down this rule, Lord *Mansfield* observed, that "Where a trust term is a mere matter of form, and the deeds mere muniments of another's estate, it shall not be set up against the real owner: it is therefore settled that a satisfied trust shall be taken to be a trust for the benefit of the heir at law. A trust shall never be set up against him for whom the trust was intended. It is a mere form of conveyance, and it is admitted, that where the term is in trust for the benefit of the lessor of the plaintiff, the defendant shall not set it up in ejectment as a bar to his recovery (*d*).

"To go a step farther third persons may have titles, and therefore the Court say, that where there is a tenant in possession under a lease which is a bar to the recovery of the lessor, he being to recover by the strength of his own title, yet to prevent this from being turned improperly against the person entitled to the inheritance whose right is not disputed by the tenant, if the lessor dispute the property only against another, and give notice to the tenant that he does not mean to disturb his tenancy, the Court will never suffer the tenant to set up the lease as a bar to the recovery (*e*).

"There is another distinction to be taken; whether supposing a title superior to that of the lessor of the plaintiff exists in a third person, who might recover the possession against him, it lies in the mouth of the defendant to say so in answer to an ejectment brought against himself by a party having a better title than his own (*f*). I found this point settled before I came into this Court, that the Court never suffers a mortgagor to set up the title of a third person against his mortgagee for he made the mortgage, and it does not lie in his mouth to say so, though such third person might have a right to recover possession. Nor shall a tenant who has paid rent, and acted as such, ever set up a superior title in a third person against his lessor in bar of an ejectment brought by him, for the tenant derives his title from him" (*g*).

Consonant to this principle, it was held that in an ejectment brought by a second mortgagee against the mortgagor, the defendant shall not give in evidence the title of the first mortgagee in bar of the second, because he is barred to aver contrary to his own act, that he had no-

(*a*) Doug. 721. 4 T. R. 682. 7 T. R. 2. (*b*) 7 T. R. 47. (*c*) 1 T. R. 758. (*d*) Ibid. [illegible] 759. (*e*) Ibid. 760. (*f*) Ibid. (*g*) 3 Salk. 152. Cowp. 601. 1 H. Bl. 2[illegible]

title in the lands when he took upon him to convey by the second mortgage (*a*).

Also, where a lessee for years had got possession of some mortgage deeds, and endeavoured to set up that title against the mortgagor: though it shewed that the plaintiff had no right to recover as against the second mortgagee, yet he was permitted to recover against the defendant in that instance, and the decision was acquiesced under (*b*).

So, the surrenderor before admittance is considered as a trustee for the surrenderee, and therefore is not permitted to set up a formal objection against the plaintiff's recovering that property which he holds for his benefit (*c*).

So, that though as a general rule, it is true, that the plaintiff in this action must recover by the strength of his own title, constant exceptions to the rule have notwithstanding been admitted (*d*).

There is an equity for the landlord, against whom judgment had been obtained in ejectment by his own negligence, to restrain his tenant, and those to whom he had attorned, from setting up the lease against his ejectment, though a year and three quarters of the term were unexpired, and it is not necessary that the ejectment should be brought before the bill actually filed (*e*).

Where several matters are necessary in order to establish a complete title, the plaintiff must prove all those requisites.

Therefore, in an ejectment for a rectory, if the plaintiff prove the taking of the tithes only, and not an entry into the glebe, he will be nonsuited. For the plaintiff ought to prove that his lessor was admitted, instituted and inducted, and that he has read and subscribed the thirty-nine articles, and declared his assent and consent to all things contained in the book of Common Prayer. But he need not prove a title in the patron; for institution and induction upon the presentation of a stranger are sufficient to bar him who has right in ejectment, and to put the rightful patron to his *quare impedit*: but presentation ought to be proved, and institution would not of itself be sufficient evidence of it, though it were recited in the letters, especially if induction or possession have not followed.—Whether proof of a verbal presentation would suffice, seems doubtful (*f*).

The books of an incumbent, respecting his tithes, may be evidence for his successor. This is the almost only instance in which the law permits the private *memoranda* of a person deceased to affect the rights of third parties (*g*).

So also, if an ejectment be brought by the assignees for lands which may have come to the bankrupt after his bankruptcy, and before the al-

(*a*) B. N. P. 110. (*b*) 3 T. R. 760. in n. (*c*) 1 T. R. 397. &c.
(*d*) Ibid. (*e*) 10 Ves. 544. (*f*) Lutch 62. B. N. P. 105.
(*g*) 3 T. R. 129. 2 Vez. 43. [illegible]

lowance of the certificate, they should give in evidence a special conveyance of this part (*a*).

Reasonable presumption, however, will be admitted in favour of a title (*b*).

Therefore where a prebendary brought this action to recover a house built upon his prebendal scite, the prebendary being called to prove the several requisites necessary by the stat 13 *Eliz.* c 12. and 13 & 14 *C* 2 c 4 the Chief Justice said, "Those shall be presumed upon sound principles of law" (*c*)

So, where the lessor claims as heir at law, as for instance of *A.* it is sufficient to prove that *A* was in possession, and that the lessor is his heir, for it shall be intended, *primâ facie*, that *A* was seised in fee, till the contrary appear (*d*), and, if there be an agreement before marriage, that a settlement shall be made of the wife's estate, reserving to her a power to dispose of it, which agreement is signed by the intended husband and wife, but not sealed, and before the marriage the wife disposes of it to the husband, who survives her and devises the estate by will, the title of his devisee is such a doubtful equity as cannot be set up in an ejectment against the title of the wife's heir at law (*e*)

So, where plaintiff produces an original lease of a long term and proves possession for seventy years, the mesne assignments shall be presumed (*f*).

However, as to the doctrine of presumption which has considerable weight in the scale of evidence, this general principle must be attended to namely, that, generally, length of time alone is nothing but presumption must arise from some facts or circumstances arising within that time (*g*) for there are two sorts of presumption, one a presumption of law, not to be contradicted, the other a species of evidence; and there can be no presumption of the nature of evidence in any case, without something from whence to make it, some ground on which to found the presumption —Every presumption may be encountered, or to speak more technically, rebutted, by contrary evidence which in the case of executors, is called rebutting an equity; as the implied revocation of a will for example, may be rebutted by parol evidence (*h*)

Thus, a demise of premises in *Westminster*, late in the occupation of *A* particularly describing them, part of which was a yard, does not pass a cellar situate under that yard, which was then in the occupation of *B* another tenant of the lessor, and the lessor in an ejectment brought to recover the cellar is not estopped by his deed from going into evidence to shew that the cellar was not intended to be demised (*i*)

In ejectment, the landlord having proved payment of rent by the de-

(*a*) 2 Fox. M. P. 43[illegible] (*b*) Run. Eject. 311 (*c*) Run. Eject. 276

(*d*) 7 T. R. [illegible]88 (*e*) 2 T. R. 6[illegible]4 (*h*) 2 P. Wms 1072 [illegible]

(*e*) [illegible] 366. (*f*) 2 Bl. R. 1228 (*g*) 1 T. R. 701

fendant, and half a year's notice to quit given to him, cannot be turned round by his witness proving on cross examination, that an agreement relating to the land in question was produced at a former trial between the same parties, and was on the morning of the then trial, seen in the hands of the plaintiff's attorney, the contents of which the witness did not know, no notice having been given by the defendant to produce that paper for though it might be an agreement relative to the land it might not affect the matter in judgment, nor even have been made between these parties (*a*).

This being an action of trespass, the ward or place mentioned in the declaration, is material.

Thus, in ejectment for a house in the parish of St. *Peter*, in the ward of *Cheap*, the defendant proved it to be in the ward of *Farringdon Within*, and that no part of the parish of St. *Peter* was in the ward of *Cheap*, and the plaintiff was nonsuited (*b*).

But if the plaintiff declare on a lease of a certain date, though his proof do not establish the lease as declared on, yet if he prove a good and subsisting lease at the time, it will be sufficient (*c*)

As where the declaration was on a lease made the 14th of *January*, 30th of *Eliz* and the evidence was a lease sealed the 13th of the same year, the evidence was held to be good, for if it was a lease sealed the 13th, it was a good lease on the 14th (*d*)

The rules respecting notice to quit, before a tenant at will, or more correctly speaking, a yearly tenant, can be ousted of his possession, and what will amount to a waiver of it pointedly apply to the present subject; for a tenancy must be determined before the day of the demise laid in the declaration, we refer the reader for information on these points to the seventh chapter of this work, where they occur as connected with the tenancy from year to year

Notice to determine a composition for tithes must be the same as between landlord and tenant (*e*).

If a man gets into possession of a house to be let, without the privity of the landlord, and they afterwards enter into a negotiation for a lease, but differ upon the terms; the landlord may maintain ejectment to recover possession of the premises, without giving any notice to quit (*f*).

An ejectment is a possessory action, in which almost all titles to land are tried (*g*) —Whether the party's title be to an estate in fee, fee tail, for life, or for years, the remedy is by one and the same action, and it is now almost the only remedy in practice for recovering land wrongfully withheld (*h*).

In this action, therefore, titles to lands arising under wills are tried. —These for the most part are cases brought by the heir at law against

(*a*) 12 East's R 237. (*b*) 1 Str 595. (*c*) 2 Esp N P. 459 (*d*) 4 Leon 14
(*e*) 2 Br R 161. (*f*) 2 Campb 505 (*g*) 1 Bur. 90. (*h*) 2 Bur. 667.

the devisee, or against the person who claims to be heir at law, on the ground of bastardy, or by a devisee claiming an estate under a will.

Where one brings an ejectment as heir at law, he ought properly to make a regular pedigree from the ancestor under whom he claims mere report of relationship, or supposition, are not sufficient, for if such evidence were admitted, the estate might be carried contrary to the rules of descent; as for example, to the paternal, instead of the maternal line (a).

The entry of the heir is necessary only, where the lands were in the actual occupation of his ancestor · for if they are held under a lease for years, and the lessee had entered under his lease, the heir will be considered as having a seisin in deed, before entry and receipt of rent, because the possession of the lessee for years is his possession (b).

In ejectments against devisees, or their heirs, the matter turns on the due execution of the will, on the testator's capacity to devise (c); or on the legality of the devise itself and though in order to effectuate the intention of a devisor, a greater latitude of construction is allowed by the Courts in the case of a will than in the construction of deeds (d), yet, words tending to disinherit the heir at law are insufficient to prevent his taking, unless the estate be given to somebody else (e) For it is a rule, that the heir at law is not to be disinherited without positive words in the will, or a plain intention in the devisor that he shall be so, to be collected from the words of the will (f).

The defendant in ejectment is entitled to the general reply, where the plaintiff, claiming by descent, proves his pedigree and stops, and the defendant sets up a new case in his defence, which is answered by evidence on the part of the plaintiff (g).

As this action sometimes turns upon the question of marriage, it may be observed, that marriages in fact may be proved either by the register or a copy of it, or by [illegible] evidence of the ceremony corroborated by circumstances identifying the parties (h). It is not necessary, however, to prove a marriage in fact a reputed marriage will be sufficient, and that may be substantiated by cohabitation, reputation, or other circumstances, from which a marriage may be inferred (i) and whoever wishes to impeach a marriage, must shew wherein it was irregular (k).

With respect to cohabitation, it is the practice to admit evidence of what the parties have been heard to say as to their being or not being married (l

In this action, therefore, proof of marriage differs from that required in a dower, in which latter action it must be tried by the bishop's certi-

(a) 2 Bl R 1099 (b) 1 Cruise's Dig [illegible] 1 s 39 1 East 15 a 3 Wils 521 7 T R 39[illegible] 8 T R. 215 (c) 2 Esp N P 467 (d) 8 T R 519 (e) Ibid 502 (f) Ibid 582 (g) 4 T R 497 (h) [illegible] 357 (i) 4 Burr 2058 (k) Ibid 360 (l) Bull. N. P. 294

ficate. However, except in cases of actions for criminal conversation, (which are in some sort penal in their nature) and prosecutions for bigamy, (in both of which an actual marriage must be proved), reputation is a good proof of marriage, and the jury may infer it from circumstances (*a*).

If the lessor of the plaintiff claim title as guardian *in socage*, he may be called upon to prove that the infant is not fourteen years of age (*b*).

In ejectment of tenants of the mortgagor, he defended, and the plaintiff proved the mortgage only, which proof was held not to be sufficient; for he should have proved the lands to be in possession of the persons to whom the ejectments were delivered, as the defendant only admits himself to be landlord to them of lands in their possession (*c*).

If tenant by *elegit* be lessor of the plaintiff, it will be necessary for him to prove the judgment, the *elegit* taken out upon it, and the inquisition and return thereupon, by which the land in question is assigned to him (*d*): and if by that it appear, that more than a moiety was extended, he cannot recover, for it would be *ipso facto* void, and not need a judgment or *audita querela* to avoid it (*e*).

So, in ejectment by the conusee of a statute-merchant, he must prove a copy of the statute, and of the *capias si facias* returned, and the extent also returned, and also the *liberate* returned, for though by the return of the extent an interest is vested in the conusee, yet the actual possession of the interest is by the *liberate* for an extent gives only a possession in law (*f*).

In ejectment for a copyhold on a forfeiture, the plaintiff ought to prove that his lessor is lord and the defendant a copyholder, and that he committed a forfeiture, but the presentment of the forfeiture need not be proved, nor the entry or seisure of the lord for the forfeiture (*g*).

If an ejectment be brought against the lessee for years of a copyholder (relying upon the lease as a forfeiture) the plaintiff must prove an actual admittance of the copyholder, and it will not be sufficient to prove the father admitted and that it descended to the defendant's lessor as son and heir, and that he had paid quit rents; for a copyholder cannot make a lease except to try a title, before admittance and an actual entry, and therefore if after admittance he were to surrender without making an actual entry, the surrender would be void (*h*).

The recital of the will in the copy of the admittance, is good evidence of the devise against the lord or any other stranger. But if the suit be between the heir of the copyholder and the devisee, the will itself ought to be produced (*i*).

(*a*) [illegible] W... 122. 125. 2 Str. 96[illegible]. [illegible] R. [illegible] 1 H. R. [illegible] R. [illegible]
(*b*) [illegible] R. [illegible] 225. (*c*) 2 Sell P. [illegible] 218. 2 [illegible] P. [illegible]
(*d*) [illegible] N. [illegible] (*e*) [illegible] 1 Ld R. [illegible] 28 (*f*) [illegible] N. P. [illegible]
(*g*) [illegible] (*h*) [illegible] (*i*) [illegible]

Whether copyholds are within the statute against fraudulent conveyances, and therefore the plaintiff claiming under a voluntary conveyance shall prevail against a defendant claiming under a subsequent purchase for a valuable consideration, is doubtful (*a*).

If the trustees of a public turnpike act, which empowers them to erect toll-houses and to mortgage, and which declares that there shall be no priority among the creditors, have made a mortgage of the toll houses and gates, which is not within their power, and an ejectment is brought against them by the mortgagee, they are not estopped by their deed from insisting that the Act gives them no such power (*b*); for the general principle, that the party granting is estopped by his deed to say that he had no interest, does not apply where trustees are acting not for their own benefit, but for that of the public; besides the deed cannot operate in direct opposition of an Act of Parliament which negatives the estoppel, and this being a Public Act, the Court are bound to take notice that the trustees had no such power (*c*).

Witnesses.—With respect to witnesses, in general a witness must testify from his own knowledge of the fact which he is called upon to prove; but he may assist his memory as to the circumstance, by *memoranda* taken at the time; yet if he does not speak from any recollection which he has, but merely from such *memoranda*, the original minutes must be produced by him at the time of examination (*d*).

The tenant is incompetent to prove the fact of possession, for he cannot be permitted to support his own possession, by his own testimony; besides he is liable for the mesne profits (*e*).

But where a witness produced to prove the lease was objected to because he had the inheritance in the land demised, it being answered that both parties claimed under the same person, he was admitted to give evidence; for under circumstances between indifferent persons, and where he has not any interest in the question, the landlord is a competent witness to prove the terms of his own demise (*f*).

In an action at the suit of a tenant claiming a right of common over a piece of waste land against the owner of an adjoining close, for not repairing an intervening fence, the landlord under whom the plaintiff holds the premises in respect of which he claims the right of common is not a competent witness to prove the right. Neither in such an action are others who have a similar right of common, competent witnesses for that purpose (*g*).

Declarations by tenants are admissible evidence after their death, to shew that a certain piece of land is parcel of the estate which they occupied, and proof that they exercised acts of ownership in it (not

(*a*) Bull. N. P. 108. Doug. 716. n. 1 Cowp. [illegible] (*b*) 2 T. R. 169. (*c*) Ibid. 171.
(*d*) Run. Eject. 293. (*e*) Cowp. 622. 1 Str. 652.
(*f*) 3 T. R. 309. Run. Eject. 251. 1 T. R. 4. (*g*) 1 Campb. 290.

resisted by contrary evidence,) is decisive.—Whether parcel or not, is always matter of evidence (*a*).

So, where the plaintiff claimed as devisee in remainder under a will twenty seven years before, under which there was no possession, declarations by the tenant who was in possession at that time, that he held as a tenant to the devisor, were admissible evidence to prove seisin in the devisor (*b*).

So, a grantee, when he appears to be a bare trustee, is a good witness to prove the execution of the deed to himself (*c*).

An heir apparent may be a witness concerning the title of the land, but the remainder-man cannot, for he has a present estate in the land, but the heirship of the heir is a mere contingency. So, tenant-in-tail, remainder in-tail, he in remainder cannot be a witness concerning the title of these lands, for he has an estate, such as it is (*d*).

In an action at the suit of a lessor against his lessee, for not cultivating the farm according to covenants contained in the indenture of lease, the sub-lessee of part of the premises is a competent witness to prove performance of the covenant on part of the defendant (*e*).

As to executors, an executor may be a witness in a cause concerning the estate, if he have not the surplusage given him by the will (*f*). It is clear therefore, that an executor in trust may be a witness; and it is now held to be no objection to an executor's testimony, that he may be liable to actions as executor *de son tort*. So an executor who takes not any beneficial interest is a competent witness to prove the sanity of his testator (*g*).

A person who had sold the inheritance without any covenant for good title or warrantry was allowed to be a witness to prove the title of the vendee (*h*).

Husband and wife cannot in any civil case be admitted as witnesses for or against each other: this is now considered as a settled principle of law (*i*).

A clerk of the Post Office accustomed to inspect franks for the detection of forgeries, was allowed to be examined to prove the handwriting of an instrument to be an imitated and not a natural hand, and also to prove that two writings suspected to be imitated hands were written by the same person (*k*). But, in a subsequent case, where similar evidence was offered to be produced, L. *Kenyon* said he could not receive it, and observed, that though such evidence was received in the preceding case, he had in his charge to the jury laid no stress upon it (*l*).

The furthest extent, his Lordship observed, to which the rule had

(*a*) 2 T. R. 53. (*b*) Ib. 55. (*c*) 1 P. Wms. 287, 290. (*d*) [illegible] 223.
(*e*) 1 [illegible] 341. (*f*) 1 Mod. 107. (*g*) Doug. 139, 141. (*h*) 1 [illegible] 223.
(*i*) 1 T. R. 678. 2 T. R. 2[illegible]. (*k*) 4 T. R. 497. (*l*) Peake [illegible] Evid. 1[illegible].

8

been carried, was to admit a person who had been in the habit of holding an epistolary correspondence with the party to prove his handwriting, from the knowledge which he acquired in the course of that correspondence; a case reported by *Fitzgibbon*, (195) was the first in which such evidence was admitted. That evidence was admitted on sound principles, for if, where letters are sent, directed to a particular person on particular business, an answer is received in due course, it is a fair presumption, that the answer was written by the person whose handwriting it purports to be: but the franks [proof of which was in question,] might be the defendant's handwriting, or they might be forgeries, for no communication on the subject of the action [a bill of exchange having on it the supposed acceptance of the defendant] was had with the defendant (*a*)

With respect to the objection of interest, which if substantiated applies to the competency of a witness, if a person who is interested, execute a surrender or release of his interest, he may be examined as a witness, although the party refuse to accept the surrender, or release: for every objection of interest proceeds on the presumption that it may bias the mind of the witness, but this presumption is taken away by proof of his having done all in his power to get rid of the interest (*b*).

An objection to the competency of a witness should be first made at the trial (*c*), for if made then, it may be shewn to have been released, or otherwise done away: therefore on motion for a new trial, no objection to a witness can be received, which was not made at the trial. Nay, an objection to the competency of witnesses discovered after trial, is not sufficient ground, of itself, for granting a new trial, though it may have some weight, if the applicant appears to have merits: and though the objection appears properly made at the trial, yet in case of doubt, it is usual to apply to the credit, rather than the competency of a witness (*d*).

Respecting the weight, as evidence, of a survey of lands, it is laid down generally by Lord C. B *Gilbert*, that an old terrier or survey of a manor, whether ecclesiastical or temporal, may be given in evidence, for there are no other ways of ascertaining the old tenures or boundaries (*e*)

Accordingly, the survey of a religious house, taken in 1563, was allowed to be good evidence to prove the vicar's right to small tithes (*f*).

But this opinion seems to relate, with regard to terriers, to such as are signed, not only by the parson, but by the churchwardens and

(*a*) Peake's L. of Evid 176 (*b*) Doug 141. (*c*) Ibid 140
(*d*) 1 T R. 719 Run Eject. 252. Bl R. 345 (*e*) 1 Str 95 *in notis*.
(*f*) 1 Wils 17[illegible]

substantial inhabitants of the parish, or at least by the churchwardens, not being of the parson's nomination: and, in respect of surveys, to such as are signed by the tenants of the manor, or appear to have been made at a court of survey. For then, being of a public nature, they cannot be supposed to have been framed and attested to serve the private interest of any individual: upon which principle also, court rolls, or at least parish books are admitted in evidence, when the rights of third persons are concerned (*a*).

But surveys, although of a private nature, have been admitted in evidence, where circumstances could be adduced to shew the improbability of their being taken to serve any interested purpose in the maker. — Thus, where two manors were in the hands of the same person, and a survey was to be taken, and afterwards one of them was conveyed to another person, and after a long time there were disputes between the lords of the two manors, this old survey was held to be evidence. So an old map of lands was allowed to be evidence, as when it came along with the writings and agreed with the boundaries [illegible] (*b*).

But where a terrier or survey is not attended with such circumstances, and is the mere private memorial of the party for whom it is made, it is [illegible] inadmissible as evidence against him (*c*).

Where a landlord has a right to enter for non-payment of rent, he cannot recover in ejectment at common law, unless he demand the rent on the day on which it became due; nor under the statute 4 G. 2. if sufficient distress be on the premises (*d*).

Of the verdict. With respect to the verdict, the plaintiff shall recover according to the title that he makes out, though not consistent with that stated in the declaration: for the true question in an ejectment is, who has the possessory right (*e*).

Therefore, where the plaintiff declared on a demise for seven years, but had title to five only, he recovered according to his title notwithstanding (*f*).

So, the plaintiff may recover as many acres as he proves title to, though he declare for more; and though the declaration goes for several things, and there is a general verdict; though the declaration be bad as to part, yet the plaintiff may recover for the remainder (*g*).

As, where ejectment was "for one messuage or tenement and four acres of land to the same belonging," the words "to the same belonging," were held to be void; for land cannot properly belong to a house, and then it is as a declaration of a messuage or tenement, and four acres of land, which though it be void for the first, it is good for

(*a*) 1 Wils. 170. (*b*) Ibid. (*c*) Ibid.
(*d*) 7 T. R. 117. (*e*) Bull. N. P. 106. (*f*) Ibid. 3 T. R. 13.
(*g*) [illegible] N. P. 420. 1 B[illegible] 330.

the land: whereupon the plaintiff released the damages and for the four acres had judgment (*a*).

In a recovery for ejectment of one hundred acres of land, twenty of pasture, &c. without mention of any house or garden, it was nevertheless held that the plaintiff should recover all the erections thereon (*b*).

The maxim however that *cujus est solum, ejus est usque ad cœlum et ad inferos*, does not apply in every case: for it has been adjudged, that the demise of premises in *Westminster*, late in the occupation of *A.* particularly describing them, part of which was a yard, did not pass a cellar situate under that yard which was then in the occupation of *B.* another tenant of the lessor (*c*).

A verdict cures a defect in setting out the title, though it cannot cure a defective title (*d*).

After verdict, if the objection be grounded upon the mere mistake of the clerk, or a trifling nicety, there is no need of any actual amendment at all: the Court will overlook the exception (*e*).

This distinction therefore must be attended to: if there be only evidence at the trial upon such of the counts as are good and consistent, a general verdict may be altered by the notes of the Judge, and entered only on those counts; but if there be any evidence applicable to the other bad or inconsistent counts, the *postea* cannot be amended: the only remedy then is by a *venire de novo* (*f*).

After verdict in ejectment for a messuage and tenement, the Court will give leave to enter the verdict according to the Judge's notes for the messuage only, pending a rule to arrest the judgment, without obliging the lessor of the plaintiff to release the damages (*g*).

Of the Judgment.—The judgment in ejectment is a recovery of the possession, (not of the seisin or freehold) without prejudice to the right as it may afterwards appear, even between the parties. He who enters under it, in truth and substance can only be possessed according to right, *prout lex postulat*. If he has a freehold, he is in as a freeholder; if he has a chattel interest, he is in as a termor; and in respect of the freehold, his possession enures according to right. If he has no title, he is in as a trespasser, and without any re-entry by the true owner, is liable to account for the profits (*h*).

Where the plaintiff declares for the whole of certain premises of which he recovered a moiety only, the judgment should not be for a moiety only, but that the plaintiff recover his term, and he must take out execution for no more than he has a right to recover (*i*).

The judgment is either against the casual ejector, or against the te-

(*a*) Cro. Eliz. 180. (*b*) Dyer, 47, a. 1 Lev. [illegible] (*c*) 1 T. R. 701, *et vide* [illegible]
(*d*) 3 Wils. 275. 1 H. Bl. 561. 6 T. R. 168. (*e*) 3 Wils. 275. (*f*) Run. Eject. [illegible]
(*g*) 8 East, 357. (*h*) 1 Burr. 114. (*i*) Ibid. 326. 366.

ment, upon a verdict, the former is generally before, the latter always after an appearance (*a*).

The casual ejector can in no case confess a verdict (*b*).

If judgment be regularly signed, but without loss of trial, it may be set aside on payment of costs, and taking notice of trial (*c*).

When the landlord is admitted defendant instead of the tenant, the judgment is entered against the casual ejector with a stay of execution till further order if the landlord be afterwards nonsuited for not confessing lease, &c. or if a verdict be given against him upon the trial, the plaintiff must move for leave to take out execution against the casual ejector (*d*), and the day of shewing cause against the motion is the proper time for the landlord to make his stand against the plaintiff's taking out execution and getting into possession It has however been held, that he may bring a writ of error, which would be a sufficient reason against taking out execution (*e*).

The plaintiff cannot have judgment against the casual ejector, till common bail is filed.

When the plaintiff is nonsuited at the trial for want of the defendant's confessing lease, &c he is not entitled to sign judgment against the casual ejector, till the *postea* comes in on the day in bank (*f*).

Of the Damages.—The damages in ejectment are merely nominal, the recovery of the term being the object of the action.

Where an action of ejectment and an action of assault and battery were joined in the same writ, after verdict it was moved in arrest of judgment, because the battery was joined with the ejectment, and the damages being entire, the plaintiff could not release the damages in the battery, to take judgment, and the execution in ejectment The reason is, that where the damages are entire, it does not appear that the plaintiff recovered by any title in ejectment, and therefore it cannot be seen by the Court, whether those two actions were not originally joined, in order that the plaintiff might have a recovery in one to save his costs in the other. But where the damages are given severally, it appears that the plaintiff had a title in both cases, and therefore if he release his damages in battery, which was misjoined with the ejectment, there is no reason why he should not take his judgment in ejectment for though the Court must judge the joinder of the action to be bad, where it appears to be a contrivance to save costs, which is the mischief of joining different actions, yet where there appears to be good cause in both cases, the joinder of the action is cured by the release, for the plaintiff should have judgment according to his right (*g*).

(*a*) [illegible]
(*b*) [illegible]
(*c*) 1 Str. 531.
(*d*) 2 Str. 1241.
(*e*) Run. Eject. [illegible]
(*f*) 2 T. R. [illegible]
(*g*) [illegible]

Of the Costs.—Incident to the judgment are the costs, or expences of the action, which are therefore, as next in order to be treated of.

If the tenant do not appear, and judgment be consequently entered against the casual ejector, the plaintiff has no other remedy for his costs, than by his action for the mesne profits, in which they are recoverable against the tenant, as consequential damages (*a*).

But if the tenant appear, and be made defendant, under the usual terms of confessing lease, *&c.* and afterwards at the trial, refuses to make that confession, he is liable, upon the rule by which he was made defendant, to the payment of costs, which if not paid, an attachment lies against him and this is all the remedy which the plaintiff has for his costs if he be nonsuited by the defendant not confessing lease, *&c.* If the tenant appear, confess lease, *&c* and a verdict be given against him upon the trial, the judgment is entered against the tenant, on which judgment the plaintiff may take out execution, as in ordinary cases. for this is not a case provided for by the rule (*b*).

Where a verdict is given for the defendant, or the plaintiff be non-suited for any other cause than that of not confessing lease, *&c* the defendant must tax his costs on the *postea*, as in other actions; and sue out a *capias ad satisfaciendum* for the same against the plaintiff, which he must shew, under seal, to the plaintiff's lessor, and at the same time serve him with a copy of the consent rule, then if the lessor being required, refused to pay the costs, the Court, on motion, will grant an attachment against him (*c*)

Though the plaintiff in ejectment be but nominal, yet if he be not found, or be not able to pay the costs, the attorney is liable, and may be committed until he pay them, or produce a sufficient plaintiff (*d*).

So, if a stranger carry on a suit in another's name, who has title, and yet is so poor that he cannot pay the costs: in case he fail, the Court, on affidavit of the circumstances, will order the person who carried on the suit to pay costs to the defendant (*e*)

So, where baron and feme were lessors, and the baron died after entering into the rule, the feme was notwithstanding held liable to the payment of costs: because they were to be paid by the lessors of the plaintiff, and both of them were in the lease

If the plaintiff has a verdict in ejectment, and costs are taxed, and an attachment issues for non-payment of them, the defendant shall not have an ejectment against the plaintiff, in the same Court, till he has paid those costs; and the Courts consider an ejectment in another, in the same light as a former ejectment in the same Court and will stay proceedings in a new ejectment till the costs of the former be paid, as

(*a*) Run Eject 144 (*b*) Ibid 415. (*c*) Ibid 416 (*d*) 6 Mod. 309
(*e*) Run. Eject. 417

well where the former ejectment was in another, as where it was in the same Court.

Proceedings in ejectment were stayed by the Court of Common Pleas, after a long delay, the day before trial, till the costs of a former ejectment in the King's Bench were paid (*a*).

So, proceedings were stayed in an ejectment by a fraudulent assignee of an insolvent debtor, till the costs of former ejectments brought by the debtor himself were paid (*b*).

So, proceedings were stayed even till the costs were paid of a former ejectment, in which the lessor of the plaintiff never entered into the consent rule (*c*).

Yet where a verdict in a former ejectment had been for the plaintiff, who upon the defendant bringing the action against him, prayed for costs before he should be compelled to plead to the new action, it was denied, because the verdict being for him, he had no vexation: but if it had been against him, or he had been nonsuited, he should not have brought another action before the costs of the first had been paid, because it was a vexation to bring a new action (*d*).—No new ejectment, however, can be brought by the defendant after a recovery against him, till he has quitted the possession, or the tenant have attorned to the plaintiff (*e*).

Where the lessor of the plaintiff was in custody under an attachment for non-payment of costs in a former ejectment, and brought a new ejectment upon the same demise, the Court refused to stay proceedings therein, till the costs of the former should be paid (*f*).

In ejectment against several, the plaintiff has his election to pay costs to which of the defendants he pleases (*g*). But if the defendants fail, each of them is answerable for the whole costs (*h*).

By stat. 8 & 9 *W.* 3. *c.* 11. in ejectment against several, if any one or more is acquitted by verdict, he shall recover his costs against the plaintiff, unless the Judge shall certify in open Court that there was good cause for making such person a defendant.

This being an action of trespass, if the judge before whom it is tried shall certify under his hand on the back of the record, that the freehold or title of the land came chiefly in question, though the damages are under 40*s.* there shall be the full costs. This is enacted by stats. 43 *Eliz. c.* 6. 21 *J.* 1. *c.* 16. 22 & 23 *C.* 2. *c.* 9. *s.* 136.

Of the Execution.—Touching the execution of the judgment, as the plaintiff in ejectment recovers only the possession of the property in question, execution of course is of the possession only (*i*).

The plaintiff having judgment to recover his term, may enter with-

(*a*) 2 Bl. R. 1153. (*b*) Ibid. 1181. (*c*) Ibid. 904. (*d*) 4 Mod. 379.
(*e*) Salk. 258. Run. Eject. 420. (*f*) Ibid. (*g*) 1 Str. 516.
(*h*) Bull. N. P. 335. (*i*) Run. Eject. 424. 1 Bur. 92. 339.

out suing out a writ of execution, which is called an *habere facias possessionem*, for where the land recovered is certain, the recoverer may enter at his own peril, and the assistance of the sheriff is only to preserve the peace (*a*).

The usual and regular way however is to make out a writ of *habere facias possessionem*, which being engrossed, signed, and sealed, and a *præcipe* being made out for it, is carried to the office of the sheriff, who issues out a warrant thereon, and will put the lessor of the plaintiff in possession (*b*). It has relation to the *teste*, therefore if *tested* the last day of the preceding term, may be sued out though the lessor of the plaintiff be since dead (*c*).

The plaintiff must take care not to take out execution for more than he hath recovered; and in order that the sheriff may not be under any difficulty in executing the writ of possession, the practice *now* is for the plaintiff himself not merely to point out to the sheriff, that of which he is to give him possession, in execution of the writ, but to take possession himself of that only to which he has title; for should he take more than he has recovered and shewn title to, the Court will, in a summary way, set it right (*d*).

Therefore, where the plaintiff in ejectment, as tenant in common, recovered possession of five-eighths of a cottage, with the appurtenances, and a writ of possession was executed by the sheriff, who turned the tenant out of possession of the whole and locked up the door, as appeared by affidavit. *Curia*.—This is wrong; the writ ought to have pursued the verdict. Let there be a rule upon the sheriff, and the lessor of the plaintiff to restore the tenant to the possession of three-eighth parts of the premises; otherwise he would be forced to bring another ejectment for the same (*e*).

If there are several messuages in possession of different tenants, the sheriff must go to all their houses and turn them out: the delivery of the possession of one tenement in the name of all, is not sufficient (*f*).

The words of the writ being *quod habere facias possessionem*, there must be a full and actual possession given by the sheriff, and consequently all power necessary for this end must be given him; if therefore the recovery be of a house, the sheriff may justify breaking open the door, if he be denied entrance by the tenant, because the writ cannot be otherwise executed (*g*).

If the officer be disturbed in the execution of the writ, the Court will, on affidavit of the circumstances, grant an attachment against the party whether he be the defendant or a stranger, for a recent ouster is a contempt; and the process is not understood to be executed complete-

(*a*) 2 Sell. Prac. 202. (*b*) Ibid. (*c*) 4 Bur. 1970. (*d*) Run. Eject. 432. 1 Bur. 366. Ind. 629. 5 Bur. 2673. (*e*) 3 Wils. 49. (*f*) 2 Sell. Pract. 203. 2 Roll. Ab. 886. (*g*) 5 Co. 91. b.

ly, till the sheriff and his officers are gone, and the plaintiff left in quiet possession (*a*).

If therefore the sheriff turns out all persons he can find in the house, and gives the plaintiff, as he thinks, quiet possession, and after the sheriff is gone, some persons appear to be lurking in the house, that is no good execution, and the plaintiff, it is said, shall have a new *habere facias possessionem* (*b*).—The new writ cannot issue, until the return of the first be expired (*c*).

An attachment was granted absolute in the first instance, against the tenant in possession, on affidavit that he had been served with a rule of Court made absolute for delivering up the possession, and had refused so to do (*d*).

The law seems, however, to make a difference where, after possession given either on the *habere facias*, or by agreement of the parties, the plaintiff is turned out of possession by the defendant, and where by a stranger. When it is done by the defendant himself, the plaintiff may have either a new *habere facias*, or an attachment, because the defendant shall never, by his own act, keep the possession which the plaintiff has recovered from him by due course of law. But where a stranger turns the plaintiff out of possession, after execution fully executed, the plaintiff is put to his new action, or to an indictment for the forcible entry, by which means the force will be punished.—The reason is, that the title was never tried between the plaintiff and the stranger, who possibly may claim the land by a title paramount to that of the plaintiff, or he may come in under him, and then the recovery and execution in the former action ought not to hinder the stranger from keeping that possession to which he may have a right. Were the law otherwise, the plaintiff might, by virtue of a new *habere facias*, turn out even his own tenants who come in after the execution is executed, whereas the possession was given him only against the defendant in the action, and not against those who were not parties to the suit (*e*).

If the execution go to the sheriff for twenty acres, he must give twenty acres, according to the common estimation of the country where the lands lie (*f*).

As the plaintiff, however, is to shew the sheriff the premises to which he has title and to take possession rightly at his peril, such a very exact description is not necessary in this action, as in a *præcipe*. An issue has been directed to try whether the sheriff had delivered possession properly, according to the recovery (*g*).

At this day, the practice is, for the plaintiff to give the sheriff secu-

(*a*) 6 Mod. 27. Salk. 322. (*b*) Leon. 145. (*c*) Run. Eject. 43[illegible]
(*d*) 2 Bl. R. 8[illegible]2. (*e*) 1 Keb. 779. 785. (*f*) Roll R. 41[illegible].
(*g*) 1 Bur. 36[illegible]. 5 Bur. 26[illegible].

rity to indemnify him from the defendant, and then for the sheriff to give execution of what the plaintiff demands (*a*).

A judgment irregularly obtained was set aside, and the possession that had been given upon the execution ordered to be restored: but the lessor of the plaintiff (who held the possession) absconding, the rule became ineffectual; whereupon it was moved on behalf of the late tenants, for a writ of restitution, which the Court awarded accordingly (*b*).

If the plaintiff neglect to sue out his writ of possession for a year and a day after judgment, he must revive the judgment by *scire facias*, as in other cases; else the Court will award a restitution *quare erronice emanavit*; unless the stay of execution be by consent of the parties for the year, not for less time, *com. sem.* or the defendant brings error and is afterwards nonsuited (*c*).

But if the delay be by injunction of the Court of Chancery there must be a *scire facias*, for an injunction not being a matter of record, a Court of law will not take notice of it: unless the party has taken out execution within the year, and continued it down by *vicecomes non misit breve*, which may be done without a breach (*d*).

If the plaintiff die within a year and a day, his executors cannot take out execution without a *scire facias*, for they are not parties to the judgment: though if execution has been regularly sued out in the life-time of the testator, the sheriff may execute it after his death, because the authority is from the Court, and not from the party (*e*).

If after judgment and before execution, the defendant in ejectment dies, and a *scire facias* goes, it must be against the terre-tenants of the land (and the heir may come in as terre-tenant), and not against the executor, without naming him terre-tenant (*f*).

Where the landlord is admitted to defend on the tenant's non-appearance, and judgment is thereupon signed against the casual ejector, with a stay of execution till further order, the lessor of the plaintiff having succeeded must apply to the Court for leave to take out execution, and in such case, if a writ of error be brought by the landlord, it may be shewn for cause, and will be a sufficient reason, against taking out execution: but if the landlord omit the opportunity of shewing it for cause, the execution is regular, and cannot be set aside (*g*).

Of the Writ of Error.

By the consent rule, as has been before observed, the defendant undertakes to appear and receive a declaration: the necessity, therefore, of

(*a*) Run. Eject. 434. (*b*) 2 S[illegible] (*c*) 2 Ld Raym. 806. Salk. 258. S. C. 6 Mod. 2[illegible]3. 2 Sell. Prac. 204. (*d*) 1 Str. 301. Salk. 322. 6 Mod. 288. (*e*) Run. Eject. 429. (*f*) 2 Sell. Prac. 204. Cro. Car. 295. 312. (*g*) Tidd's Prac. 909.

an original writ, if the proceedings are in the Common Pleas, is superseded; because as the tenant is to appear and receive a declaration, he cannot take advantage of the want of an original, unless in a writ of error but when a writ of error is brought, the plaintiff must file an original, unless it be after verdict, when it is helped by stat 38 *Eliz.* *c.* 14. (*a*).

As in the Common Pleas there is no need of an original (which also is the case in the King's Bench when the proceedings are by original), so in the King's Bench when the proceedings are by bill, there is no necessity for a *latitat*, or bill of ejectment but the party must file bail before he can proceed. He must also file a bill of ejectment besides the plea roll, in case a writ of error be brought, before errors are assigned. The reason is, that the Court has no authority to proceed in ejectment by bill, unless the defendant be in custody, therefore, by the rule, bail is ordered to be filed, that the Court may have authority to proceed (*b*)

The casual ejector cannot bring error, being a mere nominal person that writ therefore can only be brought after the defendant has appeared, and confessed lease, entry, and ouster (*c*)

So, if the landlord be permitted to defend, a writ of error cannot issue in the name of the casual ejector (*d*)

But on a writ of error from an inferior Court, in the name of the casual ejector, the Court will not order a *non pros* to be entered, though his release of errors be shewn, because inferior Courts are not competent to proceed, as before observed, by a rule confessing lease, &c. (*e*).

So, if an infant be tenant in possession, and judgment be against the casual ejector; because no laches is imputable to an infant (*f*)

The plaintiff having brought a writ of error in Parliament, the Court obliged him to enter into a rule not to commit waste or destruction during the pendency of the writ. The defendant did not oppose it, and also justified (to 400*l.*) (*g*)

By stat. 16 & 17 *C.* 2 *c* 8 *s.* 7 it is enacted, That no execution shall be stayed by writ of error upon any judgment after verdict in ejectment, unless the plaintiff in error shall become bound in a reasonable sum to pay the plaintiff in ejectment all such costs, damages, and sums of money, as shall be awarded to such plaintiff upon judgment being affirmed, or on a nonsuit, or discontinuance had, and in case of affirmance, discontinuance, or nonsuit, the Court may issue a writ to enquire as well of the mesne profits, as of the damages by any waste committed after the first judgment, and are therefore to give judgment, and award execution for the same, and also for costs of suit.

(*a*) Run. Eject. 204 (*b*) Ibid (*c*) 2 Sell Pract. 205 2 Bur 757
(*d*) Ibid (*e*) Run. Eject. 421. (*f*) Ibid. (*g*) 3 Bur. 1823.

This "reasonable sum" is generally double the rent

Under this statute the defendant is entitled by law to his writ of error, if he offers to become bound as the statute directs.

Therefore, where the lessor of the plaintiff swore that the defendant was insolvent, and also that he, the lessor, had a mortgage upon the land to more than it was worth, yet the Court held that the defendant was entitled to his writ of error, he becoming bound in double the rent (*a*).

Nothing shall be assigned for error that will make it necessary to go again into the title of the premises (*b*)

Of the Action of Ejectment where the Possession is vacant —Where a Corporation is Lessor of the Plaintiff: —and Where the Action is commenced in an inferior Court

As the old method of proceeding in this action, by sealing a lease on the premises, must still be resorted to in these cases, we have thought proper to notice them as a detached article

If the premises, the possession of which the plaintiff seeks to recover, be empty, no declaration of course can be delivered or affidavit made of the delivery of it, and consequently the Court cannot proceed to give judgment against the casual ejector (*c*).— In such case therefore the old way of proceeding must be still pursued, except in the single instance of landlord and tenant, provided for by stat. 4 G. 2 of which hereafter (*d*)

This is done by entering on the premises, and actually sealing a lease thereon, either in person or by attorney.

If the former method is preferred, the proceeding is thus:

A (the person claiming title,) must go upon the land before the essoin day of the term, and there seal and deliver a lease to *B.* (any friend of his, as tenant,) and at the same time deliver him possession. This being done, get *C.* (any other friend) to go upon the premises, and turn out *B* the tenant, by thrusting him off the premises, and whilst he continues there serve him with a declaration in ejectment, in which make *B.* the tenant plaintiff, *A* (the person claiming title) the lessor, and *C.* (the actual ejector) the defendant, and declare on the demise in the lease and subscribe a notice to appear (*e*).

The declaration is the same as usual, only the real persons are made parties, instead of fictitious names (*f*)

In order to get judgment in the Court of King's Bench, an affidavit

(*a*) 4 Bur. 2501. (*b*) [illegible] 5. (*c*) [illegible] 248. (*d*) 2 Sell. Pract. 213
(*e*) Ibid. (*f*) Ibid. 214

must be made of sealing the lease, and of the ouster by defendant, and of all the facts. This is indorsed to move for judgment against the casual ejector, and unless defendant appear and enter into the common rule, judgment may be signed as on a common ejectment.—In the Common Pleas, there is no need of any affidavit, nor any motion for judgment, but on the first day of term, give a rule to plead as in common actions, and if no appearance and plea, at the expiration of the rule, sign judgment (*a*).

If the landlord, or person claiming title, does not wish to enter himself and seal the lease, he may do it by attorney, and the proceedings are just the same; the attorney acting as the principal landlord (*b*).

To warrant the above proceedings, the premises must be vacant, they must be wholly deserted by the tenant, and the lessor of the plaintiff not be able to find out where the tenant is to serve him with an ejectment.

Therefore, where the lessee of a public-house took another and removed his goods and family, but left beer in the cellar, rent being in arrear, the landlord sealed a lease as on a vacant possession, delivered an ejectment, and signed judgment, it was set aside, the lessee still continuing in possession and a case was mentioned, where leaving hay in a barn at *Hendon*, was held to be keeping possession. It further appeared in this case, that the attorney for the plaintiff knew whither the lessee removed, and might have served him personally, which could not be done upon the premises.—So, in the case of a renting ground, to which there is no house or barn, if it be known where the tenant lives, he must be served (*c*).

In cases of a vacant possession, no person claiming title will be let in by the Courts to defend, but he that can first seal a lease on the premises must obtain possession. The person therefore claiming title must resort to his new ejectment (*d*).

But it is said that any person claiming title to the premises, and who is usually admitted by the Court, may with leave appear and enter into the common rule upon motion made for that purpose (*e*). But *quære* now?

Ejectment by a Corporation.—When a corporation is lessor of the plaintiff, they should regularly execute a letter of attorney authorizing some person to enter and seal a lease on the land, and a corporation cannot make an attorney or bailiff but by deed, nor appear but by making a proper person their attorney by deed.

As to whether the lease on which they declare need be by deed, it seems immaterial, for where the declaration stated the lease to have

(*a*) 2 [illegible] P. 214. (*b*) [illegible] P. [illegible] (*c*) 2 Str. 1064. (*d*) Bull. N. P. 9
(*e*) [illegible] K. B. 537. 2 [illegible] Pra. [illegible] 217

been made by the plaintiff under the common seal of the corporation, it was objected that the lease ought to be proved. but the objection was over-ruled by Lord *Kenyon*, who observed that, by common rule and appearance, the lease was admitted to be as stated (*a*)

If a corporation be aggregate of many, they may set forth the demise in the declaration without mentioning the Christian names of those who compose it, but if the corporation be sole, the name of baptism must be inserted, as if the demise be by a bishop (*b*).

Proceedings in an inferior Court.—Where the proceedings are in an inferior Court, the plaintiff must proceed by actually sealing a lease on the premises, and the defendant tries the title in the name of the casual ejector, to save expence: for inferior Courts are not competent to make rules to confess lease, entry and ouster, and if they were, have no power to enforce obedience to them. It seems therefore, that if the defendant in an inferior Court enter into a rule to confess lease, &c and the cause be removed by *habeas corpus*, and the Judge of the inferior Court grant an attachment against the defendant for disobedience to the rule, the superior Court will grant an attachment against the Judge for exceeding his authority and obstructing the course of the superior Court (*c*).

If an *habeas corpus* be brought to remove a cause in ejectment out of an inferior Court, the lands lying within their jurisdiction, and the lessor of the plaintiff seal a lease on the premises, the Courts above will grant a *procedendo*, because the title to the land is local, and therefore properly within the jurisdiction of the Court below, where, if it proceed regularly, it will not be prohibited: but if the lessor has not sealed a lease on the premises, the Courts above will not grant a *procedendo* (*d*).

So, if an ejectment be commenced in an inferior Court, and an *habeas corpus* be brought to remove it, and the plaintiff in ejectment declares against the casual ejector . there may be a rule to confess lease, &c as if he had originally declared in the Court above, and the Court will not grant a *procedendo* (*e*).

If the lands lie partly within the cinque ports, and partly without, the defendant cannot plead the jurisdiction of the cinque ports, above, for though the land be local, yet the demise is transitory, and triable any where and therefore though the plaintiff may lay his action for that which lies within an inferior jurisdiction in the Court below, if he take proper measures for the purpose, yet if he will proceed in a superior Court, as the demise is transitory, the defendant cannot stop his proceeding, because those Courts have competent jurisdiction (*f*).

(*a*) Run Eject 150 (*b*) Ibid (*c*) Run Eject 151, 152 (*d*) Ibid. 151 (*e*) Ibid (*f*) Ibid 152

F. [illegible]

Section III. *Of the Action for Mesne Profits.*

An ejectment being a feigned action, brought against a nominal defendant, and generally on a supposed ouster, is not a proper action for mesne profits, the action for which is wholly dependent upon facts, being brought against the real tenant, for profits which he has actually received. In the one case, therefore, the damages are merely nominal, in the other, they are such as the plaintiff has sustained by a real injury, and the fiction in the former, does not, in any manner, affect the latter (*a*). The verdict in ejectment having, in fact, established the right of the plaintiff from the time that his title accrued, the defendant is a trespasser, and the plaintiff is entitled to recover from him damages for his unjust possession, equal to the value of the lands during that time, though this point is not settled, but the *quantum* depends upon circumstances (*b*).

This action, therefore, results from the recovery in ejectment: it is an action of trespass *vi et armis*, brought by the lessor of the plaintiff, in his own name, or in the name of the nominal lessee (for it may be brought in the name of either) against the tenant in possession, to recover the value of profits unjustly received by the latter, in consequence of the ouster complained of in the ejectment (*c*).—It is usually brought by the lessor of the plaintiff in his own name, and in that case, on proving a good title in himself and an actual ouster and perception of profits by the defendant antecedent to the demise and ouster in ejectment, he will recover damages for those profits: they are seldom, however, an object of litigation, as the demise and ouster are generally laid soon after the time when the lessor's title accrued.

But the plaintiff is not bound to claim the mesne profits, only from the time of the demise: for if he prove his title to have accrued before that time, and proves the defendant to have been longer in possession, he shall recover antecedent profits (*d*).

In such case, however, the defendant will be at liberty to controvert the title, which he cannot do in case the plaintiff do not go for more time than is contained in the demise, because being tenant in possession, he must have been served with the declaration, and therefore the record is against him conclusive evidence of the title; but against a precedent occupier the record is no evidence, and therefore against such an one it is necessary for the plaintiff to prove his title, and also to prove an actual entry, for trespass being a possessory action, cannot be maintained without it (*e*).

(*a*) Run. Eject. [illegible]
(*c*) B. N. P. 87.
(*b*) 3 Bl. Com. 2[illegible].
(*d*) Ibid.
(*e*) Run. Eject. [illegible]

Yet as to actual entry, it may admit of doubt, what proof is sufficient (*a*).—It has been said that the plaintiff is entitled to recover the mesne profits only from the time he can prove himself to have been in possession, and that therefore if a man make his will and die, the devisee will not be entitled to the profits till he has made an actual entry; for that none can have an action for mesne profits unless in case of actual entry and possession (*b*). Others have holden (*c*), that when once he has made an actual entry, that will have relation to the time his title accrued, so as to entitle him to recover the mesne profits from that time; and they say, that if the law were not so, the Courts would never have suffered plaintiffs in ejectments to lay their demises back in the manner they now do, and by that means entitle themselves to recover profits, to which they would not otherwise be entitled: beside, the Court will intend every thing possible against the defendant (*d*).

Supposing, however, that a subsequent entry has relation to the time that the plaintiff's title accrued, yet certainly the defendant may plead the statute of limitations, and by that means protect himself from all but the last six years (*e*).

If one tenant in common recover in ejectment against the other, he may maintain trespass for the mesne profits (*f*).

Any one in possession of the premises after a recovery of them by action of ejectment is a trespasser and as such liable to damages, and he cannot cover himself under the licence of the defendant in ejectment, for no man can license another to do an illegal act. In this case, *Sellon*, Serj. moved for a new trial. It appeared that the plaintiff by an action of ejectment had evicted one *Mitchel* (who had been a tenant of his under an agreement for a lease), and had since brought an action against the present defendant, in which he had declared first in trespass *quare clausum fregit*, and in another count for money had and received, being in fact for the mesne profits. *Sellon* for the present defendant contended, that his client being in possession merely as the agent of *Mitchel*, who was in prison, was not liable to any action of trespass for the mesne profits, *Mitchel* himself being the only party to be looked to. But Lord *Kenyon* observed, that the plaintiff having recovered in ejectment against his tenant, any other party in possession was liable to be deemed a trespasser, and that, in action of trespass, damages ought to be given, though not amounting quite to the mesne profits. [illegible] (*g*).

If the action be brought in the name of the nominal plaintiff, the Court, on application, will stay the suit till security be given for indemnifying the costs, but will not permit such a plaintiff to release the

(*a*) [illegible] S. P. 87. (*b*) 1 Ven. 249. (*c*) 5 Mod. 384. (*d*) 3 Wils. [illegible] (*e*) [illegible] (*f*) [illegible] 121. (*g*) Gardner v. Porter, K. B. M. T. [illegible] MSS.

action; his release therefore has been set aside as a contempt of Court. and there is no distinction between a judgment in ejectment upon a verdict, or by default, for in the one case, the right of the plaintiff is tried and determined against the defendant, and in the other it is confessed (*a*).

This action may be brought pending a writ of error in ejectment and the plaintiff may proceed to ascertain his damages, and sign his judgment but the Court will stay execution till the writ of error be determined (*b*)

If the defendant bring a writ of error on the verdict against him in ejectment, and enter into a recognizance pursuant to the statute 16 & 17 *C.* 2. *c.* 8. to pay costs, the plaintiff on judgment in his favour on the writ of error, need not bring a *scire facias* or action of debt on the recognizance, but may sue out an *elegit* or writ of enquiry, to recover the mesne profits since the first judgment in ejectment (*c*).

The defendant in this action may be held to bail.

The declaration in this action for mesne profits must expressly state the several parcels of land, &c. from which the profits arose, or the defendant may plead the common bar (*d*)

The defects in a declaration in an action for mesne profits, in not stating any time when the defendant broke and entered the messuage, &c. and ejected the plaintiff from the occupation of it, and in stating only that the defendant kept and continued the plaintiff so ejected for a long space of time, without stating how long, are cured by the operation of the stat. 4. *Ann. c.* 16. after judgment by default, and a writ of inquiry of damages executed, so that no objection can be taken in arrest of final judgment for such defect in form (*e*).

In trespass for the mesne profits against the tenant in possession after a recovery in ejectment by default against the casual ejector, the tenant cannot pay the money into Court, for the action is for a tortious occupation from the time the tenant had notice of the title of the lessor of the plaintiff (*f*).

In trespass against the tenant in possession for mesne profits, either by the lessor or the nominal plaintiff, after recovery in ejectment the plaintiff need not prove a title; but it is sufficient to produce the judgment in ejectment and the writ of possession executed, and to prove the value of the profits, and thereupon he shall recover from the time of the demise laid in the declaration (*g*).

But if the judgment has been against the casual ejector, and no writ of possession executed, the defendant in possession may controvert the title, if he has not been made a defendant in the ejectment and had a

(*a*) Run. Eject. 439. Bull. N. P. 89. (*b*) 2 Sell. Prac. 226. (*c*) [illegible]
(*d*) 2 Cromp. Prac. 223. (*e*) 13 East, 407. (*f*) [illegible]
(*g*) Bull. N. P. 87. 3 Wils. 121. 1 T. R. 387.

verdict against him, and therefore the recovery in ejectment is not against him conclusive evidence (*a*).

In an action for mesne profits for one year, the declaration contained other counts for destroying fences, to which a justification was pleaded, and upon a new assignment, the general issue. An examined copy of the judgment in ejectment was proved. The trespass in respect to the fences was also proved, but the Judge (*Runnington*, Serjt.) being of opinion, that as it was committed while the defendant was in possession as tenant, the action was misconceived for that part, the jury by his direction gave no damages in respect thereof.—A rule for a new trial was obtained on the ground of the trespass having been committed after the defendant had ceased to be tenant to the plaintiff and after the recovery in ejectment; but that not appearing to be the fact, from the report as it was read from the Judge's note, the rule for a new trial was discharged (*b*).

A recovery in ejectment against the wife cannot be given in evidence against the husband and wife for mesne profits for in such case there is no evidence of the trespass but the judgment in ejectment, and the wife's confession of a trespass committed by her cannot be given in evidence to affect the husband in an action in which he is liable for the damages and costs (*c*).

Bankruptcy is no plea in bar to an action for mesne profits; for the damages occasioned by the tort are uncertain (*d*).

Where, after a recovery in ejectment and before an action of trespass for mesne profits, the defendant became a bankrupt, and the jury did not include the costs of the ejectment in their verdict in executing a writ of enquiry in the action for mesne profits, the Court refused to set aside the inquisition, because the plaintiff might have proved the costs as a debt under the defendant's commission of bankrupt (*e*).

Touching the *quantum* of damages given by the jury in this action, they are not to be bound by the amount of the rent, but may give *extra* damages indeed four times the value of the mesne profits have been known to be given in this sort of action of trespass (*f*)· and after judgment, by default, the costs in ejectment being recoverable are usually declared for as damages in this action for mesne profits (*g*).

The plaintiff can recover no farther costs in this action than were taxed in the ejectment, if it were regularly defended but it is otherwise if judgment was against the casual ejector (*h*).

(*a*) 2 Str 960 (*b*) M T 41 G 3 T's MSS (*c*) 7 T R 112
(*d*) Doug 584 (*e*) 2 T R 261 (*f*) 3 Wils 121.
(*g*) Bull N P. 88 (*h*) 1 Esp R. 358.

Section IV. *Of a second Action of Ejectment.*

A judgment in ejectment, it may be remembered, is a mere recovery of the possession without prejudice to the right [illegible], [illegible], is not final between the parties so as to protect either the defendant or plaintiff (if he succeeds) from any further suit; for the [illegible] plaintiff, if he be nonsuited, or have a verdict against him, may bring [illegible] ejectment against the same defendant, or if he succeeds in the [illegible] and gets possession, he is still liable to an ejectment from the defendant [illegible] in the former action [illegible].

This in one respect may be deemed an advantage, because the parties are not concluded by one trial, [illegible] perhaps, want of evidence, which might be [illegible] the case) happened not to be fully tried between them [illegible] another respect, much mischief may result from [illegible] litigation is thereby kept alive [illegible] (*b*).

The reason why an action of ejectment is not or cannot be final seems to be this: [illegible] is impossible, from the [illegible] of the record in this action, to plead [illegible] of another ejectment brought, [illegible] plaintiff and defendant [illegible] in most cases on record [illegible] and consequently may be changed [illegible] new action; but the identity both of plaintiff and defendant [illegible] be averred in pleading a former action [illegible] (*c*) [illegible] 2 The term demised may be laid many different ways. It has sometimes, indeed, been attempted in Chancery, after three or four ejectments, by a bill of peace to establish the prevailing party's title, yet it has always been denied: for every termor may have an ejectment, and every ejectment supposes a new demise, and the costs in ejectment are [illegible] recompence for the trouble and expence to which the possessor is put.—But where the suit begins in Chancery for relief touching pretended incumbrances on the title of lands, and that Court has ordered the defendant to pursue an ejectment at law, where after one or two ejectments tried, and the right settled to the satisfaction of the Court, the Court has ordered a perpetual injunction against the defendant, because there the suit is first attached in that Court, and never began at law (*d*), and such precedent incumbrances appearing to be fraudulent, and inequitable [illegible] the possession, it is within the compass of the Court to relieve [illegible] it [illegible].

As the costs of the ejectment are deemed the recompence [illegible] above stated (though in truth but a poor one) the Court will not [illegible] either

[illegible]

the plaintiff to bring a new ejectment, or the defendant to bring the ejectment against the successful plaintiff, until the costs of the former action are paid.—The Courts now consider a former ejectment in another Court, as one in the same Court, and will stay proceedings in a second till the costs of the former are paid (*a*).

So, though in such former ejectment the lessor of the plaintiff never entered into the consent rule, and where a rule for a new trial was obtained on the ground of the plaintiff having been nonsuited by reason of his inability to prove that the defendant had entered into the common rule to defend as landlord, the Court said, that as there had been a slip in the plaintiff not being able to prove the rule under which the defendant was let in to defend, though no blame was imputable to him as the objection could not be foreseen, yet the new trial must be on the common terms of payment of costs (*b*).—So, when an ejectment was brought by a fraudulent assignee of an insolvent debtor, the former lessor being plaintiff.—So, proceeding was stayed in error and a second ejectment, the plaintiff not being able to shew that the writ of error was brought with any other view than to delay payment of costs (*c*).

The remedy to enforce the payment of costs, after verdict, is by attachment.—But where the lessor of the plaintiff has been taken into custody upon an attachment for costs, which is in the nature of a *capias ad satisfaciendum*, there is no reason to grant the rule to stay proceedings in another action brought by the same lessor on the same demise (*d*).

So, where before trial a mistake is discovered, so as to render it necessary to serve a new ejectment, the Court will not stay proceedings till the costs of the first are paid; unless the party has been vexatious, or great expence has been incurred.

But if the lessor of the plaintiff be not known, the Court will order notice to be given where he may be found.—So, if the plaintiff loses the ejectment in one Court and brings a new action in the other (*e*).

Proceedings in a second ejectment were stayed till the special verdict in the former was determined (*f*).

When the plaintiff succeeds in an ejectment, the defendant cannot bring a new ejectment against him, until he has delivered up possession, or the tenants in possession have attorned, and, it should seem, till he has also paid the costs of the former action (*g*).

The Court will not give the plaintiff leave to discontinue after a special verdict has been had, in order to adduce fresh proof in contradiction to the verdict (*h*).

(*a*) 2 Sell. Pract. 2[illegible] [illegible] 3 K. B. [illegible] MSS.
(*d*) 2 Sell. Pract. 2[illegible]
(*f*) 2 Str. 1[illegible]
(*e*) 2 [illegible] D[illegible] [illegible] 1150 [illegible]
(*g*) 2 [illegible] 681 [illegible] 1121. [illegible] R. 4[illegible]
[illegible]

SECTION V. *Of the Action of Ejectment upon the Statute* 4 G. 2. c. 28 s. 2.

By the common law an actual entry, by the person claiming title to lands and tenements, was necessary to be made in order to support an action of ejectment, but in the case of a lease, the landlord could not enter and take the actual possession until the lease was expired: it therefore became usual to insert a proviso that in case the rent of the demised premises was behind and unpaid at a certain time, the lessor should have a right to re-enter. In parol demises, however, from year to year, the landlord could not have the benefit of such a proviso and when the right of re-entry subsisted, great inconvenience frequently happened to lessors or landlords in cases of re-entry for non-payment of rent, by reason of the many niceties that attended such re-entries at common law, and even when a legal re-entry was made, the landlord or lessor was put to the expence and delay of recovering in ejectment before he could obtain the actual possession of the demised premises (a) --It is therefore enacted,

By the 4th *G.* 2 *c.* 28. *s.* 2 "That in all cases between landlord and tenant, as often as it shall happen that one half year's rent shall be in arrear, and the landlord or lessor to whom the same is due, hath right by law to re-enter for the non-payment thereof, such landlord or lessor shall and may, without any formal demand or re-entry, serve a declaration in ejectment for the recovery of the demised premises, or in case the same cannot be legally served, or no tenant be in actual possession of the premises, may then affix the same upon the door of any demised messuage; or in case such ejectment shall not be for the recovery of any messuage, then upon some notorious place of the lands, tenements, or hereditaments, comprised in such declaration in ejectment, and such affixing shall be deemed legal service thereof, which service or affixing such declaration in ejectment shall stand in the place and stead of a demand and re-entry, and in case of judgment against the casual ejector, or nonsuit, for not confessing a lease, entry, and ouster, it shall be made appear to the Court, where the said suit is depending, by affidavit, or be proved upon the trial, in case the defendant appears, that half a year's rent was due before the said declaration was served, and that no sufficient distress was to be found on the demised premises countervailing the arrears then due, and that the lessor or lessors in ejectment had power to re-enter, in every such case, the lessor or lessors in ejectment shall recover judgment and execution in the same manner as if the rent in arrear had been legally demanded and

(a) Paine Land. & Ten. Laws 149

a re-entry made and in case the lessee or lessees, his, her, or their assignee or assignees, or other person or persons claiming or deriving under the said lease, shall permit and suffer judgment to be had and recovered on such ejectment and execution to be executed thereon without paying the rent and arrears, together with full costs, and without filing any bill or bills for relief in equity within six calendar months after such execution executed; then such lessee, &c. and all others claiming and deriving under the said lease, shall be barred or foreclosed from all relief in law or equity, other than by writ of error for reversal of such judgment in case the same shall be erroneous, and the said landlord and lessor shall from thenceforth hold the said demised premises discharged from such lease: and if on such ejectment, verdict shall pass for the defendant, or the plaintiff shall be nonsuited therein, except for the defendant's not confessing, &c. then such defendant shall recover his, her, or their full costs."

Proviso as to Mortgagees.—"Provided always, that nothing herein contained shall extend to bar the right of any mortgagee or mortgagees of such lease, or any part thereof, who shall not be in possession, so as such mortgagee or mortgagees, within six calendar months after such judgment obtained and execution executed, pay all rent in arrear, and all costs and damages sustained by such lessor, or persons, entitled to the remainder or reversion as aforesaid, and perform all the covenants and agreements which on the part and behalf of the first lessee or lessees, ought to be performed."

Of Proceedings in Equity.—By sect. 3 "In case the said lessee or lessees, his, her, or their assignee or assignees, or other person, claiming any right, title, or interest, in law or equity, of, in, or to the said lease, shall, within the time aforesaid, file one or more bill or bills, for relief in any Court of equity, such person or persons shall not have or continue any injunction against the proceedings at law on such ejectment, unless he, she, or they within forty days next after a full and perfect answer shall be filed by the lessor or lessors of the plaintiff in such ejectment, bring into Court, and lodge with the proper officer, such sum of money, as the lessor or lessors of the plaintiff in the said ejectment shall, in their answers, swear to be due and in arrear, over and above all just allowances, and also the costs taxed in the said suit, there to remain till the hearing, or to be paid out to the lessor or landlord, on good security, subject to the decree of the Court: and in case such bill or bills shall be filed within the time aforesaid, and after execution is executed, the lessor or lessors of the plaintiff shall be accountable only for so much, and no more, as he, she, or they shall really and *bonâ fide*, without fraud, deceit, or wilful neglect, make of the demised premises, from the time of their entering into the actual possession thereof; and if what shall be so made by the lessor or lessors of the plaintiff, happen to be less than the rent reserved on the said lease, then the said lessee or lessees, his, her, or their assignee or assignees, before he, she, or they shall be restored to his, her, or their possession or possessions, shall pay such lessor or lessors, landlord or landlords, what the money so by them made fell short of the reserved rent, for the time such lessor or lessors of the plaintiff, landlord or landlords, held the said lands."

Sect. 4. "Provided that if the tenant or tenants, his, her, or their assignee or assignees, shall at any time before the trial in such ejectment, pay or tender to the lessor or landlord, his executors or administrators, or his, her, or their attorney in that cause, or pay into the Court where the same cause is depending, all the rent and arrears, together with the costs, then all further proceedings in the said ejectment shall cease and be discontinued; and if such lessee, &c. or their executors, administrators, or assigns, shall, upon such bill filed as aforesaid, be relieved in equity, he, she, and they shall have, hold, and enjoy the demised lands according to the lease thereof made, without any new lease to be thereof made to him, her, or them."

Intent of the Statute.—The statute relates to ejectment for non-payment of rent, only where the landlord has a right to re-enter.—The true end and professed intention of the Act of Parliament is to take off from the landlord the inconvenience of his continuing always liable to an uncertainty of possession from its remaining in the power of the tenant to offer him a compensation at any time, in order to found an application for relief in equity, and to limit and confine the tenant to six calendar months after execution executed for his doing this; or else that the landlord should from thenceforth hold the demised premises discharged from the lease (a).

Courts of law do not lean against forfeitures, as Courts of equity relieve against them: therefore, where a landlord means to take advantage of any breach of covenant so as that it should operate as a forfeiture of the lease, he must take care not to do any thing which may be deemed an acknowledgment of the tenancy, and so operate as a waiver of the forfeiture; as distraining for the rent, or bringing an action for the payment of it, since the forfeiture accrued, or accepting such rent. So, an action for double rent on the same statute, will be barred by an acceptance of rent (b).

Therefore, where an ejectment has been brought on the stat. 4 *G.* 2. c. 28. *s.* 2. for the forfeiture of a lease, there being half a year's rent in arrear, and no sufficient distress on the premises; acceptance of rent afterwards by the landlord, has, it seems, been held a waiver of the forfeiture of the lease; which may well be: for it is a penalty, and by

(a) [illegible]

(b) B. N. P. 96. Cowp. 247. Co. 64.

accepting the rent, the party waives the penalty. Such acceptance of rent however must be with the knowledge of the forfeiture having been incurred; for otherwise it does not manifest any intention in the landlord to continue his tenant (*a*).

But though the tenant has incurred a forfeiture under the statute, yet he may stay proceedings either by tendering the rent before ejectment is delivered, or by moving for leave to pay into Court all the rent due and costs, at any time before the writ of possession is executed, even after judgment against the casual ejector (*b*).

Or it may be done by summons in vacation time.

Before the statute, proceedings would be stayed on bringing the rent in arrear and costs into Court, in an action whether of covenant or debt for rent; and it is not now confined to actions under the statute (*c*).

For, where in ejectment by a landlord, the tenant moved to stay proceedings upon payment of rent, arrears and costs. On a rule to shew cause, it was insisted for the plaintiff that the case was not within the Act, for that it was not an ejectment founded singly on the Act, but that it was brought likewise on a clause of re-entry in the lease for not repairing, and the lease was produced in Court. However the rule was made absolute, with liberty for the plaintiff to proceed upon any other title (*d*).

Where the rent was tendered before notice of the action [illegible] proceedings were set aside for irregularity; and the landlord having [illegible] directions respecting the matter to his attorney, was held to [illegible] to [illegible] (*e*).

The lessors of the plaintiff were both devisees and executors, and in each capacity rent was due to them. The defendant moved to stay proceedings on payment of the rent due to the lessors of the plaintiff as devisees, they not being entitled to bring an ejectment as executors. There appeared to be a mutual debt due to the defendant by simple contract, and the defendant offered to go into the whole account, taking in both demands as devisees and executors, having just allowances, which the lessors of the plaintiff refused. The rule was made absolute to stay proceedings on payment of the rent due to the lessors as devisees, and costs (*f*).

If the lease specifies that a demand of rent should be made, ejectment cannot be brought till such demand be made; but [illegible] such stipulation no demand is necessary; [illegible] that six months' rent should be in arrear, and no sufficient distress on the premises.— This statute, Lord *Mansfield* observed, [illegible] (*g*).

As to the question, whether an actual entry is necessary in order to maintain an ejectment on a clause of re-entry for non-payment of rent,

(*a*) Cowp. 247. [illegible] 2 Bl. R. [illegible] [illegible] 973.
(*b*) [illegible] 97. (*e*) 2 [illegible] R. 7 [illegible] (*f*) [illegible] Prac. 211.
(*c*) [illegible] 486. [illegible]

the better opinion has been, that it is not (*a*), for that an actual entry is only necessary to avoid a fine, or perhaps to prevent the operation of the statute of limitations, where tenant for life levies a fine, though it is no bar to those in remainder, yet it seems that a remainder-man must make an actual entry before he can maintain an ejectment; and where an entry is necessary, the demise must be laid after it (*b*)

In moving for judgment upon a declaration in ejectment delivered, or (in case of no tenant) affixed to the premises, according to the statute, the Courts require an affidavit that half a year's rent was in arrear before declaration served, that the lessor of the plaintiff had a right to re-enter, that no sufficient distress was to be found on the premises countervailing the arrears of rent then due, that the premises were untenanted, or that the tenant could not be legally served with the declaration (as the case is), and that a copy of the declaration was affixed on the most notorious (stating what) part of the premises else the Court will not grant a rule for judgment.—This affidavit is necessary only upon moving for judgment against the casual ejector, or after a nonsuit at the trial for the tenant's not confessing lease, entry, and ouster.

For, if the tenant appears, and the ejectment comes to trial, the matters averred in the above affidavit must be proved upon the trial (*c*).

Note The affidavit is necessary only in proceeding under the statute, but not on the common law proceeding (*d*).

The declaration in ejectment is prepared in the usual way, taking care to lay the demise after the forfeiture accrued (*e*).

The late tenant or other person, claiming title to the premises, has the same time to appear in as is allowed to tenants in possession (*f*).

After appearance the proceedings are the same as in other cases: therefore in case of no appearance, the plaintiff moves for judgment against the casual ejector on the affidavit above-mentioned, and proceeds as in ejectments at common law (*g*).

Thus, where the case comes within the statute, there is no occasion for the landlord to make an actual entry and seal a lease on the premises which, as we have before shewn, must be done in all other cases, where the premises are untenanted, nor is there any occasion to prove at the trial any actual entry or ouster; for if the defendant appear, the common consent rule is sufficiently binding (*h*)

The affidavit will in some cases be presumed, as after a long and quiet possession.

Thus where an ejectment was brought by a landlord against his tenant, under this statute, and judgment was had against the casual ejector by default, and possession thereupon delivered and nearly twenty

(*a*) Doug. 485 Salk 259 Bull N P 102 (*b*) 7 T R 433 (*c*) 1 Bur 620
(*d*) Ibid 618 (*e*) 2 Sell. Prac. 212. (*f*) Ibid. (*g*) Ibid.
(*h*) Doug 43

years after, the tenant brings an ejectment against the same landlord for the same premises. The landlord, who is defendant in this latter action, is not obliged to produce such an affidavit as this clause requires, as an essential requisite previous to his original recovery; for as it was essentially requisite, the Court will presume that such affidavit was regularly made at the time, and that the judgment was founded on it (*a*).

The landlord's remedy for rent in arrear, is by action for the mesne profits, which as has been before observed, is consequent to the action of ejectment, whereby the possession only is recovered (*b*).

If one pretending to have title to land give security to the tenants to save them harmless upon paying him the rent, and afterwards another recover in ejectment against them, they have no remedy upon the security until recovery of the mesne profits (*c*).

SECTION V. *Of the Remedy for the Landlord, under the Statute* 11 G. 2. c. 19. *where the Premises are vacant.*

The injury that the landlord would sustain in his profits by his lands lying fallow and his buildings going to decay, owing to the desertion of his tenant and the actual possession of the premises remaining in no one, is remedied by the stat. 11 *G.* 2. *c* 19 *s.* 16. which after stating that, "Whereas landlords are often great sufferers by tenants running away in arrear, and not only suffering the demised premises to be uncultivated without any distress thereon, whereby their landlords or lessors might be satisfied for the rent-arrear, but also refusing to deliver up the possession of the demised premises, whereby the landlords are put to the expence and delay of recovering in ejectments, enacts, That if any tenant holding any lands, tenements, or hereditaments at a rack-rent, or where the rent reserved shall be full three-fourths of the yearly value of the demised premises, and leave the same uncultivated or unoccupied, so as no sufficient distress can be had to countervail the arrears of rent, it shall and may be lawful to and for two or more Justices of the Peace of the county, riding, division, or place (having no interest in the demised premises), at the request of the lessor or landlord, lessors or landlords, or his, her, or their bailiff or receiver, to go upon and view the same, and to affix, or cause to be affixed, on the most notorious part of the premises, notice in writing what day (at the distance of fourteen days at least) they will return to take a second view there-

(*a*) 1 Bur. 618 (*b*) 2 Bur 668. (*c*) 6 Mod 222

of and if upon such second view, the tenant, or some person upon his or her behalf, shall not appear and pay the rent in arrear, or there shall not be sufficient distress upon the premises, then the said Justices may put the landlord or landlords, lessor or lessors, into the possession of the said deserted premises, and the lease thereof to such tenants, as to any demise therein contained only, shall from thenceforth become void."

[illegible] moved for a [illegible] directed to some magistrates of the county of [illegible], in order that they should proceed on s. 16 of the statute, to put a landlord into possession of some premises deserted by the tenant. He stated his case to be within the Act, and said the magistrates had refused to interfere, because the tenant was a [illegible]. L. *Kenyon*, on referring to the Act, asked whether the [illegible] on lease, and if there was a proviso for re-entering? [illegible]. Counsel answering in the negative, his Lordship said, in his opinion, the case was not within the Act. The preamble of the clause spoke of the expence and delay to which landlords were put in bringing ejectments, it seemed, therefore, to him, that the clause applied only to cases where the landlord could support an ejectment, as where there was a written lease with a condition to re-enter: if no such thing existed in this case, the magistrates had done right in refusing to interfere.— Rule refused (*a*).

Sect. 17. "Provided always, that such proceedings of the said Justices shall be examinable in a summary way by the next Justice or Justices of Assize of the respective counties in which such lands or premises lie, and if they lie in the city of *London* or county of *Middlesex*, by the Judge of the Courts of King's Bench or Common Pleas and if in the counties palatine of *Chester*, *Lancaster*, or *Durham*, then before the Judges thereof. and if in *Wales*, then before the Courts of Grand Sessions respectively, who are hereby respectively empowered to order restitution to be made to such tenant, together with his or her expences and costs, to be paid by the lessor or landlord, lessors or landlords, if they shall see cause for the same, and in case they shall affirm the act of the said Justices, to award costs not exceeding five pounds for the frivolous appeal."

Note. In this and all other the like cases, the Justices ought to make a record of the whole proceedings (*b*).

(*a*) East. T. 41 Geo. 3. T. v. Moss. (*b*) 1 Burn. tit. "Vagrants." [illegible]

CHAPTER XV.

Of the Remedies for and against Landlord and Tenant, (continued).

For the Landlord, for Breach of Covenants and Agreements other than for Rent.

SECTION I. By Action of Covenant.

SECTION II. By Action of Assumpsit.

SECTION I. Of the Action of Covenant.

AN action of covenant or *assumpsit*, according as the premises are demised by deed or not, lies for the recovery of damages for any injury sustained by the landlord in consequence of the tenant neglecting to repair the buildings, suffering trades to be carried on therein contrary to his covenant, treating the land in an unhusbandmanlike manner, or committing any other breach of the agreement.

An action of covenant cannot be maintained except upon a deed, and the declaration must shew that it is brought on one (*a*).

In the case of joint-lessees, if a lease be to *A* and *B.* by indenture, and *A* seals a counterpart, and *B* agrees to the lease, but does not seal, yet *B.* may be charged for a covenant broken, and this though the covenant be collateral, and not annexed to the land (*b*). The assignee of a term, however, is not liable on a mere collateral covenant (*c*).

So, if one party execute an indenture, it shall be his deed, though the other party do not execute it: but in order to make it necessary for the plaintiff to sue in covenant, the binding by deed ought to be mutual (except in the case of lessee of the King's [illegible]); for where a defendant has never sealed the indenture he cannot be sued in that form of action (*d*).

Touching the sealing of bonds or deeds, if it appear upon oyer

(*a*) 2 Ld Raym. 15[illegible]
(*b*) Cro. Jac. 43[illegible]
(*c*) C[illegible] 23[illegible]
(*d*) Co. Litt. 212. Cro. Jac. 24[illegible]

that two parties sealed it, whereas one only is sued, the law will not intend that the other sealed the deeds unless it be expressly averred that he did: and though the bond or deed upon oyer recite, "in witness whereof we have set our hands and seals," yet that does not amount to such an averment, but the defendant must shew that the bond or deed was actually sealed by the other (*a*).

There are, indeed, some words of art, such as "indenture," "deed," or "writing obligatory," which of themselves import that the instrument was sealed by the party without an averment of sealing. If, therefore, the declaration states that *J. S* by his "deed" did so and so, or by "indenture" covenanted or demised, or by his "writing obligatory" acknowledged, *&c.* without averring in either of these cases that he sealed, still the declaration is good. So, delivery, which is essential to a deed, is never averred (*b*).

But without such averment, or words of art, it is otherwise: for if it be alleged that *J S* by his "certain writing" simply, demised, or covenanted, or acknowledged, *&c.* without averring that he sealed, the Court will not intend that the writing was sealed (*c*). Neither does it follow, because the words "in witness whereof we do put our hands and *seals*," are used in the conclusion of an agreement, that therefore it was sealed by the parties: on the contrary, it has been decided that these words do not amount to an averment that the parties sealed the instrument (*d*).

Leaving the glass of windows cracked has been held to be a breach of covenant to repair.—So, not repairing a pavement is a breach of covenant to leave the premises sufficiently maintained and repaired: for it is within the intention of the covenant, and is *quasi* the building, and the not repairing may be matter of value and of such prejudice to the lessor.—So, carrying away a shelf, though not stated to be a fixture, has been held to be a breach of covenant to leave the premises in the same order, *&c.*: for it shall be intended to be fixed (*e*).

A covenant to repair during the term after three months' notice, and to leave the premises in repair at the end of the term, are distinct clauses: therefore notice is not necessary to sustain an action for non-repair at the end of the term, for the notice refers only to reparations within term, to which the lessee is not tied without notice three months before (*f*).

But a covenant to keep a house in repair from and after the lessor hath repaired it, is conditional, and it cannot be assigned as a breach that it was in good repair at the time of the demise, and that the

(*a*) 1 Sid. [illegible] r. 1. (*c*) [illegible]
(*b*) [illegible] (*f*) 1 Sa[illegible] 6[illegible]

lessee suffered it to decay; for the lessor must repair before the lessee is liable (*a*).

If a lessor covenants to let certain lands except such a close, a tortious entry by the lessee into the excepted close is said not to be a breach of a condition to perform all covenants contained in the lease (*b*).

Therefore if *H* lets a house, excepting two rooms, and is disturbed therein, covenant lies not: but if he had excepted a passage thereto, and had been disturbed in that, it would have lain; for it well lies for a thing which the lessee agrees to let the lessor have out of the demised premises (*c*).

If a copyholder in fee makes a lease for years warranted by the custom, in which the lessee covenants to repair during the term, a surrenderee of the assignee of the reversion may maintain covenant for non-repair against the original lessee, although he had assigned the term before the reversion was surrendered to the plaintiff: for a copyholder is within the stat. 32 *H.* 8. *c.* 34 (*d*).—The doubt in this case arose upon the tenure of the messuage, for if it had been freehold, it was agreed, the action might well have been brought by the assignee of a reversion against a lessee for years after he had assigned his term, notwithstanding the lessor or his assigns had accepted the rent from the assignee of the lessee; and this upon the general words of the statute which gives "the grantees and assignees of reversions of lands, tenements, and other hereditaments, the like advantage against lessees by entry for non-payment of rent as the lessors or grantors themselves might have." This clause, therefore, is not confined to a covenant for the payment of rent (*e*).

If a farm is out of repair in the life of the ancestor and afterwards the heir brings an action, he shall recover damages for the whole time, but he ought not to allege a breach in the ancestor's lifetime, because that belongs to the executor (*f*).

A recital of an agreement in the beginning of a deed will create a covenant, upon which this action will lie.

As, where on the demise of a coal mine, it was recited "that before the sealing of indenture it had been agreed that the plaintiff should have the third part dish, &c." on an action of covenant being brought on this, it was objected, that there was no covenant that the plaintiff was to have the third part: but per *Hale*—Were it but a recital that before the indenture they were agreed, it is a covenant; so, to say "whereas it was agreed to pay 20*l*." for now the indenture confirms the former agreement by such declaration, and makes it a covenant (*g*).

This action lies by the lessor against the assignee of the lessee's assignee for a breach of covenant that runs with the land, though he be

[illegible]

[illegible]

assignee of a part only of the premises demised; for he is liable while he enjoys (*a*).

A reversioner in fee of a house by one deed, and of a lease for years of land by another deed, may bring covenant on a lease against the person to whom both the house and land have been demised by the grantor of the reversions, although he derives his right from different titles (*b*).

Where this action was brought on a covenant "to permit the plaintiff, in the last year of the term, to sow clover among the defendant's barley," and the breach assigned was, that the defendant sowed so many acres with barley and so many with oats, without giving "notice" to the plaintiff, by which he was prevented from sowing the clover and grass seeds.—Plea, that the defendant did "not prevent," was upon demurrer holden good: for the covenant made no mention at all about any notice to be given: and the breach assigned, being the not permitting the plaintiff to sow grass seed, the single question was, whether the defendant did or did not prevent him? If, indeed, he had refused to give notice, or had given a wrong notice, it might have been a breach: besides, the plaintiff was the party for whose benefit the covenant was intended; therefore he ought to have used due diligence (*c*).

In covenant by an executor against a lessee, the declaration stated, that one seised in fee by will devised to *W. March* for life, remainder in tail to the said *W. M.* with power to grant leases for life reserving the best rent, that *W. M.* on *June* 9, 1773, granted to the defendant a lease for twenty years and a quarter: *W. M.* died and the premises descended to his son, who suffered a recovery, and conveyed them to the plaintiff's testator. The breaches were for non payment of rent, for not repairing, and for not putting dung upon the premises. The rent, by the *reddendum* of the lease, was 60*l. per ann.* but there was a covenant to render 64*l.* *Lawes*, of counsel for the plaintiff in error, observed, that the breach assigned was non-payment of 16*l* as a quarter's rent, which was more than the proportion of 60*l. per ann.* according to the *reddendum*. The last breach was for not laying dung upon the premises. The covenant was, that the dung should be laid each and every year during the continuance of the term. The fact was, that the plaintiff's testator purchased the estate only eight days previous to the expiration of the lease. Did his Lordship therefore think that he was entitled to the benefit of this covenant and could assign a breach for the non-expenditure of the dung which was to be laid every year upon the premises?—L. *Kenyon*, "Yes, beyond all doubt, if the testator were seised of the reversion during the continuance of the term." Judgment affirmed. The first objection as to the breach for non-payment

(*a*) [illegible] Cas. [illegible] (*b*) Cro. Ja. 329. (*c*) [illegible]

of rent was abandoned, it appearing that in the Judges copies of the paper-book, the rent reserved was 64*l*. The damages were assessed severally on each breach, which (the counsel observed), afforded a presumption that the defendant in error thought some of them not supportable (*a*)

The tenant is not estopped by the description of the lands in the lease.

Thus in covenant the plaintiff declared, that whereas he had demised to the defendant a house and several parcels of land, which were particularly described, some to be arable, some meadow, and some pasture, and especially two meadows, called *Lane's* meadows, the defendant covenanted to pay 5*l per* acre for every acre of meadow, which he should plough up during the lease, and breach assigned in ploughing up *Lane's* meadow, &c. Plea; that for sixty years past, *Lane's* meadow has been arable land, and by times ploughed up and sowed, as the tenants thereof thought proper, and traverse, that at the time of making the lease it was meadow ground, as is supposed in the declaration. To this the plaintiff demurred, on the ground that the defendant was estopped to say that what is in the lease called meadow, is of any other nature. *Sed per Curiam*; The indenture is to be construed according to the intent of the parties, and here the intention was only to covenant against the ploughing up real meadow. Every body knows that in deeds of this nature the parcels are very often taken from former deeds, without regard to every alteration of the nature of the land and it would be the hardest case in the world, that if this land had been arable at one time and laid down at another, the tenant should be concluded by calling it by either of those descriptions. This is not the essence of a deed, as what is struck at by *nil habuit in tenementis* It would be carrying estoppels too far should we extend them to this case; therefore we are all of opinion, that the defendant had a right to try the fact, whether it was antient meadow or not (*b*).

To breach of covenant for not repairing, &c. the lessee cannot plead in bar that the lessor had only an equitable estate in the premises, for that is tantamount to *nil habuit*, &c. But *Semb.* he is not estopped from shewing that the lessor was only seised in right of his wife for her life, and that she died before the covenant broken; because an interest passed by the lease (*c*).

An assignee in covenant need not name himself assignee where he shews a legal assignment (*d*)

Though a covenant be joint and several in the terms of it, yet if the interest and cause of action be joint, the action must be brought by all

(*a*) v. Davis, M [illegible] MSS (*b*) 2 Str 610 (*c*) 8 T R. 487.
(*d*) Ibid 240.

the covenantees; and on the other hand, if the interest and cause of action be several, the action may be brought by one only (*a*). So, though a man covenant with two or more jointly, yet if the interest and cause of action of the covenantees be several and not joint, the covenant shall be taken to be several, and each of the covenantees may bring an action for his particular damage, notwithstanding the words of the covenant are joint (*b*).

But where two persons covenant *jointly and severally* with another, the the covenantee may bring an action against one of the covenantors only, though their interest in the subject-matter of the covenant be joint: as, where *A* lets land to *B.* and *C.* and they covenant jointly and severally with the lessor to pay the rent or the like, he may bring an action against either of the covenantors; because they are sureties for each other for the due performance of the covenants, and it is as competent for each of them to covenant for the other, as it is for a stranger to covenant for both, which is a usual thing (*c*).

Even if the covenant were joint, and an action brought against one of the covenantors, he could take advantage of it only by a plea in abatement.—For where there are several covenantees or obligees, and one of them only brings an action, without averring in the declaration that the others are dead, the defendant may either take advantage of it at the trial as a variance upon the plea of *non est factum*, or pray oyer of the deed and demur generally. But where an action is brought *against* one of several joint covenantors or obligors the defendant can only take advantage of it by a plea in abatement; and though it should appear upon the record that there are others who ought to be joined as defendants, yet that will not be error (*d*).

For wherever any person who ought to have been joined as a defendant, is omitted, it is pleadable in abatement only: the reason is because such plea gives the plaintiff a better writ, which is the true criterion to distinguish a plea in abatement from a plea in bar (*e*).

As to what covenants shall be construed to be precedent or not, it has been laid down, that the dependence or independence of covenants was to be collected from the sense and meaning of the parties, and that, however covenants might be in a deed, their precedency must depend on the order of time in which the intent of the transaction required their performance.—Conditions therefore are to be construed to be either precedent or subsequent, according to the fair intention of the parties to be collected from the instrument, and technical words should give way to that intention (*f*).

Therefore, where in a lease for seven years, containing the usual co-

(*a*) [illegible] (*c*) [illegible] (*e*) [illegible]
(*b*) [illegible] (*d*) [illegible] (*f*) [illegible]

venants that the lessee should pay the rent, keep the premises in repair, &c. a proviso was, that the lessee might determine the term at the end of the first three or five years, giving six months' previous notice, and that then from and after the expiration of such notice, and payment of all rents and duties to be paid by the lessee and performance of all his covenants until the end of the three or five years, the indenture should cease and be utterly void. Ruled that the payment of rent and performance of the other covenants, are conditions precedent to the lessee's determination of the term at the end of the first three years, and that his merely giving six months' notice, expiring within the first three years, is not sufficient for that purpose (*a*).

Plaintiff covenanted to sell defendant a school-house, &c. and to convey the same to him on or before the first of *August*, 1797, and to deliver up the possession to him on the 24th of *June*, 1796, and in consideration thereof, the defendant covenanted to pay the plaintiff 120*l.* on or before the said first of *August*, 1797. It was holden, that the covenant to convey, and that for the payment of the money, were dependent covenants, and that the plaintiff could not maintain an action for the 120*l.* without averring that he had conveyed or tendered a conveyance to the defendant. Were it to hold otherwise, in such a case as the present, the greatest injustice might be done; for supposing, in the instance of a trader who had entered into such a contract of the sale of an estate, that between the making of the contract, and the final execution of it, he were to become a bankrupt, the vendee might be in the situation of having had payment enforced from him, and yet be disabled from procuring the property for which he had paid (*b*).

But where *A.* covenanted to build a house for *B.* and finish it on or before a certain day, in consideration of a sum of money, which *B.* covenanted to pay to *A.* by instalments, as the building should proceed, the finishing of the house was held not to be a condition precedent to the payment of the money, but that the covenants were independent, wherefore *A.* might maintain an action of debt against *B.* for the whole sum, though the building be not finished at the time appointed (*c*). It is accordingly laid down that, if a day be appointed for the payment of the money, and the day is to happen before the thing can be performed, an action may be brought for the money before the thing be done: for it appears that the party relied upon his remedy, and intended not to make the performance a condition precedent. So in this case by the terms of the contract, two several sums of money were to be paid before the thing to be done was done. The plaintiffs therefore were clearly entitled to this action for the money without averring performance, and the defendant to his remedy on the covenants (*d*).

(*a*) 6 T. R. 665. (*b*) 8 T. R. 366. (*c*) 2 H. Bl. 389.
(*d*) 1 Salk. 171. 1 Ld. Raym. 662. Com. R. 93. 12 Mod. 455.

No precise technical words, however, are required in a deed to make a stipulation a condition precedent or subsequent; neither does it depend on the circumstance, whether the clause is placed prior or posterior in the deed, so that it operates as a proviso or covenant, for the same words have been construed to operate as either the one or the other, according to the nature of the transaction: the merits therefore of a question of this kind, must depend on the nature of the contract, and the acts to be performed by the contracting parties, and any subsequent facts disclosed on the record, which have happened in consequence of the contract (*a*).

In covenant the plaintiff may assign as many breaches as he will. So in debt on bond for the performance of covenants, by stat. 8 & 9 *W.* 3. c. 11 (*b*).

On a covenant in *London* to repair houses in *Surry*, the breach must be assigned at the place where, &c. viz. at *London* (*c*).

Where there has been an assignment by deed, it is sufficient to prove the assignment by the subscribing witness without calling the witness to the original deed: for the assignment having adopted the original deed in all its parts, it is become as one deed (*d*).

In covenant, if some breaches are well assigned and some not, and there is a demurrer to the whole declaration, the plaintiff shall have judgment for those breaches which are well assigned (*e*).

A variance in setting out one of several covenants in a lease on which breaches were assigned, viz. *the Cellar Bar Field*, instead of *Aller Beer Field*, being considered as part of the description of the deed declared on, though the plaintiff waived going for damages for the breach of that covenant, is fatal (*f*).

To a count in covenant charging the defendant as executors for breaches of covenant by their testator as lessee, who had covenanted for himself, executors, and assigns, may be joined another count charging them that after the death of testator and their proving his will, and during the term the demised premises came by assignment to *D. A* against whom breaches were alleged, and concluding that so neither the testator nor the defendant after his death, nor *D. A.* since the assignment to him had kept the said covenant, but had broken the same. And *plene administraverunt* may be pleaded to both counts (*g*).

On a breach that the house was not in repair, a plea that the plaintiff agreed that the defendant should employ a person four days in and about repairing the house, in satisfaction, is bad; for the defendant was obliged to do the repairs by the original covenant (*h*).

(*a*) 1 T. R. 645.
(*b*) Cro. Car. 176.
(*c*) Cro. Jac. 446.
(*d*) 1 T. R. 21[illegible]
(*e*) 1 Saund. 235 n. 9.
(*f*) 9 East, 188.
(*g*) [illegible]
(*h*) 2 Mod. 88.

If I covenant to leave all the timber which is growing on the land when I take it, and at the end of the term I cut it down, but leave it there, it is a breach of the covenant for a covenanter shall not defeat the intent of his covenant, which is ever to be taken most strongly against himself (*a*).

A covenant is not a duty nor a cause of action, till it be broken, and therefore it is not discharged by a release of all actions; and when it is broken, the action is not founded merely upon the specialty, as if it were a duty, but savours of trespass, and therefore an accord is a good plea to it, and ends in damages (*b*)

But if the one party disable himself from performing his part, the other party is not obliged to offer performance of his part, but may have an action immediately (*c*).

As, where the lessor covenanted with the lessee to make him a new lease on surrender of the whole within twenty years, and before the twenty years expired the lessor aliened the land to another by fine it was adjudged, that the action lay immediately, for he had disabled himself to accept a surrender, and so to make a new lease (*d*).

If, however, a man have lands for a term of years, and covenant to leave them in as good a plight as he found them, although he pull down the houses, the lessor shall not have an action of covenant before the end of the term, for the covenant has relation thereto, and he may rebuild them - But if he do waste in wood, covenant lies. for he cannot repair it (*e*)

If the defendants, however, prevent the performance of a condition precedent by their neglect and default, it is equal to performance by the plaintiff's (*f*).

Performance pleaded otherwise than in the terms of the covenant, is bad (*g*), even on general demurrer to the plea of "accord and satis-"faction," in covenant (*h*), where the damages are uncertain and to be recovered, a lesser thing may be done in satisfaction, and there "accord and satisfaction" is a good plea, as to an action on a covenant to repair (*i*)

On a covenant that runs with the land, evidence that the defendant ... in as heir will support a declaration charging him as assignee (*k*).

The lessee of a coal mine, who covenants to pay a certain share of all such sums of money as the coals shall sell for at the pit's mouth, is not liable under that covenant to pay to the lessor any part of the money produced by the sale of the coals elsewhere than at the pit's mouth; and evidence of the lessee's having accounted with the lessor,

(*a*) 1 Esp. N. P. 27[illegible] (*b*) Shep. Touch. 161 n. 1 (*c*) 1 Esp. N. P. 285
(*d*) Cro. Eliz. 449 (*e*) F. N. B. 145 K [illegible] 2 Bl. Rep. 842 [illegible] C. X [illegible]
(*f*) 1 T. R. 638 (*g*) 1 Bos. & Pul. 453 (*h*) 4 Mod. 8[illegible]. (*i*) Cro. Jac. 99.
(*k*) 4 T. R. 75.

and paid him the share of the money produced by the sale of coals elsewhere, is not admissible to explain the intention of the parties (*a*).

In covenant on an indenture of demise of a coal mine made on the 8th of *July*, 1805, reserving one-fourth of the coal raised, or the value in money, at the election of the lessor, and if the one-fourth fell short of 400*l* per annum, then reserving such additional rent as would make up that annual sum, to be rendered monthly in equal portions held that the lessee having elected to take the whole in money, may declare for two years' and three months' rent in arrear but even if the money rent were reserved annually, the plaintiff may remit his claim as to the three months' rent, and enter up judgment for the two years' rent only, and having first well assigned a breach of the covenant that the lessees had not yielded monthly the one-fourth or the value in money, &c. but had refused, &c. Held, that it would not hurt on general demurrer that the count went on to allege that before the exhibiting of the plaintiff's bill, *viz.* on the 1st of *Nov.* 1797, 900*l* of the rent reserved for two years and three months was due and in arrear, for that date being before the lease made, and therefore impossible in respect to the subject-matter, must be rejected, and the general allegation that before the exhibiting of the plaintiff's bill 900*l* of the rent reserved, &c. was due, is sufficient 10 East. 139

If the breach of a covenant be assigned thus · "That the defendant "has not used the farm in an husbandmanlike manner, but on the "contrary has committed waste," the plaintiff cannot give evidence of the defendant's using the farm in an unhusbandmanlike manner, if it do not amount to waste — (*on* the former words of the breach, had they stood alone such evidence might have been given (*b*)

In covenant for non-repair (as for not repairing hedges and not ploughing land) the writ of enquiry shall be to the place where the lease was made (*c*).

Covenant lies against an assignee on a covenant not to plough, although assigns are not named in the deed for it runs with the land (*d*).

So, if *A.* leases lands to *B.* and *B.* covenants to pay the rent, repair houses, &c during the said term, and afterwards assigns to *C*, the assignee is bound to perform the covenants during the term of the first lessee, though the assignee be not named, because the covenant runs with the land made for the maintenance of a thing *in esse* at the time of the lease made (*e*).

So, if *A* demises to *B.* several parcels of land, and the lessee cove-

(*a*) 5 T. R. 564. (*b*) 3 T. R. 307. (*c*) Cro. Jac. 11. (*d*) Ibid. 125.
(*e*) Bac. Abr. tit. "Covenant," (E. 3.)

nants for him and his assigns to repair, *&c* and after the lessee assigns to *D.* all his estate in parcel of the land demised, and *D.* does not repair that to him assigned, the lessor may have an action of covenant against *D.* the assignee (*a*).

For a covenant may be dividable and follow the land; wherefore an action of covenant will lie against an assignee of part of the thing demised (*b*).

If a lessee covenants that he and his assigns will repair the house demised, and the lessee grants over the term, and the assignee does not repair it, an action of covenant lies either against the assignee at common law, because this covenant runs with the land, or it lies against the lessee at the election of the lessor, who may charge both, but execution shall be against one of them only, for if he take both in execution, he that is last taken shall have an *audita querela* (*c*).

So, the executor of a lessee is liable to the grantee of the reversion on such a covenant, though the lessee may have assigned his term and the grantee have accepted rent of the assignee (*d*).

For the personal representative of a lessee for years is his assignee, and a covenant to repair runs with the land, as it is to be performed on it, and therefore binds the assignee (*e*). So with respect to a covenant to make further assurance (*f*).

So, if there is a covenant which runs with the land and the lessee assigns over, and the assignee dies intestate, the lessor may have covenant against the administrator of the assignee and declare against him as assignee for such covenants bind those who come in by act of law, as well as by act of the parties (*g*).

As to the extent to which the lessee or assignee is liable in covenant, there is a considerable difference (*h*).

1. The lessee has, from his covenant, both a privity of contract and of estate, and though he assigns, and thereby destroys the privity of estate, yet the privity of contract continues, and he is liable in covenant notwithstanding the assignment (*i*).

2. But the assignee comes in only in privity of estate, and therefore is liable only while he continues to be in possession, and therefore has the legal estate except in the case of rent, for which though he assign over he is liable as to the arrears incurred before as well as during his enjoyment, and such assignee was made liable in equity, though the privity of estate was destroyed at common law (*k*).

(*a*) Bac. [illegible] "Covenant" ([illegible]) (*b*) Cro. Car. 222
(*c*) Cro. Jac. [illegible] (*d*) 4 Mod. 8? (*e*) 1 [illegible] 55,
(*f*) Cro. C. [illegible] (*g*) [illegible] N. P. 29? (*h*) C. N. [illegible]
(*i*) Doug. 458 764 (*k*) Bac. Abr. [illegible] Covenant (E 4), 1 Bos & P. [illegible] East's R. 58? [illegible] C. [illegible]

Assignees of a bankrupt are not liable for the rent of premises assigned to them by the commissioners unless they take possession (*a*).

Where assignees of a bankrupt advertised a lease of certain premises, of which the bankrupt was lessee, for sale by auction, without stating themselves to be the owners or possessors thereof, and no bidder offering, they never took possession in fact of the premises: held that this was no more than an experiment to ascertain the value, whether the lease were beneficial or not to the creditors, and did not amount to an assent on the part of the assignees to take the term, or support an averment in a declaration in covenant against them by the landlord, that all right, title, interest, &c. of the bankrupt in the premises came to defendants by assignment thereof (*b*).

Where the breach assigned was in two covenants, and it appeared, that for the one, the plaintiff had no cause of action, and for the other a good cause, and issue was joined on both, and found for the plaintiff in both and damages entirely assessed, the plaintiff could not have judgment.

(*c*) To an action of covenant for not pulling down part of a house called The Cherry Tree at South-gate, in *Middlesex*, which had been let by the plaintiff to the defendant's testator, the plea was that the testator had repaired and beautified other parts of the premises, at the plaintiff's request, which the plaintiff had accepted in satisfaction, replication, protesting that the plaintiff did not request the testator, to repair, and replying that he did not accept the repairs in satisfaction. It appeared that the plaintiff had demised the house to the testator, who had covenanted to pull down the corner of it for the purpose of letting the plaintiff make a cart way over the place where the corner of the house stood. Lord *Kenyon*.—The plaintiff has demised the house called the Cherry Tree, and consequently the ground on which it stood The way he claims is to be made over part of the ground on which the house so demised stood. Every deed is to be taken most strongly against the grantor If the corner of the house is pulled down, the plaintiff cannot use the ground on which it stood, because it passed by the demise. and not having reserved in the deed any right to use it unless the plaintiff had so reserved it, he cannot claim it as a way but by prescription but as the testator did covenant to pull down the corner of the house, and has not done so, there must be a verdict for the plaintiff, but only for nominal damages (*d*)

As to bringing money into Court in this action. where there are se-

(*a*) P. Wms. R. 239. (*b*) 7 Last, 265. (*c*) 2 Lev. Rep. 69?
(*d*) 1 H. Bl. 27.

veral counts or breaches in the declaration, and as to some of them, the defendant may bring money into Court, but not as to the others, he may obtain a rule for bringing it in specially. Thus, where in covenant upon a lease for non-payment of rent, and not repairing, &c. the Court made a rule, that upon payment of what should appear to be due for rent, the proceedings as to that should be stayed; and as to the other breaches, that the plaintiff should proceed as he should think fit (*a*)

Respecting relief by bill in equity, the party cannot seek for specific performance of a covenant to repair (*b*).

But upon a covenant to build, the covenantee is clearly entitled to apply to a Court of equity for a specific performance, for to build is one entire thing, and if not done prevents that security for his rent to which the lessor is entitled by virtue of a building lease (*c*).

Where a person on a building lease covenants to new build the brick messuages on the premises, the rebuilding some and repairing others was held not to be sufficient to answer the covenant, but the lessee must rebuild the whole (*d*).

Section II. *Of the Action of Assumpsit.*

If the lease be by writing without deed, or by parol demise, the landlord's remedy for the breach of such stipulations, as the terms of the agreement express or the contract implies, is by an action of *assumpsit*, for an action upon the case on *assumpsit*, (or as it is also called *on promises*) is an action which the law gives the party injured by the breach, or non-performance of a contract legally entered into, it is founded on a contract either express or implied by law, and gives the party damages in proportion to the loss he has sustained by the violation of the contract.

An agreement to leave a farm as he found it, is an agreement to leave it in tenantable repair, if he found it so, and will maintain a declaration so laid (*e*).

In an action against a tenant upon promises that he would occupy the farm "in a good and husbandmanlike manner, according to the custom of the country," an allegation that he had treated the estate contrary to "good husbandry and the custom of the country," is

(*a*) 1 Tidd's Pract 564 (*b*) 3 Atk. 51[illegible] (*c*) Ibid 3 Ves 184
(*d*) 2 Atk 512. 3 Br. R. 66 contra (*e*) 2 Bl. R. 840

proved by shewing that he had treated it contrary to the prevalent course of husbandry in that "neighbourhood," as by tilling half his farm at once, when no other farmer there tilled more than a third, though many tilled only a fourth: and it is not sufficient to shew any precise definite custom or usage in respect of the quantity tilled (*a*).

In special *assumpsit* against the tenant for not performing his agreements, the estate of the lessor is an immaterial averment, if the tenant has had the enjoyment of his lease. For the true rule is, that on the general issue in an action on the case, all *material* averments are denied and put in issue, but nothing else The estate of the plaintiff is not a material averment, for a lease by a tenant in tail (as the plaintiff in this case was) is not void, but only voidable by the issue in tail: it had not been nor could be avoided during the life of the lessor; nor does it lie in the mouth of the defendant, who has enjoyed the fruit of it, to dispute its validity. That therefore being an immaterial averment, the plaintiff, (notwithstanding he was mistaken in his title) was held to be entitled to recover on the first count of the declaration, which stated that the lands descended to him in fee on the death of his father, as son and heir (*b*).

A tenant at will even is bound to keep the premises in repair, and to use the land fairly according to the course of husbandry which the nature of the soil may require, and the custom of the country points out as being proper It seems indeed, that those covenants which are implied in a lease, (of which we have in a preceding part of this work made more particular mention,) subsist between landlord and tenant as resulting from their relative situation, by whatever means that situation is created. so that the breach of any of them is a wrong for which the law affords a remedy. an action on the case therefore will lie for damages arising from the neglect to repair (*c*).

An agreement, (as has been before observed) though not under seal, may be declared on specially, in which case it may be said to bind the parties by its own force: or the plaintiff may in some instances declare generally, and give the written contract in evidence (*d*)

A tenant from year to year is bound (as has been observed) only to fair and tenantable repairs, so as to prevent waste or decay of the premises, but is not bound to do substantial and lasting repairs (*e*).

By an agreement between plaintiffs and defendant. the defendant was to accept of the assignment of the lease of a term from the plaintiffs, and to take the fixtures and crops at a valuation; he was afterwards let into possession of the fixtures, and the crops were va-

(*a*) 4 T. R. 154. (*b*) 4 T. R. 154. (*c*) Co. L. 56. [illegible]
(*d*) 6 T. R. 319 (*e*) 2 Esp. R. 592

lued to him; but the lease was never assigned. held that *indebitatus assumpsit* would not lie for the price of the fixtures and crops, and that the plaintiff's only remedy was by a special action on the agreement (*a*).

Where an agreement between an out-going and an in-coming tenant was that the latter should buy the hay, &c. upon the farm, and that the former should allow to the latter the expense of repairing the gates and fences; and that the value of the hay, &c. and of the repairs should be settled by third persons; held that the balance settled to be due for the hay, &c., after deducting the value of the repairs, might be recovered by the out-going tenant in a count upon a general *indebitatus assumpsit* for goods sold and delivered (*b*).

(*a*) 1 Campb 472 (*b*) 12 East R 1

CHAPTER XVI.

Of the Remedies for Waste.

SECTION I. *Of Waste on the Statute of* Gloucester.

REMEDIES for waste lie at common law by prohibition of waste and action of waste in favour of the owner of the inheritance; however, the statutes of *Marlbridge*, 52 *H.* 3 *c* 23 and of *Gloucester*, 6 *E.* 1 *c* 5 provided that the writ of waste shall not only lie against tenants by the law of *England* (or curtesy) and those in dower, but against any farmer or other that holds in any manner for life or years: so that for above five hundred years past all tenants merely for life or for any less estate have been punishable or liable to be impeached for waste both voluntary and permissive, unless their leases be made, as sometimes they are, without impeachment of waste, *absque impetitione vasti;* that is, with a provision or protection that no man shall *impetere* or sue him for waste committed (*a*).

But tenant in tail, after possibility of issue extinct, is not impeachable for waste, because his estate was at its creation an estate of inheritance, and so not within the statutes. The first incident to an estate tail is, that the tenant shall not be punishable for committing waste, by felling timber, pulling down houses, opening and working mines, &c. But this power must be exercised during the life of the tenant in tail, for at the instant of his death it ceases. If, therefore, a tenant in tail sell trees, growing on the land, the vendee must cut them down during the life of the tenant in tail, for otherwise they will descend to the heir, as parcel of the inheritance (*b*).

(*a*) 2 Bl. Com. 283.

(*b*) Cruise's Digest, 2 C. 1. s. 33.

The Court of Chancery will not, in any case whatever, restrain the tenant in tail from committing waste. It is said also, that if he grant all his estate, the grantee is dispunishable for waste: so if grantee grant it over, his grantee is likewise dispunishable. Neither does waste lie for the debtor against tenant by statute, recognizance, or *elegit*, because against them the debtor may set off the damages in account: but it seems reasonable that it should lie for the reversioner expectant on the determination of the debtor's own estate, or of those estates derived from the debtor (*a*).

By the statute of *Marlbridge*, single damages only could be recovered, except in the case of a guardian: but the statute of *Gloucester* directs that tenant in dower, by the curtesy, for life, or years, shall lose and forfeit the place wherein the waste is committed, and also treble damages to him that hath the inheritance. The statute speaks of *terms of years* in the plural number, but though it be a penal law, whereby treble damages and the place wasted shall be recovered, yet a tenant for half a year, being within the same mischief, shall be within the same remedy, though it be out of the letter of the law. The expression of the statute is, that "he shall forfeit the thing which he hath wasted;" and it hath been determined that, under these words, the place is also included.—If waste be done *sparsim*, or here and there, all over a wood, the whole wood shall be recovered; or if in several rooms of a house, the whole house shall be forfeited, because it is impracticable for the reversioner to enjoy only the identical places wasted, when lying interspersed with the other. But if waste be done only at one end of a wood (or perhaps in one room of a house, if that can be conveniently separated from the rest), that part only is the *locus vastatus*, or thing wasted, and that only shall be forfeited to the reversioner (*b*).

The redress under this statute for this injury of waste is of two kinds, preventive and corrective; the former by writ of *estrepement*; the latter by action of waste.

Estrepement.—*Estrepement* from *exstirpare*, signifies to draw away the heart of the ground, by plowing and sowing it continually, without manuring or other good husbandry, whereby it is impaired; and may be also applied to the cutting down trees, or lopping them farther than the law allows. The word is used for a writ, which lies in two cases: the one by the statute of *Gloucester*, when a person having an action depending, as a *formedon*, writ of right, &c. sues to prohibit the tenant from making waste during the suit: the other is for the demandant, who is adjudged to recover seisin of the land in question after judgment and before execution sued by the writ of *habere facias possessionem*.

(*a*) Cruise's Dig. tit. 2 C[illegible] [illegible] Le[illegible]

(*b*) Co. Lit. [illegible]

to prevent waste being made before he gets into possession. By an equitable construction of the statute of *Gloucester*, and in advancement of the remedy, it is now held that a writ of *estrepement* to prevent waste may be had in every stage, as well of such actions wherein damages are recovered, as of those wherein only possession is had of the lands: for perhaps the tenant may not be able to satisfy the demandant his full damage. In an action of waste itself, therefore (of which hereafter), to recover the place wasted and also damages, this writ will lie as well before as after judgment, for the plaintiff cannot recover damages for more waste than is contained in his original complaint neither is he at liberty to assign or give in evidence any waste made after suing out the writ it is therefore reasonable that he should have this writ of preventive justice, since he is in his present suit debarred of any further remedy (*a*).

If a writ of *estrepement* forbidding waste be directed and delivered to the tenant himself, as it may be, and he afterwards proceeds to commit waste, an action may be carried on founded upon this writ, wherein the only plea of the tenant can be *non fecit vastum contra prohibitionem*, and if upon verdict it be found that he did, the plaintiff may recover damages and costs, or the party may proceed to punish the defendant for the contempt (*b*).

This writ lies properly where the plaintiff in a real action shall not recover damages by his action, and as it were supplies damages, for damages and costs may be recovered for waste, after the writ of *estrepement* is brought (*c*).

By virtue of either of these writs, the sheriff may resist those that do, or offer to do waste, and if otherwise he cannot prevent them, he may lawfully imprison the wasters, or make a warrant to others to imprison them: or, if necessity require it, he may take the *posse comitatus* to his assistance (*d*).

Writ of Waste.—The writ of waste is also an action partly founded on the common law, and partly upon the statute of *Gloucester*, and may be brought by him that hath the immediate estate of inheritance, whether it be fee-simple or fee-tail, provided the reversion continue with him, in the same state in which it was at the time of the waste done, and be not granted over, for though he take the estate back again, the action is gone, because the estate did not continue (*e*). This is a remedy and yet a penal law, and therefore shall have a favourable construction (*f*).

A purchaser (as contradistinguished from one by descent) shall have an action of waste (*g*)

([illegible]) [illegible] 3 Bl. [illegible] 228. 5 Rep. 115. ([illegible]) [illegible] 120. ([illegible]) [illegible] 2 B[illegible] 325.
([illegible]) [illegible] ([illegible]) 2 W[illegible] 251. (*f*) 3 Mod. 93. (*g*) Ibid.

So, a parson, &c. for it is the dowry of the church.

But if a lease be made to *A.* for life, remainder to *B.* for life, remainder to *C.* in fee, no action of waste lies against the first lessee during the estate in the mesne remainder, for then his estate would be destroyed; otherwise if *B.* had a mesne remainder for years, for that would have been no impediment, the recovery not destroying the term for years. But though *B.* cannot bring waste, he may have an injunction (unless it be meliorating waste, as by building houses, &c.) but the reversioner or remainder-man in fee must be made a party, for possibly they may approve of the waste (*a*).

If the lessee for years commit waste, and his term expires, yet the lessor shall have an action of waste for the treble damages (*b*). If a bishop make a lease for life or years, and die, the lessee, the see being void, doth waste, the successor shall have no action of waste (*c*). Tenant in common need not join in action of waste (*d*). This action is also maintainable in pursuance of the stat. of *Westm.* 2. (13 *E.* 1. *c.* 22.) by one tenant in common of the inheritance against another, who makes waste in estate holden in common; the equity of which statute extends to joint-tenants, but not to coparceners, because they, by the old law, might make partition; but tenants in common and joint-tenants could not, whereof the statute gave them this remedy, compelling the defendant either to make partition and take the place wasted to his own share, or give security not to commit any farther waste. But these tenants in common and joint-tenants are not liable to the penalties of the statute of *Gloucester*, which extends only to such as have life estates and do waste to the prejudice of the inheritance (*e*).

The grantee of a reversion shall have waste; therefore if the lessee of land opens a coal mine and grants all his interest, excepting the mine, waste will lie by an assignee of the reversion against the grantee for coals afterwards dug by the grantor, for the exception being of a thing with which he had not power to meddle, was void (*f*).

A proviso in a lease that the lessor shall cut down trees, is a covenant and not an exception; therefore the heir may maintain waste if they be cut down (*g*). But if a lease be made excepting the wood and timber, an action of waste will not lie against the lessee for cutting it down, because not demised. If the termor assign his term, except the trees, and afterwards the trees are cut down, waste will lie against the assignee, for the exception was void; but if tenant for life make a lease for years, he may except the trees, because he still remains tenant [illegible] waste (*h*).

Waste lies against an executor *de son tort* of a term of years or of

(*a*) 3 M[illegible] P. Wms. [illegible] (*c*) Co. Lit. [illegible] (*d*) 2 Mod. 61 [illegible] 459 (*e*) [illegible] (*g*) Ibid. 600. B. N. P. 119

other chattels, by stat. 30 *G.* 2. *c.* 7, and 4 & 5 *W.* & *M. c.* 24 *s.* 12.

An occupant shall be punished for waste.—So, if the tenant for life or years, or their assignee make a grant over, and notwithstanding take the profits, an action of waste lies against him, by him in the reversion or remainder by the statute (a).

One may have an action of waste upon several leases, and upon several grants of a reversion (b).

By the custom of *London*, waste lies at common law, for waste in houses there, and now since the statute of *Gloucester*, waste lies there in cases within the statute as well as in others, for though the statute gives an action of waste in cases where it would not lie before, and gives also treble damages *et locum vastatum*, yet it does not take away the jurisdiction of any Court that before held plea of waste.—So a writ of *estrepement* lies in *London pendente placito*, or after judgment and before execution, to stay waste (c).

No person is entitled to an action of waste against a tenant for life, but he who has the *immediate* estate of inheritance in remainder or reversion, expectant upon the estate for life. If between the estate of the tenant for life who commits waste and the subsequent estate of inheritance there is interposed an estate of freehold to any person in esse, then during the continuance of such interposed estate, the action of waste is suspended, and if the first tenant for life dies during the continuance of such interposed estate, the action is gone for ever. But though while there is an estate for life interposed between the estate of the person committing waste and that of the reversioner or remainder-man in fee, the remainder-man cannot bring waste, yet if the waste be done by cutting down trees, such remainder-man in fee may seize them, and if they are taken away or made use of before he seizes them, he may bring trover: for in the eye of the law a remainder-man for life has not the property of the thing wasted, and even the tenant for life in possession has not the absolute property of it, but merely a right to the enjoyment or benefit of it, as long as it is annexed to the inheritance, of which it is considered a part, and therefore it belongs to the owner of the fee (d).

The action of waste is a mixed action, partly real, so far as it recovers land, and partly personal, so far as it recovers damages, for it is brought for both of those purposes, and if waste be proved, the plaintiff shall recover the thing or place wasted, and also treble damages by the statute of *Gloucester* (e).

The process in the action of waste is, first a writ of summons to be made by the [illegible] of the county where the land lies, and on the return

(a) [illegible] ; (b) Co. [illegible] ; (c) Com. Dig. [illegible] (B. 1) ;
(d) [illegible]

of this writ the defendant may essoin and the plaintiff adjourn, &c. Then a *pone* is made out by the filazer of the county, on the return of which a *distringas* issues for the defendant to appear, and upon his appearing the plaintiff declares, and the defendant pleads, &c.

The writ of waste calls upon the tenant to appear and shew cause why he hath committed waste and destruction in the place named to the disinherison of the plaintiff. If the defendant makes default and does not appear at the day assigned him, then the sheriff is to take with him a jury of twelve men and go in person to the place alleged to be wasted, and there enquire of the waste done and the damages, and make a return or report of the same to the Court, upon which report the judgment is founded (*a*).—But if the defendant appears to the writ and afterwards suffers judgment to go against him by default, or upon a *nil dicit* (when he makes no answer or puts in no plea in defence), this amounts to a confession of the waste, since having once appeared, he cannot pretend ignorance of the charge. The sheriff, therefore, shall not go to the place to enquire of the fact, but shall only (as in default in other actions) make enquiry of the *quantum* of damages (*b*).

In waste the plaintiff must shew how he is entitled to the inheritance; therefore, if he counts upon a lease by himself, he must shew his seisin in fee, and demise to the defendant (*c*).

In every case the plaintiff in this action must shew his title. Thus, if he claim by fine, he must plead the fine and the uses of it; if by common recovery, he must shew the recovery and uses: so, if by grant of the reversion, he must shew how he claims by assignment; and if the husband and wife in right of the wife sue, they must allege the reversion in both: so, if the plaintiffs sue as parceners or jointenants, the declaration should shew that they are so (*d*).

If, however, the plaintiff conclude *ad exhæredationem*, it supplies the omission of the estate of which he was seised, after verdict: so if he shews the special matter it is sufficient, though he does not name himself assignee: so, if the writ is general, *cujus hæres* the plaintiff is, though he has a special inheritance (*e*).

If the plaintiff has the reversion, he shall say that the defendant holds of him: but it is otherwise, if waste be brought by him in remainder, or by the lord who has by escheat, for there is no tenure of him (*f*).

The plaintiff must always charge the defendant in the *tenet*, or in the *tenuit*, for there is no other form: and must charge him as assignee, executor, &c. So, he must charge him by virtue of the lease by which he is possessed: as, if the defendant be in by devise, he must charge

(*a*) Pig. 24. (*b*) Cro. Eliz. 18. 290. (*c*) Com. Dig. tit. "Pleader" (3 O. 2). (*d*) Ibid. (*e*) Ibid. (*f*) Ibid.

[illegible] tenant [illegible] *legem* [illegible] defendant claims by a remainder for life or for years, which is now in possession, he may be charged [illegible] a demise to him, [illegible] he be [illegible] by the statute of Uses, it is sufficient to charge him generally, without [illegible] (*a*)

The declaration [illegible] the waste conformably to the writ. For [illegible] the writ is for waste in land, and it is assigned in cutting w[illegible], it is bad (*b*)

If [illegible] be [illegible] land, [illegible] must say in what parish it lies (*c*)

It is sufficient [illegible] waste [illegible], without shewing the particular manner in which it was committed, as, if it is in gardens, it is sufficient to say, that he destroyed the gardens generally, without saying that he suffered the hedges of the wood to be neglected, whereby cattle entered and [illegible] the gardens: and if a stranger commit the waste, that fact need not be mentioned

But the declaration must particularize the [illegible] or quantity of the waste: as if it is in cutting trees, [illegible] the number of the trees. If the [illegible] other lands, [illegible] the waste [illegible] wood, parcel of the premises, it is bad, for [illegible] the premises, and also of the other lands

If trees be excepted out of a demise, waste cannot be committed by cutting them down, and therefore ejectment cannot be brought as for waste committed in or upon the demised premises (*d*)

A declaration in waste that the defendant ploughed up the land, which was pasture, *et [illegible] fecit*, was held bad for uncertainty, even after verdict (*e*) — After verdict, nothing is to be presumed but what is either expressly stated in the declaration, or necessarily implied from those facts which are stated (*f*) for a verdict will cure ambiguity only, but will not aid where the gist of the action is omitted to be laid in the declaration (*g*)

The declaration must be *[illegible]* of the plaintiff: if he be seised in right of his wife, it shall be *ad [illegible]* of the wife. So, if there are several plaintiffs, there may be summons and severance, for it is a [illegible] action, and *[illegible]* (*h*)

The general issue to an action of waste, is "no waste done," but this [illegible], but puts the whole declaration in issue, and may be pleaded [illegible] there is no waste, as if destruction happens by tempest, [illegible] the defendant plead *nul wast* [illegible], and issue is taken thereupon, the plaintiff must prove his [illegible] in the declaration: he must likewise prove the kind of waste [illegible] the declaration, and [illegible] allege waste in cutting [illegible], and [illegible] that he [illegible] them and did not cut them, [illegible]

[illegible]

variance (*a*).—Defendant may also, under the general issue give in evidence any thing which proves that it is no waste, as that it was by tempest, *&c.* as before observed, but not that it was for repairs, or that the plaintiff gave him leave to cut, or that he had repaired before the action brought. Neither will it be any defence that a stranger did it, for if the plaintiff should not have his action of waste, he would be without remedy, and the defendant may bring trespass against the stranger, and recover his damages. But it would be a good plea to say that the plaintiff himself did it (*b*).

If several wastes are assigned, and the defendant is not guilty of part of any, he may plead "no waste done" to all together, and need not say to every part severally "[illegible]" (*c*).

If the tenant repairs before action brought, it is said, the reversioner cannot have an action of waste, but the tenant cannot, in such case, plead that he did no waste, but must plead the special matter, (*d*) for

"No waste done" is no plea where the defendant has matter of justification, or excuse. Therefore, if there be a lease to *A.* for two years, and afterwards a lease to *B.* for ten years, in waste against *B.* for waste during the two years, he cannot plead "no waste done (*e*)."

The defendant may plead in justification that he took for repairs, as, for repair of the fences and other necessary uses, or, that he pulled down to rebuild and repair the house, fences, *&c.* Therefore tenant for life may justify cutting down timber upon the ground letten and repairing the house therewith, though he is not compellable to repair it if it were ruinous when the lease was made (*f*).—But it is not sufficient to say, that he took for repairs, if he does not add that he used or keeps for repairs for it is waste for a lessee to cut down timber-trees for the purposes of repairs when there is no occasion, for were it otherwise, every farmer might cut down all the trees growing upon the land under pretence that he keeps them to employ about reparations whenever such shall become necessary (*g*).

So he may plead that he took them for other necessary botes, as for wain-bote, cart-bote, plough-bote, or hedge-bote, or for gates, or stiles, or for making utensils in husbandry, or for fuel. So, he may plead that they were dead wood, bearing neither fruit nor foliage (*h*).

So, he may plead that the lease was without impeachment of waste or, that the plaintiff's ancestor made a bargain and sale of the trees to him, or, that the lessor covenanted that the lessee might cut down

(*a*) Bull N P. 119. (*b*) Ibid 120. (*c*) Com Dig tit. "Pleader" (3 O 7). (*d*) 1 Inst 282. Cro Jac 668. (*e*) Com Dig [illegible]. (*f*) Co Lit 54. (*g*) Com. Dig Waste (3 O 11). Cro. Eliz. 592. (*h*) Com Dig Waste (3 O 12).

trees.—But it is no bar, that the lessor covenanted to repair, and that he did it for him (*a*).

He may also plead, that he has rebuilt and since kept in repair; for he may plead in excuse, that he repaired before action brought, for the jury must view the place wasted; but "repaired pending the suit" is no plea. So he may plead that it was so ruinous at the commencement of his lease, that he could not repair (*b*).

So, he may plead a release from the plaintiff or one of the plaintiffs, in bar; for if waste be by two plaintiffs in the *tenuit*, a release by one is a bar to both; but where waste is in the *tenet*, a release by one plaintiff bars himself only (*c*).

So, to waste in the *tenuit*, he may plead accord with satisfaction (*d*).

So, the defendant may plead in abatement to the plaintiff's title, or that the plaintiff has nothing in reversion, but he ought to shew how the reversion is devested, for "nothing in reversion," generally, will be bad, except where waste is brought by a grantee of the reversion (*e*).

So, if the plaintiff's title fails *pendente lite*, the defendant may plead it after the last continuance.

So, he may plead that the remainder-man is still alive.

So, the defendant may plead no demise made to him; or, no demise as to part; or, that wood was excepted by the demise.—So, that he has nothing by the assignment of *B.* or that after the demise, the defendant assigned, before which assignment no waste was done (*f*).

To the plea of assignment before waste done, the plaintiff may reply, that the assignment was by fraud, and he afterwards took the profits; and if the defendant rejoins, he must traverse the pernancy of the profits, not the fraud (*g*).

In waste, if issue is joined, six jurors at the least ought to have a view of the place wasted, otherwise the trial shall be stayed; if therefore waste be assigned in several places, the jury may find "no waste done" in a place of which they had no view, and they ought, it seems, to have a view (as the *venire facias* directs them to have), though the issue be upon a collateral point, and the waste be confessed. Whether the *venire facias* be returned or not, the Court may examine as to the fact of the jury having viewed or not; for the return does not conclude the parties; but it is not necessary, that the officer return upon the *distringas juratores*, that the jury have viewed, or that he was present at the view (*h*).

If however the waste be assigned in a wood *sparsim*, it is sufficient if

(*a*) [illegible] (5 O. 41). (*b*) [illegible] (5 O. 15). (*c*) [illegible] (O. 8 1[illegible]). (*d*) [illegible] (O. 1[illegible]). (*e*) [illegible] (5 O. 19; [illegible] O. 58). (*f*) [illegible] (Com. Dig. 'Pleader,' (5 O. 21).

the jury view the wood, though they do not enter into it. So, if it be in several rooms of a house.

Of the Judgment.—Touching the judgment in waste, if there be judgment for want of an appearance upon the distringas by the stat. *W.* 2. c. 14. the sheriff taking twelve, *&c.* shall go to the place wasted and take inquisition of the damage, and upon the return thereof, there shall be damage.

When the waste and damages are ascertained, either by confession, verdict, or enquiry of the sheriff, judgment is given in pursuance of the statute of *Gloucester*, c. 5. that the plaintiff shall recover the place wasted, for which he has immediately a writ of seisin, provided the particular estate be still subsisting (for if it be expired there can be no forfeiture of the land); and also, that the plaintiff shall recover treble the damages assessed by the jury, which he must obtain in the same manner as all other damages in actions personal or mixed are obtained, whether the particular estate be expired, or be still in being (*a*).

In an action of waste upon this statute against the tenant for years, for converting three closes of meadow into garden ground, if the jury give only one farthing damages for each close, the Court (who have a kind of discretionary power therein) will give the defendant leave to enter up judgment for himself (*b*).

By stat. 8 & 9 *W.* 3. c. 11. s. 3. the plaintiff shall have costs in all actions of waste, where the damages found do not exceed twenty nobles, which he could not at common law.

Trover for Waste.—Waste is a tort, and the remedy lies at law. Therefore where timber is cut down, trover may be brought to recover the value.—In an action of waste, the place wasted is recovered; in action of trover, damages (*c*).

Trover may be brought against the executor of the person who converts the timber to his own use (*d*).

But though trover will lie at law, it may be very necessary for the party who has the inheritance to bring his bill in equity, because it may be impossible to discover the value of the timber, it being in possession of and cut down by the tenant (*e*).

Yet whether a bill for an account may be brought by the lord of a manor, or a lessor, against a tenant for timber felled, seems to be doubtful (*f*).

(*a*) [illegible] 22) (*c*) 2 Bac. & P. [illegible] (*e*) [illegible]
(*b*) [illegible] (*d*) 2 [illegible] 2[illegible] (*f*) 1 P. W[illegible]

Section II. Of the Action upon the Case in the Nature of Waste.

Since the statute of *Gloucester*, which gives no more costs than damages, it is usual to bring trespass or case in the nature of waste instead of the action of waste.

An action on the case does not lie for permissive waste (*a*).

Either an action on the case or trespass will lie, at the plaintiff's election, against his tenant for despoiling the premises; and case is the better action to recover as much as he may be damnified, because he is subject to an action of waste (*b*).

One tenant in common cannot maintain an action on the case in the nature of waste against another tenant in common (in possession of the whole, having a demise of the moiety from the first) for cutting down trees of proper age and growth for being cut, for it is no hurt to the inheritance. If however the trees were not fit to be cut, he might maintain such action (*c*).

Tenant at will has no power to commit any kind of voluntary waste, but he is not within the statute of *Gloucester*, and therefore an action of waste lies against him (*d*). If, however, a tenant at will cut down timber-trees, or pull down houses, the lessor shall have an action of trespass against him (*e*).

So, with respect to permissive waste, no remedy whatever lies against tenant at will; for he is not bound to repair or sustain houses like tenant for years (*f*).

It is so notoriously the duty of the actual occupier to repair the fences, and so little the duty of the landlord, that without any agreement to that effect, the landlord may maintain an action against his tenant for not so doing, upon the ground of the injury done to the inheritance (*g*).

A tenant from year to year is only bound to fair and tenantable repairs, so as to prevent waste or decay of the premises, not to substantial ones (*h*).

Section III. Of the Remedies in Equity, in the Case of Waste.

On the subject of waste, the Court of Chancery has, it should seem, a concurrent jurisdiction with the Courts of common law.

(*a*) 1 Bos & Pul N R 290. (*b*) Cro Car 187. (*c*) 2 T R 14[illegible]
(*d*) 1 Cruise's Dig tit 9 s 13. (*e*) 1 Inst 57 [illegible]
(*f*) [illegible] 14, 15. 3 Rep 13 b. 1 Show 268. (*g*) 4 T R [illegible]
(*h*) 2 Esp R 590.

The relief afforded by that Court, is in many cases the most eligible, and in some, absolutely necessary to be sought, in order to prevent the commission of threatened or impending waste for the Court will stay waste upon application by bill brought for that purpose praying an injunction.

At the common law, a prohibition went out of Chancery, against the tenant by the curtesy, in dower, or as guardian, at the prayer of him who had the inheritance, to inhibit waste, and that before waste committed (*a*)

Respecting the remedy of the remainder man or reversioner (or in the case of copyholds, of the lord) against the tenant about to commit, or committing waste, although a Court of Equity will not assist a forfeiture, yet the tenant in possession shall be restrained in equity from waste in all cases in which waste is punishable by law, and for this purpose, an injunction will be granted before the bill is filed. Also an injunction will be granted to stay waste in behalf of an infant *in ventre sa mere*. Equity will likewise, in some particular cases, restrain the tenant from committing waste, where he is dispunishable by law, either by the nature of the estate, or by express grant "without impeachment of waste" but where, by agreement of the parties, the lease is made without impeachment of waste, equity will not restrain the lessee from cutting timber, ploughing, opening mines, &c. though such lessee shall be restrained from pulling down houses, defacing seats, &c (*b*)

With respect to threatened or impending waste; the act of sending a surveyor to mark out trees, is a sufficient ground for an injunction (*c*).

So, a threat to open mines, entitles a party to come into this Court to restrain him (*d*). Even if a tenant for life insists on a right to do waste, and has none, the reversioner may have an injunction, though no proof of waste appear (*e*).

When a bill is filed to restrain waste or any other injury very detrimental, so that it is necessary to lose no time, an injunction may be applied for immediately after the bill is filed, by special motion supported by affidavit of the grievance (*f*).

So now an injunction shall be granted upon an affidavit of waste committed, to inhibit any waste to be committed by tenant for life or years; as to inhibit meadow, or other pasture, not ploughed within twenty years, being ploughed but not against a lessee, who had agreed to pay 20*s*. per acre *per ann* increase of rent, if he ploughed a meadow, &c.

(*a*) Com Dig tit Chancery (D 11) (*b*) 2 Eq Ca Abr 399 [illegible]
(*c*) 5 Ves jun 688 (*d*) 2 Atk. 182. (*e*) Barnard, 491
(*f*) Park An 4[illegible]

So it will be granted to inhibit antient inclosures being thrown down, or houses being pulled down (*a*)

So, against tenant after possibility, *&c* or him who in respect of a trust, *&c* is not liable to an action of waste (*b*)

So, against tenant for life, at the suit of the remainder-man in fee, though there is an intermediate remainder and if tenant for life, without impeachment of waste, or any other lessee, has cut timber, so as not to leave sufficient for repairs, the Court will restrain him from cutting any more without leave of the Court (*c*) Tenant for life, without impeachment of waste, will be restrained also from cutting down trees in lines or avenues, or ridings in a park, whether planted or growing naturally, or trees not of a proper growth to be cut (*d*), and though he be tenant for life, with liberty to cut timber "at seasonable times," he is not to cut trees planted for ornament or shelter to the mansion-house, or sapling trees not fit to be cut or felled for timber (*e*)

So, he will be restrained from pulling down the antient and capital house, and not only so, but the Court will compel him to put it in the same plight in which he found it (*f*)

But the Court of Chancery, it is said, will not decree a tenant for life to repair, or appoint a receiver with directions to repair (*g*)

However, where a jointress gave leave to the next in remainder for life without impeachment of waste, to cut timber on the jointure estate, and he dying without issue, the remainder-man over in tail having acquiesced in and encouraged the so doing, he was restrained from an action of waste against the jointress (*h*)

Where the plaintiff and defendant in possession were tenants in common, an injunction to stay waste was refused but on affidavit of the defendant's insolvency it was granted (*i*).

The Court will grant an injunction at the suit of a ground landlord to stay waste in an under lessee, who holds by lease from the original landlord, upon a certificate being produced of the waste (*k*)

So, the mortgagor may have an injunction to stay waste against the mortgagee, if he cut down timber, and do not apply the money arising from the sale in sinking the interest and principal (*l*). So, where the mortgagor commits waste, the Court will grant the mortgagee an injunction, for they will not suffer the mortgagor to prejudice the incumbrance (*m*)

So, though a rector may cut down timber for the repairs of the parsonage house or chancel (but not for any common purpose), and is entitled to botes for repairing barns and out houses belonging to the par-

(*a*) [illegible] (*c*) [illegible] (*e*) [illegible]
(*b*) [illegible] (*d*) [illegible] (*f*) Com Dig [illegible] (*g*) [illegible]
(*h*) [illegible] (*i*) [illegible] (*k*) [illegible]
(*l*) [illegible] (*m*) [illegible]

tonage, an injunction to stay waste in cutting down timber in the church-yard, will be granted till the cause be heard (*a*), and an injunction was granted to stay waste against the widow of a rector, at the suit of the patroness, during a vacancy (*b*).

An injunction to stay waste may be granted in favour of a child *in ventre sa mere* (*c*).

But where a clause "without impeachment of waste," is inserted in a lease or demise for years, it will have the same effect as when it is inserted in a conveyance of an estate for life, and the Court of Chancery will restrain the import of it, in the same manner as in the case of an estate for life (*d*).

The Court will not grant an injunction to stay waste in digging mines where the defendant sets up a right to the inheritance of the estate, till the answer is come in or the defendant has made default in not putting in his answer, for such injunctions are never granted before the hearing, unless the defendant had only a term in the estate, for years, or for life, and the reversion was in the plaintiff (*e*).

The lord of a manor may bring a bill for an account of ore dug, or timber cut, by the defendant's testator. Indeed, as to the property of the ore or timber, it would be clear even at law that if it came to the executor's hands, trover would lie for it, and if it had been disposed of in the testator's life-time, the executor, if assets are left, ought to answer for it: but it is stronger here, by reason that the tenant is a sort of fiduciary to the lord, and it is a breach of trust, which the law reposes in the tenant, for him to take away the property of the lord (*f*).

A bill, however, for a mere account of timber cut down, was dismissed by Lord *Hardwicke*, as being the proper subject of an action at law, but his Lordship added, that there were many instances where the Court had decreed an account in the case of mines, which they would not have done in that of timber, because the digging of mines is a sort of trade (*g*).

But as to the trespass of breaking up meadow, or antient pasture ground, it dies with the person; wherefore no bill will be entertained for an account thereof (*h*).

Neither is every common trespass a foundation for an injunction, where it is only contingent and temporary: but if it continue so long as to become a nuisance, in such case the Court will interfere and grant an injunction to restrain the person from committing it (*i*).

But the Court will award a perpetual injunction to restrain waste by ploughing, burning, breaking, or sowing down lands (*k*).

(*a*) 2 Atk. 217. (*b*) 2 Lev. R. 552. (*c*) 3 Atk. 211. (*d*) 1 Cruise's Dig. [illegible] 12. (*e*) 3 Atk. 4[illegible]. (*f*) 1 P. Wms. 406. (*g*) 3 Atk. 262. [illegible] (*h*) 1 P. Wms. [illegible]. (*i*) 3 Atk. 21. (*k*) 4 Br. Cas. in Parl. 377.

So, an injunction shall go to restrain the defendant from injuring fish ponds (*a*).

Where a bishop was directed by the Court of Chancery, to bring trover in order to try the right as to certain ore dug and disposed of by a tenant of a manor of which the bishop was lord, upon trial thereof it appeared that there never had been any mine of copper before discovered in the manor, wherefore the jury could not find that the customary tenant might by custom dig and open new copper mines; so that upon the production of the *postea*, the Court held that neither the tenant without the licence of the lord, nor the lord without consent of the tenant, could dig in those copper mines, being new mines (*b*).

On motion to stay waste, a particular title must be shewn, and the motion should be made upon affidavit of the title, waste committed, and a certificate of the bill filed (*c*).

(*a*) 2 L. R. 6[illegible] (*b*) 1 P. Wms. 40[illegible] (*c*) 3 Atk. 575. Com. Dig. [illegible]

CHAPTER XVII.

Of the Landlord's Remedy against third Persons

SECTION I. *By Action on the Case for Nusances, to the Injury of his Reversion.*

SECTION II. *By Action against the Sheriff, on Stat. 8. Ann. c. 14. for removing the Tenant's Goods under an Execution without paying a Year's Rent.*

SECTION III. *By Action on the Stat. 11 G. 2. c. 19. for assisting the Tenant in a fraudulent Removal of his Goods.*

SECTION I. *Action on the Case for Nusances to the Injury to his Reversion.*

AN action of trespass on the case lies for a nuisance to the habitation or estate of another, by which remedy the landlord may recover damages commensurate with the degree of injury that he has sustained by the deterioration of that property of which the reversion is in him.

Indeed, touching the remedies afforded to the landlord and the tenant respectively for a nuisance to the thing demised, an action may be brought by one in respect of his inheritance, for the injury done to the value of it, and by the other, in respect of his possession (*a*).

As, if a man have an ancient house, and another build so near as to darken his windows, he may have an action upon the case (*b*).

So, if a man build a new house, and afterwards grant the adjacent soil, and the grantee by an edifice upon it stop the lights of the other

(*a*) 4 Bac. 2141.   (*b*) Com. Dig. tit. "Action upon the Case for a Nusance," (A).

house, though it was not an antient house, for if a man build a new house upon part of his land, and afterwards sell the house to another, neither the vendor, nor any other claiming under him, may stop the lights: but if he sell the vacant ground to another, and keep the house without reserving the benefit of the lights, the vendee may build (a).

A custom that one may build upon a new foundation to the obstruction of antient lights, is void (b).

If the lights of the house be stopped up by throwing logs, *&c.* this action will lie (c).

If a man fixes a spout to his own house, from whence the rain falls into the yard of another, and hurts the foundation of his buildings, this action will lie. So, if a man dig a pit in his land, so near that my land falls into the pit (d).

So, it lies against one who erects any thing offensive so near the house of another, that it becomes useless thereby, as a swine-sty, or a lime-kiln, or a dye-house, or a tallow-furnace, or a privy, or a brew-house, or a tan-vat, or a smelting-house, or a smith's forge (e).

So, if a man erect a watch-house, stable, *&c.* and put filth in it, to the annoyance of a garden (f).

So, if a parson permit the tithes to continue upon the soil, so that the grass there is corrupted, or a vendee of hay, after the time agreed for carrying it away (g).

So if a lessee over-charge his room with weight, whereby it falls upon the cellar beneath (h).

So if a tenant who ought to inclose against my land, do not inclose, by which the cattle of his tenants enter into my land, and do damage to me. But the action must be brought against the person in possession; for it is clear that an action on the case for not repairing fences, whereby another person was damnified, cannot be supported against the owner of the inheritance, when it is in the possession of another person. Deplorable indeed would be the situation of landlords, if they were liable to be harassed with actions for the culpable neglect of their tenants (i).

So an action upon the case lies, if a man erect a mill so near to my antient mill, that the water to my mill is obstructed or diverted. So, if part only of the stream is diverted. So, if he stop a water course, whereby my land was overflowed. So, if water has been accustomed to run to his well, and from thence to his land for his use, and one diverts the stream from coming to the well (k).

So a man possessed of an antient ferry may bring an action against

[illegible]

one who sets up a new ferry near to it; for if it be an antient ferry, he is compellable to keep boats, &c. (*a*).

So, if without warrant one erect a market, to the prejudice of another market (*b*).

So, if the soil, over which another has a way, be ploughed by the tenant of the land, it is a nuisance (*c*).

If the nuisance be to the damage of the inheritance, he in reversion shall have an action for it, notwithstanding that plaintiff might have an assise, or *quod permittat* (*d*).

The action lies as well against him who continues the nuisance as against him who originally erected it: for though the party having recovered in one, cannot have another action for the same erection, he may maintain a new action for the continuance of it (*e*).

So if *A.* recover damages against *B.* for stopping his lights, and afterward *B.* assign the lands in which the nuisance was erected, *A.* may maintain another action against *B.* for the continuance of the nuisance, for before the assignment *B.* was answerable for all the consequential damages, and it shall not be in his power to discharge himself by granting it over: yet *A.* may bring the action against the assignee. Though formerly a distinction was taken, viz. where the continuance occasions a new nuisance, and where the first erection has done all the mischief, that in the first case the assignee is liable to an action, but not in the second (*f*).

So, if *A.* divert water by a pipe and cock to his house, an action lies against his wife after his death, if she lives in the house, and uses the water, for every turning of the cock is a new nuisance (*g*).

So, if a man erect a house or mill to the nuisance of another, every occupier afterwards is subject to an action for the nuisance (*h*).

So, if a man recover against *A.* for the erection of a nuisance, he may afterwards maintain an action against him, for the continuance of it, and this, although he had made a lease to another, for the plaintiff might bring the action, notwithstanding his recovery for the erection, against either the tenant for years or his under lessee, at his election (*i*).

All these cases go upon this principle, that every man should so use his own as not to dammify another: for some damage must be proved in order to sustain this action, the mere act of diverting a water-course, &c. not being sufficient, if it do no injury to the plaintiff's inheritance, or possession (*k*).

Of the Declaration.—In an action upon the case for a nuisance, the plaintiff must shew himself entitled to the thing to which the nuisance

(*a*) B. N. P. 76 [illegible] (*b*) Com. Dig. [illegible] (*c*) [illegible] (*d*) Com. Dig. [illegible] B. (*e*) 1 Ld Raym. 372 [illegible] (*f*) Bull. N. P. [illegible] (*g*) Com. Dig. [illegible] Action, &c. [illegible] [A] [illegible] (*h*) Cro. Jac. 555 (*i*) [illegible] (*k*) Bull. N. P. 76 [illegible]

was done, at the time of the nuisance: as in this action for diverting his water-course to his mill, he must shew, that he was seised of the mill at the time but a seisin in law is sufficient for this action (*a*)

Therefore, if the plaintiff allege that his father was seised and died, and a discent to himself by virtue of which he was seised, without saying that he entered, it will be well (*b*).

But in such action the plaintiff need not set forth his title to the premises, it is sufficient for him to shew that he was possessed of them (*c*)

He ought, also, to shew that the diversion was a prejudice to his mill for as damage must be proved, such allegation is material (*d*)

So, he ought to allege a continuance of the nuisance to the time of the action only, for *adhuc continuatur existit* is ill, for that goes to the time of the declaration. But, if the declaration shews a continuing nuisance, it is not material, though the first nuisance was before the plaintiff was entitled (*e*).

So, if the plaintiff allege, that his house, mill, &c. was an antient house, &c without prescribing for it, or that it was antiently erected, for that is tantamount (*f*).

So, a declaration for stopping lights is sufficient, though it do not say an antient messuage and if the plaintiff allege that he was possessed of such a house, &c. in which he ought to have so many lights, &c. without more, it is sufficient (*g*)

So, a declaration for diverting a water-course, which was used to run to a well, and from thence to his house, is sufficient, though it do not say from what place it runs to the well. This was ruled after verdict, for it ought to be proved (*h*).

So, a declaration against a man for causing water to flow through pipes near the foundation of the plaintiff's house, and neglecting to repair them, so that the water flowed through them and sapped the foundation of the plaintiff's house, is unexceptionable after verdict, though it do not expressly state that the pipes were the defendant's, that he laid them there, or that he is bound to repair them (*i*).

Touching the pleas to this action, the general issue is, not guilty, which may be pleaded where case is brought for a nuisance in overhanging the plaintiff's house, &c. or for a nuisance in stopping his lights (*k*)

So, the custom of the city of *London*, by which a man may build upon an antient foundation against the [illegible] of another, to which the plaintiff may reply by denying the custom, which shall be tried by the mouth of the Recorder (*l*).

(*a*) Com. Dig. [illegible] (*d*) [illegible] (*g*) [illegible]
(*b*) [illegible] (*e*) Ibid (*f*) Ibid. [illegible] 596
[illegible] (*c*) [illegible] (*h*) [illegible] (*k*) [illegible]

But to an action upon the case for a nuisance the defendant cannot plead, that being a blacksmith, he came to the house wherein he dwells, by the advice of the plaintiff himself, and there erected a forge for his trade (*a*)

In an action for diverting a water-course, the defendant pleaded, that he was seised of two closes through which, *&c.* and that he and all those, *&c.* had used to water their cattle in the same water-course, *&c* and the Court held that one prescription could not be pleaded against another, without a traverse: but if upon the general issue it had been proved that the water was usually drunk up by the cattle of the defendant, the plaintiff would have failed in his prescription (*b*).

If the verdict finds generally, that the house is not erected upon the antient foundation, the whole shall be abated, though it exceed only a foot (*c*).

Section II. *Of the Action on the Case against the Sheriff for removing Goods under an Execution without paying a Year's Rent, by Virtue of the Stat.* 8 Ann. c. 14.

Executions at common law took place of all debts that were not specific liens, even of rents due to landlords At length, it being thought hard that landlords should not have something like a specific lien, Parliament gave them a remedy for one year's rent, but no more, because *vigilantibus et non dormientibus jura subveniunt* (*d*)

The remedy in question is by action on the case by virtue of the stat. 8 *Ann* c. 14. for the more easy and effectual recovery of rents reserved on leases for life or lives, term of years, at will, or otherwise, by sect. 1. of which it is enacted, " That no goods or chattels whatsoever, lying or being in or upon any messuage, lands or tenements which are, or shall be leased for life or lives, term of years at will, or otherwise, shall be liable to be taken by virtue of any execution on any pretence whatsoever, unless the party at whose suit the said execution is sued out, shall before the removal of such goods from off the said premises, by virtue of such execution or extent, pay to the landlord of the said premises or his bailiff, all such sum or sums of money as are or shall be due for rent for the said [illegible] at the time of the taking such goods or chattels by virtue of such execution, provided the said arrears do not amount to more than one year's rent. and in case the said arrears

(*a*) Com Dig [illegible] (E. 2) (*b*) Bull N P 75. (*c*) Com. Dig. [illegible]
(*d*) 2 Wils 141

shall exceed one year's rent, then the said party, at whose suit such execution is sued out, paying the said landlord or his bailiff one year's rent, may proceed to execute his judgment, as he might have done before the making of the Act, and the sheriff or other officers are thereby empowered and required to levy and pay to the plaintiff, as well the money so paid for rent, as the execution money.

Sect. 8 "Provided always, that nothing in the Act contained shall be construed to extend to hinder or prejudice her [his] Majesty, her [his] heirs or successors, in the levying, recovering or seizing, any debts, fines, penalties, or forfeitures due or payable to her [his] Majesty, &c. but that it shall and may be lawful for her [his] Majesty, &c. to levy, recover, and seize such debts, &c. in the same manner as if the Act had never been made."

This statute shall have a liberal construction: and the words "party at whose suit the execution is sued out," &c. shall be construed to mean either the plaintiff or defendant, whose judgment and execution it is (*a*).

The action lies by an executor or administrator against the bailiff of a liberty for executing a *fieri facias*, and removing the goods off the premises before the landlord was paid a year's rent for the testator or intestate had an interest for which his executor or administrator may bring an action (*b*).

But, where the goods were taken and the money levied before administration taken out, it was held, that as execution was executed, that is to say, as the goods were actually sold, the administrator came too late *Powys*, J. was however of opinion, it seems, that the administration should have relation to the time of the death of the intestate, because, by the ecclesiastical law, it is not to be granted till within fourteen days of an intestate's death. but the rest of the Court denied this proposition, for relations which are but fictions in law, shall not, they said, devest any right vested in a stranger *mesne* between the intestate's death and the administration. The statute, it is true, was made for the benefit of landlords, and to prevent the tenant's setting up a sham execution to defeat him of the rent. He has still the same remedy that he had before, and if he will have the additional remedy, he must make himself capable of it, which the administrator here could not. He could not demand the rent, it not being certain that he would be administrator, for the ordinary might refuse, and the sheriff is not obliged to wait and see if any body comes and demands the rent. He cannot take notice what arrears there are, but if the landlord comes and acquaints him with it, then, and not till then, is he obliged

[illegible]

to see the year's rent satisfied before removal of the goods. If it should be otherwise, it would be in the power of him that is entitled to administration to defeat the plaintiff of his execution, for suppose he never takes administration, must the execution stand still? If the landlord himself had not demanded before removal, he had been too late: here was no landlord at all, so that there could be no demand, and it is now too late to ask it (*a*).

Therefore notice to the sheriff is necessary in order to subject him to an action for removing the goods before a year's rent be paid (*b*); for neither a plaintiff nor defendant has any right to go upon the premises, and the law gives the entry to the sheriff only by virtue of the execution: but after he has notice of rent being due to the landlord, he cannot remove the goods before he has satisfied the landlord one year's rent. The landlord shall have the like benefit of distress for one year's rent as if there had been no execution at all: unless the rent be paid, the sheriff must quit, and if he do not quit, a special action on the case lies against him after notice of the rent due (*c*).—The want of alleging notice, however, is helped by the verdict (*d*).

The landlord's rent must be paid without any deduction, the sheriff therefore cannot claim poundage of him (*e*).

The remedy, as before observed, is for one year's rent and no more. Therefore, where there are two executions, the landlord cannot have a year's rent on each: for the intent of the Act was only to continue a lien as to one year, and to punish him for his laches, if he let more run in arrear (*f*).

If the goods seized be not sold or removed by the sheriff, so as to transfer the property therein, but the defendant pays the debt and costs, the landlord, though he has given notice and demanded the rent, is not entitled in such case.

A bill of sale was made by the sheriff, and it was held to be a removal of the goods taken by a writ of *fieri facias* (*g*).

If an extent comes in, the landlord cannot claim his rent although a distress be taken the day before.—So, on extent or an outlawry, although he had distrained three days previous to the entry, and motion be made to be paid under the statute; but this is denied. If a distress be taken *October* 29, and an extent dated *November* 4, and corn, &c. seized, the landlord cannot have his rent, for no property was devested by the distress, and they were in the landlord's hands by way of pledge; but an attachment was refused, although it was a contempt to oppose the extent (*h*).

(*a*) 1 Str 97. (*b*) L. J. A. 214. (*c*) 2 Wils 141. (*d*) 1 Str 214.
(*e*) Ibid 643. (*f*) 2 Str 1024. (*g*) Barn 211.
(*h*) Imp Sheriff [illegible] Bull's Ni. Pri. [illegible] "Distress," xv.

An immediate extent against the king's debtor tested after a distress taken for rent justly due to the landlord, with notice to the tenant being the king's debtor, and appraisement of the goods and chattels, but before sale, shall prevail against the distress (*a*).

A distinction has been taken between proceedings at the suit and for the benefit of the crown, and an outlawry in a civil suit (*b*) and in the latter instance it has been ruled that "the landlord ought to be satisfied a year's rent, because a *capias utlagatum* at the suit of the party is to be considered only as a private execution," but if the outlawry be reversed, it would be otherwise (*c*).

A commission of bankrupt is not considered as an execution *quoad hoc*: therefore, as a landlord may on the one hand distrain for his whole rent after assignment or sale by the assignees, if the goods are not removed, so on the other hand, if he suffer the assignees to sell off the goods, he is not entitled to his rent, but must come in *pro rata* with the other creditors under the commission (*d*).

The ground landlord of a house, in which an under-lessee dwelt, against whom an execution was sued out, is not within the statute, which extends only to the immediate landlord (*e*).

In an action against the sheriff for taking goods without leaving a year's rent, the declaration need not state all the particulars of the demise; but if it do, and they are not proved as stated, there shall be a nonsuit. The distinction is between that which may be rejected as surplusage which might have been struck out on motion, and what cannot.—Where the declaration contains impertinent matter, foreign to the cause, and which the Master, on a reference to him, would strike out (irrelevant covenants for instance,) that will be rejected by the Court, and need not be proved. But if the very ground of the action is mis-stated, as where you undertake to recite that part of a deed on which the action is founded, and it is mis-recited, that will be fatal; for then the case decided on is different from that which is proved, and you must recover *secundum allegata et probata* (*f*).

The landlord is not always driven to this action for his remedy, for there is a shorter way, by motion to the Court, that he may have restitution to the amount of the goods the sheriff has sold, as in the principal case, in which the bailiff became a wrongdoer immediately after he had notice of rent being due to the landlord (*g*).

Instead of bringing an action against the sheriff, &c. when the goods are sold after notice, the best way for the landlord is to move the Court,

(*a*) Pri. Rev. 112 [illegible] (*e*) 7 T. R. 274
[illegible] 1 Atk. 1[illegible] [illegible] Doug. 665 [illegible] 1 T. R. 2[illegible]
[illegible] 2 Wils. 1[illegible]

that he may have restitution to the amount of the goods which the sheriff has sold, if they amount to less than a year's rent, or if they amount to more, then to have so much as will satisfy a year's rent (a).

On motion to have rent paid out of the money levied, it appeared that the sheriff's warrant on the execution, after it was sealed, had been altered, and a new bailiff's name inserted. *Per Cur.* The warrant being altered, no goods are taken in execution thereby. Let the bailiff and attorney privy to the alteration, shew cause why an attachment should not issue against them (b).

SECTION III. *The Landlord's Remedy on the Statute* 11 *Geo.* 2. c. 19. *touching Goods fraudulently carried off the Premises.*

The statute 11 *G.* 2. *c.* 19. *s.* 1. enacts that "In case any tenant or tenants, lessee or lessees, for life or lives, term of years, at will, sufferance, or otherwise, of any messuages, lands, tenements, or hereditaments, upon the demise or holding whereof any rent is reserved, shall fraudulently or clandestinely convey away or carry off or from such premises, his, her, or their goods or chattels, to prevent the landlord or lessor, landlords or lessors, from distraining the same for arrears of rent so reserved, it shall be lawful to or for every landlord or lessor, landlords or lessors, or any person or persons by him, her, or them for that purpose lawfully impowered, within the space of thirty days next ensuing such conveying away or carrying off such goods or chattels, to take and seize such goods and chattels wherever the same shall be found, as a distress for the said arrears of rent, and the same to sell or otherwise dispose of, in such manner as if the said goods and chattels had actually been distrained by such lessor or landlord, lessors or landlords, in and upon such premises for such arrears of rent."

Sect. 2. "Provided always that no landlord or lessor, or other person entitled to such arrears of rent, shall take or seize any such goods or chattels for the same which shall be sold *bonâ fide*, and for a valuable consideration, before such seizure made, to any person or persons not privy to such fraud as aforesaid."

By sect. 3. "To deter tenants from such fraudulent conveying away their goods and chattels, and others from wilfully aiding or assisting therein, or concealing the same, it is enacted that if any person or

(a) 2 Sell. Pract. 570 (b) Bar. 199

persons shall wilfully and knowingly aid and assist any such tenant or lessee in such fraudulent conveying away or carrying off of any part of his or her goods or chattels, or in concealing the same, all and every person and persons so offending shall forfeit to the landlord or landlords, lessor or lessors, from whose estate such goods and chattels were fraudulently carried off as aforesaid, double the value of the goods by him, her, or them respectively carried off or concealed as aforesaid, to be recovered by action of debt in any of his Majesty's Courts of Record at *Westminster*, or in the Courts of Session in the counties palatine of *Chester*, *Lancaster*, or *Durham*, respectively, or in the Courts of Grand Sessions in *Wales*, wherein no essoin, protection, or wager of law shall be allowed, nor more than one imparlance."

Sect 4 "Provided always, that where the goods and chattels so fraudulently carried off or concealed shall not exceed the value of 50*l.* it shall be lawful for the landlord or landlords, from whose estate such goods and chattels were removed, his, her, or their bailiff, servant or agent, in his, her, or their behalf, to exhibit a complaint in writing against such offender or offenders, before two or more justices of the peace of the same county, riding, or division of such county, residing near the place whence such goods and chattels were removed, or near the place where the same were found, not being interested in the lands or tenements whence such goods were removed; who may summon the parties concerned, examine the fact, and all proper witnesses upon oath, or if any such witness be one of the people called *Quakers*, upon affirmation required by law, and in a summary way to determine, whether such person or persons be guilty of the offence with which he or they are charged, and to enquire in like manner of the value of the goods and chattels by him, her, or them respectively so fraudulently carried off or concealed as aforesaid, and upon full proof of the offence, by order under their hands and seals, the said justices may and shall adjudge the offender or offenders to pay double the value of the said goods and chattels to such landlord or landlords, his, her, or their bailiff, servant, or agent, at such time as such justices shall appoint and in case the offender or offenders, having notice of such order, shall refuse or neglect so to do, may and shall, by warrant under their hands and seals, levy the same by distress and sale of the goods and chattels of the offender or offenders, and for want of such distress, may commit the offender or offenders to the house of correction, there to be kept to hard labour, without bail or mainprize, for the space of six months, unless the money so ordered to be paid as aforesaid shall be sooner satisfied"—Sect. 5. "Provided always that it shall be lawful for any person who thinks himself aggrieved by such order of the said two justices, to appeal to the next General or Quarter

Sessions, for the same county, who may and shall hear and determine such appeal, and give such costs to either party as they shall think reasonable, whose determination therein shall be final"—Sect. 6 "Provided also, that where the party appealing shall enter into recognizance with one or two sufficient surety or sureties in double the sum so ordered to be paid, with condition to appear at such General or Quarter Sessions, the order of the said two justices shall not be executed against him in the mean time."

By sect. 7, it is further enacted, "That where any goods or chattels fraudulently or clandestinely conveyed or carried away by any tenant or tenants, lessee or lessees, his, her, or their servant or servants, agent or agents, or other person or persons aiding or assisting therein, shall be put, placed, or kept in any house, barn, stable, out-house, yard, close or place locked up, fastened, or otherwise secured, so as to prevent such goods or chattels from being taken and seized as a distress for arrears and rent, it shall be lawful for the landlord or landlords, lessor or lessors, his, her, or their steward, bailiff, receiver, or other person or persons empowered to take and seize, as a distress for rent, such goods and chattels (first calling to his, her, or their assistance the constable, headborough, borsholder, or other peace officer of the hundred, borough, parish, district, or place, where the same shall be suspected to be concealed, who are hereby required to aid and assist therein, and in case of a dwelling-house, oath being first made before some Justice of the peace of a reasonable ground to suspect that such goods or chattels are therein) in the daytime to break open and enter into such house, barn, stable, out-house, yard, close, and place, and to take and seize such goods and chattels for the said arrears of rent, as he, she or they might have done by virtue of this or any former Act, if such goods and chattels had been put in any open field or place"

Justices either of the county from which the tenants fraudulently remove goods, or of that in which they are concealed may convict the offenders in their respective counties (*a*).

But in order to justify the landlord in seizing, under this statute, within thirty days, goods removed off the premises, as a distress for rent wherever found, the removal must have taken place after the rent became due, and must have been secret, and not open and in the face of day, as in such case the removal could not be said to be clandestine, within the meaning of the statute (*b*)

An averment in a declaration in an action of debt on Sect. 3. of this statute, to recover double the value of goods removed in order to prevent a distress. that "a certain sum was due for rent" before the goods

(*a*) [illegible] R. 156 (*b*) 2 Esp. R. 165.

were removed, need not be precisely proved as laid: for whether 5*l* or any other sum were in arrear is perfectly immaterial, the damages not being to be measured by the quantity of rent, but by the value of the goods removed. Besides, the gist of the action is the fraudulent removal of the goods from the premises in order to defeat the distress; it was therefore immaterial to the defendants whether one sum or another were due for rent, for in either case they are guilty of a tort. Where the variance, therefore, does not consist in any part of the contract, but in an averment of matter subsequent to the contract, such averment being merely a matter of inducement to the action, need not be precisely proved (*a*).

So the notice of distress may be abandoned; for a party may distrain for rent and avow for fealty (*b*).

[See also respecting this statute as it regards the duty of a magistrate, tit. *Distress*, 1 *Burn's Just.*]

(*a*) 3 T. R. 6[illegible], 6[illegible]. [illegible]

CHAPTER XVIII.

Of the Remedies for Tenants against Landlords. Of the Action of Replevin.

SECTION I. *Of the Action.*
SECTION II. *Of the Judgment, &c.*

SECTION I. *Of the Action of Replevin.*

THE action of replevin is founded upon, and is the regular way of contesting the validity of, a distress; being a re-delivery of the pledge, or thing taken in distress, to the owner, by the sheriff or his deputy, upon the owner giving security to try the right of the distress, and to restore it, if the right be adjudged against him: after which the distrainer may keep it till tender made of sufficient amends, but must then re-deliver it to the owner (*a*).

In this writ or action, both the plaintiff and defendant are called actors, the plaintiff suing for damages, and the defendant or avowant to have a return of the goods or cattle (*b*).

Replevin is an action founded on the right, and different from trespass, or detinue; and it is now held, that as no lands can be recovered in this action, it cannot, with any propriety, be considered as a real action, though the title of lands may incidentally come in question; as it may do in an action of trespass or even debt, which are actions merely personal (*c*).

In our account of this action, we shall endeavour to confine our notice of it as it regards distress for rent, or cattle damage feasant; the services of copyholders, &c being without the scope of our consideration.

Who may have Replevin.—This remedy may be said to be of common right: for if a man by his deed grant a rent with a clause of distress,

(*a*) 3 Bl. Com. 147. (*b*) Bac. Abr. tit. "Replevin," &c. (A.) (*c*) Ibid.

and grant further that the party shall keep the goods distrained against gages and pledges, until the rent be paid, yet shall the sheriff replevy the goods distrained, for it is against the nature of such a distress to be irreplevisable, and by such an invention the current of replevins would be overthrown to the hindrance of the commonwealth, and therefore it was disallowed by the whole Court, and awarded that the defendant should gage deliverance [that is, engage to deliver the distress to the owner on his pledging to try the distrainer's right thereto] or else go to prison (*a*).

It is a general rule that the plaintiff ought to have the property of the goods in him at the time of the taking. but there are two kinds of properties, a general property, which every absolute owner hath, and a special property, as goods pledged or taken to manure his lands, or the like, and of either of these replevin lies (*b*).

An executor may have a replevin for goods taken in the lifetime of his testator (*c*)

So, if the cattle or other goods of a feme sole be taken and she afterwards intermarry, the husband alone may have replevin: and if they join, judgment will not be arrested after verdict, because the Court will presume them jointly interested (as they may be, if a distress be taken of goods of which a man and woman were joint-tenants, and afterwards intermarry), the avowry admitting the property to be in the manner it is laid.—But in replevying goods which a wife holds as executrix, this action cannot be brought by either of them singly, but they must be joined (*d*)

Where cattle put on the premises for the purpose of taking possession where the tenant had held over, were distrained by the tenant on the ground of being damage feasant, on replevin being brought L. *Kenyon* said, The case is too plain for argument. Here is a tenant from year to year, whose term expired upon a proper notice to quit, and because he holds over in defiance of law and justice, he now attempts to convert the lawful entry of his landlord into a trespass. If an action of trespass had been brought, it is clear that the landlord could have justified under a plea of *liberum tenementum.*—If, indeed, the landlord had entered with a strong hand to dispossess the tenant by force, he might have been indicted for a forcible entry; but there can be no doubt of his right to enter upon the land at the expiration of the term. There is not the slightest pretence for considering him a trespasser in this case, and therefore there must be judgment for the plaintiff (*e*).

If the goods of several persons be taken, they cannot join in replevin, but every one must have a several action (*f*).

(*a*) Co. Lit. 145, b (*b*) Ibid (*c*) Bull. N. P. 53
(*d*) Ibid. Bac. Abr. tit. "Replevin," &c. (G.) (*e*) 7 T. R. 431 (*f*) Co. Lit. 145. b

Tenants, in common, therefore, should not join.—But coparceners should join, for they make but one heir: and for the same reason, so should joint-tenants (*a*).

Against whom.—Replevin lies against him who takes the goods, and also against him who commands the taking or against both (*b*).

So it lies against him who takes damage feasant, if he detains after amends tendered (*c*).

Replevin lies for what.—Replevin lies for whatever is capable of being distrained, and for nothing else; for the action is the remedy of the party whose goods are distrained.

Replevin, therefore, does not lie of things *feræ naturæ*, nor of deeds or charters; nor of money; nor of leather made into shoes (*d*).

But if a mare in foal, a cow in calf, *&c.* be distrained, and they happen to bring forth their young whilst they are in custody of the distrainer, a replevin lies of the foal, calf, *&c.* (*e*).

Replevin lies of a ship: so, of the sails of a ship (*f*).

But no replevin lies of goods taken beyond the seas, though brought hither by the defendant afterwards

In those cases in which replevin does not lie, the party may bring an action of detinue to recover the deeds, goods, *&c. in specie* (*g*).

The plaintiff having brought replevin for goods levied under a warrant of distress for an assessment, by a special sessions under the Highway Act, 13 Geo 3 chap. 78 sect. 47, on the ground of the premises for which he was assessed, being situated without the township which was liable to repair the road; the Court refused to set aside the proceedings (*h*).

The several kinds of Replevin.—Replevin may be made either by original writ of replevin at common law, or by plaint by the statute of *Marlbridge*, 52 *H.* 3. *c.* 21.

Formerly, when the party distrained upon intended to dispute the right of the distress, he had no other process by the common law than by a writ of replevin, *replegiari facias*, which issued out of Chancery, commanding the sheriff to deliver the distress to the owner, and afterwards to do justice in respect of the matter in dispute in his own County Court. But this being a tedious method of proceeding, the beasts and other goods were long detained from the owner, to his great loss and damage.

The statute of *Marlbridge*, therefore, directs, " That (without suing a writ out of the Chancery) if the beasts of any person be taken and wrongfully withholden, the sheriff, after complaint made to him thereof, may deliver them without let or gainsaying of him that took the

(*a*) Cro. Eliz. 530. Salk. 390. Bull. N. P. 53. (*b*) 2 Roll. 431. l. 5. (*c*) F. N. B. 19. G. (*d*) Bac. Abr. tit. " Replevin," &c. (F.) (*e*) Ibid. (*f*) Ibid. (*g*) Ibid. p. (*h*) 2 Bos. & Pul. N. R. 399.

beasts, if they were taken out of liberties; and if they were taken within liberties, and the bailiffs of the liberty will not deliver them, then the sheriff, for default of those bailiffs, shall cause them to be delivered."

Also, for the more speedy delivery of cattle taken by way of distress, the statute of the first of *Philip* and *Mary*, c. 12 provides, that the sheriff shall make, at least, four deputies in each county, dwelling not above twelve miles from each other, for the sole purpose of making replevins, under a penalty of 5*l* for every month such deputies shall be omitted to be provided.

When any man's goods, therefore, are distrained or impounded, he may, upon application for the purpose to one of these deputies, upon giving pledges to return the distress if judgment be against him, have a replevin, by which his goods will be restored to his possession.

But when an Act of Parliament orders a distress and sale of goods, it is in the nature of an execution, and replevin does not lie (*a*).

Out of what Courts Replevin issues.—The sheriff, upon plaint made to him without writ, may either by parol or precept command his bailiff to deliver the goods, that is, to make replevin of them; and by the words of the statute of *Marlbridge*, "after complaint made to him thereof," he may take a plaint, out of the County Court, and make replevin presently, which he is to enter in the Court (*b*).

By this statute, the sheriff may hold plea in the County Court on replevin by plaint, whatever may be the value of the subject in dispute, although in other actions he shall only hold plea where the matter is under 40*s* value; and the plaint may be taken at any time as well out of, as in Court. But if the taking be in right of the Crown, or if any thing touching the freehold come in question, or ancient demesne be pleaded, or if the distrainer claim property in the goods, and on a writ *de proprietate probanda*, they be found to be his, the sheriff can proceed no further, but must return the proceedings into the Court of K. B. or C. P. to be there, if thought adviseable, finally determined (*c*).

But either party may, by the writs of *pone*, and *recordari facias*, remove a replevin to these superior courts; the plaintiff at his election, the defendant upon reasonable cause. It is therefore usual to carry it up, in the first instance, to *Westminster Hall* (*d*).

The writ of replevin issues out of the Court of Chancery, and is returnable only into the Court of King's Bench, Common Pleas, the court of the Cinque Ports, and the County Court (*e*).

If the sheriff makes replevin he need not return the writ; but if he does, he ought to return the cause; and if he do not, an attachment

(*a*) Bac. Abr. [illegible] Replevin, &c. (C) (*b*) Bull. N. P. 52 (*c*) 2 Bl. Com. 149.
(*d*) Co. Litt. 145 b. 2 Crom. Prac. 227 (*e*) 2 Inst. 312

lies against him to the coroners, commanding them to attach the sheriff for his contempt, and in the interim make replevin (*a*).

Proceedings in replevin cannot be carried on in the Hundred Court Baron, or any other court claiming a jurisdiction over such proceedings by prescription, unless perhaps by process of the Court after a plaint entered. But it lies by plaint in *London* (*b*).

If the distress be made in a franchise or bailiwick, the sheriff is to direct the replevin to the bailiff thereof to deliver the goods upon pledges, and if he make no answer, or return that he will make no deliverance, or the like, then the sheriff may enter into the liberty, and make deliverance, and if the distress be taken without the liberty and impounded within the liberty, then the sheriff may enter and make deliverance, and need not first make out a warrant to the sheriff of the liberty (*c*).

But if a man were to presume to replevy goods, seized in order to condemnation, it would be a contempt of the Court of Exchequer, for which an attachment would be granted instantly (*d*).

The action of replevin is of two sorts. 1. in the *detinet*, 2. in the *detinuit*. Where the party has had his goods re-delivered to him by the sheriff upon a writ of replevin, or upon a plaint levied before him, the action is in the *detinuit*, "wherefore he detained the goods," &c. but where the sheriff has not made such replevin, but the distrainer still keeps possession, the action is in the *detinet*, "wherefore he detains the goods," &c.—The advantage that the plaintiff has in bringing an action of replevin in the *detinet*, instead of an action of trespass *de bonis asportatis*, is, that he can oblige the defendant to re-deliver the goods to him immediately, in case, upon making his avowry, they appear to be repleviable: but as he may more speedily have them delivered immediately after they are distrained by application to the sheriff, the action in the *detinet* has fallen into disuse, and is never brought, unless the distrainer has eloined [removed] the goods so that the sheriff cannot get at them to make replevin: whereupon, after avowry made, the plaintiff may pray that the defendant gage deliverance; or he may act as mentioned under title *the writ of Withernam* which *vide postea* (*e*).

The method of proceeding usually adopted now is by plaint, that by writ being generally disused.

The sheriff is obliged to grant replevins in all such cases as are allowed of by law, and the officer who takes the goods by virtue of a replevin, issuing for what cause soever, is not liable to an action of trespass, unless the party in whose possession the goods were claim property therein; and in all cases of misbehaviour by the sheriff or other

(*a*) 2 Sell. Pract. 244.
(*b*) 1 Ld Raym. 217; 2 Lil. Reg. 557. Bro. R. 3.
(*c*) 2 Inst. 149, 194.
(*d*) Anstr. 212.
(*e*) 2 Sell. Pract. 241.

officers in relation to replevins, they are subject to the controul of the king's superior courts, and punishable by attachment for such misbehaviour (*a*).

Where a tenant has, on coming into possession under an assignment, had notice that the lease was held under any particular person to whom the former tenant has paid rent, the title of this person cannot be contested in an action of replevin (*b*).

Of the Pledges.—The sheriff, when, upon complaint made to him, he makes replevin must take two kinds of pledges: 1st, by the common law, that the party replevying will pursue his action against the distrainer, for which purpose he puts in *plegii de prosequendo*, or pledges to prosecute at common law; and 2dly, by stat. 13. *E.* 1. *c.* 1. that if the right be determined against him he will return the distress again; for which purpose he is bound to find *plegii de retorno habendo*, or pledges to make return, if it be so adjudged (*c*).

The pledges taken must not only be sufficient in estate, *viz.* capable to answer in value, but likewise sufficient in law and under no incapacity; and therefore infants, *&c.* are not to be taken as pledges, neither are any persons politic or bodies corporate. But the sufficiency of these pledges is discretionary, and if the sheriff returns insufficient pledges, he shall answer for the price of the goods himself; for insufficient pledges are as no pledges.—The pledges when taken must be recorded in the County Court (*d*)

Upon plaint being made, and pledges found, which is done at the sheriff's office, the sheriff or one of his deputies, by stat. 1 *E.* 2. *P.* *& M.* is to make replevin of the goods or cattle distrained, which is done by granting a warrant (*e*).

There is no particular time when the replevin must be made, as the distress cannot be disposed of, but must be only kept as a pledge.

In replevin, a bond instead of pledges, taken by a sheriff to prosecute the action with effect for wrongfully taking the plaintiff's gelding, and to make return thereof if return should be adjudged, is good: but he cannot take gage instead of pledges (*f*).

If the sheriff neglect to take a replevin-bond, the party injured may have his action against him; but it is not a contempt of Court for which they will grant an attachment (*g*).

If upon such bond the plaintiff in replevin do not enter his plaint in the County Court, the bond will be forfeited, so, if afterwards he do not proceed in the prosecution; or if he be nonsuit, or has a verdict against him (*h*).

But if the plaintiff in replevin enters his plaint, and afterwards is

(*a*) Bac. Abr. tit. "Replevin," &c. (C.) (*b*) 1 Esp. R. 91 (*c*) Bac. Abr. ubi ante.
(*d*) Co. Lit. 145. 2 Inst. 340 (*e*) 2 Sell. Prac. 246 (*f*) 1 Ld. Raym. 278
(*g*) 2 T. R. 617 (*h*) Com. Dig. tit. "Replevin" (D.)

restrained by injunction out of Chancery till his death, whereby his plaint abates, the bond will not be forfeited (*a*).

The bond may be assigned, if the plaintiff in replevin do not appear at the County Court *next* after giving the bond and he may sue on the bond as assignee of the sheriff in the superior Courts, though the replevin be not removed out of the County Court (*b*).

But though if the distress be not for rent, the bond is not assignable, yet the party may apply to the sheriff for the bond and to be at liberty to sue in his name.

How to make Replevin where Distress is for Rent.

If the tenant means to replevy, he must, within five days after notice of the distress, take with him two housekeepers, living in the city or county where the distress was made, and go to the sheriff's office of such city or county, where he must enter into a bond with the two housekeepers, as sureties in double the value of the goods distrained, according to stat. 11 *G.* 2. upon which the sheriff will direct a precept to one of his bailiffs, and the possession of the goods will be restored to the tenant to abide the event of the suit in replevin (*c*).

It has before been observed, that upon making replevin, two kinds of securities were at common law taken by the sheriff, *viz.* the one for prosecuting the suit, the other, for returning the goods if a return should be awarded The first were merely nominal (*John Doe* and *Richard Roe*,) but the second should be real responsible persons. Sheriffs however gradually became remiss in their duty, and often neglected taking these pledges *pro retorno habendo*, or, if any were taken, for the most part they were found to be indigent and irresponsible people (*d*).

The stat. 11 *G.* 2. *c.* 19. *s.* 23. therefore, for the better securing the payment of rents and preventing frauds by tenants, enacts, "That to prevent vexatious replevins of distresses taken for *rent*, all sheriffs and other officers having authority to grant replevins, may and shall, in every replevin of a distress for rent, take in their own names from the plaintiff and two responsible persons as sureties, a bond in double the value of the goods distrained (such value to be ascertained by the oath of one or more credible witness or witnesses not interested in the goods or distress, which oath the person granting such replevin is hereby authorized and required to administer,) and conditioned for prosecuting the suit with effect and without delay, and for duly returning

(*a*) Com Dig tit Repl. [illegible] (D), Carth [illegible]. (*b*) 5 T R 19[illegible]
(*c*) 2 Sell. Pract 26[illegible] [illegible]

the goods and chattels distrained, in case a return shall be awarded before any deliverance be made of the distress."

For the further protection of landlords and by way of putting the remedy into their own hands, it is also ordered by the same statute, "That such sheriff or other officer as aforesaid, taking any such bond, shall, at the request and costs of the avowant, or person making conusance, assign such bond to the avowant, or person aforesaid, by indorsing the same, and attesting it under his hand and seal, in the presence of two or more credible witnesses; which may be done without any stamp, provided the assignment so indorsed be duly stamped before any action be brought thereon and if the bond so taken and assigned be forfeited, the avowant or the person making conusance, may bring an action, and recover thereupon in his own name; and the Court where such action shall be brought may, by a rule of the same Court, give such relief to the parties, upon such bond, as may be agreeable to justice and reason, and such rule shall have the nature and effect of a defeazance to such bond."

Section II. *Of the Writs in Replevin.*

The original writ in replevin issues out of Chancery, and neither that nor the *alias* replevin are returnable, but are only in the nature of a *justicies* to empower the sheriff to hold the plea in his County Court, where a day is given to the parties. But the *pluries* replevin is always with this clause, "or shew cause before us," and is a returnable process (*a*).

The *pluries* replevin supersedes the proceedings of the sheriff, and the proceedings are upon that, and not upon the plaint as they are when that is removed by *recordari*. and though there is no summons in the writ, yet it gives a good day to the defendant to appear, and if he do not appear, a *pone* issues, and then a *capias* (*b*).

Process of outlawry lies upon the *capias in withernam*, which issues upon the sheriff's return of *averia elongata* upon the *pluries*, and upon the sheriff's special return of *nihil habet* on the *withernam*, there shall go a *capias* against the person, and so to outlawry (*c*)

Capias and process of outlawry in replevin were given by stat. 25 E. 3. c. 17.

Of the Withernam.—If on the *pluries* replevin the sheriff return that the cattle are eloigned to places unknown, &c. so that he cannot deliver them to the plaintiff, then shall issue a withernam (from the *Saxon* words *wedir*, other, and *naam*, distress, signifying another distress in-

(*a*) Bac. Abr. tit. "Replevin," &c. (*b*) Ibid. (*c*) Ibid.

stead of the former which was eloigned, that is, removed,] directed to the sheriff, commanding him to take the cattle or goods of the defendant, and detain them till the cattle or goods distrained are restored to the plaintiff, and if upon the first withernam a *nihil* be returned, then an *alias* and *pluries* replevin shall issue, and so to a *capias* and *exigent* (*a*).

The writ of withernam ought to rehearse the cause which the sheriff returns, for which he cannot replevy the cattle or goods; so that it does not lie upon a bare suggestion that the beasts are eloigned, &c.— If upon the withernam, the cattle are restored to the party who eloigned them, yet he shall pay a fine for his contempt [illegible].

The withernam is but mesne process, and cannot be an execution, [illegible] it is granted before judgment (*c*).

Cattle taken in withernam may be worked, or if cows, may be milked, for the party has them in lieu of his own, and [illegible] the party is to have the use of the cattle, he is not to have any allowance or payment for the expences he has been at in maintaining them (*d*).

In [illegible] against an executor on a judgment *de retorno habendo* against his testator for a cow, but which was not executed, it was held that the plaintiff should have execution, for the defendant could not be prejudiced, inasmuch as, if the sheriff return *averia elongata*, he shall not have a withernam but of the goods of the testator, or if there are no goods of the testator, the sheriff can take nothing, but shall return [illegible], and then the plaintiff hath his ordinary way to charge the defendant, [illegible] he hath [illegible]; and it was adjudged for the plaintiff [illegible].

If [illegible] *elongata* [illegible], the defendant's cattle are taken in withernam, yet upon the defendant's appearance, and pleading [illegible], [illegible] property, the defendant shall have his cattle again, and [illegible] withernam against the plaintiff; for if the property [illegible] be in question, there is no reason that the plaintiff should have [illegible] defendant's cattle.—Both the plaintiff and defendant, indeed, may, [illegible], have a withernam ([illegible]).

Of [illegible] *of second deliverance.*—At common law, if the plaintiff had been nonsuited either before or after verdict, the defendant who distrained should have had return, but not irreplevisable [this signifies, that [illegible] not to be replevied, or set at large upon sureties] so that the plaintiff after nonsuit might have had as many replevins as he chose. To remedy which [illegible] the stat. *Westm.* 2. (13 *Ed.* 1. [illegible] c. 2.) restrains the plaintiff from any more replevins after nonsuit, but gives a writ of second deliverance, and if in such writ the plaintiff be non-

(*a*) Bac. Abr. [illegible] (*b*) Ibid. (*c*) Ibid. (*d*) Ibid.
(*e*) Ibid. (*f*) Ibid.

suited, or if the plea be discontinued, or the writ abate, or if he prevail not in his suit, return irreplevisable shall be granted (*a*).

If defendant in replevin has return awarded upon nonsuit of the plaintiff, upon which he sues a writ *de ret. hab.*, and the sheriff returns *averia elongata per querentem*, and upon this a withernam is awarded, and upon the withernam, the defendant has *tota catalla* to him delivered of the goods of the plaintiff, and thereupon the plaintiff sues a second deliverance, he shall sue it for the first distress taken, and not for the withernam, as appears by the nature and form of the writ of second deliverance (*b*).

Retorno habendo awarded to the sheriff, after a writ of second deliverance prayed by the plaintiff, is a *supersedeas* to the *ret. hab.* and closes the sheriff's hand from making any return thereon.—If the sheriff will not execute the writ of second deliverance, the party has his remedy against him (*c*).

This stat. of *Westm.* 2 gives the writ of second deliverance out of the same Court whence the first replevin was granted, and a man cannot have it elsewhere, for if he could, then he might vary from the place limited, as to this, by the statute. But though the writ cannot vary from the first in year, day, place, or number of beasts, yet if the first writ was of a heifer, the second may be of a cow, as by presumption it may in that distance of time grow to such.

Where the defendant had avowed, and plaintiff being nonsuited brought this writ, it was held that though the writ be a *supersedeas* to the *ret. hab.* it is not so to the writ of enquiry of damages, for these damages are not for the thing avowed for, but are given by the stat. 21 *H.* 8 *c.* 19. as a compensation for the expence and trouble the avowant has been at.

In error on a second deliverance, the writ must be certified, and if it vary in substance from the declaration in replevin it shall be abated (*d*).

Upon a nonsuit either before or after evidence, this writ will lie, because there is no determination of the matter, and there a writ of second deliverance lies to bring the matter in question (*e*).

But no second deliverance lies after a judgment upon a demurrer, or after verdict, or confession of the avowry, but in all these cases, judgment must be entered with a return irreplevisable, for in the case of a demurrer and verdict, the matter is determined by the law, and in that of a confession, it is determined by the confession of the party (*f*).

Note. In an avowry for rent, the second deliverance is taken away by stat. 17 *Car.* 2 *c.* 7.

(*a*) B. Abr. ut ante (1 3) (*b*) Ibid (*c*) Ibid. (*d*) Ibid
(*e*) Ibid (*f*) Ibid

Yet if the plaintiff in replevin be nonsuited for want of delivering a declaration, which happened through any cause that would have entitled him to a writ of second deliverance, as sickness of the person employed, *&c.* the Court will order the defendant to accept of a declaration on payment of costs; else the plaintiff would be remediless, the writ of second deliverance being taken away by the 17th *C.* 2. *c.* 7.

Of Writ de proprietate probandâ.—The writ *de proprietate probandâ* issues out of Chancery, or K. B. or C. P. When it issues out of Chancery, it is an original, and goes upon the sheriff's return to the *alias* replevin, when out of either of the other Courts, it is judicial and granted on the return of the *pluries*, for the *pluries* is returnable only there, the original and *alias* giving no day, but being merely viconticl (*a*).

If the defendant in replevin claim property, the sheriff cannot proceed, for property must be tried by writ. In this case, therefore, the plaintiff may have the writ *de proprietate probanda* to the sheriff, who is to give notice to the parties of the time and place of executing it, for it is an inquest of office. If it be found for the plaintiff, the sheriff is to make deliverance; if for the defendant, then he is to proceed no further, but being an inquest of office, the plaintiff may notwithstanding have a replevin to the sheriff, and if he return the claim of property, yet it shall proceed in C. P. where the property shall be put in issue and finally tried. None but he who is party to the replevin shall have the writ *de prop. prob.*

The sheriff is to return the claim of property on the *pluries*, before which time the writ *de prop. prob.* does not issue, for it recites the *pluries* (*b*).

If the defendant in replevin claim property, the plaintiff may have the writ *de prop. prob.* without continuance of the replevin, though it be two or three years after: for by the claim of property the first is determined (*c*).

If the plaintiff has property and omits to claim it before the sheriff, he may notwithstanding plead property in himself, or in a stranger, either in abatement or bar.

If it be notified to him that comes in aid of the sheriff or his officer, that claim of property is made, he at his peril ought to desist, for if he take them away, he will be a trespasser *ab initio* (*d*).

A man cannot claim property in the County Court by his bailiff or servant, for if the claim be false a fine will be imposed for the contempt. But in K. B. one may make conusance and claim property by a bailiff, for there the bailiff is not liable to a fine (*e*).

(*a*) [illegible] (*b*) Ibid. (*c*) Ibid. (*d*) Ibid.
(*e*) [illegible]

Of Writ de retorno habendo.—A replevin being granted, if the person who takes the distress "avows," or if his bailiff make "conusance," and prove the distress to be lawfully taken, or if upon removal of the plaint into the Courts above, the plaintiff whose cattle were replevied, make default or do not declare, or prosecute his action, and thereby becomes nonsuited, or if a verdict be given against him, in any of these cases, the party distraining, that is, the defendant in replevin, shall have a writ *de retorno habendo*, which being a judicial writ, and not a returnable process, if on the *pluries* the sheriff return that the cattle, goods or chattels are eloigned, he shall have a *scire facias* against the pledges according to the stat. of *Westm.* 2. and if they have nothing, then he shall have a *withernam* against the plaintiff's own cattle (*a*).

A bailiff who makes conusance may have judgment of a return, and consequently, a writ *de ret. hab.* grounded on such judgment (*b*).

Of Return irreplevisable.—Return irreplevisable is a judicial writ directed to the sheriff for the final restitution of the cattle unjustly taken by another, and so found by verdict or after nonsuit in a second deliverance (*c*).

If the plea be to the writ, or any other plea be tried by a verdict, or judged upon demurrer, return irreplevisable shall be awarded, and no new replevin shall be granted, nor any second deliverance by stat. [illegible] 2. but only upon a nonsuit.—But if upon issue joined the plaintiff does not appear on the trial, being called for that purpose, [illegible] not be awarded, but the party may have a writ of second deliverance [illegible].

If a [illegible] irreplevisable, and a beast dies in the pound, [illegible], if the beast dies before judgment (*d*).

If a [illegible] be awarded, the owner of the cattle may [illegible], and if the defendant refuse to deliver the [illegible] in the nature of a pledge, the plaintiff may have detinue [illegible].

[illegible].—By the stat. *Westm.* 2. if the party who distrains, conveys the distress into any house, park, castle, or other place of strength, and refuses to suffer them to be replevied, the sheriff may take the *posse comitatus*, and on request, and refusal, may break open such house, castle, &c. and make deliverance. If the sheriff return that the beasts are inclosed in a park among savages, &c. or [illegible], &c. [illegible], or that the bailiff will not make deliverance of the cattle, these are not good returns, for he ought to enter the franchise and make [illegible] (*e*).

[illegible] (*e*) [illegible]

If a man sue a replevin in the County Court without writ, and the bailiff return to the sheriff, that he cannot have view of the cattle to deliver them, the sheriff ought by inquest of the office to inquire of the truth thereof, and if it be found by a jury that the cattle were eloigned, &c. the sheriff may award a withernam to take the defendant's cattle: if he will not so do, the plaintiff shall have a writ out of Chancery directed to the sheriff rehearsing the whole matter, commanding him to award a withernam, and he may have an alias, and after a *pluries*, and an attachment against the sheriff, if he will not execute the king's command (*a*).

If the sheriff return *quod averia elongata sunt ad loca incognita*, it is a good return, and the party must pursue his writ of withernam, but if the sheriff return *averia elongata ad loca incognita infra comitatum meum*, he shall be amerced, for the law intends that he may have notice in his county (*b*).

Quod averia mortua sunt is a good return so, *quod nullus venit ex parte querentis ad demonstranda averia*, but it seems the sheriff is not obliged to require this (*c*).

If the sheriff come to take replevin of beasts impounded in another man's soil, if the place be inclosed and have a gate open to the inclosure, he cannot break the inclosure and enter thereby, where he may enter by the open gate: but if the owner hinder him, so that he cannot go by the open gate for fear of death, he may break the inclosure and enter there (*d*).

If the sheriff be shewn a stranger's goods and he take them, trespass lies against him, else the stranger could have no remedy. But it seems to have been held, that the action lies more properly against the person who shews the goods (*e*).

The sheriff is to return, that the cattle are eloigned, or that no person came to shew, &c. or a delivery: but he cannot return that the defendant *non cepit* the cattle, because it is supposed in the writ, and is the ground of it, which the sheriff cannot falsify (*f*).

Of the Declaration.

Although it has been holden by some, that the count of declaration in replevin should be certain and particular in setting forth the number, kinds, and qualities of the things distrained, for that otherwise the sheriff cannot tell how to make deliverance of the same, yet

It seems now to be settled, that a declaration in replevin being certain to a general intent is sufficient, especially if it be after verdict (*g*).

(*a*) [illegible] (*b*) [illegible] (*c*) [illegible] (*d*) [illegible] (*e*) [illegible]
(*f*) [illegible] (*g*) [illegible] "Replevin," [illegible]

In his count the plaintiff must allege the taking to be at a certain place, or (according to the precedents) *in quodam loco vocat'*, that the defendant may have notice as to what he is to answer, and make his title; therefore the alleging the taking *apud Dale*, or such a vill, is too general and uncertain (*a*).

In replevin both the vill and place are traversable.

Where a defendant takes cattle wrongfully at first, the wrong is continued to any place where he had them in custody, so that a place different from that where they were originally taken is well laid in the declaration, if defendant had them in custody at such other place (*b*).

A man may count of several takings, part at one day and place, and part at another day and place, for he need not shew how many he took in one vill, and how many in another (*c*).

Where the defendant counted of four oxen taken at divers days and places, and that delivery was made of two, but the other two were withheld to his damage 10*s*. this was held sufficient without any severance as to the damages (*d*).

The count, as in other actions, must agree with the writ, so that if the writ be *de averiis*, and the count *de averiis & catallis*, this is ill. In replevin the writ was in the *detinet*, and the count in the *detinuit*, and this was thought to be a material variance, but the parties agreed to amend (*e*)

Of the Pleas.

Pleas in replevin are generally of four kinds, viz. either, 1st, pleas in bar; 2dly, in justification, 3dly, by way of conusance, 4thly, by way of avowry.--The defendant may either justify or avow at his election; but if he justifies, he cannot have a return (*f*).

The general issue in replevin is *non cepit*, and one of several defendants may plead *non cepit* (*g*).

If the defendant claim property in himself, or a stranger above, as he may do, though it ought to have been before the sheriff, this does not amount to the general issue, but may be pleaded in bar or abatement, and if the plaintiff demur, the defendant shall have a return without avowing; for it appears that the beasts are not the plaintiff's. But on the issue *non cepit*, property cannot be given in evidence, for that were contrary to it (*h*)

If the defendant make conusance as bailiff to *A*. the plaintiff cannot traverse that he is his bailiff, for it is a matter of which by no intend-

(*a*) Bac. Abr. tit. "Replevin, &c." (H) (*b*) Ibid (*c*) Ibid (*d*) Ibid.
(*e*) Ibid. (*f*) Bac. Abr. ut ante (I) (*g*) Ibid (*h*) Ibid

ment he can have knowledge.—But, if in bar of the avowry the plaintiff pleads that another had made conusance as bailiff to *A* for the same cause and was barred, he need not shew that it was with the privity of *A.* for it shall be intended: and if in truth it was without, the defendant may traverse his being ever his bailiff (*a*).

In a replevin against the master and bailiff or servant, if the bailiff makes conusance as bailiff, and the master pleads that he did not take, the servant shall not have any return upon his conusance, for by the master's plea his conusance is changed into a justification (*b*).

In replevin of beasts taken at *D* the defendant pleads in abatement that they were taken at another place *absque hoc* that they were taken at *D.* and *pro retorno habendo* avows for rent on a lease for years, &c. the plaintiff replies and traverses the lease, &c. this is ill, for though the defendant, when he pleads in abatement, must also avow to have a return, yet the plaintiff cannot answer to it, but must take issue on the other matter (*c*).

[illegible], is only matter in abatement, and the plaintiff may have a new writ without being put to his second deliverance (*d*).

Of removing the Suit from the County Court, wherein of the Re. fa. lo. Also of subsequent Proceedings, and compelling the Party to proceed.

The suit remains before the sheriff, &c. though the goods and chattels, &c. distrained above the value of 40*s.*: for the replevin *alias*, and *pluries*, are all vicontiel writs, and the suit may be determined in such inferior Court: but the suit may be removed by either of the parties into the Courts of K. B. or C. P. to be there determined, and that without any cause shewn (*e*).

The method of removing it depends on the manner in which the suit was commenced below.—If replevin be in the County Court by writ, it must be removed into K. B. or C. P. by *pone*: if by plaint, by writ of *recordari facias loquelam*, (called for brevity a *refalo*.) If replevin is in a Court of Record, that may hold plea in replevin, it must be removed by *certiorari*, and not in any other manner, for a *refalo* does not go to such Court, because there the suit is already recorded. If the plaint is in the Court of another lord, it may be removed into K. B. or C. P. by *recordari* to the Sheriff commanding him *quod accedas ad curiam et in plena curia ill' recordari facias*, &c. but it is said that a replevin shall not be removed out of any which is not the King's Court, without

(*a*) Bac. Abr. [illegible] (*b*) Ibid. (*c*) Ibid. (*d*) Ibid. (*e*) 2 Sell. Pract. 248.

cause, either by the plaintiff or defendant, for the prejudice that may thereby come to the lord (*a*).

All the above writs, to remove the suit from an inferior Court, are in their nature original writs and issue out of Chancery. The suit, however, is most commonly commenced in the County Court by plaint and very rarely at this day by writ (*b*).

In order to remove it, the party makes out a *præcipe* to the cursitor of the proper county, who then makes out the writ, which must be carried to the under-sheriff of the county, who returns it of course. If the sheriff returns the *recordari, tardè*, the party shall have an [illegible], &c.

By the *recordari*, nothing is removed but the plaint, even though the issue should be joined below; and the plaint may be removed, though the plaintiff has discontinued there.

The plaint, when removed into K. B. is filed with the filazer of the county; so also when removed into C. P.

Where proceedings are removed from the County Court, the *recordari facias loquelam* (called for brevity's sake the *recordari*) being returned, and appearance of defendant entered, the plaintiff must declare *de novo*, nor need any notice be taken of the proceedings below. To the declaration, the defendant may plead in abatement or bar, or he may avow in his own right, or make cognisance in right of another, as bailiff, or may justify, and the parties go on to issue or demurrer to be tried or argued in the usual way (*c*).

But as both parties are actors in replevin, either of them may take down the record to trial, for which reason there can be no judgment as in case of a non-suit in replevin; and if the defendant gives notice of trial and does not proceed, the Court will give costs against him (*d*). But though an avowant is an actor, he cannot have a rule to discontinue, for it is the plaintiff's suit notwithstanding (*e*).

Of compelling the Party to proceed.—If the plaintiff removes the plaint, he should, upon the return of the *pone*, file it with the plaint, &c. with the filazer of the county, and search for the defendant's appearance. If the defendant has not appeared on or before the appearance day of the return of the *pone*, the plaintiff should serve him with a rule to appear, which may be had at the filazer's, and, upon his non-appearance thereto, sue out a *pone*. The *pone* is also got at the filazer's, a summons is made out thereon at the sheriff's office, and served upon the defendant by the officer. If no appearance is entered on, or before, the appearance day of the return, get the sheriff to return *nihil* on the *pone*, and sue out a *distringas*, which may likewise be at the filazer's, and proceed to levy thereon: the issues may be at next 8*l.* and so on, if the defendant

(*a*) 2 [illegible] P[illegible] 248 (*b*) Ibid. 2[illegible] (*c*) Ibid. 253 (*d*) Ibid.
(*e*) [illegible]

does not appear, proceed with *[illegible]*, *ad infinitum*. If he does afterwards appear, he must pay the costs of the *distringas*. Then (as before observed) declare *de novo*, not noticing the proceedings in the Court below.—Rules may be afterwards given to compel the defendant to avow, and so on as in common actions (*a*).

But if the defendant removes it, he must file the *re-falo* and return thereto with the filazer, and having entered an appearance, he must give a rule for the plaintiff to declare, and for want of declaration, when the rule is out, he may sign a *non-pros.* for not declaring, and immediately sue out a writ *de retorno habendo* (*b*).

If the *re-falo* is not taken by the defendant, on or before the appearance-day or the return of it, notice must be given to the plaintiff of the filing thereof by a demand in writing being made of the declaration, before *non-pros.* can be signed: but if filed on the appearance-day of the return, such demand is not necessary (*c*).

If the plaintiff has removed the cause, and does not proceed therein, or if the defendant has removed it, and after having served the plaintiff with a rule to declare, and demanded a declaration, the plaintiff does not declare or proceed therein, the defendant may sign a *non-pros.* and judgment *pro ret. hab.* and then sue out a writ *pro ret. hab.* which he may obtain of the filazer (*d*).

If the defendant has taken out the *re-falo*, and does not get it returned, and filed within two terms, the plaintiff should apply to the filazer for a certificate, that the same is not returned and filed, which certificate is a sufficient warrant for the cursitor to make out a writ of *procedendo*, which remands the cause to the County Court to be there determined (*e*).

If the *re-falo* is not returned, so as to enable the party to get it filed, the plaintiff must be ruled to return it (*f*).

The Court will not stay proceedings in an action of replevin, unless upon payment of the rent in arrear, together with all costs, though the arrears were tendered before with costs up to that time (*g*).

Where the avowry is for damage feasant, the proceedings cannot be stayed, because the Court, in such case, have no rule to guide them in ascertaining the damages (*h*).

Of Avowries.

An avowry, as has been before observed, is the setting forth, as in a declaration, the nature and merits of the defendant's case, and the shewing that the distress taken by him was lawful, which must

(*a*) 2 Sell. Pract. 250. (*b*) Ibid. (*c*) Ibid. (*d*) Ibid. 251. (*e*) Ibid.
(*f*) Ibid. (*g*) 1 Pul. & Bos. 382. 1 Tidd's Pract. 489. (*h*) Ibid.

be done with such sufficient authority as will entitle him to *retorno habendo*.

A distinction is to be observed between an avowry and a justification. An avowry always goes for a return, and therefore shews a right subsisting at the time of the avowry, as made for rent, for example; but a plea of justification does not always go for a return, as where the [illegible] was lawful, but is not so at the time of the plea pleaded (*a*).

In one respect, however, there is no difference between an avowry and a justification; for, generally speaking, whatever is set forth in either, must be maintained.

The defendant in replevin, to entitle himself to a return of the goods distrained, must make his avowry, unless it be in a case in which he claims property; so that though the plaintiff's writ abates, yet the defendant is not entitled to a *retorno habendo*, unless he had made his avowry (*b*).

The avowant is in the nature of a plaintiff, as appears, 1st. from his being called an "actor," which is a term in the civil law, signifying plaintiff; 2dly. from his being entitled to have judgment de *retorno habendo*, and damages as plaintiff, and, 3dly. from this, that the plaintiff may plead in abatement of the avowry, and, consequently, such avowry must be in the nature of an action (*c*).

An avowry, therefore, is in the nature of a declaration, and it sufficeth if it be good to a common intent. But it should shew the certainty of the place, day, and cattle, to entitle the avowant to a writ of enquiry of damages (*d*).

The avowant being, however, in the nature of a plaintiff, need not aver his avowry with a *hoc paratus est verificare*, more than any other plaintiff need aver his count, and being an actor, he shall not have a protection cast for him more than any other plaintiff (*e*).

The claim of right to distrain must be made out by the avowant against the plaintiff, who claims property in the distress; and the defendant in replevin cannot have a return of more cattle than he avows for (*f*).

With respect to avowry for rent arrear, if the clause in the lease is, "That if the rent be behind, being demanded at another place beside the land, or of the person of the lessee, that the lessor may distrain," there, if the lessor distrain without any demand, it is unlawful, for the form of the demand is different from what the law requires, and must be complied with (*g*).—But if the clause is "That if the rent be behind, being lawfully demanded, that then he may distrain," it is

[illegible] (*c*) Bac. Abr. tit. "Replevin," &c.
[illegible] Bac. Abr. tit. (A) (*f*) Ibid.
[illegible]

no more than the law speaks, and therefore the lessor may distrain without a previous demand, for the distress is of itself a demand (*a*).

But where a penalty is annexed to the non-payment of the rent and a distress is given for it, there a demand must be laid. As where the avowry was for rent and a *nomine pœnæ*, and no demand alleged, the avowry was held to be clearly ill for the *nomine pœnæ*, for want of a demand, but good for the rent, and the defendant had a return for that (*b*).

However, where the issue was on a collateral matter, *viz.* *non concessit*, though no demand of the *nomine pœnæ* was laid, it was held to be cured by a verdict (*c*).

Attending on a demand to pay the rent will not destroy the right to distrain, unless a tender of payment is actually made (*d*).

An avowry for part of a rent or penalty is bad, unless it shew how the remainder was discharged; for otherwise there may be another distress and avowry for the residue (*e*).

But an avowant may abate his own avowry for part of the rent distrained for, but not after judgment.

So, where an avowry is made for several rents, and it appears that part is not due, yet the whole avowry shall not abate (*f*).

In replevin *A.* avowed for a rent-charge, due *anno* 1600, and afterwards he continued and avowed for another part of the same rent-charge, which became due before the said year, and which was against a different tenant: in this case it was held by three Judges against a fourth, that the avowant was not estopped by his first avowry in such manner as a lessor is by giving an acquittance for the last gale of rent, but that he may, at his pleasure, avow for part of his rent at one time, and for part at another, in the same manner as the lord may command his bailiff to distrain for so much rent, and afterwards for the sum due before (*g*).

In avowry for rent, and so many hens for quit-rent, the avowant had a verdict for the whole; but it afterwards appearing upon the face of avowry, that the hens were not due at the time of the distress, the avowant had leave to release his damages as to them, and take judgment for the rent, with his costs (*h*).

If the grantee of a rent charge avows upon several under-tenants for the same rent, the Court will upon a tender pleaded by the under-tenants, make an order that the payment of the rent into Court in one action shall serve for all (*i*).

A man cannot proceed for damages upon a plea of tender after taking the money out of Court. But on a plea of tender to an avowry for rent, the plaintiff need not bring the money into Court (*k*).

(*a*) 7 Co. 28 b. (*b*) Hob. 133. (*c*) Hut. 42. (*d*) 1 Ld Raym. 619.
(*e*) Cro. Car. 104. (*f*) Bac. Abr. tit. "Replevin," &c. (C.)
(*g*) Ibid. (*h*) Ibid. (*i*) 1 Ld Raym. 429.
(*k*) Ibid. 639. Bull. N. P. 60.

Where a man is sole [illegible] to an entire rent, he should distrain for it all at once.

But if the defendant [illegible], though the avowry is for that reason bad [illegible]. As where the defendant avowed for rent due [illegible], and the distress appeared to have been made on the [illegible], which was three days before *Michaelmas*, it was [illegible] the avowry was bad (for the judgment [illegible] all the rent avowed for is paid, and so [illegible]), yet that the defendant might before judgment [illegible] so much as was claimed to *Michaelmas*, and take judgment for the rest (*a*).

But where one is not [illegible], or has not sole title to the entire rent, he cannot avow alone, for [illegible] avowry would be bad.

Therefore parceners must join in an avowry for rent or making conusance, for they make but one heir, and the rent is an entire inheritance (*b*).

Joint-tenants also should join (*c*).

One tenant in common cannot avow the taking of the cattle of a stranger upon the land damage feasant, without making himself bailiff or servant to his companion: for if one were to distrain without the other, as there could not be a double satisfaction for the same injury, the other would have no remedy. As to any supposed hardship in one denying his consent to the other avowing as bailiff to him, if he dislikes his situation he may put an end to the tenancy by a writ of partition (*d*).

In replevin against two, they made several avowries, each in his own right, and both avowries were abated: for if both the issues should be found for the avowants, the Court could not give judgment severally for the same thing (*e*).

An annuitant may distrain for a rent though the term be vested in himself to secure the payment, for the grantor will be deemed *quasi* tenant to the party at a rent to the amount of the annuity (*f*).—Where an action was brought for money had and received to the use of the assignees, and it appeared that the money was paid by the tenant of the bankrupt to the defendant as grantee of an annuity granted by the bankrupt after an act of bankruptcy and charged on the estate of which the payer of the money was tenant, L. *Kenyon* observed that the action ought to have been brought by the tenant, and said he could not transfer a chose in action, which this was, to the assignees. The tenant could not avail himself of the payment, but the assignees might

(*a*) [illegible] 5 Mod. [illegible] R. [illegible] (*b*) [illegible]
(*c*) [illegible] Rep. [illegible] K. [illegible] 2 H. Bl. R. 386 [illegible]
[illegible]

have recovered the rent notwithstanding. This was sufficient to decide the case (*a*).

Where the lessee has entered under a lease, though such entry be tortious, it does not discharge the contract for the payment of rent, for there is a great difference between replevin and ejectment (*b*).

If one distrain for rent, and before the avowry the estate on which it was reserved determine, the avowry shall be as if the estate on which it was reserved had continued, for the avowant is to have the rent notwithstanding: but if the distress were for a personal service, the defendant must have special justification, for he cannot have the service *in specie*, when the estate is determined (*c*).

The defendant in replevin need not set out his title: for the stat. 11 *G.* 2. *c.* 19. *s.* 22. enacts, "That it shall and may be lawful for all defendants in replevin to avow or make conusance generally, that the plaintiff in replevin or other tenant of the lands and tenements whereon such distress was made, enjoyed the same under a grant or demise at such a certain rent, during the time wherein the rent distrained for incurred, which rent was then and still remains due, without further setting forth the grant, tenure, demise, or title of such landlord or landlords, lessor or lessors; and if the plaintiff or plaintiffs in such action shall become nonsuit, discontinue his, her, or their action, or have judgment given against him, her, or them, the defendant or defendants in such replevin shall recover double costs of suit."

The defendant may avow in this general manner whether the plaintiff be tenant or not, for the words of the statute are in the disjunctive "plaintiff in replevin or other tenant."

Where the rent reserved at the time of entering upon the premises, was afterwards varied by agreement between the parties, yet it was holden that the landlord might avow as on a demise at a rent certain, for that such subsequent agreement operated by relation, to make it a reservation of the rent from the beginning (*d*).

The statute was made for the benefit of landlords, that after the tenant had enjoyed the land he should not be allowed to pry into the lessor's title: therefore, if the defendant avow under the statute *nil habuit in tenementis*, it is a bad and inadmissible plea, for it attempts to bring the lessor's title in question: were the premises in mortgage, for example, if this plea were allowed, the defendant could not recover his rent, which the statute never had in contemplation to prevent, but rather to assist (*e*).

So, there may be judgment in replevin though the party misrecites his title; provided he shows a good and subsisting one. As where the

(*a*) Parker Sad[illegible] [illegible] P[illegible], [illegible] Wes[illegible] [illegible] C. 3 T. MSS.
(*b*) 1 Sal. 550. (*c*) [illegible] (*d*) [illegible] (*e*) 2 W[illegible]. 208.

plaintiff entitled himself by a lease of the 3d of *March*, the defendant traversed the lease *modo et forma*, the jury found a lease of another date; yet judgment was given for the plaintiff: for the substance of the issue is, whether he has a lease or not: yet if they had found a lease from another, it would not have done. But if he had declared thus in ejectment, it had been against him, for there he is to recover the term, and is to make his title truly (*a*).

An avowry for an increased rent on a demise for every acre of the land which should be converted into tillage, is supported by the evidence of a lease for a term of years, with a covenant to pay the increased rent for every acre which should be so converted during "a part of the term," for example, for the last three years, by the stat. 11 *G.* 2. *c.* 19 (*b*).

If executors avow under stat. 32 *H.* 8. *c.* 37. for rent in fee, *&c.* due to their testator, they must shew the land in the seisin of tenant, or in those who claim under him (*c*).

If a person distrains as executor or administrator, he must bring himself within the statute under the words of which, the distress can be made only on the tenant in whose hands the lands were chargeable, or some person claiming under him, and therefore not in the hands of one claiming by title paramount, as the lord by escheat (*d*).

But where the avowry was as administratrix of rent to which the defendant was entitled in her own right, she nevertheless had judgment, that part respecting the claim as administratrix being rejected as surplusage (*e*).

The above Act gives no remedy where the testator himself has dispensed with the arrearages, or had no remedy when he died (*f*).

An avowry by husband and wife for rent due to the wife alone before the coverture, was held to be good, the supposed inconsistency being mere matter of form, for the avowry being for rent arrear, to say that it was arrear to him and his wife, is but surplusage: and although he doth not say *adhuc a retro existit*, it was held well enough in substance (*g*).

Also, if there be lessee for years, and the reversion descend on a feme covert, and afterwards the rent be in arrear, and the baron distrain, and the lessee bring a replevin, the baron ought to avow in the name of himself and his wife, and not in the name of himself only, for the avowry is to be made according to the reversion, which is in the feme (*h*).

But an avowry by a husband alone for rent due to him and his wife

(*a*) Hob. 72. (*b*) 2 H. Bl. R. 565. (*c*) Cro. Jac. 51? (*d*) Co. Litt. 162 b.
(*e*) Hob. 208. Bac. Abr. tit. "Replevin, &c." (K.) (*f*) Co. Litt. 162 b. [illegible]
(*g*) Cro. Jac. 283. (*h*) Bac. Abr. ut ante.

is good, if it appear upon the record that *he* was entitled to make the distress (*a*).

Though the defendant may be entitled to the rent, yet may the distress be tortious. As if he come on the land to distrain, and the tenant then tenders the arrears due, in such case, if he distrain the cattle, it is tortious, and the defendant may replevy (*b*). But it is not sufficient for the tenant to say that he was on the land on the day and ready to pay the rent; for if he did not make a tender *at the time of the distress made*, the taking was not tortious (*c*). The tender must be before the impounding, for when impounded they are *in custodiâ legis* (*d*).

Replevin was of cattle taken in *A.* The defendant avowed the taking in *A.* under a demise of certain premises of which *B.* was parcel, and because the cattle were damage feasant in *B.* he took them and drove them through *A.* in his way to the pound, and upon general demurrer the avowry was held to be well pleaded (*e*).

Non demisit, nothing in arrear, nothing in arrear for part of the rent and tender of the residue, are good pleas to an avowry for rent (*f*).

So, a tender and refusal may be pleaded to such avowry, without bringing the money into Court, because if the distress were not rightfully taken, the defendant must answer the plaintiff his damages (*g*).

After an avowry for rent arrear the plaintiff may pay into Court the rent for which the defendant avows, because the demand is certain: but not where the damages are unliquidated (*h*).

That the avowant afterwards used or sold the cattle or goods distrained, may also be pleaded (*i*).

So, to an avowry for rent, the tenant may plead payment of a ground-rent to the original landlord, which he paid to protect himself from a distress; for it is a payment of so much to the immediate landlord (*k*).

But the plaintiff cannot plead a set-off, because the action is founded in a tort, and the stat. 2 *G.* 2. does not extend to such actions: besides a set-off supposes a different demand arising in a different right (*l*). Neither can a mutual demand be given in evidence, where the defendant justifies under a distress.—Yet it is said, that he may plead a mutual debt of more than the rent by way of special plea to the avowry (*m*). At all events, payment may be pleaded. Therefore where to an avowry for rent, the tenant

(*a*) Cro Jac 432 (*b*) Esp N P 357 8 Co 147 a (*c*) Hut 13
(*d*) Cro Eliz 812 (*e*) 2 Bos & Pul 480 (*f*) Bac Abr *ut ante*
(*g*) Bull N P 60 (*h*) 1 H Bl R 24 (*i*) Com Dig *ut ante* (K 19)
(*k*) 4 T R 512, 14 (*l*) Bac Abr *ut ante* Bull N P 181 (*m*) Bar 450

pleaded payment of a ground-rent to the original landlord, it was holden good (*a*).

In an avowry for non-payment of rent, a plea in bar is *de injuria sua propria absque [illegible], quod prædict' R. cepit*, &c. *Non cepit* is [illegible] good traverse, but he should pursue his title, and *de injuria sua propria* is enough (*b*).

After issue joined upon a plea in bar to an avowry, the Court will not suffer the plea to be withdrawn and the avowry confessed, without consent, for the avowant will lose his costs (*c*).

As to what shall be a departure, replevin was for taking the plaintiff's goods and chattels, to wit, a lime-kiln, avowry for rent, plea in bar, that the lime-kiln was affixed to the freehold; the Court held the plea in bar bad, because it was a departure from the declaration, which had treated the lime-kiln as a chattel (*d*).

In an avowry for a distress for rent, the avowant was to shew a seisin, and such seisin by the stat. 32 *H.* 8. *c.* 2. must be alleged within fifty years before the making of the avowry or conusance: and though by stat. 21 *H.* 8. *c.* 19. the lord need not avow upon any person in certain, yet he must allege seisin by the hands of some tenant in certain, within fifty years.—Where the commencement of the rent appears, seisin is not material.

The stat. 32 *H.* 8. *c.* 2. which limits an avowry or conusance for rent, suit, or service, to a possession of fifty years next before making the avowry, &c. does not extend to a new rent created by Act of Parliament.

Of Avowry, &c. [illegible] *for Damage Feasant*.—Replevin [illegible] avowry or [illegible] for damage-feasant, if the defendant avows, or makes conusance for damage-feasant, he must shew that the place where, &c. is his freehold, or the freehold of *B.* under whom he makes conusance; and if he says that he himself or *B.* was seised, he must say of what estate, in fee, tail, or for life.

So, the bailiff who [illegible] for damage-feasant in right of a devisee, must set forth what estate the devisor had; it is not sufficient to say in general, that he was seised—the stat. [illegible] *G.* 2. applies only to avowries for rent [illegible].

In replevin [illegible] was by [illegible], and the avowry was that *A.* [illegible] of the rectory of *W.* [illegible] the lease without [illegible] that he [illegible] the Court, [illegible] would have been a good [illegible], [illegible] that he was [illegible].

The general rule [illegible] where [illegible] made

[illegible] ; R. 22)
[illegible]

under a particular estate, the commencement of that estate must be shewn, but that an estate in fee may be alleged generally (*a*)

In an avowry the issue was, whether the place where, &c was the freehold of the avowant or not, and it was found by the verdict, that it was the freehold of the avowant's wife. *Et per Cur.*—It is found against the avowant, for when he saith *his* freehold, it is to be intended his sole freehold, and in his own right (*b*).

Though the cattle of a stranger cannot be distrained unless they were levant and couchant, yet it must come on the other side to shew that they were not so (*c*).

In replevin for *bona, cattala, et averia*, a conusance of the whole and a justification for part is bad, for if a distress be entire, and it is wrong in part, it is bad for the whole (*d*)

If a man takes a distress for a thing for which he had good cause of distress, but had good cause of distress for another thing, if a replevin is brought and he comes into Court, he may avow for which he pleases (*e*).

To an avowry that the freehold was in the defendant or the party under whom he makes conusance, the plaintiff may say in bar, that it is his freehold or the freehold of *A* and by licence he put his cattle there, or, a special title by devise, fine, demise, &c (*f*)

So, the plaintiff may plead in bar to an avowry, *de son tort*, with a traverse that *locus in quo*, &c is parcel of the tenements alleged to be held (*g*)

Replevin for taking his cattle in the road, avowry for damage-feasant in the four acres, so took them there and drove them along the road to impound them plea, in bar, that the road is not parcel of the four acres, upon demurrer, the avowry was held well enough and the plea ill, for by connecting the beginning of the avowry and conusance with the latter end thereof, it appeared to be one entire transaction (*h*).

So, the plaintiff may plead in bar "tender of amends" (*i*)

If the defendant pleads that he was seised of three acres *in locus in quo*, &c it is sufficient, without saying how many acres the *locus in quo*, &c (*k*).

Where there were two issues, and one only found for the avowant, he shall [illegible] Where the parties agree in the facts, the circumstance of the jury finding otherwise is not material (*l*).

By stat 21 *H* 8 *c.* 19 all plaintiffs and defendants shall have like pleas and like advantages in all such avowries, conusances, and justifica-

[illegible]
[illegible]
[illegible]
[illegible]

tions (pleas of disclaimer only excepted,) as they might have had before the Act.

SECTION III. *Of the verdict and judgment in Replevin.*

On the execution of the writ of replevin by the sheriff, the beasts distrained are actually returned to the plaintiff, so that he hath the possession and use of the cattle pending the suit, consequently if the plaintiff in replevin hath judgment, it can only be for damages.

At common law (even before the statute of *Gloucester*) the plaintiff in replevin could recover damages, and by that statute his costs. But the avowant or defendant was not entitled to either, till the 7th *H.* 8. *c.* 4. which gives damages and costs to every avowant, and to every person making conusance, or justifying as bailiff in replevin, for any rent, custom, or service, if his avowry, conusance, or justification be found for him, or the plaintiff be otherwise barred. Also, by stat. 21 *H.* 8. *c.* 19. it is enacted, "That every avowant, and every other person or persons that make any avowry, justification, or conusance, as bailiff or servant to any person or persons in any *replegiare* or second deliverance, for rents, customs, services, or for damages-feasant, or for rent or rents, upon any distress taken in any lands or tenements, if the same avowry, or conusance, or justification, be found for them or the plaintiffs in the same be nonsuit, or otherwise barred, that then they shall recover their damages and costs against the said plaintiffs, as the same plaintiffs should have done, or had if they had recovered in the *replegiare* or second deliverance found against the defendants (*a*)."

Neither this statute, nor that of 43 *Eliz.* (if the defendant avow as overseer for a distress for a poor's rate), tie the inquisition up to the same jury as are returned or impannelled, as the stat. 17 *C.* 2. *c.* 7. (of which hereafter) does. If therefore, there is a verdict for the plaintiff, the jury usually assess the damages; or the jury after verdict may be discharged, and damages be assessed by the Justices, with the defendant's consent. For if the jury do not assess the damages, and the goods, &c. should be detained, the plaintiff may make a suggestion thereof upon the roll, whereupon a writ shall go to enquire of the value of the cattle, &c. and damages; upon which the plaintiff shall have judgment for both (*b*).

If there be judgment for the plaintiff upon a *[illegible]*, &c. or for want of a replication to his plea in bar to the avowry, or upon a demurrer, a writ of enquiry of damages

(*a*) [illegible] 2 Lill. Prac. 271 [illegible]

shall be awarded: or at the request of the plaintiff, by the assent of the defendant, the Justices may assess the damages without such writ (*a*).

But if there be judgment for the plaintiff, *quod* [illegible] by default after appearance, there shall be a special writ of enquiry for the value of the goods or cattle and damages. But where the taking was lawful, the damage shall be only for the detainer, as where goods are taken damage-feasant, and detained after amends tendered.

If the plaintiff lets judgment go by default, or becomes nonsuit, the defendant is entitled to his judgment *pro retorno*, and to a writ of enquiry, to assess his damages and cost, or if the defendant get a verdict, the jury may assess the damages, or if they omit so to do a writ of enquiry may go (*b*).

The judgment after verdict for the defendant need not express the return to be irreplevisable, because now it necessarily must be so, since the statute of *Westm.* 2. Therefore a judgment in replevin "that the defendants have a return of the cattle, and recover their damage and costs assessed by the jury," &c. is good, either as a judgment at common law, though the return be not adjudged irreplevisable, or as a judgment under stat. 21 *H.* 8. *c.* 19. which entitles the defendants to damages and costs, but not under stat. 17 *C.* 2. (*c*).

If the defendant upon the judgment *de ret. hab.* sue out a writ *pro ret. hab.* and the sheriff cannot find the cattle, he may have a *capias* in withernam upon the return of the *elongata*. But if the defendant has judgment for a return irreplevisable, if the owner of the cattle or goods tenders all that is due on the judgment and it is accepted, he shall have a writ of delivery for the goods, so if he tenders the whole upon the judgment which is ascertained upon the avowry, and is refused, he shall have detinue (*d*).

In avowry for damage feasant, defendant had a verdict, and adjudged that he shall have a *ret. hab.* for the cattle, and a *ca. sa.* for the damages; but if the party tender the costs and damages, the sheriff, after such tender, ought not to execute the *ret. hab.* But if, for want of such tender, he do execute the *ret. hab.* and afterwards the costs and damages are paid, a writ *si constare poterit* lies upon suggesting that the costs, &c. are paid, and this is to re-deliver the distress, and is called "a writ of restitution (*e*)."

It is now settled, that pleadings in replevin are within the stat. 4 *Ann.* c. 16. therefore, where some issues in the replevin are found for the plaintiff which entitle him to judgment, and some for the de-

(*a*) 2 Sell. Prac. 272.
(*b*) [illegible] 1 R. 529.
(*d*) 2 Sell. Prac. 27[illegible].
(*e*) [illegible]

fendant, the latter must be allowed the costs of the issues found for him out of the general costs of the verdict: unless the Judge shall certify that the plaintiff had probable cause for pleading the matters on which those issues are joined (*a*).

An avowant shall pay costs on the special avowries found against him, and shall not have costs on the affirmance of a judgment in his favour on a writ of error (*b*).

If the plaintiff plead several pleas in bar, upon which issues are joined, and some issues are found for the plaintiff, and some for the defendant, the latter is entitled in C. P. to such costs of the trial, as relate to the issues on which he has succeeded, as well as to the costs of the pleadings. But if a defendant after trial, and verdict for the plaintiff, obtain judgment *non obstante veredicto*, in consequence of the plaintiff's pleas in bar being bad, he is not entitled in that Court, to any costs upon the pleadings, subsequent to the pleas in bar, because he should have demurred to them: indeed if the avowant will not take advantage of a fault in the plaintiff's pleadings when he has the opportunity of so doing, he becomes *particeps criminis* (*c*).

The certificate of probable cause is not required to be made in Court, at the trial of the cause, and where the judge refuses to grant it, the Court have not a discretionary power, whether they will allow the plaintiff any costs at all; but are bound by the statute to allow him some costs, though the *quantum* is left to their discretion (*d*).

Of the Non Pros., Nonsuit, Verdict, and Judgment under Stat. 17 Car. 2. c. 7. where the Distress was for Rent.

If the cause has been removed into the superior Court by the plaintiff, and after the defendant has appeared he does not declare or proceed therein; or if the cause has been removed by the defendant, and a rule having been served on the plaintiff, he does not declare or proceed therein: the defendant may in these cases sign a *non pros.*, enter up judgment *pro retorno habendo*, and, if the original distress were made for rent, he may proceed to execute a writ of enquiry of damages, which is the better way than taking out a writ *pro retorno habendo*, because that writ may be superseded by the plaintiff suing out a writ of second deliverance, as has been seen before (*e*).

For the stat. 17 *C.* 2. *c.* 7. which is an Act for the more speedy and

(*a*) 2 Tidd Pract. 273. (*b*) Ibid. (*c*) 1 Tidd's Pract. 616. (*d*) Id. 617.
(*e*) 2 Tidd Pract. 267.

effectual proceeding upon distresses and avowries for rent, after reciting that "Forasmuch as the ordinary remedy for arrearages of rents is by distresses upon the lands chargeable therewith; and yet nevertheless, by reason of the intricate and dilatory proceedings upon replevins, that remedy is become ineffectual" by Sect. 2 enacts, "That whensoever any plaintiff in replevin shall be nonsuit before issue joined in any suit of replevin by plaint or writ lawfully returned, removed, or depending in any of the King's Courts at *Westminster*, that the defendant making a suggestion in nature of an avowry or cognizance for such rent, to ascertain the Court of the cause of distress, the Court upon his prayer shall award a writ to the sheriff of the county where the distress was taken, to enquire, by the oaths of twelve good and lawful men of his bailiwick, touching the sum in arrear at the time of such distress taken, and the value of the goods or cattle distrained; and thereupon notice of fifteen days shall be given to the plaintiff or his attorney in Court, of the sitting of such enquiry, and thereupon the sheriff shall enquire of the truth of the matters contained in such writ by the oaths of twelve good and lawful men of his county; and upon the return of such inquisition, the defendant shall have judgment to recover against the plaintiff the arrearages of such rent, in case the goods or cattle distrained shall amount unto that value, and in case they shall not amount to that value, then so much as the value of the said goods and cattle so distrained shall amount unto, together with his full costs of suit, and shall have execution thereupon by *fieri facias*, or *elegit*, or otherwise, as the law shall require; and in case such plaintiff shall be nonsuit after cognizance or avowry made, and issue joined, or if the verdict shall be given against such plaintiff, then the jurors that are impanneled or returned to enquire of such issue, shall, at the prayer of the defendant, enquire concerning the sum of the arrears, and the value of the goods or cattle distrained; and thereupon the avowant, or he that makes cognizance, shall have judgment for such arrearage, or so much thereof as the goods or cattle distrained amount unto, together with his full costs, and shall have execution for the same by *fieri facias*, or *elegit*, or otherwise, as the law shall require."

Sect. 3 gives the like remedy to the avowant or party making cognizance for any rent, upon a judgment given for him upon demurrer.

Sect. 4 enables the party or his representative to distrain again for the residue of the arrears, in case the value of the cattle, &c. taken by the first distress shall not be to the full value of the arrears distrained for.

By the above statute, in case of a nonsuit or *non pros* before issue joined, defendant may enter a suggestion upon the record, in the nature of an avowry, or conusance, and thereupon sue out a writ of enquiry. but in case of a nonsuit at the trial, or of a verdict for defendant, the jury at the trial must enquire of the rent in arrear, and the value of the goods distrained (*a*)

If [illegible] it to make such enquiry, no other jury can afterwards [illegible], no writ of enquiry therefore can go, the defendant [illegible] judgment according to the statute and proceed to [illegible] *fi fa.* or *ca. sa* but must resort to his common law [illegible] out his writ *de retorno habendo*, and thus if the [illegible] either of the rent or the value of the goods, [illegible] as the statute must be strictly complied [illegible] But this [illegible] only in cases of rent within the statute, and [illegible] in other cases [illegible] Lord *Hardwicke* has laid it down, that in every case, unless where the Court is tied up by this statute, a writ of enquiry may be granted in order to do complete justice (*c*)

If the plaintiff become nonsuit, the defendant is not bound to take his remedy under the statute, but has his option either to proceed by writ of enquiry under it, or to bring his action against the plaintiff and his sureties on the replevin bond (*d*).

Nor does the statute take away or alter the judgment at common law, it only gives a further remedy to the avowant So that after a *non pros* [illegible] may still enter his judgment *pro retorno* but it is better to make a suggestion, and proceed by writ of enquiry; because if the plaintiff sue out a writ of second deliverance, it will operate, as has been observed, as a *supersedeas* of the *ret. hab* but not so to the writ of enquiry for by this statute, the legislature intended that the proceeding by writ of enquiry, *fi fa* and *elegit*, should be final for the avowant to recover his damages, and that the plaintiff should keep his cattle notwithstanding the course of awarding a *ret hab.* which is the right judgment, and is still entered up as before the statute (*e*).

If plaintiff in replevin is nonsuited, the defendant is not bound to have his damages assessed by the jury under 17 *Car.* 2 c. 7. or to take the earliest moment to prosecute his writ *de retorno habendo* and he may again distrain the same goods for rent subsequently accrued previously to executing his *retorno habendo* without waving his action against the sureties in the bond (*f*).

(*a*) [illegible] (*c*) [illegible] (*e*) [illegible]
(*b*) [illegible] (*d*) [illegible] (*f*) 1 [illegible] 218

Where the judgment is for the defendant after verdict, if the jury have not enquired at the trial as the statute directs, it must be entered up as a common law judgment *pro. ret. hab.* But if the jury have assessed damages, but not the amount of the rent, &c. it may be entered as a judgment under stat. 21 *H.* 8. *c.* 19. and the Court will permit the defendant to amend his judgment if entered as under the statute, and not warranted thereby, to make it a common law judgment (*a*).

Where the defendant made conusance for rent in arrear, and the jury found a verdict for him, and damages to the amount of the rent claimed in his conusance, without finding either the amount of the rent in arrear or the value of the cattle distrained, and judgment was entered for the damages assessed, the Court permitted the defendant to amend his judgment, and to enter a judgment *pro. ret. hab.* after a writ of error brought (*b*).

In replevin the plaintiff avowed for a year's rent; verdict for the defendant, but no value found for the jury. It was moved for a writ of enquiry under the stat. 17 *C.* 2. *c.* 7. to ascertain the rent in arrear, and the value of the cattle. *Gould* J. doubted whether it could be granted to supply a defective verdict in case of rent, though after a judgment by default it would certainly lie, and added, that *Burrow's* note of *Andrews and James*, *M.* 29. *G.* 2. *B. R.* appeared to be a judgment by default. However, no cause being shewn, the rule was made absolute (*c*).

If there has been no avowry, the Court will set aside a writ of enquiry obtained, and the inquisition thereon, for the avowry is in the nature of a declaration, and is the only ground of an enquiry, for the defendant in replevin (*d*).

The stat. 11 *G.* 2. *c.* 19. *s.* 22. gives the defendant or defendants in replevin making avowry or conusance upon distresses for rent, relief, heriot, or other service, in case the plaintiff in the action shall become nonsuit, discontinue, or have judgment against him, double costs.—The avowry must be for taking the goods, &c. as a distress, else it will be out of the statute (*e*).

This statute does not extend to a rent-charge, or seisure for a heriot custom (*f*).

Where a statute gives double costs, they are calculated thus: 1. the common costs, and then half the common costs. If treble costs, 1. the common costs, 2. half of these, and then half of the latter (*g*).

(*a*) 1 East 271. 4 T. R. 509. (*b*) 3 T. R. 349. (*c*) 2 Bl. R. 763.
(*d*) Bac. Abr. tit. "Replevin," &c. (D) (*e*) 2 Sell. Pract. 274.
(*f*) 1 Tidd's Prac. 891. (*g*) Ibid.

SECTION IV. *Of the Remedies where the Pledges prove insufficient.*

1. *By Action against the Sheriff.*
2. *By Scire Facias against the Pledges.*
3. *By Proceeding on the Replevin Bond.*

1. *Of the Action against the Sheriff.*

The sheriff, upon making replevin, is bound, as has been before stated, to take pledges, and they must be sufficient pledges; for if they are not, an action on the case will lie against him; the Court, however, will not proceed in a summary way, by granting an attachment against the sheriff for neglecting to take a replevin bond (*a*).

In case pledges are taken and they prove to be insufficient, the party has a double remedy, viz. against the sheriff and against the bail: against the sheriff by action, and against the bail, if the distress was not for rent, by *scire facias*; if for rent, either by *scire facias*, or upon the replevin bond, assigned according to the statute (*b*).

If insufficient pledges *de retorno habendo* be taken by the officer of the C[illegible] below in the replevin, the remedy against him is by action, and the Court of Common Pleas will not order him to pay the costs recovered by defendant in replevin (*c*).

The pledges taken by the sheriff when the distress is not for rent are according to the statute of *Westm.* 2. and may be by bond, and that too of the plaintiff himself only; for the sheriff being answerable for the sufficiency of the pledges, may take the security as he pleases, since it is at his own peril (*d*).—But he cannot take money or cattle as a pawn or pledge (*e*).

The pledges taken when the distress is for rent are governed by stat. 11 G. 2. c. 1[illegible], and must be by bond with two sureties, and ought to be at least in double the value of the goods distrained. The sheriff, the under-[illegible] [illegible] ate, as has been [illegible] ob-served, an[illegible] to the [illegible] for the sufficiency of the pledges *de retorno habendo* (*f*).

The mode of proceeding on the stat. 11 G. 2. c. 19. is now generally preferred to the old remedy by *sci. fa.* where the distress was for rent, and it is not affected by the 17 G. 2. c. 7. for where, in pursuance of that statute, the avowant had judgment for want of a [illegible] [illegible] it was held that he had two methods of proceeding in his [illegible]

(*a*) [illegible] 262.
(*b*) [illegible] Gilb. L. of Rep. [illegible]
(*c*) [illegible] N. R. 292.
(*d*) [illegible] 97.
(*e*) [illegible] 96.
(*f*) [illegible]

tion: namely either to execute a writ of enquiry or to sue upon the replevin bond, the plaintiff not having prosecuted his suit with effect (*a*).

The action ought to be brought in the name of the person making conusance, where there is no avowant on record (*b*).

In the action against the sheriff some evidence must be given by the plaintiff of the insufficiency of the pledges, but very slight evidence is sufficient to throw the proof on the sheriff, for the sureties are known to him, and he is to take care that they are sufficient (*c*).

This action against the sheriff will lie without any *scire facias* previously sued out against the bail. But in the case before-mentioned, after judgment *pro ret.* and an *elegit non est* returned, the Court on motion granted a rule against the sheriff, under-sheriff, and replevin-clerk, to pay the defendant 57*l.* 15*s.* the amount of the verdict in replevin (damages and costs), together with the costs of the application (*d*).

Much doubt has been entertained, and the Courts still differ as to the *quantum* of damages which the plaintiff ought to recover in this action against the sheriff for taking insufficient pledges.

In the King's Bench it is held, that the plaintiff cannot recover beyond the value of the distress. The argument is, that the duty of the sheriff as prescribed by the Act, is to take the bond for prosecuting the suit and for a return of the goods, if a return shall be awarded, the bond therefore would be satisfied by returning the goods taken. If so, the value of these goods seems to be the true measure of damages to be given by this action. That by the stat. *Westm.* 2. it is specifically mentioned, that if any take pledges otherwise, he shall answer for the price of the beasts, and that the 11 *G.* 2. does not enlarge the sheriff's responsibility in this respect (*e*).

But in the Common Pleas the direct contrary was holden, for that Court held that the plaintiff might recover the amount of his rent, his costs in the replevin suit, the value of the goods, and whatever other damages the jury might give him, even beyond the penalty of the replevin bond, *i. e.* more than double the value of the goods distrained (*f*). However, this doctrine was shortly after over-ruled, and the Court held the sheriff liable to the extent of double the value of the goods distrained, but no farther, by analogy to the liability of the sureties (*g*).

2. *Of the Remedy by* Scire Facias *against the Pledges.*

Another remedy which the defendant in replevin has, if the plaintiff does not make a return of the goods when a return has been awarded,

(*a*) Gilb. L. of Rep. 225. 2 W[illegible] 42. (*b*) 1 Pr[illegible] 3[illegible] (*c*) [illegible] N. P. 6[illegible]
(*d*) 2 [illegible] Pract. 263. 2 P. R. 12[illegible] (*e*) 2 [illegible] Pract. 263. (*f*) Ibid. 264.
(*g*) Ibid. 547. Willes, 3[illegible]

is, by *scire facias* against the pledges. Before a *scire facias* issues, a writ *pro ret. hab.* must have been sued out, and an *elongata* or eloignment be returned by the sheriff. After which, if the names of the pledges be not known, an application may be made to the replevin-clerk, and if he refuses or delays to tell them, the Court on motion will make a rule upon him for that purpose (*a*).

If the plaint has never been removed, the defendant may sign a *non pros.* in the Court below, and have a precept in the nature of a *scire facias* (*b*).

Note. The two preceding remedies are used where the distress is not for rent, as well as where it is.

3. *Of the Remedy on the Replevin Bond.*

When goods are taken in distress for rent, and replevied, the distrainer has no lien on the goods, but is left to his remedy on the replevin bond (*c*).

The usual remedy, therefore, where the distress is for rent and a replevin bond is entered into, according to stat. 11 G. 2. c. 19. is by taking an assignment of the replevin bond, and bringing an action thereon against the pledges in the defendant's own name (*d*).

By the statute, the sheriff is ordered, at the request and costs of the avowant, or person making conusance, to make an assignment.

A replevin bond may be assigned to the avowant only, or he may bring his action upon it without joining the party making conusance (*e*).

A defendant in replevin is, indeed, entitled to an assignment of the bond, if the plaintiff in replevin do not appear in the County Court and prosecute according to the condition (*f*), which condition is not satisfied by a prosecution in the County Court, but the plaint, if removed by *refalo* into a superior Court, must be prosecuted there with effect, and a return made, if adjudged there (*g*). In such case, the defendant may sue on the bond as assignee of the sheriff in the superior Court, though the replevin be not removed out of the County Court; averring in his declaration, that the plaintiff did not appear at the next County Court and prosecute according to the condition of the bond (*h*).

The bond may be assigned four days exclusive after the time limited therein for plaintiff to prosecute his suit (*i*).

The action must be brought in the same Court in which the *refalo* is returnable. The mode of assigning and proceeding is the same as on a bail-bond (*k*).

The two sureties in a replevin bond, are together liable only to the amount of the penalty in the bond, and the costs of the suit in the bond (*l*).

(*a*) 2 Sell. Prac. 266. (*b*) 2 Wils. 41. (*c*) 1 Br. R. 427. (*d*) 2 Sell. Pract. 266.
(*e*) [illegible] (*f*) 5 T. R. 195. (*g*) 1 Pull & Bos 410. (*h*) 5 T. R. 195.
(*i*) [illegible] 266. (*k*) Ibid. 267. (*l*) 1 Taunt. 218.

CHAPTER XIX.

Remedies for Tenants against Landlords (continued).

Of the Remedies for an unfounded, irregular, or excessive Distress.

SECTION I For Rent pretended to be Arrear.

SECTION II For other supposed Right to distrain.

IT has been seen that where the goods or cattle of a person have been taken as a distress, whether on the ground that they are liable for rent arrear or damage-feasant, the party so distrained upon may contest the distrainer's right by an action of replevin. beside that action, however, the law affords other remedies where the distress is unfounded, these are by action of trespass *de bonis asportatis*, or *quare clausum fregit*, for damages, or trover for the value of the thing destroyed.

Trespass *quare clausum fregit* was the remedy commonly resorted to of old, not merely as a remedy for a distress wrongfully taken, but as a means of trying the title to lands and tenements, the title frequently coming into question in the course of that action, that action however has of late years been in some degree superseded by that of replevin in the one case, and ejectment in the other

Still, however, these actions of trespass, and that of trover, are open to the party who means to contest the validity of a distress The proceedings have in effect much similarity, but in respect to proof of title (where the distress was for damage-feasant), the action of replevin being more strict than that of trespass for taking and carrying away the goods, the latter remedy is often preferred.

Section I. *Remedies for unfounded Distress for Rent pretended to be Arrear.*

To entitle a man to bring trespass he must, at the time when the act was done which constitutes the trespass, either have the actual possession in him of the thing which is the object of the trespass, or else he must have a constructive possession in respect of the right being actually vested in him (*a*).

This action lies for an unlawful taking; as if the distress be made at night. So if beasts of the plough had been taken when other sufficient distress could have been had. So, if doors have been broken open (or enclosures thrown down), to make it, for the outer door can in no case be broken open, except under the direction of stat. 11 *G.* 2. *c.* 19. of which we have before treated.

But in distress for rent, if the outer door be open, the person distraining may justify breaking open an inner door or lock to find any goods which are distrainable (*b*).

So, even where trespass was for breaking and entering the plaintiff's house and taking his goods, and the case in evidence was that the defendant having with him a constable, had entered the plaintiff's house to make a distress for rent. After he had told his business and began to take an inventory, the plaintiff's wife tore his paper, beat him and the constable out, and then blocked up the door; about an hour after the defendant with several others returned and demanded admittance, which being refused, he broke open the doors. It was ruled by *Willes J.* that the distress having been lawfully begun and not deserted, but the defendant compelled to quit it by violence, this was a re-continuance of the first taking and so was lawful, though he could not when he first came have so broken open the doors (*c*).

Trespass, or Case.—The stat. 2 *W.* & *M.* sess. 1. *c.* 5. *s.* 5. provides, "that in case any distress and sale as aforesaid, shall be made by virtue or colour of that Act, for rent pretended to be arrear and due, where in truth no rent is in arrear or due to the person or persons distraining, or to him or them in whose name or names, or right, such distress shall be taken as aforesaid, that then the owner of such goods or chattels distrained and sold as aforesaid, his executors or administrators, shall and may, by action of trespass, or upon the case, to be brought against the persons so distraining, any or either of them, his or their executors or administrators, recover double of the value of the goods or chattels so distrained and sold, together with full costs of suit."

[illegible]

The plaintiff gave a note of hand for rent arrear, and took a receipt for it when paid, the defendant afterwards distrained for rent, the plaintiff brought trespass, and it was holden, that notwithstanding this note, the defendant might distrain, for it is no alteration of the debt till payment.—But if *A* indorse a note to *B.* for a precedent debt, and *B.* gave a receipt for it as money when paid, yet if he neglect to apply to the drawer in time, and by his laches the note is lost, it will extinguish the precedent debt, and in an action he would be nonsuited (*a*).

If a landlord accept a bond for rent, this does not extinguish it, for the rent is higher, and the acceptance of a security of equal degree is no extinguishment of a debt, as a statute staple for a bond but a judgment obtained upon a bond is an extinguishment of it (*b*)

To covenant for rent against three defendants, it was pleaded, that of rent 41*l.* was paid, that of the residue, two of the defendants had paid their shares, and that the defendant, *Mitchell*, gave the plaintiff a promissory note for his share, payable at a banker's, that such note was dishonoured, whereupon the plaintiff sued *Mitchell* and had judgment by default on such note, which judgment was still unsatisfied When the plea was pleaded, the defendant was under terms to plead issuably. The plaintiff treated it as no plea under a Judge's order and signed judgment for want of a plea. On cause being shewn, the defendant's counsel contended that the plea was good, for that the action on the covenant was merged in the judgment on the note, and the defendant had a right to avail himself of the point. L *Kenyon* "The judgment is a merger of the original cause of action where it is obtained immediately on the original cause itself; but it is no merger, where it is on a collateral point, unless the fruits of it be obtained" The defendant's counsel then said, that at any rate the plaintiff ought not to have signed judgment he ought to have demurred 3 *T. R.* 1788 L *Kenyon.* "I suspect that this plea is founded on knavery, it goes to defeat the justice of the case but I fear that the plaintiff was not justified in treating it as no plea He ought to have demurred. Rule absolute (*c*).

SECTION II. *For other supp[illegible] [illegible] to distrain*

If the distress was made for other supposed cause than under pretence of rent arrear, when in truth it was [illegible], trespass also lies for the [illegible]

After [illegible] [illegible], and [illegible] [illegible], the defendant brought trespass against the plaintiff for taking his goods, and the Court

(*a*) [illegible] (*b*) [illegible] (*c*) D[illegible] MSS

held that the action would lie; for by vacating the judgment it is as if it had never been, and is not like a judgment reversed by writ of error.—But, in such case, it would not lie against the sheriff, who has the King's writ to warrant him; but the party must produce not only the writ, but the judgment (*a*).

Where the action is transitory (as trespass for taking goods) the plaintiff is foreclosed to pretend a right to the place, nor can it be contested upon the evidence who had the right, therefore possession is justifiable enough for the defendant, and it is sufficient for him to plead that he was possessed of *Blackacre*, and that he took the goods damage-feasant without shewing title.—But it is otherwise in trespass *quare clausum fregit*, because there the plaintiff claims the close and the right may be contested (*b*).

Trespass for taking and detaining his cattle at *Teddington*, the defendant justified taking them damage-feasant at *Kingston*, and that he carried them to *Teddington* and impounded them there. It was objected on demurrer that the justification was local, and therefore the defendant ought to have traversed the place in the declaration *sed non allocatur*, for when the defendant says he carried them to *Teddington*, and impounded them there, they agree in the place, for if the defendant had not a right to take them, he was a trespasser at *Teddington* (*c*).

The general issue, in trespass, is "not guilty."

In trespass *quare clausum fregit*, the defendant may, upon "not guilty," give in evidence that he had a lease for years, but not that he had a lease at will, for that is like a licence which may be countermanded at pleasure), or that his servant put the cattle there without his assent, but he cannot give in evidence a right of common, [illegible] any other easement, nor can the defendant give in evidence that the plaintiff ought to repair his fences, for want whereof the cattle escaped, nor that he entered to take his emblements or cattle, nor that he entered in aid of an officer for execution of process, or in fresh pursuit of a felon, or to remove a nuisance, nor that it was the freehold [illegible] and that he entered by his command [illegible], for these are all matters of justification only (*d*).

So, the defendant cannot give in evidence, that the goods were seized as a heriot, or that they were distrained damage-feasant, [illegible] (*e*).

But he may give in evidence, or plead, that he was tenant in common with the plaintiff, but if he would take advantage of [illegible] being so, he must plead it in abatement, for that will not prove him not guilty. So if there be two defendants, they may plead a tenancy in common in one of them, with the plaintiff (*f*).

(*a*) [illegible] N. P. 84 (*b*) Ibid. 89 (*c*) [illegible] (*d*) [illegible] (*e*) [illegible]
(*f*) [illegible]

In case of an absolutely stinted common in point of number, one commoner may distrain the supernumerary cattle of another but not if any admeasurement is necessary, as where the stint has relation to the quantity of common land (*a*)

With respect to the plea of *liberum tenementum*, and to a new assignment, if the defendant say that the *locus in quo* is six acres in *D* which are his freehold, and the plaintiff say they are *his* freehold, and in truth the plaintiff and defendant have both six acres there, the defendant cannot give in evidence, that he did the trespass in his own soil, unless he give a name certain to the six acres, for otherwise (says *Dyer*, 23. *a* 147) the plaintiff cannot make a new assignment (*b*).

It is certain, that where the action is transitory (as for taking the plaintiff's goods), the defendant, if he would plead the *locus in quo* to be his freehold, and that he took the goods damage-feasant, must ascertain the place at his peril; because by his plea he has made that local which was at large before; for the taking of the goods is the gist of the action, and therefore the plaintiff may prove it at a different place from that laid in the declaration (*c*).

Indeed it should seem that antiently, upon a writ of *quare clausum fregit*, the plaintiff might, and may still, declare either generally, for breaking his close at *A.* or might name the close in his count, as for breaking and entering his close called *Blackacre* in *A.* or might otherwise certainly describe the same If he declared generally, and the defendant pleaded the general issue, the plaintiff might give evidence of a trespass in any part of the township of *A.* So that, for the advantage of the defendant, and to enforce the plaintiff to ascertain the place exactly, a method was devised of permitting the defendant to plead what is called "the common bar," that is, to name any place, as *Broomfield* (true or false was immaterial) in *A.* as the place where the supposed trespass happened, and then allege that such place so named was the defendant's own freehold and as the plaintiff could not prove a trespass in *Broomfield*, this drove him to a new assignment of the *locus in quo*, by naming the place in certain, as a close called *Blackacre*, to which the defendant was now to plead afresh (*d*)

In trespass, the defendant justified in a place called *A* as his freehold, the plaintiff, by way of new assignment said that the place in which, &c is called *B* It is no plea to say that *A* and *B.* are the same place, for by the new assignment the bar is at an end (*e*)

If the plaintiff make a new assignment, and the general issue be joined thereon, the plaintiff cannot prove the defendant guilty at the place mentioned in the bar for when the plaintiff makes a new

(*a*) 1 Bl R 673 (*b*) Bull N. P. 92 (*c*) Ibid (*d*) 2 Bl R. 1089
(*e*) Bull N P 92

assignment he waives that whereto the defendant pleaded in bar, so as in truth if it be the same place, he can never take advantage thereof, and therefore if it be the same, yet the defendant ought not to rejoin that it is so, but plead not guilty and take advantage of it at the trial (*a*).

A man is not obliged to justify a distress for the cause which he happens to assign at the time it was made. If he can shew that he had a legal justification for what he did that is sufficient. A man may distrain for one thing and avow for another: thus, he may distrain for rent and avow for heriot service (*b*).

On a justification for taking cattle damage-feasant, if it appear that the party distraining had not actually got into the *locus in quo* before the cattle had got out of it, the justification cannot be supported (*c*).

In trespass for taking and driving plaintiff's cattle, to which there was a justification, that defendant was lawfully possessed of a certain close, and that he took the cattle damage-feasant, plaintiff may specially reply title in another by whose command he entered, &c. and it does not vitiate the replication that it is unnecessarily proved, and farther to give colour to the defendant (*d*)

For as trespass is a possessory action, it is enough for the plaintiff in his replication to traverse the title set out by the defendant, without setting up a title in himself, for the possession admitted in the plea in giving colour is sufficient unless the defendant can make out a title in himself.—But if in trespass for taking a gelding (or other chattel), the defendant pleads that the place where is one hundred acres, and that *J. S.* is seised thereof in fee, and that he as his servant and by his express orders took the gelding (or other chattel) damage feasant; the plaintiff cannot reply *de injuria sua propria absq. tali causa*, for that would put in issue three or four things, but he must traverse one thing in particular (*e*).

If the defendant plead that it is his freehold, the plaintiff may reply three ways 1. that it is *his* freehold, and then he must always traverse the defendant's plea, except in one case, and that is where he makes a new assignment. 2. Or he may derive a title under the defendant, and then he must not deny its being the defendant's freehold. 3 He may set up a title not inconsistent with the defendant's, and then he may either traverse the defendant's title, or not, as he pleases (*f*).

It is not necessary to have an interest in the soil, to maintain trespass *quare clausum fregit*, but an interest in the profits is sufficient, as he who has *prima tonsura* So, if *J S* agrees with the owner of

(*a*) Bull. N P 92 (*b*) 7 T R 657; 3 T R 626 (*c*) 1 Esp N P 95.
(*d*) 1 T R 212 (*e*) Bull N P 92 (*f*) Ib. 94

the soil to plough and sow the ground, and for that to give him half the crop, *J. S* may have his action for treading down the corn, as the owner is not jointly concerned in the growing corn, but is to have half after it is reaped by way of rent, which may be of other things than money. though in *Co. Lit.* 142. it is said it cannot be of the profits themselves, but that (as it seems) must be understood of the natural profits (*a*).

The plaintiff may prove trespass at any time before the action brought, though it be before or after the day laid in the declaration. But in trespass with a *continuando*, the plaintiff ought to confine himself to the time in the declaration, yet he may waive the *continuando*, and prove a trespass on any day before the action brought, or he may give in evidence only part of the time in the *continuando* (*b*).

The plaintiff can only prove the taking such goods as are mentioned in the declaration; because a recovery in the action could not be pleaded in bar to any other action brought for taking other goods than those specified in the declaration. Therefore, where the declaration was for entering the plaintiff's house, and taking *diversa bona et catalla ipsius querentis ibidem inventa*, after verdict for the plaintiff the judgment was arrested (*c*).

By stat. 21 *J.* 1. *c.* 16. the defendant may to trespass *quare clausum fregit*, plead a disclaimer, and that the trespass was by negligence or involuntary, and tender of sufficient amends before the action brought; whereupon, or upon some of them the plaintiff shall be forced to join issue and if the said issue be found for the defendant, or the plaintiff shall be nonsuited, the plaintiff shall be clearly barred from the said action, and all other suits concerning the same.

Though the verdict do not agree with the plea in the manner and nature of the tenure, yet if it agrees in substance in the point for which the distress was made, that is sufficient; for there is a difference between trespass and replevin, for in replevin it behoves the avowant to make a good title *in omnibus* (*d*).

Thus in trespass for breaking and entering the plaintiff's house and taking his goods, the defendant pleaded, that the house is parcel of a half yard holden of *A.* by homage, fealty, escuage, uncertain suit of Court, enclosing his park with pales, and rent of a pound of comyn, and for three years' arrear, and for homage and fealty of the tenant, he by *A*'s command entered and took, &c. the defendant traversed the tenure *modo et formâ* Special verdict that he held of *A.* by homage, fealty, enclosing his park, rent of a pound of comyn, *et non aliter*, and judgment for the defendant (*e*).

(*a*) Bull. N. P. 85. (*b*) Ibid. 86. (*c*) Ibid. 84. (*d*) Ibid. 56. (*e*) Ibid. 55.

In trespass for taking the plaintiff's cattle, justification that they were damage feasant in the defendant's close is sufficient without setting forth a title (*a*).

If trespass for taking and selling the plaintiff's goods be brought against two persons, and the one suffers judgment to go by default, and the other justifies *the taking* on a distress for rent, by command of his co-defendant, and *the selling* by the licence of the plaintiff, and issue be taken on the licence and found for the defendant, the judgment suffered by default shall be arrested, for the case of a licence cannot be distinguished from a gift of goods, or a release, which destroys the cause of action as to all the defendants (*b*).

Trover for an irregular Distress.

Trover also lies for a distress illegally taken; as where a right to distrain exists, but the distrainer (where the distress is for rent) takes such goods as are not lawfully the subjects of a distress; as wearing apparel in use, &c.

For where cattle or goods are wrongfully taken and detained, the party may bring trespass *vi et armis*, replevin, trover, or detinue, or if they are converted into money, he may waive the tort, and bring *assumpsit* for money had and received: but the plaintiff having once made his election, cannot afterwards bring another action for the same cause, either whilst the former is depending, or after it has been determined (*c*).

If therefore a party pay money in order to redeem his goods from a wrongful distress for rent (or any other supposed ground of distress, it is presumed,) he may maintain trover against the wrong-doer (*d*).

In order to maintain trover the plaintiff must have a right of property in the thing, and a right of possession, and unless both these things concur, the action will not lie.—Therefore where goods leased, as furniture with a house, have been wrongfully taken in execution by the sheriff, the landlord cannot maintain trover against the sheriff (*e*).

For trover is a special action on the case, which one man may have against another, who hath in his possession any of his goods by delivery, finding, or *otherwise*, or sells or makes use of them without his consent, or refuses to deliver them on demand, and it is for recovery of damages to the value of the goods; and therefore a declaration ought to [illegible]

(*a*) 10 Mod. [illegible] (*b*) 8 Mod. 21[illegible] 2 Ld. Raym. 1372 [illegible] 1 S[illegible] 6[illegible]
(*c*) 1 [illegible] P. [illegible] (*d*) 6 T. R. 298. (*e*) 7 T. R. 9.

convenient certainty in the description of the things, so that the jury may know what is meant thereby (*a*).

The conversion is the gist of the action, and the manner in which the goods came to the hands of the defendant is only inducement; and therefore the plaintiff may declare upon a *devenerunt ad manus* generally, or specially *per inventionem*, (though the defendant came to the goods by delivery,) for being but inducement, such need not be proved, but it is sufficient to prove property in himself, possession to have been in the defendant, and a conversion by him. So, the declaration was holden to be good, though the conversion was laid to be on a day before the trover, for the *postea convertit* is sufficient, and the *viz.* void (*b*).

The distinction between the actions of trespass and trover is well settled, the former is founded on possession, the latter on property a special property is sufficient in order to enable the party to bring trover; and even property is sufficient without possession (*c*).

To support an action of trover, there must be a positive tortious act (*d*).

Trover being founded on a tort, "not guilty" is the general issue. A release also may be pleaded specially, and it seems is the only special plea in this action. But as the defendant cannot plead the special matter, he may give it in evidence on the general issue (*e*).

Where the goods are cumbrous, instead of allowing them to be brought into Court, the Court will grant a rule to shew cause, why on the delivery of the goods to the plaintiff and paying costs, proceedings should not be staid (*f*).

Trespass for an irregular Distress.

Trespass will also lie for any irregularity in making the distress or in the subsequent disposition of it, or conduct respecting it.

Therefore, trespass lies against a landlord, who, on making a distress for rent, turned plaintiff's family out of possession, and kept the premises on which he had impounded the distress (*g*)

But respecting a distress for rent, by stat. 11 G 2. c 19 a distress for rent shall not be deemed unlawful for any irregularity in the disposition of it afterward, nor the party making it a trespasser *ab initio*. but the party aggrieved may recover full satisfaction for the special damage he shall have sustained thereby, and no more, in an action of trespass or on the case, unless tender of amends have been before made s 19.

(*a*) Bull N P 32 (*b*) Ibid 33 (*c*) 4 T R 489 Bull N P 33.
(*d*) 2 Bos. & Pul. 439. (*e*) Bull N. P 48 (*f*) Ibid. 47 (*g*) 1 East. R. 139

Trover therefore will not lie in such case (*a*).

Trespass will not lie on an irregular distress, when the irregularity complained of is not in itself an action of trespass, but consists merely in the omission of some of the forms required in conducting the distress, such as procuring goods to be appraised before they are sold; the true construction of the provision, in 11 *G.* 2. *c.* 19. *s.* 19. that the party may recover a compensation for the special damage he sustains by an irregular distress in an action of trespass, or on the case, is that he must bring trespass if the irregularity be in the nature of an act of trespass, and case if it be in itself the subject-matter of an action on the case (*b*).

Action on the Case for an excessive Distress.

As to an excess of a distress taken, an action on the case lies for that on the statute of *Marlbridge*, 52 *H.* 3. *c.* 1. but that will not warrant an action of trespass (*c*).

Thus in trespass for breaking and entering his house, and taking an excessive distress, after judgment by default, it was holden, on error brought, that trespass would not lie, for the entry was lawful, and there is nothing subsequent to make it a trespass, as there is when the distress is abused. At common law, the party might take a distress of more value than the rent, therefore that did not make him a trespasser *ab initio*, but the remedy ought to be by a special action founded upon the statute of *Marlbridge* (*d*).

(*a*) 1 H. Bl. R. 13. (*b*) 2 Campb. 115. (*c*) 7 T. R. 658. (*d*) Bull. N. P. 81.

CHAPTER XX.

Of the Remedies for Tenants against Landlords (continued.)

Of the Tenant's Remedies by Action of Covenant or Assumpsit, according as the Lease is by Deed or without Deed.

IF the landlord commit a breach of covenant, if the lease be by deed, or violate his contract if the lease be by writing without deed, or by parol agreement, the tenant may in the one case sue him for damages in an action of covenant, and in the other in that of *assumpsit*.

A breach of covenant need not be assigned in express words: it is sufficient if it be a direct affirmative, and certain to a general intent (*a*).

Therefore, on a covenant that the defendant had a right to let for the term, a breach assigned generally that he had not a right to let is good, for the covenant being general, the breach may be assigned as general as the covenant, and it lies not in the plaintiff's notice who had the rightful estate, but the defendant ought to have maintained, that he was seised in fee, and had a good estate to demise, and then the plaintiff ought to have shewn a special title in some other; but *primâ facie* the count is good, the covenant being general, to assign a general breach (*b*).

So in assigning a breach of covenant that was for quiet enjoyment, it was held to be sufficient that at that time of the demise to the plaintiff, *A.* had lawful right and title to the premises, and having such lawful right and title entered, *&c.* and evicted him, *&c.* without shewing what title *A.* had, or that he evicted the plaintiff by legal process, *&c.* Alledging that "the party having a lawful right and title, entered," is equivalent to saying "he entered by lawful right and title (*c*)."

(*a*) Cro Jac 383 4 T R 621. (*b*) Cro Jac 304 cont. semb. 1 Mod. 66.
(*c*) Cro Eliz 212 1 Mod 101. 4 T. R 621. 8 T. R. 278.

So also, if a covenant be against the act of any particular person, interruption assigned as a breach is good, without shewing by what title (*a*).

So, if a lessor covenant for quiet enjoyment against the *lawful* let, suit, entry, &c. of himself, his heirs, and assigns, the declaration for a breach of the covenant need not expressly allege that he entered claiming title, if the disturbance complained of is such as clearly appears to be an assertion of right (*b*).

On a covenant that *A* and his wife shall enjoy, &c. a breach that *A* was ousted is sufficient (*c*).

However, to establish a breach of covenant for quiet enjoyment without incumbrance from any person, the plaintiff must shew a lawful incumbrance (*d*).

A condition that the lessee shall not molest, vex, &c. any copyholder, is not broken by any entry on the premises *vi et armis* to beat him, if he do not oust him from his copyhold (*e*).

A covenant in a lease, that the lessee should quietly enjoy the estate discharged from tithes, is broken by a suit for them after the expiration of the term (*f*).

But where in covenant for quiet enjoyment the breach assigned was, "that the defendant had exhibited a bill in Chancery against him for ploughing meadow, and obtained an injunction, which had been dissolved with 20*s.* costs; on demurrer, this was held to be no breach of covenant, for the covenant was for quiet enjoyment, and this was a suit for waste (*g*)

The seller covenants to the purchaser of an estate that he shall enjoy and receive the rents, &c. without any action, &c. or interruption by the seller or those claiming from him, or "by, through, or with his, or their acts;" this means default. Therefore, a breach was holden to be well assigned in respect of certain quit-rents in arrear before and at the time of the conveyance, though not stated to have accrued while the seller was tenant of the premises (*h*).

But to covenant for enjoyment free from arrears, plea that the defendant delivered money to the plaintiff, with intention for him to pay it over to the lessor, is good (*i*).

A covenant to surrender a copyhold to a purchaser, and to make and do all acts, deeds, &c. for the perfect surrender and assurance of the premises at the costs and charges of the seller, is not broken by the non-payment of the fine to the lord on the admission of the purchaser; for the title is perfected by the admittance of the tenant, and the fine is not due till after the admittance (*k*).

(*a*) Cro. Eliz. 212. (*b*) 1 T. R. 671. (*c*) Cro. Jac. 383. (*d*) Ibid. 425.
(*e*) Ibid. 421. Cro. Eliz. 914. 916. (*f*) Ibid. 316. (*g*) 2 Vent. 215.
(*h*) 3 East's R. 491. (*i*) 4 Mod. 249. (*k*) 1 East's R. 632. 2 T. R. 484.

In an action against executors in their own right on a covenant for "good title and quiet enjoyment against any person or persons whatsoever," contained in an assignment of a lease of the testator by way of mortgage, the declaration must shew a breach by some act of the covenantors (*a*).

Covenant by a lessee against his lessor, and breach assigned on the covenant for quiet enjoyment, for that the lessor ousted him: the defendant pleaded that he entered to distrain for rent, and traversed that he ousted him *de præmissis;* the plaintiff demurred, for that he did not traverse that he ousted him *de præmissis* or any part thereof. *Sed per Curiam,* the plea is good, and proof of any part, had the plaintiff joined issue, would have been sufficient (*b*).

Where a covenant is founded on a conveyance of an estate which proves to be void, the covenant is void also.

Thus, where the conveyance was "a grant of so much of a term as should be unexpired at the death of *A.*" and covenant for quiet enjoyment, and bond for performance of covenants: this conveyance being void, on account of the uncertainty of the time when the term was to commence and end [*Co. Lit.* 456.] the covenants were adjudged to be void as they depended on the estate (*c*).

But though a lease be void, covenant lies in certain cases for a breach of covenant before the lease became void.

Thus, upon the stat. 13 *Eliz. c.* 20. (since repealed) of leases made by parsons, that upon non-residency for eighty days the lease shall be void, yet it was adjudged, that where a parson made such a lease by indenture, in which were divers covenants on the lessee's part, and after the lease, *&c.* became void by non-residency, *&c.* for a covenant broken before, an action of covenant lay (*d*).

(*a*) 1 H. Bl. R. 84. (*b*) 1 Salk. 260. Bull. N. P. 301. (*c*) Sir T. Raym. 27. 5 T. R. 438. (*d*) Cro. Eliz. 78.

CHAPTER XXI.

Of the Remedies for Tenants against third Persons.

SECTION I. *Of Distress for Damage Feasant and Rescous.*

SECTION II. *Of Trespass for immediate Injuries to his Possession; and Case for consequential ones.*

SECTION I. *Of Distress for Damage Feasant, and Rescous.*

IF the inclosures, *&c* of the tenant be broken down, or his land injured by the cattle, *&c.* of another person, he may either bring an action of trespass for the damage done, or he may take the cattle, *&c.* as a distress feasant, for the party has his election of the two remedies; but using one of them is an utter waiver of the other, as the election of one cannot but be considered to be an implied rejection of the other, beside that *nemo debet bis vexari pro eadem causa:* a distress, therefore, taken damage feasant, as long as it is detained, is a good bar to trespass (*a*).

If a beast has done more damage than he is worth, let the injured party not distrain, but rather take his action (*b*).

This ground of distress is upon the principle of the law of recompence, which justifies the party in retaining that which occasions an injury to his property, till amends be made by the owner

Damage feasant, however, is the strictest distress that is; for the thing distrained must be taken in the very act, for if they are once off, though on fresh pursuit, you cannot distrain them, this diversity existing between distress for rent and damage feasant, that one may distrain any cattle he finds on the premises for rent, but in the other case

(*a*) 12 Mod 663. (*b*) Ibid 661

they must be actually doing damage, and are only distrainable for the damage they are then doing and continuing; for if they have done damage to-day and gone off, and come again at another time and are doing damage, and are taken for that, and the owner tender amends for that damage, the party cannot justify keeping them for the first damage (*a*).

Moreover, if ten head of cattle are doing damage, one cannot take one of them and keep it for the whole damage, but may bring trespass for the rest (*b*).

For damage feasant one may distrain in the night, otherwise it may be the beasts will be gone before he can take them; in which respect, this distress differs from that for rent, or rent-service, which must be in the day-time (*c*).

If the distress be stolen or set at large by a stranger, the distrainer shall not be answerable for it, but if in that case replevin be brought and an *elongatur* returned, as there must be, there shall be a withernam, and the distrainer is liable till he shew the matter, which, being no default of his, will excuse him (*d*).

If tender be made of damages before the taking, the taking is unlawful, if after the taking and before impounding, then the detainer after is unlawful, but tender comes too late after the impounding to make either the taking or detaining unlawful still, however, after the impounding, the distrainer may take the amends and let go the distress if he please.

If a distress damage feasant escape, or die, without any neglect of the distrainer, he may have an action of trespass against the owner.

In trespass *quare clausum fregit*, the defendant pleaded, that the plaintiff distrained his hog damage feasant for the same trespass; the plaintiff replied, that the hog escaped without his consent, and that he was not satisfied for the damage. on demurrer, it was holden, that the action would not lie, though it was admitted that if the distress had died, the action would revive; but the escape (unless the contrary be shewn) was the fault of the plaintiff (*e*).

Of Rescous.

Rescous is where the owner or other person takes away by force a thing distrained from the person distraining; but the person must be actually in possession of the thing, or else it is no rescous; as if a man come to make a distress, and he be disturbed to do it: but the party may bring an action on the case for this disturbance (*f*).

(*a*) 12 Mod. 661 (*b*) Ibid. (*c*) Co Litt 142. (*d*) 1 Mod. 660
(*e*) Bull. N. P. 84 (*f*) Ibid.

The plaintiff ought to count for what rent or services he took the distress, and the defendant may traverse the tenure (*a*).

If a man send his servant to distrain for rent, *&c.* and rescous be made, the master shall have the writ, and he may join in the writ for assault and battery of the servant; for both are torts. The joinder of action depends on the form of the action: for wherever the same plea may be pleaded, and the same judgment given on two counts, they may be joined in the same declaration (*b*).

If the defendant plead "not guilty," which is the general issue, he cannot give in evidence non-tenure of the plaintiff who distrained for rent, but he ought to plead it (*c*).

But this action is rarely brought at this day, but a special action on the case in which non-tenure may be given in evidence on the general issue (*d*).

Vide ante touching stat 2 *W. & M. c.* 5. *s.* 4. *&c.*

In an action on the case for the rescue of a distress intended for sale, the plaintiff need not state that he gave notice of the distress; nor, if the rent became due upon a lease for years, need he aver occupation: for upon a lease for years the rent is payable though the lessee never occupies; *contra* of a lease at will. Nor, though the rent was payable only during occupation, need he shew any thing more than the lessee's entry (*e*).

The venue may come from the will where the rescue was, without joining either the will where the demise was made, or the distress taken (*f*).

Section II. *Of Trespass for immediate Injuries to the Tenant's Possession.*

Where the immediate act itself occasions a prejudice, or is an injury to the house, land, *&c.* of another, trespass *vi et armis* will lie (*g*).

This is a possessory action, therefore, whoever is in possession may maintain an action of trespass against a wrong-doer to his possession (*h*).

Therefore, where a party being entitled under a lease from the Crown to the sole right of digging lead in a certain district, to the soil of which she had no right, let to the plaintiff all her right so to dig during her term: upon his bringing trespass on the case against the defendant for

(*a*) Bull N P 84 (*b*) Ibid 1 T R. 276. (*c*) Bull. N. P. 62.
(*d*) Ibid (*e*) 1 Ld Raym. 170. (*f*) Ibid. (*g*) Ibid. 79.
(*h*) Cro. Jac. 123 3 Bur. R. 1563.

taking the lead, it was held that, being in possession, he should have brought trespass *vi et armis*, wherefore he was nonsuited (*a*)

So, trespass *vi et armis* lies for one who has the profits of the soil, though not the soil itself; as *herbagium*, *pastura*, &c. (*b*).

It lies against a wrong-doer, even though the tenant's possession be void.

Therefore, one in possession of glebe land under a lease void by stat. 13 *Eliz.* c. 20. by reason of the rector's non residence, may yet maintain trespass upon his possession against a wrong-doer (*c*).

Note Where there is a demise of premises, and an entire rent reserved, if any part of the premises could not be legally demised, the whole demise is void (*d*)

As trespass is a possessory action, and possession is sufficient to maintain it against a stranger, no special title need be made (*e*).

In trespass, the plaintiff need only falsify the defendant's title, for the defendant's title being out of the case, it then stands upon the plaintiff's possession, which is enough against a wrong-doer; and the plaintiff need not reply a title (*f*).

Trespass was brought for breaking and entering the plaintiff's house, and beating, abusing, and ill-treating him · plea not guilty. The defence was, that the plaintiff being a pauper had many years before been placed by the parish officers of that time in the house, where the defendants, seven in number, committed the trespass, and that the defendants as parish officers came to the house to remove the plaintiff and his family to another house, that the plaintiff refused to quit and fastened his house against them, and that they in consequence broke open the house and by violence dispossessed the plaintiff and his family. *Plumer* for the plaintiff objected, that under the plea of "not guilty," the defendants were not at liberty to enter into evidence of this kind by way of justification. But *Le Blanc*, J was clearly of opinion that the defendants might, under not guilty, give evidence of *liberum tenementum*, and that if the plaintiff had been put into the house by the parish, he could by no length of possession whatever acquire any title, but might at any time be turned out of possession by the parish officers, and if he resisted, force might lawfully be used to dispossess him, that the evidence offered, therefore, amounted to *liberum tenementum*, and that it would be a question for the jury to decide, whether any unnecessary violence had been used in accomplishing a legal object, and to what damages, if any, the plaintiff was entitled. It being proved that great and unnecessary violence had been used, the jury, on that ground only,

(*a*) Cro Jac 123 3 Bur R. 1563 1 Ld Raym 188 (*b*) 3 Bur. R. 1827. (*c*) 1 East's R 212. (*d*) 3 Esp R 71. (*e*) Cro Jac. 123. (*f*) 2 Str. 1238.

found a verdict for the plaintiff for 40s. *Dauncey and Benyon* for the defendants (a).

At the assizes at *Hereford* on this circuit, the same question came before *Lawrence*, J. in *Worthington* v. *Buster*, and received a similar determination. This was an action of trespass for breaking and entering the plaintiff's house, and disquieting him in the possession thereof, &c. On the evidence it appeared, that the house, more than twenty years ago, had been built on a piece of waste ground at the expence of the parish for the plaintiff; that the plaintiff had ever since occupied it with his family, paying no rent to the parish or making any other acknowledgment; that lately the parish officers had made claim to the premises and put another family into the house to occupy it jointly with the plaintiff, in doing which they had committed what the plaintiff declared on as a trespass. *Lawrence* J. very early in the cause, delivered it as his clear opinion, that if the house was originally built by the parish, and the plaintiff put into it by them, no length of time would turn his possession into a title against the parish; that he could only be considered as a mere tenant at will, and that of course his right of possession ceased with the determination of that will.—Upon this opinion of the Judge's being given, the point contended between the counsel on both sides was, at whose expence the house was originally built, and on its being proved that the house was erected at the costs of the parish the plaintiff was immediately nonsuited. *Dauncey* for the plaintiff, *Williams*, Serjeant, for the defendant.

A lease was made of a farm, and also of certain allotments of common, enclosed under an Act that contained the usual clause empowering the commissioners to distrain or enter, and take the rents and profits in failure of the owner of the land to whom the allotments were parcelled out, paying his proportion of the expences of the Act; and the question was, who should defray such expence, and the expence of fencing such allotments? It was ruled that such expences were to be borne by the landlord, *Lord Ellenborough*, C. J. observing, that "The Act gives the commissioners power to oust the tenant from his occupation; and when a power is to oust the tenant of the rents and profits, there the tenant may pay in his own discharge, and for the redemption of the land (b)."

Trespass lies against a person for disturbing the plaintiff in the profits of a fair by erecting a toll-booth, without saying *quare clausum fregit* (c).

The stat. 16 & 17 *Car.* 2. says, that if in an action of trespass the plaintiff happen to omit the words *vi et armis*, or *contra pacem*, the want of those words shall not vitiate the declaration.

(a) Fox v. Oakley and others. Oxf. Sum. Ass. 1802, at Shrews. T's. MSS.
(b) Smith v. Pearce, Sitt. at Guildhall after M. T. 43 G. 3.
(c) Ibid.

If there is lessee for life or years of lands, the lessee has no property in the trees growing on the land, and even if the clause in the lease is "without impeachment of waste," it gives no property, but is merely an exemption from an action. Yet if a stranger cuts down any trees, the lessee may maintain trespass, but he shall not recover damages for the value of the trees, because the property of them is in him in reversion; but the damages shall be for cropping and breaking his close, and perhaps for the loss of shade, *&c.* (*a*).

This action also lies for not repairing fences, whereby cattle come into ground of the tenant and do damage (*b*).

Every man's ground is, in the eye of the law, fenced; and where a hedge and ditch join together, in whose ground or side the hedge is, to the owner of that land belongs the keeping of the same hedge or fence, and the ditch adjoining to it on the other side, in repair and scoured (*c*).

Where entry, authority, or licence, is given to any one by the law and he abuses it, he will be a trespasser *ab initio*; but where it is given by the party, he may be punished for the abuse, but he will not be a trespasser *ab initio* (*d*).

Where the plaintiff is in the actual occupation of the land, though he had no legal title whatever, the defendant cannot give evidence of property in a stranger under the general issue; but where land is not in the actual possession of any person, as commons and the like, the defendant, on such issue, may prove the *legal* possession to be in a third person (*e*).

It will be a trespass, if a man wrongfully enters the house, lands, or tenements of another without his consent; and therefore trespass lies *de domo sua fracta*. So, for entering his messuage or tenement. Or breaking his close. Or treading down, spoiling, eating, *&c.* his hay or corn. Or cutting down trees. Or hunting in his close. Or breaking hedges and ditches. Or throwing down or disturbing the setting of his fold. Or breaking up his pond. So if a man enters and does damage to another, though he does not keep the possession, as trespass lies *quare domum vel clausum fregit* (*f*).

The lessee for years, after his lease is expired, may have action for a trespass on the land before his lease was ended (*g*).

Where one declared in case for obstructing a water course upon his "possession" of a mill "with the appurtenances" and that "by reason of such his possession he had a right to the use of water running in a certain tunnel to the mill," such allegation was not supported by proof that the tunnel was made on the defendant's land, which he had

(*a*) Esp N P 384. 4 Co 62 a. Par Oss 188. Com Dig. tit. "Trespass" (A. 2)

(*b*) 1 Salk. 335.

(*c*) 10 Mod 140.

(*d*) Bull N P 81.

(*e*) Peake's R 67.

(*f*) F. N. B 87 D. &c.

(*g*) Esp Tresp. 436.

agreed to let the defendant have for this purpose for a certain consideration, but of which no conveyance was made by him to the plaintiff, and he had since refused assent because the plaintiff had not the water by reason of his "possession" to the mill, *&c.* but by parol licence or contract, which could not pass the title to the land, and as a licence was revokable, and revoked (*a*).

Where there is a tenant in possession, and an execution (as by *fi. fa.*) is against the landlord, whose term is to be sold, the tenant cannot, it should seem, be turned out of possession (*b*).

But it is very different where the debtor himself is in possession, in such case, *Buller*, J inclined to think that the sheriff might turn him out of possession (*c*).

The action of trespass is local (*d*)

The plaintiff may prove trespass at any time before the action brought, though it be before or after the day laid in the declaration. But in trespass with a *continuando*, the plaintiff ought to confine himself to the time in the declaration yet he may waive the *continuando*, and prove the trespass on any day before the action brought, or he may give in evidence only part of the time in the *continuando*—*Note*. That of acts which terminate in themselves, and once done cannot be done again, there can be no *continuando*, as hunting or killing a hare, or five hares, but that ought to be alleged, that *diversis diebus ac vicibus* between such a day and such a day, he killed five hares, and cut and carried away twenty trees. Where trespass is laid in continuance that cannot be continued, exception ought to be taken at the trial, for he ought to recover but for one trespass; but hunting may be continued, as well as spoiling and consuming grass (*e*).

Whether the trespass may be laid with a *continuando* or not, depends much upon the consideration of good sense, as where trespass is brought for breaking a house or hedge, it may well be laid with a *continuando*, for pulling away every brick or stick is a breach but if the declaration be that the defendant threw down twenty perches of hedge *continuando transgressionem prædictam* from such a day to such a day, this must be intended of a prosternation done at the first day, and therefore will be ill upon demurrer or judgment by default, but it will be aided by verdict, because the Court will intend that the jury gave no damage for the *continuando* (*f*).

So, trespass cannot be laid of loose chattels with a *continuando*, and if it be so laid no evidence can be given but of the taking at one day; and therefore in trespass for mesne process it ought to be laid *diversis diebus ac vicibus* Where several trespasses are laid in one declaration, *conti-*

(*a*) 4 East's R 107 (*b*) 3 T R. 298. (*c*) Ibid. (*d*) 11 Mod 181.
(*e*) 4 T. R 503 Bull. N P. 86. (*f*) Ibid.

continuando transgressiones prædictas, and some of them may be laid with a *continuando* and some not, after verdict the *continuando* shall be extended only to the trespasses which may be laid with a *continuando*. So, where the *continuando* is impossible, the Court will intend that no damages were given for it (*a*).

Though persons having only a right are not to assert that right by force, and if any violence be used it becomes the subject of a criminal prosecution, yet a person having a right of possession may peaceably assert it, if he do not transgress the laws of his country; for a person who has a right of entry may enter peaceably, and being in possession may retain it and plead that it is his soil and freehold (*b*). The common plea of *liberum tenementum* proves this (*c*).

It is impossible to suggest the possession of a certain term that is not the subject matter of a seizure by the sheriff under a *fieri facias* (*d*); and as in a deed of assignment the sheriff need not specify the particular interest which the party had, so, if he can convey a title in general words, it is equally sufficient to justify in the same general words in an action of trespass (*e*).

It is a general rule in pleading that the party justifying must shew and admit the fact (*f*).

A special justification must be of matter of fact, and not of record; for matter of record must be pleaded even by an officer (*g*).

Regularly, indeed, by the common law, matter of excuse or justification must be pleaded specially, as in trespass to real property, a licence, or that the beasts came through the plaintiff's hedge, which he ought to have repaired; or by reason of a rent-charge, common or the like (*h*).

A justification in trespass must, it is said, answer the whole trespass as laid in the declaration.

Thus, in trespass for breaking and entering plaintiff's house and expelling him, the plea justified the breaking and entering, shewing a good cause for it, and it was held to be a full answer to the count; for the breaking and entering are the gist of the action, and the expulsion is only matter of aggravation (*i*). If the plaintiff had wished to take advantage of the expulsion, he should have shewn the special matter in a new assignment, for according to the six carpenters' case, he should shew in reply that such makes the party a trespasser *ab initio* (*k*).

Therefore, where trespass was for going over the plaintiff's close with horses, cows, and sheep, and the defendant justified that he had a way for horses, cows, and sheep, and said, that such a day he went

(*a*) 4 T R 503. Bull N P 86. (*b*) 3 T R 295. (*c*) 7 T R 431.
(*d*) 3 T R. 295. (*e*) Ibid 298. (*f*) Ibid. (*g*) 6 Mod 40.
(*h*) Tidd's Pract. 597. (*i*) 3 T R. 297. (*k*) 8 T. R 216.

over with horses; upon demurrer it was adjudged ill, for it was a justification for horses only (*a*).

In trespass, the value of the damages must be stated and proved (*b*).

Judgment recovered against another for the same injury is a good plea in bar to this action (*c*).

Of the judgment and damages.—In actions of tort, as trespass, *&c.* where the wrong is joint and several, the distinction seems to be this, that where the plea of one of the defendants is such as shews that the plaintiff could have no cause of action against any of them, there if this plea be found against the plaintiff, it shall operate to the benefit of all the defendants, and the plaintiff cannot have judgment or damages against those who let judgment go by default, but where the plea merely operates in discharge of the party pleading it, that it shall not operate to the benefit of the other defendants, but notwithstanding such plea be found against the plaintiff, he shall have judgment and damages against the other defendants (*d*).

If there be a demurrer to part and an issue upon the other part, or, in an action against several defendants, if some of them demur and others plead to issue, the jury who try the issue shall assess the damages for the whole, or against all the defendants. In this case, if the issue be tried before the demurrer is argued, the damages are said to be contingent, depending upon the event of the demurrer. But where the issue, as well as the demurrer, goes to the whole cause of action, the damages shall be assessed upon the issue, and not upon the demurrer (*e*).

Where there are several defendants who sever in pleading, the jury who try the first issue shall assess damages against all, with a *cesset executio*, and the other defendants, if found guilty, shall be contributory to those damages. In trespass against several defendants who join in pleading, if the jury on the trial find them all jointly guilty, they cannot assess several damages. But they may find some of them guilty and acquit others, in which case the damages can be assessed against those only who are found guilty, or they may find some of the defendants guilty of the whole trespass, and others of part only: or some of them guilty of part, or at one time, and the rest guilty of the other part, or at another time, in either of which cases, they may assess several damages (*f*).

Also, where in an action against several defendants the jury by mistake have assessed several damages, the plaintiff may cure it, by entering a *nolle prosequi* as to one of the defendants and taking judgment against the others; or he may enter a *remittitur* as to the lesser damages,

(*a*) 11 Mod. 219 (*b*) 6 Mod. 153 (*c*) Cro. Eliz. 30. (*d*) 2 Tidd's Pract 805
(*e*) Ibid. (*f*) Ibid. 805

or, even without entering a *remittitur*, he may take judgment against all the defendants for the greater damages (*a*).

Where the jury upon the trial of an issue have omitted to assess the damages, the omission may in certain cases be supplied by writ of inquiry. Where they give greater damages than the plaintiff has declared for, it may be cured by entering a *remittitur* of the surplus before judgment (*b*).

Of the Costs.—As to costs, the stat. 22. 23 *Car.* 2. *c.* 9. enacts, That in all actions of trespass, wherein the Judge, at the trial of the causes shall not find and certify, under his hand, upon the back of the record, that the freehold or title of the land mentioned in the plaintiff's declaration was chiefly in question, the plaintiff, in case the jury shall find the damages to be under the value of forty shillings, shall not recover or obtain more costs of suit than the damages so found shall amount unto.

The construction (*c*) of this statute, which now prevails, is that the statute is confined to actions of assault and battery, (which action is comprised in it) and actions for *local* trespasses, wherein it is possible for the Judge to certify that the freehold or title of the land was chiefly in question. In actions, therefore, for local trespasses, the statute applies, whenever an injury is done to the freehold, or to any thing growing upon or affixed to the freehold, and in a modern case it was carried still further.—That was an action of trespass *quare clausum fregit*, the first count stated, that the defendants broke and entered the close of the plaintiff's, and the grass of the plaintiff's there then growing, with the feet in walking, trod down, spoiled, and consumed, and dug up and got divers large quantities of turf, peat, sods, heath, stones, soil, and earth of the plaintiffs, in and upon the place in which, &c. and *took and carried away* the same, and converted and disposed of the same to their own use. Another count was upon a similar trespass in another close. The defendants pleaded the general issue to the whole declaration, and two special pleas to the second count. On the trial, a verdict was found for the plaintiffs on the general issue, with one shilling damages, and for the defendants on the special pleas, and the Judge had not certified. *Per* Lord *Mansfield.*—"The question on this record is, whether the plaintiff are entitled to any more costs than damages under the stat. 22 & 23 *C.* 2. *c.* 9.? There is a puzzle and perplexity in the cases on this part of the statute, and a jumble in the reports; and as the question is a general one, we thought it proper to consult all the Judges, and they are all of opinion, that this case is within the statute, and that the plaintiffs ought to have no more costs than damages. You will observe, that

(*a*) 2 Tidd's Pract. 805. (*b*) Ibid 806. (*c*) Ibid 880.

what has been called an *asportavit* in this declaration is a mode or qualification of the injury done to the land. The trespass is laid to have been committed on the land by digging, *&c.* and the *asportavit* as part of the same act, and on the trial of the issue, the freehold certainly might have come in question. This is clearly distinguishable from an *asportavit* of personal property, where the freehold cannot come in question, and which therefore is not within the Act. Thus after trees are cut down, and thereby severed from the freehold, if a trespasser comes and carries them away, that case is not within the statute, because the freehold cannot come in question; here it might (*a*)."

Where an injury is done to a personal chattel, it is not within the statute; nor where an injury to a personal chattel is laid, in the same declaration, with assault and battery, or a local trespass; consequently, in these cases, though the damage be under forty shillings, the plaintiff is entitled to full costs, without a certificate.—But then it must be a substantive and independent injury: for where it is laid or proved merely in aggravation of damages, as a mode or qualification of the assault and battery, or local trespass, or there is a verdict for the defendant upon that part of the declaration which charges him with an injury to a personal chattel it is within the statute (*b*)

The certificate required by this statute need not, it seems, be granted at the trial of the cause.—The award of an arbitrator is not tantamount to a Judge's certificate under this statute.

It has been determined in several cases, that if the defendant, in trespass *quare clausum fregit*, plead a licence or other justification, which does not make title to the land, and it is found against him, the plaintiff is entitled to full costs, though he do not recover 40*s* damages; the principle on which these determinations have proceeded is, that where the case is such, that the judge who tries the cause cannot in any view of it grant a certificate, it is considered to be a case out of the statute. So on a plea of not guilty to a new assignment of *extra viam*, the plaintiff obtaining a verdict for less than 40*s.* damages is entitled to full costs, without a judge's certificate; unless the way pleaded be set forth by metes and bounds: and when the plaintiff is entitled to costs upon the new assignment, he is entitled to the costs of all the previous pleadings (*c*).

The stat. 4 & 5 *W.* & *M.* *c.* 23. *s.* 10. after reciting that great mischiefs ensue by inferior tradesmen, apprentices, and other dissolute persons, neglecting their trades and employments, who follow hunting, fishing and other games, to the ruin of themselves and damage of their neighbours, enacts, " That if any such person shall presume to

(*a*) Doug. 780. (*b*) Ibid. 882. (*c*) Ibid. 884

hunt, hawk, fish or fowl, (unless in company with the master of such apprentice, duly qualified by law,) such person shall be subject to the penalties of this Act, and shall or may be sued or prosecuted for his wilful trespass, in such his coming on any person's land: and if found guilty thereof, the plaintiff shall not only recover his damages thereby sustained, but his full costs of suit; any former law to the contrary notwithstanding." The words "inferior tradesman" extend, it seems, to every tradesman, not qualified to kill game: but this was doubted in a subsequent case, wherein the Judges were divided in opinion upon the question, whether a surgeon and apothecary should be considered as an inferior tradesman (*a*).

So, by the stat. 8 & 9 *W.* 3. *c.* 11. *s.* 4. for the prevention of wilful and malicious trespasses, it is enacted, "That in all actions of trespass, to be commenced or prosecuted in any of his Majesty's courts of record at *Westminster*, wherein at the trial of the cause it shall appear, and be certified by the Judge under his hand upon the back of the record, that the trespass, upon which any defendant shall be found guilty, was wilful and malicious, the plaintiff shall recover not only his damages, but his full costs of suit; any former law to the contrary notwithstanding." The certificate, required by this statute, need not be granted at the trial of the cause; and if it appear on the trial that the trespass, however trifling, was committed after notice, and the jury give less than 40*s.* damages, the Judge is bound to certify that the trespass was wilful and malicious, in order to intitle the plaintiff to his full costs (*b*).

In an action of trespass, brought by a pauper against the overseers of the poor, for entering his house and taking away his bed, it was proved that on the defendants' entering the house, the plaintiff desired them to go away, notwithstanding which they persevered in accomplishing their purpose. *Heath, J.* ruled this to be a wilful trespass, and though he reprobated the action as an improper one, under the circumstances in evidence, yet, he said he had no discretion, but was bound to certify that the trespass was wilful (*c*).

Where the declaration consists of several counts, the plaintiff in the Court of *K. B.* is only entitled to the costs of such as are found for him; and neither party is allowed the costs of those which are found for the defendant. Where the plaintiff's declaration consisted of two counts, to one of which the defendant pleaded the general issue, which was found for the plaintiff, and to the other a justification, to which the plaintiff demurred, and judgment was thereupon given for the defendant; the Court agreed that the defendant could have no costs upon the

(*a*) Doug. 586. (*b*) Ibid. 887. (*c*) Oxf. Sum. Ass. 1800. T. MSS.

demurrer (*a*).—But if there be two distinct causes of action, in two separate counts, and as to one the defendant suffers judgment to go by default, and as to the other takes issue, and obtains a verdict, he is entitled to judgment for his costs on the latter count notwithstanding the plaintiff is entitled to judgment and costs on the first count. So where the declaration in trespass consisted of one count only, to which there were several pleas of justification on which issues were taken, and a new assignment on which judgment passed by default, and a *venire* was awarded, as well to assess the damages on the judgment by default, as to try the issues, all the issues being found for the defendant, it was holden that he was entitled to the costs of them (*b*).

Of Trespass on the Case.

For injuries to his possession, an action on the case will also lie in most cases where trespass would be maintainable, and in others where it would not.

An action on the case lies for consequential damages where the act itself is not an injury. It is now indeed a settled distinction, that where the immediate act itself occasions a prejudice, or is an injury to the plaintiff's person, house, land, *&c.* trespass *vi et armis* will lie; but where the act itself is not an injury, but a consequence from that act is prejudicial to the plaintiff's person, house, land, *&c.* trespass *vi et armis* will not lie, but the proper remedy is an action on the case (*c*). The difference, therefore, between trespass and case is, that in the trespass the plaintiff complains of an immediate wrong; and in case, of a wrong that is the consequence of another act (*d*).

Fixing a spout, therefore, so as to discharge water upon the land of another, is only consequentially injurious, and the party who sustains the damage must bring case in order to get a compensation (*e*).

So, if a man who ought to enclose against my land, do not enclose, whereby the cattle of his tenants enter into my land, and do damage to me, I may have this remedy (*f*)

So, case lies for breaking the fences of a third person, whereby my cattle escape into his land and are distrained (*g*).

If a house of office be separated from other premises by a wall, and that wall belongs to the owners of the house of office, he is of common right bound to repair it, and an action on the case will lie.

In such action by a lessee for years against the owner of the adjoining house, for not repairing a party-wall, by which the plaintiff's house

(*a*) Oxf. Sum. Ass. 1800. T.'s MSS. 888. (*b*) Ibid. 889. (*c*) Bull. N. P. 74. 2 Ld. Raym. 1402. 8 Mod. 275. 6 T. R. 449. (*d*) 1 Str. 635. (*e*) 2 Ld. Raym. 1399. (*f*) Bull. N. P. 74. (*g*) 1 Ld. Raym. 273.

was damaged, it is not necessary to state that he was bound by prescription to repair the wall; it is sufficient to declare that he was possessed of a messuage for a certain number of years, and that the defendant ought to repair the wall (*a*).

Note. If the owner of the house is bound to repair it, he and not the occupier is liable to an action on the case for an injury sustained by a stranger from the want of repair (*b*).

But an action on the case for not repairing fences, whereby another party is damnified, can only be maintained against the occupier, and not against the owner of the fee, who is not in possession (*c*).

Case may be maintained by a lessee for years, for obstructing the lights of an antient messuage. A declaration, that the defendant was, and yet is possessed of a house and a void piece of land, and erected buildings thereon, and thereby stopped the light coming by the said windows into his house, whereby his house was totally darkened, and he much prejudiced by such stopping, is good (*d*).

So in an action for stopping the plaintiff's lights, it is sufficient to declare that he was possessed of such a messuage for years and had and ought to have such light, without stating that the messuage and lights were antient (*e*).—Not lengthening windows, or making more lights in the old wall than formerly, was thought by L. *Hardwicke* not to vary the right of persons. Indeed a contrary doctrine might create innumerable difficulties in populous cities (*f*).

A prescription of antient lights is to the house, and not to the person (*g*).

Special matter may be given in evidence on the general issue in an action on the case for stopping lights (*h*).

This action lies for damage done to the plaintiff's colliery, by what the defendant has done to his own colliery, within his own soil, though several other collieries lie between them: and trespass *vi et armis* does not lie, for the damage is not immediate, but consequential (*i*).

Case does not lie for a mere trespass: as, for pulling down a wall, and taking down the tiles from a house, unless it be alleged that the timber was thereby rotted (*k*).

A possessory right is sufficient to maintain an action of trespass or case, though not a replevin. But trespass and case cannot be joined, for the judgments differ, that in trespass being a *capiatur*, and that in case, though *vi et armis*, a *misericordia* (*l*).

As this action arises from the special damage, any thing may be given in evidence on the general issue that destroys the right of action (*m*).

(*a*) 8 Mod. 312. 2 Ld. Raym. 1089. (*b*) 2 H. Bl. R. 349. 12 Mod. 168. 3 T. R. 766.
(*c*) 4 T. R. 318. (*d*) Cro. Car. 325. (*e*) 6 Mod. 116. (*f*) Atk. 83.
(*g*) Cro. Car. 326. (*h*) 1 Ld. Raym. 752. (*i*) Com. Dig. tit. "Action on the Case" (A.)
(*k*) Ibid. (B. 6.) (*l*) 1 Ld. Raym. 273. 10 Mod. 25. 1 Ld. Raym. 272. 12 Mod. 235.
(*m*) Bull. N. P. 78.

A declaration for stopping up a watercourse, without shewing how, is bad upon demurrer. but unobjectionable after verdict (*a*).

Case lies against the proprietor of tithes for not taking them away. But trespass *vi et armis* will not; because it is only a non-feasance and not a mal-feasance (*b*). The declaration may state that the plaintiff set out the tithes, and the defendant refused to take them away; or the plaintiff may declare with a *per quod* the grass did not grow where the tithes lay, and he could not put his cattle into the close to pasture the residue of the grass, lest they should hurt the tithes; for though the proprietor of tithes does not remove them in convenient time, the owner of the land cannot put in his cattle and eat them, for to permit if the corn be not removed at the day, to put in his cattle and eat all the corn, would be a much greater loss to the parson than that which the plaintiff hath sustained by the continuance of the corn upon the land, besides that it is much more reasonable to permit the plaintiff to bring an action against the parson, and so the Court to be the judge of the reasonableness of the time, and that the recompence be proportionable to the loss sustained (*c*).—In such a case, the owner's remedy is either by distress or action (*d*).

Case will not lie against a parson for not taking away his tithe, unless they have been properly set out: it is, therefore, not maintainable for not taking away the tithe of hay where it was not set out in swathe (*e*).

A parson is not entitled to carry his tithes home by every road which the farmer himself uses for the occupation of his farm. *Semble* that he may only use such road as the farmer does for the occupation of the close in which the tithes grow (*f*).

For other points respecting this action, we refer our readers to Chap. XVII.

(*a*) 1 Ld. Raym. 452 (*b*) 3 Bur. 189 (*c*) 2 Ld Raym 167, 9
(*d*) 3 T. R 72. (*e*) 3 Esp. R. 31 (*f*) 2 Bos. & Bull N R. 466

CHAPTER XXII.

Of Remedies against third Persons; wherein of Forcible Entry and Detainer.

FORCIBLE entry and detainer are offences at the common law; and the prosecutor, if he pleases, may proceed in that way: but then the indictment ought to express, not only the common technical words *with force and arms*, but also such circumstances, as that it may appear upon the face of the indictment to be more than a common trespass (*a*).

But the safest and most usual way is, to proceed upon the statutes. Concerning which, it may be premised, that "they who keep possession with force, in lands and tenements, whereof they or their ancestors, or they whose estate they have in the same, have continued their possession of the same, by three whole years next before without interruption, shall not be endamaged by force of any of the statutes concerning forcible entry." 8 *H.* 6. *c* 9. *s.* 7.

Forcible Entry, what.—By the 5 *R* 2. *c.* 8. "None shall make any entry into any lands or tenements (or benefice of the holy church, 15 *R.* 2 *c.* 2. or other possessions, 8 *H.* 6. *c.* 9. *s.* 2) but where entry is given by the law; and in such case, not with strong hand, nor with multitude of people, but only in peaceable and easy manner, on pain of imprisonment and ransom at the King's will"

Or other possessions.] It seems clear, that no one can come within the danger of these statutes, by a violence offered to another in respect of a *way*, or such like easement, which is no possession. And there seems to be no good authority, that an indictment will lie on this case for a *common* or *office* (*b*).

Not with strong hand, nor with multitude of people] It seems certain,

(*a*) 3 Bur. 1698, 1731.

(*b*) 2 Burn's Just. 1 H P. C. c. 64. s. 31.

that if one, who pretends a title to lands, barely go over them, either with or without a great number of attendants, armed or unarmed, in his way to the church or market, or for such like purpose, without doing any act, which either expressly or impliedly amounts to a claim upon such lands, he cannot be said to make an entry thereinto (*a*)

But it seemeth, that if a person enter into another man's house or ground, either with apparent violence offered to the person of any other, or furnished with weapons, or company, which may offer fear, though it be but to cut or take away another man's corn, grass, or other goods, or to fell or crop wood, or do any other like trespass, and though he do not put the party out of his possession, yet it seemeth to be a forcible entry. But if the entry were peaceable, and after such entry made, they cut or take away any other man's corn, grass, wood, or other goods, without apparent violence or force, though such acts are accounted a disseisin with force, yet they are not punishable as forcible entries (*b*).

But if he enter peaceably, and there shall, by force or violence, cut or take any corn, grass, or wood, or shall forcibly or wrongfully carry away any other goods there being, this seemeth to be a forcible entry punishable by these statutes (*c*).

So also shall those be guilty of a forcible entry, who, having an estate in land, by a defeasible title, continue with force in the possession thereof, after a claim made by one who had a right of entry thereto (*d*).

But he who barely agrees to a forcible entry made to his use, without his knowledge or privity, shall not be adjudged to make an entry within these statutes, because he no way concurred in, or promoted, the force (*e*).

Indeed, in general, it seemeth clear, that, to denominate the entry forcible, it ought to be accompanied with some circumstances of actual *violence* or *terror*, and therefore that an entry which hath no other force than such as is implied by the law, in every trespass whatsoever, is not within the statutes.

As to the matter of *violence*, it seems to be agreed, that an entry may be forcible, not only in respect of a violence actually done to the person of a man, as by beating him if he refuse to relinquish his possession, but also in respect of any other kind of violence in the manner of the entry, as by breaking open the doors of a house, whether any person be in it or not, especially if it be a dwelling-house, and perhaps also by an act of outrage after the entry, as by carrying

(*a*) 2 Burn's Just 1 H P. C. c. 64. s. 20. (*b*) Dalt c 126 (*c*) Ibid.
(*d*) 1 H. P C. c 64. s 23. (*e*) Ibid s. 24

away the party's goods. But it seems, that an entry is not forcible by the bare drawing up a latch, or pulling back the bolt of a door, there being no appearance therein of being done by *strong hand* or *multitude of people*, and it hath been holden, that entry into a house through a window, or by opening a door with a key, is not forcible (*a*).

In respect of the circumstances of *terror*, it is to be observed, that wherever a man, either by his behaviour or speech, at the time of his entry, gives those who are in possession just cause to fear that he will do them some bodily hurt, if they will not give way to him, his entry is esteemed forcible, whether he cause such a terror by carrying with him such an unusual number of attendants, or by arming himself in such a manner, as plainly intimates a design, or by actually threatening to kill, maim, or beat those who should continue in possession, or by giving out such speeches as plainly imply a purpose of using force, as if one say that he will keep his possession in spite of all men, or the like (*b*).

But it seems that no entry shall be judged forcible from any threatening to spoil another's *goods*, or to destroy his cattle, or to do him any other such like damage, which is not personal (*c*).

However, it is clear that it may be committed by a single person, as well as by twenty (*d*).

But, nevertheless, all those who accompany a man, when he makes a forcible entry, shall be judged to enter with him, whether they actually come upon the land or not (*e*).

Forcible Detainer, what.—The same circumstances of violence or terror which will make an entry forcible, will make a detainer forcible also, and a detainer may be forcible, whether the entry were forcible or not (*f*).

How punishable by Action.—By stat. 8 *H.* 6. *c.* 6. "If any person be put out or disseised of any lands or tenements in a forcible manner, or put out peaceably, and after holden out with strong hand, the party grieved shall have assize of novel disseisin, or writ of trespass against the disseisor, and if he recovers he shall have treble damages, and the defendant moreover shall make fine and ransom to the king."

The Party aggrieved shall have Assize, &c.] But this action being at the suit of the party, and only for the right, is only where the entry of the defendant was not lawful, for if a man entereth with force, where his entry is lawful, he shall not be punished by way of action, but yet

(*a*) 1 H. P. C. c. 64. s. 26. (*b*) Ibid. s. 27. (*c*) Ibid. s. 28. (*d*) Ibid. s. 29.
(*e*) Ibid. s. 22. (*f*) Ibid. s. 30.

he may be indicted upon the statute, for the indictment is for the force and for the king, and he shall make fine to the king, although his right is never so good (*a*).

Treble Damages.] And this he shall recover as well for the mesne occupation as for the first entry, and albeit he shall recover treble damages, yet he shall recover costs, which shall be trebled also; for the word *damages* includeth costs of suit (*b*).

How punishable at the Sessions.—The party grieved, if he will lose the benefit of his treble damages and costs, may be aided and have the assistance of the justices at the general sessions, by way of indictment, on the statute of 8 *H.* 6 which being found there, he shall be restored to his possession, by a writ of restitution granted out of the same Court to the sheriff (*c*).

In the caption of which indictment, it will be sufficient to say, "*justices assigned to keep the peace of our lord the king,*" without shewing that they have authority to hear and determine felonies and trespasses; for the statute enables all justices of the peace, as such, to take such indictments (*d*).

The tenement in which the force was made, must be described with convenient certainty, and the indictment must set forth that the defendant actually entered, and ousted the party grieved, and continueth his possession at the time of finding the indictment; otherwise he cannot have restitution, because it doth not appear that he needeth it (*e*). But if a man's wife, children, or servants, do continue in the house or upon the land, he is not ousted of his possession, but his cattle being upon the ground do not preserve his possession (*f*).

A repugnancy in setting forth the offence in an indictment upon any of the statutes, is an incurable fault (*g*).

An indictment for forcible entry was quashed therefore for not setting forth that the party was seised or disseised, or what estate he had in the tenement; for if he had only a term for years, then the entry must be laid into the freehold of *A.* in the possession of *B.* (*h*).

How punishable by a Justice.—By 8 *H.* 6. *c.* 9. for a more speedy remedy, the party grieved may complain to any one justice, or to a mayor, sheriff, or bailiff within their liberties. But although one justice alone may proceed in such cases, yet it may be adviseable for him, if the time for viewing the force will suffer it, to take to his assistance one or two more justices.

(*a*) 2 Burn's Just Dalt c 129 (*b*) 1 Inst. 257 (*c*) Dalt c 129
(*d*) 1 H P C c 64 s 36 (*e*) Ibid s 37 41. (*f*) Dalt. c. 132.
(*g*) 1 H P. C. c 64 s. 39 (*h*) 3 Salk. 169. 3 Bur. 1732.

Concerning which power of one justice it is enacted as follows; "After complaint made to such justice, by the party grieved, of a forcible entry made into lands, tenements, or other possessions, or forcibly holding thereof, he shall, within a convenient time, at the costs of the party grieved, (without any examining or standing upon the right or title of either party), take sufficient power of the county, and go to the place where the force is made." 15 *R.* 2. *c* 2 8 *H.* 6. *c* 9. *s* 2. (*a*).

Complaint —— by the Party grieved] Yet these words do not inforce any necessity of such a complaint; for it is holden, that the justice may and ought to proceed, upon any information or knowledge thereof whatsoever, though no complaint at all be brought unto him, by any party grieved thereby (*b*).

Power of the County] All people of the county, as well the sheriff as others, shall be attendant on the justices, to arrest the offenders, on pain of imprisonment and fine to the king. 15 *R.* 2. *c.* 2

And if the doors be shut, and they within the house shall deny the justice to enter, it seems he may break open the house to remove the force (*c*).

And if after such entry made, the justice "shall find such force, he shall cause the offenders to be arrested." 15 *R.* 2 *c* 2. 8 *H.* 6. *c.* 9. *s* 2.

He shall also take away their weapons and armour, and cause them to be appraised, and after to be answered to the king as forfeited, or the value thereof (*d*).

Also such justice ought to "make a record of such force by him viewed," which record shall be a sufficient conviction of the offenders, and the parties shall not be allowed to traverse it, and this record, being made out of the sessions by a particular justice, may be kept by him; or he may make it indented, and certify the one part into the King's Bench, or leave it with the Clerk of the Peace, and the other part he may keep himself. For this view of the force by the justice, being a judge of record, maketh his record thereof, in the judgment of the law, as strong and effectual as if the offenders had confessed the force before him · and touching, the restraining of traverse, more effectual than if the force had been found by a jury, upon the evidence of others. (This is, as to the fine and imprisonment, but not as to restitution.) 15 *R.* 2. *c.* 2. (*e*).

Shall be put in the next Gaol.---The offenders being arrested (as before said), shall be put in the next gaol, there to abide convict by the record of the same justice, until they have made fine and ransom to the king. 15 *R.* 2. *c.* 2.

(*a*) Dalt c 44 (*b*) Lamb 147 (*c*) Dalt. c. 44. (*d*) Ibid
(*e*) Ibid. 1 H. P. C. c 66 s 8

But it is said, that the justice hath no power to commit the offender to gaol, unless he do it upon his own view of the fact, and not upon the jury finding the same afterwards (*a*).

And if such offenders, being in the house at the coming of the justice, shall make no resistance, nor make shew of any force, then the justice cannot arrest or remove them at all upon such view.

If however the force be found afterwards, by the inquiry of the jury, the justice may bind the offenders to keep the peace, and if they be gone, he may make his warrant to take them, and may after send them to the gaol, until they have found sureties for the peace (*b*)

[Until they make Fine.] If the justices convict a man of a forcible detainer, they ought to set the proper fine upon him. But this they are not bound to do upon the spot, but they may take a reasonable time to consider of the fine: for by the words of the Act, the commitment is to be until he has paid the fine (*c*).

The fine must be assessed upon every offender severally, and not upon them jointly. And the justice ought to estreat the fine, and to send the estreat into the exchequer, that from thence the sheriff may be commanded to levy it for his majesty's use. But upon payment of the fine to the sheriff, or upon sureties found (by recognizance) for the payment thereof, it seemeth that the justice may deliver the offenders out of prison again at his pleasure (*d*).

So much concerning removing the force. But the party ousted cannot be restored to his possession by the justice's view of the force, nor unless the same force be found by the inquiry of a jury.

Concerning which it is enacted as follows: "And though that the persons making such entry be present, or else departed before the coming of the justice; he may notwithstanding, in some good town next the tenement so entered, or in some other convenient place by his discretion (and that though he go not to see the place where the force is), have power to inquire by the people of the county, as well of them that make such forcible entry, as of them which hold the same with force." 8 *H.* 6. *c.* 9. *s.* 3

In order to which, "the justice shall make his precept to the sheriff, commanding him, in the king's behalf, to cause to come before him sufficient and indifferent persons, dwelling next the lands so entered, to inquire of such entries, whereof every man shall have lands or tenements of 40*s*. a year, above reprises. And the sheriff shall return issues on every of them, at the day of the first precept returnable 20*s*. and at the second day 40*s*. and on the third day 100*s*.

(*a*) Dalt. c. 44. 1 H. P. C. c. 64. s. 8. (*b*) Dalt. c. 44. 2 B... Ju... (*c*) ... 79. 2 Ld Raym. 1514. 1 Sess. Cas. 280. (*d*) Dalt. c. 44.

and at every day after double. And the sheriff making default, shall, upon conviction of the said justice, or before the judge of assize, forfeit 20*l* half to the king and half to him who shall sue, with costs, and, moreover, shall make fine and ransom to the king." s. 4, 5.

An inquisition for a forcible entry is good, although it be not stated that the jurors were then and there sworn and impannelled (*a*).

Before the same Justice.] The justice may proceed against the sheriff for this default, either by bill at the suit of the party, or by indictment at the suit of the king (*b*).

The defendant, if he is not present, ought to be called to answer for himself, for it is implied by natural justice in the construction of all laws, that no one ought to suffer any prejudice hereby, without having first an opportunity of defending himself (*c*) and it seems to be settled at this day, that if the defender tender a traverse of the force, the justice ought not to make any restitution till the traverse be tried (*d*).

The defendant may also by the 31 [illegible] 11. plead "*three years' possession*," whereby it is enacted, "That no restitution upon an indictment of forcible entry, or holding with force, shall be made, if the person indicted have had the occupation, or been in quiet possession for three years together next before the indictment found, and his estate therein not determined and restitution shall stay till that be tried and if it is found against the party indicted, he shall pay such costs and damages as the judges or justices shall assess, to be recovered as costs and damages in judgment on other actions."

It hath been holden, that the plea of such possession is good, without shewing under what title, or of what estate, such possession was because it is not the title, but possession only, which is material in this case (*e*).

It was holden in *Leighton's* case, that if the defendant either traverse the entry or the force, or plead that he has been three years in possession, the justice may summon a jury for the trial of such traverse, for it is impossible to determine it upon view and if the justice have no power to try it, it would be easy for any one to elude the statute by the tender of such a traverse, and therefore by a necessary construction the justice must needs have this power as incidental to what is expressly given him (*f*) and this traverse must be tendered in writing, and not by a bare denial of the fact in words, for thereupon a [illegible] must be awarded, a jury returned, the issue tried, a verdict found, and judgment given, and costs and damages awarded, and there must be a re-

(*b*) Dalt. c. 44

(*e*) 1 H. P. C. c. 64 s. 60

(*c*) 1 H. P. C. c. 64 s. 57

(*f*) Ibid. s. 3

cord, which must be in writing, to do all this and not a verbal plea. Upon which traverse tendered, the justice shall cause a new jury to be returned by the sheriff, to try the traverse; which may be done the next day, but not the same day (*a*).

It seemeth, that he who tendereth the traverse, shall bear all the charges of the trial and not the king, or the party prosecuting.

And "if such forcible entry and detainer be found before such justice, then the justice shall cause to reseise the lands and tenements so entered or holden, and shall restore the party put out to the full possession of the same." 8 *H.* 6 *c.* 9. *s.* 3.

The said Justice.] It seems to be agreed, that no other justices of the peace, except those before whom the indictment shall be found, shall have any power, either at the sessions or out of it, to make any award of restitution (*b*).

Shall cause to reseise.] And the justice may break open the house by force, to reseise the same, and so may the sheriff do, having the justice's warrant

Reseise.] That is, shall remove the force, by putting out all such offenders as shall be found in the house, or upon the lands, that entered or held with force (*c*).

And shall restore the Party put out.] And this he may do in his own proper person: or he may make his warrant to the sheriff to do it (*d*).

And by 21 *J. c.* 15. it is enacted, "That such judges, justices, or justice of the peace, as may give restitution unto tenants of any estate of freehold, may give the like unto tenants for term of years, tenants by copy of court-roll, guardians by knight's service, tenants by *elegit*, statute merchant and staple, of lands or tenements by them so holden, which shall be entered upon by force, or holden of them by force."

How punishable on a certiorari.—Although regularly the justices only who were present at the inquiry, and when the indictment was found, ought to award restitution, yet if the record of the presentment or indictment shall be certified by the justice or justices into the King's Bench, or the same presentment or indictment be removed or certified thither by *certiorari*, the justices of that Court may award a writ of restitution to the sheriff, to restore possession to the party expelled, for the justices of the King's Bench have a supreme authority in all cases of the crown (*e*).

Also where upon removal of the proceedings into the King's Bench the conviction shall be quashed, the Court will order restitution to the

(*a*) Dalt c 133 (*b*) 1 H. P. C. c. 64 s 50 (*c*) Dalt. c 150
(*d*) 1 H. P C. c 64 s. 49 (*e*) Dalt. c. 44.

party injured. As in the case of the *K* v. *Jones*, *M.* 8 *G.* a conviction of forcible entry was quashed for the old exception of *messuage* or *tenement*, by reason of the uncertainty, but the restitution was opposed, on an affidavit that the party's title (which was by lease) was expired since the conviction. But the Court said, they had no discretionary power in this case, but were bound to award restitution on quashing the conviction (*a*).

How punishable as a Riot.—If a forcible entry or detainer shall be made by three persons or more, it is also a riot, and may be proceeded against as such, if no inquiry hath before been made of the force (*b*).

For Precedents of the Forms, see 2 *Burn's Justice.*

(*a*) 1 Str. 471. (*b*) Dalt. c. 44.

CHAPTER XXIII.

Of Remedies against third Persons, wherein of Obstruction of a Right of Way

A WAY, or a right of going over another man's ground has been before noticed in *Chap.* V. *Sect* II. among other incorporeal hereditaments.

In such private ways a particular man may have an interest and a right, though another be the owner of the soil (*a*).

This may be grounded on a special permission, as when the owner of the land grants to another a liberty of passing over his grounds, to go to church, to market or the like; in which case the gift or grant is particular and confined to the grantee alone, it dies with the person, and if the grantee quit the country he cannot assign over his right to any other, nor can he justify the taking another person in his company (*b*).

A way may also be by prescription, as if all the inhabitants of such a hamlet, or all the owners and occupiers, of such a farm, have immemorially used to cross such a ground, for such a particular purpose; for this immemorial usage supposes an original grant, whereby a right of way thus appurtenant to lands or houses may be clearly created (*c*).

A right of way may also arise by act and operation of law; for if a man grants me a piece of ground in the middle of his field, he at the same time tacitly and impliedly gives me a way to come at it; and I may cross his land for that purpose without trespass; for when the law doth give any thing to one, it giveth impliedly whatsoever is necessary for enjoying the same (*d*). Therefore when one, (even as trustee) conveys land to another to which there is no access but over the grantor's land, a right of way passes of necessity as incidental to the grant. So also, if the owner of the closes, having no way to one of them but over the other, part with the latter without reserving the way, it should seem that it will be reserved for him by operation of law. So also under a grant of a free and convenient way for the purpose of conveying oats, among other articles, the grantee has a right to lay a framed waggon-way (*e*).

(*a*) 2 Bl. Com. 35. (*b*) Ibid. (*c*) Ibid. 36. (*d*) Ibid. (*e*) 8 T. R. 50.

Disturbance of ways principally happeneth when a person who hath a right of way over another's grounds, by grant or prescription, is obstructed by enclosures or other obstacles, or by ploughing across it; by which means he cannot enjoy his right of way, or at least not in so commodious a manner as he might have done (*a*).

If this be a way annexed to his estate, and the obstruction is made by the tenant of the land, this brings it to another species of injury; for it is then a nuisance for which an assize will lie (*b*).

But if the right of way, thus obstructed by the tenant, be only in gross (that is, annexed to a man's person, and unconnected with any lands or tenements), or if the obstruction of a way belonging to a house or land is made by a stranger, it is then in either case merely a disturbance: for the obstruction of a way in gross is no detriment to any lands or tenements, and therefore does not fall under the legal notion of a nuisance which must be laid *ad nocumentum liberi tenementi*, and the obstruction of it by a stranger can never tend to put the *right* of way in dispute (*c*).

The remedy therefore for these disturbances is not by assize or any real action, but by the universal remedy of action on the case to recover damages (*d*).

Case and trespass for disturbing a right of way.—A right of way, however, is as often contested in an action of trespass.

In an action on the case for spoiling the plaintiff's way with the defendant's carriages, the defendant may justify going along the way with the carriages of a third person having a right to go along the way (*e*).

But under a right of way over a close to a particular place, a man cannot justify going beyond the place.

Therefore if a defendant justify passing along a private way under a right of way to a close called *A*. the plaintiff may reply that he went beyond *A* (*f*).

So, it is not a good justification in trespass that the defendant has a right of way over part of the plaintiff's land, and that he had gone upon the adjoining land, because the way was impassable from being overflowed by a river: for he who has the use of a thing ought to repair it, and in the principal case, for aught that appeared, the overflowing might have happened by the neglect of the defendant; and it did not appear that the defendant had no other road (*g*).—Highways, however, are governed by a different principle: they are for the public service, and if the usual tract is impassable, it is for the general good that people should be entitled to pass in another line (*h*).

(*a*) 3 Bl. Com. 341 (*b*) Ibid (*c*) Ibid (*d*) Ibid. 242 (*e*) Lutw. 114. 1 Ld. Raym. 75 (*f*) Ibid (*g*) Doug 745. (*h*) 1 T. R 570

A man may prescribe for a way for himself and all those whose estate he hath, without shewing that the way is appurtenant to his estate · and if he states that he was seised of two closes, and that he and all those, *&c* had a right of way "*tanquam ad tenementa spectantem,*" the Court will reject these words as surplusage (*a*).

In trespass, where no evidence appeared to shew that a way over another's land had been used by leave or favour or under a mistake of an award which would not support the right of way claimed, such an usage for above twenty years exercised adversely and under a claim of right, is sufficient to leave it to the jury to presume a grant which must have been made within twenty-six years, as all former ways were at that time extinguished by the operation of an Inclosure Act (*b*).

A claim of a prescriptive right of way from *A.* over the defendant's close into *D.* is not supported by proof that a close called *C.* over which the way once led, and which adjoins to *D.* was formerly possessed by the owner of close *A.* and was by him conveyed in fee to another, without reserving the right way; for thereby it appears that the prescriptive right of way does not, as claimed, extend unto *D.* but stops short at *C* (*c*).

But where in trespass *quare clausum fregit* the defendant prescribed for an occupation way *from* his own close "unto, through and over" the *locus in quo* "to and unto" a certain highway, *&c.* such plea may be sustained, though it appeared that one out of several intervening closes was in the possession of the defendant self (*d*).

However, under a grant of a way from *A* to *B.* "in, through and along" a particular way, the grantee is not justified in making a transverse road across the same (*e*)

Quare obstruxit.—Another remedy which the law affords in cases of a similar kind, is by writ of *quare obstruxit.*

This writ lay for him who, having a liberty to pass through his neighbour's ground, could not enjoy his right, because the owner had so obstructed it (*f*).

It lies in the nature of a writ of right close, (*de recto clauso*, directed to the lord or bailiffs of a manor of ancient demesne (*g*).

(*a*) 1 Ld Raym 75 (*b*) 3 East's R 294 ( ) 1 East's R 377
(*d*) Ibid 381 (cited) et vide 8 T R 80 (*e*) 1 T R 560 (*f*) Fleta, L. 4 c 26.
(*g*) F.N.B. 11 J 2 Com Dig in voce

CHAPTER XXIV.

Of Liability to repair a Church, and of Right to Pews therein.

OF common right, that is, by the ancient canon and civil law, the parson ought to have repaired the whole church, and it is by the custom of England only that the parish repairs the body (*a*).

In one case the Court said, that the repairing of the church is a real charge upon the land, let the owner live where he will (*b*).

But in a subsequent case it was holden, that the occupier of land in a parish shall be rated to the repairs of the church, and not the landlord living out of the parish. So, it was said, if a man take a lease of a stall in a market-town where he uses once a week to sell his wares, but lives in another parish, he shall not be charged towards the repairs of the church in that market-town (*c*).

So, church ornaments are a personal charge upon the inhabitants, and not upon those who live elsewhere, though they occupy lands in that parish (*d*).

The paying towards the repairs of a chapel of ease will not prevent the churchwardens from proceeding in the spiritual court for non-payment of a rate for repairing the mother church (*e*). The making of church-rate is a subject of ecclesiastical jurisdiction, wherefore a *mandamus* to the churchwardens to make such rate was refused (*f*).

A libel was entered in the Episcopal Court at *Exeter*, against one for not paying a church-rate at *Totness*. Plea that the corporation of *T* was bound to repair, and it appeared that this was the first rate ever made. A prohibition had been moved for on the ground that the plea put in issue matter of prescription. *Gibbs* shewed cause. Lord *Kenyon* said, an individual may be subject to the repair of the aisle, or any other part of a church, by prescription, so *com. semb* of the whole church, so that the parishioners may not be rateable, and so of a corporation (*g*). If therefore certain funds, vested in a corporation who have always been accustomed to the repair of the church, prove inadequate to that pur-

(*a*) 12 Mod 83. (*b*) 3 Mod 211. (*c*) 4 Mod 148. (*d*) 3 Mod 211.
(*e*) Ibid. 264. (*f*) 5 T R 364. (*g*) MSS. Eas. T. 30 G. 3.

pose, the inhabitants are not *com. semb.* liable to a rate, but the funds must be applied as far as they will go, and the aid of Parliament be resorted to for relief in respect to the sum wanted; in which case Parliament would probably create a rate on the parishioners, if any, and if there were none, would grant a certain sum (*a*).

An individual may have a prescriptive right to a seat, *&c.* in a church which might be in respect to his house, and its inhabitants, even though it be situated in another parish; and not in respect to his lands, and the sheep and horses thereon but the right to repair a part or the whole of the church, may well be in respect of lands (*b*).

A person may prescribe for a pew in the chancel of a church (*c*).

But there cannot be a gift of a pew without a faculty: and a faculty to a man and his heirs is bad (*d*).

However, if a faculty be annexed to a messuage, it may be transferred with the messuage to another person (*e*).

A faculty may be granted even for exchanging seats in a church (*f*).

A seat in a church may be annexed to a house either by a faculty, or by prescription, and from long uninterrupted usage a faculty may be presumed (*g*).

It is impossible to determine *à priori*, what evidence will or will not be sufficient to support such a right; it must vary in each particular case.

Evidence of continued possession for thirty-six years, where the pew was claimed as appurtenant to a messuage, was deemed good presumptive evidence of a faculty (*h*).

So, uninterrupted possession of a pew in the chancel for twenty-eight years, unexplained, is presumptive evidence of a prescriptive right to the pew, in an action against a wrong doer, which presumption however, may be rebutted by proof that prior to that time the pew had no existence (*i*).

But possession alone of a pew in a church, though for above sixty years, was, in an antecedent case, holden not to be a sufficient title to maintain an action on the case even against a wrong doer, for disturbance in the enjoyment of it: but that the plaintiff must prove either a prescriptive right or a faculty, and should claim it in his declaration as appurtenant to a messuage in the parish. For bare possession can never give a right, because every parishioner has a right to go into the church and therefore it was the plaintiff's own fault if he did not gain to himself a complete title to a pew, which he might do either by applying to the ordinary for a faculty, or to the minister or churchwardens to allot him a seat in the church. If bare possession were

(*a*) Cro Eliz 659 Note—There is nothing in the Case [illegible]

(*b*) Cro Jac 366 (*c*) 5 T R 297. (*d*) 1 T R 431 [illegible] 432 (*e*) [illegible] 431.

(*f*) Ibid (*g*) 5 T R 2[illegible] (*h*) 1 T R 431. [illegible] (*i*) 5 T. R. 297.

allowed to be a sufficient title, it would be an encouragement to commit disorders in the church; for disputes would frequently arise respecting the possession (*a*)

Note.—Trespass will not lie for entering into a pew, because the plaintiff has not the exclusive possession; the possession of the church being in the parson; wherefore in case for such disturbance, a right by prescription or faculty must be proved (*b*).

But though the possession of the church is in the parson (for the whole church and church-yard are the rector's freehold,) yet, where a rector was cited in the episcopal consistorial court to shew cause why the ordinary should not grant to a parishioner a faculty for stopping up a window in a church, against which it was proposed to erect a monument, to the grant of which the rector dissented, notwithstanding which the court below were proceeding to grant the faculty with the consent of the ordinary, it was held to be no ground for a prohibition: but mere matter of appeal if the rector's reasons for dissenting were improperly over-ruled; for as yet, no common law right was touched which called upon the Court to prohibit the ecclesiastical court from proceeding to grant a faculty; which faculty was no more than a licence from the ordinary himself to do the act proposed, and would not bind the rector against his consent, if by law his consent were material (*c*).

(*a*) 1 T R. 430. (*b*) Ibid. (*c*) 3 East R. 217.

APPENDIX.

PRECEDENTS OF AGREEMENTS, &c.

Agreement for granting a Lease of a House and Field.

MEMORANDUM of an agreement entered into this day of 1804, between *A. B*, of of the one part and *C. D.* of of the other part, whereby the said *A. B.* agrees by indenture to be executed on or before Michaelmas day next, to demise and let to the said *C. D.* a messuage or tenement, with the garden and appurtenances thereto belonging, situate, lying, and being in in the parish of in the county of now or late in the occupation of together with all that field or close, situate, lying, and being in aforesaid, called or known by the name of now or late in the occupation of to hold to the said *C. D* his executors, administrators, and assigns, from Michaelmas day aforesaid for and during the term of years, at or under the clear yearly rent of pounds, payable half yearly, clear of all taxes and deductions except the land tax. In which lease there shall be contained covenants on the part of the said *C D.* his executors, administrators, and assigns, to pay the rent, and to pay all taxes, rates, and assessments (except the land tax), to repair the premises (except damages by fire), to deliver the same up at the end of the term in good repair (except as last aforesaid), with all other usual and reasonable covenants, and a proviso for the re-entry of the said *C D.* his heirs or assigns, in case of non-payment of the rent for the space of days after either of the said rent days, or the non-performance of the covenants.—And there shall also be contained a covenant on the part of the said *A. B.* his heirs and assigns, for quiet enjoyment. And the said

C. D. hereby agrees to accept of the said lease on the terms aforesaid.—And it is mutually agreed that the costs of this agreement, and of making the said lease and a counterpart thereof, shall be borne by the said parties equally.

In witness, &c.

Agreement for granting a Farming Lease.

MEMORANDUM of an agreement made this day of in the year between *A. B.* &c. of the one part, and *C. D.* &c. of the other part, whereby it is agreed, that the said *A. B.* shall, on or before the 25th day of March now next ensuing, make and execute unto the said *C. D.* his executors, administrators, and assigns, a good and valid lease of all that messuage, &c. and all those several closes, pieces, or parcels of land, &c. with the appurtenances thereunto belonging, for the term of years, from the said 25th day of March, at the yearly rent of pounds, payable half yearly clear of all deductions for taxes, or any other account whatsoever (except the land tax), the first payment of the said rent to be made at Michaelmas day next, and at or under the further yearly rent of 5*l* for every acre, and so in proportion for a less quantity, of meadow or pasture ground which shall be ploughed or converted into tillage contrary to a covenant to be contained in the said lease, as hereinafter directed: the first payment of the last-mentioned rent to be made on the first half yearly rent day after such ploughing and conversion into tillage as aforesaid; and in the said lease there shall be contained covenants on the part of the said *C. D.* his executors, administrators, and assigns, to pay the aforesaid rents, and to pay all taxes, rates, and assessments (except the land tax),—for doing all manner of repairs to the said buildings, hedges, ditches, rails, and other fences (the said *A. B.* his heirs or assigns, providing upon the premises, or within miles thereof, rough timber, bricks, tiles, and lime, for the doing thereof, to be conveyed by the said *C. D.* his executors, administrators, or assigns).—For permission for the said *A. B.* his heirs or assigns, at all seasonable times, to view the state of repairs. That the said *C. D.* his executors, administrators, or assigns, shall not plough or convert into tillage any of the closes of meadow or pasture ground

At a yearly rent

And a further rent per acre for ploughing.

The lease to contain covenants on the part of the tenant

To pay rent and taxes

For repairing (landlord finding timber, &c.)

For permission to view state of repairs

Not to plough meadow

without the licence of the said *A. B.* his heirs or assigns, in writing first obtained.—That the said *C. D* his executors or administrators, shall not carry off from the farm any hay, straw, or other fodder, and that the said *C. D.* his executors, administrators, or assigns, shall spread on some part of the said lands in an husbandlike manner, all the dung, manure, and compost, which shall arise from the said farm, and shall in all respects manage and cultivate the same in an husbandlike manner, and according to the usual course of husbandry used in the neighbourhood, and shall leave all the dung, manure, and compost of the last year, for the use of the landlord or succeeding tenants.—That the said *C D.* his executors, administrators, or assigns, shall not cut or plash any of the quick hedges under years growth, and shall cut or plash those at seasonable times in the year, and at the time of doing thereof shall cleanse the ditches adjoining thereto, and guard and preserve the hedges, which shall be so cut and plashed as aforesaid, from destruction or injury by cattle, and shall also at all times guard and preserve all young hedges and young trees from the like destruction or injury.—That the said *C. D.* his executors, administrators, or assigns, shall, in the summer immediately preceding the determination of the said term to be granted as aforesaid, prepare for seed in an husbandlike manner such part of the land as shall be in a course of fallow and fit to be sown with a crop the ensuing season, and lay down with clover-seed and rye-grass acres of the arable land which shall be then in tillage, sowing upon each acre thereof pounds of the best clover-seed and bushels of the best rye grass seed. And in the said lease there shall be contained a proviso for re-entry by the said *A B.* his heirs or assigns, in case of non-payment of rent for the space of days, or non-performance of the covenants, or in case the said *C D* his executors, administrators, or assigns, shall assign, under-let, or otherwise dispose of the said premises, or any part thereof, or do commit or suffer any act or deed whereby, or by means whereof the said premises, or any part thereof, shall be assigned, under-let, or disposed of, without the consent in writing of the said *A. B* his heirs or assigns, first obtained.—And there shall be contained covenants on the part of the said *A. B.* his heirs and assigns, for quiet enjoyment.—That the said *A. B.* his heirs or assigns, shall,

Not to carry off fodder, &c

To spread dung on the premises.

And manage same in an husbandlike manner

To leave dung of last year.

Not to cut hedges under certain growth

To cleanse ditches, &c.

To prepare fallow lands at the end of the term for a crop.

To lay down part with clover, &c

And to contain a proviso for re-entry.

And covenants on the part of the landlord for quiet enjoyment.

executors, administrators, and assigns, upon the premises, or within miles thereof, all such rough timber, bricks, tiles, and lime, as shall be necessary for the repair of the premises. the said materials to be conveyed at the expence of the said *C D.* his executors, administrators, and assigns.—That the said *A B.* his heirs and assigns, shall permit the said *C. D.* his executors, administrators, or assigns, to have the use of the great barn, the stable for four horses adjoining, and the stack-yard and farm-yard, until after the expiration or determination of the said term, for the convenience of thrashing out the last year's crops of corn and grain, and feeding his or their cattle with the straw and fodder, so that the same may be made into manure to be left on the said premises as aforesaid; and also some convenient room in the farm-house for his or their servants to lodge and diet in, until the time aforesaid, without any recompence being made for the same respectively.

To permit tenant to have the use of the barn, &c at the end of the term

In witness, &c.

Agreement for Lodgings.

MEMORANDUM of an agreement entered into this day of 1804, by and between *E F* of, *&c* and *G. H.* of, *&c.* whereby the said *E. F.* agrees to let, and the said *G. H.* agrees to take, the rooms or apartments following: that is to say, an entire first floor, and one room in the attic story or garrets, and a back kitchen and cellar opposite, with the use of the yard for drying linen, or beating carpets or clothes, being part of a house and premises in which the said *E. F.* now resides, situate and being in To have and to hold the said rooms or apartments, and the use of the said yard as aforesaid, for and during the term of half a year, to commence from next after the date hereof, at and for the yearly rent of pounds of lawful money of Great Britain, payable quarterly, by even and equal portions; the first quarterly payment to be made on next ensuing the date hereof: and it is further agreed, that at the expiration of the said term of half a year, the said *G H* may hold, occupy, and enjoy the said rooms or apartments, and have the use of the said yard as aforesaid, from quarter to quarter, for so long a time as the said *G. H* and *E. F.* may and shall agree, at the rent of for each quarter, and that each party be at liberty quit possession, on giving to the other a quarter's notice in writing or warning And it is also further agreed between the said parties, that when the said *G H.* shall quit the premises, he shall leave them in as good condition and repair as they shall be in on his taking possession thereof, reasonable wear excepted.

As witness, *&c.*

An Agreement to let a ready furnished Lodging.

MEMORANDUM of an agreement entered into this day of in the year of our Lord by and between *J. K.* of *&c* of the one part, and *L. M.* of *&c.* of the other part, by which the said *J. K.* agrees to let to the said *L. M.* a room or apartment up pair of stairs forwards in his the said *J. K.*'s house, situate in street, in the parish and county aforesaid, ready furnished; together with the use and attendance of his servant, in common with the other lodgers, at such hours and times when he himself can spare And also the use of a cellar, at the rent of pounds of lawful money of Great Britain *per* quarter. And the said *L M.* agrees to take the said room or apartment, with the use of the servant and cellar as aforesaid, at the rent aforesaid, and also to find and provide for himself, all manner of linen and china or crockery ware whatsoever, that he shall have occasion for, and that if he shall break or damage any part of the furniture of the said *J. K.* he will make good or repair the same, or pay her sufficient to enable her to put the same in the same plight and condition as they now are in And it is further agreed, that if either party shall quit or leave the premises, he or she shall respectively give or take a quarter's notice or warning.

As witness, *&c.*

A Lease for Years of a House and Lands in the Country with an Exception of Trees, and Special Covenants.

THIS INDENTURE made the day of in the year of our Lord and in the year of the reign of our Sovereign Lord George the Third, between

The parties — *A. A.* of the one part, and *B. B.* of the other part, *witnesseth*, that for and in consideration of the rents, covenants, provisoes, and agreements hereinafter reserved and contained, and which on the part and behalf of the said *B. B.* his executors, administrators, and assigns, are to be paid, done, and performed, he the said *A. A. hath* demised, granted, and to farm letten, and by these presents *doth* demise, grant, and to farm let unto the said *B. B.* his executors, administrators, and assigns, *all* that messuage, tenement, or farm-house, late in the possession of *E. B* and those two cottages or tenements, now or late in the possession of *F F* and *G. G.* or their assigns, with the appurtenances, situate, standing, and being in the parish of *C* and *H.* or one of them, in the said county of *D.* together with all and singular the yards, gardens, orchards, backsides, barns, stables, out-houses, edifices, and buildings thereunto belonging, and also all those several closes, pieces, or parcels of arable land, meadow, pasture, wood, and wood ground, containing by estimation acres (be they more or less), lying and being in several parishes, fields, precincts, and territories of *C.* and *H.* or one of them, in the said county of *D.* to the said messuage, tenement or farm-house belonging, and therewith held, used, occupied, and enjoyed, as part and parcel thereof (*except*, and always reserved out of this present lease, unto the said *A A* his heirs and assigns, all timber and timber-like trees, and all other trees whatsoever, but the fruit trees for their fruit only, and the pollard trees for their lops and tops only, which now are, or at any time or times hereafter shall be standing, growing, and being in, upon, and about the said leased premises, or any part thereof, with free liberty of ingress, egress, and regress, to and for the said *A. A.* his heirs* and assigns, servants and workmen, from time to time, and at

Margin notes: The consideration. — The demise — The parcels. — General words — More parcels — [illegible] — …ress, &c …ror &c

* Where the *lessor* has the *freehold*, make the *exception, reservation*, &c. to *him*, his *heirs* and *assigns*, and not *heirs, executors, administrators*, and *assigns*, so he may covenant for *himself*, his *heirs* and *assigns*, and it is sufficient, *executors* and *administrators* are superfluous, they are his *assigns* in law of course, but have nothing to do with the freehold as such. But where the *lessor* has *not* the *freehold*, then make the *exception, reservation*, &c to *him*, his *executors, administrators*, and *assigns*, and the covenants from *him*, his *executors, administrators*, and *assigns*, though here it is usual to make *him* covenant for *himself*, his *heirs, executors, administrators*, and *assigns*, that *he*, his *executors, administrators*, and *assigns*, shall and will, &c in which case the *heir* will be bound.

all times during the term hereby leased, the same to fell, stock up, cut down, hew, and carry away, in and through the said leased premises, or any part thereof, doing no wilful hurt or damage to the grain and grass of the said *B. B.* his executors, administrators, and assigns, and also except to the said *A. A.* his heirs and assigns, at all time during the term hereby leased, free liberty to enter into, and upon the said premises, and every part thereof, to view the condition of the repairs thereof) *to have and to hold* the said messuage, tenement, or farm-house, closes, pieces, or parcels of arable land, meadow, pasture ground, and premises, with their and every of their appurtenances, (except as before excepted) unto the said *B. B.* his executors, administrators, and assigns, from the feast of next ensuing the date hereof, for and during, and unto the full end and term of years, thence next ensuing, and fully to be complete and ended, *yielding and paying* therefore yearly, and every year during the said term, unto the said *A. A.* his heirs or assigns, at or in his now dwelling-house, situate, *&c.* the yearly rent or sum of *l.* of lawful money of *Great Britain*, at the two most usual feasts or days of payment in the year, that is to say, the feasts of and in every year, the first payment thereof to begin and be made on the feast day of next ensuing the date hereof, and also *yielding and paying* thereof yearly, and every year during the said term, unto the said *A. A.* his heirs and assigns, at or in his now dwelling-house, situate, *&c.* the yearly rent or sum of *l.* of lawful money of *Great Britain* at the two most usual feasts or days of payment in the year, that is to say, the feasts of and in every year, the first payment thereof to begin and be made on the feast day of next ensuing the date hereof, and also *yielding and paying* therefore yearly, and every year during the said term, unto the said *A. A.* his heirs and assigns, on the days and place, and in manner, aforesaid, (over and above the said yearly rent of *l.* hereinbefore reserved,) for every acre of meadow or pasture ground hereby leased, that the said *B. B.* his executors, administrators or assigns, shall plough, dig up, or convert into tillage, the sum of *l.* of like money, and so proportionably after that rate, for every greater or less quantity than an acre, the first payment of the said *l.* per acre to be made on the first day of the said feasts, which

And liberty to view, &c.

Habendum.

For years.

For years.

Payment to lessor's dwelling-house a certain rent.

And an additional rent for ploughing.

Proviso on non-payment.

Or assignment by the lessee without consent, the lessor may re-enter.

The lessee covenants for payment of rents.

And for repairs.

shall next happen after the ploughing or digging up any part of the same meadow or pasture ground. *Provided always*, nevertheless, that if it shall happen that the said yearly rents, hereby reserved, or either of them, or any taxes, levies, and assessments, which shall be rated or assessed on the said hereby leased premises, (except land tax) shall be behind and unpaid by the space of twenty-one days, next over or after either of the said feasts or days of payment, whereon the same ought to be paid as aforesaid, (being lawfully demanded,) or if the said *B. B* his executors, or administrators, shall assign over, or otherwise depart with this indenture, or the premises hereby leased, or any part thereof, to any person or persons whatsoever, (except the said two cottages,) without the consent of the said *A. A* his heirs and assigns, first had and obtained in writing, under his or their hands and seals for that purpose, then, and in either of the said cases, it shall and may be lawful to and for the said *A A* his heirs or assigns, into the said premises hereby leased, or any part thereof in the name of the whole, to re-enter, and the same to have again, retain, and repossess, and enjoy, as in his and their first and former estate or estates, any thing herein contained to the contrary thereof, in anywise notwithstanding. *And* the said *B B.* doth hereby for himself, his heirs, executors, administrators, and assigns, covenant, promise, and agree, to and with the said *A A.* his heirs and assigns, in manner following, (that is to say,) that he the said *B B.* his executors, administrators, and assigns, shall and will well and truly pay, or cause to be paid unto the said *A A* his heirs and assigns, the said yearly rent of *l.* and also the said rent of *l.* per acre, *per annum*, for ploughing up any meadow, or pasture, as aforesaid, at the days, times, and places, and in such manner as are hereinbefore limited and appointed for payment thereof, according to the respective reservation thereof, and the true intent and meaning of these presents. *And also* that the said *B. B.* his executors, administrators, and assigns, shall and will, at his and their own proper costs and charges, well and sufficiently repair, maintain, amend, scour, cleanse, preserve, and keep in repair the said messuage, tenement or farm-house, and all other the houses, out houses, edifices, buildings, barns, stables, dove-houses, gates, rails, pales, stiles, hedges, fences, and mounds, belonging to the said hereby leased premises, from time to time during this present lease, (he the said *A. A.* his heirs and assigns, upon request and notice to them made, finding and allowing on the said premises, or within four miles' distance thereof, all rough timber, brick, lime, tiles, and all other materials whatsoever (except straw) for doing thereof, to be carried to the said hereby leased premises, at the charge of the said *B B* his executors, administrators, or assigns.) And the same premises, so repaired, amended, and kept in repair, as aforesaid, at the end, expiration, or other sooner determination of this present lease, shall and will yield up unto the said *A. A.* his heirs or assigns. *And also* that the said *B. B* his heirs, executors, administrators, or assigns, shall not, nor will at any time during this present lease, crop, or sow, above two years together, any of the arable lands and closes hereby leased, but every third year permit the same to lie fallow and unsown *And* that it shall and may be lawful, to and for the said *A A.* his heirs and assigns, with servants, horses, ploughs carts, and other necessaries, at day next preceding the expiration of the present lease, to enter upon such closes and grounds, parcel of the said hereby leased premises, as then ought to lie fallow and unsown, and the same to plough, fallow, and manure, and to have the grass, herbage, sheep walks, and sheep commons thereof, and also to enter upon the dung which shall be then in the yard or yards, and at the same time to have the dung in the dove-house, and the hen-dung in the hen-house And also to have some convenient place in the said dwelling-house, for his and their servants to lodge and diet in, and some convenient place to lay hay and chaff in, and some convenient stable for their horses to stand and be in, without extinguishment of any of the yearly rents herein beforereserved, and without giving or making any allowance or satisfaction for the same. *And further*, that the said *B. B.* his executors, administrators, and assigns, shall not at any time or times during the last two years of the said term, sell, give away, or otherwise dispose of any of the straw which shall be growing and arising upon the said leased premises, and shall not burn any straw, except it be for the necessary singeing of his and their hogs, for the use of their own families. *And* that the said *B B.* his executors, administrators and assigns, shall and will lay in and in-

The landlord to find all rough timber

The tenant covenants not to sow the same above two years together, and that the lessor may enter within the term to plough the fallow ground.

And to have the dung, and lodging for servants, &c

The lessee not to dispose of straw within the last two years

And to in-barn the corn upon the premises.

barn all the crops of grain, which shall be growing and arising upon the said hereby leased premises, in every year of the said term, in the barns and rick-yards belonging to the said leased premises, and not elsewhere, and the same there thrash out, and the straw and stover

And to use the straw there

which shall arise therefrom and thereby, turn into the yard and yards, and the same feed up with his or their cattle, for the better increase and making of dung, and the dung and soil which shall arise thereby, lay, spread and bestow upon the hereby demised premises, in a husband-like manner, and not elsewhere; and shall and will leave unto, and for the use of the said *A. A.* his heirs or assigns, all the dung and compost which shall be made on the said leased premises the three last years of the said term, which shall arise from the two last crops of corn and grain, for manuring the premises, or otherwise to be disposed of as he the said *A. A.* his heirs and assigns, shall think fit and convenient, and that the said *B. B.* his executors, administrators, and assigns, shall sow the three last years of this present lease, one

To sow peas, &c. in the latter years

third part of the edge crop with peas or vetches. *And* that the said *B. B.* his executors, administrators, and assigns, shall and will, at all times, during the term

To preserve doves

hereby leased, endeavour to preserve and keep the dove-house, with a good flight of pigeons, dove-house like, and at the end, expiration, or other sooner determination of the said term of years, shall and will give up the same, so preserved and kept, unto the hands of the said *A. A.* his heirs and assigns. *And* that the said *B. B.* his executors, administrators, and assigns, shall and will, at all times during the said term of years hereby leased, bear, pay, and discharge all such taxes, levies,

To pay taxes, &c.

and assessments whatsoever, as shall be taxed, rated, levied, or assessed upon the said hereby leased premises, land tax only excepted. *And* that he the said *B. B.* his executors, administrators, and assigns, shall not nor will, at any time or times during this present lease, cut, plash,

Not to cut hedges under a certain growth, &c.

or new-make any of the hedges belonging to the hereby leased premises, but such as shall be of twelve years' growth, and those only at seasonable times in the year and when the closes and ground to which such hedges belong shall be sown with wheat, rye, or barley, on a summer's tilth, or be closes of old pasture, and after the same shall have been cut, plashed or new-made, as aforesaid, the same preserve and keep from biting, or destruction by cattle or otherwise, and shall and will, at such cutting and plashing thereof, cleanse and scour the ditches, against such hedge or hedges, where ditches have been heretofore, and do lie next to any lane or highway, and the offal wood which shall arise by the cutting or plashing of such hedges, faggot and make up, and carry unto the said leased messuage, or farm house, there to be spent by way of fire wood, and not to be sold or disposed of in any other manner whatsoever. *And* that the said *A. A.* his executors, administrators, and assigns, shall not, nor will, at any time or times during the term hereby leased, lop, top, shred, or cut, any of the trees or spring wood belonging to the said leased premises, but such pollard trees, and spring wood, as have been usually lopped, and cut by former and other tenants, and those only of twelve years' growth, and the lops which shall arise and come therefrom, carry into the said hereby leased messuage or farm house, there to be spent by way of fire bote, and not to be sold or disposed of in any other way whatsoever, and shall not, nor will at any time or times during this lease, inordinately burn or waste any of the fire-wood, which is so allowed to be spent by way of fire boot, as aforesaid, and shall preserve and keep the said pollard trees, as also all the fruit trees, and spring wood, belonging to the said hereby leased premises, from all wilful or negligent waste. *And* the said *A. A.* doth hereby for himself, his heirs, and assigns, covenant, promise, and agree, to, and with the said *B. B.* his executors, administrators, and assigns, in manner following, (that is to say) that he the said *A. A.* his heirs, and assigns, shall and will from time to time, and at all times during this present lease, at seasonable times for cutting timber, find, provide for, and allow unto the said *B. B.* his executors, administrators, or assigns, on the said premises hereby leased, or within reasonable distance therefrom, necessary rough timber, brick, lime, and tiles, and all other materials whatsoever, for the repairing and amending thereof (except straw), within forty days after notice of the want thereof, and demand of the same made by the said *B. B.* his executors, administrators, or assigns, the said materials to be carried to the said leased premises at the expence of the said *B. B.* his executors, &c. *And* also shall and will from time to time, and at all times during this present lease, allow unto the said *B. B.* his

And to spend wood in the house.

Not to lop trees except pollards.

The lops to be spent in the house.

executors, administrators, or assigns, timber to be had and taken off and from the said hereby leased premises, (if any such there be) for necessary plough-bote, to be used and spent upon the said premises, and not elsewhere, and to be set out for that purpose by the said *A. A.* his heirs, or assigns on such notice as aforesaid of the want thereof; and that the said *A. A.* his heirs and assigns, shall and will permit and suffer the said *B. B.* his executors, administrators, or assigns, to have the use of all the barns, yards, and granaries hereby leased, for the laying in, and threshing out of his or their crop of corn or grain, which shall be growing and being upon the premises in the last year of the said term hereby leased, for the spending of the straw and fodder which shall arise therefrom, with horses, cows, bullocks, and other cattle, until the feast of next after the end, expiration, or other sooner determination of the said term of years, and also to have some convenient rooms in the said hereby leased messuage or farm house, for his or their servants to lodge and diet in, and some convenient place for his and their horses to stand and be in, and some convenient place to lay hay and chaff in, until the said feast day of next after the determination of the said term. *And lastly*, that it shall and may be lawful, to and for the said *B. B.* his executors, administrators, and assigns (paying the rent hereinbefore reserved, and performing the covenants and agreements hereinbefore mentioned and contained, and which on his and their part and behalf, are or ought to be paid, done and performed) peaceably and quietly to have, hold, occupy, possess and enjoy, all and singular the said hereby leased premises, with the appurtenances during the said term of years hereby demised, without any molestation or interruption whatsoever, of or by him, the said *A. A.* his heirs or assigns, or of or by any other person or persons lawfully or equitably claiming or to claim, by, from, or under him, them, or any of them

In witness, &c.

An Indorsement for continuing a Lease for a Longer Term after the Expiration of the Present.

THIS INDENTURE, &c. between the within named *A. B.* of the one part, and the within named *C. D.* of the other part, *witnesseth*, that for and in consideration of the rent hereby reserved, and of the covenants, conditions, and agreements respectively, herein after contained, which on the part and behalf of the said *C. D.* his executors, administrators and assigns, are to be paid, done and performed, the said *A B hath* demised, leased, set, and to farm let, unto the said *C D.* his executors, administrators and assigns, *all* that piece or parcel of ground, with the messuage or tenement, thereon erected and built, and all and singular other the premises respectively, comprised in the within written lease, and thereby demised to the said *C. D* (except as therein is excepted), *to have and to hold* the said piece or parcel of ground, and messuage or tenement, and all and singular other the premises hereby leased, set, and to farm let, or mentioned, or intended so to be (except as aforesaid), unto the said *C. D.* his executors, administrators and assigns, from the day of , which will be in the year of our Lord , and when the said within written lease will expire, for and during, and unto the full end and term of years longer, from thence next ensuing, and fully to be complete and ended, subject to, and under the like rent, and payable in like manner, as is within mentioned, for and in respect of the rent reserved, in and by the said within written lease, and subject to the like power of entry as well on non-payment of rent, as on the happening of any of the other incidents mentioned in the within written proviso or condition of re-entry, *and* it is hereby declared and agreed, by and between the said parties to these presents, that they, and their respective heirs, executors, administrators and assigns, shall and will, by these presents, during the continuance of the additional term of years hereby granted, stand, and be bound, for and in respect of the said hereby demised premises with the appurtenances, in such and the like covenants, conditions, and agreements, respectively, as they the said parties and their respective heirs, executors, administrators and assigns, do now stand bound in and by the said within lease, for and during the now residue unexpired of the within mentioned term hereby granted, it being the intent and meaning thereof, that this present endorsed lease, and the additional term hereby granted, shall be upon such and the like footing, and all the covenants, clauses, conditions and agreements, respectively therein contained, be equally available, take place, and have the like force and effect, to all intents and purposes, as if every such clause, matter and thing, contained in the said within lease, were inserted and contained in this present indenture.

In witness, *&c.*

A Building Lease.

THIS INDENTURE, made, *&c.* between *A B &c.* of the one part, and *C. D* of the other part, *witnesseth*, that the said *A B* for and in consideration of the rents, covenants and agreements, hereinafter reserved and contained, by, and on the part and behalf of the said *C. D.* his executors, administrators and assigns, to be paid, done, and performed, *hath* demised, leased, set, and to farm let, and by these presents *doth* demise, lease, set, and to farm let, unto the said *C D* his executors, administrators and assigns, *all* that piece or parcel of ground, situate, lying and being, on, *&c.* in the said parish of containing in breadth on the north side thereof and in depth on the east side thereof be the same more or less, and on the west side thereof east and from thence south and from thence east, be the same more or less, together with the messuages or tenements, and other the erections and buildings thereon, which the said *C. D.* shall have full liberty to pull down, and to take to and for his own use, which said piece or parcel of ground abuts north on aforesaid, south on gardens to some houses on the north side of belonging to the said *A B* now on lease to east on buildings, *&c.* and west, *&c.* and is more fully delineated and described in the plan or ground plot thereof, in the margin of these presents, together with all erections and buildings to be erected and built thereon, and all ways, paths, passages, drains, water, water-courses, easements, profits, commodities, and appurtenances, whatsoever, belonging, and which shall belong to the said hereby demised premises, or any part or parcel thereof, *to have and to hold* the said piece or parcel of ground, messuages, or tenements, erections, buildings, and premises hereby demised or intended so to be, with their and every of their appurtenances, unto the said *C. D* his executors, administrators and assigns, from the day of last past, before the date thereof, for and during, and unto the full end and term of years, from thence next ensuing, and fully to be complete and ended, *yielding and paying* therefore for the first year of the said term hereby demised, the rent of a pepper corn on the last day thereof, if demanded, and yielding and paying therefore yearly, and every year, for and during the remaining years of the said term hereby demised, unto the said *A B.* his heirs and assigns, the yearly rent or sum of l of lawful money of the United Kingdom of *Great Britain* and *Ireland*, current in *Great Britain*, by half yearly payment, on the and in each year, by even and equal portions, the first payment thereof to begin and be made on in the year of our Lord the said several rents to be paid and payable from time to time, on the several feasts aforesaid, during the said term, free and clear of all rates, taxes, charges, assessments, and payments whatsoever, taxed, charged, assessed, or imposed upon the said hereby leased premises, or any part thereof, by authority of parliament or otherwise howsoever, during the term hereby granted. *And* the said *C. D* for himself, his heirs, executors, administrators, and assigns, doth covenant, promise, and agree, to and with the said *A B* his heirs and assigns, by these presents, in manner following (that is to say), that the said *C. D.* his heirs, executors, administrators, and assigns, shall and will yearly, and every year during the last years of the said term hereby granted, well and truly pay, or cause to be paid unto the said *A B* his heirs and assigns, the said yearly rent or sum of l of lawful money of the United Kingdom of *Great Britain* and *Ireland*, current in *Great Britain*, on the several days and times, and in the manner hereinbefore limited and appointed for payment thereof, without making any deduction or abatement thereout, for, or in respect of any rates, taxes, assessments, duties, charges, or impositions whatsoever, taxed, charged, assessed, or imposed upon the said hereby demised premises, or any part thereof, during the said term hereby granted; all which rates, taxes, assessments, duties, charges, or impositions, he the said *C D* his executors, administrators, or assigns, shall and will bear, pay, and discharge, and therefore, and therefrom, acquit, save harmless, and keep indemnified the said *A B.* his heirs and assigns *And* that he the said *C D* his executors, administrators or assigns, shall and will, before the expiration of the first year of the term hereby granted, at his and their own proper costs and charges, erect, build, complete, and in a workman-like manner finish, one or more good and substantial brick messuages or tenements, upon some part of the ground hereby demised, and shall and will lay out and expend therein the sum of   *l.* or upwards, and also that he the said *C. D.* his executors, administrators and assigns, shall and will, from time to time, and at all times, from and after the said messuage or tenement, erections and buildings, on the said piece of ground hereby demised, shall be respectively completed and finished, during the remainder of the said term hereby granted, when, where, and as often as need or occasion shall be and require, at his and their own proper costs and charges, well and sufficiently repair, uphold, support, maintain, pave, purge, scour, cleanse, empty, amend, and keep the said messuage or tenement, messuages or tenements, erections and buildings, and all the walls, rails, lights, pavements, grates, privies, sinks, drains, and watercourses, thereunto belonging, and which shall belong unto the same, in, by, and with all and all manner of needful and necessary reparations, cleansings and amendments whatsoever. *And* that he the said *C. D.* his executors, administrators and assigns, shall not, nor will, during the said term hereby granted, permit or suffer any person or persons to use, exercise, or carry on, in and upon the said hereby demised premises, or any part thereof, any trade or business which may be nauseous or offensive, or grow to the annoyance, prejudice, or disturbance of any of the other tenements of the said *A. B.* near adjoining thereto, and the said messuage or tenement, messuages or tenements, erections, buildings, and premises, with the walls, pavements, sewers, and drains belonging thereto, being in every respect so well and sufficiently repaired, upheld, supported, sustained, maintained, paved, purged, scoured, cleansed, emptied, amended, and kept, shall and will, at the expiration, or other sooner determination of the said term hereby granted, peaceably and quietly leave, surrender, and yield up unto the said *A. B.* his heirs and assigns, together with all the doors, locks, keys, bolts, bars, wainscots, chimney-pieces, slabs, foot-paces, windows, window-shutters, partitions, dressers, shelves, pumps, water-pipes, rails, and all other things which shall be any ways fixed and fastened to, and shall be standing, being, and set up, in and upon the said premises hereby demised, or any part thereof within the last   years of the said term hereby granted. *And* that the said *C. D.* his executors, administrators, and assigns, shall and will, at his and their own proper costs and charges, from time to time sufficiently insure all and every the messuages or tenements, erections and buildings, which shall be erected and built upon the said piece or parcel of ground hereby demised, or any part thereof, from casualties by fire, during the then remainder of the said term hereby granted, in some one of the public offices kept for that purpose, in *London* or *Westminster*, and in case the said messuages or tenements, erections and buildings, or any of them, or any part of any of them, shall, at [illegible] times during the said term, be burnt down, de[illegible] from time to time, [illegible] sufficiently [illegible] may be lawful, to and for the said *A. B.* his heirs and assigns, or any of them, with workmen or others, in his, them, or any of their company, or without, to enter or come into and upon the said demised premises, and every part thereof, at seasonable and convenient times, in the day time, as well at any time or times, during the last seven years of the said term hereby granted, to make an inventory or schedule of the several fixtures and things then standing and being, in and upon the said hereby demised premises, which are to be left at the end of the said term, to and for the use of the said *A. B.* his heirs and assigns, pursuant to the covenant hereinbefore in that behalf contained, as also twice or oftener in every year, during the said term hereby granted, to view, search, and see the defects and want of reparations of the said premises, and all defects and want of reparations, which upon every or any such view or search shall be from time to time found, to give or leave notice or warning thereof in writing, at or upon the said demised premises, unto, and for the said *C. D.* his executors, administrators or assigns, to repair and amend the same. *And* that the said *C. D.* his executors, administrators or assigns, shall and will, within three months next after every such notice or warning shall be given or left, at his and their own proper costs and charges, well and sufficiently repair, amend, and make good, all and every the defects and want of reparations, whereof such notice or warning shall be so given or left as aforesaid. *Provided always*, nevertheless, and these presents are upon this condition, that if the said yearly rent, or sum of *l.* hereby reserved, or any part thereof, shall be behind and unpaid by the space of days, next after either of the said feasts or days of payment, whereon the same ought to be paid as aforesaid (being lawfully demanded), or if the said *C. D.* his executors, administrators or assigns, shall not well and truly observe, perform, fulfil and keep, all and every the covenants, articles, clauses, conditions and agreements, in these presents expressed and contained, on his and their part and behalf to be performed and kept according to the true intent and meaning thereof, then, and from thenceforth, in either of the said cases, it shall and may be lawful, to and for the said *A. B.* his heirs and assigns, into, and upon the said demised premises, or any part thereof in the name of the whole, wholly to re-enter, and the same to have again, retain, repossess and enjoy, and in his, and their first and former estate, and the said *C. D.* his executors, administrators or assigns, and all other tenants or occupiers of the said premises, thereout, and from thence utterly to expel, put out, and amove, and that from and after such re-entry made, this present lease, and every clause, article and thing, herein contained on the lessor's part and behalf, from thenceforth to be done and performed, shall cease, determine, and be utterly void, to all intents and purposes whatsoever, any thing hereinbefore contained to the contrary thereof in anywise notwithstanding. *And* the said *A. B.* for himself, his heirs, and assigns, doth hereby covenant, promise, and agree, to and with the said *C. D.* his heirs, executors, administrators, and assigns, paying the said yearly rent hereby reserved, in manner and form aforesaid, and observing, performing and keeping, all and singular the covenants and agreements, hereinbefore mentioned, on his and their parts and behalf to be performed and kept, shall and may lawfully, peaceably and quietly have, hold, occupy, possess, and enjoy the said piece or parcel of ground and premises hereby demised, with their and every of their appurtenances for and during the said term of years hereby granted, without any let, suit, trouble, denial or interruption of or by the said *A. B.* his heirs or assigns, or any other person or persons, lawfully claiming or to claim, by, from, or under him, them, or any of them.

In witness, &c.

Lease of a House in a Town.

THIS INDENTURE, &c. between *A. [illegible]* of &c. of the one part, and *H. H.* of, &c. of the other part, *witnesseth*, that for and in consideration of the yearly rent,

[illegible]

and of the covenants, provisoes and agreements, hereinafter reserved and contained, by and on the part and behalf of the said *H H* his executors, administrators and assigns, to be paid, observed, and performed, he the said *A A* hath demised and leased, and by these presents doth demise and lease unto the said *H. H* his executors, administrators, and assigns, *all* that messuage or tenement and dwelling house, situate and being on the side or part of street, in the parish of in the city of London, together with *here describe the particulars of the premises*, and also all ways, passages, lights, easements, rooms, vaults, cellars, areas, yards, water-courses, profits, conveniences, hereditaments, and appurtenances, whatsoever, to the said messuage, or premises hereby demised, belonging or in any way appertaining, or reputed or known to be part, parcel, or member thereof all and singular which said messuage and premises are now, or lately were, in the occupation of *G G* his assignee or assigns to *have and to hold* the said messuage or tenement and premises, with the appurtenances hereby demised, or so mentioned to be unto the said *H H.* his executors, administrators, and assigns, from the 25th day of December last past, for and during the term of twenty-one years, thence next ensuing, and fully to be complete and ended, determinable nevertheless at the expiration of the first seven or fourteen years thereof, upon such conditions as are hereinafter mentioned he the said *H H* his executors, administrators, and assigns, yielding and paying yearly and every year during the said term, unto the said *A A* his executors, administrators and assigns, the yearly rent or sum of pounds, of lawful money of the United Kingdom of *Great Britain* and *Ireland*, current in *Great Britain*, the same to be paid by equal quarterly payments on the respective days following namely, on the 25th day of *March*, the 24th day of *June*, the 29th day of *September*, and the 25th day of *December*, in every year, (save and except, at all times during the said term, such proportionable part of the said yearly rent of pounds as shall or may grow due during such time, as the messuage or tenement hereby demised, shall without the hindrance of the said *H. H* his executors, *&c* be and remain uninhabitable by reason of accidental fire) and to be clear of all and all manner of parliamentary, parochial and other taxes, assessments, rates and deductions whatsoever, the first quarterly payment thereof to commence and be made on the 24th day of *June* next ensuing the date of these presents. And the said *H. H.*

Covenant to pay rent.

doth hereby for himself, his executors, &c. covenant, promise and agree to and with the said *A. A.* his executors, &c. that he the said *H. H.* his executors, &c. shall and will yearly and every year during the continuance of the said term hereby demised (save and except as aforesaid,) well and truly pay, or cause to be paid unto the said *A. A.* his executors, &c. the said yearly sum or rent of pounds, of lawful money of the United Kingdom of Great Britain and Ireland, current in *Great Britain*, on the respective days, and in the manner the

And taxes (except land tax.)

same is hereinbefore mentioned to be payable. And also shall and will well and truly pay, or cause to be paid, all and all manner of taxes, rates, duties, and impositions whatsoever, parliamentary, parochial or otherwise, (the land tax only excepted,) which now are, or shall at any time during the continuance of the said term hereby demised, be assessed, rated, or imposed on the said demised messuage or tenement, and premises, or any part thereof, or on the said yearly rent hereby reserved, or any part thereof, or on the said *H. H.* his executors,

Covenant that lessee shall paint every 3d year.

&c. on account thereof. And also that he the said *H. H.* his executors, &c. shall and will at his and their own

And do other repairs.

proper costs and charges, cause to be well and sufficiently painted, all the outside wood and iron work belonging to the said messuage or tenement and premises hereby demised, every third year during the continuance of the said term, and at his and their like proper costs and charges, shall and will at all times during the continuance of the said term, keep in a good, sufficient, and tenantable state of repair, as well all and singular the glass and other windows, wainscots, beams, floors, partitions, ceilings, tilings, walls, rails, fences, pavements, gutters, sinks, privies, drains, vaults, and watercourses, as also all and every other the parts and appurtenances of the said messuage or tenement and pre-

Power to lessor to enter and view state of repairs.

mises hereby demised, (damage happening by casual fire only excepted.) And further, that it shall be lawful for the said *A. A.* his executors, &c. either alone or with others, twice in every year during the said term hereby granted, at such times of the year as to him or them shall seem meet, to enter at seasonable times of the day into and upon the said messuage or tenement and premises hereby demised and every part thereof, and there to view and examine the state and condition thereof, notice of such intention to view being at all times previously given unto the said *H. H.* his executors, &c. one day at least before the same shall take place, and in case any decay or want of reparation be found on such view, the said *H. H.* for himself, executors, &c. doth hereby covenant, promise and agree, to and with the said *A. A.* his executors, &c. to cause the same to be well and sufficiently repaired and amended within the space of [illegible] months after notice thereof in writing shall have been given to him or them for that purpose. And the said *H. H.* doth for himself, his executors, &c. promise, covenant, and agree, to and with the said *A. A.* his executors, &c. that he the said *H. H.* his executors, &c. at the end or earlier determination of the said term hereby granted, shall and will leave and yield up unto the said *A. A.* his executors &c. all and singular the said messuage or tenement and premises with their appurtenances, in such good, sufficient and tenantable state of repair as aforesaid, together with all and every the doors, locks, keys, bolts, bars, chimney-pieces, dressers, shelves, water-pipes, and other things mentioned in an inventory or schedule, * hereunder written or hereunto annexed, in as good plight and condition as the same now are, (reasonable use and wear thereof and casualties happening by fire only excepted,) Provided always, and these presents are upon this express condition, that if the said yearly rent hereby reserved, or any part thereof, shall be in arrears and unpaid for the space of [illegible] days next after any of the days whereon the same is hereinbefore covenanted to be paid as aforesaid, (it being first lawfully demanded,) or if the said *H. H.* his executors, &c. shall not well and truly observe, perform and keep, according to the true intent and meaning, all and every the covenants, clauses, provisions and agreements by him and them to be observed and kept, then and from thenceforth in either of the said cases, it shall be lawful for the said *A. A.* his executors, &c. to re-enter into and upon the said hereby demised messuage or tenement and premises, or any part thereof, in the name of the whole, and the same to have again, repossess, retain, and enjoy, as his and their former estate, and the said *H. H.* his executors, &c. and all other tenants and

After notice.

Covenant for lessee to quit at the end of the term and to leave the premises in repair, &c.

Proviso for lessor to re-enter [illegible]

* This [illegible]

occupiers of the said premises, thereout utterly to eject and remove, and that from and after such re-entry made, this lease, and every clause and thing herein contained, shall determine, and be utterly void to all intents and purposes, any thing herein contained to the contrary notwithstanding. And the said *A. A.* for himself, his executors, &c. doth covenant, promise and agree, to and with the said *H. H.* his executors, &c. by these presents, in manner following, that is to say, that he the said *H. H.* his executors, &c. paying the rent hereby reserved in manner aforesaid, and performing the covenants and agreements herein contained and by him and them to be performed, shall and lawfully may peaceably and quietly hold, occupy, and enjoy the messuage or tenement, and all other the premises hereby demised, for and during the said term of twenty-one years hereby granted, without any lawful action, suit, or interruption of the said *A. A.* his executors, &c. or any other person lawfully claiming by, from, or under him or any of them, and that freed and discharged, or otherwise by the said *A. A.* his executors, &c. saved harmless and indemnified from the rents and covenants reserved and contained in a certain indenture of lease, bearing date the   day of   in the year of our Lord   whereby the said *A. A.* holdeth the said messuage or tenement and premises hereby demised, from the date thereof   for the term of sixty-one years, and from all claims and demands whatsoever in respect thereof. And the said *A. A.* doth hereby further covenant, promise and agree to and with the said *H. H.* his executors, &c. that the said *A. A.* his executors, &c. shall and will, before the expiration of this present lease, on the request, and at the costs and charges of the said *H. H.* his executors, &c. grant and execute unto him and them, a new and fresh lease of the messuage or tenement, and all other the premises hereby demised, with their appurtenances, for the further term of   years, to commence from the expiration of the term hereby granted, the same to be at the same yearly rent, payable in like manner, and under and subject to the like covenants, provisoes and agreements, (except a covenant for the renewal thereof at the end of such further term,) as are contained in these presents, such new lease however to be granted and be valid, only on condition that the said *H. H.* his executors, &c. do execute a counter part thereof, and also pay unto the said *A. A.* his executors, *&c.* the sum of pounds of lawful money, *&c.* at the time of executing the said lease, as and by way of fine or premium for the renewal thereof, *And also*, that if the said *H. H.* his executors, *&c.* shall be desirous to quit the said messuage or tenement and premises hereby demised, at the expiration of the first seven or the first fourteen years of the term of twenty-one years hereby granted thereof, and of such his or their desire, shall give notice in writing to the said *A. A.* his executors, *&c.* six calendar months before the expiration of the said first seven or fourteen years, (as the case may be) then and in such case, (all arrears of rent being duly paid, and the said messuage or tenement, and all other the premises hereby demised, being in such repair as they are hereinbefore covenanted to be maintained and left in,) this lease and every clause and thing herein contained, shall, at the expiration of such first seven or first fourteen years of the said term of twenty-one years hereby granted, (which ever be in the said notice expressed,) determine and be utterly void to all intents and purposes, in the same manner as if the whole term of twenty-one years had been out and expired, any thing in these presents contained to the contrary notwithstanding. In witness whereof the said parties have hereunto set their hands and seals, the day and year first above written.

A. A. (Seal)
H. H. (Seal)

Sealed and delivered in the presence of
B. B. of
C. C. of

An Indorsement to continue the Term of an expiring Lease.

THIS INDENTURE made the day of in the year of our Lord and in the year of the reign of our Sovereign Lord George the Third, *&c.* between the within named *K. L.* of the one part, and the within named *M. N.* of the other part, *witnesseth*, That in consideration of the rent hereby reserved, and of the covenants, provisoes and agreements herein contained, by and on the part and behalf of the said *M. N.*

to be paid, observed and performed, the said *K. L.* his executors, &c. *M.* that piece or parcel of ground, with the messuage or tenement thereon erected, and all and singular other the premises comprised in the within written lease, and thereby demised or mentioned so to be. To have and to hold the said piece or parcel of ground, or messuage or tenement, and premises, unto the said *M. N.* his executors, &c. from the day of which will be in the year of our Lord when the within written lease will expire and determine, for and during, and unto the full end and term of years thence next ensuing, subject to and under the same rent, as in the within written lease is reserved, and also subject to the like power of re-entry on the non-payment of the rent, or the happening of any other of the incidents mentioned in the proviso for re-entry within written. And it is hereby declared and agreed, by and between the parties to these presents, that they and their respective executors, &c. shall and will, during the continuance of the additional term of years hereby granted, stand to and be bound by such and the like covenants, provisoes and agreements, as they, their respective executors, &c. are now bound by according to the within written lease, in respect of the said messuage or tenement and premises thereby and hereby granted, it being the intent and meaning of the parties hereto that this indorsed lease and the additional term hereby granted, shall be upon such and the like footing as is the lease within written, and that all the covenants, provisoes, and agreements in the within written lease contained be equally applicable and have the like force and effect to all intents and purposes as if the same and every thing in the said lease contained were repeated and inserted in these presents.

Habendum

In witness, &c.

Covenant by the Lessee not to use or assign the Premises for any offensive Trade.

AND also that the said *C. D.* his executors, &c. shall not nor will, at any time during the continuance of the said term hereby granted, use or carry on, or suffer or permit to be used or carried on, in the said demised messuage or tenement and premises, or assign over the present indenture of lease, or set over, let or assign any part of the said messuage or tenement and premises, to any person or persons using or carrying on the trade, business or calling of a maker of sedan or other chairs, baker, brewer, butcher, currier, distiller, dyer, founder, smith, soap-boiler, school-master or school-mistress, sugar-baker, auctioneer, pewterer, tallow-chandler or tallow-melter, cooking brazier, tinman, tripe-boiler, pipe-maker, pipe-borer, plumber, or any other noxious or offensive trade, business, or calling whatsoever, without the consent in writing of the said *A. B.* his executors, &c. first had and obtained for that purpose, nor shall nor will, without such consent as aforesaid make or cause to be made any addition or alteration whatever, in, upon, or about the said messuage or tenement and premises, or any part thereof.

An Assignment of a Leasehold Interest by Deed-poll indorsed on the Lease.

KNOW all men by these presents, that I the within named *A. B.* for and in consideration of the sum of five shillings of lawful money of the United Kingdom of *Great Britain and Ireland* current in *Great Britain* to me in hand paid by *N. O.* of [illegible] gent. at or before the ensealing and delivery of these presents, the receipt whereof I do hereby acknowledge, have bargained, sold, set over, and assign unto the said *N. O.* all and singular the messuage or tenement, yard, garden, coach-house, stables, out-houses, and hereditaments, in and by the within written indenture demised or mentioned so to be, with their appurtenances, and also all that small garden at the end of and adjoining to the aforesaid garden, with the summer-house and mount which were leased or agreed to be leased to me by the within named *E. F.* by agreement between us dated the day next before the day of the date hereof for twenty-one years or such other term as is therein mentioned, at the yearly rent of ten pounds of said lawful money of the United Kingdoms of *Great Britain* and *Ireland*, current in *Great Britain* payable quarterly, that is to say, at the feasts of [illegible] also all my estate, right, title, interest, term of years, claim and demand whatsoever, of, into, or out of the same messuage and other the premises, or any or either of them or otherwise howsoever, together with the same indenture and agreement and all the benefit thereof, To have and to hold the said messuage or tenement, buildings, gardens, summer-house, mount, and other the premises hereby assigned or mentioned so to be, with the appurtenances, unto the said *N. O.* his executors, administrators, and assigns, from henceforth, for all the now residue of the within mentioned term of twenty-one years, and of such other term or terms as I the said *A. B.* now have or ought to have therein respectively, subject nevertheless to the rents, covenants, and agreements in the said indenture and agreement respectively reserved and contained and agreed upon, and which from henceforth on the tenant's or lessee's part are or ought to be paid, done and performed.

In witness whereof, &c.

Forms of Notices to quit Possession of the Premises, Repair, &c.

[They need not be stamped.]

Notice by the Landlord to his Tenant.

Sir,

I Hereby give you notice to quit the premises which you hold of me situate at in the county of on next, or at the expiration of the current year of your tenancy*.

Yours, &c.

[*the date.*] *A. B.* [*the landlord.*]

To *I. K.* [*the tenant in possession.*]

Another Form, more particularly describing the Premises.

Sir,

YOU are hereby required to quit possession of the Premises which you hold of me, namely, a messuage and garden with the appurtenances, [*describing the*

* [illegible]

Premises] situate in the parish of in the county of now occupied by you on next, or at the expiration of the current year of your tenancy.

Dated this day of 18—.

B. E. [*the landlord*] or *C. F.* agent
To *C. E.* [*the tenant.*] for *B. E.* legally authorized.

A third Form.

Mr *C. D.*

I Hereby give you notice to quit and deliver up to me on *Christmas-day* next, the peaceable and quiet possession of all those two messuages, tenements, and dwelling-houses with their appurtenances, situate in in the parish of in the [*city, borough, or county*] of which you lately held under Messrs. and which you now hold of me, as tenant from year to year, provided your tenancy originally commenced at *Christmas* or otherwise, that you quit and deliver up to me the peaceable and quiet possession of the said premises, at the end of the year of your tenancy, which shall expire next after the end of half a year from the date hereof.

Dated this day of 18—. *A. B.*

This seems to be the proper form of a general notice to quit, and is according to the form which was deemed sufficient in the case of *Doe ex dem.* [illegible], 2 [illegible] R. 559.

Notice to quit lodgings.

Sir,

I Hereby give you notice to quit and deliver up on or before next, the rooms or apartments, and other tenements which you now hold of me in this house [*as the case is.*]

Witness my hand, this day of in the year

To *E. N.* [*the lodger.*] *E. F.* [*the landlord.*]

Notice to the Tenant either to quit the Premises, or pay double Rent.

Sir,

I Hereby give you notice to quit and yield up, on the day of next, possession of the messuage with its appurtenances, lands, tenements, and hereditaments which you now hold of me, situate at in the parish of and county of in failure whereof I shall require and insist upon double the value of the said premises according to the statute in such case made and provided. Dated this day of

To *A. B* [*tenant*] *E. N* [*landlord*]

Notice to quit by the Tenant.

SIR,

I Hereby give you notice that on day of I shall quit possession of the messuage or tenement, and premises which I now hold of you, situate at in the parish of in the county of Dated this day of 18—.

Yours, &c.

To *T. E.* [*landlord*] *A B* [*tenant*]

Notice by the Tenant to quit Lodgings.

SIR,

THIS is to give you notice that on day of next I shall quit and deliver up possession of the rooms or apartments and other tenements which I now hold of you in this house.

Witness my hand, this day of 18 –.

N O. [*the lodger*]

Notice to Tenant to repair

SIR,

YOU are hereby required to put in good and tenantable repair, all and singular the messuage or tenement and premises which you now hold of me, situate at, &c. Particularly the servant's hall in the said messuage or tenement, and the tiling or roof at the northern end thereof [*as the case may be.*]

Witness my hand, this day of

To *E. N.* [*tenant*] *P. L.* [*landlord*]

Notice to Tenant to pay Rent.

SIR,

THIS is to warn you that unless you pay, or cause to be paid unto me, on or before the day of next, the sum of being a year's rent due on the day of for the messuage or tenement and premises which you now hold of me, at the yearly rent of situated, &c. I shall claim and insist upon such forfeiture thereof, as I may be by law entitled to.

Witness my hand

X. Y. [*landlord.*]

To *I. K.* [*tenant.*]

How to make a Distress for Rent Arrear, and of the Sale of the same.

THE landlord himself, or any other person, as his bailiff, by an authority from him in writing, may make the distress. The warrant or authority may be in the following form: "To Mr. A. B. my bailiff, greeting.—Distrain the goods and chattels of C. D. (the tenant), in "the house he now dwells in (or on the premises in his "possession), situate in in the county of for " pounds, being one year's rent, due to me for the "same at Christmas-day last, and for your so doing this "shall be your sufficient warrant and authority. Dated "the day of 18—. "*J. S.*" — Written authority to distrain.

Being legally authorized to distrain, you enter on the premises, and make a seizure of the distress. If it be made in a house, seize a chair or other piece of furniture, and say, "I seize this chair, in the name of all the goods "in this house, for the sum of pounds, being one "year's rent due to me (or to *J. S.* the landlord) at "Christmas-day last, by virtue of an authority from the "said *J. S.* for that purpose (*provided you distrain as bailiff*)." — How to make distress.

Then take an inventory of so many goods as you judge will be sufficient to cover the rent distrained for, and also the charges of the distress. Make a copy thereof, as follows:

"An inventory* of the several goods and chattels distrained by me *A. B.* this day of in the "year of our Lord in the houses, out-houses, and — The inventory.

* This inventory is liable to a 6d. stamp-duty, stat. 37 G. 3. c. 90. s. 1.

"lands (*as the case is*), of *C D* situate in in the "county of by the authority and on the behalf of "*J. S.* (*provided you distrain as bailiff*), for the sum of " pounds, being one year's rent due to me, or to "the said *J S.* (*as the case is*), at Christmas day last.

"In the dwelling-house, two tables, two chairs, &c.

"In the barn, six hurdles, and so on."

At the bottom of the inventory, subscribe the following notice to the tenant:

"Mr. *C D.*

[illegible] "Take notice, that I have this day distrained (or that "as bailiff to *J. S* your landlord, I have this day dis- "trained) on the premises above mentioned, the several "goods and chattels specified in the above inventory, for "the sum of pounds, being one year's rent, due to "me (or to the said *J. S*) at Christmas day last, for the "said premises, and that unless you pay the said rent, "with the charges of distraining for the same, within "five days from the date hereof, the said goods and chat- "tels will be appraised and sold according to law. Given "under my hand, the day of in the year of "our Lord "*W. T.*"

[illegible] A true copy of the above inventory and notice must either be given to the tenant himself, or left at his house, or, if there be no house, on the most notorious place on the premises. And it is proper to have a person with you when you make the distress, and also when you serve the inventory and notice, to examine the same, and to attest the regularity of the proceedings.

[illegible] The goods may be removed immediately, and in the notice the tenant may be acquainted where they are removed, but it is now most usual to put a man in possession, and let them remain on the premises till you are entitled by [illegible] law to sell them*, which is on the sixth day inclusive, after the distress made, *i. e.* goods distrained on the Saturday, may be removed and sold on the Thursday afternoon following. *Wallace* v. *King* and another, 1 *H. Bl.* 13.

* [illegible] law, a distress was merely a pledge, and [illegible] not be sold [illegible] in the recovery of their rent, the st[illegible] 2 *W. & M.* [illegible] the sale of goods distrained for rent, after five days from [illegible] the distress.

If the tenant require further time for the payment of the rent, and the landlord chuses to allow it, it is best to take a memorandum in writing from the tenant; "That "he does consent that he should continue in possession "of his goods and chattels in his house (or upon the premises), for such a time longer, you having agreed not "to sell them for that time, and that he will pay the expences of keeping possession." This memorandum prevents the landlord from being deemed a trespasser, which, after the expiration of five days, he otherwise would be, and might have an action of trespass brought against him for staying longer upon the premises.

How, if further time required.

Agreement for that purpose.

If there be no allowance of, or agreement for, further time, search at the expiration of the five days at the sheriff's office to see if the goods have been replevied; if not, and the rent and charges still remain unpaid, send for a constable* and two sworn appraisers, who having viewed the goods, the former must administer to the latter the following oath:

How to search [illegible] and proceed to sale.

"You, and each of you, shall well and truly appraise "the goods and chattels mentioned in this inventory "(holding it in his hand), according to the best of your "judgment. So help you God."

Appraisers' oath.

Then indorse on the inventory the following memorandum.

"Memorandum; that on the day of in the "year of our Lord *A. B* of, &c. and *C. D.* of, &c. "two sworn appraisers, were sworn upon the Holy "Evangelists, by me *J. K.* of, &c. constable, well and "truly to appraise the goods and chattels mentioned in "this inventory, according to the best of their judgment,

"As witness my hand,

"Present at the time "*J. K* Constable."

"of swearing the said

"*A. B.* and *C. D.* as

"above, and witness

"thereto.

"*L. M.*

"*O. P.*"

Memorandum thereof.

* It should be a constable of the hundred, parish or place, where such distress was taken, and not one out of the district. *Walter* v. *King*, 1 [illegible] *Bla.* 14

After the appraisers have valued the goods, continue the indorsement on the inventory as follows

Appraisement.

"We, the above named *A B.* and *C. D.* being sworn "upon the Holy Evangelists, by *J. K.* the constable "above named, well and truly to appraise the goods and "chattels mentioned in this inventory, according to the "best of our judgment; and, having viewed the said "goods and chattels, do appraise the same at the sum of " pounds. As witness our hands the " day of in the year of our Lord .

A. B.
C. D } Sworn Appraisers."

How disposed of.

When the goods are thus valued, it is usual for the appraisers to buy them at their own valuation, and a receipt at the bottom of the inventory, witnessed by the constable, is usually held a discharge. But if the distress be of considerable value, it is much more adviseable to have a proper bargain and sale between the landlord, the constable, the appraiser, and the purchaser.

The goods being disposed of, deduct the rent in arrear, and all reasonable charges attending the distress, and return the overplus (if any) to the tenant.

If the produce is not sufficient to cover the demand, you may distrain again.

Form of a Tenant's Consent to the Landlord's continuing in Possession upon the Premises, when he requires further Time for Payment.

I *E T.* do hereby consent that *A B* my landlord, who on the day of distrained my goods and chattels for rent due to him, shall continue possession thereof on the premises for the space of seven days from the date hereof, the said *A. B.* undertaking to delay the sale of the said goods and chattels for that time, in order to enable me to discharge the said rent.

Witness my hand, this day of 18—.

E. T.

Notice to the Sheriff when in Possession on an Execution.

IF the sheriff is in possession of the tenant's goods on an execution, the landlord need not make a distress, but should forthwith serve him with the following notice:

To *N O.* and *E F* } Esqrs Sheriffs of Middlesex [*as the case may be.*]

TAKE notice, that the sum of for one year's [*as the case is*] rent due at last, is now due from *E N.* the person to whom the goods belong of which you are now in possession, by virtue of his Majesty's writ of returnable [*state the writ and return*]

As witness my hand, this day of 18—.

Note The man in possession of the goods, *&c* is to be paid 2s. 6*d.* *per diem*, if the tenant keep him: and 3*s.* 6*d* if he keep himself.

Precedents of Pleadings in Replevin.

THE King, *&c* We command you that justly, and without delay, you cause to be replevied the cattle of *B* which *D* took and unjustly detains, as it is said, and afterwards thereupon cause him justly to be removed, that we may hear no more clamour thereupon for want of justice, *&c.* Writ of replevin

A. B complains against *C. D* in a plea of taking and unjustly detaining his cattle against sureties and pledges, *&c.* Plaint

Pledges to prosecute, { *E F.* and *G H.* }

——to wit. *C. D.* was summoned to answer unto *A B* of a plea: wherefore the said *C. D.* took the goods and chattels [or cattle] of the said *A B* and unjustly detained the same against sureties and pledges, until, *&c.*, and thereupon the said *A B.* by *E. F.* his attorney, complains that the said *C. D.* on the day of in the year Narr Declaration of our Lord at the parish of in the county of in a certain dwelling-house there [or place there] called took the goods and chattels [or cattle] to wit, [*here set out the goods, or cattle, as the case may be.*] and unjustly detained the same against sureties and pledges until, &c., wherefore the said *A. B* says that he is injured, and hath sustained damage to the value of *l.* and therefore he brings his suit, &c.

Trinity Term, 44 *G.* III.

No. II. Plea of *non cepit.*

C. D. v. *A. B.* And the said *C. D.* by *G. H.* his attorney, comes and defends the wrong and injury, when, &c. and says, that he did not take the said goods and chattels [or cattle] in the said declaration mentioned, or any part thereof, in manner and form as the said *A. B.* hath above thereof complained against him, and of this he, the said *C. D.* puts himself upon the country, &c.

Trinity Term, 44 *G.* III.

No. III. Avowry [illegible] 11 G. 2. c. 19.

C. D. v. *A. B.* And the said *C. D.* by *G. H.* his attorney, comes and defends the wrong and injury, when &c. and well avows [*or if a cognizance say,* as bailiff of *C. D.* well acknowledges] the taking of the said goods and chattels, in the said declaration mentioned in the said dwelling-house, in which, &c. and justly, &c., because he says that the said *A. B* for a long space of time, to wit, for the space of next before and ending on the day of in the year of our Lord and from thence, until, and at the said time, when, &c. held and enjoyed the said dwelling-house, in which, &c. with the appurtenances as tenant thereof to him, the said *C. D.* by virtue of a certain demise thereof to him, the said *C. D.* theretofore made up, and under the yearly rent of *l.* payable quarterly, on the day of the day of the day of and the day of in every year, by even and equal portions; and because *l.* of the rent aforesaid, for the said space of ending as aforesaid on the said day of in the year aforesaid, and from thence until, and at the said time, when, &c. were due and in arrear from the said *A. B.* to the said *C. D.* he the said *C. D.* well avows [*or* as bailiff of the said well acknowledges] the taking of the said goods and chattels, in the said dwelling-house, in which, &c. and justly, &c. as for and in the name of a distress for the said rent so due and in arrear as aforesaid, and which said rent still remains due and in arrear to him the said *C. D.* (or to the said *G H.*) and this he, the said *C. D.* is ready to verify. Wherefore he prays judgment and a return of the goods and chattels, together with his damages, *&c.* according to the form of the statute in such case made and provided, to be adjudged to him, *&c.*

And the said *A. B* says, that the said *C D.* by reason of any thing in his said avowry [or cognizance] above alleged ought not to avow [or acknowledge] the taking of the said goods and chattels, in the said dwelling-house, in which, *&c* and justly, *&c.* Because he says, that the said *A. B.* did not hold and enjoy the said dwelling house in which, *&c* as tenant thereof to the said *C D* in manner and form as the said *C D.* hath above in his said avowry [or cognizance] in that behalf alleged, and this he the said *A. B.* prays may be inquired of by the country, *&c.* No. IV. Pl[illegible] bar [illegible]

Because he says, that no part of the said rent in the said avowry [or cognizance] mentioned at the said time, when, *&c.* was due, or in arrear, to the said *C. D.* in manner and form as the said *C. D.* has above in his said avowry [or cognizance] in that behalf alleged, and this he prays may be inquired of by the country, *&c.* No. V. Ple[illegible] rent in arrear

C D. } *ads.* *A B.* } And the said *C. D* by *G. H* his attorney, comes and defends the wrong and injury, when, *&c* and well avows the taking of the said cattle in the said place, in which, *&c.* and justly, *&c* because he says, that the said place now is, and at the said time when, *&c.* was the soil and freehold of him, the said *C. D.* and because the said cattle, at the same time when, *&c.* were wrongfully in the said place, in which, *&c.* eating up and depasturing the grass there then growing, and doing damage there to the said *C. D.* he the said *C. D.* well avows the taking of the said cattle in the said declaration mentioned, in the said place, in which, *&c.* and justly, *&c.* so there doing damage as aforesaid, as for and in the name of a distress for the said damage so there done and doing, and this he the said *C. D* is ready to verify. Wherefore he prays judgment and a return of the said cattle, together with his damages, *&c* according to the form of the No. VI. A[illegible] statute in such case made and provided, to be adjudged to him, *&c.*

No. VII. [illegible]

——to wit. *C. D.* puts in his place *G. H.* his attorney, at the suit of *A. B.* in a plea of taking and unjustly detaining the goods and chattels of the said *A. B.* against sureties and pledges, *&c.*

——to wit. *C. D.* was summoned to answer *A. B.* of a plea, wherefore he took, *&c.* [*the goods and chattels in the plaint*] of the said *A. B.* and unjustly detained them against sureties and pledges, *&c.* And hereupon the said *C. D.* in his proper person, offers himself on the fourth day, against the said *A. B.* in the plea aforesaid, but the said *A. B.* although solemnly called, comes not, but makes default, nor does he further prosecute his writ against the said *C. D.* Therefore it is considered, that the said *A. B.* take nothing by his said writ, but that he and his pledges to prosecute be in mercy, *&c.* and that the said *C. D.* do go thereof without day, *&c.* and that he have a return of the said goods and chattels, *&c.* It is also considered by the Court here, that the said *C. D.* do recover against the said *A. B.* [illegible] for his costs and charges by him laid out, about his defence in this behalf, by the said Court here adjudged to the said *C. D.* and with his assent, according to the form of the statute in such case made and provided, and that the said *C. D.* have execution thereof, *&c.*

No. VIII. [illegible]

——to wit. *A. B.* puts in his place *E. F.* his attorney, against *C. D.* in a plea of taking and unjustly detaining the goods and chattels of the said *A. B.* against sureties and pledges, *&c.*

——to wit. The said *C. D.* puts in his place *G. H.* his attorney, at the suit of the said *A. B.* in the plea aforesaid.

——to wit. *C. D.* was summoned to answer unto *A. B.* of a plea, *&c.* [*here copy the declaration and cognizance, and proceed as follows.*] and upon this the said *C. D.* prays that the said *A. B.* may plead in bar of the said cognizance, and thereupon a day is given to the said *A. B.* before our Lord the King, until wheresoever our said Lord the King shall then be in *England*, that is to say, for him the said *A. B.* to plead in bar of the said cognizance, *&c.* The same day is given to the said *C. D.* there, *&c.* At which day, before our said Lord the King at *Westminster*, comes the said *C. D.* by his attorney aforesaid, and offers himself against the said *A. B* in the plea aforesaid; but the said *A B* although solemnly called, comes not, but makes default, nor hath he pleaded in bar of the said cognizance, nor does he further prosecute his writ against the said *C. D* · therefore it is considered, &c [*as in the last*].

No IX. Writ of [illegible] of the [illegible] 17 Car. 2. c. 7. [illegible] in the nature of a [illegible]

George the Third, &c to the sheriff of greeting · whereas *C D* was summoned to appear in our Court before us, on wheresoever we then should be in *England*, to answer unto *A B.* of a plea wherefore he took the goods and chattels of the said *A B.* and unjustly detained the same, against sureties and pledges, until, &c. And the said *C D* offered himself in our said Court before us, on the fourth day, against the said *A B* in the plea aforesaid, and the said *A B.* although solemnly called, came not but made default · therefore it was considered by the same Court, that the said *A. B.* and his pledges to prosecute should be in mercy, &c And the said *C D.* offered himself in our said Court before us, on the fourth day, against the said *A B* in the plea aforesaid, and the said *A B* although solemnly called, came not, but made default therefore it was considered by the same Court, that the said *A B* and his pledges to prosecute should be in mercy, &c. and that the said *C D* should go thereof without day, &c and have a return of the said goods and chattels, and thereupon it hath been suggested in our said Court before us, by the said *C. D.* that he the said *C. D* took the said goods and chattels of the said *A B.* as aforesaid, at in the said county, in a certain messuage or dwelling-house there, and that he took the same as bailiff of *E F* for that the said *A. B.* for the space of one year, next before and ending on the day of in the year of our Lord and from thence until and at the time of taking the said goods and chattels, held and enjoyed the said messuage or dwelling-house and premises, with the appurtenances, amongst other things, as tenant thereof to the said *E. F.* at and under the yearly rent of *l.* And because *l.* of the rent aforesaid, for ending as aforesaid, on the said, &c. and from thence until and at the time of taking the said goods and chattels, were due and in arrear from the said *A. B* to the said *E. F.* he the said *C D.* as bailiff to the said *E. F.* took the said goods and chattels, as for and in the name of a distress for the said rent, so due in arrear from the said *A. B.* to the said *E. F.* as aforesaid, and the said *C. D.* according to the form of the statute in such case made and provided, prayed our writ to be directed to you, to inquire of the arrears of the rent aforesaid, and of the value of the said goods and chattels, and it was granted to him, which as by the record and proceedings thereof, still remaining in our said Court before us, at *Westminster* aforesaid, fully appears: therefore we command you, that according to the form of the statute aforesaid, you diligently inquire by the oath of twelve good and lawful men of your bailiwick, how much of the yearly rent aforesaid, at the time of taking and distraining the said goods and chattels, was in arrear and unpaid, and how much the said goods and chattels so as aforesaid taken and distrained were worth, according to the true value of the same, and the inquisition which you shall thereupon take, make appear to us on wheresoever we shall then be in *England*, under your seal and the seals of those by whose oath you shall take the said inquisition, and have there the names of them by whose oath you shall take the said inquisition, and this writ.

Witness, *Edward*, Lord *Ellenborough*, &c.

[illegible] George the Third, &c. to the sheriff of greeting: whereas *C. D.* lately in our Court before us at *Westminster*, was summoned to answer *A. B.* of a plea wherefore he took the goods and chattels of the said *A. B.* and unjustly detained them against sureties and pledges, &c. whereupon the said *A. B.* by his attorney, complained that the said *C. D.* theretofore, to wit, on, &c. at, &c. in your county, in a certain place there, called had seised and taken the goods and chattels of the said *A. B.* to wit, [illegible] and unjustly detained the same against sureties and pledges, until, &c. And the said *C. D.* appearing in our said Court before us, at *Westminster* aforesaid, by his attorney, well avowed the taking of the said goods and chattels, &c. [*here state the whole of the avowry, and proceed as follows.*] And such proceedings were thereupon had in our said Court before us, at *Westminster* aforesaid, that it was afterwards considered in the same Court, that the said *A. B.* should take nothing by his writ aforesaid, but that he and his pledges to prosecute should be in mercy, &c. and that the said *C. D.* should go thereof without day, &c. and have a return of the said goods and chattels, and thereupon the said *C. D.* according to the form of the statute in such case made and provided, prayed our writ, &c. [*as in the* [illegible], *to the end.*]

[*As in No. 8, to the end of the judgment for a return, and then as follows.*]

No. XI. The [illegible] on the stat. 17 C. 2. c. 7.

And hereupon the said *C. D.* according to the form of the statute in such case made and provided, prays the writ of our said Lord the King, to be directed to the sheriff of to inquire of the arrears of the rent aforesaid, and of the value of the said goods and chattels; and it is granted to him, &c. Therefore it is commanded to the said sheriff of according to the form of the statute aforesaid, that he diligently inquire, by the oath of twelve good and lawful men of his bailiwick, how much of the yearly rent aforesaid, at the time of taking and distraining the said goods and chattels, was in arrear and unpaid, and how much the said goods and chattels so as aforesaid taken and distrained were worth according to the value of the same; and that the inquisition which the said sheriff shall thereupon take he make appear to our said Lord the King, on [illegible] wheresoever our said Lord the King shall then be [illegible] under his seal and the seals of those by whose oath he shall take the said inquisition, together with the writ of our said Lord the King to him thereupon directed [illegible] to the said *C. D.* &c. At which day before our said Lord the King at *Westminster*, cometh the said *C. D.* by his attorney aforesaid, and the sheriff of [illegible] in the said county, on the day of in the year of the reign of our said Lord the King by the oath of twelve good and lawful men of his county, whereby it appears, that the sum of of the said yearly rent was in arrear and unpaid [illegible] owing from the said *A. B.* to the said *C. D.* at the time in the said cognizance mentioned, and of the distress taken; and that the goods and chattels so distrained were worth according to the value thereof the sum of *l.* Therefore it is considered that the said *C. D.* do recover against the said *A. B.* the said sum of *l.* being the arrearages of the said rent, by the said inquisition in form aforesaid found, and also *l.* by the Court of our said Lord the King now here adjudged to the said *C. D.* and at his request, for his costs and charges by him about his suit in this behalf sustained, according to the form of the statute in such case made and provided: which said damages, costs and charges, in the whole amount to *l.* and that the said *C. D.* have execution thereof, *&c.*

And execution.

No XII
[illegible]

Therefore it is considered, that the said *C. D.* do recover against the said *A. B.* the said *l.* parcel of the rent aforesaid, by the said inquisition in form aforesaid found, and his damages by reason of the premises to *l.* by the Court of our said Lord the King now here adjudged to the said *C. D.* and at his request, for his costs and charges by him in this behalf sustained, according to the form of the statute in such case made and provided, which said value, costs and charges, in the whole, amount to *l.* And that the said *C. D.* have execution thereof, *&c.*

Execution.

No XIII
[illegible]

George the Third, *&c.* to the sheriff of greeting whereas *C. D.* was summoned to be in our Court before us, to answer *A. B.* of a plea wherefore he took the cattle, goods and chattels, of the said *A. B.* and unjustly detained them against sureties and pledges, as it is said and the said *A. B.* afterwards in our same Court before us made default, wherefore it was considered in our same Court, that he and his pledges to prosecute should be in mercy, *&c.* and that the said *C. D.* should go thereof without day, *&c.* and that he should have a return of the said cattle, goods and chattels therefore we command you, that without delay you cause the said cattle, goods and chattels, to be returned to the said *C. D.* and that you do not deliver them on the complaint of the said *A. B.* without our writ, which makes express mention of the judgment aforesaid, and in what manner you shall execute this our writ, make appear to us on wheresoever we shall then be in *England*, and have there this writ. Witness, *&c.*

[illegible]

—— to —— to wit *C. D.* by his attorney offered himself on the fourth day against *A. B.* of a plea wherefore he the said *C. D.* took the cattle, goods and chattels, of the said *A. B.* and unjustly detained them against sureties and pledges, *&c.* and the said *A. B.* being solemnly called, came not: and was the plaintiff, *&c.* therefore it is considered, that he and his pledges to prosecute be therefore in mercy, *&c.* and that the said *C. D.* go thereof without day, *&c.* and that he have a return of the said cattle, goods and chattels, *&c.* and let the names of the pledges be inquired, *&c.* and in what manner, *&c.* let the sheriff make appear to our Lord the King, on wheresoever, *&c.*

No XIV

George the Third, *&c.* to the sheriff of greeting: whereas *C D* was summoned to be in our Court before us, to answer *A. B.* in a plea wherefore the said *C. D* on the day of in the year of our Lord at the parish of in the county of in a certain place there called took the cattle, goods and chattels, of him the said *A. B.* to wit, *&c.* [*here set out the cattle and goods, as in the declaration*] and unjustly detained the same against sureties and pledges, until, *&c.* as it was said and the said *C D* appearing in our said Court before us, for certain causes by him alleged in our same Court, as bailiff of *E F.* well acknowledged the taking of the said cattle, goods and chattels, in the said place in which, *&c.* and unjustly, *&c.* for damage there done, [or for certain arrears of rent, to wit, for the sum of *l* due and in arrear from the said *A B* to the said *C. D.* for the said place in which, *&c.* with the appurtenances, held and enjoyed under, and by virtue of, a certain demise thereof, made by the said *C. D.* for the space of next before and ending on the day of in the year of our Lord] whereupon the said *A. B* being afterwards solemnly called in our said Court before us, came not, nor did he further prosecute his writ aforesaid: wherefore it was considered in our said Court before us, at *Westminster*, that the said *A. B* should take nothing by his writ aforesaid, but that he and his pledges to prosecute should be in mercy, *&c.* and that the said *C. D.* should go thereof without day, *&c.* and that he should have a return of the said cattle, goods and chattels: therefore we command you, that without delay you cause the said cattle, goods and chattels, to be returned to the said *C. D* and that you do not deliver them on the complaint of the said *A B.* without our writ, which makes express mention of the judgment aforesaid: and in what manner you shall have executed this our writ, make appear to us, on wheresoever, *&c.* and have there this writ Witness, *&c.*

No XV

George the Third, *&c.* to the sheriff of greeting Whereas *C D.* was summoned to be in our Court before us, &c. [*as in the last, to the end for a return, and then as follows*] and also that the said *C. D.* ought to recover against the said *A. B.* his damages on occasion of the premises, according to the form of the statute in such case made and provided. Therefore we command you, that without delay you cause the said cattle, goods and chattels to be returned to the said *C. D.* &c. [*as in the last, to* "wheresoever, &c.,"] and also that by the oath of honest and lawful men of your county, you diligently inquire what damages the said *C. D.* hath sustained, as well on occasion of the premises, as for his costs and charges, by him about his suit in this behalf expended: and the inquisition which you shall thereupon take, make appear to us at the aforesaid time, wheresoever, &c. under your seal and the seals of those by whose oath you shall take that inquisition, and have there the names of them by whose oath you shall take that inquisition, and this writ. Witness, &c.

Proceedings in Ejectment.

No. I. Original writ.

GEORGE the Third, by the grace of God of the united kingdom of *Great Britain* and *Ireland*, king, defender of the faith, to the sheriff of greeting. If *A. B.* shall give you security to prosecute his claim, then put by gage and safe pledges *C. D.* late of yeoman, so that he be before us on the morrow of *All Souls*, wheresoever we shall then be in *England*, to shew wherefore with force and arms he entered into one messuage, with the appurtenances, in which *E. F.* esquire hath demised to the aforesaid *A. B.* for a term which is not yet expired, and ejected him from his said farm, and other enormities to him did, to the great damage of the said *A. B.* and against our peace. And have you there the names of the pledges, and this writ. Witness ourself at *Westminster*, the day of in the year of our reign.

Pledges to prosecute, { *John Doe,* *Richard Roe.*

The within named *C. D.* is attached by pledges, { *John Den,* *Richard Fen.*

In the *King's Bench*,

Easter Term, in the 44th year of the reign of *George* the Third

——to wit, *C. D.* late of yeoman, was attached to answer unto of plea wherefore the said *C. D.* with force and arms, &c. entered into messuages, &c. [*here describing the premises*] with the appurtenances, situate and being in the parish of in the county of which *E. F.* had demised to the said *A. B.* for a term which is not yet expired; and ejected him from his said farm, and other wrongs to the said *A. B.* there did, to the great damage of the said *A. B.* and against the peace of our Lord the now King, &c. And thereupon the said *A. B.* by his attorney, complains, that whereas the said *E. F.* on the day of in the year of our Lord at the parish aforesaid, in the county aforesaid, had demised the said tenements with their appurtenances to the said *A. B.* to have and to hold the same unto the said *A. B.* and his assigns, from the day of the said month of for and during, and to the full end and term of seven years, from thence next ensuing, and fully to be complete and ended By virtue of which demise, the said *A. B.* entered into the said tenements with the appurtenances, and was thereof possessed for the said term so to him thereof demised, and the said *A. B.* being so thereof possessed, the said *C. D.* afterwards, to wit, on the day of in the year aforesaid, with force and arms, &c. entered into the said tenements with the appurtenances, which the said *E. F.* had demised to the said *A. B.* in manner and for the term aforesaid, which is not yet expired, and ejected the said *A. B.* from his said farm, and other wrongs to the said *A. B.* then and there did, to the great damage of the said *A. B.* and against the peace of our said Lord the now King, whereofore the said *A. B.* saith, that he is injured and hath sustained damage to the value of *l.* and therefore he brings his suit, &c.

Mr

I am informed that you are in possession of, or claim title, to the premises in this declaration of ejectment mentioned, or to some part thereof. And I being sued in this action as a casual ejector only, and having no claim or title to the same, do advise you to appear on the first day of next *Trinity term* [in town or in the country, " in next *Trinity Term*"], in his Majesty's Court of *King's Bench*, wheresoever his said Majesty shall then be in *England*, by some attorney of that Court, and then and there by rule of the same Court to cause yourself to be made defendant in my stead Otherwise I shall suffer judgment therein to be entered against me by default, and you will be turned out of possession.

Yours, &c.

C. D.

No III [illegible] —— *ss.* *A. B.* complains of *C. D.* being in the custody of the marshal of the *Marshalsea* of our Sovereign Lord the King himself for that whereas *E F.* on the day of in the year of the reign of our Lord the now King, at in the county of had demised, to the said *A.B.* messuages, *&c* [*reciting the several parcels*] with the appurtenances, situate, lying and being, in the parish of in the said county of to have and to hold the said tenements, with the appurtenances, to the said *A.* and his assigns, from the day of then last past, to the full end and term of five years from thence next ensuing, and fully to be complete and ended, by virtue of which said demise, he the said *A.* entered into the said tenements, with the appurtenances, and was thereof possessed until the said *C.* afterwards, that is to say, on the day of in the year aforesaid, with force and arms, *&c.* entered into the said tenements with the appurtenances which the said *E F.* had demised to the said *A.* in manner aforesaid, for the term aforesaid, which is not yet expired, and ejected the said *A.* out of his said farm and then and there did other wrongs to the said *A.* against the peace of our said Lord the King, and to the damage of him the said *A.* of twenty pounds, and thereupon he brings his suit, *&c.*

Pledges to prosecute, { *John Doe,* *Richard Roe.*

The notice to this declaration is the same as the last, only instead of the words, " wheresoever, *&c.*" must be substituted " at *Westminster.*"

In the *King's Bench.*

Easter Term, 44*th Geo.* III.

[illegible] —— to wit. *C. D.* late of yeoman, was attached to answer unto *A. B.* of a plea wherefore the said *C. D.* with force and arms, *&c.* entered into messuages, &c. [*describing the premises*] with the appurtenances, situate and being in the parish of in the county of which E. F. had demised to the said A. B. for a term which is not yet expired and ejected him from his said farm. And also, wherefore the said C. D. with force and arms, &c. entered into other messuages, &c. with the appurtenances, situate and being in the parish aforesaid, in the county aforesaid, which G. H. had demised to the said A. B. for a term which is not yet expired, and ejected him from his said last mentioned farm, and other wrongs to the said A. B. and against the peace of our Lord the now King, &c. And thereupon the said A. B. by his attorney complains, that whereas the said E. F. on the day of in the year of our Lord at the parish aforesaid, in the county aforesaid, had demised the said tenements first above mentioned, with the appurtenances, to the said A. B. to have and to hold the same unto the said A. B. and his assigns, from the day of the said month of for and during and unto the full end and term of seven years, from thence next ensuing, and fully to be completed and ended. And also, that whereas the said G. H. on the day of in the year of our Lord at the parish aforesaid, in the county aforesaid, had demised the said tenements secondly above-mentioned, with the appurtenances, to the said A. B. to have and to hold the same unto the said A. B. and his assigns, from the day of the said month of for and during, and unto the full end and term of seven years from thence next ensuing, and fully to be complete and ended, by virtue of which said several demises, the said A. B. entered into the said tenements first and secondly above-mentioned, with the appurtenances, and was thereof possessed for the said several terms so to him thereof demised, and being so thereof possessed, the said C. D. afterwards, to wit, on the day of in the year aforesaid, with force and arms, &c. entered into the said tenements first and secondly above-mentioned, with the appurtenances, which he the said E. F. and G. H. had so respectively demised to the said A. B. in manner, and for the several terms aforesaid, which are not expired, and ejected the said A. B. from his several farms, and other wrongs to the said A. B. then and there did, to the great damage of the said A. B. and against the peace of our said Lord the now

King; wherefore the said *A B.* saith, that he is injured and hath sustained damage to the value of *l.* and therefore he brings his suit, *&c.*

Notice as before.

In the *King's Bench.*

No. V. Trespass with two counts.

Easter Term, 44th *Geo* III

—— to wit *C. D.* late of yeoman, was attached to answer unto *A. B.* of a plea wherefore the said *C. D.* with force and arms, *&c.* entered into messuages, *&c.* [*describing the premises*] with the appurtenances, situate and being in the parish of in the county of which *E. F.* had demised to the said *A. B.* for a term which is not yet expired; and ejected him from his said farm. And also, wherefore the said *C. D.* with force and arms, *&c.* entered into other messuages, *&c.* with the appurtenances, situate and being in the parish aforesaid, in the county aforesaid, which *G. H.* had demised to the said *A. B.* for a term which is not yet expired, and ejected him from his said last mentioned farm, and other wrongs to the said *A. B.* then did, to the great damage of the said *A. B.* and against the peace of our Lord the now King, *&c.* And thereupon the said *A. B.* by his attorney complains, the said *E. F.* on the day of in the year of our Lord at the parish aforesaid, in the county aforesaid, had demised the said tenements first above-mentioned, with the appurtenances, to the said *A. B.* to have and to hold the same unto the said *A. B.* and his assigns, from the day of then last past, for and during, and unto the full end and term of years, from thence next ensuing, and fully to be complete and ended. By virtue of which said demise the said *A. B.* entered into the said tenements with the appurtenances first above-mentioned, and became, and was thereof possessed, for the said term so to him thereof granted and the said *A. B.* being so thereof possessed, the said *C. D.* afterwards [to wit.] on the day of in the year aforesaid, with force and arms, *&c.* entered into the said tenements with the appurtenances first above-mentioned, which the said *E. F.* had demised to the said *A. B.* in manner, and for the term aforesaid, which is not expired, and ejected the said *A. B.* from his said first mentioned farm. And also, that whereas the said *G. H.* on the day of in the year aforesaid, at the parish aforesaid, in the county aforesaid, had demised the said tenements with the appurtenances secondly above-mentioned, to the said *A. B.* to have and to hold the same, unto the said *A. B* and his assigns, from the day of then last past, for and during, and unto the full end and term of seven years, from thence next ensuing, and fully to be complete and ended By virtue of which said last-mentioned demise, the said *A B.* entered into the tenements with the appurtenances secondly above-mentioned, *&c* and became, and was thereof possessed, for the said term so to him thereof granted, and the said *A. B.* being so thereof possessed, the said *C D* afterwards, [to wit.] on the said day of in the year aforesaid, with force and arms, *&c.* entered into the said tenements with the appurtenances secondly above-mentioned, which the said *G H* had so demised to the said *A B.* in manner, and for the term last aforesaid, which is not yet expired, and ejected the said *A B* from his said last-mentioned farm, and other wrongs to the said *A B* then and there did, to the great damage of the said *A B.* and against the peace of our said Lord the now King Wherefore, the said *A B* saith that he is injured, and hath sustained damage to the value of *l* and therefore he brings his suit, *&c.*

Notice as before.

In the *King's Bench.*

No VI. Affidavit of service of declaration, and notice, [illegible]

Between { *A. B.* on demise of *E. F.* plaintiff, and *C. D.* - - defendant. }

S S of, *&c.* maketh oath, and saith, that he this deponent did, on the day of last, deliver a true copy of the declaration and notice hereunto annexed, to *W. T* tenant in possession of the premises in the said declaration mentioned, and at the same time, told him it was a declaration in ejectment, and that unless he did appear thereunto, by some attorney of this Honourable Court, on the first day of the present Term, judgment would be entered against the said defendant by default, and the said *W T.* would be turned out of possession, [or words to that or the like effect]

Sworn *&c.* *S. S.*

No. VII.
Similar affidavit, where there are several tenants.

S. S. of, *&c.* maketh oath and saith, that he this deponent did on, *&c.* last, deliver a true copy of the declaration and notice hereunto annexed, to *W. T.* tenant in possession of part of the premises in the said declaration mentioned, and did also, on the same day, deliver another copy of the said declaration and notice to *D.* the wife of *I. T.* tenant in possession, of the residue of the premises in the said declaration mentioned, she the said *D.* then being thereon. And this deponent further saith, that he told them *severally* that it was a declaration in ejectment, and that unless they did *severally* appear thereto, by some attorney of this Honourable Court, on the first day of this present   term, judgment would be entered against the said defendant by default, and they the said *W. T.* and *I. T.* would be *severally* turned out of possession, [or words to that or the like effect.]

Sworn, *&c.*   *S. S.*

A. on a demise of *F.* against *C.*

No. VIII.
Rule for judgment.

Unless the tenant in possession of the premises in question shall appear and plead to issue on *Tuesday* next after, *&c.* (*time tenant is to appear in*) LET judgment be entered for the plaintiff against the now defendant *C.* by default upon the motion of Mr. *D.*

By the Court.

Note. If plaintiff does not move for judgment the same Term tenant had notice to appear, the court will not grant such rule.

Note. When you move for a rule for judgment you annex the affidavit of service to a copy of the declaration stamped, and give it to counsel with 10*s.* 6*d.* fee to move. The clerk of the rules files the affidavit and declaration on such motion, therefore keep by you another copy on stamp, or if judgment go against the casual ejector for want of tenant's entering into the rule, you must have an office copy of the declaration from the clerk of the rules in order to enable you to sign judgment.

The Common Rule of Court.

Hilary Term, the twenty-ninth year of King *George* the Second.

Smith v. *Stiles*, for one messuage with appurtenances in Sutton, on the demise of *John Rogers*.

Berkshire to wit. It is ordered by the Court, by the assent of both parties, and their attornies, that *George Saunders*, gentleman, may be made defendant in the place of the now defendant *William Stiles*, and shall immediately appear to the plaintiff's action, and shall receive a declaration in a plea of trespass and ejectment of the tenements in question, and shall immediately plead thereto, not guilty, and, upon the trial of the issue, shall confess lease, entry, and ouster, and insist upon his title only. And if, upon trial of the issue, the said *George* do not confess lease, entry, and ouster, and by reason thereof the plaintiff cannot prosecute his writ, then the taxation of costs upon such *non-pros* shall cease, and the said *George* shall pay such costs to the plaintiff, as by the Court of our Lord the King here shall be taxed and adjudged for such his default in non-performance of this rule, and judgment shall be entered against the said *William Stiles*, now the casual ejector, by default. And it is further ordered, that, if upon trial of the said issue a verdict shall be given for the defendant, or if the plaintiff shall not prosecute his writ, upon any other cause than for the not confessing lease, entry, and ouster, as aforesaid, then the lessor of the plaintiff shall pay costs, if the plaintiff himself doth not pay them.

By the Court.

When the proceedings are by *bill*, and not by *original*, the words "*and file common bail*" should be inserted after the words requiring the tenant's appearance, and the word *bill* should stand in the room of the word *writ*, throughout.

A. on the demise of *F.* against *C.*

K. B.

No X

A notice of the premises the defendant defends for

SIR,

Take notice that I defend a title for a messuage and garden, with the appurtenances, in the parish of in the county of now in possession of the

said *L. F.* or his under-tenant. Dated the
day of 1804

To Mr *R. F.*
the plaintiff's attorney,
These.

Yours, *&c.*
P. P.
defendant's attorney.

No. XI. [illegible]

As yet of term, *&c.* to wit. *John Doe* on the demise of *A. B* puts in his place *L. F* his attorney, against *Richard Roe*, in a plea of trespass and ejectment.

—— to wit the said *Richard Roe* in person, at the suit of the said *John Doe*, in the plea aforesaid.

—— to wit. Be it remembered, that in Term last past, before our Lord the King at *Westminster*, came *John Doe* by *L. F.* his attorney, and brought into the Court of our said Lord the King himself then there, his certain bill against *Richard Roe*, being in the custody of the marshal of the marshalsea of our said Lord the King before the King himself of a plea of trespass and ejectment: and there are pledges for the prosecution thereof to wit *John Doe*, and *Richard Fenn*, which said bill follows in these words, that is to say: *John Doe* complains of *Richard Roe* being in the custody, *&c.* (*here copy the declaration to the end, omitting the pledges and notice, and then proceed on a new line as follows.*)

And now at this day that is to say, on next after in this same Term until which day the said *Richard Roe* had leave to imparl to the said bill, and then to answer the same, *&c* before our said Lord the King at *Westminster*, come as well the said *John Doe* by his attorney aforesaid as the said *Richard Roe* in his proper person, and the said *Richard Roe* defends the force and injury when, *&c.* and says nothing in bar or preclusion of the said *John Doe*, whereby the said *John Roe* remains therein undefended against the said *Richard Roe*, therefore it is considered that the said *John Doe* recover against the said *Richard Roe* his said term yet to come of and in the tenements aforesaid with the appurtenances and also his damages sustained by reason of the trespass and ejectment aforesaid and hereupon the said *John Doe* freely here in Court remits to the said *Richard Roe*, all such damages costs and charges as ought to be adjudged to him the said *John Doe*, by reason of the trespass and ejectment aforesaid. Therefore let the said *Richard Roe* be acquitted of those damages, costs and charges, *&c.* And hereupon the said *John Doe* prays the writ of our said Lord the King to be directed to the sheriff of the county aforesaid, to cause him to have possession of his said term yet to come of and in the tenements aforesaid with the appurtenances: and it is granted to him, returnable before our said Lord the King at *Westminster* on next after , the same day is given to the said *Richard Doe* there, *&c.*

(*Entry of warrant's of attorney, as in the last.*)

—— to wit. *Richard Roe* was attached, *&c* [*here copy the declaration to the end, and then proceed as follows.*]

And the said *Richard Roe* in his proper person, comes and defends the force and injury when, *&c.* and says nothing in bar or preclusion, *&c.* [*as before, making the writ of possession returnable on a general return day*].

[*To the end of the issue, and then as follows.*]

No XII Judgment with a remitter of part of the damages.

At which day, before our said Lord the King at *Westminster*, come the parties aforesaid, by their attornies aforesaid, and hereupon the said *C. D.* relinquishing his said plea by him above pleaded, says that he cannot deny the action of the said *A. B.* nor but that he the said *C. D.* is guilty of the trespass and ejectment above laid to his charge, in manner and form as the said *A. B* hath above thereof complained against him; and he confesses and admits that the said *A. B* hath sustained damages, by reason of the said trespass and ejectment, to the sum of one penny, besides his costs and charges, by him about this suit in this behalf expended. And hereupon the said *A. B.* freely here in court remits to the said *C D.* the residue of the damages in the said declaration mentioned, and prays judgment and his term yet to come of and in the tenements aforesaid with the appurtenances, together with his said damages so confessed, and his costs and charges aforesaid, to be adjudged to him, *&c.* Therefore it is considered, that the said *A. B.* do recover against the said *C. D.* his said term yet to come of and in the tenements aforesaid with the appurtenances, together with the damages aforesaid, to the sum of one penny, in form aforesaid confessed, and also *l.* for his said costs and charges, by the court of our said Lord the King, now here adjudged to the said *A. B.* and with his assent, which said damages, costs and charges

Judgment signed, &c.

in the whole, amount to l. And hereupon the said *A. B.* prays the writ of our said Lord the King, to be directed to the sheriff of aforesaid, to cause him to have possession of his said term yet to come, of and in the tenements aforesaid, with the appurtenances; and it is granted to him, returnable before our said Lord the King, on wheresoever, &c.

[*To the end of the issue, and then as follows.*]

No XIII The like for the plaintiff as to part of the premises, and for the defendant on a *noli prosequi* as to the residue

At which day, before our said Lord the King at *Westminster*, come the parties aforesaid, by their attornies aforesaid, and hereupon the said *C. D.* as to parcel of the tenements in the said declaration mentioned, relinquishing his said plea, by him above pleaded, says, that he cannot deny the action of the said *John Doe*, nor but that he the said *C. D.* is guilty of the trespass and ejectment above laid to his charge, in manner and form as the said *John Doe* hath above thereof complained against him And upon this, the said *John Doe* says, that he will not further prosecute his suit against the said *C D.* for the trespass and ejectment in the residue of the tenements aforesaid, and he prays judgment and his term yet to come, of and in the said with the appurtenances, parcel, *&c.* together with his damages, costs and charges, by him in this behalf sustained. Therefore it is considered, that the said *John Doe*, do recover against the said *C. D* his said term yet to come, of and in the said with the appurtenances, parcel, *&c.* and also l. for his said damages, costs and charges, by the Court of our said Lord the King now here adjudged, to the said *John Doe*, with his assent, and the assent of the said *C. D* And let the said *C D.* be acquitted of the said trespass and ejectment, in the residue of the tenements aforesaid, and go thereof without day, *&c.* And the said *John Doe* prays the writ of our said Lord the King to be directed to the sheriff of aforesaid, to cause him to have possession of his said term yet to come, of and in the said with the appurtenances, parcel, *&c.* and it is granted to him, returnable before our said Lord the King, on whatsoever, *&c.*

Judgment signed, &c

Special verdict.

Afterwards, that is to say, on the day and at the place within contained, *&c.* [*as in a common postea, to the finding of the jury, which varies according to facts of the case, and concludes as follows.*] but whether or not upon the whole matter aforesaid, by the jurors aforesaid in form aforesaid found, the said *C. D.* is guilty of the trespass and ejectment within specified, the jurors aforesaid are altogether ignorant, and hereupon they pray the advice of the Court of our said Lord the King, before the King himself; and, if upon the whole matter aforesaid, it shall seem to the said Court, that the said *C. D.* is guilty of the trespass and ejectment aforesaid, then the jurors aforesaid, upon their oath aforesaid, say, that the said *C. D.* is guilty thereof, in maner and form as the said *John Doe* hath within thereof complained against him, and in that case, they assess the damages of the said *John Doe*, on occasion of the trespass and ejectment aforesaid, besides his costs and charges by him about his suit in that behalf expended, to *l.* and for those costs and charges to *s.* But if upon the whole matter aforesaid, it shall seem to the said Court, that the said *C. D.* is not guilty of the trespass and ejectment aforesaid, then the jurors aforesaid, upon their oath aforesaid say, that the said *C. D.* is not guilty thereof, in manner and form as he hath within in pleading alleged. And because, &c.

No XIV. The like where part is found for the plaintiff and part for the defendant.

Therefore it is considered, that the said *John Doe* do recover against the said *C. D.* his said term yet to come of and in the tenements aforesaid with the appurtenances, and his said damages to *l.* by the jurors aforesaid in form aforesaid assessed, and also *l* for his said costs and charges by the Court of our said Lord the King now here adjudged of increase to the said *A. B.* and with his assent, which said damages, costs and charges, in the whole, amount to *l.* And let the said *C. D.* be taken, &c. And hereupon the said *John Doe* prays the writ of our said Lord the King to be directed to the sheriff of the county of aforesaid, to cause him to have possession of his said term yet to come of and in the tenements aforesaid with the appurtenances, and it is granted to him, returnable before our said Lord the King, on wheresoever, &c.

No XV. The like for the plaintiff as to part of the premises, and for defendant as to the residue

George the Third, &c. To the sheriff of greetting. therefore it is considered, that the said *John Doe* do recover against the said *C. D* his said term yet to come of and in the said parcel, &c. with the appurtenances, and the damages, costs and charges, aforesaid, by the jurors aforesaid, in form aforesaid assessed, and also *l.* for his said costs and charges, by the Court of our said Lord the King now here adjudged of increase to the said *John Doe*, and with his assent; which said damages, costs and charges, in the whole, amount to *l.* And let the said *John Doe* be amerced, for his false claim against the said *C. D* as to the residue of the tenements in the said declaration mentioned, whereof the said *C. D* is acquitted in form aforesaid and the said *C. D.* go thereof without day, &c. and hereupon the said *John Doe* prays the writ, &c. (*as in the last*).

No. XVI. Habere fac. possessionem.

Whereas *A. B.* lately in our Court before us at *Westminster*, by bill without our writ (*or if by original*, by our writ), and by the judgment of the same Court, recovered against *C. D.* his term then and yet to come of and in two dwelling-houses, &c. (*as in the declaration in ejectment*), with the appurtenances, situate, lying and being, in the parish of in your county, which *E. F.* on the day of in the year of our reign, had demised to the said *A. B.* to hold the same to the said *A. B.* and his assigns, from the day of then last past, for and during, and unto the full end and term of years from thence next ensuing, and fully to be complete and ended, by virtue of which said demise, the said *A. B.* entered into the said tenement with the appurtenances, and was possessed thereof until the said *C. D* afterwards, to wit, on the day of in the year aforesaid, with force and arms, &c. entered into the said tenements with the appurtenances, which the said *E. F.* had demised to the said *A. B* in manner and for the term aforesaid, which was not then, nor is yet, expired, and ejected the said *A. B* from his said farm, whereof the said *C. D.* is convicted, as appears to us of record: therefore we command you that without delay you cause the said *A. B* to have the possession of his said term yet to come of and in the tenements aforesaid with the appurtenances. and in what manner you shall have executed this our writ, make appear to us at *Westminster*, on next after and have there then this writ. Witness, &c.

Note. This writ must be engrossed on parchment. Make a *præcipe* for the office thus

—— to wit. Writ of possession for *A. B* on the demise of *E. F.* against *C. D.* for a messuage, with the appurtenances, situate at in the county of

Returnable [*the return*].

R. R. attorney.

Note. Carry the *writ* and *præcipe* to the officer who signs the writs in this Court, pay him for signing the same 1*s.* 8*d* sealing at the seal office 7*d.* the sheriff's warrant thereon 2*s.* 4*d* his fee for executing the same is 1*s.* in the pound, in the yearly value of the premises, if the same does not exceed 100*l per annum*, and 6*d.* in the pound for every 20*s* above, and 2*s.* returning the writ. Officer's fee executing writ usually 1*l.* 1*s*

If the proceedings are by *original*, the writ of possession differs only from the above in the introductory part, and in the return. It is signed by the filacer, and sealed as the above writ.

No XVII. The like on a double demise.

George the Third, &c. To the sheriff of greeting whereas *A B.* lately in our Court before us at *Westminster*, by bill without our writ [or *by original*, by our writ], and by the judgment of the said Court, recovered against *C D* his term then and yet to come of and in two dwelling-houses, &c [*as in the declaration in ejectment*] with the appurtenances, situate, lying and being, in the parish of in your county, which *E. F.* on the day of in the year of our reign, had demised to the said *A. B* to hold the same to the said *A. B.* and his assigns, from the day of in the year aforesaid, for and during, and unto the full end and term of years, from thence next ensuing, and fully to be complete and ended, and also his term then and yet to come of and in two other dwelling-houses, &c. with the appurtenances, which *G H* on the day of in the year aforesaid, had demised to the said *A B.* to hold the same to the said *A B* and his assigns, from the day of in the year aforesaid, for and during, and until the full end and term of years from thence next ensuing, and fully to be complete and ended, by virtue of which said several demises, the said *A B.* entered into the said several tenements with the appurtenances, and was possessed thereof, until the said *C. D* afterwards, to wit, on the day of in the year aforesaid, with force and arms, &c. entered into the said several tenements, with the appurtenances, which the said *E. F* and *G. H.* had respectively demised to the said *A. B.* in manner and for the several terms aforesaid, which were not then, nor are yet, expired, and ejected the said *A. B* from his said several farms: whereof the said *C. D.* is convicted, as appears to us of record: therefore we command you, that without delay you cause the said *A. B.* to have the possession of his said several terms yet to come of and in the said several tenements, with the appurtenances; and in what manner you shall have executed this our writ, make appear to us at *Westminster*, on next after and have there then this writ Witness, *&c.*

No XVIII The like out of a county-palatine

George the Third, *&c.* To our chancellor of our county-palatine of *Lancaster* or to his deputy there, greeting whereas, *&c.* [*as in the last writ, to the words* "as appears to us of record," *then as follows*] therefore we command you that by our writ under the seal of our said county-palatine to be duly made, and directed to the sheriff of the same county, you command the said sheriff that without delay he cause the said *A. B.* to have the possession of his several terms aforesaid, yet to come of and in the several tenements aforesaid with the appurtenances, and in what manner the said sheriff shall execute our said writ, let him certify to you, so that you may make the same known to us at *Westminster*, on next after and have there then this writ, Witness, *&c*

No XIX The like, and fieri facias for costs

George the Third, *&c.* To the sheriff of greeting, whereas *&c* [*as in the* habere facias, *to the return day, then proceed as follows:*] we also command you that of the goods and chattels of the said *C. D.* in your bailiwick you cause to be made *l.* which the said *A. B.* lately in our said Court before us at *Westminster* aforesaid, recovered against the said *C. D.* for his damages which he had sustained as well on occasion of the trespass and ejectment aforesaid, as for his costs and charges by him about his suit in that behalf expended; whereof the said *C. D.* is also convicted as appears to us of record, and have you the said monies before us at *Westminster* on the return day aforesaid, to render to the said *A. B* for his damages aforesaid; and have there then this writ. Witness *&c.*

No XX The like, and capias ad satisfaciendum for costs

George the Third, *&c* To the sheriff of greeting whereas, *&c.* [*as in the* habere facias possessionem, *to the return day, and then as follows*] we also command you, that you take the said *C D* if he shall be found in your bailiwick, and him safely keep, so that you may have his body before us at *Westminster*, on the return day aforesaid, to satisfy the said *A B.* *l.* which in our said Court before us at *Westminster* aforesaid, were adjudged to the said *A. B.* for his damages which he had sustained, as well on occasion of the trespass and ejectment aforesaid, as for his costs and charges by him about his suit in that behalf expended; whereof the said *C. D* is also convicted, as appears to us of record, and have there then this writ. Witness, &c.

No XXI Declaration by bill for the mesne profits and costs in ejectment, after judgment by default against the casual ejector.

—— to wit. *A. B.* complains of *C. D.* being in the custody of the marshal of the *Marshalsea* of our Lord the now King before the King himself, for that he the said *C. D.* on the day of in the year of our Lord with force and arms, &c. broke and entered messuages [*describing the premises as in the declaration in ejectment*] with the appurtenances, of him the said *A. B.* situate and being in the parish of &c. in the said county of and then and there ejected and expelled, put out and removed the said *A. B.* from the possession, use, occupation and enjoyment thereof, for a long space of time, to wit, for the space of then next following; and during all that time there took, had and received to his own use all the rents, issues and profits of the said tenements, with the appurtenances, being of a large yearly value, to wit, of the yearly value of *l.* By reason whereof the said *A. B* for and during all that time not only lost and was deprived of all the profits, benefit and advantage of the tenements aforesaid, but was also thereby forced and obliged to lay out and expend, and did necessarily lay out and expend a large sum of money, to wit, the sum of *l.* in and about recovering and obtaining possession of his tenements aforesaid, with the appurtenances, to wit, at the parish aforesaid, and other wrongs to the said *A B* then and there did against the peace of our said Lord the now King, and to the damage of the said *A B.* of *l.*, and therefore he brings his suit, &c.

Pledges to prosecute { *John Doe,* *Richard Roe.*

No XXII. The like, by original.

—— to wit. *C. D.* late of in the county of yeoman, was attached to answer *A. B.* of a plea wherefore, with force of arms, he broke and entered messuages, &c. with the appurtenances, in in the county of aforesaid, and expelled, put out and removed the said *A. B.* from the possession and occupation of his said tenements, and kept and continued the said *A. B* so ejected, expelled, put out and removed from the possession and occupation of the same for a long space of time; and, during all that time, there had and received to his own use, all the rents, issues and profits of the said tenements, being of a large yearly value; and other wrongs to the said *A B* there did, to the great damage of the said *A. B.* and against the peace of our Sovereign Lord the King, *&c*, and hereupon the said *A B* by *E. F* his attorney, complains that the said *C. D.* on the day of in the year of the reign of his present Majesty, with force and arms, broke and entered the said tenements, &c. with the appurtenances, in aforesaid, in the said county of and ejected, expelled, put out and removed the said *A B* from the possession and occupation of his said tenements, and kept and continued the said *A. B* so ejected, expelled, put out and removed from the possession and occupation of the same, for a long space of time, that is to say, from the said day of in the year aforesaid, until the day of suing out the original writ of the said *A B.*, and, during all that time, there had and received to his own use, all the rents, issues and profits of the said tenements, being of a large yearly value, to wit, of the yearly value of *l.*, and other wrongs to the said *A B.* then and there did to the great damage of the said *A. B* and against the peace of our said Sovereign Lord the King wherefore the said *A. B.* says that he is injured, and hath sustained damage to the value of fifty pounds, and therefore he brings suit, *&c.*

No XXIII. Pleas thereto, viz 1 Not guilty, and 2, Not guilty within six years.

And the said *C. D.* by *G. H* his attorney, comes and defends the force and injury when, *&c.* and says, that he is not guilty of the supposed trespass above laid to his charge, in manner and form as the said *A. B.* hath above thereof complained against him; and of this he puts himself upon the country, and the said *C. D* doth the like. And for a further plea in this behalf, the said *C. D* by leave of the Court here, for this purpose had and obtained, according to the form of the statute in such case made and provided, says, that the said *A B.* ought not to have his aforesaid action thereof against him, because he says that he was not guilty of the supposed trespass aforesaid, above laid to his charge, at any time within six years next before the day of exhibiting the bill [or suing out the original writ] of the said *A B.* against the said *C. D.* in the manner and form as the said *A. B.* hath above thereof complained against him the said

C. D. and this he the said *C. D.* is ready to verify; wherefore he prays judgment if the said *A. B.* ought to have his aforesaid action thereof, against him, *&c.*

C. R.

And the said *A. B.* as to the said plea of the said *C. D.* by him lastly above pleaded in bar, says, that he, by reason of any thing by the said *C. D.* in that plea alleged, ought not to be barred from having his aforesaid action thereof against him; because he saith that the said *C. D.* was guilty of the trespass aforesaid, above laid to his charge, within six years next before the day of exhibiting the bill [or suing out the original writ of the said *C. D.* against the said *C. D.* in manner and form as he the said *A. B.* hath thereof complained against him the said *C. D.* and this he the said *A. B.* prays may be enquired of by the country; and the said *C. D.* doth the like, *&c.* No XXIV. Replication and issue.

INDEX.

Rr 2

LEASE.

THE END.

Lightning Source UK Ltd.
Milton Keynes UK
UKHW051627180223
416791UK00043B/143